T0389482

Rekindling the Strong State in Russia and China

International Comparative Social Studies

VOLUME 45

The titles published in this series are listed at *brill.com/icss*

Rekindling the Strong State in Russia and China

Domestic Dynamics and Foreign Policy Projections

Edited by

Stefano Bianchini
Antonio Fiori

BRILL

LEIDEN | BOSTON

The research included in this book was made possible by a generous grant from the Cariforlì Foundation (Fondazione Cassa dei Risparmi di Forlì).

Cover illustration: John Tallis (1851). Tibet, Mongolia and Manchuria. Source: Wikimedia Commons, the free media repository.

Library of Congress Cataloging-in-Publication Data

Names: Bianchini, S. (Stefano), editor. | Fiori, Antonio, 1972- editor.
Title: Rekindling the strong state in Russia and China : domestic dynamics
    and foreign policy projections / edited by Stefano Bianchini, Antonio
    Fiori.
Other titles: Russia e Cina nel mondo globale. English
Description: Leiden ; Boston : Brill, 2020. | Series: International
    comparative social studies, 1568-4474 ; vol.45 | Includes index.
Identifiers: LCCN 2020007746 (print) | LCCN 2020007747 (ebook) | ISBN
    9789004328488 (hardback) | ISBN 9789004428898 (ebook)
Subjects: LCSH: Russia (Federation)--Foreign relations. | China--Foreign
    relations--21st century. | Geopolitics. | Russia (Federation)--Politics
    and government--1991- | China--Politics and government--2002-
Classification: LCC DK510.764 .R853213 2020 (print) | LCC DK510.764
    (ebook) | DDC 327.47--dc23
LC record available at https://lccn.loc.gov/2020007746
LC ebook record available at https://lccn.loc.gov/2020007747

Typeface for the Latin, Greek, and Cyrillic scripts: "Brill". See and download: brill.com/brill-typeface.

ISSN 1568-4474
ISBN 978-90-04-32848-8 (hardback)
ISBN 978-90-04-42889-8 (e-book)

Contents

Acknowledgments   IX
List of Maps, Tables and Figures   XI
List of Abbreviations   XIII
List of Contributors   XVI

1   Introduction: Reshaping International Norms and State Models? China and Russia's New Role in the World Arena   1
     Stefano Bianchini and Antonio Fiori

PART 1
Managing State–Society Relations in Russia and China

2   In Search of "New Roots": Towards a Situational Ideology in Putin's Russia   17
     Marco Puleri

3   Towards the "Great Rejuvenation": State Nationalism, Shifting Identities, and Foreign Policy Choices in Contemporary China   40
     Andrea Passeri

4   Reframing Human Rights in Russia and China: How National Identity and National Interests Shape Relations with, and the Implementation of, International Law   61
     Marco Balboni and Carmelo Danisi

5   The Emerging Influence of the Chinese Strong-State Model   79
     Mingjiang Li and Mahalakshmi Ganapathy

6   Envisioning the Russian Welfare State Model: The New Political Economy of Gender and the Labour Market   98
     Rosa Mulè and Olga Dubrovina

7   Reshaping the Strong-State Model: Dmitrii Medvedev's "Failed Modernisation"   117
     Evgeny Mironov

8   State and Social Protests in China   135
        Yongshun Cai

9   Migration Flows between Russia and China: Legal and Social
        Implications   157
        Vasil Sakaev

        PART 2
        *China and Russia in the Changing World: Opportunities and
        Sources of Competition*

10   Global Shocks, Regional Conflicts and the Quest for Stable Prosperity:
        Which Way Forward for China and Russia?   185
        Eugenia Baroncelli

11   NATO-Russia Relations through the Prism of Strategic Culture   223
        Nicolò Fasola and Sonia Lucarelli

12   The Western Decline, Multipolarity and the Challenges of Identity in the
        Making of Russian Foreign Policy   249
        Stefano Bianchini

13   BRICS and Development Alternatives: Russia and China   271
        Stanislav L. Tkachenko

14   Engaging with European (Dis-)Integration: Russia in Dialogue with
        Europe/s   298
        Marco Puleri

15   Looking at the EU from the Russian and Chinese Perspectives   323
        Vitaly Kozyrev

16   The Fight against Human Trafficking in the European Union and
        Russia   344
        Marco Borraccetti

PART 3
Russia and China in Contested Regional Theatres: Some Case Studies

17   The Disputed Ukrainian Knot   365
      Francesco Privitera

18   Central Asia in China's Energy Strategy   378
      Antonio Fiori

19   The Convergence of Differences: Russia and China in the Middle East
      and North Africa   404
      Massimiliano Trentin

20   The Chinese Penetration in Sub-Saharan Africa: The Case of
      Tanzania   429
      Arrigo Pallotti

21   Relations with the West: The Case Study of the EEC-USSR, as Viewed by
      the Community (1950–1991)   450
      Giuliana Laschi

22   Postface: Europe's Response to Challenges from China and
      Russia   470
      Michael Leigh

23   Concluding Remarks   478
      Stefano Bianchini and Antonio Fiori

      Index   485

Acknowledgments

International relations are currently undergoing a deep transformation, and the increasingly assertive role of Beijing and Moscow's leaderships requires special consideration by scholars, policy makers, journalists, activists, and people at large. These general considerations were the impetus in 2015 for the launch by our unit of the Department of Political and Social Science of the Forlì Campus of the University of Bologna of a three-year international research project on state and society in China and Russia. The aim of the research was twofold. On the one hand, we sought to scrutinise the two countries' most relevant domestic dynamics in relation to the evolution of their external projections. On the other hand, we aspired to strengthen the research teamwork of our department, while attracting the contribution of prominent scholars with great international reputations, in order to promote a vivid exchange of views that their active participation in the project would definitely ensure.

During this long period of research, we held a workshop in Forlì every year. These were excellent occasions to jointly determine the general research design, distribute the research tasks, and mutually update the interim findings of our investigations, including the outcomes of our fieldwork. Methodologically, as the reader will realise in the chapters of this volume, the interdisciplinary approach to the research topic has been particularly stimulated by involving scholars from different disciplines: historians, political scientists, economists, lawyers, area studies experts and IR specialists. As a result, the structure of the international research team offered a variety of views, sometimes complementary and sometimes dissimilar or unconventional, but for this reason able to reflect, through different lenses, the complexity of the countries under scrutiny.

Statistics and, generally speaking, data collection has been originally monitored and elaborated by the individual authors. Interviews with local experts, public administrators, and policy makers were regularly conducted, also thanks to our scholarly mobility program. Furthermore, public statements, documents, and reports from a wide variety of sources have been critically examined by resorting to the contextual interpretation, while the empirical work has been supervised through critical observation.

This three-year project was made possible by a generous grant by the Cariforlì Foundation (Fondazione Cassa dei Risparmi di Forlì), which was willing to support the research activity of the Forlì Campus of the University of Bologna, where national and international teaching programs have already achieved a recognised international reputation.

Stefano Bianchini
Antonio Fiori

Maps, Tables and Figures

Maps

1   People's Republic of China   XXV
2   Russian Federation   XXVI

Tables

9.1   Demographic development of Russia   160
9.2   Employment pattern of Chinese migrants in Russia, %   165
9.3   Number of tourist trips to the Russian Federation by Chinese citizens (thousands)   167
9.4   Number of Chinese citizens in the Russian Federation in 2010   168
9.5   Crimes committed by foreign citizens in the Russian Federation (%)   171
10.1   Top World Exporters, 2005 and 2015   189
10.2   Top World Importers   190
A1   Major World Economies by GDP   212
A2   China Trade/GDP Shares 1991–2015   213
A3   Russia Trade/GDP Shares 1991–2015   214
A4   Research and development Spending as a share of GDP (%): BRICS and other advanced economies   215
A5   FDI, net inflows   216
A6   FDI, net outflows   217
A7   Military expenditures: BRICS vs selected transatlantic allies, 1995–2015   218
13.1   China and Russia: economic and social indicators (end of 2016)   289

Figures

8.1   Social Protests in China (2000–2015)   136
8.2   Stages of the Evolution of Popular Contention   140
10.1   The BRICS and the US: Trends in GDP growth and GDPpc   187
10.2   BRICS and the US: Exports as a share of GDP   193
10.3   BRICS vs US: R&D in GDP   194
10.4   BRICS vs US: High-Tech Exports in Manufactured Exports   194
10.5   BRICS vs US: FDI inflows and outflows in GDP (%), 1990–2015   196

10.6   BRICS poverty trends   199
10.7   China and Russia: political openness 1990–2015   200
10.8   BRICS, the US and the EU: Trends in military spending   205
19.1   China's Export and Import to Saudi Arabia and Iran (1992–2015)   410

Abbreviations

ABMI	Asian Bond Markets Initiative
ADIZ	Air Defence Identification Zone
AEM	Asia-Europe Meeting
AICHR ASEAN	ASEAN Intergovernmental Commission on Human Rights
AIIB	Asian Infrastructure Investment Bank
ANC	African National Congress
APEC	Asia Pacific Economic Cooperation
ARF ASEAN	ASEAN Regional Forum
ASEAN	Association of Southeast Asian Nations
ASP	Afro-Shirazi Party
BC	Beijing Consensus
BRI	Belt and Road Initiative
BRICS	Brazil, Russia, India, China and South Africa
CASCF	China-Arab States Cooperation Forum
CCP	Chinese Communist Party
CICA	Conference on Interaction and Confidence-Building Measures in Asia
CIS	Commonwealth of Independent States
CMI	Chiang Mai Initiative
CNOOC	China National Offshore Oil Corporation
CNPC	China National Petroleum Corporation
CoE	Council of Europe
CPRF	Communist Party of the Russian Federation
CSCAP	Council on Security Cooperation in Asia and Pacific Region
CSTO	Collective Security Treaty Organisation
DDR	Deutsche Demokratische Republik
DPRK	Democratic People's Republic of Korea
EAEU	Eurasian Economic Union
EAS	East Asia Summit
ECHR	European Convention on Human Rights
ECSC	European Coal and Steel Community
ECtHR	European Court of Human Rights
EDC	European Defence Community
EEC	European Economic Community
EPC	European Political Cooperation
EPRS	European Parliamentary Research Service
ETIM	East Turkestan Islamic Movement

EU	European Union
FDI	Foreign Direct Investment
FoRGO	Foundation for Civil Society Development
FPC	Foreign Policy Concept
FRELIMO	Frente de Libertação de Moçambique
GDP	Gross Domestic Product
GEP	Greater Eurasian Project
GRETA	Group of Experts on Action against Trafficking in Human Beings
GCC	Gulf Cooperation Council
HEI	Higher Education Institution
ICT	Information and Communication Technology
IMEMO	Institute of the World Economy and International Relations
IMF	International Monetary Fund
IMU	Islamic Movement of Uzbekistan
ISEPR	Institute for Socio-Economic and Political Studies
IT	Information Technology
LNG	Liquefied Natural Gas
MDGS	Millennium Development Goals
MENA	Middle East and North Africa
MERCOSUR	Mercado Común del Sur
MNCS	Multi-national corporations
MPLA	Movimento Popular de Libertação de Angola
NATO	North Atlantic Treaty Organisation
NBP	National Bolshevik Party
NDB	New Development Bank
NEACD	Northeast Asia Cooperation Dialogue
NGO	Non-Governmental Organisation
NOCS	National Oil Companies
NSS	National Security Strategy
OAU	Organisation of African Unity
OBOR	One Belt One Road
OECD	Organisation for Economic Cooperation and Development
OHCHR	Office of High Commissioner on Human Rights
OPEC	Organisation of the Petroleum Exporting Countries
PAC	Pan-Africanist Congress of Azania
PECC	Pacific Economic Cooperation Council
PfP	Partnership for Peace
PLAN	People's Liberation Army Navy
PRC	People's Republic of China
P4M	Partnership for Modernisation

Rosstat	Russian Federal State Statistics Service
RUR	Russian ruble
SCO	Shanghai Cooperation Organisation
SEZ	Special Economic Zone
SINOPEC	China Petroleum & Chemical Corporation
SLOCS	Sea lines of communication
SOE	State-owned enterprise
TEU	Twenty-foot equivalent unit
TFEU	Treaty on the Functioning of European Union
THB	Trafficking in Human Beings
TPP	Trans-Pacific Partnership
TTIP	Transatlantic Trade and Investment Partnership
UAE	United Arab Emirates
UN	United Nations
UPR	Universal Periodic Review
US	United States
USSR	Union of Soviet Socialist Republics
WB	World Bank
WTO	World Trade Organisation
ZANU	Zimbabwe African National Union
ZAPU	Zimbabwe African People's Union
ZNP	Zanzibar National Party

Contributors

Marco Balboni

is Professor of European Union and International Law at the University of Bologna, where he is also the Program Director of the Degree in *International Relations and Diplomatic Affairs*. His research interests include, among others, international refugee law and EU migration law, international and EU non-discrimination law and the role of the EU in promoting and protecting human rights worldwide. Among other activities, he is member of the Editorial board of the journal "Diritto, Immigrazione, Cittadinanza", co-director of the University of Bologna's multidisciplinary research network on gender studies Almagender–IRT, and has been Senior legal adviser for the EU Fundamental Rights Agency.

Eugenia Baroncelli

is Associate Professor of Political Science at the University of Bologna. Between 2001 and 2006 she has consulted for the World Bank on trade, tariff and intellectual property rights policies. Her research interests are in International Political Economy, International Relations, European Union and Global economic governance studies. She has published, among others, several articles and books on the IPE of trade, democracy and security and neo-Kantian theories, the India-Pakistan peace dividend from SAFTA trade preferences, the global economic crisis, the World Bank and the EU in development policies, neo-Gramscian theories of development and Susan Strange's thought. Among her most recent publications, *The European Union, the World Bank and the policymaking of aid* (Abingdon, Routledge 2019); "The World Bank in the Post-Crisis Landscape: Stasis and Change after the Post-Washington Consensus", in Poletti, A. and Raudino, S. (eds) *Global Economic Governance and Human Development* (Abingdon, Routledge 2018).

Stefano Bianchini

is Professor of East European Politics and History at the University of Bologna and Rector's delegate for relations with Eastern Europe. Former director of the two-years Interdisciplinary Master of Arts in East European Studies (MIREES), a joint diploma of the Universities of Bologna, St. Petersburg, Vytautas Magnus at Kaunas, and Corvinus of Budapest. He is Visiting professor of the State University of St. Petersburg and holds a H.D. in Humanities of the Vytautas Magnus University, Kaunas. From 2001 to 2018 he was also the co-director of the European Regional Master in Democracy and Human Rights for SEE (ERMA) awarding a double diploma of the Universities of Sarajevo and Bologna. He is a member of the Executive Committee and former Vice president of the Association for Studies of Nationalities (ASN) based at the Harriman Institute, Columbia University (New York), Executive Editor of the blind peer-review journal "Southeastern Europe", published by Brill, and other academic journals. He is the author, among others, of *Liquid Nationalism and State Partitions in Europe* (London-New York, Edward Elgar 2017), *Eastern Europe and the Challenges of Modernity 1800–2000* (Abingdon-New York, Routledge 2015), *Partitions. Reshaping States and Minds*, written with Sanjay Chaturvedi, Rada Ivekovic and Ranabir Samaddar (London, Frank Cass 2005 and 2015); *Sarajevo, Le Radici dell'odio. Identità e Destino dei Popoli Balcanici* (Roma, Edizioni Associate 2003); *La Question Yougoslave* (Paris, Castermann 1996) and co-editor of *Regional Cooperation, Peace Enforcement and the Role of the Treaties in the Balkans*, together with Joseph Marko, Craig Nation and Milica Uvalic (Ravenna, Longo 2007).

Marco Borraccetti

is Associate Professor in European Union Law at the University of Bologna, where he teaches EU Law and EU Migration Law. He is co-director of the European Regional MA Programme in Democracy and Human Rights in South East Europe (University of Bologna and University of Sarajevo), where he teaches Migration and Human Rights. He is member of the Editorial board of the journal "Diritto, Immigrazione, Cittadinanza". His current main research interests include migration, trafficking in human beings and human rights; the EU external borders policy; the judicial protection of fundamental rights in the EU. He is a member of CONREP, a network of excellence on Refugee Externalisation Policies; GLOBUS, a H2020 research project that critically examines the European Union's contribution to global justice; ESPON 2020 Programme ECTG, on Territorial and Urban Potentials Connected to Migration and Refugee Flows; AMIF, Arts Together, Integrating migrant children at schools through artistic expression. He was Visiting scholar at the European Union Center of the University of Illinois at Urbana-Champaign (2015), and Visiting professor at Université Libre de Bruxelles – Institut d'Etudes Européennes (2011).

Yongshun Cai

is Chair Professor at the division of Social Science of the Hong Kong University of Science and Technology. His current research interests include social movements and collective action, legal institution building, and cadre management in China. His research has appeared in *British Journal of Political Science, Political Science Quarterly, China Quarterly,* and *China Journal.* His paper "Disaggregating the State: Networks and Collective Action in Shanghai" (with Fayong Shi) won the Gordon White Prize for the most original article published in *China Quarterly* in 2006. His book, *Collective Resistance in China: Why Popular Protests Succeed or Fail* (Stanford, Stanford University Press 2010), examines the conditions under which Chinese citizens are able to stage successful collective action. His current research focuses on how the Chinese state authority manages the vast number of state agents by concentrating on the use of discipline.

Carmelo Danisi

is Research Fellow at the University of Sussex (UK) and Adjunct Professor of International Law at the University of Bologna (Forli Campus). After obtaining a PhD in International Human Rights Law from the University of Genova in 2012, he has been post-doc fellow at the University of Bologna (2012–2015). In 2015, he was awarded with an Endeavour Research Fellowship at the Australian National University, with a project on the principle of the best interests of the child in the context of migration. At the University of Sussex he has joined the SOGICA Project's Research Team (an ERC funded project). He is the author of several publications in the field of international and European Union (EU) law, especially in relation to human rights, non-discrimination and migration in the framework of the European Convention on Human Rights (ECHR) and the EU. He has participated in several national and international research projects, involving also legal analysis for the EU Agency for fundamental rights, on a range of different topics (e.g. international refugee law, Western Sahara and the principle of self-determination, EU external policy, gender-based violence and Brexit).

Olga Dubrovina

obtained her PhD degree from Modena and Reggio Emilia University in 2015 with a thesis on "Images of Soviet Union in fascist Italy" and in 2017 she obtained her second PhD degree from Moscow State University Lomonosov with a thesis on "Construction's mechanism of representations about Soviet Russia in Italy: 1922–1943". From 2015 to 2018 she was Adjunct Professor at Modena and Reggio Emilia University, where she lectured on Russian history and culture. Among her publications, *In the reflection of the enemy...Representations of Soviet Russia in Italy during the interwar period* (Moscow, Stepanenko 2019, in Russian), *Battles in Russia. Don and Stalingrad 75 years later* (Milano, Edizioni Unicopli 2018).

Nicolò Fasola

is Doctoral Researcher in the Department of Political Science and International Studies (POLSIS) of the University of Birmingham. He was Associate Researcher of the Institute of International Relations (IIR) in Prague. His research focuses on Russia's foreign and security policy, NATO-Russia relations, post-socialist transition(s), and IR theory. Before joining POLSIS, he served at the Italian Embassy in Estonia and NATO Supreme Headquarters Allied Powers Europe (SHAPE), working on the Ukraine portfolio. He regularly contributes to "East Journal", an Italian online magazine focused on Eastern Europe.

Antonio Fiori

is Associate Professor of History and Institutions of Asia at the University of Bologna and Adjunct Professor at Korea University (International Summer Campus). He is the Degree Program Director in *International Politics and Economics* (Forlì Campus) and Rector's Delegate for relations with Asia and Oceania. He has been Visiting fellow at the United International College (Zhuhai, PRC), East-West Center (Honolulu, USA), and at the Kyunjanggak Institute of Seoul National University (Republic of Korea). He has published widely on China's foreign policy, inter-Korean relations, and North Korea's domestic and foreign policy. His most recent co-edited book is titled *The Korean Paradox. Domestic Political Divide and Foreign Policy in South Korea* (London & New York, Routledge 2019).

Mahalakshmi Ganapathy

is a PhD student in the Comparative Asian Studies (CAS) Program at National University of Singapore. She locates her research interests within the broad spectrum of Sino-Indian relations, with special attention to China and India's resource geopolitics in Southeast Asia, diaspora politics, soft power strategies and effects of popular nationalism and national interest in contemporary Sino-Indian relations. She has published several articles in renowned magazines, policy briefs and conferences proceedings. She has previously worked as a Visiting associate in the China Program at Rajaratnam School of International Studies (RSIS) in Singapore. She received the Chinese Government Scholarship (CSC) to pursue an MA in Chinese Politics at East China Normal University (ECNU) in Shanghai (2015–2017). She is also a recipient of the ECNU Excellent Graduate Award (2017).

Vitaly Kozyrev

is Professor of Political Science and International Relations at Endicott College, Beverly, MA (USA). He studies international relations and foreign policy in Eurasia. In 2003–2018 he taught at Amherst College, the University of Delaware, Feng Chia University (Taiwan), and Yale University. As Endicott faculty he held fellowships at Harvard University, East-West Center (Washington, D.C.), and National University of Singapore. He is also affiliated with the Fairbank Center for Chinese Studies at Harvard University as Associate in Research. Among his recent publications, *Harmonizing "Responsibility to Protect": China's Vision of a Post-Sovereign World* ("International Relations", 30.3, 2016) and "Russia's New Global Vision and Security Policy in Asia" (in Tsuneo Akaha, Anna Vassilieva – eds., *Russia and East Asia: Informal and Gradual Integration*, New York, Routledge 2014).

Giuliana Laschi

is Associate Professor at the University of Bologna, where she teaches Contemporary History and History of European Integration. She is Jean Monnet Chair *ad personam*, President of the Scientific Committee of Punto Europa Forlì (Europe Direct Centre of European Commission since 2007 and Jean Monnet centre of Excellence since 2014). Her main research field is the history of the European integration, with a special focus on the political history of Common Agricultural Policy and the external relations of the European communities. Among her publications, *L'Italia e il processo di integrazione agricola europea* (Frankfurt am Main, Peter Lang 1999), and *L'Unione europea* (Roma, Carocci, 2005). She edited with Mario Telò, *Europa, potenza civile o entità in declino?* (Bologna, Il Mulino 2007) and *L'Europa nel sistema internazionale* (Bologna, Il Mulino 2009). Her latest book is titled *L'Europa e gli altri. Le relazioni esterne della Comunità dalle origini al dialogo Nord-Sud* (Bologna, Il Mulino 2015).

Michael Leigh

is senior Adjunct Professor at the Paul H. Nitze School of Advanced International Studies (SAIS) of Johns Hopkins University in Bologna and Senior fellow at the German Marshall Fund (GMF) of the United States. He was recently an Erskine fellow at the University of Canterbury, New Zealand. He has written and lectured extensively about the EU and transatlantic relations. Sir Michael Leigh served as director-general for enlargement at the European Commission after a career of more than 30 years in the European institutions. He holds a Bachelor's degree in Philosophy, Politics and Economics from Oxford University and a PhD in Political Science from Massachusetts Institute of Technology.

Mingjiang Li

is Associate Professor at S. Rajaratnam School of International Studies (RSIS), Nanyang Technological University (Singapore) and also the Coordinator of the

China Program at RSIS. He received his PhD in Political Science from Boston University. His main research interests include Chinese foreign policy, Chinese economic statecraft, the Belt and Road Initiative, Chinese politics, China-ASEAN relations, Sino-U.S. relations, and Asia-Pacific security. He is the author (including as editor and co-editor) of 13 books. His recent books are *China's Economic Statecraft* (Singapore, World Scientific 2017) and *New Dynamics in US-China Relations: Contending for the Asia Pacific* (lead editor, Abingdon, Routledge 2014). He has published papers in various peer-reviewed outlets including *Asian Security, Oxford Bibliographies, Journal of Asian Security and International Affairs, Journal of Strategic Studies, Global Governance, Cold War History, Journal of Contemporary China,* the *Chinese Journal of International Politics,* the *Chinese Journal of Political Science, China: An International Journal, China Security, Harvard Asia Quarterly, Security Challenges,* and *The International Spectator.* He frequently participates in various track-two events on East Asian regional security.

Sonia Lucarelli

is Associate Professor at the University of Bologna and Director of research at the Forum on the Problems of Peace and War in Florence. She has been Resident Member of the Bologna Institute for Advanced Studies, Jean Monnet Fellow at the European University Institute and participant in the International Visitors Programme of the U.S. Department of State. Her areas of expertise include the EU foreign policy and external image, European security, NATO, European identity and Foreign Policy, Migration and Global Justice. She is Team Leader in the project GLOBUS: *Reconsidering European Contributions to Global Justice* (2016–2020, Horizon 2020), and has been Lead Scientist in the project PREDICT (NATO grant), in the Network of Excellence GARNET (EU VI FP) and in the Research project EU-GRASP (EU VII FP). She has also received grants for individual research projects from NATO, the Volkswagen Stiftung, the Italian Ministry of Foreign Affairs and the Institute for International Affairs in Rome.

Evgeny Mironov

is Deputy Director of the Institute of Social Sciences and Professor at the Russian Academy of National Economy and Public Administration (RANEPA). His main research interests include the history of Russian culture of the Soviet and post-Soviet period, the transformation of the value and emotional attitudes of Russian society in the Soviet and post-Soviet period, and the reflection of these processes in the texts of literature and cinema. Engaged in applied and theoretical aspects of the development of innovative and interdisciplinary forms of education in the humanities and social sciences, he was the creator and for several years the dean of the Liberal Arts College of the RANEPA, headed the working group on the creation and implementation of the Federal educational standard "Public Policy and Social Sciences".

Rosa Mulè

is Associate Professor of Political Science at the University of Bologna. Her main research interests focus on comparative political economy, comparative welfare systems, welfare state, globalisation and nation-states, gender and political economy. She has published several books and articles on political parties, subsidiarity, gender and political economy, regional political economy, welfare states. Among her recent publications, *Lo studio della politica, l'individuo e la libertà. Scritti in onore di Angelo Panebianco*, (Bologna, Il Mulino 2019, with Sofia Ventura).

Arrigo Pallotti

is Associate Professor of History of Africa at the University of Bologna (Forlì Campus) and Research Fellow at the Centre for Africa Studies at the University of the Free State (South Africa). He is the author of 2 monographs (*Alla ricerca della democrazia. L'Africa sub-sahariana tra autoritarismo e sviluppo*, Soveria Mannelli, Rubbettino 2013; *Regionalismo, sicurezza e sviluppo in Africa sub-sahariana. Storia e politica della Southern African Development Community*, San Marino, Aiep editore 2005), co-author of 3 books and has edited 2 books and 3 special issues of the Italian peer-reviewed journal "Afriche e Orienti". He is also the author of more than 30 chapters or articles in journals and edited books in both Italian and English. His research interests focus primarily on democratisation in sub-Saharan Africa, the decolonisation of Southern Africa, and relations between Africa and the European Union.

Andrea Passeri

is Research Fellow and Adjunct Professor at the Department of Political and Social Sciences of the University of Bologna, where he teaches the course "Democracy and Authoritarianism in Asia". He holds a PhD in International Relations of East Asia from the University of Cagliari (Italy). His articles have appeared on leading international journals devoted to East Asian politics, including "The Pacific Review" and "The Korean Journal of Defence Analysis". His main research interests include nationalism in East Asia, alignment strategies, and Myanmar politics. He regularly collaborates with renowned think thanks located both in Italy and abroad, such as the East-West Center, the Istituto per gli Studi di Politica Internazionale (Italian Institute for International Political Studies – ISPI), and Treccani.

Francesco Privitera

is Associate Professor of East European History at the University of Bologna (Forlì Campus). His research interests include the history of the Balkans and Russia in the 19th and 20th Centuries, current institutional and political problems of the transition processes in Eastern Europe, the idea of State, and the modernisation process in the Balkans, Russia, and Eastern Europe. Among his publications, the monograph *Jugoslavia* (Milano, Unicopli 2006), the edited volume *Self-Determination. From Versailles to Dayton: its Historical Legacy* (Ravenna, Longo 1999) and the research article "Uniti nella diversità: le transizioni politiche postbelliche croata e serba e l'integrazione europea" (in Arianne Landuyt – ed., *L'Italia e i Balcani tra interessi nazionali e leadership europea. Il ruolo italiano nel processo di allargamento comunitario nell'area balcanica*, QCR, 1/2015).

Marco Puleri

is Research Fellow in Post-Soviet Studies and Adjunct Professor of History of Eastern Europe, Nation Building and Protection of Minorities at the Department of Political and Social Sciences of the University of Bologna. His research interests include contemporary Russian and Ukrainian sociocultural developments and nation-building in the post-Soviet area. He is the author of the monograph *Narrazioni ibride post-sovietiche* (Firenze, Firenze University Press 2016) and has published several articles on the Ukrainian and Russian cultural and social history. He has extensively worked on the integration and nation building process in Post-Soviet Ukraine as a Research fellow at the Kyiv-Mohyla Academy (2014) and Visiting fellow at the Ivan Franko National University of L'viv (2018).

Vasil T. Sakaev

is Associate Professor at the Department of International Relations, World Politics and Diplomacy of the Kazan Federal University (Russian Federation). Former Head of Political Science Department of the Kazan Federal University Campus in Naberezhnye Chelny and former Head of Centre for Monitoring of Inter-ethnic and Inter-religious Relations in the Republic of Tatarstan. He is the author of *Politics and Demography: the problems of Interaction and Interdependence* (Kazan, Kazan University Press 2017), which was awarded as the best book in Political Science by the Russian Political Science Association.

He develops an educational online course project in Political Demography under the support of the Vladimir Potanin Charity Foundation.

Stanislav Tkachenko

is Professor of International Political Economy and Director of the MA Programme in *Diplomacy of Russian Federation and Foreign States* at Saint-Petersburg State University. His main research interests are political economy of development, economic diplomacy, and Russian foreign policy. He has published 11 books and 140 articles on monitoring of elections, development diplomacy of Russian Federation, and regional political economy. Among his recent publications, *La Russia, i BRICS e l'ordine internazionale* (Roma, Edizioni nuova Cultura 2015, with Anton Giulio de Robertis), *Monitoring of democracy: development of democracy* (St.Petersburg, IPA CIS 2016), *Coercive diplomacy in Russian security strategy* (New York, Routledge 2019).

Massimiliano Trentin

is Associate Professor of History and Institutions of Asia at the University of Bologna. He focuses on the international history of Western Asia, with a special focus on the interplay between diplomacy, economics and development. Among his works, *Engineers of Modern Development: East German Experts in Ba'thist Syria, 1965–1972* (Padova, Cleup 2010), *La Guerra fredda tedesca in Siria. Diplomazia, politica ed economia, 1963–1970* (Padova, Cleup 2015) and edited volumes as *The Middle East and the Cold War* (Newcastle Upon Tyne, Cambridge Scholars Publishing 2012), *Counter-shock. The Oil Counter-Revolution of the 1980s* (London, IB Tauris 2018), *L'ultimo Califfato. L'organizzazione dello stato islamico in Medio Oriente* (Bologna, Il Mulino 2018). His works appeared in several academic journals, among which *Diplomatic History, Cold War History, Foro Internacional*.

Maps

MAP 1   People's Republic of China

MAP 2   The Russian Federation

Introduction: Reshaping International Norms and State Models? China and Russia's New Role in the World Arena

Stefano Bianchini and Antonio Fiori

At the beginning of the twenty-first century western enthusiasm surrounding the "third wave of democracy" (Huntington 1991) started to vanish, given the slowdown in the pace and extent of political transitions around the world. As a result, democratic regimes and the notions of political rights and civil liberties were strongly challenged by new types of authoritarianism and hybrid regimes (Diamond et al. 2016).

Meanwhile, the increasingly globalised and interdependent world was marked by a growing diversification of players, aiming to take advantage of the new opportunities offered by their economic achievements. Within this context, a variety of countries including India, Iran, Saudi Arabia, South Africa, Turkey and Brazil demanded new space for expressing their potential, both at the regional level and within international organisations. On top of that, the powerful rise of China as well as the rapid recovery of Russia after the fall of the Soviet Union, have been highly significant. Although in different respects, both these *land powers* have remodelled their pattern of development and have expressed the ambition to reinforce their normative role in reshaping international law, covenants and conventions.

As a result, and despite the peculiarities and differences characterizing these two countries, Russia and China deserve a special comparative analysis, given their convergence in disputing the dominance of the US and the EU (Sakwa 2017). Russia and China, in fact, increasingly refer to the need to recognise the coexistence of multiple civilisations, by leveraging their deep military, social, and economic transformations. In so doing, they are also challenging the normative power of the West, which is, moreover, less cohesive than during the second half of the twentieth century and particularly in more recent times, since the Trump administration has taken office.

As stressed in the chapters of the present book, the motivations that have encouraged Russia and China to identify forms of convergence in a variety of fields arise from a plurality of sources. To a large extent, they originate from developments in either their domestic policies or external projections.

Historically, these two states' relations have oscillated from narrow cooperation and vicinity to distrust, mutual suspicion and even clashes. However, the
authors of this volume basically agree that 2012 can be considered a turning
point in Moscow-Beijing relations: indeed, since then their cooperation has
constantly expanded and deepened in several fields, even though some mutual
apprehension still persists.

The self-confidence of strong and stable state-building seems likely to have
influenced these countries' own perception of world dynamics and their own
role within it, particularly since the beginning of the new millennium. In
December 1999, for example, when Russia was still trapped in a chaotic transition, after years of corruption and humiliation that peaked with the great
financial collapse of 1998, newly appointed president Vladimir Putin (who was
elected just a few months later) repeatedly referred in a speech to the "strong
state" as a key goal to be achieved to renew Russian power and its respectability around the world (Putin 1999, in Sakwa 2004: 258–259). In China, the
impressive transformation that started with Deng Xiaoping's reforms in the
1980s, consolidated further socially, ideologically and nationally at the turn
of the new millennium, leading the Chinese leadership to outline its "strong
state model" for other international players. Here, as with Russia, state and
nation-building processes have been largely informed by China's competitive
and often antagonistic relations with the West, thus paving the way for an increasingly nationalistic posture centred on the narrative and traumas of the
so-called "century of humiliation".

Admittedly however, how to measure a "strong state" was and still is a matter of debate among scholars. Some sociological studies since the 1960s have
concentrated analysis on comparative relations between strong and weak
states, with a special focus either on the relation between the state and revolutions or on post-colonial Africa (particularly the sub-Saharan region). Even
Davidheiser (1992: 464–465) for example, elaborated a theoretical approach to
assessing the strength of the state by suggesting three criteria: the "depth of
social penetration by policy institutions; the breadth of societal penetration by
policy institutions; and the penetration, or permeability, of the state by society", by confronting the Russian, German and Swedish experiences between
the nineteenth and twentieth centuries. However, other works of western international social science literature have stressed the relevance of additional
key factors, like democratic stability, the respect of human rights and the rule
of law, the basic availability of public goods and economic growth, as crucially
relevant to guaranteeing the strength of the state (Hillel & Vom Hau 2008; Acemoglu 2005; Tilly 1993). These studies, however, mainly focused on Africa and
Latin America (with some rare, questionable comparative attention to the

Central European post-communist transition), where weak states are predominantly marking the macroregional context (Di John 2010; Linz & Stepan 1996; Boone 2003). Recently, some researchers have pointed out the importance of empirical differentiation, while considering the impact of subtypes such as bureaucracy, territorial reach, and autonomy from non-state factors in the analysed case-studies (Giraudy 2012).

Scholars of Russian studies, on the contrary, have often measured the model of strong state in Eastern Europe in relation to the Byzantine legacy (in terms of form of governance, religiosity, irrationality) or to the role played by leaders as "guarantors of stability" (Shevtsova 1999). More radically, some authors have emphasised the absolutist tradition of Tsarist autocracy and the subjugation requested by the Orthodox Church to authorities in power, as the identifying aspects of the "Russian Strong State" (Walicki 1979; Pipes 2005). Others have seen some of these elements encoded (a) in the Soviet organisation of power, either since Stalin or since Lenin himself (Pipes 1996), (b) in the ability to expand borders as a factor of security policy (Nation 1992), or (c) in the control of internal borders, in order to maintain stability among nations (Martin 2001). Most of these aspects have been filtered and applied in the international literature in the scholarly (and political) assessment of Putin's political decisions. Putin himself, in describing his idea of "strong state" in the mentioned document of 1999, mixed different features by emphasizing the relevance of an efficient economy and financial system, the rule of law, an effective federal state, the authority of the judiciary, together with the emphasised role of the "Russian idea". This definition has been extensively discussed in several chapters of this book, but basically the convergence of patriotism, statism (that is, in his words, the "restoration of the regulative role of the state"), and social solidarity had to be incorporated in the new representation of the Russia's greatness, identified with the untranslatable word of *Derzhavnost'*.

By the same token, in China the idea of a "strong state", capable of penetrating society and its local institutions, displays ancient roots. In fact, the Chinese communist state originated with the confluence of three traditions: the late-imperial and republican one; the political and administrative tradition acquired during the civil war and the management of areas occupied by communist forces; and the Soviet model. When the Chinese Communist Party (CCP) seized power in 1949, it already had a long history of governing its territories. Despite the profound differences and friction between the Maoist nomenclature and Stalin's USSR, when the Chinese had to consider the creation of a new state the only political and economic institutional model that seriously influenced them was the Soviet one. The importation of this model, based on the centralisation of power, was one of the fundamental elements of this process, as it was for the introduction of a planned economy. A further consequence of the revolutionary period was the intimate relationship between the army and the party, characterised by a process of politicisation of soldiers and strong control exerted by the political power over the armed forces. According to Mao, in fact, the political power had to keep supremacy, without running the risk of being "controlled by the rifle". The revolution, therefore, left to the Maoist state diverse legacies: a disciplined and normatively regulated party but also a charismatic leader endowed with the prestige and authority to modify those norms whenever necessary (Teiwes 2000). Against this backdrop, the People's Republic of China has constantly represented an example of "strong state and weak society". Even in the wake of modifications introduced by Deng Xiaoping and Jiang Zemin, the dominance of party/state institutions and the elitist nature of China's politics have not changed much, although certain power decentralisation phenomena have become evident in the realms of domestic politics and foreign economic policy (Lampton 2001).

The advent of Xi Jinping, however, has demolished the efforts of the political post-Maoist tradition, according to which a collective leadership had to be favoured in order to prevent the possibility of another Maoist-like dictatorship. As a result, with Xi's ascendance at the helm of both the party (2012) and the state (2013), China has showcased an increasingly assertive and uncompromising behaviour, both domestically and in terms of its international projection, which – according to some scholars – has been characterised by a "strident turn" (Zhao 2013). The evidence of this shift is abundant, especially if one considers the recent reform of the Chinese constitution that abolished presidential term limits, the vast anti-corruption campaign unleashed by Xi, and the ongoing rift with Hong Kong in the attempt to reassert China's sovereignty over the former British colony. Furthermore, this shift is exemplified by the unveiling of the "Belt and Road Initiative" (BRI), and, last but not least, the dangerous "trade war" with the Trump administration. In the meantime, state control is increasingly being asserted through the digital domain, where Chinese policymakers are finding unprecedented avenues to strengthen their tools of repression and propaganda vis-à-vis the indigenous population. Hence, China's ongoing metamorphosis poses further challenges to scholars who seek to categorise and compare its political system. In general terms, the People's Republic of China (PRC) is considered variably as a dictatorship or an authoritarian state. The presence of a single party and the repression of human rights contributes to this somewhat simplistic depiction of the country. However, according to other analysts, things are much more complicated: China's regime has abandoned its "totalitarian paradigm" and should be considered differently. Following Larry Diamond's six-fold categorisation of the various forms of regimes (liberal democracy; electoral democracy; ambiguous regime; competitive authoritarian; hegemonic electoral authoritarian; and politically closed authoritarian), Wang (2006) contends that China cannot be considered a "politically closed authoritarian" system, which would perfectly apply to the North Korean case, but should be labelled a "hegemonic electoral authoritarian" regime. According to this scholar, the fact that all important government offices are "elected" – albeit not in a competitive form – and, above all, that free, fair and competitive elections are held both at the village and township levels, is a visible confirmation that forms of open elections exist, even though in a "minimalist" way.

By contrast, the quality of the Russian system is likely to be a more contested subject among scholars. Admittedly, the debate is largely influenced by the neoliberal and US perception of international reality, encoded in Freedom House's or the Economist Intelligence Unit's democracy indexes. On the one hand, by taking as indicators Freedom House's criteria based on political rights – defined as the "extent that the people have a choice in determining the nature of the system and its leaders" – and civil liberties – i.e. "freedoms to develop views, institutions, and personal autonomy apart from the state" – Russia is classified as "not free". Similarly, Human Rights Watch and Amnesty International show huge deficits in Russia's political and civil freedoms. Therefore, according to these organisations the fact that the country does not satisfy the formal requirements of a democratic regime is quite evident. This has been explained by some scholars by referring to the political culture of the country and its legacy: following this line of reasoning, Russia's tradition of centralised rule – from Tsarism to the Soviet experience – has deeply marked a cultural inclination towards a strong state (because of its socially pervasive institutions and military power), while Russian society has been traditionally weak in terms of independent sources of political expression (White et al. 2010).

This limited predisposition to democratic values helps to shed light on the challenges of democratic transition. Moreover, El'tsin's administration seems to have reinforced such a posture towards democracy, given that his transition to that regime resulted in political and economic turmoil. This has contributed to convincing Russians of the validity of their view of democracy, focused on security and stability more than on individual freedom (Remington 2012). Apart from the political "heritage" however, Russia also satisfies additional criteria that could make it a textbook example of *hybridity*. Despite the fact that formal democratic institutions and procedures exist – like holding periodic elections and the presence of several political parties – the Russian system is characterised by a variety of deficiencies such as electoral manipulation, which Hale (2011) defines as "coercing and buying votes", media manipulation, the use of political violence and intimidation, and the introduction of laws favouring incumbents. These characteristics are all features of a relatively consolidated hybrid regime (Schedler 2001; Shul'man 2015).

Contrary to the abovementioned stances, other scholars highlight a diversified picture, marked by recent reforms that, for example, have lowered the threshold for entering Duma, thereby increasing competition between parties and their representatives in Parliament; reinstated gubernatorial elections; far-reaching civic initiatives involving millions of Russians in voluntary activities; the critical role played by the most important newspapers (like *Nezavisimaia Gazeta*, *Vedomosti*, or *Kommersant*) or some TV channels like RBK or *Telekanal Dozhd* (Rain TV); changes in criminal justice, which have expanded the rights of defendants, introduced a jury and separate juvenile justice, raising public confidence in the courts (Petro 2018; Cohen 2012).

Moreover, the short-term presidency of Medvedev was initially regarded in the West as an interesting approach to distancing Russia from the strategies pursued by Putin during his second mandate. This new situation, in fact, was seen as likely to lead in 2010 to the revitalisation of the P4M program (Partnership for Modernisation), which was defined alongside the EU already in 2003. However, the administrative and judicial reforms that the EU warmly supported were soon frustrated by the two partners' incompatible viewpoints. Indeed, the outlined cooperation did not achieve its goals, mostly because the Russian expectation of investments and high-tech transfers collided with the normative modernisation that the EU was expecting and urging. This approach, instead, was rejected by Moscow as a form of intrusion in its sovereignty.

In the end, over the last two decades the ambiguity of the Russian system has been often categorised according to the notion of "hybridity", which encompasses a "certain functional and territorial mix". In a way, the Russian system should have been classified as a "genuine advance from the past [i.e. authoritarianism] and a significant step in the long-range process of building democracy" (Karl 1995: 74). According to Furman (2008: 39) however, hybrid systems arise when the "conditions in a given society are not ripe for democracy, and yet there is no ideological alternative to it".

In this context, when the domestic political, social, and economic systems as well as demography are so different, what brings China and Russia together? Why should these two countries be comparatively analysed?

Essentially, there are many reasons that suggest such an approach. Despite differences, it is a fact that a convergence between Moscow and Beijing is strengthening not only at the international level, but also in terms of values.

Geopolitically, in fact, western sanctions on Russia have accelerated the Kremlin's quest to identify alternative partners in the world arena. This originated, in particular, with the worsening relations between the West and Moscow starting with Putin's criticism of the unipolar world at the Munich Security Conference in 2007, and aggravated by the Georgian war, the Crimean incorporation, and the war in Eastern Ukraine. On the other hand, China – which has adopted a rather diplomatic behaviour while intensifying its economic penetration of Africa, Central Asia, and the Balkans – has been facing multiple tensions both in Hong Kong and the South China Sea, and with the United States because of the growing custom confrontations, with a relevant impact on the world economy.

Subsequently, the riots that affected the Arab world after 2011, the military operations of western countries in Libya and Syria, the war in Yemen, the endless military clashes in the Near East, and the confrontation in the Persian Gulf with Iran have, to a large extent, contributed to affecting the moral authority of the West, unable to establish stable democratic regimes after its interventions.

These circumstances have had an unprecedented impact on values perceptions in the two *land powers.* Indeed, they have alarmed both Moscow and Beijing, whose leaderships politically and culturally reject the normative supremacy of the West. As a result, they have felt encouraged to demand negotiations on an equal basis (of the international legal order), thus challenging the western approach that recognises human rights and its own sphere of values (encompassing democracy, rule of law, respect of diversity, gender equality, etc.) as a universal centrality. In other words, Russia's and China's persistent demand for multipolarity (also supported by other organisations of which the two are members, such as the BRICS) is not only a veiled critique of US/western unipolarity (which often leads to a stalemate in the Security Council and other international institutions), but also a strategic effort aimed at juxtaposing a different set of values, as an expression of the equality of civilisations.

These synthetic considerations, developed under different themes in the chapters of this volume, actually mirror some crucial international aspects that characterise increasing world disorder, while encouraging Russia and China, each for its part and through bilateral consultations, to claim greater influence in normative approaches.

As a result, this book inevitably looks both to the management of state-society relations and the dynamics that mark the external projections of two new/old key players of the world arena. Although some of the most relevant features are presented here in two different sections of the volume for reasons of clarity, they are, in fact, deeply interconnected, as the reader will easily grasp by scrolling through the pages of this volume. Furthermore, we have included in the volume a third section focused on some case-studies. The aim is to offer additional insights into key geopolitical directions that Russia and China are nurturing and developing in different world contexts.

Consistently, the first section deals with new narratives involving the identity reconstruction of Russia and China, since both the search for "new roots" (Puleri) and inputs for "great rejuvenation" (Passeri) manifest domestic and international implications, related to the self-assurance of these two global powers in terms of internal consensus and external projection. Admittedly, their reframing of human rights (Balboni and Danisi) is part of efforts to build alternative (conservative) values of which both Moscow and Beijing are confident. Under this context, Russia and China have emerged as representatives of new economic "models", commonly known under the label of "authoritarian modernisation", "state capitalism" or "Strong State model" (Li and Ganapathy; Mironov). Therefore, this book investigates the main characteristics of these models and to what extent they might be attractive, by scrutinizing the quality of the welfare state (Mulè and Dubrovina), the impact of migration (Sakaev), and relations between power and social protests (Cai).

The effort is to offer powerful insights to the reader to enable a better understanding of how the leaderships of these global powers perceive themselves and imagine their international role. In fact, the central advocating role of the strong state, through the reforms passed for its implementation (however questionable they may be in the eyes of western political cultures), is viewed by Russian and Chinese leaderships as the crucial agent able to meet their global expectations. Therefore, domestic policies and external projections are tightly intertwined, the former promoting the development of the latter and vice versa. This connection is not a peculiarity of Russia and China, since it can be identified in most national contexts around the world. Nonetheless, in our case, it takes a specific stance, given the unique historical and cultural legacies of these countries, whose dynamics are discussed not only in the first section, mainly focused on state-society relations, but also in the second one. In the latter, our authors have conjectured whether shifting boundaries, in contexts that are suffering from global shocks and regional conflicts, do represent a real opportunity for Russia and China's exercise of power politics or a risk that can affect world peace.

As a result, the second section gives specific relevance to the strategic alternatives that both Moscow and Beijing are pursuing in search of stable prosperity (Baroncelli), by bridging some gaps that still characterise the western international literature. For example, this is the case of the role of BRICS (Tkachenko), which is rarely analysed. By contrast, the Eurasian Economic Union (EAEU) has been often minimised, despite the potential radical impacts that might affect either Russia's pendular behaviour between Europe and Asia or the Central Asian transition, as soon as its elder leaderships vanish (Bianchini). Furthermore, the section deals with the military integration of the Shanghai Cooperation Organisation (SCO) and the regional alliance represented by the Collective Security Treaty Organisation (CSTO). Within this framework, the section has also considered the prospect of collaboration, or rivalry, between our two actors under scrutiny, and relations with both the EU (Puleri; Kozyrev; Borraccetti) and NATO (Lucarelli and Fasola). Indeed, there are many reasons why these aspects require particular attention.

Firstly, the US factor (but also NATO, at least for Russia) plays a key role in shaping relations between Moscow and Beijing. Although for both countries relations with Washington remain crucial, both are highly dissatisfied with the existing international order. They demand equal treatment, and – paradoxically – are looking with concern at the impact of protectionist trends prevailing under the Trump administration. Secondly, China has made impressive inroads in Central Asia, with particular regard to the former Soviet Republics, as well as in Africa, contrasting, in that continent, with the models of cooperation implanted by western countries and dependent on the adoption of "good governance" measures while introducing an alternative pattern of collaboration. Thirdly, Russia's presence in the Asia-Pacific region remains weak, even though Moscow has tried – while maintaining friendly relations with Beijing – to develop ties with other countries like Japan, India and ASEAN countries. In the future, the Kremlin might translate this approach into a "containment strategy" against China's rise. And finally, the crucial question remains the following: will there be competition or cooperation between these new Global Powers in the foreseeable future?

Consistently, in light of these recent global dynamics and the rise of new competing economic and political partnerships, the third section offers some additional insights by focusing on some case studies of potential or real "battlefields", that have been identified in different regions of the world.

For example, China's energy strategy (Fiori) and its long-term penetration into sub-Saharan Africa (Pallotti), the protracted instability in the Middle East (Trentin), the confrontations with the West in Ukraine (Privitera) and the enduring legacies of European integration and the Kremlin (Laschi) represent, in our approach, a true testing ground for the "reshaped powers" of Russia and China. In particular, the controversial relations with the EU have undergone important and shifting turning points, complicating every attempt to formulate an organic description of their respective interactions. On the other end, the EU – despite its internal divisions – has recently acquired a more autonomous position regarding the US. For example, the proximity recorded on climate change strategy, the preservation of the nuclear agreement with Iran, reactions to the "protectionist war" driven by the Trump administration, all these events have encouraged either Russia or China to see the EU as a valuable partner. Inevitably, these changes are symptomatic of the rapid, albeit largely unexpected global re-positioning of key great powers, granting both Moscow and Beijing wider room for manoeuvre, potentially higher international prestige and, prospectively, new opportunities to readjust the rules of the international legal order that both now consider out of date.

As a result, this book explores different narratives, either diachronically or synchronically, in order to offer the reader a comprehensive view of the complexity of ways in which the EU, Russia, and China are looking at each other, with mutual suspicion and interest, stemming from the awareness that dialogue is still needed on a number of strategic issues, from trade to economic growth, from fighting criminality and human trafficking to infrastructure and new technologies.

Nonetheless, the general framework of these relations remains open to a variety of developments, in which the prospect of confrontation and cooperation remains at the stake. In particular, the unpredictable effects of American trade protectionism to the detriment of EU and Chinese exports might lead to a reconsideration of the feasibility of the Greater Eurasian Project, that attracted the interest of De Gaulle, Gorbachev, and is currently endorsed by important German foundations, as for example the Bertelsmann Stiftung.

Then, the set of international relations would take a far-reaching turn, whose dimensions at the moment are impossible to imagine.

Bibliography

Acemoglu, D. (2005). 'Politics and economics in weak and strong states', *Working paper, 11275*, April, http://www.nber.org/papers/w11275.

Armony, A.C., and Schamis, H.E. (2005). 'Babel in Democratization Studies', *Journal of Democracy*, 4(16): 113–128.

Balzer, H. (2003). 'Managed Pluralism. Vladimir Putin's Emerging Regime', *Post-Soviet Affairs*, 19(3): 189–227.

Bauman, Z. (2000). *Liquid Modernity*. Cambridge: Polity Press.

Boone, C. (2003). *Political Topographies of the African State. Territorial Authority and Institutional Choice*. Cambridge: Cambridge University Press.

Cohen, S.F. (2012). 'Stop the Pointless Demonization of Putin', *Reuters*, 7 May, http://blogs.reuters.com/great-debate/2012/05/07/stop-the-pointless-demonization-of-putin/.

Davidheiser, E.B. (1992). 'Strong States, Weak States: The Role of the State in Revolution', *Comparative Politics*, 4(24): 463–475.

Di John, J. (2010). 'The Concept, Causes and Consequences of Failed states: a Critical Review of the Literature and Agenda for Research with Specific Reference to Sub-Saharan Africa', *European Journal of Development Research*, 22(1): 10–30.

Diamond L., Plattner M.F., Walker C. (eds.) (2016). *Authoritarianism Goes Global. The Challenge to Democracy*. Oxford: Johns Hopkins University Press.

Diamond, L. (1996). 'Is the Third Wave Over?', *Journal of Democracy*, 7(3): 20–37.

Diamond, L., Linz, J.J. and Lipset, S.M. (eds.) (1995). *Politics in Developing Countries*. Boulder, CO: Lynne Rienner.

Furman, D. (2008). 'Imitation Democracies. The Post-Soviet Penumbra', *New Left Review*, 54, November-December: 29–47.

Gabuev, A. (2016). 'Friends with Benefits? Russian-Chinese Relations After the Ukraine Crisis', *Carnegie Moscow Center*, 29 June, http://carnegie.ru/2016/06/29/friends-with-benefits-russian-chinese-relations-after-ukraine-crisis-pub-63953.

Giraudy A. (2012). 'Conceptualizing State Strength: Moving Beyond Strong and Weak States', *Revista de Ciencia Política*, 3(32): 599–611.

Hale, H.E. (2011). 'Hybrid Regimes', pp. 23–45 in Brown, N.J. (ed.). *The Dynamics of Democratization: Dictatorship, Development, and Diffusion*. Baltimore: The Johns Hopkins University Press.

Huntington, S. (1991). *The Third Wave. Democratization in the Late Twentieth Century*. Norman, OK: University of Oklahoma Press.

Klein, K. (2010). '"New Authoritarianism" in China: Political Reforms in the One-Party State', *Telos*, 151: 30–56.

Koch-Weser, I. and Murray, C. (2014). 'The China-Russia Gas Deal: Background and Implications for the Broader Relationship', U.S.-China Economic and Security Review Commission, 9 June, https://www.uscc.gov/sites/default/files/Research/China%20Russia%20gas%20deal_Staffbackgrounder.pdf.

Lampton, D. (2001). *The Making of Chinese Foreign and Security Policy in the Era of Reform: 1978–2000*. Stanford, CA: Stanford University Press.

Levitsky, S., and Way, L.A. (2010). *Competitive Authoritarianism: Hybrid Regimes After the Cold War*. Cambridge: Cambridge University Press.

Linz, J. and Stepan, A. (1996). *Problems of Democratic Transition and Consolidation: Southern Europe, South America, and Post-communist Europe*. Baltimore, MD: Johns Hopkins University Press.

Lo, B. (2015). *Russia and the New Worlds Disorder*. London/Washington, D.C.: Chatham House and Brookings Institution Press.

Luhn, A. and Macalister, T. (2014). 'Russia signs 30-year deal worth $400bn to deliver gas to China', *The Guardian*, 21 May, https://www.theguardian.com/world/2014/may/21/russia-30-year-400bn-gas-deal-china.

Martin, T. (2001). *The Affirmative Action Empire*. Ithaca, NY: Cornell University Press.

O'Donnell, G.A. (1994). 'Delegative Democracy', *Journal of Democracy*, 5(1): 55–69.

Pei, M. (2000). 'China's Evolution Toward Soft Authoritarianism', pp. 75–81 in Friedman, E. & McCormick, B.L. (eds.). *What If China Doesn't Democratize? Implications for War and Peace*. Armonk, NY: ME Sharpe.

Munck, G.L. (2001). 'The regime question. Theory building in democracy studies', *World Politics*, 54(1), October: 119–144.

Nathan, A.J. (2008). 'China's Political Trajectory: What Are the Chinese Saying?', pp. 25–43 in Cheng Li (ed.). *China's Changing Political Landscape: Prospects for Democracy*. Washington, D.C.: Brookings Institution Press.

Nation, C.R. (1992). *Black Earth, Red Star: A History of Soviet Security Policy 1917–1991*. Ithaca, NY: Cornell University Press.

Petro, N. (2018). 'Are we Reading Russia Right?', *The Fletcher Forum of World Affairs*, 42(2): 131–154.

Pipes, R. (2005). *Russian Conservativism and Its Critics*. New Haven, CT: Yale University Press.

Pipes, R. (1996). *The Unknown Lenin*. New Haven, CT: Yale University Press.

Putin, V. (1999). 'Russia at the Turn of the Millennium', 29 December, pp. 251–262 in Sakwa, R. (2004). *Putin: Russia's Choice*. London: Routledge.

Remington, F.T. (2012). *Politics in Russia* (7th ed.). London: Longman.

Sakwa, R. (2017). *Russia against the Rest. The Post-Cold War Crisis of World Order*. Cambridge: Cambridge University Press.

Schedler, A. (2001). 'Measuring democratic consolidation', *Studies in Comparative International Development*, 36(1): 66–92.

Schedler, A. (2002). 'Elections without democracy: The menu of manipulation', *Journal of Democracy*, 13(2): 36–50.

Schedler, A. (2006). 'The Logic of Electoral Authoritarianism', pp. 1–23 in Schedler, A. (ed.). *Electoral Authoritarianism. The Dynamics of Unfree Competition*. Boulder, CO: Lynne Rienner Publishers.

Shevtsova, L. (1999). *Yeltsin's Russia: Myths and Reality*. Washington, D.C.: Carnegie Endowment.

Shul'man, E. (2015). 'Avtoritarnye rezhimy: mutanty, bastardy, gibridy', *Slon*, 3 March, https://republic.ru/posts/48948.

Soifer, H. & and Hau, M.v. (2008). 'Unpacking the strength of the state: the utility of state infrastructure power', *Studies in Comparative International Development*, 3–4(43): 219–230.

Stronski, P. and Ng, N. (2018). 'Cooperation and Competition: Russia and China in Central Asia, the Russian Far East and the Arctic', *Carnegie Endowment for International Peace*, 28 February, http://carnegieendowment.org/2018/02/28/cooperation-and-competition-russia-and-china-in-central-asia-russian-far-east-and-arctic-pub-75673.

Teiwes, F.C. (2000). 'The Chinese State During the Maoist Era', pp. 105–160 in Shambaugh, D. (ed.). *The Modern Chinese State*. Cambridge: Cambridge University Press.

Terry, L.K. (1995). 'The Hybrid Regimes of Central America', *Journal of Democracy*, 6(3): 72–86.

Tilly, C. (1990). *Coercion, Capital and the European States*. Cambridge & Oxford: Blackwell.

Walicki, A. (1979). *A History of Russian Thought*. Stanford, CA: Stanford University Press.

Wang, Z. (2006). 'Hybrid Regime and Peaceful Development in China', pp. 117–138 in Guo, S. (ed.). *China's 'Peaceful Rise in the 21st Century'*. Aldershot: Ashgate.

White, S. et al. (2010). *Developments in Russia Politics*. Basingstoke: Palgrave Macmillan.

World Bank (2018). *China Overview,* April, http://www.worldbank.org/en/country/china/overview.

Zakaria, F. (1997). 'The Rise of Illiberal Democracy', *Foreign Affairs,* 76(6): 22–43.

Zhao, S. (2013). 'Foreign Policy Implications of Chinese Nationalism Revisited: the strident turn', *Journal of Contemporary China*, 22(82): 535–553.

PART 1

Managing State–Society Relations in Russia and China

∵

In Search of "New Roots": Towards a Situational Ideology in Putin's Russia

Marco Puleri

...in order to better understand a political system, we should take seriously – and therefore pay close attention to – the stories that its political
actors tell about themselves and their system. This is not a Russo-specific
assertion. To understand the United States, we need to be cognizant of
narratives representing the US as the leader of the free world and pro-
moter of democracy. To understand the EU, we must acknowledge its
developing story of ever-closer union. These narratives are repeated,
believed, and enacted. They highlight factors that matter within a political system. They reveal self-conceptualizations that play into policy
development.

> BACON 2015: 230

As stressed by Edwin Bacon in the above-mentioned excerpt from his study
Perspectives for Russia's Future: The Case for Narrative Analysis, "in order to better understand a political system, we should pay close attention to the stories
that its political actors tell about themselves and their system". In the case of
Russia, this entails mainly the need to reconsider the historical legacies coming from imperial and Soviet times. As stressed by Fedor Luk'ianov:

It was long believed that Russia could progress only by rejecting its Soviet
past [...] But today Russia follows the path chosen by its main partner,
China: the past is not only legitimated, but some of its main experiences
are glorified.

> LUK'IANOV 2014: 95[1]

Along these lines, we could describe the Russian political discourse as a process involving a pervasive "look at the past". Looking at the recent conceptuali-
sations of the Russian national idea, we can observe how the discourse flow

---

1 Unless otherwise indicated, translations from Italian and Russian are the author's.

© KONINKLIJKE BRILL NV, LEIDEN, 2020 | DOI:10.1163/9789004428898_003

enacted by the Kremlin follows the dynamics of a "balancing game" in the domestic ideological market (Laruelle 2017b), by "promoting the multinationality of the Russian nation and simultaneously exalting the Russianness of Russia's cultural and historical symbols" (ivi). On the one hand, the set of symbolic resources adopted by the Kremlin "certainly includes 'conservative elements' if it is understood as a wish to lean on 'traditional values' [...] and religion" (Malinova 2014). On the other hand, as stressed by Olga Malinova (ivi) "the problem is that in the Russian context it is not easy to identify a 'tradition' that could be used as a reference point" and, at the same time Orthodoxy cannot represent the core of "a secular and multiconfessional state". As observed by Sergei Sergeev in his latest monograph emblematically entitled *The Russian [russkaia] nation, or the story of its absence* (2017), "behind this fact stands the very logic of Russian history", whereas "it is not by accident that Russian historiography prefers to describe the history of the Russian [rossiiskogo] state, rather than the history of the Russian [russkogo] people".[2] Most likely, "several factors complicate a more universal acceptance of an *ethno-national* identity" (Blakkisrud 2016: 267) in the Russian "multinational state", as defined by Putin in 2012:[3] above all, the ethno-federal structure inherited by the Russian Federation[4] and the legacy of the Soviet ethno-political discourse.[5]

---

2   "Here we have to immediately explain that by using the word 'nation' the author does not mean a specific ethno-cultural community (which Russians undoubtedly were and are), but an ethnopolitical community, i.e. a people acting as a political subject with legally fixed rights [...] Thus, throughout their history, with the exception of the brief period of 1905–1917, Russians were not a political nation. They were and remain a 'sovereign's', serving people, on whose shoulders all the incarnations of the Russian state – the Moscow Tsardom, the Russian Empire, the Soviet Union – were held, and now the Russian Federation is holding" (Sergeev 2017).

3   This is the definition adopted by Vladimir Putin in an article entitled *Russia: the national question*, published in *Nezavisimaia Gazeta* shortly before his re-election as the President of the Russian Federation in 2012: "Russia emerged and has been developing for centuries as a multinational state. A state characterised by an ongoing process of mutual adjustment, mutual understanding, and unification of people through families, friendship and work [...] The rod that binds the fabric of this unique civilization is the Russian people and the Russian culture" (Putin 2012).

4   As observed by Laruelle (2017), "Russian nationalism is a more risky tool that can generate stronger reactions from the 20 percent of the population that doesn't consider itself ethnically Russian and belongs to a national minority, and it can become a mobilizing slogan against the regime for some ethnically Russian grassroots movements".

5   "According to the Soviet self-understanding, the 'nationality question' had been resolved [...] The reluctance to acknowledge the ethnic Russians as the 'state-forming nation', as well as

Accordingly, only in recent years has a new hybrid "Russian idea" come to be defined. It responds to the need to make the current political system "conceivable", whereas following Ekaterina Shul'man's definition (2014), we describe the Russian system as a "hybrid regime":[6]

> But where can we find the fortune of hybridity? It is more flexible and adaptable than autocracy [...] As far as the purpose of a hybrid regime is not to conquer the world, but its own survival, it cannot bear the shackles of ideology. The regime should be free and convey something vague, in order to crawl back or jump over a little at any moment for the sake of self-preservation.
>
> SHUL'MAN 2017a

Actually, we are dealing with a "situational ideology". While throughout the last decades, the discourse of the Russian political elite has focused on several key concepts, such as "a strong state" (2000), "sovereign democracy" (2005), and "modernisation" (2009), which different actors have used in different ways (see Tolz 2001; Petro 2009; Koteyko 2014), nowadays we witness the creation of "floating signifiers" (Laruelle 2015a), to cope with the challenges posed by domestic and foreign affairs. In particular, the translation of the ideas of the Russian World [*Russkii Mir*] and Eurasia into the regime's ideological language works within blurred boundaries. This is the result of the specific dynamics involved in the Russian process of self-representation, which is still working between supranational and national dimensions. Within this framework, the state itself does not need to create a full-fledged ideology: nationalism, imperialism, and conservatism are all included in a situational narrative which answers the needs of the state and cannot be identified as the unique code of self-representation. Most fundamentally, it also responds to the other competing actors in the Russian political space, by appropriating their voices and stances.

---

the fact that the old Soviet slogan about the 'friendship of peoples' found its way into the final version of the new State strategy on Nationalities Policy, further testify to the resilience of traditional Soviet political correctness (Blakkisrud 2016: 269).

6 Recently, the use of this conceptual framework in comparative politics, rather than widespread definitions such as "electoral authoritarianism" (Gel'man 2015) or "personalist autocracy" (Geddes 1999, 2003), has been highly debated and contested by Russian political scientists (see also Golosov 2015, 2017; Shul'man 2015; Ponomareva 2017).

As stressed by Olga Malinova (2014), if the new narrative relies mainly on populism,[7] patriotism[8] and anti-westernism,[9] this "system of meanings can hardly be viewed as a full-fledged ideology offering a coherent worldview", but "it is a fragmented ad hoc construct based on available symbols and primarily intended for consolidating Putin's new majority". Thus, the description of the hybrid and situational nature of the Russian elite's narrative represents the main tool for looking at the latest developments in the contemporary political discourse. In the aftermath of the Ukrainian crisis we witnessed the concrete birth of a new "social contract" signed by both the Kremlin and Russian citizens: this came to be based on the consolidation of "securitized spiritual bonds" (Malinova 2014). As stressed by the Russian political analyst Aleksandr Morozov (2014), three main points are to be symbolically included in the contract: "Firstly, the passage from Putin to 'non-Putin' is not possible as long as Putin is alive ('Non-Putin means non-Russia') [...] Secondly, isolationism [...] Thirdly, the country will not be reformed without Putin".[10]

Along these lines, this chapter will focus on the framework of ideological benchmarks adopted by the Russian elite during Putin's third mandate (2012–2018), in an attempt to understand and interpret the internal dynamics which reshaped the political discourse in the Russian Federation. In a dynamic and culturally oriented approach, we will deal with the processes which have led to political transformation and the consensus-building strategies put in place by the Russian political establishment. We will also focus on the patterns and origins of the current dominant political orientations in Russia through the lens of the main cultural parameters and geopolitics. The research structure will be built around the analysis of official documents and public speeches published and held mainly in 2014–16, and surveys and sociological research on Russian

---

7   "Putin's new ideology has an element of populism suggesting a formal appeal to Demos and democratic principles. Declarations proclaiming the priority of interests of a patriotic majority over the minority critical of the government, or speculation about international norms being non-democratic can serve as examples. As an auxiliary tool, this element lends democratic respectability to the authorities' actions" (Malinova 2014).

8   "'Patriotism' and imperial nationalism have been crucial ingredients of the state support system of beliefs from the very beginning, as they assert the importance of keeping Russia's status of a great power for the well-being of its citizens at present and in future" (ivi).

9   "[...] anti-westernism actually makes up the core of Putin's new ideology, leaning on a well rooted repertoire of stereotypes. It is easily mobilized and has a good consolidating effect [...] Also, anti-westernism helps finalize a body of 'traditional values' which are easier to define as being different from others, rather than by proving their real historical continuity" (ivi).

10   This idea was reflected in the statements by Viacheslav Volodin, chairman of the State Duma, on the occasion of the 2014 edition of the Valdai Club in Sochi (see Izvestiia 2014).

society elaborated by the main research centres in the Russian Federation throughout Putin's third term. Along these lines, we will also pay close attention to other instruments implemented by Russian elites, including legislative measures and government funding.

1   The Road to a New "Political Style": Neo-conservatism (2012–2018)

> The Kremlin's response during Putin's third term has been to deliberately blur the boundaries between the civic *rossiiskii* and the ethnic *russkii* identities. The civic identity has become more explicitly Russian, with the Kremlin holding up the Russian language, culture and traditional values as the core of this identity.
>
> BLAKKISRUD 2016: 267

When dealing with Putin's Russia we usually tend to overestimate the external projection of the Russian role in contested and conflicting world areas by accepting Russian elite self-representation as an internally coherent and cohesive realm, while underestimating the space for contestation in the domestic sphere of the Russian Federation. Nonetheless, even the everlasting failure to normalise Ukrainian-Russian relations has shown us that a central issue that political and cultural analysts often need to take into consideration when studying post-Soviet societies consists of questioning the unresolved national identities which arose in the aftermath of the Soviet collapse.

Along these lines, it was in the aftermath of the contested annexation of Crimea to Russia in March 2014, that the national public debate in the Russian Federation opened up to a more dynamic and polyphonic system of interrelations. Ethnicity, language, and collective memory have been subjected to an intense process of resignification, undertaken mainly by the political elite. The short period of "openness" following the "Crimea campaign" highlighted the rise of heterogeneous voices in the national political debate. Neo-imperialist, nationalist and liberal discourses on Ukraine found their common ground in the Russian geopolitical imagination, whereas "Ukraine is not a political subject but an arena of contestation among geopolitical players" (Zhurzhenko 2016). Thus, only recently has a large part of the internally heterogeneous national intelligentsia come to embrace the so-called "increasingly conservative and nationalistic ideology" (Kolesnikov 2015) proposed by the Kremlin.

In a wider perspective, this is the result of a long-term process which has occurred throughout the last decades, whereas the administrative and economic consolidation which has taken place in the Russian Federation under

Putin's presidential terms has given way to the rise of a new political discourse. At the core of the contemporary intellectual debate lies the construction of a narrative focusing on a renewed post-Soviet "national renaissance" (De Lazari 2014). According to its promoters, the roots of this model are to be found in the so-called historical "Russian political mission", at the crossroads between the West and the East (Basics of State Cultural Policy 2015: 4). This national narrative conveys new benchmark values, bringing together the elements of the Russian Federation's "neoconservative" vision of its role in domestic and foreign affairs.

In following the internal dynamics characterising the Russian Federation throughout the last years, it is worth noticing that the "unexpected" outburst of protests in Moscow and St. Petersburg in 2011–2012, in the aftermath of the State Duma elections, marked the rise of a new important benchmark to be traced in the national narrative: an "ethnic turn" in the elite's discourse, apt to distinguish between "real patriots" and "other" Russians. As observed by Blakkisrud, "in addition to being the biggest manifestations of political opposition since the collapse of the Soviet Union", the 2011–12 demonstrations embodied "a breakthrough for cooperation across ideological divides, with western-oriented liberals overcoming some of their traditional distaste for the Russian ethnonationalists" (Blakkisrud 2016: 255). In response to this, the Russian elite decided to "co-opt some of their rhetoric" (ivi 2016: 255). Thus, following Shul'man's reflections, we could consider the "external projection" of this internal conflict throughout Putin's third mandate, i.e. the neo-conservative shift and the Ukrainian campaign, as a direct answer to the 2011–12 protests:

> I consider the entire Crimean and East Ukrainian story as a consequence or a response of the authorities to the 2011–12 protests. These protests were an objective sociopolitical process: they became a manifestation of the conflict between the society and the system of government [...] The differently directed development of both the "productive forces" and "relations of production", using the language of Marxism [...] led to a conflict that found its realisation in the 2011–12 mass protests.
>
> SHUL'MAN 2017b

Thus, in order to respond to internal conflicts and public mobilisation "from below", throughout the first years of Putin's third mandate we witnessed the ratification of several federal laws which regulated the terms of public discourse, following neo-conservative stances: i.e. the federal law on public meeting (June 2012), the law on "foreign agents" and its direct outcomes for NGOs (July 2012), the law on protecting the religious feelings of Russian citizens against insults or malicious acts (July 2013), and the law banning swearing in arts and media (May 2014). These legislative measures came to be legitimate in the symbolic narrative carried on by the Russian elite on the new "clash of ci-vilisations" between Russian traditional values and the "spiritual decay of the West". It is no coincidence that in his address to the Federal Assembly in De-cember 2013 Putin referred to the philosopher Nikolai Berdiaev (1874–1948), quoting his statements on the decay of western civilisation in the early 20th century:

> We know that there are more and more people in the world who support our position on defending traditional values that have made up the spiri-tual and moral foundation of civilisation in every nation for thousands of years: the values of traditional families, real human life, including reli-gious life, not just material existence but also spirituality, the values of humanism and global diversity. Of course, this is a conservative position. But speaking in the words of Nikolai Berdiaev, the point of conservatism is not that it prevents movement forward and upward, but that it pre-vents movement backward and downward, into chaotic darkness and a return to a primitive state.
>
> PUTIN 2013

As observed by Laruelle (2017), "fostering conservatism provides a much easier ideological framework" for the Kremlin.[11] Throughout the Russian Federation's recent history state actors have been stuck in an ideological impasse, alterna-tively shifting their focus from a civic *rossiiskii* to an ethnic *russkii* understand-ing of the Russian national idea (see Shevel 2011; Blakkisrud 2016). Even during the Ukraine crisis, Putin's address on the inclusion of Crimea and Sevastopol as subjects of the Russian Federation in March 2014 was considered a crucial shift to an ethnic conceptualisation of the "Russian question".[12] Nonetheless, only

---

11   "The presidential administration therefore succeeded in developing an *explicit* but blurry narrative of conservatism – embodied by anti-westernism, anti-liberalism, and the pro-motion of so-called traditional moral values – and in offering an *implicit* ideological di-versity available for collective consumption. These doctrinal products are elaborated by different groups of ideological entrepreneurs who have room to act [...] Their fragile en-trepreneurship must work in permanent negotiation and tension with competing groups and the presidential administration itself" (Laruelle 2017b).

12   Such is the perspective claimed by the Norwegian scholar Helge Blakkisrud: "[...] Putin went even further in linking the fate of the ethnic Russians and Russian statehood [...] Putin consistently used the term *russkii* rather than rossiiskii [...] In other words, bringing the peninsula back under Moscow's control was not only legitimised by Crimea historically

through the lens of the much more flexible pattern of conservatism can we observe how the national question has been recently reframed. Evidence comes from the 2013 Valdai Club meeting, whose results were published in February 2014, on the eve of the Ukraine crisis. The report *National identity and the Future of Russia* better testifies to the main core of the new directions recently undertaken in the Russian "struggle for meanings". In the section emblematically entitled *Culture as the basis of Russian identity*, conservatism and identity find their common ground in "Russian culture" – as selectively conceptualised by the editors of the report:

> Any attempt to formulate national identity through the ethnic or religious prism contradicts the entire history of *Rossiiskii/Russkii* civilisation [...] Historically in Russia the dominant culture is the Russian [*russkaia*]. The Russian [*rossiiskaia*] national identity should be built on the principle of a common cultural field, with vivid national fragments enriching the basic culture. We are not a nation-state or an empire. In the long term, the hybrid form of a cultural-civic nation is the closest one to Russia as a country. The links lying in the cultural field, which were codified in the great Russian literature, music, painting, architecture and cinema, are the most lasting integrator for all the people who connect themselves with Russia.
>
> VALDAI 2014: 30–31

In the framework of the conservative shift, which can be considered "a deliberate attempt to 'neutralise' liberal Russians" (Bennetts 2017) in the aftermath of the 2011–12 protests, nowadays Orthodox and radical nationalist groups "are permitted to exist by the authorities", representing the "marginal, extreme side of the state's official dialogue" (ivi). It was mainly the "patriotic mobilisation" in 2014 that deeply influenced the co-optation of radical actors in the state discourse. Specifically, it was among the nationalistic and imperialistic segments of the Russian cultural milieu that the Russian intervention in Crimea came to reconcile the internal fracture with state-actors, as claimed by the fantasy writer and historian of Belarusian origin Kirill Benediktov in February 2014:

> I do not understand my colleagues, the Russian nationalists, who rejoice in the victories of the rebels in Kiev, looking at it only as Putin's defeat

---

having been part of the Russian Empire and the RSFSR – the peninsula was also considered ethnic Russian lands" (Blakkisrud 2016: 259).

and humiliation. Comrades, Putin will leave but the Russian people will remain. And the Russophobic, Western Ukraine, that you are welcoming now, will also remain [...] Therefore, I am, of course, for Russia's intervention in the Ukraine Crisis. And I am with those who call for intervening in defence of the Russians in Crimea and in the Southeast with "all power and glory".

BENEDIKTOV 2014

Benediktov is the editor in chief of the online platform "*Russkaia* Idea – Site on conservative political thought", which was sponsored by the Institute for Socio-Economic and Political Studies (ISEPR), a new influential think tank founded in 2012, soon after Putin's re-election, and financed with presidential grants until late 2015. According to its editors, the platform "is devoted to the issue of 'political conservatism' in relation to the new ideology for Russia" (Russkaia Idea 2014).

Within this framework, it is worth noting that following Putin's election in 2012, by creating new non-governmental organisations and think tanks under the direction of figures close to the presidential administration, the position of "experts" in the decision making process gained a primary role in codifying the new ideological lines in the Kremlin's public communication. In the Russian "struggle for meanings", institutions such as ISEPR and FoRGO – the Foundation for Civil Society Development, which was also founded in 2012 – came to bridge the gap created by the lack of ideological representativeness played by political parties in the Russian Federation. The former in particular has been engaged in promoting neoconservative values and categories. The newly established ISEPR was behind the organisation of three conferences in 2014, which were held in Moscow and Crimea, devoted to "Berdiaev Readings". On the occasion of his opening speech at the Forum Dmitrii Badovskii, Chairman of the Board of Directors of the ISEPR Foundation and member of the Civic Chamber of the Russian Federation, stressed that "conservatism is not so much an ideology", but a "political style" (ISEPR 2014):

> [...] Crimea's reunification with Russia the way it happened demonstrated that Russia has one of the greatest potentials for so-called soft power. But it is important for us that our "smart power" grows. For this to happen researchers should discuss ideas of what modern conservatism can be like, what conservative strategy should be in modern politics. I'd call the modern position that our country and President Vladimir Putin defend "a polite conservatism" [...]

Most fundamentally, the functioning of ideological platforms such as ISEPR testifies to the constant reshaping of cultural benchmarks and identity markers in the contemporary Russian Federation, marking a new point of intersection between state and non-state actors. This testifies to how social mobilisation during the Ukraine crisis "also strongly influenced Russian society and public discourse" (Kolstø 2016: 702), especially affecting the cultural *milieu*. As Benediktov observed in February 2014, on the eve of the Crimean annexation to Russia, "the events of the last days in Ukraine have extremely aroused the creative part of our society" (Benediktov 2014). Especially for the nationalistic segments of the Russian cultural milieu, the Russian intervention in Crimea acted to reconcile their internal fracture with state-actors. Notable fantasy writers such as Sergei Lukianenko immediately assumed a pro-Kremlin stance, while only recently the Russia's PEN Center lost some of its most prominent liberal members, such as Sviatlana Aleksievich and Boris Akunin, who disapproved of the "conformist" and "servile" position taken by the institution.[13]

The shifting political positions assumed by the segment of Russian imperial nationalists can further shed light on the alternative outlooks endorsed by the intellectual environment throughout the crisis.[14] Among these, the experiences of the Russian writers Eduard Limonov and Zakhar Prilepin, respectively the leader and a prominent member of the National Bolshevik Party (NBP), clearly reflect the subtle nuances of social mobilisation that occurred during the different phases of the crisis. In his article emblematically entitled *The Journey of National Bolsheviks towards Putin and Back Again*, Il'ia Azar (2017) retraces the origins and the recent story of one of the most relevant parties of the opposition groups which "have seen their ideological stance challenged during the Ukrainian Crisis" (Laruelle 2017: 92). Appearing in the 1990s, and labelled "imperial nationalists" (Kolstø 2016: 707), the so-called *Limonovtsy* "created a vivid youth counterculture around music, aesthetics, dress codes, and street violence targeting official institutions, such as police headquarters and the judicial administration" (Laruelle 2017: 91). It was not until 2014 that the NBP partly reconciled with the Kremlin:

---

13   Only on September 20, 2017, the St. Petersburg PEN centre, a liberal branch of the Russian PEN centre, was elected an independent member of the International Pen Club. This was on the occasion of the 83rd World Congress which was held in L'viv, to which the leadership of the Russian PEN centre was not invited.

14   In his *Crimea vs. Donbas: How Putin Won Russian Nationalist Support and Lost it Again*, Kolstø (2016) highlighted how the situational and floating ideological references used by state actors deeply affected the unstable directions undertaken by non-state actors in the public debate.

The National Bolsheviks – once the most vivid of the opposition forces to Putin – after the annexation of Crimea to Russia believed in the revival of the Russian imperial project. They sent around 2000 volunteers to the Donbass along with the "Interbrigada" and fought the war. But the dream of the DNR [Donetsk National Republic] as a country where National Bolsheviks could engage in politics holding weapons and build new social justice quickly collapsed.

AZAR 2017

While in the aftermath of the Crimean annexation "Eduard Limonov attacked his former allies in the Russian opposition for their failure to welcome Crimea into Russia" (Kolstø 2016: 718), it was the prolonged and bloody war in Donbas that again distanced the NBP from the Kremlin. In contrast to Limonov, Zakhar Prilepin has even recently maintained a pro-Kremlin stance. In early 2017, he reached the battlefield in Donbas with his own volunteer battalion (Kots 2017). By calling on the tradition of Russian "literary spetsnaz",[15] Prilepin's decision has emblematically received the public praise of Sergei Lavrov, the Russian minister of Foreign Affairs (Ukraïns'ka Pravda 2017).

2   A New (Old?) National Cultural Code: Translating *Russkii Mir* and *Eurasia* into the Regime Language

Adherence to culture and values is seen as more important than ancestry and genes when it comes to defining who is in and who is out. The boundaries of the *russkii* identity are opened up so as to include members of other ethnic groups that subscribe to the values-based identity now promoted by the Kremlin [...] The new take on national identity thus not only contributes to rallying considerable support for the regime within the Russian Federation, it also opens up for reaching out to the Russian and Russified diaspora in the neighbouring states.

BLAKKISRUD 2016: 267–271

---

15   "In general, when I began to reflect on this topic, this phrase came to my mind: 'We have special forces of Russian literature behind us'. We certainly knew that Gumilev, Lev Tolstoi were serving somewhere... But in fact this list is huge. In Russia, since the 18th century, I counted more than a hundred among poets and writers, whose life was directly connected with military service. Over here impostors of Russian literature began to prove, that the Russian writer is such a little prick on thin legs which always speaks of children's tears or other touching things" (Kots 2017).

As shown by the legislative provisions adopted by the Russian elite, the institutionalisation of Russian culture and conservatism as the main benchmarks in defining the national idea was codified in December 2014, with the ratification of the "Basics of State Cultural policy", which are considered to be "an integral part of the Russian Federation National Security Strategy" (Basics of State Cultural Policy 2015: 3). This new passage in the contemporary political discourse leads to the crystallisation of the Kremlin situational narrative in a concrete normative policy. The document follows the main lines of the draft project published in May 2014 by Sergei Ivanov (see Basics of State Cultural Policy 2014), the head of the presidential administration until August 2016. Here, finally the national "cultural code" comes to have a normative value:

> The national "cultural code" is "a system of distinctive, dominant social values, meanings and attitudes (knowledge, skills, intellectual, moral and aesthetic development, philosophy of life, forms of communication, spiritual enlightenment), which took shape in the process of historical civilisational development, and which is adopted as common standard for self-identification of people regardless of their ethnicity and is transmitted from generation to generation through upbringing, education and training".
>
> Basics of State Cultural Policy 2015: 26

As observed by Il'ia Kalinin (2015), "in this new language of the Russian cultural policy, 'patriotism' stands for loyalty to the politics undertaken by the state, 'love for the homeland' stands for support of the current elite, 'cultural tradition' stands for tradition of the Russian strong and autocratic statuality [...] This normativization has its foundations in the idea of nation and in the approval of unity as the main national value". Within this normative frame, the "national roots" and the national culture come to represent the core of the new Russian idea: according to Kalinin (2015), the pragmatic aspect of this extreme change of direction lies in "the use of culture for strategic interest, adopting it as the main subject in foreign politics and the main tool in order to consolidate the electorate".

Most fundamentally, here we come to an important distinction to make between "pure" cultural categories and their political use – and normativisation – in the contemporary Russian elite's discourse. The ambiguous path followed by the Russian elite in appropriating different – and often contradictory – cultural references, in order to react to critical junctures in internal and foreign politics, is the answer to the search for a balance between state controlled "patriotism" and the radical stances taken up by other social subgroups in the public discourse.[16] On the one hand, this approach lies behind the constant process of translating nationalistic and imperialistic stances in a more functional way (i.e. a way that needs to function for the regime to consolidate consensus), which was undertaken by the Russian political establishment in recent years. On the other hand, the legitimation of conservative stances followed the externalisation of the internal conflict *beyond* the borders of the Russian Federation, but *within* the blurred boundaries of the "Russian cultural space".

The "Crimean euphoria" also served as a catalyst for new external projections of the Russian idea, mostly answering the need for ideological promotion and legitimation in the regional and international arena. Specifically, the conceptual appropriation and institutionalisation within state agencies of the Russian World [*Russkii Mir*] and Eurasian conceptual frames, both claiming the existence of a Russian-led "civilisation", works exactly within blurred boundaries. As for the former, Laruelle retraced the origins of the current post-Soviet term in the work of "image-makers" such as Gleb Pavlovskii and Petr Shchedrovitskii back in the 1990s, in the framework of conceptualisation of CIS policy. *Russkii Mir* was then adopted in the 2000s by state actors for strategic interests, mainly referring to "Russia's policy for its Near Abroad", "Russia's interaction with Russian diasporas in the world" and "Russia's brand, both as a public-relations project and a messianic project" (Laruelle 2015a: 6). We are dealing with a conceptualisation of Russian identity as a "transnational community" gathering together those who are united by Russian language and culture. It is no coincidence that on the occasion of the address to the Federal Assembly in April 2007, significantly in the aftermath of the EU's eastward enlargement and the "colour revolutions" in Georgia and Ukraine, Vladimir Putin highlighted the symbolic importance of the Russian language for demarcating the boundaries of "Russianness":

> Russian is the language of a historical fraternity of peoples, a true language of international communication. The Russian language not only preserves an entire layer of truly global achievements but is also the living space for the many millions of people in the Russian-speaking world, a community that goes far beyond Russia itself.
>
> PUTIN 2007

---

16   As for the broader repertoire of philosophical and literary references adopted by the Kremlin, the Russian elite alternatively shifted from the philosophers Nikolai Berdiaev and Ivan Il'in, to historians and statesmen such as Nikolai Karamzin and Petr Stolypin. For further reading, see Laruelle 2017a; Schillinger 2015.

Following a blurred balance between a purely cultural and a political understanding of the concept, the Russian elite then created the Russkii Mir Foundation in June 2007, through the joint efforts of the ministries of Foreign Affairs
and of Education and Science, significantly "opening up to all those interested
in supporting Russia in the world" (Laurelle 2015a: 13). This works in parallel
with Russia's other foreign policy projects, such as the Compatriots' (*sootechest-
venniki*) project directed at the Near Abroad (see Shevel 2011), and the term
Russian World was emblematically used by Vladimir Putin in the March 2014
address on Crimea.[17] Since the outbursts of the 2011–12 protests and Putin's re-
election in 2012, the concept has emblematically become "less associated with
dispersed people – bearers of 'Russianness' – and more with territories and
historical legacies" (Suslov 2016: 295). As observed by Mikhail Suslov, even in
the national Orthodox geopolitical imagination, since Patriarch Kirill became
the head of the Russian Orthodox Church in 2009, this began to signify, along
with the twin concept of Holy Rus, "an ethnically and religious united landmass, comprised of Russia proper, Belarus, Ukraine, and, depending on the
geopolitical appetites of ideologues, parts of other post-Soviet republics" (ivi).
According to Laruelle, even if it "is poorly articulated", the Russian world concept "functions in almost complete harmony with the Kremlin's new conservative agenda", whereas "both repertoires advance the idea or assumption that
Russia represents a unique civilization" (Laruelle 2015a: 20).

Moreover, the rather fluid civilisation conceptualised under the Russian
World umbrella "is simultaneously broader and smaller than the Eurasian one"
(ivi: 18),[18] another relevant ideological tool included in the situational narrative which was constructed by the Russian elite. The idea of a civilisation embracing Europe and Asia, which came to be clearly upheld in the Basics of State

---

17   While supporting the aspiration for self-determination of Crimean people, the Russian
     president addressed the Western counterpart, comparing the 2014 annexation of Crimea
     to German reunification in 1990: "I believe that Europeans will understand me, and first of
     all Germans. Let me remind you that in the course of political consultations on the unifi-
     cation of the FRG and DDR [...] not all the representatives of the countries which are and
     were then allies of Germany supported the idea of unification. And our country, on the
     contrary, unequivocally supported the sincere, overwhelming aspiration of Germans for
     national unity. I am certain that you have not forgotten it, and I expect that German citi-
     zens will also support the aspiration of the Russian world (*Russkogo mira*), of historical
     Russia to restore unity" (Putin 2014).
18   As emblematically stressed by Laruelle (2015a: 18), the Russian world concept "is broader
     because its founding principle is to structure Russia's voice in the world [...] It is smaller
     because within the post-Soviet space, it focuses mostly on Russian ethnic minorities and
     Russian speakers [...] In contrast the Eurasian narrative puts so-called 'titular' and Rus-
     sian-speaking populations on the same level, without discrimination" (Laruelle 2015a: 18).

Cultural Policy (2015), is deeply rooted in the Russian intellectual tradition, but in the case of the post-Soviet "revival" of Eurasia we should again refrain from a purely cultural understanding of the term.[19] As suggested by Laruelle (2015), today we should consider "Eurasia without Eurasianism", i.e. we should differentiate between the intellectual constructs of Russian intellectuals of the 1920s and 1930s, laying the foundation of the Eurasian movement, and the recent revival of the term. Similarly to the Russian World, in the Russian political elite's discourse Eurasia was also translated into a "floating" ideological signifier, but differently from the former – which mainly addresses society – it directly affects the "institutional, economic and strategic reality" (Laruelle 2015a: 18). On the one hand, this is the case of the Eurasian integration project – under the umbrella of the Eurasian Economic Union – which was officially ratified in 2014 by the leaders of Belarus, Kazakhstan and Russia, and later the same year joined by Armenia and Kyrgyzstan, or the Greater Eurasian strategy, claimed by Putin in 2016 as the country's new geopolitical framework embracing the entire Eurasian landmass – and significantly opened to both China and the EU (see Prezident Rossi 2016); on the other hand, this is the case of the Eurasian model of economic modernisation, which – as emphasised by Lissovolik (2015) for the Valdai Forum platform – can be pursued as a gradual integration into the world economy, i.e. combining integration efforts in Europe and Asia, or as a tool for prioritizing multilateralism in the world economy.

Also in this case, the creation of ideological platforms such as the Izborskii Club, founded at the end of 2012 by Aleksandr Prokhanov, Vitalii Aver'ianov, and Andrei Kobiakov, claiming and supporting neo-Eurasianism as the ideological doctrine for the Russian state, "reveals the existence of autonomous spaces" in the public discourse which are "authorized by the regime, sometimes supported, some marginalized" (Laruelle 2016: 644). Significantly, this "confirms the progressive structuring of a field of 'think tanks' in Russia whose function is to occupy different ideological niches and offer a range of 'products' that the authorities can sample, make official, or reject" (ivi). As emphasised by

---

19   In the introduction to the all-encompassing research work entitled *Russian Eurasianism. An Ideology of Empire* (2008), Laruelle clearly explains the paradoxical dynamics of the Eurasian revival in the 21st century: "Since the beginning of the 2000s [...] the term 'Eurasia' has undergone a profound transformation. It has grown beyond the purely intellectual circles to which it had been confined for about a decade, entering a larger public space. The idea of 'Eurasia' has become the victim of its own success, because it is now being used as a catchall vision of Russia. Though Eurasianist theories as such remain little known, the idea of a Eurasian entity encompassing the center of the Old Continent, in which Russia would be 'at home', is becoming ever more widespread" (Laruelle 2008: 1–2).

Laruelle, today the term Eurasia responds to different claims arising in both the domestic and international arena:

> Under the label "Eurasia", it is in fact possible to express a geopolitical principle – that is, Russia's claim to be the "pivotal" state and "engine" of the post-Soviet world [...] But the term can also be used to designate a philosophical principle – that is, Russia's status as the "other Europe" [...] Lastly, the term "Eurasia" also points to a third dimension, that of memory, mourning, and commemoration. Through it Russian society can understand the imperial and Soviet experiences [...].
>
> LARUELLE 2015: 191

It is no coincidence that in the aftermath of the diplomatic paralysis between Russia and the EU the term has become more central in the Kremlin's narrative, while the Russian World concept is losing its focus. This is the case of the recent Ukraine crisis: whereas the supporters of the Euromaidan revolution clearly opted for the European integration model – thus discarding the Eurasian option, the Kremlin invoked the defence of the rights of the Russian and Russian-speaking minorities in the neighbouring country and the right of the Russian World "to restore unity" (Putin 2014), while later switching again to the broader Eurasian ideological "container" in the face of the "clash of civilisations" with "liberal" Europe – and its "crumbling" integration process. Eventually, borrowing Laruelle's definition, we can conclude that "the Russian World, in the sense of Russian minorities, is invoked when Eurasia fails" (Laruelle 2015a: 18), and vice versa. This still significantly reveals the reactive – more than strategic – use of ideological benchmarks in the Russian Federation elite's discourse: if, on the one hand, it is aimed at influencing developments in regional – i.e. in other post-Soviet republics – and international arenas – i.e. Russia as the herald of an alternative model of integration, on the other hand it also responds to the need to find a point of intersection between the different actors in the domestic ideological market – i.e. alternatively mobilizing and demobilizing the electorate.

3   "Rebounding" Ideologies: A Fluid Repertoire for Reactive Use

In conclusion, the main research question at the core of the scientific debate around the nature of the contemporary political discourse in the Russian Federation can be reframed as follows: Is it possible to define a unique – and unifying – state ideology in the Russian Federation? Following the lines suggested in this study, we can assume that today it is exactly the fluidity of the ideological repertoire – provided by "experts" and adopted by state actors – that responds to the situational dimension of Russia's on-going process of self-representation. Eventually, looking at the concrete questions posed by international geopolitical issues throughout the first decades of the 21st century, the redefinition of the role of the Russian Federation in national, post-Soviet and global arenas follows a specific path which – adopting the definition proposed by D. Arel and B.A. Ruble (2006) – could be described as a constant identity-transition or negotiation: "Identities 'rebound' rather than becoming resolved" (*ibid.*: 336).

In light of the above described assumptions, here we deal with a plurality of discourses and movements, which establish a specific kind of relation to the state narrative. Under Putin's third term the ideological framework proposed by the Kremlin succeeded in distancing the public consensus on the elite from the economic and social prospects of Russians, thus creating a significant gap between the image of the country offered by the power and social claims. This is evident from the data included in the social-economic indices published by Levada Centre, a non-governmental sociological research centre in Russia (see Levada): while the government still boasts high ratings, the indices show how the worsening economic situation in the aftermath of the Ukraine crisis has clearly affected social expectations.

Nonetheless, as noted by Denis Volkov (2017) in his commentary emblematically entitled *"Crimea" does not work: Why people are coming back to the streets*, throughout 2017 this gap eventually began to be contested and recognised on the occasion of the March and June protests against corruption in the Russian government. These demonstrations differed significantly from the 2011–12 protests: they took place only in Moscow and a few other cities; they were mainly supported by younger generations; and they took shape on social networks, such as Facebook and Vkontakte. As observed by Konstantin Gaaze, the new protesters found in Aleksei Naval'nyi, a Russian blogger and politician already active in the 2011–12 demonstrations, "a symbol for claiming a new form of politics for those who see present life too cramped and stuffy" (Mikhalchenko 2017). The 2017 events were "therefore not a revolution but rather a sort of petition for substantive revision of the social contract" (Kolesnikov 2017). Most fundamentally, it was the June protests in Moscow against the urban renovation plan initiated by mayor Sergei Sobianin that showed how the Russian elite is not yet ready to manage a political mobilisation from below coming from that part of Putin's electorate which is "satisfied with him overall as a symbol of Russia's renewed grandeur", but "dissatisfied with their social standing or the actions of the authorities" (Kolesnikov 2017).

This was the prelude to Putin's re-election in 2018, whereas in the forthcoming mandate "the real challenge will be the mismatch between the expectations of the Russian people and the decisions that the regime will have to make after the election" (Makarkin 2017). After an extended period of speculation on the regime transition towards the elections, Vladimir Putin confirmed his candidacy only on December 6, 2017 during a meeting with workers at the Gor'kii Automobile Factory in Nizhnii Novgorod. On the occasion of his annual televised press conference held a week later, Putin then confirmed his decision to run for re-election as an independent candidate, significantly underscoring "the Kremlin's determination to cast him as a leader who has grown far beyond ordinary politicians" (Hille 2017). Confident in his high approval ratings, which in November 2017 were around 80% (see Levada ratings), the current Russian president looked for a great legitimation in the elections, aiming also at a high turnout at the polls in March 2018. It is no coincidence that the most credible opponent to Putin's re-election, Aleksei Naval'nyi, while officially barred from running in the 2018 presidential elections, called on his supporters to boycott the election in response (see Vishnevskii 2018).[20]

Looking at the shaping of the new (old?) ideological framework which preceded the election, a controversial portrait of the Russian leader seemed to emerge: on the one hand, significantly far from the "Crimean euphoria", we witnessed the rise of a Putin-"peacemaker" (Nikol'skii et al. 2017), announcing the withdrawal of Russian troops from Syria and facilitating a prisoner swap between Ukrainian authorities and the separatists in Donbas (The Moscow Times 2017); on the other hand, this happened while great-power sentiment in Russia reached a historic high (Mukhametshina 2017). This can perhaps be explained by interpreting the message delivered by Vladimir Putin in his last public speech before the election: in his March 1 address to parliament, we witnessed how the Russian elite's ambition came to be mainly reframed as "building an economic and technological 'West' inside Russia, while continuing an aggressive posture towards the West on the outside" (Baunov 2018).

---

20   As part of the "authorised opposition", as Ekaterina Shul'man (2017) highlighted, "little Naval'nyis" emerged, whereas among the new candidates we had: Pavel Grudinin, the new presidential candidate of the Communist Party – even though the leader Gennadii Ziuganov headed his campaign headquarters; Ksenia Sobchak, daughter of Anatolii Sobchak and liberal journalist who standed as a "protest candidate" – even if observers criticised her candidacy as Kremlin-backed; and Boris Titov, a business ombudsman representing the Party of Growth, who – although he is a figure strictly tied to the presidential administration – was the voice of Russia's leading liberal minds.

Emblematically, even in light of the results of the 2018 elections, Putin's outstanding victory can now be read as the time for the "sacralisation of Post-Crimea Russia" (Stanovaia 2018) – or as the final act in the successful reshaping (or rebounding) of Russian "roots and values" throughout Putin's third mandate, in order to regain power to eventually mobilise the majority of Russians from the top. At the time of writing (July 2018) we can value the ability of the Russian political elite to neutralise the space for contestation in the domestic sphere, by creating a shared ideological space with other factions of Russian society, such as ethnonationalists and Orthodox fringes, integrating and reframing their claims in the state discourse. It is exactly the proper functioning of the current social contract between state and society that can explain Putin's high approval rating throughout the last years (Kalegina 2017).

Bibliography

Arel, D., and Ruble B.A. (2006). *Rebounding Identities*. Baltimore: The John Hopkins University Press.

Azar, I. (2017). 'Puteshestvie natsbolov k Putinu i obratno', *Novaia Gazeta*, 12 March, https://www.novayagazeta.ru/articles/2017/03/12/71752-puteshestvie-natsbolov-k-putinu-i-obratno.

Bacon, E. (2015). 'Perspectives for Russia's Future: The Case for Narrative Analysis', pp. 229–237 in Pikulicka-Wilczewska, A., and Sakwa, R. (eds.), *Ukraine and Russia. People, Politics, Propaganda and Perspectives*. Bristol: E-International Relations Publishing.

Basics of State Cultural Policy. (2014). 'Osnovy gosudarstvennoi kul'turnoi politiki (Proekt)', *Ministerstvo Kultury Rossiiskoi Federatsii*, 16 May, http://kremlin.ru/events/administration/21027.

Basics of State Cultural Policy. (2015). 'Osnovy gosudarstvennoi kul'turnoi politiki', *Ministerstvo Kultury Rossiiskoi Federatsii*, http://mkrf.ru/info/foundations-state-cultural-policy/.

Baunov, A. (2018). 'A Hi-Tech Russian Doll: Putin's Fourth-Term Reboot', *Carnegie Moscow Center*, 9 March, http://carnegie.ru/commentary/75751.

Benediktov, K. (2014). 'Esli zavtra voina', *Vzgliad*, 22 February, https://vz.ru/columns/2014/2/22/673796.html.

Bennetts, M. (2017). 'From here to eternity', *Eurozine*, 4 September, http://www.eurozine.com/from-here-to-eternity/.

Blakkisrud, H. (2016). 'Blurring the boundary between civic and ethnic: The Kremlin's new approach to national identity under Putin's third term', pp. 249–274 in

Blakkisrud, H. and Kolstø, P. (eds.), *The New Russian Nationalism. Imperialism, Ethnicity and Authoritarianism 2000–15*. Edinburgh: Edinburgh University Press.

De Lazari, A. (2014). 'Russkaia ideia "po-putinski"', *Gefter*, 21 May, http://gefter.ru/archive/12304.

Geddes, B. (1999). 'What Do We Know about Democratization after Twenty Years?', *Annual Review of Political Science*, 2: 115–144.

Geddes, B. (2003). *Paradigms and Sand Castles: Theory Building and Research Design in Comparative Politics*. Ann Arbor: The University of Michigan Press.

Gel'man, V. (2015). *Authoritarian Russia. Analyzing Post-Soviet Regime Changes*. Pittsburgh: Pittsburgh University Press.

Golosov, G. (2015). 'Rossiia: "Elektoral'nyi avtoritarizm" ili "gibridnyi rezhim"?', *Slon*, 24 February, https://republic.ru/app.php/posts/1607.

Golosov G. (2017). 'Est' demokraticheskie rezhimy i est' avtoritarnye. Nuzhno li znat' chto-to eshche?', *Republic*, 10 January, https://republic.ru/app.php/posts/78343.

Hille, K. (2017). 'Russian President Putin to run for re-election as an independent', *Financial Times*, 14 December, https://www.ft.com/content/fd9ac41b-85da-3562-b07b-4c819978766b.

ISEPR. (2014). 'The ISEPR Foundation held the first "Berdyaev Readings"', 19 May, http://www.isepr.ru/en/news/The+ISEPR+Foundation+held+the+first+%E2%80%98Berdyaev+Readings%E2%80%99/.

Izvestiia. (2014). 'Est' Putin – est' Rossiia, net Putina – net Rossii', *Izvestiia*, 22 October, https://iz.ru/news/578379.

Kalegina, M. (2017). '"Levada-tsentr": Elektoral'nyi reiting Putina dostig istoricheskogo maksimuma', *life.ru*, 29 May, https://life.ru/t/%D0%BD%D0%BE%D0%B2%D0%BE%D1%81%D1%82%D0%B8/1012200/lievada-tsientr_eliektoralnyi_rieitingh_putina_dostigh_istorichieskogho_maksimuma.

Kalinin, I. (2015). 'Kul'turnaia politika kak instrument demodernizatsii', *Polit.ru*, 15 February, http://polit.ru/article/2015/02/15/cultural_policy/.

Kolesnikov, A. (2015). 'Russian Ideology after Crimea', *Carnegie Moscow Center*, 22 September, http://carnegie.ru/2015/09/22/russian-ideology-after-crimea/ihzq?mkt_tok=3RkMMJWWfF9wsRohu6zOZKXonjHpfsX56OosW6S2lMI/0ER3fOvrPUfGjI4HS8BrI%2BSLDwEYGJlv6SgFSrnAMbBwzLgFWhI%3D.

Kolesnikov, A. (2017). 'New Protests Question Russia's Social Contract', *Carnegie Europe*, 16 June, http://carnegieeurope.eu/strategiceurope/71283.

Kolstø, P. (2016). 'Crimea vs. Donbas: How Putin Won Russian Nationalist Support – and Lost it Again', *Slavic Review*, 75(3): 702–725.

Koteyko, N. (2014). *Language and Politics in Post-Soviet Russia*. London-New York: Palgrave Macmillan.

Kots, A. (2017). 'Zakhar Prilepin sobral v DNR svoi batal'on', *Komsomol'skaia Pravda*, 13 February, http://www.kp.ru/daily/26642.5/3661046/.

Laruelle, M. (2008). *Russian Eurasianism: An Ideology of Empire*. Baltimore: John Hopkins University Press.

Laruelle, M. (2015). 'Postface. The Paradoxical Legacy of Eurasianism in Contemporary Eurasia', pp. 187–193 in Bassin, M., Glebov, S., Laruelle, M. (eds.), *Between Europe and Asia: The Origins, Theories and Legacies of Russian Eurasianism*. Pittsburgh: Pittsburgh University Press.

Laruelle, M. (2015a). *The 'Russian World'. Russia's Soft Power and Geopolitical Imagination*. Washington, D.C.: Center on Global Interests.

Laruelle, M. (2016). 'The Izborsky Club, or the New Conservative Avant-Garde in Russia', *The Russian Review*, 75: 626–644.

Laruelle, M. (2017). 'Is Nationalism a Force for Change in Russia?', *Deadalus*, 2: 89–100.

Laruelle, M. (2017a). 'In Search of Putin's Philosopher', *Intersection*, 3 March, http://intersectionproject.eu/article/politics/search-putins-philosopher.

Laruelle, M. (2017b). 'Putin's Regime and the Ideological Market: A Difficult Balancing Game', *Carnegie Endowment for International Peace*, 16 March, http://carnegieendowment.org/2017/03/16/putin-s-regime-and-ideological-market-difficult-balancing-game-pub-68250.

Levada. 'Sotsial'no-ekonomicheskie indikatory', http://www.levada.ru/indikatory/sotsialno-ekonomicheskie-indikatory/ (11/2017).

Levada ratings. 'Indicators: Putin's approval rating', Levada Center, https://www.levada.ru/en/ratings/ (11/2017).

Lissovolik, Ya. (2015). 'Russia's Eurasian Model of Modernization', *Valdai Discussion Club*, 2 December, http://valdaiclub.com/a/highlights/russia-s-eurasian-model-of-modernization/.

Luk'ianov [Luk'janov], F. (2014). 'Ritorno alle origini', *Limes*, 12: 93–100.

Makarkin, A. (2017). 'The Test for Russia is Not the 2018 Election But What Follows', *Carnegie Moscow Center*, 25 May, http://carnegie.ru/commentary/70077.

Malinova, O. (2014). '"Spiritual Bounds" as State Ideology', *Russia in Global Affairs*, 18 December, http://eng.globalaffairs.ru/number/Spiritual-Bonds-as-State-Ideology-17223.

Mikhalchenko, E. (2017). 'Deti Putina na razvalinakh Kremlia, ili Chto novogo v novykh protestakh?', *Colta.ru*, 14 June, http://www.colta.ru/articles/society/15110.

Morozov, A. (2014). 'Obshchestvo bez tormozov, ili novyi kontrakt Putina s Rossiei', *Vedomosti*, 26 December, http://www.vedomosti.ru/opinion/articles/2014/12/26/bez-tormozov.

Mukhametshina, E. (2017). 'Velikoderzhavnye nastroeniia v Rossii dostigli istoricheskogo maksimuma', *Vedomosti*, 21 December, https://www.vedomosti.ru/politics/articles/2017/12/21/746009-velikoderzhavnie-nastroeniya.

Nikol'skii, A. et. al. (2017). 'Putin idet na vybory kak mirotvorets', *Vedomosti*, 17 December, https://www.vedomosti.ru/politics/articles/2017/12/11/744880-putin-mirotvorets.

Ponomareva, A. (2017). 'Ukraina, Somali, Zimbabve', *Radio Svoboda*, 5 January, http://www.svoboda.org/a/28215609.html.

Petro, N.N. (2009). 'The Great Transformation: How the Putin Plan Altered Russian Society', *ISPI – Policy Brief*, 132: 1–6.

Prezident Rossii. (2016). 'Plenarnoe zasedanie Peterburgskogo mezhdunarodnogo ekonomicheskogo foruma'. 17 June, http://kremlin.ru/events/president/news/52178.

Putin, V. (2007). 'Annual Address to the Federal Assembly', *President of Russia*, 26 April, http://en.kremlin.ru/events/president/transcripts/24203.

Putin, V. (2012). 'Rossiia: Natsional'nyi vopros', *Nezavisimaia Gazeta*, 23 January, http://www.ng.ru/politics/2012-01-23/1_national.html.

Putin, V. (2013). 'Poslanie Prezidenta Federal'nomu Sobraniiu', *Prezident Rossii*, 12 December, http://www.kremlin.ru/events/president/news/19825.

Putin, V. (2014). 'Obrashchenie Prezidenta Rossiiskoi Federatsii', *Prezident Rossii*, 18 March, http://kremlin.ru/events/president/news/20603.

Russkaia Idea. (2014). 'O proekte', http://politconservatism.ru/about.

Schillinger, L. (2015). 'The Rise of Bulgakov Diplomacy', *Foreign Policy*, 31 August, http://foreignpolicy.com/2015/08/31/the-rise-of-bulgakov-diplomacy-russian-literature-vladimir-putin-read-russia/.

Sergeev, S. (2017). 'Kak vozmozhna russkaia natsiia?', *Gefter*, 8 February, http://gefter.ru/archive/21085.

Shevel, O. (2011). 'Russian Nation-building from Yel'tsin to Medvedev: Ethnic, Civic or Purposefully Ambiguous?', *Europe-Asia Studies*, 63 (2): 179–202.

Shul'man, E. (2014). 'Tsarstvo politicheskoi imitatsii', *Vedomosti*, 15 August, http://www.vedomosti.ru/opinion/articles/2014/08/15/carstvo-imitacii.

Shul'man, E. (2015). 'Avtoritarnye rezhimy: mutanty, bastardy, gibridy', *Slon*, 3 February, https://republic.ru/posts/48948.

Shul'man, E. (2017). 'Ekaterina Shul'man: Vlast' predlagaet neskol'kikh "malen'kikh Naval'nykh" vmesto odnogo bol'shogo', *The Insider*, 26 December, https://theins.ru/opinions/schulman/86026.

Shul'man, E. (2017a). 'Gibka, kak gusenitsa, gibridnaia Rossiia', *Rosbalt*, 2 January, http://www.rosbalt.ru/russia/2017/01/02/1579820.html.

Shul'man, E. (2017b). 'Prisoedinenie Kryma – otvet vlastei na protesty 2011–2012 godov', *Snob*, 22 March, https://snob.ru/selected/entry/122061?preview=print.

Stanovaia, T. (2018). 'Ni vybory, ni referendum: kogo i zachem pobedil Vladimir Putin', *Moscow Carnegie Center*, 19 March, http://carnegie.ru/commentary/75831.

Suslov, M. (2016). 'The "Russian World" Concept in Online Debates During the Ukrainian Crisis', pp. 295–316 in Suslov, M. and Bassin, M., *Eurasia 2.0: Russian Geopolitics in the Age of New Media*. Lanham-Maryland: Lexington Books.

Tolz, V. (2001). *Russia. Inventing the Nation*. New York: Oxford University Press.

Ukraïns'ka Pravda. (2017). 'Lavrov: Prilepin na Donbasse nalazhivaet normal'nuiu zhizn", 21 February, http://www.pravda.com.ua/rus/news/2017/02/21/7136032/.

Valdai. (2014). 'Natsional'naia identichnost' i budushchee Rossii. Doklad Mezhdunarodnogo diskussionnogo kluba'. February, vid1.rian.ru/ig/valdai/doklad_identich nost_RUS_ISBN.pdf.

Vishnevskii, B. (2018). 'Boikotiruia zdravyi smysl', *Novaia Gazeta*, 10 January, https:// www.novayagazeta.ru/articles/2018/01/10/75107-boykotiruya-zdravyy-smysl.

Volkov, D. (2017). 'Krym ne rabotaet: pochemu liudi vozvrashchaiutsia na ulitsy', *Rbk*, 27 March, https://www.rbc.ru/opinions/politics/27/03/2017/58d8db2f9a7947ba863 b71ba.

Zhurzhenko, T. (2016). 'Hybrid Reconciliation', *Eurozine*, 8 April, http://www.eurozine .com/hybrid-reconciliation/.

CHAPTER 3

Towards the "Great Rejuvenation": State Nationalism, Shifting Identities, and Foreign Policy Choices in Contemporary China

Andrea Passeri

In recent years, while the People's Republic of China (PRC) was committed to portraying itself as a pragmatic and increasingly integrated stakeholder in the global arena, several events underscored the tangible resurgence of nationalism as a powerful driving force in shaping the course of contemporary Chinese politics, both in their domestic manifestations and external repercussions. As a consequence, Beijing's diplomatic posture has started to experience a slow yet steady evolution from a generally conciliatory, flexible, and "low-profile" attitude to a more assertive, emotional, and muscular stance, which became particularly evident in the aftermath of the 2008 financial crisis and gained further momentum in late 2012, with the unveiling of Xi Jinping's ideological manifesto the "Chinese dream". Since then, the PRC has not only demonstrated a more vigorous orientation in dealing with relevant foreign policy challenges, by reacting with mounting animosity to any possible infringement of its national pride, interests, and sovereignty, but it has also showcased an unprecedented degree of self-esteem in advocating larger responsibilities on the international stage. Accordingly, many commentators have warned about the perils brought about by China's ongoing quest to embody a credible alternative to Western models around the globe, pointing to the gradual dismissal of several precepts and guiding principles associated with Beijing's political trajectory since the inception of Deng's reformist era, such as his signature mantra of "hiding real capabilities and never claim the lead", so as to bide time and concentrate on domestic development (Clover 2017).

Yet, notwithstanding the importance of the positive shocks prompted by the global economic meltdown and the almost simultaneous ascendance of a new generation of political leaders, Beijing's growing disillusionment with the West and its anti-foreign tendencies display ancient roots, drawing upon a consolidated narrative that dates back to the first half of the 19th century and the inauguration of China's "century of humiliation". During this highly traumatic stage, ignited in 1839 with the First Opium War, the Chinese population had to endure humiliating setbacks and painful privations, including the forced opening of its ports to European imperialists, the progressive disintegration of the imperial court, and the stripping of vast portions of the mainland that fell under the control of Japan, a rising Asian power traditionally considered as a subordinate actor subject to China's cultural primacy. At the same time, however, the higher strata of its intellectuals were also exposed to an unprecedented influx of foreign innovations, scientific discoveries, and revolutionary notions in the fields of science and technology, warfare, philosophy, and statecraft, all potentially capable of turning a crumbling empire into a modern State. Among the ground-breaking concepts the reached China's shores through so-called "gunboat diplomacy", the prism of nationalism rapidly emerged as the most popular, controversial, and attractive, inspiring the genesis of the very idea of a Chinese nation endowed with specific political prerogatives and aspirations.[1]

In subsequent decades the local discourse on nationalism assumed a highly transformative and oscillating trajectory that stretched up to present days, marked by mixed fortunes and also by the progressive appearance of a series of distinctive features, such as China's almost unique transition from culturalism to the paradigm of a post-Westphalian nation-state able to enlist people's loyalty. Its historical evolution, in particular, has been strongly influenced by the appearance of three major "golden eras", punctuated by a long season of retrenchment and decline during the founding years of the PRC: the already mentioned "embryonic phase" (1839–1919), the post-Tiananmen "patriotic revival" (1989–2001) kick-started by the appearance of a crucial shift in the sources of China's state legitimacy, and the current stage (2007–), ignited by the global financial collapse and spearheaded by Xi Jinping's political apparatus. Completely overshadowed by the Maoist orthodoxy for more than three decades, nationalist sentiments and appeals have in fact re-emerged from the ashes of the Cold War with great momentum, uniting under the same banner the apical echelons of the central government and expanding portions of China's civil society.

Such a tangible revival of the idea of "Chineseness", as could be expected, has reverberated its massive impact both internally, by providing a new ideological foundation for the Chinese Communist Party (CCP) during a period of tumultuous reforms, and also in terms of Beijing's perceptions of its status and role in the current international system, through a systematic recovery of a "victim mentality" that strives to redeem China's past setbacks by bringing the

---

1   Since its very inception, moreover, China's own idea of nationalism and its intimate liaison with the concept of State – which will vividly emerge in the post-Tiananmen era – have been eloquently exposed even from a mere etymological standpoint. Unsurprisingly, the Chinese term usually employed to refer to nationalist ideals is *aiguozhuyi* ("patriotism"), which literally means "loving the State" (see Wu 2008).

country back to its ancient splendour and rightful place in the global arena (Zhao 2013: 101–103). Its foreign policy implications, moreover, have mirrored the changing attitude displayed by the Chinese regime in managing the sources of its own legitimacy and popularity, by shifting from a merely pragmatic, reactive, and instrumental reliance on patriotic values under Jiang Zemin and Hu Jintao, to the far more genuine, enthusiastic, and proactive embrace of China's exceptionalism pursued by the fifth generation of CCP's cadres. As a result, the powerful convergence between State propaganda and popular chauvinism has gradually transformed Chinese nationalism from an effective tool in the hands of central authorities to channel domestic discontent, to a "double-edged sword" able to expose both the State and the party to the growing scrutiny of public audiences, with the effect of reducing room for diplomatic manoeuvre and accommodation when dealing with the traditional targets of Beijing's historical grievances, such as Japan and the US.

Building upon this puzzling scenario, the following chapter explores the intimate relationship between the changing domestic strategies employed by the Chinese government to safeguard political consensus and national cohesion, the evolving official narrative related to China's perceptions and self-perceptions in the global arena, and its shifting attitude in the diplomatic realm. Accordingly, the analysis will first be devoted to acquainting the reader with the notion of nationalism from a theoretical standpoint, by recalling the scholarly debate on its roots, variants, and outcomes from an IR perspective, as well as the unique features pertaining to China's own representation of such a concept. The subsequent section looks at the pivotal turning points in the historical process of inception, diffusion, and metamorphosis of the Chinese political discourse on nationalism, with the aim of scrutinizing the key features entailed in its three fundamental waves: the nascent stage culminated in two revolutions between 1911 and 1949, the post-Cold War era characterised by the ascendance of state-led patriotism as an antidote to the dismissal of the official ideology, and the ongoing phase marked by an unprecedented confluence of "top-down" and "bottom-up" nationalist appeals. Finally, the concluding paragraph investigates the consequences stemming from the aforementioned phenomena in the field of China's foreign policy, with a focus on the case-study provided by the recent deterioration in Sino-Japanese ties.

1   Nationalism, Interstate Relations, and the "Burden of History":
         A Theoretical Overview

Since its advent as an historical by-product of the Modern era, nationalism has embodied a prominent driving force behind the rapid ascendance of a post-Westphalian world, centred on the consolidated primacy of nation states as the main protagonists in the international arena. Labelled by many as a "relic of the past" in the aftermath of the global proliferation of multilateral and supranational institutions, at the turn of the last century the prism of nationalism appeared severely undermined in all its basic tenets, and thus fated to be rapidly eclipsed by a smaller, interconnected, and truly globalised community (Halliday 1997: 441–442). Yet, the actual praxis of current interstate relations portrays a very different diagnosis, that seems to openly discard these simplistic views. Nationalist and even chauvinistic tunes are still vivid both in the advanced societies of the West and among numerous developing countries, while the periodic revival of past grievances and "national traumas" fuels recurrent diplomatic spats between highly interdependent and interlocked actors. To a large extent, the case of northeast Asia is no exception in the global picture, showcasing the enduring relevance of similar factors in shaping the external trajectories of key political entities such as Japan, South Korea, Taiwan, and the PRC. Due to its frequent skirmishes, in fact, this area has usually been described as a hostage of the "burden" of history, considering the persistence of regional tensions linked to longstanding territorial disputes in the South and East China Seas, or generated by conflicting memories over specific events, as epitomised by the long-lasting impact of the "comfort women" and "history textbook" issues in setting the tone of contemporary ties between Tokyo, Seoul, Beijing, and Taipei. However, before jumping into a more detailed exploration of the impact of nationalism on China's foreign policy choices when dealing with its regional neighbours, it is crucial to briefly conceptualise it from a basic theoretical perspective, while recalling the scholarly debate surrounding the origins, variants, and political implications of such a puzzling social phenomenon. In a nutshell, nationalism must first be understood as a principle or ideology which prescribes how modern societies should be ruled, by calling for a high degree of congruence between political and national entities. States boundaries, to put it differently, should carefully coincide with national ones, so to safeguard peace and stability both at the domestic and international level (Gellner 1983: 1). From a normative standpoint, the idea of nationalism thus presupposes the pivotal assumption that humanity is naturally divided along the fault lines of nationality, and each nation reflects a peculiar character and array of values. Secondly, this notion is also generally conceived as a sentiment, or movement, that acts in accordance with its basic principles, while striving to attain and promote "the autonomy, unity, and identity for a population which some of its members deem to constitute an actual or potential nation". (Smith 2001: 9).[2] This dual understanding of the concept, moreover,

---

2 Hence, if the ultimate source of sovereignty rests on national collectivities, its fullest manifestation must be pursued within the framework of a nation-State, in which the collectivity

underscores several additional features, especially in terms of the causal links entailed in the relation between the genesis of nationalist values and the formation of modern nation states, suggesting – as brilliantly argued by Ernst Gellner – that "it is nationalism which engenders nations, and not the other way around" (Gellner 1983: 55). Given that nations stem from the consciousness of belonging to a wider aggregation amalgamated by a specific identity, it is crucial to depict them through a combination of objective criteria – such as territory, institutions, ethnicity, language and customs, etc. – and intersubjective features, capable of reflecting their impalpable nature of "imagined political communities" (Anderson 1983: 6). Therefore, by relying on a mixture of the two it is possible to formulate an accurate definition of nation, as a way of connoting a named human polity located in a specific homeland, united by common myths, history, and culture, as well as organised around a single economy with shared rights and duties for all its members (Smith 2001: 13).

Building upon the aforementioned idea of nation, the bulk of the scholarly debate has traditionally revolved around the modalities through which national identities can be triggered, nurtured, and mobilised. This process has led to the emergence of two distinct strains of literature, resting on the so-called "functionalist theories" and on the "primordialist" ones, which have been further complemented in recent years by the formulation of a third conventional explanation, based on constructivist assumptions. According to the former, nationalism primarily embodies the functional outcome of specific historical phenomena, related to the epochal transition towards modern and industrial societies and the parallel spread of mass education programs coordinated by nascent nation states. Primordialist or ethno-symbolist accounts, conversely, consider collective identities as given, rather than flexible and malleable features, emphasizing the role of pre-modern identity factors such as kinship, ancient myths, and memories that can be rediscovered and reinterpreted by political élites (Smith 2000: 9). Hence, in contrast with the view advanced by instrumentalist explanations, states can harness pre-existing ethnic and cultural identities by means of these symbols and ideals, in order to boost their legitimacy. Constructivism, at the opposite of the spectrum, holds that nations are essentially fabricated and "imagined" communities, while toning down the impact of past ethnic cores (Anderson 1983: 4–7). Consequently, the rise of nationalist sentiments is portrayed as a direct result of purposeful and deliberate

---

can survive and prosper in exchange for the loyalty of its adherents to the institutions erected by the community itself. For a further exploration on the relation between nationalism and the concept of nation state, see Smith 1983.

strategies of cultural manipulation implemented by political leaders, aimed at holding a community together through mass education and political socialisation (Tang & Darr 2012: 812–813). As opposed to functionalism, the blossoming of similar beliefs is thus intended as part of a calculated power struggle among societal elites, and not as a mere reverberation of historical phenomena linked to the emergence of the Modern era, even though both schools agree on the fluid nature of collective identities and also on the role of standardised education and print capitalism as the main binding elements in the nation-building process.

Theoretically, another useful differentiation that comes in handy in the attempt of untangling the peculiarities of the Chinese discourse on nationalism revolves around the agents involved in the transmission of such sentiments. If nationalism as a movement ultimately entails the framing and promotion of a shared collective identity, which in turn leads to the formation of new political entities, it must be noted that similar dynamics can unfold in two opposite ways: through "top-down" directives, with the state actively committed to nation-shaping and unifying efforts as the supreme interpreter of collective interests, or as "bottom-up" dynamics, mirroring the "state-seeking" and "state-shaping" nationalism of oppressed or dissatisfied social groups (Tilly 1994: 133). More specifically, the development of an apical "state-led nationalism" requires the successful ascendance of a regime that speaks for the whole citizenship, while attracting its loyalty and self-identification in spite of any competing interest. In terms of its aspirations and *modus operandi*, accordingly, the general narrative embraced by state-sponsored nationalism is infused with a patriotic tone capable of surrounding any aspect of state policy, so that development and modernisation become truly national causes involving both the population and the official propaganda apparatus, entrusted with the task of celebrating the country's achievements and key milestones (Zhao 1998: 291).

The scrutiny of such notions, moreover, requires some further considerations on the role of history as the crucial raw material in the creation of national identities. As highlighted both through the idea of nations as "imagined communities" and by Tilly's definition of "state nationalism", the genesis and diffusion of nationalist sentiments rests on intersubjective and socially constructed processes, ultimately aimed at binding a human group together by instilling a sense of "we-ness" in its members, that can be further perpetuated to future generations. In trying to accomplish this ambitious task, historical narratives and collective memories of the past often stand out as the primary references not only in clarifying who is a community member and what such membership means, but also in indicating the group's enemies, while schools become the primary venues in which states articulate their official "self-image" and mould loyal citizens.[3] Finally, similar processes can also unleash a powerful impact in the international arena, by modelling patterns of interaction among different nations and their mutual attitudes, given that foreign policy choices are directly shaped by national interests, the scope and hierarchy of which is generally motivated by means of identity factors. Therefore, due to the political manipulation of shared memories regarding a country's past achievements and traumas, painful experiences embedded in national history can affect interstate relations up to present times, fuelling enduring animosities among different populations rooted in mutual prejudices, enmities, and resentments.

Under such circumstances, political elites may also opt to emphasise certain "chosen traumas" and "chosen glories" within a general framework that underlines the common yet exceptional historical path undertaken by a specific population, and also its bond with the motherland, with the effect of legitimizing their aspirations to revive the country's former splendour (Volkan 1997: 48–49; Zerubavel 1995: 214). As could be expected, the foes who antagonised this collective ascension to glory are often portrayed as the incarnation of the "chosen trauma" itself, adding substance to historical rivalries and setting the stage for their intergenerational perpetuation. Notwithstanding its numerous specificities, the case of China tends to perfectly validate the argument that sees in nationalism an essentially intersubjective and socially constructed phenomenon, often ignited by the state through political socialisation; which, in turn, is designed to attentively manipulate the historical and cultural heritage of the local population with the goal of promoting an idealised collective narration. In the PRC, as highlighted in the pages ahead, this strategy has largely drawn upon Beijing's problematic relation with its past, thus consolidating a "victim mentality" that traditionally blames foreign actors for China's own setbacks. Paradoxically, however, what seemed until recently a mere instrumental tool to boost the domestic legitimacy of a pragmatic and "agnostic" regime, is now increasingly turning into a "boomerang" – or a "double-edged sword" – capable of severely affecting the Chinese strategic calculus, by means of an unprecedented convergence of popular and apical nationalist appeals which demands further scrutiny.

---

3   On the relationship between history, collective memories and nationalism, see Eller 1999; Evans 2003; and Nozaki 2008.

2   The Genesis and Historical Evolution of China's Political Discourse on Nationalism

The brief exploration conducted throughout the most crucial paradigms and concepts associated with the inception and unravelling of nationalist ideals has underscored a series of distinctive theoretical features, which loom very large in the charting of China's evolving discourse on nationalism. In this case, in fact, the very idea of a Chinese nation endowed with specific rights and aspirations was firstly cultivated as a "bottom-up" and "state-seeking" sentiment shared by growing fractions of local intellectuals, to be then progressively embraced by the higher strata of the political élite through the materialisation of a rather sophisticated form of "state-led" nationalism. In turn, this set the stage for the last metamorphosis, centred upon the mounting and ongoing convergence between official propaganda and popular chauvinism. As emphasised in the previous pages, moreover, China's peculiar understanding of nationalism and its adherence to similar sentiments seems to strongly validate the assumption that sees in history, and especially in major past traumas, a primary binding element behind the establishment of shared collective identities, which draw upon the selection of recurrent foes and enemies to better clarify the group's boundaries and membership.

Historically, in fact, the genesis and advancement of the Chinese discourse on nationalism has intimately reflected the evolution of Beijing's interactions with the West, which entered into a drastically new era in the early 19th century following the advent of European imperialism in East Asia, the forced opening-up of many indigenous societies through so-called "gunboat diplomacy", and the resulting colonisation of significant portions of the region. Up to that moment, the concept of "Chineseness" had been relentlessly portrayed by local rulers and intellectuals by insisting on cultural, ideational, and moral prerogatives, rather than ethnic or political ones. The power of attraction of the former had proven extremely successful both internally, as the ultimate source of people's loyalty, and externally, in charming, incorporating, and eventually assimilating new ethnic groups under the imperial court. The severe blow to China's self-image and sense of superiority inflicted by the humiliating debacles against the Westerners, however, set in motion an epochal process of metamorphosis in its collective identity, or, as labelled by Townsend, a "culturalism-to-nationalism" transition capable of experiencing numerous twists and turns (Townsend 1992).

Building upon this swerving trajectory, it is thus possible to construct a basic periodisation of Chinese nationalism based on the three distinct "golden ages" that have ultimately shaped the indigenous approach towards this elusive paradigm: the embryonic stage (1839–1919), the post-Tiananmen patriotic revival (1989–2001), and the current decade (2007–2018) characterised by Beijing's assertive shift. The fundamental trigger and turning point, as already mentioned, resides in the country's progressive descent into the abyss of the "century of humiliation" (bǎinián guóchǐ), a highly dramatic period kick-started in 1839 with the outbreak of the First Opium war. Following the crushing defeat suffered at the hands of the British, China was subjugated and partitioned into different spheres of influence controlled by distant powers, prompting an irreversible "crisis of identity" of the Qing dynasty, increasingly confronted by the dilemma of whether or not to embrace and emulate foreign models. In parallel, as this clash of civilisations resulted in the forced opening of China's ports to international trade, goods, and capital, growing portions of the local population were progressively introduced to Western scientific knowledge, especially in the fields of philosophy and statecraft. The "immovable" empire was therefore compelled to acknowledge the primacy of the West not only from a technological and military standpoint, but also in terms of the resilience and efficiency of its political institutions, centred around the paradigm of a post-Westphalian nation-state.

During this embryonic stage, China effectively embarked on a highly delicate process of change that lasted until 1949, laying the foundations for the appearance of a unique historical example of empire-turned-nation-state, or, as argued by Pye, of "a civilization pretending to be a nation-state" (Pye 1990: 58). Confucianism lost ground in coping with the ideational challenge posed by Western science and religions, as demonstrated by the Taiping (1851–64) and Boxer (1900) rebellions, while the mortifying Chinese setback in the Second Opium War (1856–60) further consolidated Beijing's subaltern position vis-à-vis foreign powers through the signing of a long list of "unequal treaties". Simultaneously, the declining Qing dynasty faced an additional threat provided by China's historical nemesis, namely Japan, which unveiled its thirst for territorial expansionism in the Chinese mainland with the first Sino-Japanese War (1894–95). At the end of the conflict, the Treaty of Shimonoseki ratified a decisive shift in the regional balance of power by setting the stage for the gradual assimilation of the Korean peninsula under Tokyo's orbit and for the Japanese annexation of Taiwan and the Senkaku/Diaoyu islands.

Mortified and confounded by the shadow of territorial disintegration at the hands of foreign invaders, a considerable fraction of China's intellectual elite turned towards the adoption of European paradigms, ideals, and technology, seeking to defend the very existence of the Chinese nation and to transform it from a quite loose and inclusive cultural community to a political one.

Economic and military reforms inspired by Western models were the first to gain momentum, as epitomised by the emergence of the "Self-Strengthening" movement during the late stages of the Qing era, which reflected the attempt to reverse China's backwardness vis-à-vis foreign powers by combining several pivotal features of its former structure, such as dynastic rule and the primacy of Confucianism, with unprecedented practices and innovations borrowed from abroad. Then, with the collapse of the empire and the establishment of the Republic of China (ROC) in 1912, the highly pragmatic and compromising attitude of the "Self-Strengthening" movement was progressively replaced by a stronger and more genuine commitment to emulating Western paradigms. Nascent state institutions were increasingly tailored after European models, while the appearance of the "New Culture" and "May Fourth" movements on the eve of the Versailles Peace Conference held in the spring of 1919 under-scored the visible impact of nationalism among the local population. Besides their explicit anti-Western character in denouncing all the abuses experienced by China over the course of the "century of humiliation", these bottom-up forc-es gained the forefront in laying the foundations for China's modern political discourse on nationalism, by pushing forward the standardisation of vernacu-lar Chinese, the re-examination of Confucian precepts and texts, as well as the introduction of new political formations and procedures.

Accordingly, this initial stage of popularity of nationalist ideals strongly contributed to the restructuring of the Chinese collective identity, providing a powerful cement to hold the country together against all odds. From the early 1930s, however, the main target of Beijing's acrimonies and frustrations shifted from the West to Japan, following Tokyo's expansionist conduct on the Chinese mainland and the outbreak of Second Sino-Japanese War (1937–45). The aston-ishing price paid by China in resisting such an existential threat to its survival as a sovereign actor included millions of casualties, the systematic depreda-tion of ample portions of its territory, the quagmire of a brutal civil war be-tween nationalist and communist fronts, and the formal loss of the "renegade province" of Taiwan. Nevertheless, in the autumn of 1949 the Chairman of the CCP, Mao Zedong, grandiosely announced in front of a vast audience that his people "had finally stood up", putting a decisive end to the "century of humili-ation" by pushing its internal and external foes out of the country. Hence, with the establishment of the People's Republic, China's victim mentality was rap-idly eclipsed by an unprecedented "victor's narrative" inspired by the "class struggle theory", and ultimately designed to celebrate the CCP as the vanguard and supreme saviour of the Chinese nation (Wang 2008: 789). As a conse-quence, for more than three decades nationalist appeals were completely over-shadowed by the strength of the new official ideology both at the apical and popular level, whereas communist historiography extensively re-interpreted China's past traumas by toning down foreign responsibilities, while blaming the backwardness, incompetence, and corruption of the late imperial court.

This tangible decline in the local discourse on nationalism was gradually reversed with the death of the "Great Helmsman" in 1976, which opened up the Pandora's box of a comprehensive reassessment of the Maoist ideology. The initial response put forward by his successors Deng Xiaoping and Jiang Zemin officially kick-started the "Reform and Opening-up" era, a period of tumultuous changes for Chinese politics and economics aimed at accomplishing the "four modernisations" in the fields of agriculture, industry, national defence, and scientific development. In the following years however, the double shock to the external and domestic outlook of the PRC triggered first by the Soviet collapse, and then by the outbreak of the Tiananmen protests, dramatically exposed the "bankruptcy" of the official ideology, persuading the communist leadership to engage in a wider and deeper metamorphosis. This further transformation was thus directed at providing a new ideological foundation for state legitimacy and people's loyalty, so as to counter the crisis of faith experienced by the Chinese system especially in attracting the sympathies of younger generations (Zhao 1998: 288–289). Accordingly, the official apparatus profoundly restructured its self-image, mission, and *modus operandi*, while downplaying the traditional Maoist narrative centred on the party as the forerunner of the Chinese proletariat and the architect of a truly communist society. In order to re-enlist mass support, in the aftermath of the Tiananmen demonstrations Jiang Zemin started to portray the CCP as "the firmest and most thoroughgoing patriot", by re-introducing the values and ideals of nationalism among the local population: the popular narrative revolving around the "century of humiliation" was therefore re-discovered and celebrated once again, this time with the aim of emphasizing the role of the communists in putting an end to China's most traumatic historical stage (Wang 2012: 133–135). Under this general banner, the third generation of party cadres also endorsed a new paramount goal for the decades ahead, pledging to "revitalise" the nation and to bring the country back to its rightful place in the global arena, as a strong, prosperous, and revered actor.

Consequently, the years between 1976 and 1991 can be considered a highly delicate transitional stage characterised by China's search for a new identity, which resulted in the tailoring of a revised official ideology based on state-sponsored nationalism. The fullest manifestation of this process was embodied in August 1991 by the unveiling and implementation of the "patriotic education" campaigns, a wide-ranging series of cultural and educational efforts essentially targeted at China's youth with the aim of reviving nationalism as the new glue that would hold the local society together, while perpetrating the dominant position of the CCP. The party's Central Committee, under the strict guidance of Jiang Zemin, was entrusted with the task of formulating the strategy's manifesto in the "Outline on Implementing Patriotic Education", which stated that:

> The objectives of conducting patriotic education campaign are to boost the nation's spirit, enhance cohesion, foster national self-esteem and pride, consolidate and develop a patriotic united front to the broadest extent possible, and direct and rally the masses' patriotic passions to the great cause of building socialism with Chinese characteristics.
>
> WANG 2012: 99

As a consequence, the genesis of this second golden age for the Chinese discourse on nationalism entailed a three-pronged approach in the fields of education, tourism, and audio-visual arts that sought to re-ignite the patriotic fervour and historical awareness of the population, especially in terms of the traumas endured during the "century of humiliation". In doing so, the campaign also advanced a powerful rebut against the advocates of a proto-democratic transition, not only by instructing ordinary Chinese citizens about the uniqueness and exceptionalism of the country's national conditions, but also in depicting Western-style liberal models as profoundly unfit for the PRC (Zhao 2008: 5). Accordingly, local schools – from kindergartens to China's most renowned universities – were invested by a series of directives aimed at strengthening and updating history curricula, so as to better disseminate the CCP's revised narrative regarding the national struggle for independence. Simultaneously, the introduction of new textbooks underscored a vast recovery of the old mentality that blames China's traditional nemesis – namely Japan and the West – for all the sufferings and hardships experienced by the motherland, while museums, cultural relics, and other memory sites complemented such endeavours by attracting growing crowds of visitors. On top of that, the third arrow of the strategy looked at modern media that could effectively convey patriotic values to Chinese youth, through a program of public funding of hundreds of songs, books, and movies which sold millions of copies across the whole country.

To a large extent, the rise of State-nationalism in post-Tiananmen China can be thus conceived as an instrumental, "agnostic", and essentially defensive attempt to channel domestic tensions outside, as well as to erect a powerful wall vis-à-vis foreign criticism based on the mantras of democracy and human rights promotion. In line with this view, under Jiang Zemin the PRC successfully managed to advance its "peaceful development" strategy in a generally conciliatory and non-antagonistic framework, by steering a middle course in international politics between foreign pressures and rising popular demands for a more assertive and confident diplomacy. Over the short term, most notably, the negligible impact of state-led nationalism in making Beijing's external projection more war-prone was first epitomised in 1999 – with the accidental bombing of the Chinese embassy in Belgrade during the NATO airstrikes on Yugoslavia – and then in 2001, following the controversial collision over the Hainan Island between an American EP-3 spy plane and a Chinese fighter jet. On both occasions, the Chinese government opted for an essentially pragmatic and assuaging response, notwithstanding the eruption of mass demonstrations in the country calling for a tougher stance against the US, while endeavouring to keep in check or at least tone down public chauvinist manifestations that could potentially escalate (Cabestan 2005: 11). In the long run, however, the re-emergence of vocal anti-foreign sentiments among the Chinese population as the principal by-product of the "patriotic education campaigns" laid the foundations for another significant twist in the local discourse on nationalism, whose main repercussions would be highly visible in the years ahead with top-down and state-sponsored inputs being gradually replaced by an unprecedented convergence of apical and popular demands for a stronger China.

3   Nationalism and Foreign Policy Choices in Xi's China: The Case of Contemporary Sino-Japanese Ties

As anticipated, the turn of the last century marked a decisive shift in the nature and structure of Chinese nationalism, nurturing a steady transition from a reactive and generally flexible approach coordinated by a pragmatic regime in search of new sources of political legitimacy, to a far more proactive and emotional attitude, advocated both by societal groups and the top echelons of the fifth generation of the CCP's leaders. Under such circumstances, the party's paramount mission concerning the "rejuvenation" and re-ascendance of the country to its rightful place among other nations has been further reconfirmed and emphasised by a political elite that – rather than resorting to nationalist calls as mere tactical tools to divert domestic discontent towards external rivals – seems to be genuinely attached to similar values and beliefs. This process, in turn, has paved the way for wider spillovers on China's diplomatic trajectory and foreign policy choices, by means of a gradual dismissal of the conciliatory and peaceful posture of the Jiang Zemin's era, conducive to the adoption of a more unilateral, impulsive, and "strident" stance in the advancement of Chinese core interests such as territorial integrity (Zhao 2013a). As a consequence, over the course of the last decade Beijing has appeared more sensitive than ever to any possible infringement of its sovereignty and national aspirations, as epitomised by recurrent diplomatic spats arising with East Asian neighbours over territorial disputes, or vis-à-vis Western countries with regard to the management of their ties with Taiwanese and Tibetan authorities, while, domestically, the party's leadership appears targeted by the mounting scrutiny of increasingly vocal nationalist constituencies.

The epochal watershed that triggered a new stage in the Chinese discourse on nationalism, and its steady metamorphosis into a "double-edged sword" for the PRC, reflects a by-product of the interplay of external and domestic dynamics. As far as the former are concerned, a first major shock was prompted by the 2008 financial crisis, which persuaded Beijing to put aside its traditional "low-profile" attitude by embracing a bolder and more muscular posture. Simultaneously, China's anti-crisis agenda successfully insulated its market from the most virulent effects of the global meltdown, outperforming the responses of Western stakeholders and leading, two years later, to the leapfrogging of Japan as the second-largest economy in the world. Inside the country, the growing perception that the international balance of power was finally leaning towards the PRC – despite America's attempts to "keep Beijing down" – fuelled numerous calls for a less accommodative diplomacy, as demonstrated by the widespread success of "China is Not Happy", a popular chauvinist essay published in 2009 which sold millions of copies over the course of the following months (Zhao 2013a: 543–545). From a political standpoint, the stage was thus set for the appearance of a younger generation of party cadres who could effectively embody the soaring nationalist orientation of the general public, by pushing forward the country's quest for prosperity and development with unprecedented resolve.

Against this backdrop, the ascension of Xi Jinping's charismatic leadership in late 2012 has de facto projected China's nationalist posture into a whole new era, under the state-sponsored banner of the "Chinese dream". Conceptually, Xi's signature manifesto inaugurates a further stage in China's nationalist narrative as it was shaped since the outbreak of the "century of humiliation", revolving around an extremely ambitious project of national "rejuvenation". The idea behind this recurrent buzzword, in fact, seeks to depict Beijing's regained centrality as a return to its traditional status, rather than a take-off from nothing, while calling on the local population to work hand in hand with the party to achieve several important milestones. Among them, the overarching aim is to equip the country with the tools required to assert itself politically, economically, and militarily, so as to become a "moderately well-off society" by 2021 and a "fully developed nation" by 2049, in concomitance with the hundredth anniversaries of the CCP and the PRC, respectively. As a result, it can be argued that the unveiling of the "Chinese dream" blueprint has marked a confrontational turn in the advancement of Beijing's regional agenda, destabilizing the management of its interaction especially with the traditional targets of Chinese historical acrimony, namely Japan and the US.

With regard to the latter, China's changing mood has been vividly epitomised by Xi's recurrent calls to frame Sino-American ties within a "new model of great power relations"; which, according to Chinese diplomats, should be based on the principle of equality and parity between the two counterparts, so as to denote Washington's implicit recognition of the epochal achievements attained during the last decades by the PRC in its astonishing rise (Perlez 2013). Moreover, China's dissatisfaction with the West on issues ranging from US arms sales to Taiwan, to the Dalai Lama's diplomatic tours across European capitals, is currently coupled by the periodic revamp of tensions with several East Asian neighbours, mostly fuelled by territorial disputes. In the South China Sea, Beijing's recent muscle-flexing has entailed a sharp increase in the presence and activities of the People's Liberation Army Navy (PLAN) in the waters of the Spratly and Paracel archipelagos, further complemented by the realisation of several artificial islets, ports, airstrips, and radar installations at China's major strongholds in the area, such as the Johnson South Reef and the Fiery Cross Reef (Paul 2016). As could be expected, these developments have sparked vocal reactions from countries like Vietnam and the Philippines, which have emerged as the fiercest opponents of Chinese territorial claims.

Yet, notwithstanding the importance of the South China Sea conundrum the tangible deterioration of China's generally conciliatory diplomacy during the years of the "peaceful development" and "good-neighbourhood" strategies is nowhere more visible than in the ongoing disruptive spiral of Sino-Japanese relations, following the almost simultaneous elections of Xi and Shinzo Abe to the helms of the two countries. Due to the strong nationalist credentials of their leaders, Tokyo and Beijing have thus entered a new and unprecedented stage in their bilateral ties, bringing an end to the previous era based on the principle of "shelving controversies and pursuing joint development". The course taken since the early 2010s, on the contrary, has been characterised by the harsh revamp of the Senkaku/Diaoyu dispute in the East China Sea, by deepening reticence at the official level between the counterparts, and by a mounting display of historical acrimony and chauvinist sentiments among various strata of the general audience, both in the PRC and Japan. In contrast to the cases of the Belgrade bombing and the EP-3 incident, in fact, the worrisome turn in Sino-Japanese ties reveals two interlocking trends of this third golden era of Chinese nationalism that are worthy of further consideration:

the increasing effectiveness of bottom-up forces in affecting the government's posture and behaviour on specific foreign policy issues, and the equally growing reluctance of official authorities and party cadres to contain similar expressions of popular anger.

Hence, in the eyes of Chinese leaders, the nationalist constituencies that emerged from the patriotic campaigns of the post-Tiananmen period to channel domestic unrest are progressively turning into a "double-edged" sword, due also to their growing effectiveness in drawing strength from the internet to then establish a stronger presence on Chinese streets, at rallies, and protests. Under such circumstances, China's political establishment seems progressively caught between a rock and a hard place. On the one hand, these groups' mounting scrutiny of the alleged "weakness" of the country's responses to external provocations is currently persuading Beijing to adopt a more assertive stance, in an attempt to consolidate domestic support. In doing so, however, the Xi administration's room for diplomatic accommodation and flexibility appears to be significantly undermined, as is China's space for manoeuvre when dealing with the targets of its historical acrimony. With Japan, a first relevant example of this was the bilateral row that ignited in September 2010: on this occasion, the detention of a Chinese skipper involved in a collision near the Senkaku between his fishing trawler and a Japanese Coast Guard's patrol boat triggered a massive wave of anti-Japanese protest in many Chinese cities, aimed at pressuring the government in Beijing to adopt a firm and tough response. As a result, the PRC opted for a sudden halt in the shipment of rare earth exports to Japan, as opposed to the pragmatic and conciliatory approach that informed China's posture in 1999 and 2001 in the aftermath of both the Belgrade bombing and the EP-3 incident (Bradsher 2010).

Two years later, Tokyo's nationalisation of three islets pertaining to the Senkaku/Diaoyu archipelago triggered another bilateral spat, setting the stage for the outbreak of the widest and most violent anti-Japanese protests in the country's recent history, marked by the looting and burning of many Japanese restaurants and companies. For several days, Chinese authorities *de facto* turned their eyes away from popular protests, while escalating the crisis by sponsoring hardline commentaries on state media and imposing a national boycott of Japanese goods. In subsequent weeks, the PLAN sent another unprecedented signal by dispatching multiple warships in the Senkaku/Diaoyu perimeter, so as to contest the effects of Tokyo's nationalisation and reassert China's claims in the area (Gries et al. 2016: 264–265). Interestingly enough, such a vehement and unprecedented reaction by Chinese authorities was criticised by numerous local netizens for being too weak and restrained (Buckley 2012). Then, over the course of the last years this antagonistic turn has been marked by further episodes and skirmishes that led to growing tensions, as epitomised in November 2013 by the establishment of the Chinese Air Defence Identification Zone (ADIZ) that covers significant portions of the East China Sea, or, in December 2013, following Abe's first official visit as prime minister to the Yasukuni Shrine, that spurred widespread anger and outrage both in China and South Korea.[4] In the military realm, moreover, frequent scrambles between Chinese and Japanese jet fighters over the Senkaku/Diaoyu islands have recently raised the risk of dangerous incidents on the two sides, whereas the precarious state of such a pivotal bilateral relationship from a political standpoint was vividly exposed in November 2014, in the frosty and embarrassed handshake between Xi and Abe on the sidelines of the APEC summit, their first personal encounter in almost two years in office. Once again, the rapid succession of such events underscores the relevance of nationalism in setting the tone of China's posture vis-à-vis its most important neighbour and historical rival, through a powerful convergence between the official narrative endorsed by the fifth generation of Chinese leaders and the evolving orientation of the general public. If Sino-Japanese ties are progressively sliding down the slippery slope of mutual confrontation, an important part of the explanation descends from the evolving sources of state legitimacy in the PRC, that are providing powerful incentives for the materialisation of a more unilateral approach in the advancement of Beijing's national interest.

4   Concluding Remarks

The exploration conducted in the previous pages through the evolution of Chinese nationalism has moved from a basic premise: structural variations in the overall distribution of power at the international level, and Beijing's growing stakes of global resources and wealth, can only partially account for the recent assertive turn in its diplomatic behaviour, inasmuch as they tend to overlook a set of major, albeit intangible transformations that have occurred inside the country over the course of the last decades. Therefore, in order to untangle the

---

4   The shrine commemorates those who died since the Meiji restoration as part of the establishment and expansion of the Japanese Empire, including hundreds of prisoners of war convicted at the end of World War Two for war crimes while operating in occupied countries such as China and Korea. For a timely analysis of this controversy and its enduring impact on Sino-Japanese relations, see Cheung 2017.

roots of China's ongoing muscle-flexing, the present analysis has sought to consider its evolving belief systems, national narratives, and ideational factors as analytically relevant and noteworthy as the material implications of its ascending path, whilst endeavouring to clarify the correlation between Beijing's domestic consensus strategies and foreign policy choices. Building upon this three-pronged investigation in the theory, history, and empirical manifestations of Chinese nationalism, it is now possible to draw some conclusions that can shed additional light both on the genesis and future directions of Beijing's primary ideological reference. As far as the former is concerned, the evidences collected suggest that constructivist accounts appear to be the most suited to capturing the essence and defining traits of the indigenous discourse on nationalism since its very inception, especially in light of their emphasis on the intersubjective and socially constructed nature of similar phenomena. The case of the PRC, furthermore, seems to corroborate several additional corollaries of the constructivist approach, such as the importance accorded to historical narratives and past traumas, which can provide powerful raw material not only for framing collective identities, but also for indicating possible friends and foes of a certain population, with the effect of establishing a membership based on specific criteria and strong boundaries. Similarly, the pivotal role played by the state since the post-Tiananmen era in bolstering popular national fervour through sophisticated strategies as the "patriotic education campaigns" validates the constructivist assumption that sees Chinese nationalism as the by-product of purposeful efforts of cultural manipulation, deliberately implemented by political leaders. Against this backdrop, the current course of Sino-Japanese ties vividly illustrates the detrimental impact of conflicting memories and historical grievances in hampering the establishment of constructive interactions among two highly interdependent actors, due also to the revamp of their clash of identities in the East China Sea.

In parallel, the antagonistic stance recently embraced by Tokyo and Beijing allows for some additional considerations on the future trajectories and dilemmas confronting China's foreign policy. Among them, the paramount puzzle for the fifth generation of CCP leaders as the country grows stronger and more influential is likely to be the choice between globalism and parochialism, or, to put it in other words, between the status of a global stakeholder with growing responsibilities vis-à-vis the international community, and a narrow-minded reliance on nationalism aimed at aggressively pursuing China's core interests both domestically and externally. On the one hand, the PRC finally appears confident enough to make a systematic bid as the new forerunner of economic globalisation, by presenting its own take on paramount issues such as global trade, climate change, and sustainable growth, as highlighted by Xi Jinping's anti-protectionist speech at the World Economic Forum held in Davos in January 2017. On the other, however, bottom-up nationalist appeals are undoubtedly on the rise among the local population, fuelling the emergence of controversial social phenomena such as China's "angry youth", usually consisting of urban netizens who have been exposed since a very early age to state-sponsored patriotic propaganda, and now take to the streets either to protest against perceived foreign adversaries – as epitomised by the massive anti-Japanese rallies of 2012 – or to push the government towards bolder diplomatic conducts. As a result, Chinese central authorities currently face the emergence of a nascent and quite peculiar "two-level game" based on the mounting scrutiny of public opinion, which rewards the mounting assertiveness of Beijing's foreign policy and severely limits the room for flexibility and accommodation when dealing with foreign interlocutors on highly sensitive matters.

Nationalism, hence, increasingly stands out as tricky boomerang for the leadership of the PRC, since it has endowed the government with a powerful instrument to keep domestic tensions at bay, but, at the same time, it has also equipped ordinary citizens with new standards to evaluate China's diplomatic choices and performances. Significantly, the paternalistic and populist rhetoric endorsed both in the apical and in the wider strata of the indigenous society has already undermined several central tenets entailed in Beijing's "peaceful development" strategy, by raising the emotional and unilateral stakes of Chinese foreign policy. As a consequence, a host of regional actors have found common ground in endeavouring to keep in check China's muscle-flexing, as exemplified by the already mentioned cases of Japan, Vietnam, and the Philippines, which have recently upgraded their security capabilities to better cope with the rising assertiveness displayed by the PRC, thanks also to extensive assistance by the US. These developments have, in turn, nourished a dangerous vicious cycle, by reinforcing the arguments of those Chinese citizens who believe that the Western powers and their Asian allies are still committed to encircling and keeping the country down, as traditionally argued by Beijing's deep-rooted victim mentality. In this scenario, given that state legitimacy increasingly rests on its ability to deliver continued growth and erect a strong, united, and prosperous country, the potential emergence of a major shock following a sudden economic slowdown or a new diplomatic crisis would certainly represent a vital threat, both for China's continuous pursuit of its core interests and for the current regime, forcing its leaders to strike a new compromise between domestic and foreign policy imperatives.

Bibliography

Anderson, B. (1983). *Imagined Communities: Reflections on the Origin and Spread of Nationalism*. London: Verso.

Bradsher, K. (2010). 'Amid Tension, China Blocks Vital Exports to Japan', *The New York Times*, 22 September, http://www.nytimes.com/2010/09/23/business/global/23rare .html.

Buckley, C. (2012). 'Chinese leaders may come to regret anti-Japan protests', *Reuters*, 19 September, https://www.reuters.com/article/us-china-japan-politics/analysis-chinese-leaders-may-come-to-regret-anti-japan-protests-idUSBRE88I0AU20120919.

Cabestan, J.P. (2005). 'The Many Facets of Chinese Nationalism', *China Perspectives*, 59, http://journals.openedition.org/chinaperspectives/2793#quotation.

Cheung, M. (2017). *Political Survival and Yasukuni in Japan's Relations with China*. Abingdon: Routledge.

Clover, C. (2017). 'Xi Jinping Signals Departure from low-Profile Policy', *The Financial Times*, 20 October, 2017, https://www.ft.com/content/05cd86a6-b552-11e7-a398 -73d59db9e399.

Eller, J.D. (1999). *From Culture to Ethnicity to Conflict: An Anthropological Perspective on International Ethnic Conflict*. Ann Arbor: University of Michigan Press.

Evans, R. (2003). 'Redesigning the Past: History in Political Transitions', *Journal of Contemporary History*. 38(1): 5–12.

Gellner, E. (1983). *Nations and Nationalism*. Ithaca: Cornell University Press.

Gries, P., Steiger, D. and Wang, T. (2016). 'Popular Nationalism and China's Japan Policy: the Diaoyu Islands protests, 2012–2013', *Journal of Contemporary China*, 25(98): 264–276.

Halliday, F. (1997). 'Nationalism', pp. 441–455 in Baylis, J., and Smith, S. (eds.), *The Globalisation of World Politics*, Oxford: Oxford University Press.

Nozaki, Y. (2008). *War Memory, Nationalism and Education in Postwar Japan*. Abingdon: Routledge.

Paul, M. (2016). 'A Great Wall of Sand in the South China Sea? Political, Legal and Military Aspects of the Island Dispute', *SWP Research Paper*, 8, July.

Perlez, J. (2013). 'Chinese President to Seek New Relationship with U.S. in Talks', *The New York Times*, 28 May, http://www.nytimes.com/2013/05/29/world/asia/china-to-seek-more-equal-footing-with-us-in-talks.html.

Pye, L. (1990). 'China: Erratic State, Frustrated Society', *Foreign Affairs*. 69(4): 56–74.

Smith, A. (1983). *Theories of Nationalism*. London: Duckworth.

Smith, A. (2000). *Myths and Memories of the Nation*. Oxford: Oxford University Press.

Smith, A. (2001). *Nationalism. Theories, Ideology, History*. Cambridge: Polity Press.

Tang, W. and Darr, B. (2012). 'Chinese Nationalism and its Political and Social Origins', *Journal of Contemporary China*, 21(77): 811–826.

Tilly, C. (1994). 'States and Nationalism in Europe 1492–1992', *Theory and Society*, 23(1): 131–146.

Townsend, J. (1992). 'Chinese Nationalism', *The Australian Journal of Chinese Affairs*, 27: 97–130.

Volkan, D.V. (1997). *Bloodlines: From Ethnic Pride to Ethnic Terrorism*. New York: Farrar, Straus & Giroux.

Wang, Z. (2008). 'National Humiliation, History Education, and the Politics of Historical Memory: Patriotic Education Campaign in China', *International Studies Quarterly*, 52: 783–806.

Wang, Z. (2012). *Never Forget National Humiliation: Historical Memory in Chinese Politics and Foreign Relations*. New York: Columbia University Press.

Wu, G. (2008). 'From Post-imperial to Late Communist Nationalism: Historical Change in Chinese Nationalism from May Fourth to the 1990', *The Third World Quarterly*, 29(3): 467–482.

Zhao, S. (1998). 'A State-Led Nationalism: The Patriotic Education Campaign in Post-Tiananmen China', *Communist and Post-Communist Studies*, 31(3): 287–302.

Zhao, S. (2008). 'Chinese Pragmatic Nationalism and Its Foreign Policy Implications', Paper presented at the 2008 Annual Meeting of the American Political Science Association, 28–31 August.

Zhao, S. (2013). 'Chinese Foreign Policy as a Rising Power to find its Rightful Place', *Perceptions*, 18(1): 101–128.

Zhao, S. (2013a). 'Foreign Policy Implications of Chinese Nationalism Revisited: the Strident Turn', *Journal of Contemporary China*, 22(82): 535–553.

Zerubavel, Y. (1995). *Recovered Roots: Collective Memory and the Making of Israeli National Tradition*. Chicago: University of Chicago Press.

CHAPTER 4

Reframing Human Rights in Russia and China

How National Identity and National Interests Shape Relations with, and the Implementation of, International Law

Marco Balboni and Carmelo Danisi

1   Introduction

In 2016 Russia and China issued a *Joint Declaration on the Promotion of International Law* in an attempt to "systematise" their approach to international law.* By reaffirming long-held views, both countries sent a clear message to the entire international community: Russia's and China's "own political identity" needs to be integrated into the interpretation of every field of international law.[1]

The analysis carried out in this chapter on the role and understanding of human rights "as a matter of international law" in Russia and China stems, and cannot be read apart, from this important official stance, as well as from the position conferred by both countries to individuals in society.

In order to analyse the common aspects, as well as specific features, of the Russian and Chinese approaches in this field, our analysis will consider the dynamics emerging from the participation of both countries in the human rights systems set up at the regional and international level. In this respect, Russia and China are characterised by diverse levels of integration in these systems with important implications for the protection afforded in their domestic orders.

Starting with Russia, this country replaced in the 1990s the USSR in its universal international treaty obligations and joined the more sophisticated European human rights system.[2] As a member state of the Council of Europe, in

---

* The authors contributed equally to the introduction and the concluding remarks of this chapter. Section 2 was written by M. Balboni, while Section 3 was authored by C. Danisi.

1 See *Joint Declaration on Promotion and Principles of International Law*, 25 June 2016, available at www.mid.ru/en/foreign_policy/news/-/asset_publisher/cKNonkJEo2Bw/content/id/233 1698.

2 Russia is party to 11 out of 18 UN human rights treaties (see http://indicators.ohchr.org). See also the CoE's dedicated online section on Russia for key figures on its participation in the European system at www.coe.int/et/web/portal/russian-federation.

1998 Russia ratified the European Convention on Human Rights (ECHR), whose respect is supervised by the European Court of Human Rights (ECtHR).[3] China, instead, acceded to its first international human rights treaty – the United Nations (UN) Convention on the Elimination of All Forms of Discrimination against Women – in 1980, and today it has joined only "some" international human rights treaties and mechanisms, i.e. those that seem more in line with its strategic aims.[4] Moreover, China does not belong to any regional framework of human rights protection. In fact, while Asia lacks a human rights mechanism that is comparable to the European, African or American ones, China is not even involved in the first attempt to establish a rather weak regional human rights institution based on so-called Asian values (Renshaw 2013; Neo 2017).[5]

Yet, for both countries, the interaction with the international arena has led to remarkable outcomes. As for Russia, dialogue with the ECHR's protection system is resulting in an attempt to defend a "national appreciation" of human rights, in opposition to the way these rights are protected and interpreted at international level. As for China, its more isolationist approach goes hand in hand with the elaboration of its own interpretation of human rights law, which pays greater attention to the Chinese model of economic and social development.

With this background in mind, the chapter is therefore organised as follows. Section 2 examines both countries' approaches to international law. This analysis sets the stage for addressing the Russian and Chinese positions towards human rights and for explaining why these countries cannot be easily

---

3   *Convention for the Protection of Human Rights and Fundamental Freedoms*, signed in Rome, 4 November 1950. The Council of Europe (CoE) unites 47 European States that are all bound by the Convention and are subject to the ECtHR as its supervising mechanism. As we explore below, the ECtHR plays a key role in the interpretation of the Convention as a "living instrument" to meet today's human rights challenges. See, for instance, ECtHR, 24 January 2017, *Khamtokhu and Aksenchik v. Russia*, Applications nos. 60367/08 and 961/11, para. 73. On Russia's compliance with the ECtHR's judgments, among others J. Lapitskaya, *ECHR, Russia, and Chechnya: Two is not Company and Three is Definitely a Crowd*, in *International Law and Politics*, Vol. 43, 2011, 479–547.

4   See data provided by the Office of High Commissioner on Human Rights (OHCHR) at http:// indicators.ohchr.org. Interestingly, these commitments are related mostly to the rights of specific groups (women, children, and people with disabilities).

5   See the so-called ASEAN Intergovernmental Commission on Human Rights (AICHR), established in 2009 in accordance with Article 14 of the Association of Southeast Asian Nations (ASEAN)'s Charter, and the subsequent ASEAN Human Rights Declaration adopted on 18 November 2012, available at www.asean.org/storage/images/ASEAN_RTK_2014/6_AHRD_ Booklet.pdf.

described as human rights' opponents.[6] Section 3 scrutinises, for each country, the kind of dialogue established with the human rights mechanisms to which they belong. The chapter ends with some conclusive remarks on the common aspects as well as distinctive features of Russia and China in the field of international human rights law.

2 A Traditional Approach to International Law

Russia and China share some common views on the role of international law in international relations, which, in turn, are at the heart of their renewed willingness to influence in a certain way its development. These common aspects shaped the above-mentioned 2016 *Declaration*.

Through this common position, Russia and China have stressed their adherence to the UN Charter, as well as the need for all members of the international community to pay attention to the most traditional principles of international law thereby affirmed – i.e. state sovereignty, states' equality and non-intervention in internal or external affairs.[7]

In light of the centrality of the principle of sovereign equality for the stability of international relations, Russia and China also made clear that all states have the right to participate "in the making of, interpreting and applying international law on an equal footing" (point 2), while stressing the need to take into account each state's political identity in this process. As international human rights law is a branch of international law, a country's identity should also have an impact in this field. In this respect, it is worth noting that the *Declaration* makes no mention whatsoever of human rights. This striking "silence", taken together with the need to "contextualise" the rules of international law,

---

6 The chapter does not address or analyse the "human rights' record" of these countries. In this respect, see the results of the last cycles of the Universal Periodic Review related to Russia and China in the framework of the Human Rights Council: respectively, *Report of the Working Group on the Universal Periodic Review – Russian Federation*, 12 June 2018, doc. A/HRC/39/13, and *Report of the Working Group on the Universal Periodic Review – China*, 26 December 2018, doc. A/HRC/40/6. Other non-institutional resources include Human Rights Watch's 2017 World Report on Human Rights for both countries, respectively at www.hrw.org/world-report/2017/country-chapters/russia and www.hrw.org/world-report/2017/country-chapters/china-and-tibet.

7 It is no coincidence that specific references are made to the 1970 Declaration on Principles of International Law concerning Friendly Relations and Cooperation among States, where all these principles are "codified", and to the "Five Principles of Peaceful Coexistence". See UN General Assembly's Resolution 24 October 1970, doc. A/RES/25/2625, and the Principles affirmed in the Panchsheel Treaty, signed on April 29, 1954.

shows a sort of criticism of the western "use" of international law to strengthen the protection of individual fundamental rights and freedoms (Wuerth 2016; Malskoo 2016).

Yet, this is not equal to saying that these countries oppose the respect of human rights as such. Rather, in the Russian and Chinese vision of international law, it is the western focus on human rights protection and fulfilment as a key value of the contemporary international community that can be problematic when it is not balanced with the above traditional core principles[8] or when it jeopardises international and internal stability and/or a country's own identity. As a consequence, Russia and China may be defined as strong guardians and supporters of international law in its most traditional terms, as it is essentially aimed at ensuring peaceful coexistence between sovereign states.

Interestingly, this common position does not reflect an equal common constitutional framework in these countries. In fact, historical, social and cultural factors have shaped very differently the way Russia and China regulate the relationships between international law and their internal legal orders, with significant implications for human rights. This state of affairs certainly supports the view that international law is also a "political project" in which history and culture influence the way it is domestically understood and applied (Bianchi 2016). Let us therefore explore these two countries' internal frameworks separately.

2.1   *Russia: A Consent-based Approach to International Law*
After the USSR's disintegration, there was a widespread belief that Russia had no choice but to make western values its own (Baaz 2016: 264; Juviler 1992). The new Russian constitutional system set up during that time supported this view. In fact, the 1993 Constitution referred not only to sovereignty and territorial integrity and inviolability, which needed to be protected by Russian authorities (see Articles 1, 4, 10 of the Constitution). It also mentioned classical democratic principles, such as democracy, the rule of law and human rights, and set out a remarkable openness to international law.[9] Hence, if the former Soviet Union was characterised by considerable closure to international law, as it had never

---

8   The reference to "The Russian Federation and the People's Republic of China fully support the principle of non-intervention in the internal or external affairs of states, and condemn as a violation of this principle any interference by states in the internal affairs of other states with the aim of forging change of legitimate governments" may be seen as a concrete example of this vision (see *Joint Declaration*, point 4).

9   See *Constitution of the Russian Federation*, adopted on 12 December 1993. An English version is available at www.mid.ru/en/foreign_policy/official_documents/-/asset_publisher/CptICk-B6BZ29/content/id/571508.

before been considered as something that might be invoked or enforced by its domestic courts (Danilenko 1998: 5), the new Russian constitutional framework included this openness to the international order within its fundamental principles (see Chapter 1 of the Russian Constitution).

More specifically, as provided by Art. 15.4 of the 1993 Constitution, universally recognised principles and norms of international law, as well as international agreements of the Russian Federation, are an integral part of its legal system. According to the same provision, if an international agreement of the Russian Federation establishes rules which differ from those stipulated by domestic law, then the rules of the international agreement shall be applied. As a result, the Russian Constitution marked the prevalence of international law over domestic law, although this prevalence is not related to the entire range of obligations binding Russia but is limited only to international treaties. At the same time, as affirmed in Art. 2 of the Constitution, human rights are assumed as the legal order's supreme values and, as such, need to be respected and protected by the state. Interestingly, in the Russian Federation these rights are recognised and guaranteed according to the universally recognised principles and norms of international law as well as to its Constitution (see Art. 17 and Chapter 2 of the Russian Constitution).[10] Finally, while Art. 79 of the Constitution allowed the participation of Russia in international organisations, as well as the transfer of sovereign powers to them, this participation or transfer cannot entail restrictions on human rights and cannot conflict with the basic principles of the Russian constitutional order.

This generally open approach was later confirmed by Federal Law no. 101-FZ, adopted in 1995, on Russia's international treaties, which also granted the Constitutional Court the power to verify the preliminary compatibility of international treaties with the Russian Constitution when the former are not yet in force (see Art. 34). This openness to international law emerged also from the domestic case law. The Constitutional Court has frequently used international law to support a specific interpretation of national provisions (see *Collective Labour Disputes Case*, 1995; *Case Concerning Art. 42 of the Law of the Chuvash Republic on the Election of the Deputies of the State Assembly of the Chuvash Republic*, 1995; see also Danilenko 1998) or as an additional argument for achieving a particular conclusion (see, in relation to the death penalty, judgment 19 November 2009, or to political representation, judgment 21 December 2005). For its part, the Supreme Court also stated the direct applicability of

---

10   As we will see below, this reference to universally recognised principles has not remained ineffective, as it has been essential for subsequent developments in the interaction between Russia and the human rights systems to which it belongs.

international treaties in some cases, affirming that national citizens may derive rights and obligations from them (see Supreme Court decision no. 5/2003).

However, this legal framework, which is indeed similar to many western countries, has been gradually interpreted and used in a way that ensures the superiority of the Constitution and the internal values defining the country's identity over Russia's international obligations (Malksoo 2015). This is especially true as far as the Constitution's "fundamentals" are concerned (Marochkin 2017; Marochkin & Popov 2011). Not surprisingly, this position has gone hand in hand with an increasing emphasis on the importance of international law as the guarantor of a state's sovereignty, meant as "indivisible" and "unlimited" (Malksoo 2015). Put this way, international law is primarily understood as connected with the protection of national security and territorial control. Rather than enhancing states' cooperation in "sensitive" fields such as human rights, the first aim of the international community is to ensure the conditions for peaceful coexistence among equal and sovereign states. In such a traditional view, states' consent is the fundamental basis for any relationship established at the international level and ruled by international law.[11]

This multifaceted approach has influenced the role assigned by Russia to international human rights law. International obligations in the field of human rights are embraced *when* they are consistent with the principle of non-intervention in internal affairs, as well as Russia's prevailing national values. It is no coincidence that, when the international understanding of human rights was perceived as interference in domestic affairs, Russia's participation in human rights systems of protection was questioned. The Russian Constitutional Court's case law is instructive in this respect, as we will analyse below.

2.2 China: A Critical Approach to International Law

The experience of China shows even more clearly that historical and ideological factors have played a great role in the definition of its approach to international law. Although China, along with Russia, seems progressively willing to play the role of "norms shaper" within the contemporary international community, it has always been sceptical of international law. This aspect has hugely influenced both its participation in the international community, as well as the openness of its internal order to international law. It seems that the Chinese leadership is still dominated by "an enduring mentality" according to which China has always been a victim of international law (Chan 2015: 16). The

---

11   It is no coincidence that the mentioned prevalence of international law, as established by
        Art. 15.4 of the Constitution, is affirmed only in relation to international treaties in light of
        the need to provide clear consent to be bound by such international obligations.

imposition of the so-called "unequal treaties" by western countries to take advantage of the Chinese market is at the heart of this position, which in turn radically conditioned the drafting of China's Constitution (Wang 1990: 237).

It is no coincidence that no references to international law were included in the 1982 Constitution[12] and no significant changes were introduced by subsequent reforms, even during the period characterised by greater openness to the international community. Only the well-known five key general principles ruling relations with other states are made explicit in its Preamble. These include mutual respect for sovereignty and territorial integrity, mutual non-aggression, non-interference in each other's internal affairs, equality and mutual benefit, and peaceful coexistence in developing diplomatic relations and economic and cultural exchanges with other countries. While it is true that these principles cannot rule the effects of international law in China's internal legal order (Rossi 2016: 431), they are nonetheless important as they show that China supports a traditional view of the role of international law in the life of the international community.

Nevertheless, it is worth recalling that Chinese legislation, such as the Law on the general principles of civil law (Art. 142), includes some references to international obligations undertaken by China and to their prevalence over conflicting internal norms. However, there is no agreement on the effects of such provisions. This is probably due to the lack in the Constitution of explicit references to the effects of international law within the domestic system, as well as to the general approach of domestic courts that do not seem disposed to apply international law, with some exceptions perhaps in the economic field (Sanzhuan 2009).

All these factors play an important role in defining the country's position on international human rights law. Despite its involvement in specific international human rights mechanisms, China is still characterised by a substantial "closure" to international law. By the same token, although a constitutional reform in 2004 included, for the first time, a new Article 33 providing that "the State respects and preserves human rights", this was not meant to allow the application of international human rights treaties at the domestic level (Ahl 2010: 379).

---

12   The only exception relates to the identification of national authorities called on to conclude and ratify international treaties. See Articles 67, 81 and 89 of the Constitution. All versions, starting from the first Constitution adopted in 1982, are available at www.npc .gov.cn/englishnpc/Constitution/node_2824.htm. Considering that no references are made even to customary international law, the Chinese Constitution has been identified as a *unicum* within contemporary national constitutions. See A. Cassese, *Modern Constitutions and International Law*, in *Recueil des cours*, vol. 192, 1985, at 437.

This comprehensive approach gives rise to the framework that permits China to "protect" its own view of human rights as well as its internal order from the prevailing understanding of human rights at the international level, as we will explore below.

3   Between Universalism, Regionalism and National Values

Despite their shared views on the role of international law, Russia and China show a different approach to the issue of human rights. If, as seen above, both countries tend to allow collective interests to prevail over individual rights, in contrast to the balance commonly shown in the West, each country takes a different approach to achieving that balance. While Russia pays great attention to the protection of the values on which its identity is framed, China recognises a primary weight to its strategic aims as a regional and global power. These distinctive features emerge clearly from the dialogue of both countries with the international systems of human rights protection to which they belong.

3.1   *Russia: "National Identity First"*
As a matter of principle, Russia shares the idea that individuals have rights that may be claimed directly before a judge. This explains why, after the fall of the Soviet Union, it was easy for Russia to join the international systems of human rights protection, including the ECHR and its enforcement mechanism set up in the Council of Europe's framework. This position is well expressed also in the Russian Constitution which, in Article 46, recognises even an individual right to submit a claim to an international mechanism for protecting one's rights, provided that all internal remedies have been exhausted.

Yet, Russia's involvement in these international frameworks has encountered some difficulties. Let us consider the example of death penalty. It is widely known that a preliminary condition to join the Council of Europe is the abolition of death penalty. While Russia promised to abolish this kind of punishment and to ratify the additional Protocol no. 6 to the ECHR elaborated for this purpose, after almost twenty years it was eventually able only to grant a *de facto* moratorium.[13] According to some scholars, this demonstrates that Russia was not ready to undertake such international obligations (Malskoo 2012: 363).

---

13   See the Amnesty International, *Death Sentences and Executions*, 2017, p. 43. As it may be verified through the CoE Treaty Office's website, *Protocol no. 6 to the Convention for the Protection of Human Rights and Fundamental Freedoms concerning the Abolition of the Death Penalty*, opened for signature on 28 April 1983, was only signed by Russia in 1997.

Its membership in the European human rights protection system was therefore aimed primarily at causing a positive "Strasbourg effect", which still seems far from having been fully produced (if not even dwindling now: Malskoo & Benedek 2018: 4–6; 24; 399).

The ongoing dialogue between domestic judges, especially the Constitutional Court, and the ECtHR is instructive in this respect. While it is true that, since the ratification in 1998, Russia's internal order has been influenced positively by interaction with the ECtHR (Lapitskaya 2011; Caligiuri 2016; Malskoo & Benedek 2018),[14] in the last years internal courts have begun to identify the ECtHR's activity as a sort of repetitive and illegitimate interference in their own conceptualisation of human rights and freedoms.

The first occasion in which such discontent emerged was the ECtHR's decision in the *Markin* case.[15] The application, which dealt with an army employee claiming family benefits that were granted only to his female colleagues, called into question the Russian idea of family and gender roles. By deciding in favour of the applicant and his right to enjoy childcare leave without discrimination based on his sex, the ECtHR advanced its idea of equality between men and women and its anti-stereotyping vision of gender roles in family and society (Timmer 2011). Due to a more traditional understanding of the same concepts, Russian authorities opposed the ECtHR's interpretation of the relevant ECHR's provisions, as well as the execution of this judgement. Yet, called to take a position on the internal developments of the *Markin* case, the Russian Constitutional Court was able to reconcile the ECtHR's reading with Russian values by stressing that both systems are based on the same concept of human rights (Vaypan 2014).[16]

---

14 See also Russian Constitutional Court, judgment no. 4-P, 26 February 2010, and Supreme Court of the Russian Federation, order 10 October 2003, no. 21 (*On the Application by Courts of General Jurisdiction of the Convention on the Protection of Human Rights and Fundamental Freedoms from 4 November 1950 and the Protocols Thereto*), on the obligation of domestic Tribunals to consider the interpretation given by the ECtHR when implementing the ECHR.

15 ECtHR, Grand Chamber, 22 March 2012, *Konstantin Markin v. Russia*, no. 30078/06. As noticed also by some scholars (Malskoo & Benedek 2018), at least two other cases have significantly marked the general relationship between Russia and the ECtHR: ECtHR, 21 October 2010, *Alekseyev v. Russia*, nos. 4916/07, 25924/08 and 14599/09; ECtHR, Grand Chamber, 19 October 2012, *Catan and Others v. Moldova and Russia*, nos. 43370/04, 8252/05 and 18454/06.

16 See Russian Constitutional Court, judgment no. 27-P, 6 December 2013, related to the consequences of the *Markin* case.

In light of growing criticism of the ECtHR, which reached perhaps its highest peaks with the judgment in the *Yukos* case,[17] the Constitutional Court eventually adopted a more defensive approach aimed at ensuring that Russia's idea of "human rights" would always prevail vis-à-vis its international law commitments (Filippini 2016: 386; Malskoo & Benedek 2018). Thus, in 2015, the Constitutional Court affirmed that Russian interaction with the ECHR's system of protection cannot be possible in conditions of "subordination"[18] to the latter. Building on the principle of "sovereign equality of States", recalled as a *jus cogens* norm (Kleinlein 2017), the Constitutional Court fundamentally affirmed that Russia is entitled to avoid complying with its international duties when the ECtHR's own reading of the ECHR does not respect the Russian "national constitutional identity" or, alternatively, is not admissible in light of Russian values.[19] While pushing for the introduction of an important legislative reform (Guazzarotti 2016: 383), with this decision the Constitutional Court essentially supported the idea that the "specificity" of Russian society should be protected against "external" interpretations of human rights, unless Russia ensures its express consent.

It is no coincidence that soon after, an internal institutional reform was adopted to ensure that the Russian Constitutional Court can prioritise Russian values over the obligations arising under the ECHR, including the execution of the ECtHR's judgments and how such judgments should be executed.[20]

Hence, in *Anchugov and Gladkov*, the first judgment adopted after this law entered into force, the Constitutional Court got the chance to clarify the above position in a case related to prisoners' right to vote, previously examined by the ECHtR. In the Russian authorities' view, the interpretation given by the ECtHR to the right to vote, protected under Art. 3, Protocol no. 1 to the ECHR, created

---

17   ECtHR, 31 July 2014, *Yukos v. Russia*, no. 14902/04, giving rise to one of the biggest amount of money to be paid to a victim (almost 2 billion of Euros) in the history of the ECHR.

18   See Russian Constitutional Court, judgment no. 21-П, 2015.

19   See Venice Commission, Opinion 13 June 2016, no. 832/2015, para. 59–73.

20   See Law of the Russian Federation amending the Law on the Constitutional Court no. 1-FKZ of 21 July 1994, which entered into force on 15 December 2015. According to this Law, a federal executive authority, "which has competence for protecting the interests of the Russian Federation in litigations before an inter-state body on the protection of human rights and freedom", may ask the Constitutional Court to declare that an international judgment should not be executed if it is based on an interpretation of the international treaty which is deemed to be in contrast with the Constitution. As a result, substantially the Constitutional Court has been given the powers to declare an international decision "non-executable", to identify how to execute an international judgment, as well as to assess the constitutionality of an individual measure of execution, such as an order to pay just satisfaction.

a conflict between the European Convention and the Russian Constitution. In fact, the latter denies the right to elect and to be elected to citizens who are kept in places of imprisonment (see Art. 32 of the Russian Constitution). According to the Constitutional Court, when Russia ratified the ECHR such a divergence did not exist. It has been, instead, the result of the subsequent ECtHR's own reading of the European Convention. Although deemed "exceptional", in such a situation Russia can advance its own interpretation of human rights as embedded in its Constitution and refuse the execution of the ECtHR's judgments. Despite the Constitutional Court stressed its willingness to reach lawful compromises with the ECtHR in the future, in the subsequent *Yukos* case[21] it again refused to execute the ECtHR's relevant judgment (Marochkin 2017).

In this process, it is notable that, in order to support its arguments on the relationship between the duty to enforce international human rights obligations and the protection of national values, the Russian Constitutional Court referred to the case law of the Italian and German Constitutional Courts. On some occasions, these Courts have indeed embraced different interpretations of human rights or have refused the execution of international obligations in order to let the protection of individual rights, as read at the domestic level, prevail.[22] However, the two situations do not appear comparable. While the Italian and German Constitutional Courts privilege dialogue with the international judge in order to create better mutual understanding and achieve common results, in the Russian case dominant domestic social conceptions prevail for protecting supposed collective identity values.[23] In doing so, the Russian Constitutional Court essentially stresses the need to comply with traditional principles of international law, such as sovereignty, non-intervention in internal affairs and equality of States, in line with the analysed approach to international law.

Hence, while it may be said that it substantially confirms its adherence to the ECHR system, the Constitutional Court's case law makes clear two points. First, it grants Russian authorities the "last word" on some specific "sensitive" issues for Russian society.[24] In this way, a wide range of situations may be

---

21 See Russian Constitutional Court, judgment 19 January 2017.

22 See for instance Italian Constitutional Court, 22 October 2014, judgment no. 238, on which among many others R.P. Mazzeschi 2015; Cataldi 2015.

23 See also Venice Commission, Opinion 11 March 2016, which pointed out the flimsiness of the comparison made by the Constitutional Court of the Russian Federation with the German and Italian Constitutional Courts.

24 According to some, this might be justified in line with the principle of subsidiarity on which the entire international human rights system is based (Shelton 2013 and *High Level*

protected as expressions of Russia's national identity, such as the patriarchal idea of society or the heterosexual nature of the family. Second, it points out how Russia strikes a balance between conflicting interests. While it does not deny the protection of individual rights, Russia allows the prevalence of domestic collective and moral values that shape its national identity over such individual rights. However, in turn, this eventually leads to giving a different meaning to the same human rights, thus undermining the consolidation of their universal, and even regional, understanding.

3.2 China: "People First"

According to the Chinese approach, human rights are "aspirational goals" to be promoted progressively, instead of enforceable individual rights. This probably explains why if compared to Russia, China is characterised by a lower degree of integration in international human rights mechanisms. This is true even at the regional level, where a feeble human rights framework based on some shared values is promoted by ASEAN.[25] At the same time, this has also prevented the acceptance of relevant international human rights treaty-bodies' competence in receiving applications from individuals subject to China's jurisdiction.

Yet, this limited participation in the universal human rights machinery, which started soon after the inauguration of its "open-door" economic reform policies at the end of 1978, has resulted in the definition of its own concept of human rights. In contrast with Russia's defensive approach, China has advanced a specific proposal in this field in order to avoid being at odds in the international arena as well as to promote its core interests: ensuring favourable international conditions for its economic growth, preserving political and social stability and defending its territorial integrity (Sceats & Breslin 2012). Put in the context of the history of China's international relations, this general approach seems to be based on the need to "regain" a central role in the international arena after the long period "of shame" (Onnis 2011).

Historical factors are important in this process. While China's initial adherence to international efforts to promote and respect human rights did not lead to any significant domestic changes, it put pressure on the country to express

---

Conference on the Future of the European Court of Human Rights – Brighton Declaration, 19–20 April 2012, where this principle is particularly stressed) and does not differ from the approach supported by other States bound by the ECHR (Malskoo & Benedek 2018). However, this can only apply where the right, as protected at the European level, leaves room for a margin of appreciation by the Contracting States, which is a situation that is far from the Russian case law analysed here.

25   See Plan of Action to Implement the Joint Declaration on ASEAN-China Strategic Partnership for Peace and Prosperity (2016–2020), point 1.6.

its position in the field (Foot 2000). It is no coincidence that China's own vision of the matter was expressed only after the 1989 events in Tiananmen Square, through the publication of the first White Paper on Human Rights in 1991 and the subsequent adoption of a few National Human Rights Action Plans.[26] Already on that occasion, some essential aspects emerged as distinctive features of the Chinese proposal in the field of human rights. Subsequently reaffirmed and further elaborated in international *fora*, these aspects may be here analysed.

Firstly, although Chinese authorities accept the idea of the universality of human rights, China supports a vision based on the idea that human rights are not subjective legal entitlements directly enforceable before a judge. Human rights are understood as "causes" to be promoted in line with each state's social and economic development (Xue 2012: 144). As such, in China's view, social, cultural and historical particularities are fundamental parameters for promoting some "universal" rights instead of others in order to grant the country's general wellbeing. That is why, in one of the last national Human Rights Action Plans, China affirmed the principle of "pursing practicality": this is meant as the need to develop the human rights "cause" on "a practical basis" in light of China's conditions as a country.[27] In this respect, for instance, the death penalty is still considered necessary in light of its level of socio-economic development, but it may be superfluous in the future.[28]

Secondly, on all occasions in which human rights are discussed in international fora, Chinese authorities stress the collective dimension of this development paradigm (Subedi 2015: 439). It is no coincidence that human rights are not referred to as belonging to the individual human being but are promoted as "the rights of people". That is why, in China's view, individual rights should not prevail or be prioritised over the interests of the country and may be sacrificed in light of the common goals pursued by the society as a whole. Indeed, the rights of individuals and of minority groups may be restricted for ensuring the peaceful coexistence of the national (and international) community, as this is the preliminary condition for ensuring the country's development. Following this *rationale*, it is not uncommon for China to identify what is described externally in terms of human rights violations as tools for ensuring the

---

26 For a detailed analysis of these policy instruments, see A. Pisanò, *Human Rights and Social Development in the Chinese White Papers on Human Rights*, in *Peace Human Rights Governance*, 2018, 301–330.

27 *National Human Rights Action Plan 2012–2015*, 2011.

28 See *Report of the Working Group on the Universal Periodic Review – China*, points 15; 22 ff. See also footnote 6.

country's social stability and security and, ultimately, for reaching higher standards of protection.[29]

A few consequences may be drawn from this general proposal. First, China usually supports collective rights, such as the right to self-determination or the right to development, while stressing individual duties. For example, in the 1991 White Paper on human rights, Chinese authorities made clear that the right to subsistence is the primary "cause" to be promoted "by the State", while in international *fora* they emphasise the reduction of poverty as China's main human rights achievement. Second, China prioritises socio-economic rights over civil and political rights, thus questioning the principle of the indivisibility of human rights as one of the core characteristics of the international human rights' framework. It is no coincidence that China has not yet ratified the International Covenant on Civil and Political Rights but only the International Covenant on Economic, Social and Cultural Rights.[30] This limited move, however, has not ensured that socio-economic rights could become enforceable by individuals under Chinese jurisdiction. In fact, it seems that only on a few occasions have international human rights treaties ratified by China been applied by domestic courts.[31]

This "Chinese vision" of human rights also finds expression within the UN system. For instance, China seems to use the UN bodies to emphasise its goals when human rights are at stake. In this regard some scholars have underlined an "unordinary" activism within the General Assembly, which has been aimed, together with Russia, at promoting discussions on international security and human rights, including issues around the restriction of the use of internet for granting national social stability (Sceats & Breslin 2012: 37). By the same token,

---

29   For some scholars, this explains China's ambivalent attitude on the international level towards the events of the so-called Arab spring and the gross human rights violations in Syria (Sceats & Breslin 2012: 27 ff.). See also the records of the Human Rights Council's discussion during its 18th session in Geneva, when China delivered one of its few statements on the "duties of States to maintain public security, public order and social stability". The same approach was pointed out for Russia (Dannreuther 2015: 77 ff.).

30   China ratified the International Covenant on Economic and Social Rights in 2001. This treaty protects, among others, the right to self-determination and the right of everyone to an adequate standard of living and to the continuous improvement of living conditions, including the "fundamental" right of everyone to be free from hunger. See www.ohchr .org/en/professionalinterest/pages/cescr.aspx.

31   More specifically, the national judge at stake used the international Convention on the Rights of the Child, ratified by China in 1993, to handle a dispute between two parents over their children's custody recalling the duty to protect involved children in line with their best interests. See Popular Court of Jing'an District, *F.D. v. Dong*, no. 1816/2012 and Popular Intermediate Second Court of Shanghai, *F.D. v. Dong*, no. 1661/2013. As affirmed elsewhere, these cases are identified as exceptional: see Rossi 2016: 441.

China has used the periodic review mechanism set up by the UN Human Rights Council, the so-called Universal Periodic Review (UPR), to stress its re-interpretation of human rights. In the documents related to the UPR of the country carried out in 2013, China stated its necessity to build "a moderately prosperous society"[32] and to establish "a robust system of human rights safe-guards" in the "framework of socialism with Chinese characteristics".[33] The Chinese motto "putting people first" was thus emphasised in order to stress the idea that only a "fairer and more harmonious society" ensures the enjoyment of "a life of ever-greater dignity, freedom and well-being" for every citizen.[34]

4   Concluding Remarks

This chapter has shown that Russia and China have their own vision of inter-national law, based on the respect of their most traditional principles such as the equality of states and non-interference in domestic affairs. This position was confirmed in the joint official 2016 *Declaration*, which both countries are trying to use to influence the development of international law. This position has equally influenced the degree of openness of Russia's and China's internal legal orders and, in turn, their understanding of international human rights law in terms of role and content as well as how they strike a balance with com-peting interests.

As analysed above, notwithstanding the common approach to the role of international law, these countries' participation in international human rights systems has enabled the emergence of some distinctive features. Despite the fact that both countries stress the collective dimension of human rights, Russia pays great attention to the protection of values that shape its national identity while China advances its own concept or, even better, its own reinterpretation of human rights for pursuing its national strategic aims.

More broadly, the approach of these two countries to international law sheds light on the difficulty of reaching a "universal" understanding of international

---

32   See *Report of the Working Group on the Universal Periodic Review – China*, 4 December 2013, doc. A/HRC/25/5 point 6. It also stressed the need to: strike a balance between re-form, development and stability; place great emphasis on poverty reduction; work hard to improve well-being and promote inclusive development; and enhance environmental and ecological protection (point 83).

33   See also the report discussed by XI Jinping on 18 October 2017 at the XIX National Con-gress of the Chinese Communist Party.

34   *National report submitted in accordance with paragraph 5 of the annex to Human Rights Council resolution 16/21 – China*, 5 August 2013, points 4 and 5, doc. A/HRC/WG.6/17/CHN/1.

norms and values. International law is often perceived as a Western/European projection that needs to be renegotiated to take into account other or different traditions. If this push to renegotiate international law is governed by a genuine interest in human dignity, it does not seem to be a problem in itself, in light of the potential positive long-term effects on the international community. In fact, the more international norms and values are shared, the easier their consolidation, respect and/or implementation.

To this end, considering the role of Russia and China, a stable and structured dialogue is certainly beneficial for the international community as a whole and should be further promoted to ensure fruitful "traffic in both directions" (Baaz 2016: 275).

Bibliography

Ahl, B. (2010). 'Exploring Ways of Implementing International Human Rights Treaties in China', *Netherlands Quarterly of Human Rights*, 28(3): 361–403.

Baaz, M. (2016). 'International Law is Different in Different Places: Russian Interpretations and Outlooks', *International Journal of Constitutional Law*, 14(1): 262–276.

Bianchi, A. (2016). *International Law Theories. An Inquiry into Different Ways of Thinking*. Oxford: Oxford University Press.

Bowring, B. (2015). 'What's in a Word: "Sovereignty" in the Constitutional Court of Russian Federation', *Russian Journal of Communications*, 7(3): 328–336.

Caligiuri, A. (2016). 'La recente giurisprudenza costituzionale russa sui rapporti tra Convenzione europea dei diritti umani e ordinamento interno', *Diritti umani e diritto internazionale*, 10(3): 703–711.

Cassese, A. (1985). 'Modern Constitutions and International Law', Collected Courses of the Hague Academy of International Law, vol. 192. Leiden, Boston: Brill Nijhoff.

Cataldi, G. (2015). 'La Corte costituzionale e il ricorso ai "contro-limiti" nel rapporto tra consuetudini internazionali e diritti fondamentali: oportet ut scandala eveniant', *Diritto internazionale e diritti umani*, 11(1): 41–50.

Chan, P.C.W. (2015). *China, State Sovereignty and International Legal Order*. Leiden, Boston: Brill Nijhoff.

Danilenko, G.M. (1998). 'Implementation of International Law in Russia and Other CIS States', NATO research paper, www.nato.int/acad/fellow/96-98/danilenk.pdf.

Dannreuther, R. (2015). 'Russia and the Arab Spring: Supporting the Counter-Revolution', *Journal of European Integration*, (37)1: 77–94.

Filippini, C. (2016). 'La Russia e la Cedu: l'obiezione della Corte costituzionale all'esecuzione delle sentenze di Strasburgo', *Quaderni costituzionali*, 36(2): 386–389.

Foot, R. (2000). *Rights Beyond Borders. The Global Community and the Struggle over Human Rights in China*, Oxford: Oxford University Press.

Guazzarotti, A. (2016). 'La Russia e la CEDU: i controlimiti visti da Mosca', *Quaderni costituzionali*, 36(2): 383–386.

Juviler, P. (1992). 'Human Rights in the Ex-Soviet Successor States: A Case of the Bends', *Nationalities Papers*, 20(2): 15–24.

Kleinlein, T. (2017). 'Jus Cogens Re-examined: Value Formalism in International Law', *European Journal of International Law*, 28(1): 295–315.

Koskenniemi, M. (2010). 'What is International Law for?', in M.D. Evans (ed.), *International Law*, 4th Edition. Oxford: Oxford University Press.

Lapitskaya, J. (2011). 'ECHR, Russia, and Chechnya: Two is not Company and Three is Definitely a Crowd', *International Law and Politics*, 43(2): 479–547.

Malksoo, L. (2012). 'Russia and European Human-Rights Law: Margins of the Margin of Appreciation', *Review of Central and East European Law*, 37(2): 359–369.

Malksoo, L. (2015). *Russian Approaches to International Law*. Oxford: Oxford University Press.

Malskoo, L. (2016). 'Russia and China Challenge the Western Hegemony in the Interpretation of International Law', *EJIL Talk!*, 15 July, www.ejiltalk.org/russia-and-china-challenge-the-western-hegemony-in-the-interpretation-of-international-law/.

Malskoo, L. and Benedek, W. (eds.) (2018). *Russia and the European Court of Human Rights. The Strasbourg Effect*. Cambridge: Cambridge University Press.

Marochkin, S.Y. (2017). 'A Russian Approach to International Law in the Domestic Legal Order: Basics, Development and Perspectives', *Italian Yearbook of International Law*, 26: 15–40.

Marochkin, S.Y. and Popov, V.A. (2011). 'International Humanitarian and Human Rights Law in Russian Courts', *Journal of International Humanitarian Legal Studies*, 2(2): 216–249.

Neo, J.L. (2017). 'Realizing the Right to Freedom of Thought, Conscience and Religion: The Limited Normative Force of the ASEAN Human Rights Declaration', *Human Rights Law Review*, 17(4): 729–751.

Onnis, B. (2011). *Le relazioni internazionali della Cina*, Roma: Carocci.

Pisanò, A. (2018). 'Human Rights and Social Development in the Chinese White Papers on Human Rights', *Peace Human Rights Governance*, 2(3): 301–330.

Pisillo Mazzeschi, R. (2015). 'La sentenza n. 238 del 2014 della costituzionale ed i suoi possibili effetti sul diritto internazionale', *Diritto internazionale e diritti umani*, 11(1): 23–40.

Renshaw, C.S. (2013). 'The ASEAN Human Rights Declaration 2012', in *Human Rights Law Review*, 13(3): 557–579.

Rossi, P. (2016). 'L'adattamento al diritto internazionale nell'ordinamento giuridico della repubblica Popolare Cinese', *Rivista di diritto internazionale*, 99(2): 425–453.

Sanzhuan, G. (2009). 'Implementation of Human Rights Treaties by Chinese Courts: Problems and Prospects', *Chinese Journal of International Law*, 8(1): 161–179.

Sceats, S. and Breslin, S. (2012). *China and the International Human Rights System*, London: The Royal Institute of International Affairs.

Shelton, D. (ed.). (2013). *The Oxford Handbook of International Human Rights Law*, Oxford: Oxford University Press.

Subedi, S.P. (2015). 'China's Approach to Human Rights and the UN Human Rights Agenda', *Chinese Journal of International Law*, 14(3): 437–464.

Timmer, A. (2011). 'Toward an Anti-Stereotyping Approach for the European Court of Human Rights', *Human Rights Law Review*, 11(4): 707–738.

Vaypan, G. (2014). 'Acquiescence affirmed, its limits left undefined: The Markin judgement and the pragmatism of the Russian Constitutional Court vis-à-vis the European Court of Human Rights,' *Russian Law Journal*, 2(3): 130–140.

Wang, T. (1990). 'International Law in China: Historical and Comparative Perspectives', Collected Courses of the Hague Academy of International Law, vol. 192. Leiden, Boston: Brill Nijhoff.

Wuerth, I. (2016). 'China, Russia and International Law', *Lawfare*, 11 July, www.lawfare blog.com/china-russia-and-international-law.

Xue, H. (2012). *Chinese Contemporary Perspectives on International Law*. Leiden, Boston: Brill Nijhoff.

CHAPTER 5

The Emerging Influence of the Chinese Strong-State Model

Mingjiang Li and Mahalakshmi Ganapathy

The rise of China has been astonishing. The economic achievements that the country has made in the past 40 years are unprecedented in human history. Many analysts believe that the Chinese experience in modernization has now successfully created a China model or "Beijing consensus". Chief among the features of the China model is a strong state which spearheaded the socio-economic transformations in China in the past decades.

This chapter analyzes the role of a strong Chinese state in shaping the evolution of China's political economy since the 1990s. We discuss how the Chinese Communist Party (CCP) managed to maintain its monopoly of power in China while allowing for some features of a hybrid politico-economic system to exist. We use the term "hybrid" to show the coexistence of political authoritarianism and economic liberalism, though economic liberalism in the Chinese context is quite different from that of many Western countries. We examine how the ruling elites have undertaken political and ideological reforms, dealt with state-society relations, handled political dissidents, and managed new socio-political changes brought about by new social media platforms. We will analyze how a strong Chinese state has played a dominating role in economic reform and opening up, in social welfare policy reform, and in macro-economic policy management. We will also assess how these socio-economic policies and achievements have, in turn, sustained the CCP's legitimacy and power. In the concluding section, we will summarize the key arguments in the chapter and briefly discuss the potential global influence of the Chinese model.

1 The CCP's Efforts in Maintaining and Enhancing a Strong Party-State

The introduction of economic reform in the late 1970s under Deng Xiaoping was the first step towards the re-establishment of CCP legitimacy. After Mao died in 1976, the elites replaced his "techniques of mass mobilization and ideological indoctrinations" with a "performance-oriented paradigm" (Weatherly

2006: 109), to be achieved with aggressive economic goals. The argument of economic growth was used as a tool to revive ailing party fortunes (at the same time, the Chinese leaders made it very clear that the reform program should not undermine CCP rule in any manner). Deng Xiaoping specifically highlighted the need to observe the Four Cardinal Principles: sticking to the socialist path, maintaining the ruling position of the CCP, insisting on the dictatorship of the proletariat, and following the guidance of Marxism, Leninism, and Mao Thought. From the very beginning, economic reform was carried out within these political boundaries.

In the face of various political limitations, Chinese incremental reform began to deliver impressive results within a short period of time. Between 1978–2012 the average growth rate of real GDP has been 9.4 percent (Cheremukhin et al. 2015: 3). China has also made unprecedented progress in addressing the issues of poverty alleviation. Based on China's official poverty line, the absolute level of poverty incidence fell from 33 percent in 1978 to less than 3 percent in 2004. Based on the World Bank's US$ 1/day (in terms of purchasing power parity) poverty line, the incidence of rural poverty also fell from more than 30 percent in the early 1990s to about 8 percent in 2004 (Huang et al. 2006.) Average annual growth rates of 9.7 percent between 1985 and 1995 also enabled China to achieve self-sufficiency in grain production for the first time since 1949.

Rapid economic development restored the CCP's credibility, enabling it to take the lead in delivering growth and improving living standards. Paradoxically, as the pace of reform gained momentum, the CCP was confronted with two fundamental questions: (1) How could the CCP continue to rely on Marxist ideology as the source of its authority when there was a clear contradiction between Marxism and market economics? (2) To what extent would the CCP be willing to reform the political system without threatening its monopoly on power? (Weatherly 2006: 109). The CCP now had to reconcile reform with the core Marxist ideology and come up with a Marxist explanation for economic reform.

Party leaders decided to re-interpret orthodox Marxism in the context of China's need to address those questions. In the mid-1980s, the CCP declared that China had entered a new phase of development called the "Socialist Commodity Economy", in which state-owned enterprises (SOEs) would enjoy greater independence than before and were allowed to sell "an increasing number of commodities in the market place" (Weatherly 2006: 111). Making a case for markets, party theorists argued that a limited role for market forces was not only useful but also essential to China's socialist development.

Another attempt at making current economic reform conform to China's Marxist ideology was undertaken by Zhao Ziyang (a former party general-secretary). Zhao in the 1980s claimed that even though China was a communist country, it was still an underdeveloped nation and remained in the "primary stage of socialism" (Chai 2003: 168). Before the shift to communism, the first priority was to achieve rapid development of the means of production by means of capitalist measures. In 1987, Zhao argued before the 13th National Congress that "the Chinese people cannot take the socialist road without going through the stage of fully developed capitalism", nor could China "jump over the stage of highly developed productive forces" (Wang 2002: 60).

Reform and opening up in the 1980s, amid growing political activism and ideological confusion among Chinese intellectuals (partly prompted by socio-economic problems of corruption and inflation), eventually led to the Tiananmen movement in 1989. Many Chinese social elites and young students took to the streets in protest against corruption, calling for democratic reform. The CCP leaders brutally suppressed the movement to demonstrate its resolve to rule in China and continue with reform characterized by gradual economic liberalism and tight political control.

In the aftermath of the 1989 Tiananmen demonstrations, there was a conservative turn in economics. Deng, seeking to reverse what he felt was a roll-back of reform, gave a series of speeches in the early 1990s to champion further reform. In his speeches, he introduced a theory known as the Criterion of Productive Forces (similar to Zhao Ziyang's theory) which defined all reform-enhancing methods, whether it be the central plan or the open market, as socialist (Fewsmith 2001: 133). In January 1992, he made a highly symbolic visit to the southern Chinese cities of Shenzhen and Zhuhai, the Special Economic Zones (SEZs) of China which most closely signified the achievements of economic reform.

Dismissing his rivals' claims that lopsided reform led to the Tiananmen crisis, Deng held that the opposite was true. According to him, it was economic reform that saved the CCP after the tumultuous Cultural Revolution and helped it overcome the crisis in 1989. He argued that the real threat to China's future came from conservatives in the CCP who sought to take China back to the pre-reform days of ideological campaigns and class struggle. Deng then called upon Guangdong to catch up economically with the wealthy "dragons" in East Asia (namely Taiwan, South Korea, Singapore and Hong Kong) within 20 years (Fewsmith 2001: 137).

Economic reform continued to be treated as a panacea even after the 1989 Tiananmen crisis, with added emphasis on accelerated reform. Like the demonstrations in Tiananmen Square, the collapse of socialism in Eastern Europe and the subsequent break-up of the Soviet Union underscored that reform that led to economic development could also lead to political collapse. But Deng, pressing forward with reform, was convinced that China could handle the potential fallout arising from market reform. He insisted that while socialist reform would lead to economic development, capitalist reform would lead to the collapse of socialism. When a renewed emphasis on socialist market economy became the norm in 1992, the CCP sought to wrap capitalist modes of production in socialist terms (Fewsmith 2012: 7). In the subsequent 20 years, the Chinese economy experienced a remarkable transformation. The GDP continued to increase at a phenomenal rate and improved the lives of the majority of Chinese people.

Besides economic performance, other ideological and political policies also played a pivotal role in maintaining CCP rule by enhancing socio-political stability in China. Forward-looking economic policies, stagnant political reforms, and emphasis on nationalism were used as tools of legitimacy. Perry (2007: 8), in explaining how China held onto and enhanced a strong party-state since the 1990s, points to the "retention and reinvention" of many elements of China's revolutionary heritage. For example, to move from Maoist Communism to post-Mao authoritarianism, the leaders mixed old revolutionary practices to form a robust brand of "revolutionary authoritarianism". Further, Nathan (2003: 10) explains the "resilience" of China's authoritarian system with regime theory. The CCP has focused on the regime's institutionalization for its survival. There is a "norm-bound succession politics", whereby a peaceful, orderly succession from one generation of leaders to the other has been institutionalized. Few authoritarian regimes, Nathan asserts, have managed to conduct orderly, peaceful, and stable leadership transitions. Second, Deng Xiaoping in the 1980s gave instructions to senior party leaders to undertake a "four-way transformation" of cadre corps by finding and promoting cadres around the age of 40 who were "revolutionary, younger, more educated and more technically specialised". Third, there has been an "institutional differentiation within the regime" with the separation of policy and ideology. State Council members and provincial–level officials are selected increasingly for their policy-relevant experience whereas large enterprises were either removed from state ownership or placed under joint state-private ownership.

2   Political and Ideological Reforms during the Eras of Jiang Zemin
        and Hu Jintao

Jiang Zemin and Hu Jintao, two successors designated by Deng, continued the economic reform and pursued greater routinization of politics to strengthen the CCP's legitimacy. Jiang Zemin, who took over from Deng in 1989 and ruled until 2002 is credited for introducing informal norms into China's elite politics. Elite politics during the Jiang era became more "rational, normal and predictable" (Shambaugh 2001: 101). He advanced the new concept of the Three Represents to augment Deng's "socialism with Chinese characteristics". According to Jiang, the party now represented "three forces" in Chinese society: "the most advanced social productive forces" (including China's growing urban middle class of entrepreneurs, professionals, and high technology specialists), "the most advanced culture" (which now includes foreign and traditional Chinese culture), and "the fundamental interests of the broad masses of the people" (Bao 2002). The CCP's formal recognition of the new and emerging middle class in China ("the most advanced social productive forces") sought not only to move away from the Mao era's disdain for the moneyed class but to actively represent their interests in the post-Mao market era, along with those of their traditional voting block, the working classes, and peasantry.

The second and more important element of this strategy was the active recruitment of entrepreneurs and other professionals into the CCP. This is seen as a strategy of co-opting a potential source of opposition "into" the system. This strategy provides a key explanation for the CCP's survival – the ability to recruit, monitor, and reward the political elite (Brødsgaard 2004: 57–91). According to China's scholars, such co-optation has worked in favor of the CCP, where neither the rising class of entrepreneurs nor the declining class of workers demand political reform. As the elite are increasingly bound to the CCP through policies and institutions, they show more interest in political stability than in political reform.

Given this stability and renewed legitimacy, both Deng's theory and Jiang Zemin's Three Represents paved the way for China's adoption of pragmatism and multilateralism as its outlook for the twenty-first century (Zhang 1998: 169). This new outlook led to China's participation in multilateral economic arrangements that accelerated China's development in the 1990s. China took an active role in the Asia Pacific Economic Cooperation (APEC), the Association of Southeast Asian Nations (ASEAN), the Pacific Economic Cooperation Council (PECC), and eventually the World Trade Organization (WTO). China also participated in many regional security dialogues like the ASEAN Regional Forum (ARF), the Conference on Interaction and Confidence-BuildingMeasures in Asia (CICA), the Council on Security Cooperation in Asia and Pacific Region (CSCAP), and the Northeast Asia Cooperation Dialogue (NEACD). China's decision to become a member of the World Trade Organization in 2002, in particular, signified China's deeper integration into the world economy.

Ideological adaptations continued during the Hu Jintao era. Hu was elected general secretary of the CCP in November 2002. He proposed the "Scientific Concept of Development" as an antidote to the growing ills of income disparity and inequality that arose due to far-ranging economic reforms. It emphasised the "scientific" (*kexue*) nature of the new concept, signifying the CCP's innovative capacities and strategies for tackling these social ills. The "scientific" nature was espoused in the so-called "five co-ordinations" that included overall coordination of urban and rural development, regional development, economic development, and social development. The focus was on integrating humanism with the "five co-ordinations" to achieve harmonious development between man and nature while coordinating development and further opening up to the world (People's Daily 2004).

The Harmonious Socialist Society (*Shehui zhuyi hexie shehui*) was another formula introduced by Hu Jintao to better underscore the social expectations contained in the Scientific Outlook on Development. The concept of a harmonious society was first mentioned in the resolution of the 16th National Congress in November 2002 and defined at the Fourth Plenary Session in September 2004 as a society built on "democracy and rule of law, justice and equality, trust and truthfulness, amity and vitality, order and stability, and a harmonious relation with nature" (China Daily 2010).

The concept acknowledged the existence of serious social contradictions that had arisen during the reform era, increasing economic inequality, the growing material and cultural needs of the people, and the lessening hold of party ideology to influence them. Hu expounded on the concept's relevance where he stated that the ideas contained in the harmonious socialist society were essential for consolidating the party's foundation to govern, thus drawing attention to the legitimacy of the Party.

This trend of ideological adaptation continued even after Xi Jinping took over political power in 2012. He successfully consolidated his power through a series of dazzling political moves such as an anti-corruption campaign, rectification activities within the party, and "campaigns to discredit Western democracy" (ChinaFile 2013). He was officially recognized as the core of the party's leadership during the 19th National Congress in 2017. The "Xi Jinping Theory on Socialism with Chinese Characteristics for the New Era" was written into party and state constitutions. With the growth of Xi's personal power, the CCP is better poised for greater intervention in China's political economy as compared to past decades. Political and ideological control has been tightened in China. Xi has a grand blueprint for China's grand national rejuvenation. The Xi leadership has also called for a new round of reform and opening up for the coming decades. It appears that Chinese politics is becoming more inward-looking and conservative while economic development takes the same path of state-dominated market reforms.

3   Managing Changing State-Society Relations since the 1990s

One notable feature of the reform programs initiated by the CCP since the late 1970s has been the expansion of social organizations. While Western scholars tend to talk of the term "civil society" for organizations that are "outside" of the state, in the case of China, this definition does not hold true; hence, "social organizations" would be a better nomenclature because it encompasses a wide range of associations, forums, and organizations. In 2009, there were 414,614 social organisations, including private non-enterprise units and foundations (Xu & Zhao 2010: 12).

In the reform and growth era, the CCP faced a dilemma. While continuous growth was necessary for its own survival, this meant further lay-offs. Downsizing the government bureaucracy and keeping the SOEs lean and competitive would lead to greater instability as people would lose jobs and social security. To prevent social instability and unrest, social organisations were increasingly encouraged by the CCP to take on these functions on behalf of society.

While the role played by social organisations cannot be downplayed, as a Leninist party, ceding power outside of its control would be unthinkable. While civil autonomy has not emerged, a new mode of state control has taken shape. Kang Xiaoguang and Han Heng (2008: 49) call the key feature of this new state-society relationship a "graduated mode of control" whereby the state controls society purposefully, flexibly, and selectively. Such control is intensive and strong when the state deems it necessary but lax or absent when unnecessary. The extent of control varies according to the challenges the social organisations pose to the state.

To qualify this further, Tony Saich (2000: 127) argues that the state tries to manage these state-society relations by binding them to organizations that are dependent on patronage. It tries to prevent mass opposition by attempting to extend its organization, co-ordination, and supervision. It fixes the boundary between the state and society to prevent overreach by social organisations as a frontal point of attack by disenfranchised groups. In this regard, the 1998 "Regulations on the Registration and Management of Social Organizations" provides a clear case of the state's attempt to limit its reach within existing party-state structures. It requires an organisation to find a sponsor and gain its approval after which it is sent to the Ministry of Civil Affairs (Saich 2000: 129). Second, similar organizations are not allowed to co-exist at various administrative levels to prevent collusion. Third, the CCP has reactivated the use of party cells within non-party organizations to ensure control and monitoring. In this way, the CCP is able to effectively control newer state-society relations arising from the process of economic reform by using it as a tool to sustain its own legitimacy.

In keeping with the trend of reforming the economy and developing state-society relations and social organisations, there has also been a rising trend of rights consciousness among the citizens of China. The rights defense movement (*Weiquan yundong*) emerged in the late 1990s together with a renewed push by citizens to engage with the state. He Qinglian (2013) identified a direct correlation between the types of protest and the specific industries that fueled the economic development of China. He added that contention arose mainly from issues related to land, environment, corruption of grassroots cadres, and the miscarriage of justice.

While China's growth and development accelerated, social and economic inequality also steadily rose. Protests, often termed "mass incidents", increased tenfold. Between 1993 and 2005, these incidents grew from 8,700 to 87,000 (Cai 2005: 777). The aim of the rights defense movement was to defend economic and social rights with peasants' uprising against excessive taxes, levies and forced seizure of farmland; workers' strikes against low pay and poor working conditions, laid-off urban workers' demonstrations against unfair dismissal by their employers, as well as homeowners' protest against forced eviction by government and developers, and protests against environmental pollution (Feng 2013: 34–35).

To tackle the rise in mass incidents, the Chinese State introduced a "stability maintenance" system and an extensive budget for funding many law enforcement agencies (including state security police) to specifically target "potential" threats to social stability. These threats include rights activists, political dissidents, religious believers, and ethnic minority groups. Under this "stability maintenance" project, huge investments were made to the extent that the CCP's total spending on domestic security exceeded defense spending in 2013 (Radio Free Asia 2016).

The ruling elites took prevention measures. On July 13, 2009, the central government enacted the "accountability system" for officials above the county level, including members of the central government. The accountability system established that if the "misconduct of officials" resulted in the outbreak of any mass incident or official mishandling of the mass incident, they would be held accountable. Depending on the seriousness of the incident, the officials would be expected to apologize publicly, tender resignation, or face dismissal (Tong & Lei 2010: 9). As part of "Chinese cadre management practice" (Minzner 2006: 135), the responsibility system (*zeren zhuijiu zhi*) is used for "evaluating the performance of local cadres in the areas of economic development, environmental protection, and social order". While success in performance is reflected in career rewards, failure leads to loss of promotion, suspension, criticism, or loss of party membership.

In order to prevent mass incidents, local governments also designed the harmony bonus scheme. If a village had no mass incident during a land requisition process, in addition to land and relocation compensation, every family would receive a harmony bonus of 8,000 RMB each, to be delivered in installments in two and a half years (Minzner 2006: 135). If there were mass incidents during this period, then the entire village had to forsake the harmony bonus.

To divert blame for excesses away from the system and the current form of government, shifting blame from the central government to local governments has been promoted. Besides this strategy, the central government was portrayed as the saviour of problems "created" by local government. In the process, any kind of petition or activism taken to Beijing would be repressed. While the normal approach to addressing protest has been to suppress them and detain and arrest individuals who instigated the protest, the state also gives certain concessions by facilitating strategies of "rightful resistance" among the petitioners and mediation institutions and judging practices from the Mao era.

4   Coping with Social Media Challenges in the Information Age

Deng Xiaoping's economic reform that started in 1978 also had an impact on the media in China. In 1979, the Central Propaganda Department, the organ responsible for media, lifted restrictions and encouraged media to write and report more on the economic transformation and help rebuild the propaganda system. While still under party control to serve CCP interests, newer voices were encouraged. This led to the proliferation of the media with a large increase in print media from 1,116 newspapers and magazines in 1978 to 7,298 in 1987, signaling a 654 percent increase in the number of available print media (Esarey 2005: 48).

After a brief suppression of the media during the 1989 Tiananmen movement, the media became increasingly commercialized after Deng's Southern Tour in 1992. The tour concluded that economic reform was needed to reinforce CCP legitimacy. This economic reform was also extended to the media sector and since then, the economic basis of the Chinese media has been effectively transformed from a system of state subsidies to one based on advertisement subsidies. Chinese media was increasingly encouraged to obtain external funding through advertising and increased sales. The shift in funding further promoted investment and profit orientation of media outlets. Media reform was thus characterized by changes in management, financing, and ownership, and the combination of these changes resulted in the marketization (or commercial liberalization) of the media (Stockmann and Gallagher 2008: 5).

Zhao (2004: 179–212) notes that the once state-subsidized and party-controlled propaganda organs rapidly transformed themselves into advertisement-based and market-driven capitalistic media enterprises under party ownership. Thus the Chinese media system, while increasingly becoming a platform for profit making, started to speak on behalf of the ruling party elite, the rising business class, and the urban middle class. She further argues that party control in the political domain and liberalization in the economic, media, and lifestyle spheres are two sides of the same coin that serve the interest of the political and economic elite. China's information revolution is an integral part of the country's modernization path that began in 1978.

The commercialization of media in China showed that the media was dependent on CCP direction. The party now had in place multiple tools of legitimacy. Examples included the renewed push for economic reforms, Jiang Zemin's opening of the CCP to entrepreneurs and the middle class, and the commercialization of media that the party could use to relay its growth story effectively. All these tools were created and sustained by the party for its legitimacy.

The Chinese media, while open to economic ideals, could hardly break free of the ideological blinds that controlled it. After the Tiananmen demonstrations in 1989, instead of suppressing public opinion, Jiang Zemin espoused the "guidance of public opinion" (*yulun daoxiang*) as the focus of CCP propaganda work at a national work conference in 1994 (Chan 2007: 548). The guidance of public opinion model was introduced as a response to the crisis of the propaganda model in the mid-1980s, to better deal with public opinion. Recognising its inability to control what people think, the party state shifted its focus from political ideology to social agenda. The role of media was necessary to guide public opinion "correctly", to boost morale and to promote political unity and social stability.

Starting in the mid-1990s, more and more Chinese people began to use the Internet. In subsequent years, various Internet communication tools and social media platforms through mobile electronic devices became popular. The emergence of these new social media outlets posed a significant challenge to the party's ability to control public opinion and political activism among some netizens. In this context, the party-state developed a comprehensive approach towards managing media and public opinion. According to Vi L. Nhan

(2008: 36), print media, social media, and cyberspace are managed by the party through four main approaches: legal, political, economic, and technological means.

Legal and Institutional Approach: The state exercises many legal and institutional methods to control the flow of information and to restrict media's ability to operate independently. Article 35 of the 1982 Constitution guarantees the Chinese citizenry "freedom of speech, of the press, of assembly, of association" (People's Daily Online 2004). However, several other articles in the constitution effectively nullify the previously granted rights. Article 38, for example, calls for elevation of the collective interests of the nation, society and the freedoms enjoyed by other citizens above those of the individual. Article 54, for example, states that citizens are prohibited from veering from their duty to protect the "security, honour and interests of the motherland" etc.

Political approach: The government exerts great political control over the content of news media through the structure and organization of its media regulatory bodies. The Central Propaganda Department, the central coordinator of the media, is directly under the Political Bureau and its Standing Committee. The Central Propaganda Department's function is to promote the party's ideologies and project its legitimacy (Zhao 2004: 42). It wields immense power over the media market that includes books, magazines, newspapers, TV, radio, and IP addresses. The Central Organization Department and the Central Propaganda Department also use the nomenklatura system for appointments to keep a hold over the media by directly selecting managers of national media (Esarey 2006: 3). These managers are responsible for the content of their organizations and are expected to censor content deemed unfavourable to the government.

Economic approach: It uses the commercialization of media to its advantage by promoting the creation of powerful profitable domestic media conglomerates under party control that can influence opinion abroad (Esarey 2006: 6). Some of the leading official media organizations, such as Xinhua News Agency, People's Daily, and China Central Television (CCTV), receive strong financial support from the government for the purpose of strengthening their role in shaping and guiding public opinion in the context of the growing influence of various social media outlets.

Technological approach: The party exerts tight control over the Internet due to its potential for threatening the party narrative and challenging its legitimacy. Regulations have been designed and introduced to restrict online content and enable state monitoring such as requiring website operators and ISPs to keep records of their content and user identities and hand them over to authorities as and when asked for. The Great Firewall, a massive censorship apparatus, blocks out content that the party deems "harmful information" and websites.

5   The Chinese Model and Its Growing Influence in the World

The analyses in the above section suggest that China has indeed undergone a conspicuously different trajectory in its socio-political and economic development in the past decades. In 2004, Joshua Cooper Ramo coined the term "Beijing Consensus", arguing that China has successfully created a development model that is diametrically different from the "Washington Consensus". Ramo may not have been the first person to make references to the "China model" concept. In fact, in the 1980s, the late Chinese leader Deng Xiaoping used the term "Chinese model" to distinguish his opening up and reform program from what Gorbachev was doing in the former Soviet Union's reforms. Deng encouraged his people to explore a Chinese development path instead of following an existing model or Moscow's approach. In any case, after 2000, discussion and debate on the "Chinese model" became a popular topic among political pundits and scholars throughout the world.

The Chinese model can be understood as the entirety of major Chinese institutions and policy approaches in response to the challenges and problems in China's own reforms and opening up and globalization in the past four decades. The Chinese institutions and policies were all aimed at achieving rapid socio-economic development and ultimately realizing China's grand national rejuvenation. It is commonly recognized that a predominant state has been a main feature in the Chinese model. The state has supplied various institutions in the social, economic, and political arenas in a top-down fashion.

Many scholars have attempted to explain the main features of the Chinese model. Zheng Yongnian (2016) points out that the Chinese model contains various major elements such as mixed economy, political openness, policy uniqueness, gradualism in reforms, and incremental improvement in the political and economic systems. A Chinese scholar, Zhang Weiwei (2015), has strongly argued that China has successfully created a unique model for its development in the decades since the late 1970s' initiation of reforms and opening up. Zhang argues that China has established a meritocracy system that combines selection and election. He further points out the major differences between China and the West in the economic and social arenas. Economically, the Chinese system, which is officially called "a socialist market economy", allows for the roles of the government and the market. Socially, the society and the state enjoy positive interaction, unlike the confrontational relations between the society and the state in Western countries. He asserts that the Chinese system can compete with the Western system.

The China model, however, is not short of flaws and even defects. Pessimists use these shortcomings to question the effects of the model in influencing other countries. Many analysts believe that the downside of this strong-state approach lies in the occasional shortage or untimely supply of institutions, thus intensifying social conflicts. The current lack of strong momentum in reforms is a clear demonstration of the negative result of this kind of institutional transformation in China. Also, in the past decades, it has been clear that the Chinese model led to a few major shortcomings in China's development. Examples include corruption, resource depletion, environmental degradation, insufficient domestic consumption, slow innovation progress, and slow income growth. All these problems eventually hinder China's further development. It is commonly believed that these problems have been caused by the imbalance in China's economic structure, the imbalance between social and economic development, and the imbalance between society and the state.

These challenges have been in existence for quite some time, but their negative effects have, to some extent, been mitigated by rapid economic growth rate and nationwide prosperity. With the accumulation of these problems and a slower growth rate, it has become imperative for the party-state to seriously address these problems. At the Third Plenary Session of the 18th Central Committee in 2013, the ruling elites rolled out a comprehensive document for the deepening of reforms. The document highlighted two new major policy directions. First, the market should eventually play a decisive role in resource reallocation, though the government will continue to play an important role in managing the macro-economy, rule of law, supervision, and industrial policy designs. Second, the government's role should be improved, particularly in the social arena.

The government is supposed to enhance social security by formulating more effective policies to provide more social benefits: (a) minimum livelihood, pension, and unemployment benefits for lower-income people, and (b) medicare, compulsory education, and public housing for ordinary people. The Fifth Plenary Session of the 18th Central Committee passed China's 13th Five-Year Plan. According to the new plan, China should strive for a medium-to-high growth rate. New concepts such as innovation, balanced development, green development, openness, and shared benefits were emphasized. This clearly indicates that the Chinese political elites recognize the need to revise the Chinese model (Zheng 2013: 67–92).

Despite the on-going evolution and flaws in the Chinese development trajectory, in the 2000s many scholars began to argue that the Chinese model may become influential in other parts of the world. In his book *When China Rules the World*, Martin Jacques (2012) opines that partly because of the growing appeal of the Chinese model, China may become a key player in the world. He believes that China would not follow the model of Western democracy but will continue to adhere to its own way of development. Hu Angang (2012) notes that China's success will eventually transform the country into a mature and responsible global superpower by 2020 and that its rise will be peaceful and will achieve a win-win outcome for China and for the outside world. Daniel Bell (2016), in his book *The China Model: Political Meritocracy and the Limits of Democracy*, praises the Chinese political system for allowing the most capable leaders to be selected to guide the nation's development. He argues that the Chinese political system allows democracy at the grassroots level, experiments at the middle level, and meritocracy at the central level.

To what extent can the Chinese model influence the rest of the world? Such a question remains debatable. There is no clear sign of the Chinese government's intention of promoting its development model in other countries. In fact, Chinese leaders have repeatedly vowed not to promote its development model in other parts of the world. However, two observations warrant a close watch over the possible attraction the Chinese model may have in other parts of the world, particularly developing countries.

First, the 19th National Congress political report clearly states that the Chinese experiences may provide an alternative option for other countries' development. Second, the Chinese ruling elites have been emphasizing that they should be more and more confident in their own ideology, developmental path, institutions, and culture. This suggests that China may be interested in seeing greater appreciation and even acceptance of its model (at least some elements of the model) in other countries. It is quite possible that the Chinese media outlets may become more active in introducing Chinese experiences in the coming years. Given the fact that China does provide significant training programs for bureaucrats from many developing countries, it is also quite plausible that the Chinese model will at least tacitly influence the politics and policies of many countries in the developing world.

The 19th Party Congress is particularly noteworthy given China's expanding economic and global governance ambitions. Moving past the Deng Xiaoping maxim of keeping a low profile, under Xi Jinping, China is positioning itself at the forefront of global change be it as the defender of globalization or on issues of trade and climate change. In fact, Xi in his Davos speech stated that China is now "taking a driving seat" when it comes to fighting climate change (Huang &

Lahiri 2017). Xi has also indicated that there is a Chinese model – the path of "socialism with Chinese characteristics" that offers a "new option" for developing countries to accelerate their development while maintaining their independence. This suggests a newfound confidence in the developmental process of China and its wider applicability in the world (Peng 2017).

In a study session attended by members of the Bureau of the CCP Central Committee in 2016, Xi stated his intentions to reframe the world order "as the international balance of power has shifted and global challenges are increasing, global governance system reform has emerged as a 'trend of [the] times'"(XinhuaNet 2016). In the same meeting he stressed the need for China to improve its ability to participate in rule-making, agenda setting, publicity and coordination in global governance. Moreover, Xi has linked this objective to the overall goals of establishing a "community of common destiny" and "a new model of international relations with win-win cooperation as the core" (Boao Forum 2015).

China is seeking to influence the changing global world order in a multiplicity of ways but primarily by participating and integrating into global economic aid mechanisms and institutions and playing a key role in UN-led bodies, while selectively using some of these multilateral institutions for its own economic development. China has placed a heavy emphasis on sustaining and building new institutions and also reforming from within those institutions that will help propel its growth, enhance its international image and also add to its decision making and global power ambitions, commensurate to its rise.

As one of the BRICS states, China today is increasingly making use of its enhanced economic and soft power to successfully launch the Asian Infrastructure Investment Bank (AIIB) and the New Development Bank (NDB) and "articulate what is arguably a global vision with Chinese characteristics, given form in the ambitious project of constructing 'one belt, one road'(OBOR)" (Zhang 2016).

6   Conclusion

Chinese political economy in the past decades has demonstrated a hybrid system, quite different from many other hybrid systems and authoritarian regimes. Political power in China is highly centralized, yet there exists much decentralization and even fragmentation in politics and policy-making. The party appears to be omnipotent and omnipresent, but at the same time the society can enjoy many forms of socioeconomic freedom. In the information age, with the proliferation of new technologies and new social media, the scrutiny of public opinion and society can no longer be ignored by the political elites. Well-established institutions coexist with many informal socio-political norms and very often work together to influence the ultimate political and policy outcomes. The economic area is particularly obvious in terms of mixed features. By and large, the Chinese economy runs on a market basis, but at the same time the government plays a very strong role in macro-economic design and regulation. There is a significant state-owned sector and parallel to that, there is a dynamic and still growing private sector.

This Chinese hybrid system has so far proven a success in supporting China's economic development. All the major policy approaches and institutions that have been adopted under this hybrid system in the past decades have led to the emergence of a Chinese model of development. Nevertheless, the Chinese model is not complete and mature simply because the Chinese success story has not reached its end. Despite tremendous success in the past decades, China still faces enormous challenges in its further development. In the words of Chinese leaders themselves, China has now entered an era of "deep-water reform". Whether the CCP can lead China to overcome the "middle-income trap" while significantly improving its governance remains to be seen in the coming decades.

With the apparent failure of the "Washington Consensus" in many developing countries and growing socio-political challenges in some Western countries, the Chinese model appears to be gaining more traction in the world and is already a significant factor in world politics. The Chinese model has the potential to become a meaningful alternative to neo-liberalism, the old Soviet-model, and the social democracy model. Of course, the actual influence of the Chinese model will depend on the ultimate success of the Chinese political economy in the coming decades.

Bibliography

Bao, T. (2002). 'Three Represents: Marking the End of an Era', *The Wall Street Journal*, September 5, http://online.wsj.com/public/resources/documents/a-baotong 20020827.html.

Bell, D.A. (2016). *The China Model: Political Meritocracy and the Limits of Democracy*, Princeton: Princeton University Press.

Brødsgaard, K.E. (2004). 'Management of Party Cadres in China', pp. 57–91 in K.E. Brødsgaard and Y. Zheng (eds.), *Bringing the Party Back: How China is Governed*, Singapore: Eastern Universities Press.

Cai, Y. (2005). 'China's Moderate Middle Class: The Case of Homeowners' Resistance', *Asian Survey,* 45(5): 777.

Chai, W. (2003). 'The Ideological Paradigm Shifts of China's World Views: From Marxism-Leninism-Maoism to the Pragmatism-Multilateralism of the Deng-Jiang-Hu Era', *Asian Affairs: An American Review,* 30(3).

Chan, A. (2007). 'Guiding Public Opinion through Social Agenda-Setting: China's Media Policy since the 1990s', *Journal of Contemporary China,* 16(53): 547–559.

Cheremukhin, A; Golosov, M; Guriev, G and Tsyvinski, A. (2015). 'The Economy of the People's Republic of China from 1953', *NBER Working Paper Series,* no. 21397, https://www.nber.org/papers/w21397.pdf.

China Daily (2010). 'Harmonious Society', 16 September, http://cpcchina.chinadaily .com.cn/2010-09/16/content_13918117.htm.

China Daily (2016). 'Xi calls for reforms on global governance', 28 September, http://www.chinadaily.com.cn/china/2016-09/29/content_26931697.htm.

ChinaFile (2013). 'Document 9: A ChinaFile Translation', 8 November, http://www .chinafile.com/document-9-chinafile-translation.

Esarey, A. (2005). 'Cornering the Market: State Strategies for Controlling China's Commercial Media', *Asian Perspective,* 29(4): 37–83.

Esarey, A. (2006). 'Speak No Evil: Mass Media Control in Contemporary China', *Freedom at Issue: A Freedom House Special Report,* https://freedomhouse.org/sites/default/files/inline_images/Speak%20No%20Evil-%20Mass%20Media%20Control%20in%20Contemporary%20China.pdf

Feng, C. (2013). 'Preserving Stability and Rights Protection: Conflict or Coherence?', *Journal of Current Chinese Affairs,* 42(2): 21–50.

Fewsmith, J. (2001). *China since Tiananmen: The Politics of Transition,* Cambridge: Cambridge University Press.

Fewsmith, J. (2012). 'China Politics 20 Years Later', in N. Bandelj and D.J. Solinger (eds.), *Socialism Vanquished, Socialism Challenged: East Europe and China, 1989–2009,* New York: Oxford University Press.

He, Q. (2013). 'Stability Maintenance and China', 10 July, http://hqlenglish.blogspot .com/2013/07/stability-maintenance-and-china.html.

Hu, A. (2012). *Zhongguo 2010: Yige xinxing chaoji daguo [China in 2010: A new superpower],* Hongzhou: Zhejing Renmin Press.

Huang, J., J. Yang, and S. Rozalle (2006). 'China's Rapid Economic Growth and Its Implications for Agriculture and Food Security in China and the Rest of the World', *The Food and Agriculture Organization,* http://www.fao.org/docrep/009/ag088e/AG088E03.htm.

Huang, E. and Lahiri, T. (2017). 'Xi Jinping to China: "Any harm we inflict on nature will eventually return to haunt us"', *Quartz,* 18 October, https://qz.com/1105119/

watch-what-xi-jinpings-19th-chinese-communist-party-congress-work-report-said-on-climate-change/.

Jacques, M. (2012). *When China Rules the World: The End of the Western World and the Birth of a New Global Order,* London: Penguin Books.

Kang, X. and H. Han (2008). 'Graduated Controls: The State-Society Relationship in Contemporary China', *Modern China,* 34(1): 36–55.

Minzner, C.F. (2006). 'Xinfang: An Alternative to Formal Chinese Legal Institutions', *Stanford Journal of International Law,* 42(1):103 https://papers.ssrn.com/sol3/papers.cfm?abstract_id=1548577.

Nathan, A.J. (2003). 'China's Changing of the Guard: Authoritarian Resilience', *Journal of Democracy,* 14(1): 6–17.

Nhan, V.L. (2008). 'Media in China: Methods of State Control', *The Orator,* 3:36, http://students.washington.edu/nupsa/Docs/Volume3/Vi_L_Nhan_Media_in_China.pdf.

Perry, E.J. (2007). 'Studying Chinese Politics: Farewell to Revolution?' *The China Journal,* 57(8):1–22.

People's Daily Online (2004). 'Constitution of The People's Republic of China', 22 March, http://en.people.cn/constitution/constitution.html.

People's Daily Online (2003). 'Premier Wen Highlights Scientific Development Concept', 22 February, http://en.people.cn/200402/22/eng20040222_135467.shtml.

Peng, T.H. (2017). '19th Party Congress: 7 key themes from President Xi Jinping's work report', *The Straits Times,* 18 October, https://www.straitstimes.com/asia/east-asia/19th-party-congress-7-key-themes-from-president-xi-jinpings-work-report.

Radio Free Asia (2016). 'China to Spend "At Least" U.S.$25 Billion on "Maintaining Stability"', 8 March, http://www.rfa.org/english/news/china/china-security-03082016144158.html.

Saich, T. (2000). 'Negotiating the State: The Development of Social Organizations in China', *The China Quarterly,* 161: 124–141.

Shambaugh, D. (2001). 'The Dynamics of Elite Politics during the Jiang Era', *The China Journal,* 45: 101–111.

Stockmann, D. and M.E. Gallagher (2011). 'Remote Control: How the Media Sustain Authoritarian Rule in China', *Comparative Political Studies,* 44(4): 436–467.

Tong, Y. and S. Lei (2010).'Chinese Government Learning to Live with Social Protests', *EAI Background Brief,* 521, Singapore: East Asian Institute, http://www.eai.nus.edu.sg/publications/files/BB521.pdf.

Wang, J.C.F. (2002). *Contemporary Chinese Politics,* Upper Saddle River, NJ: Prentice Hall.

Weatherly, R. (2006). *Politics in China Since 1949: Legitimizing Authoritarian Rule,* New York: Routledge.

Xi, J. (2015), 'Towards a Community of Common Destiny and a New Future for Asia', *Boao Forum for Asia,* 8 April, http://english.boaoforum.org/hynew/19353.jhtml.

Ying, X. and L. Zhao (2010). 'China's Rapidly Growing Non-Governmental Organizations', *EAI Background Brief*, 514, Singapore: East Asian Institute, http://www.eai.nus.edu.sg/publications/files/BB514.pdf.

Zhang, W. (2015). 'The Chinese path and its implications', *Guancha* [Observer Network], 29 May, http://www.guancha.cn/ZhangWeiWei/2015_05_29_321353_3.html.

Zhang, Y. (1998). *China in International Society since 1949: Alienation and beyond.* New York: St. Martin's Press.

Zhao, Y. (2004). 'The State, the Market and Media Control in China', pp. 179–212, in P. Thomas and Z. Nain (eds), *Who Owns the Media?: Global Trends and Local Resistances*, New York: Zed Books.

Zheng Y. (2013). *Weiji huo chongsheng-quanqiuhua shidai de Zhongguo minyun* [Danger or revitalization: China's destiny in the globalization era]. Hongzhou: Zhejiang renmin Press.

Zheng Y. (2016). *The Chinese Model: Experiences and Challenges* [Zhongguo moshi: Jingyan yu tiaozhan]. Beijing: Zhongxin Press.

Zhang, Yongjin. (2016). 'Introduction: Dynamism and Contention: Understanding Chinese Foreign Policy Under Xi Jinping', *International Affairs*, 92(4): 769–772.

CHAPTER 6

Envisioning the Russian Welfare State Model: The New Political Economy of Gender and the Labour Market

Rosa Mulé and Olga Dubrovina

Global economic integration remodels patterns of political and economic development in both democratic and authoritarian countries, creating new opportunities but also new social risks. Russia is a big and complex country with a history of command political economy, where the state was responsible for social and care services. While the communist welfare state was inspired by Marxist ideology and underpinned by the command economy (Inglot 2008), in the past twenty–six years Russia has been charting new paths towards democracy as well as towards a market-oriented economy.

This pathbreaking shift has made Russia representative of a new economic model based on the reconfiguration of business-state-society relations, most notably through the privatisation of state-owned firms and the dismantling of public social services. Privatisation brought an end to the era of lifetime employment and egalitarian labour compensation in Russia. Under the command economy, lifetime employment, centrally controlled wage structures and comprehensive social services meant that women could bear the double burden of work and family duties without suffering substantial wage losses as a result of their care-giving role.

In an increasingly globalised and interdependent world, the new opportunities offered by Putin's Russia, involved in the process of reintegration since 2000, have challenged the status of women in the labour market. Putin's idea of a "strong state" as expressed in 1999 has had an impact on social politics in terms of enhancing the state's role in social and care services for women and families. The views regarding welfare policies have changed compared to the El'tsin years, giving way to new interactions between women's needs and state necessities. Putin has made attempts to resolve the "women's issue" by increasing social benefits. However, financial assistance to women has been more likely to meet the requirements of the demographic situation, rather than a real desire to improve women's position in the labour market.

Our research question is whether international economic integration, the transition to a new economic growth model and the remoulding of state-society relationships in Russia have positively or adversely affected women's opportunities in the labour market. The chapter charts the trajectories of some key institutional changes which have occurred in the Russian welfare state in the face of global challenges and the shaping of a new economic model, focusing on gender and the labour market. It maps out the transformation of the welfare state in terms of laws, social services and benefits as well as exploring women's participation in the labour market. Labour markets are systematically and directly influenced by welfare states because working life and social policy are mutually interdependent institutions.

Despite the dramatic changes in Russia and other hybrid political systems such as China, these political-economic systems have systematically been marginalised in mainstream welfare state theories. Reasons for exclusion are manifold. In general, social scientists focusing on the welfare state chiefly work in European or Anglo-American universities. Language difficulties are a further obstacle for assembling primary and secondary sources to carry out empirical research. But perhaps the main reason is that the literature has been too exclusively focused on those democratic mechanisms that explain the origins, development and consolidation of welfare states in European and Anglo-American countries (Marshall 1950; Esping-Andersen 1990; Gunther et al. 2006).

The point to note is that focusing on democratic mechanisms can account for only part of the story pertaining to authoritarian hybrid political economy regimes. Hybrid systems of political economy face different challenges and constraints to welfare state development. Moreover, historians stress that the democratic process has not always been a precondition for welfare state development (Briggs 1961). Rimlinger (1971) argues that the functions of social security serve different goals under a liberal market economy or under a centrally planned economy. In the latter, the provision of welfare benefits may be in the interest of political elites if it positively impacts productivity, economic growth and development (Wintrobe 1998). Authoritarian welfare states are characterised by paternalism (the elites know better than the masses); state interests take precedence over group interests; and welfare state benefits aim at securing loyalty to the political elites.

In addition, welfare state developments in authoritarian and emerging countries encounter different pressures than those experienced during the 20th century by European countries. European welfare states emerged under relatively closed national boundaries, whereas today the international economic integration erodes the protective barriers that shield domestic political economies. Emerging countries have generally reduced public expenditures in social services and provisions and adopted neo-liberal, market-conforming welfare models. Consequently, the enormous transformation in the political economy sphere of these countries has altered the relationship between state, market and society.

Like in other industrialised countries, these changes shape "new risks" in people's lives (Bonoli 2006). One prominent sector where new social risks are pervasive is the labour market. Technological progress in production reduces the share of unskilled labour, while stricter competition promoted by international economic integration and globalisation has advanced labour market flexibility. These trends contribute to radically altering labour markets in transition economies, with far-reaching implications for gender equality.

In Russia the transition process has progressively eroded the institutional mechanisms that protected women's reproductive role under central planning. Most notably, the dismantling of the socialist welfare system has led to a substantial decline in care provision in the form of subsidised childcare, shifting care responsibilities predominantly to the family. The literature suggests that in Russia firms are increasingly reluctant to accommodate employees' care-giving needs (Carpinelli 2004).

How does gender map onto contemporary Russia's post-communist welfare regime? Our argument is that the gender transformation of the welfare state in Russia is moulding a hybrid neofamilist model with neoliberal and paternalistic elements and the gradual erosion of state support for social services, childcare and elderly care. On the one hand, Russia's authoritarian modernisation in welfare policies (Cook 2015) appears to be converging towards neofamilist patterns shaped by the male/breadwinner-female/carer model and by demographic pressures. On the other hand, economic constraints, historical legacies and family values have shifted towards individualism, materialism and consumerism, thus limiting the implementation of neofamilist policies.

The chapter is structured as follows. Section two briefly illustrates the welfare state transition from Soviet Russia to the Russian Federation. Section three sets out the theoretical approach adopted in this work. Section four elaborates on the application of the neo-familistic model to the Russian case study. Section five centres on social policy. Section six elaborates on the implications of the new authoritarian welfare state and offers some concluding remarks.

1   Welfare State Transition from Soviet Russia to the Russian Federation

It is worth stressing that Bolshevik legislation made Soviet Russia one of the most progressive nations in the world on issues of gender. The right to divorce, legalisation of abortion, access to higher education, political participation through the Women's Section of the Communist Party (Zhenotdel) and socialisation of housework made the image of the Soviet woman very attractive for western feminists. Even if the number of day-care centres and the quality of canteens could not address the needs of Soviet families, it still allowed women to enter the professional sphere. But real gender equality was not created since the Soviet state drew women into active public and political life but did not really liberate them from domestic burdens. The liberalisation of family and gender policy ceased in the Stalinist period under the demographic pressure that led to the strengthening of the state's role in the private lives of Soviet citizens. Motherhood was no longer a personal choice but was transformed into a woman's duty to the state. The institutionalisation of the "working mother" gender contract led to the phenomenon of the "double burden"; parallel to this process was the marginalisation of males from childcare, household and state family policy that led to the establishment of gender asymmetry.

The last Soviet period continued to be characterised by this pronatalist policy but in a more liberal legal context. During "perestroika" the traditional family model was strengthened: every policy initiative aimed to encourage women to bear and raise children, rather than to help them to advance in their career or combat discrimination in the workplace. Moreover, financial allowances, services and facilities were designed for mothers and children, thus making women "social disables". As long as the command economy involved centralised job allocation and a system of social protection, female oriented social policy was not an obstacle in women's professional achievement. As a result, three generations of Soviet people became used to the state being "obliged" to solve many problems such as job hunting, recruitment, social entitlements, welfare benefits, etc. They have been schooled in a regime of social protection that allows people not to be too concerned about earning a living. These women had no previous experience of the economic and psychological pressure of unemployment (Mezentseva 1994: 78). The situation changed dramatically in the early post-communist period. According to some scholars, because of the paternalistic state policy, Soviet women were no longer used to competing in the labour market with men. Hence feminist oriented social researchers argued for the renunciation of the state's protectionist policy with regard to women in the new free market conditions (Khotkina 1996). Nonetheless, for some of the most vulnerable social categories state support was crucial. For example, single mothers who felt unprotected as mothers and workers lacking both male support and, especially, the support of the state (Utrata 2015).

The communist welfare state was deeply entrenched in the economic model of state planning of human and material resources. This model was based on a political economy system that mobilised high levels of female labour force participation. Family policies encouraged female participation in the labour force, especially maternity leave and state-sponsored childcare. This meant that women's participation rate was similar to men's. Under the command economy jobs were allocated almost exclusively by the state and the communist party/state made considerable efforts to support female labour force participation. Furthermore, in the communist political economy welfare services and the firm were highly integrated. Firms provided kindergartens for children as well as housing for families.

Since the 1990s one consequence of globalisation and the transition process has been the retreat of the state, decreasing state responsibility in the social sphere. Hefty cuts in social services mean that women have less public and institutional support for family and childcare. In addition to this, privatisation of state-owned firms implied that private employers were expected to take up, at least in part, financial responsibility for maternity benefits and childcare facilities. Consequently, it is more difficult today for women of reproductive age to find jobs because employers are reluctant to pay such benefits and women are becoming less desirable employees.

2 The Collapse of the Soviet Union as a Critical Juncture in the Russian Development of the Welfare State

The major reconfiguration of the Russian political economy offers a unique opportunity to scrutinise if and how the new restructuring of the labour market has influenced gendered patterns. New patterns raise two crucial questions regarding the conditions of the female labour supply: (1) what determines whether women stay or exit from the labour market? (part-time work, sheltered employment, retraining, unemployment benefits); (2) under what conditions can women exercise their own choices under the contract, in particular do they benefit from paid absence from work? (sickness, maternity leave etc.).

Theoretically, this paper contributes to the literature by applying the recent theories of the political economy of institutional change to explain key transformations of the Russian welfare state. This research programme asks questions about what kinds of institutional changes take place, propelled by what kinds of political and economic processes (Mahoney & Thelen 2015; North 1990). In this chapter we build on recent scholarship to specify the analytical benefits of applying institutional theory to understanding welfare state change and continuity in Russia.

We will employ the insights of this new wave of research to highlight the peculiarities of welfare state transformation in Russia. We argue that the source of welfare state change is explicable in terms of punctuated equilibrium analysis (Mahoney & Thelen 2015). Like in other command political economies such as China after the 1989 Tiananmen uprising, in Russia institutional welfare change is the result of abrupt events, which are concentrated in short periods of time.

Emerging new patterns of state-market-family relations reveal considerable strains and tensions. In particular, the boundaries between public and private responsibility for family members are undergoing significant rethinking and reshaping, with some social services shifting from public control to private contracts in crucial fields, including care, education, and health. Several public policies can potentially influence the labour supply of women. However, family policies and especially care, aimed at providing financial support or social services are of primary significance (Daly 2002). For this reason, the empirical part of this work focuses on the provision of care services.

Punctuated equilibrium analysis helps understand welfare state change in Russia. The punctuated equilibrium conception of institutional change is a discontinuous process, in which long periods of stability are interrupted by abrupt events. There is no doubt that the collapse of the Soviet Union in 1991 represents an episode of abrupt and rapid transformation, a critical juncture that radically altered the status quo of the Russian political economy. Critical junctures are defined as "moments in which uncertainty as to the future of an institutional arrangement allows for political agency and choice to play a decisive causal role in setting an institution on a certain path of development" (Capoccia 2015: 148). Critical junctures induce discontinuous and radical reorganisation because of an in-built capacity to overcome institutional stasis. In this view, change in the political economy results from a breakdown of continuous dynamics in the organisation, bringing about new patterns and configurations. Critical junctures generate uncertainty by disrupting the institutional status quo. In times of uncertainty, when multiple options are available to key actors, the expectation is that the organisational scenario of politics creates space for political and economic innovation (Capoccia 2015).

One important defining feature of a critical juncture is relevant in the Russian political economy of the early 1990s: inducing discontinuous and radical reorganisation. As the Russian Federation moved into market transition during the early 1990s, its inherited systems of broad social provision increasingly came under attack. The periodisation in the development of the post-Soviet welfare state in Russia has been divided in three different phases of liberalisation (Cook 2015). The first phase between 1991 and 1993 liberalisation was non–negotiated; the second phase between 1994 and 1999 was marked by contested liberalisation; and the third phase between 2000 and 2004 liberalisation was negotiated within the elite. Reformers demanded a liberal paradigm of reduced subsidies and entitlements and social sector privatisation. Social services and provisions were to move away from the state and towards the market.

However, some aspects of the Soviet welfare system are still in place. Russian labour laws are similar to previous Soviet laws in both the gender and family spheres. Russian labour Law (Federal Law N. 197-30 December 2001) replaced the USSR labour Law of 1971 (KZoT RSFSR). Russian law rather strongly protects working women when they have a child: they are entitled to paid maternity leave, partially paid childcare leave, allowance for registering with an obstetrician during the first twelve weeks of pregnancy, etc. Some articles of the labour law are addressed directly at protecting motherhood and regulating the relationship between mother and employer. It should be noted that such strong and severe legislation can have a negative impact on returning to work after maternity leave: it makes female hiring and earning the subject of discrimination. Taking into account very weak law enforcement and the poor culture of defending rights in Russia, it is possible to conclude that employers have often broken the law with regards to working mothers (Karabchuk & Nagerniak 2013: 29). Labour market practices included "informal contracts" and can be seen as the most common unofficial response of the Russian labour market to rigid labour regulations as well as a sign of adaptation to new market conditions, through non-punishable violations of institutional norms and rules (Teplova 2007: 313).

During the transition period difficulties in the job market drastically increased, especially for women. For the majority of Russian women, the end of the Soviet system brought about a dramatic decline in living standards and millions lost their jobs. However, in the scholarly work concerning female unemployment there is disagreement about the precise figures. Some Russian scholars estimate that women constituted around 70–80% of the unemployed in the mid-90s (Khotkina 1994: 98). However, figures from 1998 show roughly equal proportions of male and female unemployed (13.7 % and 13.3 % respectively) (Alpen Engel 2004: 258). In fact, the Russian scholar Khotkina even used the expression "the female face of unemployment" arguing that some 70 to 80% of registered unemployed were women as well as professionals with higher and secondary education. On the other hand, the Russian sociologist Zubarevich claimed that gender differences compared with the Soviet period increased slightly: the proportion of women *out of the employed population* dropped from 50% to 48–49%. At the very beginning of the transition period the female employment rate dropped faster than the male one. But as the labour market deteriorated further, the employment of both males and females fell at approximately the same rate (Zubarevich 2008). Despite similar gender employment rates, in practice women had to face more hardship than men due to their gender, such as unfair dismissals, preference for hiring males, sexual harassment and the gender salary gap.

One reason for the gender wage gap is that the management of factories and firms tried to keep qualified male workers while reducing the number of working days for women and therefore their wages. It also led to female loss of work skills and to their lower level of competitiveness compared to men. Women featured more on dismissal lists, issued by the administration, in an attempt to get rid of young women with children and women of retirement age (Khotkina 1994: 100).

The research carried out by the American scholar Jennifer Utrata on single mothers shows that nearly every mother with young children described widespread discrimination in the job market. Repeatedly the scholar heard from Russian women: "no one wants to hire a woman with a small child" (Utrata 2015: 62). Men and women faced the process of recruitment differently: it was rather longer for women than for men for a number of reasons. First of all, the majority of unemployed women were professionals with higher education (engineers, office-workers, accountants and book-keeping staff, scientists, lecturers, managers and secretaries). They all became "unwanted" in the job market (Khotkina 1994: 102). According to the statistics there were more women with higher or secondary education than men (40% against 25%). In the 1990s the labour market favoured "blue-collars" and the demand for highly educated women dropped. Even in cases of suitable vacancies a lot of businesses that contacted an employment service specified a preference for male workers even if it was not justified by the specific characteristics of the workplace (Khotkina 1996). Secondly, the high level of formal education was not maintained through women's working lives, since there was no system in Russia for continuing education. And thirdly, many women's social entitlements and preferential terms made them an unattractive proposition for employers (Khotkina 1994: 102).

In view of the above, we can distinguish at least two specific features of female behaviour in the labour market: fear to face dismissal even if their wage is very low or not regular, and readiness to accept any position they find with a low salary. A former woodworker, who was working in the 1990s as a hospital worker after the closure of her furniture factory, captured a common view of the differences between men and women in the labour market: "All the women who were sacked from the factory are working as a rule, even if not in their profession. But lots of the men have taken to the bottle, and are simply waiting around for the sun to come out, 'enduring'. Husbands are enduring in the sense of suffering, and their wives are enduring in the literal sense of getting through life and feeding their families" (Ashwin 2006: 87–133). In part men's behaviour can be explained in terms of a dual pressure that they had to face: a personal need to maintain their professionalism, and a strong social obligation to perform as breadwinners. Women are expected only to be "second order" breadwinners, and in this sense can "afford" to work in poorly paid professions without any threat to their status in the household (Ashwin 2006: 215–217). According to the English researcher Sarah Ashwin women's readiness to accept unfavourable working terms led to reinforcing women's second-class status in the labour force and increased the risk of discrimination by employers (Ashwin 2000: 63–72).

Recent social and economic data indicate gender asymmetry in the professional sphere. According to the Federal statistical service (Rosstat) in 2016 out of 72m active workers 35m were women and 37m men (48.5% of women) (Rosstat 2016). The average age of female workers is 39.5 (one year older than male workers). Females' educational level is higher than the male one (62% of female workers have a university degree or have vocational training compared to 50% of men). There is more male unemployment than female (the total unemployment rate in 2015 was 5.6%, 5.8% of men and 5.3% of women) (Rosstat 2016). Nonetheless, women represented more than half of state employees (56.2%). In state institutions strong segregation is very evident: women occupy the lower positions of the administrative hierarchy. Only 4.7% of top-level officials are women, while at the "junior" level they make up 80.6%. In the penultimate convocation of the Duma there were 13.6% women (61 women out of 450 seats) and 15.8% in the last Seventh Duma (71 women) that placed Russia in 129th place in the world just before Jordan and Egypt (United Nations Women 2017).

Employers' stereotypes regarding women are still very strong and include ideas about the inferior value of women as a working resource; hence a phenomenon of "glass ceiling" persists: female wages are almost 1/3 less than male ones and the higher the work position (role, wage, etc.) the more likely the job will be occupied by a man. According to the Global Gender Gap Index Report in 2017 the Russian Federation occupies 71st place (compared to 75th place the previous year) in the world ranking that evaluates the gender gap in social, economic and political sectors (Global Gender Gap Report 2017: 10). However, when comparing Russia to China it appears that the Russian Federation performs much better in terms of both global gender gap index (71st place against 100th)[1] and the sub index of economic participation and opportunity (41st against 86th).

Still, both Russia and China are a long way from gender equality. The McKinsey Global Institute Report of September 2015 entitled "The power of parity: How advancing women's equality can add US$ 12 trillion to global economy", suggests that gender inequality is not only a pressing moral and social issue, but also a critical economic challenge. The report estimates that fully closing the global gap between men and women on labour-force participation, hours worked, and the sector mix of employment could boost annual GDP by 26 percent over business-as-usual forecasts for 2025. This maximum potential is equivalent to 2.2 percentage points of incremental global GDP growth per year.

It is worth noting that this chapter cannot do justice to the complexities of the political-economy transition process in Russia. One important omission is the discussion of the urban-rural divide. Like in China, it is well known and documented that there are stark differences of employment rates, gender pay gaps and income inequality between rural and urban areas in Russia. This is an important and interesting research agenda that, however, lies outside the scope of our work; it is hoped that the topic will be addressed in future.

3   Social Family and Gender Policy

In the post-communist period motherhood has become a private choice and responsibility rather than a public duty and a social interest. In the transition process, hefty cuts in social services meant that women had less public and institutional support for family and childcare. In the 1990s financial allowances were strictly addressed only to very poor families with the lowest incomes (Chernova 2013: 143). The childcare support system that during the Soviet period was highly integrated with firms, was overhauled. From 87,900 preschool institutions in 2000 only 51,300 remained (Rosstat 2016: 186). In the conditions of a liberal market economy firms were no longer willing to provide social services, while the state endured drastic cuts in the public sphere. Privatisation of childcare services has pushed women to leave the labour market and return to more traditional roles as housewives. Therefore, as consumers of welfare services, women have been penalised with less public service support.

---

1   The gender gap index measures the gap between women and men in several variables such as health outcomes, the gap in educational attainment, the gap in economic participation and political empowerment.

From the beginning of 21st century the demographic problem was raised by Putin's government and a set of measures were undertaken in order to allow women to have more children. In 2006 during his annual discourse Putin proposed to resolve the birth rate decline through a programme aimed at increasing the number of births with financial support for young families, childbearing and childcare. The government increased maternity and childcare allowances, established educational compensation for preschool age-children and, most significantly, introduced the programme "maternity capital" (Elizarov 2012). Politicians and the media called these measures aimed at improving the demographic situation a "new national project" (Zorina 2007: 180).

According to the programme "Maternity capital",[2] which the Duma passed as a law in December 2006, women who gave birth to (or adopted) a second or more children from 1 January acquired the right to an economic allowance from the federal budget. A mother receives this amount in the form of a certificate after the child is three years old. The fact that the use of the certificate is strictly limited represents one of the critical points of this social support. The most relevant criticism levelled at the Maternity Capital programme concerns the population's general mistrust in state initiatives, insufficient funding to resolve the housing problem, unnecessary bureaucratic procedures and excessively "female oriented" measures (Borozdina et al. 2014). The "Maternity capital" programme was extended to 2021 but without annual index-linking to inflation. Petrova (2017) shows that the gender wage gap per female age group increases by 4 percentage points from 21% to 25% between 25 and 29 years and peaks at 33% between 35 and 39 years during the most intense period of motherhood, indicating that employers consider a woman as a potential mother and treat her as such on a professional level.

To sum up, it appears that the abrupt institutional change and transition process to a market–oriented economy in the Russian Federation has increased the burden of care on women and consequently reduced their career opportunities. On the bright side, thanks to education and high-level work skills women have become an important resource for small and medium sized businesses in Russia. Moreover, the introduction of international companies characterised by the diversification of human resource policies has contributed to promoting females' working status in Russia (Khotkina 2014). High education skills and economic internationalisation have meant that after the end of the transformation period between 1998 and 2012 the number of female top managers has fluctuated between 35.2 and 39.6%. This increase is due to

---

2   In 2017 is 453,026 rub., or about 7,000 euros.

the development of the tertiary sector where a majority of small and medium sized firms are managed by women. In 2017 female senior managers were 47% of the total, which places Russia in the first position in the world according to the Grant Thornton International Rating (Women in Business 2017), while in China female senior managers are 31%. According to the Grant Thornton Report these figures place both Russia and China in the top ten economies worldwide.

4 The Advent of a Neofamilist Welfare State Model in Russia?

As the previous sections indicate, the transition to a new growth model has two important implications for female labour force participation in Russia. Women are more economically dependent on families' and men's incomes, undermining the communist era "dual breadwinner" model throughout Russia (Pascall & Lewis 2004). Despite a high percentage of women holding managerial positions, most positions are in less paid jobs such as services; in addition, the gender pay gap is higher than the European average and the difficulties in reconciling work-family duties and responsibilities, the three year maternity leave and the paucity of kindergartens mean that men are often the breadwinners. Russia has witnessed an erosion of the social support system, especially in childcare and elderly care, offloading care responsibilities on women. These policies mark a sharp return to traditional gender roles in Russia (Chandler 2008).

It is important to note that the introduction of "maternity capital" was in line with conservative paternalistic policies. One additional factor that exacerbated the less favourable position of women with respect to men in the labour market was the increasingly patriarchal attitude. This patriarchal attitude was expressed in direct appeals to reduce female employment and convince women to return home. Supporters of such views base their arguments on their desire to reduce working women's overall burden, to enable mothers to give more time and attention to bringing up their children – which, they say, would strengthen family relationships and contribute to reducing the number of divorces (Mezentseva 1994: 76). Yet according to some scholars, the real reason for this patriarchal policy towards women was to hide female unemployment and to increase the birth rate. Still, the problem persisted because the "double burden" did not disappear but instead intensified: the number of day care centres dropped, laundries closed and the majority of previous services and facilities was curtailed. Confronted with the economic crisis on the one side and political instability on the other side, women became increasingly reluctant to engage in childbearing. The abortion rate was very high in the 1990s, though it has steadily declined from 100 per 1,000 women of reproductive age in 1991, to 55 in 2000 (Rivkin-Fish 2013: 573). What is more, not all women wanted or were able to stay at home. A high percentage of women wanted or had to work (Zdravomyslova 2003), so the patriarchal policy was carried out against women's willingness to work.

In recent years the problem of work-family balance has persisted and the state has not contributed to resolving it at the institutional level. Conservative neofamilist policy runs up against young generations' representation of the balance between family and career and women's role in the labour market. The first generation born in the context of a liberal economy lives in conditions of professional freedom, flexible work schedules, high wages, individual economic and housing independence (in some geographical and professional spheres) (Chernova 2013: 175). Their life strategies are radically different from those of their parents. The life strategies of this first generation are based on self-sufficiency and weak reliance on public social services, pushing young individuals to postpone marriage and childbirth and focus instead on career opportunities and professional success (Semeinye strategii 2009). Social values towards the family changed in the period from 1994 to 2014: preferences for career-building and job ambitions delay childbearing and contribute to declining numbers of children in the family (Zhuravleva & Gavrilova 2017: 145). The same trend is indirectly confirmed by the increasing number of women in the last two decades who refuse to have children (Grigor'eva et al. 2014: 30). Arguably, Russian state policy is inadequate: pronatalism does not resonate with the target audience (Chernova 2013: 175). This is akin to the development of the DINK family in China, "double income with no kids" family structure.

The majority of women in Russia remains excluded from the labour market during the childbearing and childcare period despite their desire to continue to work (Karabchuk & Nagerniak 2013: 41). The lack of preschool institutions, low wages, allowances that do not cover all needs and often the absence of family support force women to stay at home for three years and even more in case of a second child. Public perceptions about female roles as mother first of all and worker then, also influence women's choices.[3] Moreover, the exclusion of men from domestic chores and childcare duties in Russian families is still

---

3   See for example the survey results of "30-year milestone: gender roles and stereotypes" conducted in August 2015 by Levada center. https://www.levada.ru/2015/08/26/30-letnij-rubezh-gendernye-roli-i-stereotipy/.

significant and there is no tendency towards the gender neutralisation of household work (Kravchenko & Moteiunaite 2008: 197).

The problem of work-life balance for women surfaced in the Russian government's policy agenda in 2012. One of the measures aimed at stimulating employers to organise family-friendly work places. But such measures seem to have merely symbolic relevance and do not include economic incentives (Chernova 2017: 99).

In comparative terms, the shift from the dual breadwinner model to a neo-familist model of care in Russia draws on the male/breadwinner-female/carer model typical of southern European welfare states (Ferrera 1996). Generally speaking, it is not possible to find a unified criterion which defines and specifies what is meant by "familialism" as a feature of a given welfare state model (Leon & Migliavacca 2013). The term has been applied to south European welfare states to account for the key role that the family plays in developing strategies to protect and increase the welfare of its members, acting as the main provider of care and welfare for children and dependent individuals (Mulé 2016). These strategies include pooling incomes from different sources and providing income as well as protection to dependent family members. The male/breadwinner-female/carer model is characterised by low female participation in the labour market and provision of care to dependent family members, including children, elderly and members with disabilities, by female family members. In this model the welfare of individuals relies on family arrangements and networks rather than on state or private provisions.

The process of welfare state recalibration in terms of distributive and institutional features has been characterised by a return to traditional female/male roles in Russia (Teplova 2007). An incomplete revolution took place that has provoked unwelcome disequilibria. Gender discrimination, the dilemma of reconciling work and family responsibilities and the feminisation of poverty are among the most pressing new social risks facing the political economy transition. The economic reforms in Russia appear to have been the harbinger of new inequalities, with a return to a more traditional male/breadwinner-female/care model. This neo-familistic trend suggests a convergence among countries as different as the Russian Federation and southern Europe concerning the diffusion of new social risks in modern societies.

Welfare state institutions in contemporary Russia manifestly neglect relevant provisions of family policy. Like some countries in southern Europe such as Italy, maternity leave is quite generous, however public policies and programmes aimed at economic and service support for child care and gender equity are few and far between.

5   Conclusion

As representative of a new economic model under the label of authoritarian modernisation, the reconfiguration of the Russian welfare state is underpinned by rapid urbanisation and industrialisation that is creating new social risks. These new social risks stem from the massive transformation of the political economy landscape over the past twenty years. This transformation has altered the relationship between the state-market-society, deeply affecting labour market opportunities for women.

In Russia, the complex interaction of international economic integration and the return to traditional patterns of social care is moulding a neo-familistic welfare state. In the transition to a market economy, the former communist welfare state has been retrenched and liberalised, with an erosion of the social support system.

In such circumstances, policy makers should engage in formulating and implementing family-work reconciliation policies with the aim of moving beyond gender roles (Mulé 2016). Men and women should be considered "working citizens", within the "adult worker family model". One way forward is to implement policies for the "de-familialisation" of care or supported familialism. De-familialisation concerns the satisfaction of one's own needs independently from family support. It implies that the services women provide within the family and for family members are partly outsourced to the market or to the state or to a mix of private/public services. The debate revolves around which policies are more apt to advance de-familialisation. Policies should acknowledge the work needed for caring for family members, children, dependent adults, and elderly parents, as an activity that gives entitlement to financial support, such as allowances and care leaves. Finally, policies could support and favour men's family care responsibility via parental leave.

Another question is which public policies support gender equity in paid work and care. The issue is not merely about gender inequality and the way it affects job market opportunities or the gender division of paid and unpaid work in the family. As Saraceno and Keck (2011) argue, the problem in many ways is deeper. Relevant policies include social services, parental leave, income support and fiscal instruments, de-familialisation and supported familialism. Social policies that relieve families from responsibilities in the care of dependent family members are central to the decline of familialism.

Finally, our findings regarding the impact of the political economy transformation in Russia during the past twenty-six years suggest that if the transition from a command economy to a market economy involves cuts in public service jobs and public care services, this may have detrimental effects on women's employment opportunities as well as on their ability and willingness to raise children. The reconfiguration of the political economy in Russia has entailed the restructuring of the labour market which has in turn significantly influenced gendered patterns, unfortunately deepening the gender divide. With the privatisation of welfare services, the gender divide is becoming more obvious. To help change public perceptions of both genders, government should provide more welfare services that would help modify public perceptions very gradually, working through education and on the identity of female-male workers. In rekindling the "strong state" in Russia, policymakers may improve the identity reconstruction of Russia by promoting welfare policies that could rebalance the deep gender divide in the long run.

Acknowledgments

The authors wrote this chapter together but Rosa Mulé is responsible for paragraphs 1, 3, and 6, while Olga Dubrovina is responsible for paragraphs 2, 4, and 5. We are grateful to Irina Semenenko for constructive comments.

Bibliography

Abdusalamova, M. and Ramadanov M. (2015). 'Zhenshchiny na rynke truda: statisticheskoe izmerenie'. *Aktualnye problemy gumanitarnykh i estestvennykh nauk*, 1: 120–124.

Ashwin, S. (2000). 'Vliianie sovetskogo gendernogo poriadka na sovremennoe povedenie v sfere zaniatosti', *Sotsiologicheskie issledovaniia*, 63–72.

Ashwin, S. (ed.) (2006). *Adapting to Russia's New labour Market: Gender and Employment Strategy*. London; New York: Routledge Curzon.

Bonoli, G. (2005). 'The politics of the new social policies. Providing coverage against *new social risks* in mature welfare states', *Policy and Politics*, 33: 431–450.

Borozdina, E., Rotkirch, A., Temkina, A. and Zdravomyslova, E. (2014). 'Using maternity capital: citizen distrust of Russian family policy', *European Journal of Women's Studies*, 23(1): 60–75.

Briggs, A. (1961). 'The welfare state in historical perspective'. *European Journal of Sociology*, 2(2): 221–258.

Caiazza, A.B. (2002). *Mothers and Soldiers: Gender, Citizenship, and Civil Society in Contemporary Russia*. New York: Routledge.

Capoccia, G. (2015). 'Critical Junctures and Institutional Change', pp. 147–179, in Mahoney, J., and K. Thelen (eds.), *Advances in Comparative Historical Analysis*. Cambridge: Cambridge University Press.

Carpinelli, C. (2004). *Donne e povertà nella Russia di El'cin*. Milano: Franco Angeli.

Chernova, Z. (2013). 'Sem'ia kak politicheskii vopros: gosudarstvennyi proekt i praktiki
privatnosti', *Gendernaia Seriia* 4. Sankt-Peterburg: Evropeiskii universitet v Sankt-
Peterburge.

Chernova, Z. (2017). 'Rabochee mesto, druzhestvennoe sem'e: politicheskie initsiativy,
pozitsiia rabotodatelia i tipy podderzhki rabotnikov s semeinymi obiazannostiami',
The Journal of Sociology and Social Anthropology, xx, 1(89): 93–113.

Cook, L. (2010). 'Eastern Europe and Russia', pp. 671–688, in F. Castles et al. (eds.), *The
Oxford Handbook of the Welfare States*, Oxford: Oxford University Press.

Daly, M. (2002). 'A fine balance: women's labour market participation in international
comparison', pp. 467–510, in F. Scharpf and V. Schmidt (eds.), *Welfare and Work in
the Open Economy, Volume II*. Oxford: Oxford University Press.

Elizarov, V. (2012). 'Stimulirovanie rozhdaemosti i podderzhka semei s det'mi v sovremennoi Rossii'. *Demoskop*, 495–496, http://www.demoscope.ru/weekly/2012/0495/
analit02.php.

Engel Alpern, B. (2004). *Women in Russia, 1700–2000*. Cambridge: Cambridge University
Press.

Esping-Andersen, G. (1990). *The Three Worlds of Welfare Capitalism*. London: Polity
Press.

Ferrera, M. (1996). 'The "southern model" of welfare in social Europe', *Journal of European Social Policy*, 6(1), 17–37.

Grigor'eva, N., Diupra-Kushtanina, V. and Sharova, M. (2014). 'Sotsial'naia politika v
oblasti roditel'stva: sravnitel'nyi analiz (Rossiia-Frantsiia)', *Zhurnal issledovanii
sotsial'noi politiki*, 12(1): 21–38.

Gunther, R., Nikiforos Diamandouros P. and Sotiropoulos, D.A. (2006). *Democracy and
the State in the New Southern Europe*. Oxford: Oxford University Press.

Hacker, J. Pierson, P. and K. Thelen (2015). 'Drift and Conversion: Hidden Faces of Institutional Change', pp. 180–208, in J. Mahoney and K.A. Thelen (eds.), *Advances in
Comparative-Historical Analysis*. Cambridge: Cambridge University Press.

Inglot, T. (2008). *Welfare States in East Central Europe, 1919–2004*. Cambridge: Cambridge University Press.

Karabchuk, T. and Nagerniak, M. (2013). 'Determinanty zaniatosti dlia materei v Rossii',
Zhurnal issledovanii sotsial'noi politiki, 11: 25–48.

Khotkina, Z. (1994). 'Women in the labour market: yesterday, today and tomorrow',
pp. 85–108, in A. Posadskaya-Vanderbeck (ed). *Women in Russia: A New Era in Russian Feminism*. New York: Verso.

Khotkina, Z. (1996). 'Gendernye aspekty bezrabotitsy i sistemy sotsialnoi zashchity naseleniia', pp. 74–83, in *Gendernye aspekty sotsialnoi transformatsii*. Moskva: Institut sotsial'no-ekonomicheskikh problem narodonaseleniia RAN.

Khotkina, Z. (2014). 'Strana umnits. Gendernye aspekty kariery'. *Polit.ru*, 23 August, https://polit.ru/article/2014/08/23/career/.

Kravchenko, Zh. and Moteiunaite A. (2008). 'Zhenshchiny i muzhchiny na rabote i doma: gendernoe razdelenie truda v Rossii i Shvetsii', *Zhurnal issledovanii sotsial'noi politiki*, 6(2): 177–200.

León, M. and Migliavacca, M. (2013). 'Italy and Spain: Still the Case of Familistic Welfare Models?', *Population Review*, 52: 25–42.

Mahoney, J. and Thelen, K. (eds.) (2015). *Advances in comparative-historical analysis*. Cambridge: Cambridge University Press.

Marshall, T.H. (1950). *Citizens and Social Class and Other Essays*. Cambridge: Cambridge University Press.

McKinsley Global Institute (2015). 'The power of parity: How advancing women's equality can add $12 trillion to global economy', September, https://www.mckinsey .com/~/media/McKinsey/Featured%20Insights/Employment%20and%20Growth/ How%20advancing%20womens%20equality%20can%20add%2012%20tril lion%20to%20global%20growth/MGI%20Power%20of%20parity_Full%20report _September%202015.ashx.

Mezentseva, Y. (1994). 'What does the future hold? Some thoughts on the prospects for women's employment', pp. 74–84, in A. Posadskaya-Vanderbeck (ed). *Women in Russia: A New Era in Russian Feminism*. New York: Verso.

Mulé, R. (2016). 'The South European Welfare State in the new Millennium: Constraints, Challenges and Prospects for Europeanization', *Mirovaia ekonomika i mezhdunarodnye otnosheniia*, 60(7): 25–36.

North, D. (1990). *Institutions, institutional change and economic performance*. Cambridge: Cambridge University Press.

Pascall, G., and Lewis, J. (2004). 'Emerging gender regimes and policies for gender equality in a wider Europe', *Journal of Social Policy*, 33(3): 373–394.

Petrova, N. (2017). 'Zarplata zhenskogo roda. Pochemu voznikaet diskriminatsiia na rynke truda'. *Kommersant*, 30 September, https://www.kommersant.ru/doc/3423623.

Pushkareva, N. (ed.). (2013). *Rossiiskaia povsednevnost' v zerkale gendernykh otnoshenii: sbornik statei*. Moskva: Novoe literaturnoe obozrenie.

Rivkin-Fish, M. (2013). 'Conceptualizing Feminist Strategies for Russian Reproductive Politics: Abortion, Surrogate Motherhood, and Family Support after Socialism', *Signs*, 38(3): 569–593.

Rhein, W. (1998). 'The Feminization of Poverty: Unemployment in Russia', *Journal of International Affairs*, 52(1): 351–365.

Rimlinger, G.W. (1971). *Welfare policy and industrialization in Europe, America and Russia*. Chichester: Wiley and Sons.

Rosenberg, C. (1989). *Women and Perestroika*. London: Bookmarks.

Rosstat, (2016). Statistical yearbook.

Rzhanitsyna, L. (2001). 'Working women in Russia at the end of the 1990s', *Russian Social Science Review*, 42(4): 52–63.

Semeinye strategii. (2009). *Semeinye strategii sovremennoi rossiiskoi studencheskoi molodezhi. Reshenie konflikta 'rabota-sem'ia'*. Subregional'noe biuro MOT dlia stran Vostochnoi i Tsentral'noi Azii. Available at: https://www.ilo.org/wcmsp5/groups/public/---europe/---ro-geneva/---sro-moscow/documents/publication/wcms_312488.pdf.

Teplova, T. (2007). 'Welfare state transformation, childcare and women's work in Russia', *Social Politics*, 14(3): 284–322.

Utrata, J. (2015). *Women without Men: Single Mothers and Family Change in the New Russia*. 1st Edition. Ithaca: Cornell University Press.

Wintrobe, R. (1998). *The Political Economy of Dictatorship*. Cambridge: Cambridge University Press.

Women in business. (2017). 'New perspectives on risk and reward', *Grant Thornton*, March, https://www.grantthornton.co.uk/globalassets/1.-member-firms/united-kingdom/pdf/publication/women-in-business-new-perspectives-on-risk-and-reward.pdf.

Wright, S. (2014). 'Devolution and Social Policy', pp. 70–89, in H. Bochel and G. Daly (eds.), *Social Policy*, 3rd ed., Abingdon: Routledge.

Zhuravleva, T., and Gavrilova, I. (2017). 'Analiz faktorov rozhdaemosti v Rossii: chto govoriat dannye RMEZ NIU VShE?', *Ekonomicheskii zhurnal VShE*, 21(1): 145–187.

Zorina, E. (2007). 'Vozmozhnosti i napravleniia sotsial'noi podderzhki sem'i v Rossii i Germanii', *Zhurnal sotsiologii i sotsial'noi antropologii*, 1: 180–189.

Zubarevich, N. (2008). 'Regional'nye rynki truda Rossii: skhodstvo nepokhozhikh'. *Polit. ru*, 30 June, https://polit.ru/article/2008/06/30/demoscope337/.

CHAPTER 7

Reshaping the Strong-State Model: Dmitrii Medvedev's "Failed Modernisation"

Evgeny Mironov

In September 2009, assessing the content of Dmitrii Medvedev's article "Russia, forward!" and some alternative proposals for the development of the Russian economy, analyst and expert Kirill Rogov argued that "in the Russian elite, there was practically a consensus on the exhaustion of the development model that was formed in the past 5–6 years" (Rogov 2009). The point was that the "rental and debt model of development", based on the export of hydrocarbons as the main source of state revenues "is incompatible with innovation and diversification". Dmitrii Medvedev himself did not talk about changing the development model (for Kirill Rogov this implied above all a change in the political system). But he repeatedly emphasised the danger of dependence on the oil price situation, and precisely in connection with this danger, he considered the ultimate strategic goal of modernisation the diversification of the economy and the move first to interact with international partners in the development of high-tech production, and then to Russia's leadership in certain areas of high-tech. To what extent has this main goal of modernisation announced by Medvedev been realised?

During 2017 the price of oil rose, reaching US\$ 60 per barrel in October. For the fourth consecutive quarter, Russia's GDP has also grown, having accumulated 1.8% by the end of the third quarter of 2017. The main contribution to GDP, as before, was mining, and the manufacturing sector was declining (Centre for Development 2017). From 2002 to 2016 the share of extractive industry and oil refining in GDP in current prices increased by 2.6 percentage points of GDP, while the share of processing (with refining) decreased by 2.8 percentage points, and in 2017 this trend continued. This is a direct consequence of rising oil prices. According to Ruvinskii (2017): "It seems that the economic results of the three quarters of 2017 retain all those unfavourable structural trends that were formed in the 2000s against the backdrop of rising oil revenues". Thus, having passed through the period of the economic crisis that almost coincided with the period of Dmitrii Medvedev's tenure as president, the Russian economic model has remained the same. Moreover, against the backdrop of GDP growth, a return to the oil rent model is taking place, "with the difference that now it is not distributed across the economy, but settles in the budget and the extractive companies" (Ruvinskii 2017). With the growth of oil revenues, budget expenditures practically are not increasing, the real incomes of the population continue to fall and turnover stagnates. This situation can be viewed as the implementation of Dmitrii Medvedev's pessimistic forecasts of the period 2008–2009, when he explained the need for modernisation with this kind of perspective. Thus, the main goal of the modernisation process announced by Dmitrii Medvedev has not been achieved.

The period 2008–2012 has been described by many experts as a turning point, although the conceptualisation of this break only reduces the significance of the initiatives taken by Dmitrii Medvedev. The same Kirill Rogov proposed a model of three cycles in Russia's post-Soviet history: transformation (1990), stabilisation (2000s) and the third, beginning with the crisis of 2008–2009. In his interpretation, the chance for serious transformation was missed: the crisis of 2008–2009 did not cause structural changes in the economy, and the rapid recovery in oil prices led to the fact that post-crisis growth in many respects repeated the previous scenario. If this assumption is correct, "we are in the phase of maturing a new structural crisis associated with the impossibility of further sustained economic growth without a new stage of structural adjustment" (Rogov 2012a).

Another interpretation of the crucial nature of the period has been made by sociologist and journalist Konstantin Gaaze. From his point of view, "at the turn of 2009 a new political form appeared in Russia, which did not exist before". This form he calls "President Putin's court", implying that as a result of the transfer of power to Dmitrii Medvedev, the formal "Putin team" actually ceased to exist, but was replaced by an informal network of business ties, which after 2012 turned into a mechanism of government. If Konstantin Gaaze is right, we are talking, if not about archaisation, then at least about an anti-modernisation trend in the evolution of the political system (Gaaze 2017).

The analysis by Dmitrii Travin and Boris Gel'man of Russian modernisation in a broader historical perspective, taking into account the change of generations in Russia's social and political history as the basic factor of transformation, generally discounts modernisation efforts: "In any case, the period of Russia's radical economic and political modernisation, which started in 1985, was completed at the end of the twentieth century. The events of the 2000s and early 2010s have not changed (at least not yet) the outlines of the economic and political system formed during the transformations of the 1980s and 1990s. In this respect the assertion that the processes of Russian modernisation in 2000–2010 almost stopped where they were completed by the 'seventies' generation in the late 1990s, does not look exaggerated" (Travin & Gel'man 2013).

Thus, the problems that clearly appeared in the period 2008–2012 precisely because of the unresolved modernisation problems, continue to be relevant for Russia. A number of topics have arisen in recent public discussions indicating a return to the need to address the problems posed in 2008–2009 (talk about the digital economy, and the need to encourage small businesses) and the likelihood that the main tools for solving these problems will also be similar (the idea of establishing a second Skolkovo) (Koriakin 2017). The economic, political and social context in which "Medvedev's modernisation" took place, its assessment and criticism in the discussions of that period, including the reflection about the possible reasons for its failure, are topical issues for modern Russia, not only in an historical and theoretical sense, but also a practical sense. This article is devoted to the analysis of these issues.

1 Medvedev's Modernisation Program

As first vice-premier of the Russian Federation and a presidential candidate, Dmitrii Medvedev presented his economic program for the development of the country for 4 years at an economic forum in Krasnoiarsk in February 2008. He formulated four main directions and seven tasks on which Russia should concentrate. This program became known as the four "I's" – institutions, infrastructure, innovations, and investments. Seven tasks that Medvedev declared needed to be addressed in these four areas were to overcome legal nihilism, a radical reduction in administrative barriers, a reduction in the tax burden, the transformation of the rouble into one of the regional reserve currencies, modernisation of transport and energy infrastructure, formation of the foundations of a national innovation system and implementation of the country's social development program. Among the important priorities for the next four years was to ensure the independence of the Russian judicial system and ensure the real independence of the media. There was talk about protecting businesses from raid seizures and removing administrative barriers, and clear regulation of government agencies.

All these goals and tasks remained on Dmitrii Medvedev's agenda throughout the entire period of his presidency, but until 2009 the term "modernisation" was not central to his speeches. As such, he coined the motto "Russia, forward!" Then in a more detailed Annual Address to the Federal Assembly of 2009, he proposed a modernisation program envisaging five priority areas in which Russia was expected to achieve significant progress, to then achieve leading positions in the world market. Medvedev spoke about the effective use of energy; nuclear technologies; information technologies; medical technologies and pharmaceuticals; and space technology in combination with telecommunications. Achievements in these areas were seen as a means of attaining the main goal of economic diversification and thereby removing dependence on external factors, primarily on fluctuating oil prices. At the same time, Medvedev repeatedly stressed that the failure to fulfil this task would be fraught with serious risks and dangers in the future.

This idea was not new. Vladimir Putin also talked about the need for diversification, and in 2005 Putin's prime minister Mikhail Fradkov warned about excessive dependence of the economy on raw materials exports; in 2007 Deputy Prime Minister Sergei Ivanov said that without diversification, the Russian economy would sooner or later face collapse. The novelty was rather in an attempt to make this thesis the starting point for the whole program of activities, as well as the critical pledge in which this idea was voiced. The president, in particular, argued that in the previous period not enough had been done to achieve this goal, and the development of the economy was based on the Soviet technical heritage (rapidly becoming obsolete) and revenues from oil exports.

The enunciation of these priorities immediately aroused criticism of the president in terms of presenting a purely technological understanding of modernisation. There were certainly grounds for such an assessment, however, at least in public speeches Medvedev repeatedly stressed the connection between technical modernisation and improving the economic and political system. However, this connection has never been clearly analysed by him, nor has a clear definition of modernisation been given. As a result, in a broad interpretation, one can see in the various speeches of Medvedev a comprehensive modernisation plan, but also the lack of clear priorities and the tendency to substitute rhetoric for the program. Both versions were present in the public discussion of that period. Nevertheless, the priority of developing high technologies and related scientific research in this program was obvious. What factors in this area could help or hinder the president's plans?

2   Science and Technology in Post-Soviet Russia

The USSR once had a well-developed infrastructure for integrating science and technology. This infrastructure was based on state orders and was focused mainly on the need to ensure national defence and national security, as well as on the implementation of large-scale industrial projects. After the collapse of the Soviet Union, the demand for Russian science and technology in Russia almost disappeared. Many talented scientists either left the country, or left the field of science. There was a scientific diaspora, but its potential was practically not used in Russia. The integration of Russia into the world's high-tech markets was also insufficient due to extremely weak mechanisms for commercialising inventions. Russia had significant competitive advantages in terms of intellectual and human capital, especially in physics and mathematics, as well as in such sectors as space and nuclear energy.

In the period under review, the reform of higher education began, the aim of which was to focus on international standards, as well as to develop research in universities (for this purpose, "research universities" receiving special state funding were established). The Russian leadership started to create new physical infrastructure aimed at stimulating entrepreneurship – "incubators", special economic zones and technology parks. In addition, the Russian leadership stimulated investment by creating development institutions. An important restriction was the system of state procurement and price orientation as opposed to the quality of products, and this therefore did not encourage innovative products. Often, the choice was in favour of large or state-owned companies or, as many suspected, in favour of giving the maximum "rollback". In the 1990s, when the process of Russia's integration into the world economy was just beginning, enterprises that had enough money to modernise, did so by acquiring imported equipment. In those sectors where Russian products initially had competitiveness potential, entry to international markets was hampered by lack of knowledge of foreign business culture and practice, the poor quality of advertising and packaging materials, lack of compliance with technical standards, lack of required certificates and licenses, unclear ownership of intellectual property, and payment schemes. An exception in this period was the sphere of offshore programming, in which Russian companies were able to successfully gain a foothold in international markets (Pavese et al. 2010).

In the 1990s multinational companies became the main source of demand for Russian brains. Many talented Russian scientists, researchers and mathematicians moved to the US or Europe. Subsequently, the most far-sighted international companies that sought to use Russian intellectual resources established their own research centres in Russia, integrating them into the overall scheme of their activities. These companies included Intel, Boeing, Cisco, EMC, Motorola, Schlumberger and Price Waterhouse. Employing a large number of Russian employees, these transnational companies created a pool of people who were engaged in international business and production activities, thereby directly or indirectly contributing to the creation of Russia's new technological and entrepreneurial potential.

During the years of economic growth that followed the 1998 crisis, Russia spent much less on modernising its economic infrastructure than its developing competitors. For the period 2000–2007, the volume of Russian investment in fixed assets was about 20% of GDP, while in China this figure averaged 40%, and in India 30%. This led to a lag in the demand for modern equipment and innovative products in the private sector of the domestic market. Most Russian businessmen are not inclined to invest in their own production assets, but prefer to maximise short-term profits. They try to avoid long-term investments both because of uncertainty in the future, and because they manage to get sufficient profit with existing capacities. Limited competition in the domestic market also allows companies to avoid improving efficiency, which could be achieved by investing in innovation. In such circumstances, public financing becomes one of the key engines of domestic demand for innovation.

Due to the fact that one of the key elements in the implementation of the modernisation plan was the commercialisation of scientific developments as a model, in particular for the Skolkovo project, successful samples of technological clusters existing near leading universities (in particular Stanford and MIT) were observed. In Russia, the closest thing to this type of model inherited from the USSR was a system in which the centres of fundamental research were the institutes of the Russian Academy of Sciences. However, universities in the USSR were higher educational institutions, not research centres. Only the most advanced universities and institutes were integrated with the scientific research institutes of the Academy of Sciences of the USSR for conducting fundamental research. This system was reformed during the presidency of Dmitrii Medvedev, and in particular, federal and research universities were established. At the same time, within the framework of the budget reform of the 2000s, regional authorities lost the right to directly provide financial support to local higher education institutions (HEIs). This hindered local initiative, flexibility and opportunities for additional financial support from the progressive governments in the regions. On the other hand, however, the modernisation plans also entailed a law adopted in 2009 allowing Russian universities to create their own commercial enterprises.

Another important legacy of Soviet science was the presence of geographically dispersed and classified science cities, created to solve fundamental research problems. During the entire Soviet era, more than fifty such closed cities were built. Most of them were located near ordinary settlements, but were separated from the local infrastructure by a strict security system and were not connected with the surrounding reality. These cities were clusters of scientists supported directly by the state. Integration into the general economic system was done through ministries within the framework of a planned economy. In view of the complete absence of an independent economic base after the collapse of the Soviet Union, they also faced extremely difficult times, and many of them lost their potential. However, some science cities – Dubna, Obninsk, Sarov, Koltsov, Chernogolovka, Troitsk – attempted to modernise in the 2000s and this experience (as a rule, not very successful) can be considered a reference point for the Skolkovo project.

In Russia there was already a system for allocating grants to the Russian Foundation for Fundamental Research to support scientific research, similar to other countries. However, as a rule, this system is characterised by a high level of formalities in assessing the results of activities for which a grant can be issued, and has often been another form of budget financing, rather than an instrument for obtaining specific scientific results.

In addition, in the context of large-scale modernisation, it is important that science and scientists are completely out of the public space. According to the results of the VTSIOM poll held in 2010, 81% of citizens could not name any modern Russian scientist (VTSIOM 2009).

3 The Economic Context of Modernisation

The goals of modernisation were primarily declared to be economic. What are the implications of this decision? After the transformations of the 1990s, Russia entered a period of steady economic growth which began in 2000 and lasted until the global economic crisis of 2008. The main reason for this growth was the rise in the price of oil and other minerals and the subsequent increase in personal consumption in the large cities. During the crisis the Russian economy declined by 13%, but in 2010 there was already 6% growth. The blow was mitigated by the presence of the state reserve fund which was used to cover the budget deficit, increase social payments to pensioners, especially veterans, and to provide support for systemically important financial and industrial groups. The model of the economy formed in the pre-crisis years was based on the fact that the constantly growing revenues from commodity trade were transformed into an increase in incomes and domestic demand. External loans were available and stimulated the growth of demand, and it was not difficult for enterprises to respond to this demand:

"Enterprises took out loans to produce goods, and consumers took out loans in order to buy these goods" (Rogov 2009a). This model allowed millions of people to improve their well-being and gave a powerful impetus to the development of trade and services infrastructure. Many branches invested heavily in renewing their facilities and machinery: the share of machinery and equipment in imports was about 50% in recent years. But this model also had long-term negative effects: the rapid strengthening of the rouble, accelerated growth of domestic prices and high inflation. All of these factors were directly related to the fundamental condition for economic growth – an ever-growing inflow of external capital. This economic model was socially effective, but at the same time it worked against modernisation. For example, in 1999 the share of fuel and energy products in exports was 44%, and in 2007 it was 62%; in general, raw materials exports including metals, timber and hard coal accounted for ¾ of all Russian exports in 2007. The share of machinery and equipment in exports decreased from 8.8% in 2000 to 5.6% in 2007. While the value of exports increased 3.5 times from 2000 to 2007, the volume of imports increased 5 times, which indicated that Russian industry was losing its position in the domestic market (ibid).

The fundamental problem of the Russian economy, directly related to the modernisation problem, is that Russian industrial products are largely uncompetitive.

> The prospects for expanding Russian industrial exports are limited by the relatively high cost of labour and inflated social standards, while across the world more and more cheap labour is involved in the process of mass industrial production. This fact can be considered one of the incentives for trying our luck in the field of high-tech products, having skipped the competitiveness phase in traditional industry and hoping for a higher return on human capital in knowledge-intensive industries.
>
> ROGOV 2009

Another important feature of the Russian economy which hinders modernisation efforts is the key role of large corporations with a large share of state participation. At the same time, access to the market for small and medium-sized players, as well as access to capital, is difficult. It is small and medium-sized players that are most affected by the shortcomings of the institutional environment, the weakness of legal regulation, and have difficulty accessing financial resources. "Large enterprises have either adapted to these conditions or even "rule" them, that is, they have learned to use these institutional flaws for their own interests. Such a decline in the level of domestic competition will inevitably affect the global competitiveness of Russian companies. And this is already having an effect in the form of accelerated growth of costs ... While initiators and engines of development and innovation are usually just small companies" (Rogov & Freinkman 2008).

The economic crisis of 2008 became an important part of the economic context of the transformation. On the one hand, Dmitrii Medvedev directly pointed out that the crisis should stimulate the search for ways to improve economic efficiency. On the other hand, the anti-crisis program of the Russian government envisaged an extensive system of measures designed to alleviate the consequences of credit overheating in previous economic years for various economic subjects and groups of the population, but did not say anything about stimulating the economy. This program strengthened the trend according to which "the state acts as the largest owner and manager of economic processes" (Rogov 2009a), and at the same time assumed high social obligations and supported large, completely unprofitable and uncompetitive industries, such as the auto industry (Dragunskii 2010).

4   State Innovation Management

Three supreme bodies were established in Russia to manage innovative processes, two of which are related to the Administration of the President and the third to the Government of the Russian Federation. First of all, we are talking about the Commission under the President of the Russian Federation for Modernisation and Technological Development of the Russian Economy. Chairman of the Commission was the President himself, Dmitrii Medvedev. The Commission consisted of working groups on energy efficiency, nuclear technologies, strategic computer technologies and software, medical equipment and pharmaceuticals, and space and telecommunications. Secondly, there was the Governmental Commission on High Technology and Innovation. The Head of the Commission was Chairman of the Government of the Russian Federation Vladimir Putin. The Commission was responsible for the development of the state modernisation policy and the use of new technologies in the process of economic development. In addition, a Council was set up under the President of the Russian Federation for the Development of the Information Society. The Council monitored the creation of e-government and the use of modern information technologies in the field of health care, social protection, culture, education and science, and ensuring life safety. The Council also dealt with the problem of overcoming the digital divide existing between Russia's regions, examining the international experience of developing an information society and contributing to the overall development of the information industry. In addition, the innovation policy was implemented by a number of ministries accountable to the Chairman of the Government of the Russian Federation, including the Ministry of Education and Science of the Russian Federation, which developed a document entitled "Strategy for the Development of Science and Innovations in the Russian Federation for the Period until 2015". This document aimed to create an effective innovation system: the formation and expansion of a competitive research and development sector, the provision of legal protection of research and development results and the modernisation of the economy based on technological innovation. However, the Ministry does not bear formal responsibility for the commercialisation of research. The Ministry of Economic Development, including the Department of Special Economic Zones and Project Finance, acted within the framework of the "Concept of long-term social and economic development of the Russian Federation for the period until 2020" and "The main activities of the Government of the Russian Federation for the period until 2012". The tasks of the Ministry in the innovation sphere are stimulation of innovation activity of operating enterprises, assistance in the creation of new innovative companies, increasing demand for innovative products, and supporting the innovative direction of the science and education sector. The Ministry approved the "Action plan to stimulate the innovative activity of enterprises". The Ministry of Communications and Mass Communications is responsible for the administration of the network of technology parks, the program for the creation of e-government and the provision of broadband internet access throughout the country. This set of institutions did not lead, however to a breakthrough in the change of the innovation environment. The main problem here was the coordination of activities:

> At first glance, the duties of these ministries include all aspects of the spread of innovation in Russia. However, in practice, no one takes personal responsibility for the innovation ecosystem as a whole, nor for the introduction of new technologies in public institutions and state companies. As a result, the practical actions carried out by these and other ministries and departments contribute little to innovative development.
>
> PAVESE et al. 2010

During the decade that preceded the beginning of the presidency of Dmitrii Medvedev, measures were taken to build new infrastructure to support the creation of new enterprises. This infrastructure includes business incubators, special economic zones and technology parks. Business incubators have become widespread in Russia, but their effectiveness and generally the feasibility of the establishment is not always obvious. In most cases, incubators are state institutions rather than self-sufficient enterprises, and are more interested in reporting indicators than in the commercial success of the companies they serve, which, of course, is not attractive to entrepreneurs.

In an attempt to emulate the Indian model implemented in Bangalore, the Government of the Russian Federation established a special economic zone (SEZ) as a closed territory, with special rules encouraging entrepreneurship.

SEZ residents are subject to special time-limited tax privileges, including a reduction of profit tax, exemption from customs duties, property and land taxes. The law provides for several types of SEZs, including industrial-production, technology-promotional, tourist-recreational and port areas. A number of SEZs have been created (production facilities in the Lipetsk region, the Republic of Tatarstan, technical and innovative ones in St. Petersburg, Zelenograd, Dubna and Tomsk, etc.). But they have had rather limited success in terms of creating start-ups. The reason is the complexity of the procedure for entering the SEZ, the rather inconvenient internal procedures and the system of decision-making, oriented to the interests of state managers, and not to the interests of investors. As a result, SEZs have achieved much greater success in supporting industrial and assembly production and, in some cases, subsidiaries of large Russian companies.

In addition to SEZs, the Russian leadership has developed a program to create a network of high-tech parks or techno-parks. It was assumed that techno-parks would be small towns with a population of 10–15,000 people and become full-scale scientific and technical clusters, in which the distance between science, education and business would be minimised. In the techno-parks there are housing complexes designed to improve the living conditions of researchers and scientists. Each techno-park develops around a large educational institution or a leading scientific institute. Unlike the Special Economic Zones, techno-parks do not provide any special customs or tax incentives, being an open commercial environment.

Inconsistent state support and the introduction of the program for the construction of techno-parks led to the fact that only two of the planned network operated in 2010 – in Novosibirsk and Kazan, and to a limited extent (without housing) (Pavese et al. 2010).

5   The Social Context

Critics of Medvedev's program repeatedly pointed out that the plan for creating the conditions for innovation was based on non-obvious assumptions about the existence in the society of a desire for entrepreneurship in the innovation sphere and a large number of relevant ideas held back by unfavourable legal and institutional conditions, and changing these conditions could lead to a qualitative leap. To assess these assumptions, it is necessary to consider the following. Entrepreneurship began to appear in Russia with the collapse of the Soviet Union. As a result of privatisation of state property, a small number of extremely successful people began to monitor the conduct of business in all sectors of the economy. For those scientists and engineers who went into business, it was at least to some extent natural, because in the Soviet period they had the notion of competition (which was carried out, however, in a completely non-market context), but for most, small businesses emerged simply out of need. Therefore, Russian business was initially characterised by short-term thinking, the desire to enrich oneself with rapid turnover of goods and the persistent desire to conceal revenues from state and tax structures. So, although in Russia a class of entrepreneurs appeared, such entrepreneurship had little to do with the long-term management of the innovation process. As a result, the number of successful entrepreneurs who linked their activities with technologies that required serious scientific research in the country was small, and, accordingly, there were few mentors able to convey the experience to young people. During twenty years of reform scientists and engineers were often perceived as freaks and dreamers; many successful people either did not advertise themselves, or left with their companies to the West. Only a few projects of commercialisation and transfer of technology have been crowned with considerable success, and on the whole, the experience of transforming the intellectual potential of a particular person into real status and wealth in Russia was practically unknown to the general public.

On the other hand, the expectation of changes in the domestic policy vector was noticeable by 2008 and could have become a social modernisation resource. That was the vector,

> which can be designated by the word "soft" and which implies institutional renewal, the improvement of the legal regime, the democratization of economic life, the rejection of the concentration of resources in the hands of the state and the return of faith in the initiative of private capital. The vector, in which Russia's strategic interests on the foreign arena do not boil down to the interests of gas geopolitics, the law enforcement system is not a repressive mechanism that protects those in power, and state corporations look like a historical anomaly.
>
> ROGOV 2008

But even purely technical innovations were considered necessary for the country's prosperity by 63% of the respondents polled by VTSIOM in 2008 (VTSIOM 2008). Of course, such expectations were typical, first of all, for educated and active residents of large cities, most likely not the majority of the inhabitants of Russia. But it is also clear that it was the intellectual potential and social capital of this stratum that was targeted by Medvedev's modernisation project. It was this social stratum that became involved in the protest activity of 2011–2012. Obviously, the goals of the program proposed by the president were broader than purely technical modernisation and this layer of people supported it, but its implementation caused disappointment. And the matter, apparently, was not just in not fully implementing the declared plans, but in the contradictory nature of the power politics. And the first gap between the modernising president and an active layer of urban residents, most likely began almost immediately after the beginning of Medvedev's presidency, during the Russian-Georgian armed conflict. Comparing the consequences of the situation resulting from this conflict with the arrest of Mikhail Khodorkovskii, Kirill Rogov wrote:

> [...] recognition of the independence of South Ossetia and Abkhazia is a choice that will determine the scope of the possible development of Russia for many years ... This bomb laid under relations with the West and cooperation, especially in the business sector, is almost impossible to overcome.
>
> ROGOV 2008

While Dmitrii Medvedev sought to use the conflict with Georgia to establish his image as a resolute and strong-willed leader in the public space, it was this conflict, and above all the way it was covered by the Russian media, that seriously weakened support for the president from those who could support the modernisation process:

> The way the conflict in Georgia was covered made the situation in the main Russian media more and more obvious. By their information policy, they only increase the distance of distrust between the authorities and the educated part of society. It is impossible to fill the information space with such "information" and simultaneously ... think about modernisation.
>
> KAPLUN 2008

But to overcome this problem to the displeasure of the "creative class" would be wrong. Investigations of the Levada Centre in the fall of 2011 showed that the demand for change arose in the broader social strata. The problem, however, is that according to sociologists, this request was addressed to Putin. "It comes from an audience that does not yet see an alternative to him as president ... these people do not want to change Putin for anyone else (and vote for him), but they are waiting for Putin to become different" (ibid). At the same time, if we consider the Skolkovo project as the most complete practical embodiment of Dmitrii Medvedev's modernisation model, we can talk about the attempt to modernise in general without attracting any broad social layers and this choice should be taken into account when evaluating the modernisation strategies of that period.

6   Criticism of the Modernisation Program

For most independent experts there was broad support for the idea of the need for major changes, but almost all aspects of the preparation of the program and the logic of this program were critically evaluated. Thus Dmitrii Travin, one of the leading Russian experts on the history and theory of modernisation, pointed out that the experience of analysis and conceptualisation of the modernisation phenomenon existing in the modern scientific literature was not taken into account by the team of developers of Medvedev's program. According to Travin, if the changes in the country are focused on technical and infrastructural updating, then actual modernisation (necessarily assuming the transformation of political and economic institutions), in fact, becomes impossible, because obsolete and ineffective governance mechanisms will only be strengthened (Travin 2010)

As a rule, the word "modernisation" among Russian citizens is associated with the formation of a scientific centre in Skolkovo, but not with the rationalisation of consciousness, the development of democracy, strengthening of the market nature of the economy, an increase in social, psychological and geographical mobility, as well as other processes cited in the scientific literature which develops the theory of modernisation (Rogov 2012). Attention was also drawn to the fact that the planning horizon itself was limited to a ten-year period and does not allow us to speak about the existence of a genuine strategy and reduces modernisation to a set of tactical steps (Travin 2010).

The main critical point in assessing the program proposed by Medvedev is the ratio of technological and political modernisation. And here, first of all, attention was drawn to the absence in the program statements of the President of the assessment of the current political system. Pointing to serious problems in the economic sphere, Dmitrii Medvedev nevertheless presented them as flaws in the system, which, in general, worked successfully. In contrast to this view, many analysts saw the main obstacle to modernisation in the essence of Russia's political system:

It was about the notion of a "power vertical" in which the politico-bureaucratic model looks more like a matryoshka doll or a big pyramid built of many small pyramids. The principle of relationships established at the top is repeated and reduplicated on the lower floors... The vertical structure is not capable of transmitting down certain impulses (for example, the impulses of modernisation), but is only capable of transmitting the principle of its existence.

ROGOV 2009

At the same time, by ignoring the main problem, the program did not offer a reasonable focus on any breakthrough problem, but suggested acting immediately in many different ways:

Another problem with the proposed model is its ambitiousness, which leads to the defocusing of the goal. It's not just about increasing sales in the markets of high-tech products, but also about achieving technological leadership in a number of areas. These two tasks are consistently achievable in the strategic perspective of "modernisation", but are unlikely to be compatible within the framework of tactical goal-setting.

RUBTSOV 2013

Objections were also raised about the way priorities were set in the modernisation program. In particular, the proposal to immediately gain competitiveness in high-tech industries, passing up more traditional production:

Classic examples of successful modernisation of the 20th century were built in the opposite way: from the production of low-tech products to the production of increasingly technological products, from copying samples to copying technologies, and then – development institutions and the introduction of innovations... without the skills to control the effectiveness of investments, we are going to make a leap in directions where such control looks particularly difficult.

ROGOV 2009b

There were also doubts that even if successful, the modernisation plan would seriously change the situation in the economy at all:

this sphere of high technology is very small in terms of the labour market. In fact, this will mean that the majority of the country's population will still be engaged in the production of non-competitive goods, as well as in the public services sector. This, in turn, will mean the need to transfer export revenues in favour of a mass of uncompetitive population. And as a result – the inability to accumulate resources for further development (weakening competitive advantages). And also the preservation of the current model of the domestic market, where the expansion of domestic demand is mainly covered by imports.

IBID

7   Conclusion

The conclusion made by the team of the New York Academy of Sciences in preparing the plan for the modernisation of the Russian economy in 2010 is still topical: "The reforms of old innovative institutions have been launched, new ones have been created, and laws aimed at stimulating innovation have been adopted. However, Russia has not yet managed to create an independent self-replicating system based on new technologies – an innovative ecosystem" (Pavese et al. 2010). The main embodiment of the modernisation program is still Skolkovo, a successfully developing city with an innovative environment, but existing not only in parallel with the rest of Russia, but also opposed to it, implementing in practice everything that does not exist in other places, from energy-saving technologies to transport infrastructure, a special tax base and its own security service, its own customs and financial services and a multi-level education system. Many residents of Skolkovo are successful at developing and commercialising technology. However, the presence of such a large-scale project obviously does not solve Russia's economic problems and does not affect in any significant way the diversification of the economy. Given that most of the ideas declared by Medvedev during his tenure as President were to some extent rooted in already existing development trends and even in specific projects, it can be assumed that the modernisation program could continue with great success even after the end of his presidency. The economic goals of the modernisation plan were not achieved. However, the social effect, which was not really predicted or approved by the initiators of the modernisation project, was significant. The experience of Medvedev's modernisation gave the active part of society hope for changes, a sense of involvement in these changes and, as a result, opportunities to influence power. It is no coincidence that the protests of 2010–11, which marked the start of the new period of Vladimir Putin's presidency, were associated by many analysts with the expectations and hopes formed during the Medvedev "thaw" period, which created in the minds of many people in Russia a landmark, in relation to which the subsequent period almost immediately came to be viewed as a period of anti-modernisation "cooling".

Bibliography

Center for Development. (2017). 'Kommentarii o gosudarstve i biznese', *Tsentr Razvitiia – Natsional'nyi issledovatel'skii universitet Vysshaia shkola ekonomiki*, 4–31 October, https://dcenter.hse.ru/mirror/pubs/share/direct/211464400.

Dragunskii, D. (2010). 'Modernizatsiia v stile Steampunk', *Neprikosnovennyi zapas*, 6(74), http://magazines.russ.ru/nz/2010/6/dd18.html.

Gaaze, K. (2017). 'Dvor vmesto politbiuro. Chto proiskhodit s okruzheniem Putina', *Moskovskii Tsentr Carnegi*, 25 August, http://carnegie.ru/commentary/72910.

Kaplun, V. (2008). 'Kolbasa ili zhizn': perspektivy rossiiskoi modernizatsii posle vooruzhennogo konflikta v Gruzii', *Neprikosnovennyi zapas*, 5(61), http://magazines.russ.ru/nz/2008/5/ka12.html.

Koriakin, K. (2017). 'Skolkovo razmnozhaetsia. Zachem Rossii eshche odin tsentr tekhnologii', *Kommersant FM*, 18 October, https://www.kommersant.ru/doc/3441890.

Pavese, K.E., Hayter, C. and Satinsky, D. (2010). 'Iaroslavskii Plan 10–15–20', *The New York Academy of Sciences*, https://www.hse.ru/data/2011/02/07/1208875319/Yaroslavl%20Roadmap_Russian_Print.pdf.

Rogov, K. (2008). 'Vektor: khard end soft', *Vedomosti*, 27 August, https://www.vedomosti.ru/newspaper/articles/2008/08/27/vektor-hard-jend-soft.

Rogov, K. (2009). 'Vertikal' vlasti sebia izzhila', *Vedomosti*, 23 September, https://www.vedomosti.ru/opinion/articles/2009/09/23/vertikal-vlasti-sebya-izzhila.

Rogov, K. (2009a). 'Antikrizisnaia strategiia: Neftianaia anasteziia', *Vedomosti*, 4 June, https://www.vedomosti.ru/newspaper/articles/2009/06/04/antikrizisnaya-strategiya-neftyanaya-anesteziya.

Rogov, K. (2009b). 'Model razvitiia: verticalnye grabli', *Vedomosti*, 23 September, https://www.pressreader.com/russia/vedomosti/20090923/281565171804696.

Rogov, K. (2012). 'Stsenarii "Rossiia-1"', *Vedomosti*, 8 February, http://www.vedomosti.ru/opinion/articles/2012/02/08/strategiya_rossiya1.

Rogov, K. (2012a). 'Gipoteza tret'ego tsikla', *Russia-2020: scenarios of development*, 135, Moscow: Rosspen.

Rogov, K. and Freinkman, L. (2008). 'Vyzovy krizisa: Smena modeli', *Vedomosti*, 6 October, https://www.vedomosti.ru/newspaper/articles/2008/10/06/vyzovy-krizisa-smena-modeli.

Rubtsov, A. (2013). 'Filosofiia opasnosti. Ugrozy i riski v formate strategicheskogo planirovaniia', *Otechestvennye zapiski*, 2(53), http://www.strana-oz.ru/2013/2/filosofiya-opasnosti.

Ruvinskii, V. (2017). 'Kogda neft' ne pomogaet. Rossiiskaia ekonomika vozvrashaetsia k neftianoi modeli', *Vedomosti*, 8 November, https://www.vedomosti.ru/opinion/articles/2017/11/08/740836-neft-pomogaet.

Travin, D. (2010). 'Medvedevskaia modernizatsiia i gorbachevskaia perestroika', *Neprikosnovennyi zapas*, 6(74), http://magazines.russ.ru/nz/2010/6/tr11.html.

Travin, D. and Gel'man V. (2013). '"Zagoguliny" rossiiskoi modernizatsii: smena pokolenii i traektorii reform', *Neprikosnovennyi zapas*, 4(90), https://magazines.gorky.media/nz/2013/4/zagoguliny-rossijskoj-modernizaczii-smena-pokolenij-i-traektorii-reform.html.

VTSIOM 2008. 'Innovatsii: spasut li oni Rossiiu?', 27 March, https://wciom.ru/index.php?id=236&uid=3089.

VTSIOM 2011. "Sovremennaia nauka: chem i komu ona interesna", 22 March, https://wciom.ru/index.php?id=236&uid=1716.

CHAPTER 8

State and Social Protests in China

Yongshun Cai

Authoritarian regimes are characterized by the lack of political opportunities for collective action, but popular contention is not absent in such regimes (Schock 2005). China has witnessed numerous instances of social protests in the past twenty years. These protests are caused by a variety of sources of grievances (Chung et al. 2006), deficiencies of dispute-resolution mechanisms (Lee 2007; Chen 2012), and protestors' mobilization capacity (O'Brien & Li 2007; Cai 2010; Chan & Pan 2009). Regardless of the causes, these persistent protests place significant pressure on the government because the reoccurrence of protests not only disrupts social order but also encourages more protests.

While much research has focused on how social grievances have caused protests, it merits exploring how popular contention becomes a cause of changes in state institutions. Slater (2010: 5) writes that "the recent profusion of research on contentious politics has almost universally treated it as an outcome to be explained – as a product instead of a producer of political institutions". In other words, contentious politics should also be treated as a factor that shapes state institutions. "Contentious politics is the independent variable. States, militaries, and ruling parties are dependent variables arising from contentious politics, as well as intervening variable that influence authoritarian durability in turn" (Slator 2010: 20).

The China case can thus shed light on how popular contention shapes state behaviour and more importantly, on institution building. An examination of social protests in China not only reveals how the Chinese government responds to specific protests, but also helps understand how the state changes itself in the process of dealing with popular contention. This chapter examines how popular contention – as an explanatory variable – has shaped the state's behaviour, political learning, and organizational response in dispute resolution, or more broadly, institution building as a result of responding to social conflict.

The Chinese government's monopoly of power makes it both the major target and mediator in popular contention. However, popular contention does not necessarily weaken the state because the state has been able to collect information and gain information advantages over the people, reduce pent-up grievances especially among large groups, and strengthen and extend the

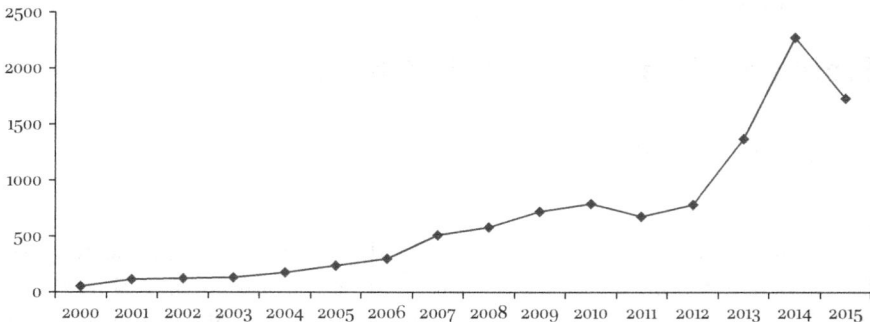

FIGURE 8.1   Social protests in China (2000–2015)
SOURCE: AUTHOR'S COLLECTION

reach of the state. State penetration can significantly enhance the state's capacity to manage social protests. Nevertheless, the government's success in containing social protests does not necessarily relieve all the pressure it faces. A weak institutionalization of conflict resolution creates the possibility of persistent popular contention.

1   Social Protests as a Form of Pressure in China

Social protests have persisted in China over the past 20 years. Systematic data on protests are lacking because the government has been reluctant to release such information. Figure 8.1 presents the data on social protests from 2000 to 2015 we collected from online sources. The frequency of social protests rose steadily in China from 2000 to 2014, but then began to decline in 2015. We are unable to assess whether these cases are representative of the general tendency of social protests in China, but these incidents at least indicate the persistence of protests. Persistent protests have become an important concern of the Chinese government and have prompted it to allocate a large amount of resources to ensure social stability. Maintaining social and political stability has become the top priority of Chinese central and local governments, and the interaction among the central state, local state, and protestors has been significantly shaped by this priority. Protest management reveals how the Chinese government has achieved social stability while the society has undergone significant socioeconomic changes. It also reflects the political rationale behind governance in an authoritarian context where the government prioritizes its political survival over other issues.

The fast and dramatic socioeconomic changes in China have generated a large quantity of social conflict. The weak dispute-resolution mechanisms also contribute to people's choice of protests as a mode of pursuing their interests. As a result, social protests have been staged by various social groups in China. In rural areas, peasants protested because of heavy taxes (before 2004), loss of land, pollution, and other disputes with local authorities or the business. In urban China, workers protested against poor working conditions, low salaries, and delayed payment of salaries, among others. Urban residents protested because of conflict with the government in land use, housing developers, and property management companies. Other groups, such as schoolteachers, demobilized soldiers, and students, have also staged protests. The persistence of protests has generated pressure on the government not only because the government is directly targeted, but also because the government is treated as a mediator of conflict.

1.1   *State as the Target*

Widespread protests in China are generally tied to the central and local policies. From the late 1990s to the early 2000s, waves of protests staged by laid-off workers from public firms and pensioners resulted from the government's reform of pubic firms, because the reform was conducted "in the absence of an adequate welfare system" (Cai 2006: 19). "As the Communist Party withdrew from its old role of working-class vanguard, SOE [State-Owned Enterprise] workers were abandoned by their political champion and revolutionary master" (Hurst 2009: 139). Many aggrieved workers found themselves going back and forth between passivity, depression, and even self-destruction, on the one hand, and outbursts of rage, desperation, and heroic acts of collective defiance, on the other (Lee 2007: 69–70).

National policies have also triggered nationwide protests indirectly. The 1994 fiscal reform that allowed the central government to collect more tax revenue than local governments has significantly affected the latter's interaction with the people in both rural and urban areas. The fiscal crisis at the township level and the related worsening of the peasant burden were predominantly caused by the 1994 tax reform. "Diminished sources of revenue compelled township officials to squeeze the peasants even harder, particularly in the agricultural provinces" (Chen 2008: 303). When local officials became predatory, direct conflict between officials and peasants arose. As Bernstein and Lu suggest, tax collection had become the most difficult task faced by local officials in agricultural areas (Bernstein & Lu 2003).

Fiscal pressure has also led to conflict between local governments and the people in land use. Strongly motivated by generating revenues from land sales or attracting external investors, local governments have turned farmland into non-agricultural use while ignoring peasant interests. Given the importance of land to peasants, resistance to land occupation has persisted as the land seizure continues. Conflicts have arisen between farmers and village cadres or other land users who are either local governments or the business supported by local governments (Zweig 2007; Cai 2010). Because of local governments' high stake in land use, peasants often face great difficulties in wrestling concessions from the government.

Similarly, land development in cities because of urban renewal or commercial purposes has become conflict ridden. Land development and urban renewal often lead to the relocation of residents and the demolition of their housing. Housing demolition has remained the major source of conflicts in urban China because local governments often fail to provide sufficient compensation (Cai 2007).

Some other protests occur not because of the central government's behaviour but because of local governments' practices. Environmental protection has become a goal of popular contention in many cities and villages in China (Jing 2000; van Rooij 2000; Deng & Yang 2013; Zhong & Hwang 2016). People protest either because the government's approval of (possibly) polluting projects or because the government fails to stop polluting projects. Other protests are tied to local governance. For example, riots arising from conflicts between vendors and city management people have occurred in a number of cities because city governments' attempts to stop vendors' business activities.

1.2   *State as the Arbitrator or Mediator*
The Chinese government is also targeted by protestors as the arbitrator or mediator. The concentration of power in the hand of the government leads it to shoulder most of the responsibility of conflict resolution. The government has become an arbitrator of disputes between its lower-level counterparts and the people or between social actors. When local residents find that their interests have been encroached upon or fail to be protected by local authorities, they often approach, or seek the intervention of, higher-level authorities for redress.

The concept "rightful resistance" well captures how the discrepancies between high authorities' policies or laws and local practices have shaped people's strategy of resistance. O'Brien and Li (2007: 2–3) write that rightful resistance "is a kind of partially sanctioned protest that uses influential allies and recognized principles to apply pressure on those in power who have failed to live up to a professed ideal or who have not implemented some beneficial measure". Rightful resisters seek the assistance of upper-level authorities when defending their interests against local agents. Upper-level authorities become the arbitrator or mediator between local authorities and farmers.

The effectiveness of rightful resistance is thus less determined by the "rightful-ness" of a grievance, but by the support rightful resisters receive from upper-level authorities.

The party-state's monopoly of political power and its mass-line propaganda make it deeply involved in the resolution of civil disputes. The so-called mass line has indeed encouraged people to stage collective action (Chen 2012). For example, the petition agencies in China have received a significant portion of civil disputes not caused by the government (Wang & Chen 2015). Local governments are pressured to intervene in civil disputes partly because of their worry that social disputes may escalate into incidents that threaten local stability or damage the image of local governments. Because of the people's expectation of the government's intervention in conflict resolution, they often seek government intervention sometimes by bypassing the formal channels of conflict resolution. One example is the disputes between residents and the business in urban residential communities. When disputes between homeowners and developers or property management companies occur, homeowners may stage protests in order to attract the attention of the local government (Cai 2005; Shi & Cai 2006).

Labour disputes are another source of social protests in China, especially in places like Guangdong province that attract a large number of external labour (Lee 2007; Zhang 2015). Workers complain about poor work conditions and management's violations of laws or government rules. Migrant workers' collective actions involve their conflict with management at the point of production. Worker's collective action did trigger local governments' intervention, but the government may face a dilemma. On one hand, the local government needs to pressure the management to abide by the law and pacify the workers. However, continual rise of the legal wage would undermine the competitiveness of their localities against other regions or countries (Chen & Pun 2009).

Labour disputes also point to an important cause of social protests in China – the inadequacies or ineffectiveness of existing sanctioned or legal channels of dispute resolution (Gallagher 2006). Migrant workers' collective actions often have a legal basis, but their disputes are not necessarily solved in sanctioned channels. The inefficient or even corrupt bureaucracy and legal system often fail to address labour disputes. Instead, their failures may trigger protests (Lee 2007).

2 Government Response

In China, contentious politics has shaped behaviour of both the ruling elite and local governments. Thus far, the most challenging collective action to the

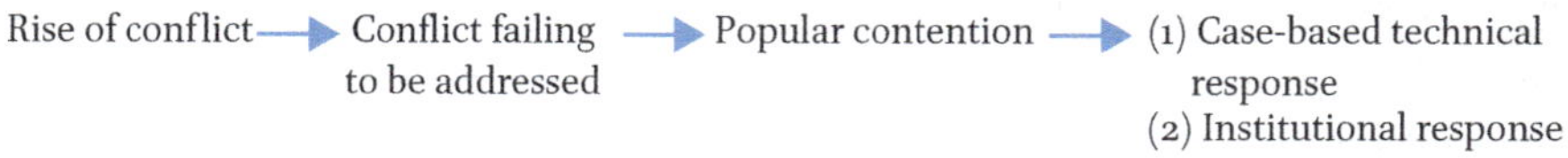

Rise of conflict──▶ Conflict failing ──▶ Popular contention ──▶ (1) Case-based technical
                to be addressed   response
                                                          (2) Institutional response

FIGURE 8.2 Stages of the evolution of popular contention

party-state is the 1989 Tiananmen incident. The most serious lesson drawn by the ruling elite from this incident is the importance of the solidarity among the leadership. In the aftermath of the incident, Deng Xiaoping stressed the importance of a united leadership. In 1990, Deng (1993: 365) said:

> The core issue of China is that the Chinese Communist Party has a good Politburo, especially a good standing committee of the Politburo. As long as the committee does not have a problem, China will be as steady as a rock (*wen ru taishan*)...The critical issue is the presence of a united core leadership. If we maintain such a leadership for 50 or 60 years, a socialist China will be invincible.

Elite solidarity directly affects the political opportunities faced by protestors. In China, elite solidarity has not been a serious issue since the 1989 student movement, although power struggle has persisted. However, social protests still generate direct pressure on the authoritarian government because such protests directly or indirectly challenge social stability. More importantly, social protests may diffuse and escalate into political action. The Chinese government is sensitive to social protests and has therefore exerted tremendous efforts to deal with these protests in order to limit the effect of the protests.

Figure 8.2 presents the evolution of protests in China. A large number of studies have examined the issues in each of the stages, often focusing on specific groups as mentioned above. Although there are also collective actions staged by religious sects and separatists (Mackerras 2012), such protests are much smaller in number compared with the vast number of non-political protests stated by various social groups (Chung, Lai & Xia 2006; Chen 2009). The government influences the development of social protests in each of the stages. The government may directly cause social protests, or it may cause protests because it fails to address the grievances.

Not surprisingly, the government has taken measures to pre-empt protests or reduce their effect. It silences protests by making concessions or resorting to repression; it tries to pre-empt social protests by strengthening information collection, creating dispute-resolution institutions, and exercising stricter control over public employees. Although these efforts do not necessarily achieve the institutionalization of conflict resolution, they reduce the pressure faced by the government at least in the short run.

2.1 Technical Response

A government generally oscillates between repression and concessions when dealing with popular contention (Piven & Cloward 1977). The Chinese government's responses can be divided into the following categories: concessions, concessions with discipline, tolerance, ignorance, and repression (Cai 2010). The choice of a particular mode of response is tied to protestors' power and the cost involved in making concessions or mete out repression on the part of the government. Hence, the government is less likely to make concessions in zero-sum games between itself and protestors.

The concrete measures taken by Chinese local governments in resolving social conflict are various. Lee and Zhang suggest three micro-foundations for Chinese local governments to maintain social stability: non-zero-sum bargaining, legal-bureaucratic absorption, and patron-clientelism (Lee & Zhang 2013). Non-zero-sum bargaining that involves "buying stability" is the most prevalent means of pacifying the aggrieved in labour, land rights, and property disputes. "Buying stability" involves the use of a combination of tactics, including unrest and emotion control, fragmentation and co-optation, framing of citizens' rights in practical senses, and the use or threat use of force.

The legal-bureaucratic absorption is an important method that consumes the energy of the aggrieved and weakens their determination because of bureaucratic inefficiency and irresponsiveness. The government has also tried to cultivate patron-clientelist ties to help resolve social conflicts in their jurisdictions: communist party members, civil servants, the elderly and retirees, and former protest leaders and participants. But these patronage ties are both instrumental and affective, illustrating the many guises and fragility of state power (Lee & Zhang 2013: 1502). Thus, government response may be meaningless to other protestors.

Repression remains crucial to authoritarian rule. Art (2012: 353) writes that "our understanding of the coercive institutions of modern authoritarian and hybrid regimes is pretty thin". Levitsky and Way (2010: 57–58) divide repression in authoritarian regimes into two types: high-intensity coercion and low-intensity coercion. The former refers to high-visibility acts that target large number of people, well-known individuals, or major institutions, whereas the latter refers to surveillance, low-profile physical harassment (but not necessary less severe), denial of employment, scholarships, or university entrances, denial of public service ice, and use of tax, regulatory or other state agencies to investigate and prosecute opposition people.

Repression has been used or remained to be a credible threat employed by the Chinese government (Wang 2014). Repression can be divided into three categories: (1) repression with legal charges; (2) repression through illegal measures; and (3) relational repression. Collective action is by and large illegal in China, and legal charges are a convenient way of repression. When legal charges are not used, local authorities can resort to illegal detention and harassments, sometimes with the assistance of hired thugs. Repression may take a subtler form. Deng and O'Brien (2013) find that Chinese local officials have employed "relational repression" to demobilize protesters. Local officials investigate activists' social ties, locate individuals who might be willing to help stop the protest. These people include protestors' relatives, friends and fellow townspeople.

Authoritarian governments' protest management must go beyond repression. Although the Chinese central government rarely addresses individual cases of protests directly, it does pay serious attention to social conflict in the country. When certain national policies have caused nationwide conflict, the central government comes under the pressure of revising or revoking the policy. The central government speeded up the establishment of welfare system for workers in the late 1990s and the early 2000s and abolished the agricultural tax in 2004 partly because of the widespread and persistent popular contention (Cai 2010). The government prevents the accumulation of grievances among fixed groups in order to avoid the "revolutionary constraints". Acemoglu and Robinson (2006: 118) contend that "an important issue in non-democracies is to ensure that no group is unhappy enough to attempt to overthrow the regime or take other political or economic actions detrimental to the utility of the group in power".

A combination of these modes of response helps maintain social stability by accommodating some protestors, silencing others, and thereby creating fragmentation among the aggrieved. By removing deep-seated sources of grievances, the government prevents the accumulation of grievances among fixed groups. By denying or repressing some of the protestors, the government deters protestors or lowers their expectations of when staging protests to pursue their interests.

2.2   *Information Collection*
Authoritarian governments can be better prepared to deal with regime-threatening collective action if they are able to gain information about popular grievances. Yet, authoritarian regimes tend to rely on repression and exercise control over information flow. These measures create superficial legitimacy or "pluralistic ignorance" – citizens pretend to accept the political system, thereby

creating a popular belief that many others accept or support the rule (Kuran 1991). However, an authoritarian government's control over information does not always benefit itself because the government may fail to know the true preference of the people or the severity and scope of people's grievances. Without this knowledge, the government is unable to assess the opposition it faces. There is thus a possibility that the government overestimates the support it enjoys.

In China, the problem with the flow of information faced by the central government is alleviated because of the multiple channels of information collection. One channel is people's petition. Research on petitions in China suggests that citizens' petitions are not only a channel for dispute resolution (Chen 2012; Minzer 2006), but also a channel through which the central authority gains information on local society. Over the years, the complaints departments at both the central and local levels have developed a records system to file people' petitions; "this has become the basis for providing information to the authorities concerned" (Cai 2004: 441). At the central level, some letters and recorded petitions are directly forwarded to national leaders, whereas others are included in internal publications submitted pertinent leaders and organizations for reference.

A second channel is the central government's own agencies. Chung suggests that the Chinese government has tried to establish nationwide surveillance and the intelligence networks at both the central and local levels. At the central level, public-security-related ministries and agencies engage in gathering intelligence and monitoring local situations, including the Ministry of Public Security, the Ministry of National Security, and the Stat Council Information Office. These units report directly to the State Council and Premier. The government units also work the Party's organizations, such as the Central Commission for Comprehensive Management of Public Security, the office of Stability Preservation Leading Group, and the Central Commission on Political and Legal Affairs. The Stability Preservation Leading Group is the nucleus in terms of managing collective protests. Serious cases of collective protests are discussed and solutions are sought in its meetings (Chung 2012: 33).

Third, protests themselves are suggested to have become a source of information because of its signalling function. Lorentzen (2013: 152) writes:

> Authoritarian governments have limited sources of information about either the actions of the officials at their lower levels or the discontent of their citizens. Permitting protests provides information about both, helping to limit corruption and to bring discontented communities out in the open rather than driving them underground.

However, the central government may tolerate local non-political protests, but this is no empirical evidence to suggest that the central government encourages such protests. As Chung suggests, absolute stability or zero protest was an impossible goal to achieve. Allowing local protests can reduce the base for more violent and better-organized anti-government protests (Chung 2012: 32). Thus, protests are less a source of information on grievances than an indication of the severity of problems giving rise to protests. As O'Brien and Li (2007: 112) also point out, popular contention "first alerts concerned officials to poor policy implementation and sometimes prompts them to take corrective steps". Exposure of local protests can pressure local governments to tackle the source of conflict.

The government also establishes its one networks of information collection. In recent years, Chinese local governments commonly adopt the so-called grid-management. Specifically, a local government divides the area under its jurisdiction into a number of pieces, with each piece being monitored by a specialized person. These people responsible for surveillance are required to report information to upper-level authorities regularly. For example, in one district in eastern China we visited, the government received 23,460 tips in January 2016, and more than 94.4 percent of the tips were collected by the government through its own networks, whereas the remaining were reported by residents.

The advent of new information and communication technologies (ICTs) was initially seen as an important challenge to authoritarian governments that allow citizens' conditional access to the Internet. Yet, a growing body of literature on new ICTs in authoritarian regimes has found that authoritarian governments can adjust well to the new environment (Morozov 2011; Gunitsky 2015). In China, although new ICTs have become a tool of coordinating collective action (Cai & Zhou 2016), they are not particularly challenging to the government.

The Chinese government has instituted a sophisticated online monitoring system to censor information detrimental to the regime (King et al. 2013). Compared with citizens, the government is better equipped to collect information through new ICTs because of its resources and regulatory power over Internet companies. Consequently, people who orchestrate collective action by using new ICTs face the common-knowledge constraint: the information on a proposed protest that protesters release to potential participants can also be known to the government (Cai & Zhou 2016). Consequently, the government can make preparations to reduce or pre-empt collective action.

The Chinese government thus enjoys informational advantages over the citizens in two ways. First, the central government is better equipped to collect nationwide information than individual regime opponents or critics. Second, the government creates information asymmetries between itself and the people by concealing certain information from the people. In other words, while the government may know the scale and severity of popular grievances, this knowledge is not available to the public. This information asymmetry benefits the regime by undermining the confidence of the opposition forces.

Kuran contends that in repressive regimes, people who alienate themselves from the regime do not know how widely their alienation is shared or how many of their fellow citizens favour a change in the regime. Government-controlled press exploits this ignorance by stressing the unity of the society and its solidarity in supporting the party. "Insofar as such propaganda led potential revolutionaries to underestimate the prevalence of discontent, it weakened their incentives to join the minuscule opposition" (Kuran 1993: 30). Hence, the government can gain informational advantages by manipulate or control information flow while collecting information it needs.

2.3   *Organizational Response*

In China, a number of agencies are involved in dispute resolution, but these agencies are found to be ineffective or inefficient. For example, in the mediation of labour disputes, the grassroots judiciary bureaus, mediation committees, labour bureaus, labour dispute arbitration offices, and petition bureaus in a locality are given the tasks of resolving conflicts. Yet, as Lee and Zhang (2013: 1495) find, "the protracted and arduous processes of petition, arbitration, and litigation demobilize collective action by consuming aggrieved citizens' time, emotion, energy, and solidarity through endless rounds of red tape, paper chases, interminable waiting, and appeals".

Chinese local governments come to realize the need of pooling resources and coordinating state agencies in order to enhance the efficiency and effectiveness of dispute resolution. An increasing number of local agencies have been created or required to participate in maintaining social stability. These agencies include the political-legal affairs committee, the stability-preserving office, the court, the procuratorate, the police, the justice bureau, and the civil affairs bureau. Some local governments have established the so-called Comprehensive Social Management Centre which includes the following member institutions: the petition office, the comprehensive social management office, the police, the mediation office, the justice bureau, the community information centre, and the social worker station (Ieong 2016; Su & He 2010).

The coordination among state agencies helps alleviate the problems arising from fragmented authority in conflict resolution. The inefficiency of the multiple but separated agencies has led local governments to adopt the so-called grand mediation. Hu (2011) suggests that grand mediation relies on mediation but links various social and governmental resources together aiming at resolving conflict more effectively. The grand mediation involves legal institutions or the court, government agencies, and the people's mediation committee.

Grand mediation has become a mechanism for coordinating all pertinent state and social institutions involved in conflict management. These institutions include local administrative e agencies, the legal system, the police, the petition department, and so on. The basic function of grand mediation is to "provide an alternative channel for ordinary people to pursue remedy rather than to appeal through collective actions so as to prevent the mass grievances from the grassroots level, which can minimize the potential challenges to the political order" (Ieong 2016: 97).

Coordination for conflict resolution is not limited to different local agencies within a government; it also occurs across governments of different levels that share the same sources of social unrest. Therefore, the efforts of the government in maintaining social stability "are regularized, bureaucratized, routinized and neatly integrated into the regime's daily operations and system-wide workflow" (Yan 2016: 420).

Coordination among state agencies in conflict resolution has strengthened state penetration or extended the reach of the state in two significant ways. One is strengthening local authorities' direct monitoring and information collection. Yan (2016) finds that in the county of his research, different levels of the stability-preservation offices extended great efforts to screen and detect social conflict. The screening was conducted once a week at the village level and twice a week at the township level. Such activities include field investigation, information gathering and analysis, household visits and discussions with pertinent parties. The Chinese government has instituted roadside patrol, 24-hour surveillance, and rapid-reaction forces in cities. In rural areas, police are assigned to monitor peasants, associations are formed for the monitoring purpose, and volunteers are recruited for information collection (Chung 2012: 33–34).

Second, coordinated action allows the government to solve and pre-empt disputes at the grassroots level. In China, disorganized contention usually takes the form of isolated conflict and disputes. The local state has developed strong mechanisms for case-base-case dispute resolution. Consequently, disputes are handled by different modes of settlement or government agencies in coordinated and collaborative ways to secure quick and effective solutions and prevent them from escalating and spreading. This mode of conflict resolution has, in turn, strengthened the state's penetration into the society:

> [T]o cope with the pervasiveness, unexpectedness and randomness of disorganized contention, conflict management institutions have evolved

into a network of social monitoring agents involving information gathering, risk assessment and the micro-governance of communities. This reinforces the government's capacity to reach out into grassroots society and prevent and pre-empt social conflicts.

CHEN & KANG 2016: 611

Yan (2016: 420) similarly finds that "the Party-state's efficient, localized and mundane efforts in extending its reach to China's grassroots society have enabled the incumbent political regime to build its strength and consolidate the durability of its socio-political basis".

The state's penetration can be subtle, including ideological elements. For example, conflicts in urban China are contained by the gated structures of the neighbourhoods to prevent systemic challenges to the government. The penetration of the state is achieved not only through organizational network but also through state discourses on the need of maintaining social stability. As a result, contained conflicts in the neighbourhood are institutionalized through a definition of the rules of interaction, territorial order, and the shard imposition of political boundaries as well as through the presence and involvement of neighbourhood institutions (Tomba 2014: 178).

The party-state has not only strengthened its reach but also extended its reach. For example, the party is extending its presence and influence to urban residential communities, including grassroots NGOs in neighbourhoods. After the weakening of the work-unit system, the party-state began to establish primary party organizations to extend and maintain its presence in society. Various territories or spaces, such as office buildings, business districts, become the new supporting institution for its party building. In this way, "the highly mobile new social strata in the non-state sector can be partially 'stabilized' in various territories/spaces through the organizational networks of the CCP" (Zhang 2015: 662).

The extended and strengthened reach of the state becomes the institutional base for the state's presence and influence. Local state's organizational building and coordination prepare itself for addressing subsequent popular contention. In other words, local authorities' efforts in Stage 4 (Table 1) strengthen their ability to deal with issues arising from the four stages in subsequent periods. More broadly, the government's institution building, coordination, and organizational penetration enhance its capacity in conflict management.

2.4   *Dependent Citizens and Organizational Control*

Maintaining social stability in China has gone beyond protest management. As Geddes (1999: 138) writes, "Authoritarian governments need some support and a good deal of acquiescence to remain in power". While the organizational network discussed above allows state penetration, both traditional and new mechanisms of social control have also been created to help maintain the authoritarian control in China. As the government controls a large public sector, it creates the economic dependence on the regime on the part of a large number of citizens; this dependence undermines their willingness to criticize or oppose the regime.

About 30 years ago, Walder (1986: 12) pointed out the organized dependence of Chinese workers on their work units: "economic and social dependence on the enterprises; political dependence on the party and management; and personal dependence on supervisors". Although economic reform and marketization have weakened the control of the work unit, its influence over the people remains. People who work in the public sector still rely heavily on their particular work units for welfare and other resources. For example, most universities are dependent on the government for funding in China, and university professors are economically dependent on the regime.

The dependence of public employees on the state has two important implications for regime stability. One is that public employees are beneficiaries of the political regime, and the lack the incentive to overthrow the regime. For example, a survey of about 1,500 middle-class people in Beijing, Shanghai, and Guangzhou between 2014 and 2015 shows that over 40 percent of them worked in public sectors, including state agencies and public firms (Liang 2015). As beneficiaries of the political system, they are unlikely to oppose the regime, although they may have other types of grievances against the government.

In explaining the lack of protesting activities against the government in China after 1989, Perry (2016) highlights the various control mechanisms that lead to campus quiescence. Ensuring that college campuses are tightly monitored and that intellectual energies are channelled into system-supportive rather than system-subversive activities is therefore a critical element in the regime's comprehensive scheme for "stability maintenance". The Chinese government has created organizational dependence on the state on the part of university professors who can receive benefits, honours or funding from the government. There is thus an interest alignment between the state and university faculty members in building the so-called world-class universities.

Second, because of their dependence on their employers or the government, public employees face threats when taking action against the will of the government. Public employees may have grievances against the government, but it can be risky if they take action against the latter. For example, environmental pollution is a common source of grievance among Chinese people regardless of the type of their employment. Community disputes between homeowners and property management companies or local governments are also common in urban China as mentioned above. In dealing with such protests, local governments can require public employers to limit their employees' participation in collective action. Some local governments also require private companies to prevent their employees from participating in protests (Cai and Zhou 2016). Although these measures are not necessarily sufficient to stop protests, they sometimes help reduce the size and thereby effects of protests.

3   Remaining Challenges

Although the Chinese government has, thus far, succeeded in preventing the numerous social protests from threatening social or political stability in the country, it still faces two significant challenges. One is the costs required for maintaining social stability, and the other is the party-state's dilemma between its need of rule by law and its rule-breaking practices in dispute resolution. A lack of the institutionalization of conflict resolution generates constant pressure on the government because it creates space for social protests.

3.1   *Financial Resources and Regime Stability*
The current practices of maintaining social stability in China relies heavily on the state's provision of financial resources. Buying stability inevitably requires consistent input of money. Chen (2013: 61) suggests that the cost of maintaining the current system is believed to be "enormous and rising". The high cost casts doubt on whether the system can be sustained. Thus far, local governments do not seem to have financial difficulties in maintaining the system. It indeed remains unclear how financial capacity has affected local governments' practices of dispute resolution.

China has not experienced long economic downturns since the 1980s. The reform of state-owned enterprises in the late 1990s and the early 2000s was not carried out at a time of economic downturn. The viable private sector, the state's financial support, its efforts in establishing social welfare network, and the fragmentation among the laid-off workers all contributed to the success of the massive retrenchment. The financial crisis in 2008 did not lead to a lasting economic downturn because of the government's stimulus package.

One issue is thus whether the system can be sustained during economic downturns.

The government is likely to face pressure arising from economic recessions. First, local governments may become predatory during such downturns in order to extract financial resources from the society, and their extractive behaviour can be a source of grievances and conflict. Peasants' financial burdens before 2004 exemplified local governments' predatory practices under financial pressure. Second, a decline in revenue makes it difficult for the state apparatus to operate and for local governments to "buy stability". Third, a more serious problem faced by the government is whether it is able to continue to provide economic benefits to various social groups, thereby sustaining their acceptance of the authoritarian rule.

Geddes (1999: 139) finds that "single-party regimes have been remarkably resilient even in the face of long, severe economic crises". Repression will certainly become a crucial approach of unprecedented importance to sustaining authoritarian rule during economic crises. Yet, repression may not be the only measures adopted by the government. Therefore, it remains to be examined how the Chinese government will deal with challenges to its rule in economic downturns if there is one.

3.2   *The Party's Dilemma*

The Chinese party-state faces a plight in addressing social dispute. The pressure of preserving local stability forces local governments to become extensively involved in dispute resolution. Nevertheless, its heavy involvement creates problems for itself. First, the government's heavy involvement requires time, energy, and financial resources that can be heavy burdens. Second, the government creates a trap for itself when it becomes involved in conflict resolution. Local governments sometimes accommodate protestors' (unreasonable) demands in order to end social disruptions quickly. But government accommodation produces an encouraging effect among the aggrieved, sustaining their belief in the effectiveness of disruptive action and in the moral responsibility of the government. This belief is detrimental to the formation of a culture conducive to rule of law.

This dilemma between the need of rule by law and a quick resolution of dispute has been well reflected in the operation of the petition system. As Chen (2012: 119–120) writes, "on the one hand, they [CCP leaders] encourage the judicial system to play a bigger role in conflict resolution; on the other hand, administrative powers reserve the right to intervene in cases where significant political interests at stake". The Chinese central government allows the citizens present petitions to different levels of governments, but it is reluctant to see people present their petitions in Beijing. With a belief in central authorities, some people approach national authorities without going through local governments. In 2009, the petition office of the Supreme Court received 670,000 petitions, an increase of 24.5 percent when compared to 2008. Skip-level petitions accounted for 47 percent of the total number, and 70 percent of these petitions were repeated ones (Wang & Li 2010).

In order to institutionalize dispute resolution, the central government has taken two measures. One is to encourage people to have their disputes resolved in courts instead of petition offices if the disputes fall into the legal purview. The second is discouraging "skip-level" petitions. In 2014, the National Complaints Bureau issued a stipulation that requires petitioners to present their petitions level by level. People working in the Bureau claimed that "If the Center is treated as a responsive saviour, people will be encouraged to come to Beijing" (Cheng 2014). He claimed that in the past, the bureau accepted 90 percent of the petitions submitted by petitioners. With the new policy taking effect, the bureau only accepted 10 percent of the petitions. In the past, 90 percent of the petitions were "skip-level" ones, and 80 percent were repeated. In May 2014, the number of petitioners who approached central governments agencies decreased by 56 percent, when compared with that of 2013.

The central government's new policies seem to signal that the state is withdrawing its commitment to the mass line and is moving to rule by law. However, it is possible that the withdrawal may prove to be ineffective as long as the government monopolizes political power. Indeed, the government's withdrawal may also become a new source of citizens' grievances. Rule of law requires constraining the power of both public and private actors. It remains to be examined to what extent the party-state is determined to restrain its own power in governance and in dispute resolution.

4   Conclusion

Svolik (2012) contends that authoritarian governments face two ruling issues. One is the "problem of authoritarian control" that arises from the conflict between "a small authoritarian elite and the much larger population over which it rules". Authoritarian governments have to institute effective mechanisms in order to prevent mass riots. The other issue is "power-sharing" among the ruling elite. Although many dictators were removed by regime insiders who are from the dictator's inner circle, the government, or the repressive apparatus instead of the people, authoritarian rulers cannot afford to ignore the threat from the masses.

The authoritarian government is sensitive to popular contention because of the challenges it poses. First, popular contention can directly threaten regime survival, constituting a revolution from below (Huntington 1991). Second, popular contention reveals sources of grievances or the problems with the regime, although it does not necessarily threaten regime survival. Protests signals the regime's weakened control because anti-regimes are not expected to rise in such regimes (Davenport 1995). At a time when a large number of people become dissatisfied, such signals can trigger large participation (Kuran 1993). Finally, popular contention contributes to organizational building and the accumulation of experience on the part of regime opponents, facilitating collective action when opportunities arise (Laba 1991).

Authoritarian governments are never passive in ensuring regime survival, and they naturally protect themselves with resources at their disposal. They will try to pre-empt regime-threatening protests by demobilizing opponents or preventing their coordination.

Government efforts may shape the behaviour of both protestors and themselves. In his research on contentious politics in Southeast Asia, Salter (2012: 5) suggests that authoritarian governments can form coalition to deal with threatening contention. In China, the elite have learned a lesson from the 1989 Tiananmen movement, which is preventing public split within them.

The government's response to popular contention also shapes protestors' behaviour. In China, popular contention is generally localized, and local governments assume the primary responsibility of addressing social conflict in their jurisdictions. Because of the heavy duty of preserving local stability, local governments have mobilized, created, and coordinated a large number of state institutions to participate in stability preservation. Local governments' efforts have led to a significant consequence that enhances the party-state's capacity to protect social order – the state's presence and deep penetration in the society. The state's reach compounds coordinated collective action among the people even within local communities, not to mention across provinces, although exceptions of non-regime-threatening protests do occur.

Yet, the government still faces two challenges in managing social protests. One is the rising costs of maintaining social order. An important way of reducing the cost is the adoption of new technologies. The other challenge faced by the government is that its responses have not achieved the goal of institutionalizing social conflict. The Chinese government may therefore face a predicament it creates for itself. On one hand, its power leads to abusive state authorities that cause grievances and protests. On the other hand, local authorities are unable to prevent the mobilization of the aggrieved. It thus remains to be seen how the central and local governments in China will deal with this predicament.

Bibliography

Acemoglu, D. and J. Robinson. (2006). *Economic Origins of Dictatorship and Democracy.* New York: Cambridge University Press.

Art, D. (2012). 'What Do We Know about Authoritarianism after Ten Years?', *Comparative Politics,* 44(3): 351–373.

Bernstein, T. and Lu X. (2003). *Taxation without Representation in Contemporary China.* New York: Cambridge University Press.

Cai, Y. (2004). 'Managed Participation in China', *Political Science Quarterly,* 119(3): 425–452.

Cai, Y. (2005). 'China's Moderate Middle Class: The Case of Homeowners' Resistance', *Asian Survey,* 5: 777–799.

Cai, Y. (2006). *State and Laid-Off Workers in China: The Silence and Collective Action of the Retrenched.* London: Routledge.

Cai, Y. (2007). 'Civil Resistance and Rule of Law in China: the Case of Defending Home Owners' Rights', pp. 174–195, in E. Perry and M. Goldman (eds.), *Grassroots Politics in China.* Cambridge: Harvard University Press.

Cai, Y. (2010). *Collective Resistance in China: Why popular protests succeed or fail.* Stanford: Stanford University Press.

Cai, Y. and Zhou T. (2016). 'New Information Technologies and Social Protest in China: Information as Common Knowledge', *Asian Survey,* 56(4): 731–753.

Chan, C.K., and Pun N. (2009). 'The Making of a New Working Class? A Study of Collective Actions of Migrant Workers in South China', *China Quarterly,* 198: 287–303.

Chen, A. (2008). 'The 1994 Tax Reform and Its Impact on China's Rural Fiscal Structure', *Modern China,* 34(3): 303–343.

Chen, C. (2009). 'Growing Social Unrest and Emergent Protest Groups in China', pp. 87–106, in H. Huang, M. Hsiao and C. Lin (eds.), *Rise of China: Beijing's Strategies and Implications for the Asia-Pacific.* London: Routledge.

Chen, F. (2000). 'Subsistence Crisis, Managerial Corruption and Labor Protests in China', *China Journal,* 44: 41–63.

Chen, F. and Y. Kang. (2016). 'Disorganized Popular Contention and Local Institutional Building in China: A Case Study in Guangdong', *Journal of Contemporary China,* 25(100): 596–612.

Chen, X. (2012). *Social Protest and Contentious Authoritarianism in China.* New York: Cambridge University Press.

Chen, X. (2013). 'The Rising Cost of Stability', *Journal of Democracy,* 24(1): 57–64.

Chung, J.H. (2012). 'Managing Political Crises in China', pp. 25–42, in J.H. Chung (ed.), *China's Crisis Management.* London: Routledge.

Davenport, C. (1995). 'Multi-Dimensional Threat Perception and State Repression: An Inquiry into Why States Apply Negative Sanctions', *American Journal of Political Science*, 39: 683–713.

Deng, Y. and K. O'Brien. (2013). 'Relational Repression in China: Using Social Ties to Demobilize Protesters', *China Quarterly*, 215: 533–552.

Deng, Y. and G. Yang. (2013). 'Pollution and Protest in China: Environmental Mobilization in Context', *China Quarterly*, 214: 321–336.

Deng, X. (1993). *Deng Xiaoping Wenxuan* [A Collection of Deng Xiaoping's works]. Beijing: Renmin chubanse.

Gallagher, M. (2006). 'Mobilizing the Law in China: "Informed Disenchantment" and the Development of Legal Consciousness', *Law & Society Review*, 40(4): 783–816.

Geddes, B. (1999). 'What Do We Know about Democratization after Twenty Year?', *Annual Review of Political Science*, 2: 115–144.

Gunitsky, S. (2015). 'Corrupting the Cyber-Commons: Social Media as a Tool of Autocratic Stability', *Perspectives on Politics*, 13(1): 42–54.

Hu, J. (2011). 'Grand Mediation in China: Mechanism and Application', *Asian Survey*, 51(6): 1063–1089.

Huang, H., S. Boranbay-Akan, and L. Huang. (2019). 'Media, Protest Diffusion, and Authoritarian Resilience', *Political Science Research and Methods* 7(1): 23–42.

Huntington, S. (1991–1992). 'How Countries Democratize', *Political Science Quarterly*, 106(4): 579–616.

Hurst, W. (2009). *The Chinese Workers After Socialism*. New York: Cambridge University Press.

Ieong, M.U. (2016). 'The Development of Grand Mediation and its Implications for China's Regime Resilience: The Li Qin Mediation Office', *China Review*, 16(1): 95–119.

King, G., J. Pan, and M. Roberts. (2013). 'How Censorship in China Allows Government Criticism but Silences Collective Expression', *American Political Science Review*, 107(2): 1–18.

Kuran, T. (1991). 'Now out of Never: The Element of Surprise in the East European Revolution of 1989', *World Politics*, 44: 7–48.

Laba, Roman. (1991). *The Roots of Solidarity: A Political Sociology of Poland's Working-Class Democratization*. Princeton: Princeton University Press.

Lee, C.K. (2007). *Against the Law: Labor Protests in China's Rustbelt and Sunbelt*. Berkeley: University of California Press.

Lee, C.K. and Y. Zhang. (2007). 'The Power of Instability: Unraveling the Microfoundations of Bargained Authoritarianism in China', *American Journal of Sociology*, 118(6): 1475–1508.

Levitsky, S. and L. Way. (2010). *Competitive Authoritarianism: Hybrid Regimes after the Cold War*. New York: Cambridge University Press.

Lorentzen, P. (2013). 'Regularizing Rioting: Permitting Public Protest in an Authoritarian Regime', *Quarterly Journal of Political Science*, 8(2): 127–158.

Li, L. and K. O'Brien. (2008). 'Protest Leadership in Rural China', *China Quarterly*, 193: 1–23.

Liang, Y. and Zhang H. (2015). 'Beijing, Shanghai Guangzhou shehui zhongjian jieceng diaocha baogao' [A survey report on the middle class in Beijing, Shanghai, and Guangzhou], pp. 189–218, in Li P., G. Chen and Y. Zhang (eds.), *2016 zhongguo shehhi8 xingshi fenxi yu yuce* [Analysis and prediction of Chinese society]. Beijing: Shehui kexue wenxian chubanshe.

Mackerras, Colin. (2012). 'Managing Ethnic Minority Crises: The Tibetan areas and Xinjiang', pp. 65–86, in J.H. Chung (ed.), *China's Crisis Management*. London: Routledge.

O'Brien, K. and L. Li. (2007). *Rightful Resistance in Rural China*. New York: Cambridge University Press.

Perry, E. (2008). 'Chinese Concepts of "Rights": From Mencius to Mao-and Now', *Perspective on Politics*, 6(1): 37–50.

Perry, E. (2016). 'Higher Education and Authoritarian Resilience: The Case of China, Past and Present', manuscript.

Piven, F. and R. Cloward. (1977). *Poor People's Movements: Why They Succeed, How They Fail*. New York: Pantheon Books.

Shi, F., and Y. Cai. (2006). 'Disaggregating the State: Networks and Collective Action in Shanghai', *China Quarterly*, 186: 314–332.

Slater, D. (2010). *Ordering Power: Contentious Politics and Authoritarian Leviathans in Southeast Asia*. New York: Cambridge University Press.

Su, Y. and X. He. (2010). 'Street as Courtroom: State Accommodation of Labor Protest in South China', *Law & Society Review*, 44(1): 157–184.

Sun, X. and R. Huang. (2015). 'Extension of State-Led Growth Coalition and Grassroots Management: A Case Study of Shanghai', *Urban Affairs Review*, 52(6): 917–943.

Svolik, M. (2012). *The Politics of Authoritarian Rule*. New York: Cambridge University Press.

Tomba, L. (2014). *The Government Next Door: Neighborhood Politics in Urban China*. Ithaca: Cornell University Press.

Van Rooij, B. (2010). 'The people vs. pollution: understanding citizen action against pollution in China', *Journal of Contemporary China*, 19(63): 55–77.

Walder, A. 1986. *Communist Neo-Traditionalism: Work and Authority in Chinese Industry*. Berkeley: University of California Press.

Wang Y. and C. Peng. (2015). 'Shesu xinfang de jiben leixing jiqi zhili yanjiu' [A research on petitions that can be solved through the legal channel], *Shehuixue pinglun* [Sociological Review], 3(2): 16–33.

Wang, Y. 2014. 'Coercive capacity and the durability of the Chinese communist state', *Communist and Post-Communist Studies,* 47(1): 13–25.

Yan, X. 2016. 'Patrolling Harmony: Pre-emptive Authoritarianism and the Preservation of Stability in W County', *Journal of Contemporary China,* 25(99): 406–421.

Zhang, H. (2015). 'Party Building in Urban Business Districts: Organizational Adaptation of the Chinese Communist Party', *Journal of Contemporary China,* 24(94): 644–664.

Zhang, L. (2015). *Inside China's Automobile Factories: The politics of labor and worker resistance.* New York: Cambridge University Press.

Zhong, Y. and W. Hwang. (2016). 'Pollution, Institutions and Street Protests in Urban China', *Journal of Contemporary China,* 25(98): 216–232.

Zhuang, W. and F. Chen. (2015). '"Mediation First": The Revival of Mediation in Labor dispute Resolution in China', *China Quarterly,* 222: 380–402.

CHAPTER 9

Migration Flows between Russia and China: Legal and Social Implications

Vasil Sakaev

Migration between Russia and China countries has a rich history: the joint development of the Far East in the 19th – early 20th century, and the mass exodus of remnants of Kolchak's army to China after the Civil War. Migration virtually ceased during Soviet times after a series of border clashes. The new Russian government proclaimed visa-free policies for tourists from China after the collapse of the USSR. As a result, some Chinese migrants illegally remained in Siberia and the Far East, as well as in Moscow and other cities. The massive influx worried the Russian authorities and led to the restriction of migration, but it did not stop migration completely.

This is why the topic of Chinese migration to Russia attracted researchers during the 1990s and 2000s such as V. Gel'bras, A. Larin, V. Larin, V. Diatlov, S. Luzianin and others. They investigated some aspects of Chinese migration, but the new challenges (in the 2010s) are beyond the scope of their research.

Here we should make a few remarks aimed at correctly understanding the importance of the problem of Chinese migration for modern Russia, as well as the nature of its perception in Russian society. This is necessary because, among other things, the problem affects the processes of state strengthening in Russia and state-public relations.

First, the issue of Chinese migration is extremely important in light of the Russian and Chinese political leaders' statements about the combination of the Eurasian Economic Union and the Silk Road Economic Belt, as well as in connection with the new demographic challenges facing Russia including depopulation, ageing of the population and the shrinkage of labour resources. As is known, China is actively seeking to develop the Eurasian space. Paradoxically, this does not cause much enthusiasm among a significant part of Russian elites, who are actually "tacitly sabotaging" similar initiatives.[1] It is also not popular among the Russian population, as shown by a series of conflicts

---

1 For further information see: Gabuev 2015, 2015a; Piontkovskii 2015; Evstaf'ev 2019; Polonskii 2019.

between Chinese companies and their employees with the local population.[2] In most cases this is due to fears of Chinese economic expansion and labour migration. In fact, in the current situation only certain regional and local authorities are actually really interested in attracting Chinese companies and, accordingly, the arrival of foreign labour. Thus, these economic projects and related problems of Chinese labour migration provoke certain tensions in society and conflicts with lobbyists of Chinese interests.

Another aspect of this problem is connected with stereotypes of citizens from the PRC in Russian society. Most of these stereotypes were formed in the 1990s and portray Chinese citizens as low-skilled, uneducated, and low-paid workers. These stereotypes on the one hand have taken the form of contempt because Chinese citizens had low social status, and on the other hand, fear of possible competitors in labour market. However, now the average citizen of the PRC is actually richer than the average Russian.[3] Their economic opportunities have recently increased significantly. In particular, we are witnessing a massive flow of Chinese tourists to Russia, while at the same time a reduced flow of Russian tourists to the PRC. We are also witnessing a diminishing flow of unorganised Chinese labour migration to Russia and, in contrast, there is an emerging movement of Russian expats to the PRC. Thus, these stereotypes are in contradiction to the aspirations of the countries' political leaders and indeed, objective economic reality.

Finally, the third aspect of the problem stems from different perceptions of the PRC's image by different generations of Russians. Now among Russian youth there is a huge increase in interest in learning the Chinese language and Chinese culture, while at same time there is a significant fear of China and possible Chinese expansion especially among middle-aged and older people. This contradiction in the perception of the image of the PRC can also create serious difficulties for the cooperation of the two countries.

Therefore, the current problem of Chinese migration includes several research questions: How many Chinese citizens are now in Russia? What are the main types of Chinese migration into Russia? Does Russia have enclaves of Chinese migrants already? What is the influence of Chinese migration on the Russian economy? Is there a significant volume of crime by Chinese migrants?

---

2   The details of these conflict situations are described in the following: Gorod 2018; Priemskaia 2019; Varnavskaia 2019; Dao 2019.

3   Despite the fact that GDP per capita is higher in Russia than in China, Engel's laws show that Russians spend a higher share of their incomes on food than people in China. For more details see: Iukhansen 2017; Bashkatova 2017.

What are Chinese migrants' opinions about Russia and about their plans in Russia? What are the future prospects of Chinese migration flows into Russia?

The main aim of our research is a complex and comprehensive analysis of the current situation of Chinese migration. This analysis includes historical background, consideration of economic and demographic predictors, investigations of social and legal aspects and an attempt to forecast the future prospects of migration. These topics are described in the subtitles of the chapter. The sources of research were based on new statistical databases and current publications; the methodology includes historical and logical approaches.[4]

1   Russian Demographic and Economic Predictions of Chinese Migration

Russia's development in the 21st century will be mainly influenced by migration. Depopulation and a dramatic reduction in the labour force (in the next 10 years the country's working population is supposed to decline by roughly 1 million every year) will increase the importance of immigration. By 2060 the total demographic load on 100 working people will have risen from 38.6 to 70.9.[5] Demographic development will be possible only with contribution of immigration; the impact of the demographic dividend of the young structure of the population is now over.

Furthermore, the Siberian Federal district and the Far Eastern Federal district have experienced rapid depopulation during the last decades. In 2010 the Siberian Federal district had a population of only 19.3 mln, while in the Far Eastern Federal district – 6.3 mln (VPN 2010). Compared to 1989 the population of the Siberian district decreased by more than 7.5%, while the Far Eastern district shrank by more than 19%. These indicators were higher than for the whole of Russia.

The population of the Asian part of the country during the period between the Census of 1989 and the Census of 2010 decreased on 3170 thousand people, and as a result the share of the population living in Asian Russia fell from 21.8% to 20.3%. In 2011–2015 years, the share of the population living in the Asian part of the country fell to 20.2%. The losses of population were determinated by the

---

4 We had some difficulties with statistical information after 2011 when the statistical method of studying migration was changed and after 2016 when the Federal Migration service was re-organized and absorbed into the Ministry of Internal Affairs.

5 Data from Bulletin "Naselenie i obshchestvo". Available at: http://demoscope.ru/weekly/app/app40der.php.

TABLE 9.1   Demographic development of Russia

Period	Natural growth	Migration balance
2010	-239,568	+158,078
2011	-129,091	+319,761
2012	-4,251	+294,930
2013	+24,013	+295,859
2014	+30,336	+299,990
2015	+32,038	+245,384
2016	-2,286	+261,948
2017	-135,818	+211,878
2018	-224,566	+124,854

SOURCE: ROSSTAT. AVAILABLE AT: HTTP://WWW.GKS.RU

continuing migration outflow. In the period from 2011 to 2015 the migration balance of the Siberian Federal District amounted to minus 39 thousand people, and the migration balance of the Far Eastern Federal District amounted minus 120 thousand people (Zakharov 2017: 45–46). And the tendency is continuing now: every year near 20,000 inhabitants have left the Far East (Khramova & Bezverbnyi 2017: 242).

Immigration is able to soften the negative consequences of demography. One can say that mass migration is inevitable in our country; it is a chance for the country. Russia's future is as a country of mass migration whether we like it or not. There is no other future for Russia. Concerning the required number of migrants, approaches differ. According to S.V. Riazantsev and L.L. Rybakovskii's estimates, to sustain the current Russian population it would be necessary to accept about 490,000 migrants annually until 2025 (Riazantsev & Rybakovskii 2007). A.G. Vishnevskii states that to keep the Russian population at its current level it is important to intensify the involvement of immigrants, and after 2025 their number should exceed a million people annually (Vishnevskii 2004). According to the World Bank, to compensate for Russian labour resources it is urgent in the next 20 years to have more than 600,000 people per year (Kommersant-Vlast' 2010). The "Conception of state demographic policy in the RF until 2025" proposes to provide for a migration influx of 200,000 people annually until 2015, and in 2016–2025 – more than 300,000 (Prezident Rossii).

How many migrants are now in Russia? The National Census of 2010 revealed that between 2002 and 2010 more than 2,939,200 migrants had moved into the country (on average more than 360,000 people annually) (VPN 2010). Since 2010 migration flows have lessened, but are still significant.

These figures testify, on the one hand, to Russia's magnetism for immigrants, and on the other hand, to Russian employers' interest in the foreign labour force. Therefore, Russia cannot avoid mass migration. Further positive Russian demographic and economic development obviously depends on mass population inflows.

2   Chinese Background of Migration

The size of the able-bodied Chinese population has grown rapidly during the last years and could have reached almost 190 million people in the period 2000–2015 (Mikheev 2005: 297–298). This has led to unemployment in the country, including both hidden and partial unemployment. At the beginning of 2008, according to Chinese experts' estimates, 184 million workers were unemployed or underemployed (Larin 2009: 350–351). This has boosted the mobility of the population, both within and outside the country.

Another important aspect is the problem of social differentiation and poverty in China (for example, 122m of the rural population in 2012 had an income lower than 1 US$ per day; 8% of the urban population or 50 mln in 2009 had an income of only 1.07 – 1.2 thousand US$ per year) (Ivanov 2011) and the difference in living standards between Russia and China is significant (real per capita GNI in terms of purchasing power parity in 2016 in US$: Russia – 23,162 and China – 15,534).[6]

Russia is one of the most important destinations for Chinese migration because of its resource wealth and low population density in the Siberian and Far Eastern regions (Van 2017: 62). The population of the Far Eastern Federal District, with an area of 6.2 million square kilometres, amounts to 6.2 million people, whereas three of China's North-Western provinces (Heilongjiang, Jilin, and Liaoning), with a total area of 804,000 square kilometres, have a population of about 110 million people (Gabuev 2014).

Mass migration from China is certainly beneficial for the Chinese government as it contributes to the modernisation of the country, improves the wellbeing of citizens and reduces tension in the domestic labour market. According to some experts, the Chinese government is pursuing a purposeful policy to promote the export of the labour force (Larin 2013: 205; Anokhina 2012: 192–194).

---

6   Data from World Bank. Available at: http://www.worldbank.org/en/publication/reference.

These factors create the significant demographic, geographic, geopolitical and economic preconditions for migration flows from China into Russia.

3   The Number of Chinese Migrants in Russia

The problem with studying Chinese migration in modern Russia becomes more complicated due to the lack of accurate data about its scale. Unfortunately, there is no accurate system for recording statistics on international migrants in Russia and the data provided by different departments often show significant discrepancies.

The large Chinese community which existed in the Far East at the beginning of the 20th century was liquidated during the Soviet period. Most of these Chinese citizens were deported to their homeland in the 1930s; some of them were subjected to repression. Chinese students and graduate students who came to the USSR in the 1950s were recalled due to the deterioration of relations between the USSR and China in 1959–1960. In fact, there was practically no Chinese community on Soviet territory at the time the collapse of the USSR. Following the 1989 census, the number of Chinese in Russia amounted to only 5,000 people. Thus, the current Chinese population in Russia was formed solely as a result of migration flows in the 1990s-2000s.

The best estimate in the expert community (obtained by summing the estimates of the number of Chinese people in various locations) is considered to be a figure of about 400,000–500,000 people (including illegal migration as well) (Gel'bras 2001: 39–40).

However, this figure was calculated almost 10 years ago and since then no extensive studies have been carried out in relation to the number of Chinese. Anyway, most experts do not believe that the number of Chinese migrants is in the range of several million people and that there is a threat of demographic expansion.

4   Features of the Dynamics of Migration Flows from China

Until 2000 the main channels for the arrival of Chinese citizens were group tourist trips (according to the agreement of 18 December 1992, they were carried out for a period of up to 30 days on a visa-free basis). The vast majority of Chinese tourists brought consumer goods from China (primarily clothing and footwear) and were engaged in retail trade in Russian markets. In the late

1990s, for example, up to 95% of Chinese tourists traded on markets in the Amur region (Anokhina 2012: 189).

Since 2000, migration controls of tourism have increased (the visa-free period for tourist trips for Chinese citizens has been reduced to 15 days and the requirements for tourist groups have been increased). Simultaneously, since 1st July 2002 in China "The regulations for tourist trips of Chinese citizens abroad" entered into force, establishing strict requirements for timely reporting of non-return of tourists from a trip abroad, imposing sanctions for failure to inform, with a maximum penalty of cancellation of tour operators' licenses. These measures have led to a situation in which the main channel of migration has become commercial and business visits using a visa based on the invitation of Russian firms, sometimes fictitious (Anokhina 2012: 61). At the same time, the majority of Chinese citizens have not been permanent residents but temporary workers who came for several months, and the rest were entrepreneurs in the field of trade. According to some data, the share of Chinese traders in the markets of the Central Federal District was estimated at about 80% in the mid-2000s (Larin 2013a). According to the Russian Union of Consumer Societies published on January 30, 2007, about 61% of traders in all Russian markets were Chinese citizens (Anokhina 2012: 183–184).

Since 2007 when foreign citizens were banned from retail trading in open markets (Federal Law "On retail markets and amendments to the Labour Code of the Russian Federation" dated 22 December 2006), the nature of Chinese migration has changed significantly. A substantial number of Chinese returned to their homeland (the Association of Chinese citizens in Vladivostok, in 2007, claimed that 100,000 Chinese traders left the Far East) (VL 2007) while the share of construction and agricultural workers increased. The structure of Chinese migration was also affected by increased taxes and duties on raw timber in 2007 and 2009 resulting in an outflow of raw timber buyers from the Far East. On the other hand, China has started to consider projects to develop woodworking industries in Russia requiring Chinese workers for wood processing (Anokhina 2012: 183–184). In addition, the number of Chinese people holding a residence permit has increased.

5   The Structure of Chinese Migration

As we have mentioned above, Chinese migration consists of several components: labour migration, migration for the purpose of studying, tourism, migration with the purpose of long-term or permanent residence in the territory of the Russian Federation, and illegal migration, including transit. Let us examine them in detail.

Labour migration is one of the most important components. In the 1990s, labour migration was primarily spontaneous and derived mainly from the poorest populations of the North-Eastern China. The situation changed in the 2000s and migration generally came under the control of Chinese companies and organizations carrying out business in Russia.

The distribution of the Chinese labour force across the Russian territory was quite uneven in the 1990s. In some regions the share reached a considerable size and in other regions there were no workers from China. Thus in 1995 the share of all Chinese workers in the 2 regions of Primorskii Krai and Khabarovsk territories accounted for 42%. Significant numbers of them were also in Irkutsk, Cheliabinsk, Kemerovo, Moscow region and Moscow, whereas there were no Chinese workers in the other 34 regions of the Russian Federation and no more than 10 people in 21 other regions (Anokhina 2012: 190).

In the 2000s the majority of Chinese migrant workers was still concentrated in the Central Federal District (Moscow) and in the southern regions of Siberia and the Far Eastern Federal Districts. 81.2% of all Chinese migrant workers were in 10 regions of the Russian Federation in 2008, including 25.3% in Moscow, 25.3% in Siberia and 18.0% in the Far East (Larin 2013: 205).

Up until 2008 the number of Chinese migrants gradually increased but then due to the economic crisis it began to decline: the growth of net migration (excess of entry over exit of Chinese citizens) in 2000–2008 amounted to 199,100 and during the period 2009–2011 it decreased to 180,500. At the same time, the number of Chinese migrant workers decreased as well: 331,000 in 2007, 281,700 in 2008, 269,900 in 2009, and 186,500 in 2010 (Larin 2010: 35–36; Larin 2013: 205). More recently, it was 76,300 in 2014 and only 40,500 in 2016 (FSGS 2016). The importance of Chinese migrants in relation to the Russian economy has gradually decreased (influenced both by economic difficulties after 2008 and by the influx of migrants from Central Asia). This finding is confirmed by the data on the change in the share of Chinese citizens in the total number of citizens registered in the FMS as foreign migrant workers: 20.4% in 2004, 20% in 2006, 15.5% in 2007, and 10.4% in 2010 (Molodikova & Diuvel' 2009: 186; Larin 2010: 35–36). The only exceptions were the regions of the Far East, where the share of Chinese workers out of the total number of foreign labour migrants hardly changed, due to geographical proximity. Thus, in Primorskii Region the share of Chinese workers was 49% in 2008 (ToRpPK 2009: 68).

As regards the employment pattern of Chinese migrants in the 1990s, we only have data for Primorskii Region (1997). At that time the region had 42% of

TABLE 9.2   Employment pattern of Chinese migrants in Russia, %

Industries	2005	2009
trade	62.3	33.4
construction	13.6	31.5
agricultural sector	7.6	17.7
manufacturing sector	3.7	6.5
Other industries	12.8	10.9

SOURCE: DATA FROM ZAIONCHKOVSKAIA 2010, 2011[a]

a   Unfortunately, we do not have more recent data on the labour
    structure of Chinese migrants in Russia

all Chinese workers in construction, 30% was involved in agriculture, 10% in trade, and 8% in industry (Larin 2009: 154). More recent data for all Russian regions is in Table 9.2.

A comparison of figures in 2005 and 2009 reveals that the share of Chinese migrants involved in trade has gradually decreased while there has been a considerable increase in those working in construction and agriculture. Services provided by Chinese (hotels, catering, repair shops, medical services) and initially intended for Chinese migrants have over time come to be used by Russian citizens as well. Chinese migration to Russia differs from Chinese migration to the United States and other countries, in that Chinese in Russia tend to go into trade and services rather than industry (Anokhina 2012: 192). At the same time, the employment pattern of Chinese people in the border regions of the Russian Federation may differ. In the Far Eastern regions Chinese labour is mainly engaged in services and agriculture (Motrich & Izotov 2017: 230). But in the Amur region the employment of Chinese citizens in the forestry industry, the extraction of natural resources and the agricultural sector is now prohibited (Druziaka 2014: 288–289). For the Zabaikal'skii region, 2/3 of Chinese migrants were involved in construction, while no more than 10% were engaged in trade (Kozykina 2010: 55).

When characterising different groups of Chinese economic migrants, it should be noted that trading mainly consisted of so-called "people's trade" – small and medium-sized businesses. Now, however, Chinese citizens are prohibited from trading in Russian markets and the specialised Chinese markets have disappeared, including the closure of the largest one, the "Cherkizovskii market" in Moscow in 2009 (the only exceptions were the border cities between

China and Russia, for example, Blagoveshchensk) (Diatlov & Grigorichev 2013: 185). However, Chinese citizens have been able to get around this law because it does not regulate trade in covered shopping malls; furthermore, Chinese migrants have begun to do business using front RF citizens (Diatlov et al. 2009). As a result, Chinese citizens have continued to conduct retail trade, albeit in reduced numbers.

Generally, the Chinese labour force in the construction industry is known by experts for its low professional capacity. Agricultural workers are generally involved in Eastern Siberia and the Far East (the cultivation of vegetables, fruits, soya, etc.), and their activity is seasonal.

Migration for the purpose of studying. Chinese students started to come to Russia after the collapse of the USSR and their numbers increased during the 1990s. Many of them combined study in Russian universities with work or business activities in the 1990s. Now, Chinese students make up the second-largest contingent of foreign students in Russia (18,200 students in 2013–2014, 26,000 students in 2014–2015) (Malykhin 2015; Ria Novosti 2015). At the same time, their number in the RF has not changed significantly over the past 10 years (e.g. in 2008–2009 it amounted to 17,500) and is only 1.5–2% of the total number of Chinese citizens studying abroad (Ivanov 2013: 44). Therefore, there is no significant increase in the contingent of foreign students, and the attractiveness of Russian education is relatively low. These are mostly students with poor results or coming from poor families (the overwhelming majority of them pay for the cost of education in Russian universities themselves). The largest number of students from China is studying at the universities in the Far Eastern Federal District (mostly residents of border provinces: Heilongjiang, Jilin, Liaoning), and a slightly smaller number is studying at universities in Siberia, the Urals and the Volga regions as well as in both capitals.

Tourism. There were particularly large flows of tourists from China to Russia in the 1990s, including in the context of illegal immigration. However, the illegal aspects were minimised after immigration control strengthened in the 2000s.

In recent years we have seen a renewed increase in the intensity of Chinese tourists, reaching its peak for the entire period in 2015–2016. However, it should be noted that the total number of trips of Chinese citizens has risen slightly: the number of tourist trips in 2015 rose by 65.3%, and the total number of trips only by 20.3%, i.e. an increase in the number of tourist trips accompanied by a reduction in the number of other types of travel (e.g., traveling for a private visit).

If we compare data on the number of tourist trips with the number of Chinese citizens admitted as tourists to the Russian Federation, we find a significant discrepancy. The number of tourists from China for the previous years is usually 3–4 times less than the number of tourist trips of Chinese citizens

TABLE 9.3   Number of tourist trips to the Russian Federation by Chinese citizens (thousands)

	Tourism	Total number of all trips
2004	283.8	813.2
2005	204.2	798.7
2006	157.4	765.3
2007	129.8	765.1
2008	127.2	815.5
2009	115.9	718.6
2010	158.1	747.6
2011	234.1	845.6
2012*	276.3	768.5
2013	372.3	1071.5
2014	409.8	1125.1
2015	677.6	1353.1
2016	916.4	1227.0
2017	1051.2	1386.6
2018	1295.4	1733.6

SOURCE: ROSSTAT. AVAILABLE AT: HTTP://WWW.GKS.RU; MINISTRY
OF INTERNAL AFFAIRS OF RUSSIA. AVAILABLE AT: HTTPS://XN--
B1AEW.XN--P1AI/DELJATELNOST/STATISTICS/MIGRACIONNAYA
*   Figures only for 9-month period in 2012

recorded (for example, in 2014 there were only 106,500 tourists, but 409,800 touristic trips).[7] Thus, tourist trips often include travel for other (labour, commercial) purposes and obviously are the most intensive in the border regions between China and Russia. The situation changed in 2015: 677,600 trips compared to 566,600 Chinese tourists. Thus, in 2015 there was a real "influx of tourists" from China. The question is what is the cause? Perhaps this is the result of a major devaluation of the rouble, which took place in late 2014, leading to a reduction in the cost of tourist trips to Russia.

Migration with the purpose of long-term or permanent residence in the territory of Russia is also an important component of Chinese migration. But what is its size, and has it led to the emergence of a permanent Chinese community in the country?

---

7   Data from Rosstat. Available at: http://www.gks.ru/dbscripts/cbsd/dbinet.cgi.

TABLE 9.4   Number of Chinese citizens in the Russian Federation in 2010

	Number of citizens of the PRC	Share, %
Totally in Russia	28,382	100.0
Central Federal District	6,682	24.0
North-West Federal District	1,576	6.0
Southern Federal District	884	3.0
Volga Federal District	942	3.0
Urals Federal District	1,963	7.0
Siberian Federal District	7,122	25.0
Far Eastern Federal District	9,082	32.0

SOURCE: ROSSTAT (VPN 2010)

The Chinese community in Moscow in the early 2000s amounted to about 30,000–40,000 people (Gel'bras 2001: 39–40). In 2003, some scientists estimated the number of Chinese citizens living in Moscow at 50,000, and in the Primorskii Region – 40,000 people (VL 2008). Several experts in the mid-2000s estimated the number of Chinese citizens in the Far East at 65,000–70,000 people (Larin 2011: 108).

Here we must mention two pronounced trends in the nature of this type of Chinese migration: (1) a concentration of Chinese citizens primarily in Moscow and the Far East; and (2) a gradual increase in the number of this population.

It is known that in the period 1997–2006 6,886 Chinese citizens were included in the composition of the permanent population of the Russian Federation (migration growth in persons having the right to a long-term stay in the country); in the period 2007–2014 this number had already grown to 17,923 Chinese citizens. However, in 2015, apparently in connection with the tightening of migration legislation and due to the difficult economic situation, this number decreased (9,043 arrived, 9,821 retired, -778 – migration growth).

Some data on the number of ethnic Chinese and Chinese citizens are given by the Russian Population Census of 2010, but this data is known to be incomplete (Table 9.4).

The population census in 2010 revealed that the largest groups of citizens of the PRC were in Moscow – 5,505, St. Petersburg – 1,444, Novosibirsk region – 1,811, Krasnoiarsk region – 1,747, Primorskii Krai – 4,005, Khabarovsk Krai – 3,468 (VPN 2010).

It should be noted however, that more than 4.1 million people did not mention their nationality in the census, possibly including a significant group of immigrants from China. Only 28,900 people called themselves ethnic Chinese in the census, but people from China can be categorised as a part of the 153,000 Koreans, as well as part of the Dungan, Uighur, Mongolian, Manchzhu, Kazakhs and others (VPN 2010). Furthermore, 5.6 million people did not declare their ethnicity in the census. Thus, the actual number of Chinese citizens or ethnic Chinese with Russian or other citizenship could be greater in reality.

Many Russian experts agree that currently there is no fully realised Chinese diaspora in Russia, although there is a permanent Chinese population (Anokhina 2012: 192–194). The absence of a Chinese diaspora is related to the fact that the sustainable Chinese communities in Russia are relatively small in number and the majority of Chinese migrants are characterised by high mobility. So, N.V. Kozykina stresses that the Chinese population has a tendency to become permanent, but with a floating composition. In addition, Chinese people do not tend to integrate, understanding that their stay in Russia is affected by many factors (Kozykina 2010: 57).

There is no organization in Russia that unites all the Chinese people in the country, as Chinese communities in Russia are based on commercial interests, which often do not coincide for different representatives of China, so we can only speak about the process of formation of Chinese diasporas in Russia (Anokhina 2012: 192–194).

Illegal migration, including transit. The analysis of entry mechanisms for illegal immigrants from China shows that in general, the process of entering is legal and only afterwards is followed by a change of objectives, status and transformation of legal migrants into illegal. This allows them to be in the country for quite a long time and then, to attempt to either extend the period of legal stay or to go into hiding while evading a timely departure. One of the legal ways to enter the country for Chinese citizens is to enter as tourists on a visa-free basis; this status is then used for commercial purposes and illegal labour activities. This was the channel for the largest share of illegal migration of Chinese citizens in the 1990s as well as partly in the 2000s. The other options for illegal migration are Russia-China joint ventures which are usually small businesses involved in consumer services, primary industries and agricultural production (Repetskaia 2012).

What is the number of Chinese migrants, including its illegal part? As mentioned above, the most respected Russian researchers of Chinese migration tend to estimate that simultaneously there are no more than 500,000 Chinese citizens in the Russian Federation (Larin 2010: 35–36; Vitkovskaia & Panarin

2000: 209). About one-half or more of this population make up the legal labour migrants, students from China, tourists, and people on private or official visits. The number of illegal immigrants is difficult to determine. It is obvious that most of them are those who either violate the conditions for staying in the territory of the Russian Federation (migrants who enter the country legally, but then use all possibilities for illegal employment) or overstay their visa. The population of such illegal migrants from China seems to be low and the figure is likely to be in the tens of thousands.

Levels of illegal migration were also seriously affected by the new Chinese law on passports, which came into force in January 2007. This law contains a ban on the issuance of passports for a period of 6 months to 3 years for those who have violated the border regulations as well as repatriated illegal migrants, staying or working there illegally (Larin 2009: 367–368).

Regarding illegal transit migration, it can be noted that the Russian route for illegal migration to EU member-countries seems to be very attractive. A.G. Larin, referring to Chinese publications, mentions the presence of Chinese organised crime groups (known as "snakeheads") engaged in these activities in Russia (Larin 2008a: 57–61).

6   The Impact of Chinese Migration on Crime Rates

It should be noted that while promoting the economic activity of its citizens in Russia and considering China's call for outward investment, made at China's third session of the National People's Congress in early 2000 (Druziaka 2014: 246), the Chinese authorities have officially called on their citizens to strictly observe Russian law. In case of violation of Russian legislation by citizens of China, Chinese officials support the implementation of justice.

However, in case of unlawful infringement of the interests of citizens of the PRC, the Chinese representatives come down on their side, but at the same time, they show restraint and flexibility as well as the desire to localise the conflict and a willingness to resolve it through study and discussion, without prejudice to the development of bilateral relations (Portiakov 2006).

Information from the UN Office on Drugs and Crime for 2011 showed a lower level of crime in China than in the Russian Federation: 14,574 murders (10.2 per 100 thousand of population) were registered in Russia, in China – 13,410 murders (1.0 per 100 thousand people) (GPRF 2011). Similar results were also demonstrated in a report by the International Centre for Prison Studies for 2012, which pointed to the 697,800 prisoners in the Russian Federation (487 per 100,000 population) (GPRF 2012) and 1.64 million prisoners in the PRC (121 per 100,000 inhabitants). Thus, crime rates in China are several times lower

TABLE 9.5 Crimes committed by foreign citizens in the Russian Federation (%)

	Crimes committed by all foreign citizens	Crimes committed by citizens of CIS member states	Proportion of crimes committed by citizens of CIS member states
2014	44.4	38.4	86.4
2015	46.4	40.3	86.9
2016	43.9	38.5	87.6
2017	41.0	36.2	88.3
2018	38.6	34.3	88.7

SOURCE: RUSSIAN MINISTRY OF INTERNAL AFFAIRS. AVAILABLE AT: HTTPS://XN--B1AEW.
XN--P1AI/DELJATELNOST/STATISTICS

than in Russia. It can be concluded that the population of China is more law-abiding, and it should be assumed that arriving Chinese immigrants are more law-abiding than Russian citizens.

However, one of the main stereotypical attitudes in Russia against migration is linked to fears of rising crime. As rightly stated by one of the most authoritative sinologists A.G. Larin:

A lot of angry revelatory publications are devoted to the criminal activity of Chinese people, where truth is mixed with fiction, sometimes with a marked preponderance in favour of the latter. This phenomenon can be explained in part by the limited factual material that the relevant authorities find it possible to share with the public, and partly, this is the apparent preference of the authors.

LARIN 2010: 34

How does migration relate to the crime rate in the country? There is no doubt that Chinese migrants (as well as any other workers who find themselves in a foreign environment) are not immune to committing criminal acts. But what is the extent of crime among Chinese migrants in the Russian Federation?

In 2018 foreign citizens in Russia committed 38,600 crimes (3.5% of total number of investigated crimes); the percentage of crimes committed by citizens of the CIS (primarily citizens from Uzbekistan, Tajikistan and Kyrgyzstan) amounted to 89% of the total (MVDRF 2019). The share of citizens of countries outside the CIS (including Chinese citizens) consisted of only 4,300 crimes. Thus, the criminality of Chinese migrants has no significant effect on the crime situation in the country. Although there is some evidence that such crimes are not adequately recorded (particularly when they are committed by citizens of the People's Republic of China against other Chinese citizens).

Of course, these data show general information throughout Russia and the situation in the east of the country may be quite different. Data for the regions of Siberia and the Far East show a higher level of Chinese crime compared to the average figure for Russia, which is quite understandable because that is where the main contingents of Chinese citizens are located. However, even there, for example in the Irkutsk region, statistics show a small number of registered crimes by Chinese citizens, and most of them are related to forgery of various documents (Repetskaia 2012).

Reports about the detention of illegal Chinese migrants, arrests of contraband goods, and the suppression of illegal business activities of Chinese entrepreneurs on Russian territory are periodically published in the mass media. However, apparently not every such crime committed by Chinese citizens becomes known to the law enforcement authorities and the public, as all these types of offenses are related to the corruption of administrative, supervisory and control, and law enforcement officials. The other criminal offenses (extortion, robberies, murders) committed by Chinese migrants, as a rule, in their environment, do not become known to the police and therefore do not have a major impact on crime statistics.

What are the key factors behind Chinese crime in the Russian Federation? Researchers mention both socio-economic causes (desire for rapid enrichment), and the severity of sentences for similar crimes in the People's Republic of China as some of the reasons for Chinese crimes. For example, in contrast to Russia, deforestation is prohibited in China, killing an Amur tiger is punished with a sentence of 10 years while in Russia it is punished only with a fine; drug trafficking is punishable by death in China, whereas in contrast, in Russia there is a moratorium on the death penalty (Diadiun 2012). The high level of corruption in Russia and the low level of legal awareness of Russians themselves are mentioned as other reasons (Larin 2010: 39–40).

What are the main types of crimes committed by PRC citizens? A.G. Larin identifies the following most common types of illegal activities of Chinese migrants: violation of the rules for entry across the border, stay (residence) and labour activity; economic crimes related to the trafficking of goods across the border: illegal trafficking, usage of shady schemes for customs clearance; illicit business on the territory of Russia: illegal business activities (illegal logging, illicit extraction of various natural resources, etc.), tax evasion, bribery of officials, withdrawal of funds abroad through underground banks, poaching etc.; criminal offenses: robbery, extortion, abduction, murder, and as a rule, all of these committed in their own environment (Larin 2010: 35). As we can see, some of these types of crimes are of an economic nature, and apparently related to organised crime activities.

Is there organised crime among Chinese citizens within the territory of Russia? Some experts deny the existence of Chinese criminal organizations in Russia, whereas other experts believe the opposite. Sergei Laptev, for example, stated in early 2000:

> The Chinese community lacks not only the organization, but even the minimum degree of consolidation. There is no "Chinese mafia" in Russia. On the contrary, the Chinese themselves are often subjected to attacks and robberies by some ethnic criminal groups.
>
> LAPTEV 2002

V.A. Nomokonov and other competent experts, on the other hand, believe that Chinese organised crime has operated in the Far East and Siberia since the early 1990s. Indeed, a number of Russian research works mention substantial facts pointing to the existence of Chinese mafia formations (so-called "triads") among the Chinese communities in Russia, which ensure "the indissolubility and integrity of Chinese business" (Zolotukhin 2012). Thus, according to estimates by S.E. Leliukhin, the share of identified Chinese organised crime groups in the Far East is 32.2%, and in Eastern Siberia it is 34.3%, in relation to all ethnic organised crime groups operating in the mentioned regions (Leliukhin & Nomokonov 2009).

According to S.E. Leliukhin, the "triads" in the Far East are engaged in the following illegal activities: smuggling and distribution of illegal drugs; smuggling and export of raw materials from Russia to China; smuggling of consumer goods of Chinese production into Russia; the organization of illegal financial systems and laundering of "dirty" money; organization of illegal channels for migration from China to other countries through the territory of the Russian Federation; and trafficking in women for purposes of sexual exploitation (Leliukhin & Nomokonov 2009).

The "triads" constitute a flexible network, the structure of which varies depending on the type of criminal activity. Some types of criminal activities are specific just for "triads", for example, drug trafficking (90% of synthetic drugs and psychotropic substances imported to the Far East get there from China); support for illegal migration of Chinese citizens (including transit through Russia to the EU; having entered the territory of Russia legally, these migrants then get counterfeit visas in Moscow for entry into the EU); the sale of Chinese citizens into slavery and, on the contrary, trafficking of Russian women for purposes of sexual exploitation in China (which some sources estimated to be not less than 15,000 Russian women); smuggling of raw materials from Russia to China, such as ferrous and nonferrous scrap metal, gold, timber, fish and seafood, agricultural products, etc. (Nomokonov 2001).

In areas with a high proportion of Chinese population, the "triads" are engaged in the racketeering of Chinese entrepreneurs, usually merchants and owners of catering enterprises (Nomokonov 2001; Diatlov 2014). In some cases, Chinese criminal groups organise robberies against their nationals as well as abductions for ransom. Moreover, they are good at exploiting the reluctance of victims and their relatives to contact Russian law enforcement bodies because of their ethnic loyalty and fear of having problems with the migration authorities. For this reason, it is almost impossible to identify witnesses of crimes committed by members of "triads".

There are reasons to believe that in the territory of the Russian Far East there is a system of illegal money transfer called "hui kuan" ("transfer of funds") or "fei chien" ("flying cash"). The point of this system is that the money will never leave the place where it has been paid, and an equivalent amount of money can be received anywhere in the world where the ethnic Chinese community is. However, the money transfer operations leave no paper trail that could be investigated by international law enforcement agencies.

Some researchers hypothesise that Chinese criminal organizations operating on the territory of Russia can be controlled by the Chinese security services and other government agencies. This is evidenced by the fact that the heads of firms engaged in this type of illegal business are often former employees of the Chinese secret service in Russia. There is also a connection between Chinese provincial officials and leaders of Party committees residing in Russia, and Russian criminal businessmen (Leliukhin & Nomokonov 2009).

In many cases, researchers note a process of "matching" of Chinese and Russian criminal organizations within a large community. In any case, Chinese criminal groups quickly establish informal relationships with corrupt Russian officials and law enforcement agencies (police, customs, etc.).

Are Chinese migrants themselves targeted as such or not? According to Russian Ministry of Internal Affairs statistics, the number of crimes committed against foreign citizens is growing: in 2014 it amounted to 14,000 crimes, in 2015 – 16,500, in 2016 – 15,700, in 2017 – 14,679, in 2018 – 15,816, and in 2019 – 16,810 crimes.[8] As mentioned above, the majority of crimes against Chinese people are committed by Chinese citizens themselves. As for crimes committed by

---

8 Data from Russian Ministry of Internal Affairs. Available at: https://xn--b1aew.xn--p1ai/Deljatelnost/statistics.

Russian citizens against Chinese people, according to A.L. Repetskaia, in the Irkutsk region the main crime is theft, with a gradually decreasing frequency, also owing to the fact that the victims of crime are engaged in illegal business and are loath to seek protection from the police (Repetskaia 2012).

Thus, Chinese migration has an impact on the crime rate in Russia, even if the criminal statistics do not reflect it. Often the migrants themselves are the target of criminal attacks as well as being involved in illegal activities or staying illegally in Russia. The concomitant factor for Chinese migration has become Chinese organised crime, carrying out illegal activities and strongly promoting criminalization of the Chinese diaspora in the host country. The role of Chinese officials in organizing illegal migration and the activities of Chinese criminal communities on the territory of its "northern neighbour" is also not clear. Although Beijing has officially condemned these activities, there is no denying the objective benefits for China from illegal migration and illegal businesses in Russia.

7 Future Prospects of Migration for Russia

For the first time China is now facing the problem of an aging population and the prospect of a decreasing able-bodied population. Although China's population is still slowly growing, its age structure is changing rapidly. Together with an ageing population, the share of the population which is potentially ready to migrate is gradually decreasing. In 2000, the population aged 20–40 was estimated at 448.6 million people (36.1% of the total population), and in 2007 there were 397.7 million people (30.8%) (Larin 2009: 346–347). According to population projections, starting from 2015 the increase in working age population (15–64) will be negative, and economic forecasts indicate a decreasing trend in unemployment (this figure with an economic growth rate of 7% a year should mean that there are up to 10 million new jobs annually) (Larin 2009: 353–354). By 2050 the aging population is expected to rise substantially: the share of workers under the age of 30 years will decrease by more than one and half times (compared with 1990) and the proportion of workers aged 45–49 will more than double (Berger 2009: 294). Actually, the most mobile group under the age of 35 years, comprehensively, may be in demand in China itself.

Experts confirm that massive Chinese migration abroad will continue in the coming years, but it will have a falling trend and by 2030 China may well become a host country, rather than a country which is sending the migrants. Also, in 2017 the PRC created a new strategy for attracting labour migrants to China (Nezhdanov 2017).

The problem of poverty in China is decreasing (according to official statistics in 2015 the level of poverty decreased from 7.2% to 5.7% and the number of poor population decreased from 70.17 mln to 55.75 mln) (CRI 2016). The difference in living standards between Russia and China is slowly decreasing (real per capita GNI in terms of purchasing power parity in 2016 in US$: Russia – 23,162 and China – 15,534; in 2014 it was 24,710 and 12,600)[9] and new Chinese migrants often prefer to search for a job in the Chinese megapolises rather than abroad. Russia's financial and economic crisis and the devaluation of the rouble made the Russian labour market less attractive. Indeed, the share of Chinese citizens in the total number of foreign migrant workers registered in Russia is decreasing every year, but it is also the biggest contingent of foreign workers in Russia from non-CIS countries (40,500 Chinese workers out of 118,600 foreign workers from non-CIS countries at the end of 2016 and only 2.4% of the total number of foreign workers in Russia) (FSGS 2016).

Thus, the weight of the demographic and economic preconditions for migration will gradually decline, while the importance of other factors may increase focused management of migration flows, environmental problems or political instability in the PRC, or armed conflict in border countries (for example, North Korea) caused by new flows. The growth of Chinese migration is constrained by economic weakness in Russia's regions, low demand for Chinese labour and Chinese investments, as well as legal restrictions, migrant phobia, the rise of nationalism and differences in political systems. The sociological polls show that the majority of Chinese labour migrants do not want to have Russia as a permanent residence (Larin 2008). There are no "Chinatowns" in Russia now.

Chinese labour migrants have found their place in some sectors of the Russian economy (trading, construction and agriculture), and they are well integrated into Russian society now, for example, 66.9% of them have good Russian language skills (Motrich & Izotov 2017: 230). Indeed, China is the optimal economic partner for the Russian Far East and Siberia due to geographical proximity, economic characteristics, significant financial resources, and surplus labour (Van 2017). But Russian society generally feels that Chinese immigration is primarily a threat. Currently Russian society has a conservative attitude toward China's participation in the development of Siberia and the Far East. There is a fear that Chinese capital will control the economy of these regions, and the flow of Chinese labour will create the threat of separation (Diatlov 2016). The Russian authorities (both federal and regional) have proclaimed a

---

9   Data from World Bank. Available at: http://www.worldbank.org/en/publication/reference.

policy of good neighbourliness and partnership relations with China, but at the same time they are not creating favourable conditions for the development of such relations and for an increase in Chinese immigration. In any case, there is still no alternative to replacing Chinese workers in the Russian Far East and Eastern Siberia (Van 2017). Chinese migration has become a source of economic benefit for the Russian population living in the border regions and a significant part of the Russian population in the border regions has begun to consider Chinese people not as a threat, but as an important resource, which needs to be valued and preserved, including by "Moscow" (Panarin 2016: 141).

The flow of Chinese migrants (tourists and workers) is also likely to grow once the bridge over the Amur River which divides Russian territory from the Chinese Province Heilongjiang (the main supplier of Chinese migrants), is completed in 2019. The project "One belt, one road" will promote migration flows from China into Russia also, especially if it entails the creation of a Free Trade Zone between Russia and China (Luzianin & Larin 2017: 65–66). The Chinese authorities have been promoting this initiative for the last 15 years, but the Russian authorities have consistently refused their proposals.

8   Conclusion

Thus, the character of Chinese migration has undergone significant change since the 2000s and now it does not represent a real geopolitical threat for the Russian state and society. Currently we do not have information on enclaves of Chinese migrants apart from those in the main cities (Moscow, Vladivostok and others). The majority of Chinese migrants are temporary migrants; they usually do not want to live in Russia permanently (due to corruption, low level of economic development, legal limitations, climatic conditions and other reasons). However, there are Chinese migration networks in several regions of Russia. There is no data on the significant influence of Chinese migration on the level of criminality, but many facts prove the presence of Chinese organised crime groups in the Far East and Siberia. The impact of Chinese migration on the Russian economy is also highly correlated with certain regions (in the Far East regions such as the Jewish Autonomous district, Primorskii krai and Khabarovsky krai it is more visible). The future of Chinese migration is not clear now and depends on economic, geopolitical, demographic and other factors. Of course, it will continue, but forecasting the volume and character of migration is difficult. Many arguments (political and economic) attest to the fact that the current character of migration will be preserved during the next few years (excluding extreme challenges).

Bibliography

Anokhina, E.S. (2012). *Novaia kitaiskaia migratsiia i politika KNR po ee regulirovaniiu.* Tomsk: Tomskii gosudarstvennyi universitet.

Bashkatova, A. (2017). 'Kitaitsy stali sostoiatel'nee rossiian', *Nezavisimaia gazeta*, 17 October, http://www.ng.ru/economics/2017-10-17/1_7096_china.html.

Berger, Ia. M. (2009). *Ekonomicheskaia strategiia Kitaia.* Moscow: ID 'Forum'.

CRI. (2016). 'Kolichestvo bednykh v Kitae sokratilos' na 14,42 mln chelovek', 1 March, http://russian.cri.cn/881/2016/03/01/1s575290.htm.

Dao, B. (2019). 'Guan'cha (Kitai): obosnovanno li rossiiane boiatsia zakhvata Baikala kitaitsami?', *InoSMI*, 16 February, https://inosmi.ru/politic/20190216/244511094 .html.

Diadiun, K.V. (2012). 'Migratsiia i prestupnost': vzaimosviaz' prichin i uslovii', *Gumanitarnye issledovaniia v Vostochnoi Sibiri i na Dal'nem Vostoke*, 2: 109–114.

Diatlov, V., Zhuravskaia, T., Okhotnikov, A., Perevalova, L. and Sobennikova, E. (2009). 'Kitaiskie rynki rossiiskikh gorodov – "ukhodiashchaia natura"?', pp. 249–288, in Diatlov, V.I. (ed.), *Transgranichnye migratsii i prinimaiushchee obshchestvo: mekhanizmy i praktiki vzaimnoi adaptatsii.* Ekaterinburg: Izdatel'stvo Ural'skogo Universiteta.

Diatlov, V.I. and Grigorichev, K.V. (eds.) (2013). *Pereselencheskoe obshchestvo Aziatskoi Rossii: migratsii, prostranstva, soobshchestva.* Irkutsk: Ottisk.

Diatlov, V.I. (2014). 'Kitaiskii rynok "Shankhai" v Irkutske: rol' v zhizni gorodskogo soobshchestva', *Izvestiia Irkutskogo gosudarstvennogo universiteta*, 10: 103–119.

Diatlov, V. (2016). 'Kitaiskie migranty i dinamika kitaefobii v Rossii', pp. 230–249, in Malakhov, V.S., Simon, M.E. (eds.), *Transnatsional'nye migratsii i sovremennoe gosudarstvo v usloviiakh ekonomocheskoi turbulentnosti.* Moscow: Delo.

Druziaka, A.V. (2014). 'O nekotorykh problemakh global'noi kitaiskoi migratsii', pp. 239–294, in Kuznetsov, D.V. and Buiarov, D.V. (eds.), *Sovremennyi Kitai i ego okruzhenie*, Moscow: URSS.

Evstaf'ev, D. (2019). 'Sblizhenie Rossii i Kitaia: takticheskaia neizbezhnost' na fone strategicheskoi neodnoznachnosti', *Zvezda*, 13 June, https://zvezdaweekly.ru/news/ t/2019610160-8B0VN.html.

FSGS. (2016). 'Sotsial'no-ekonomicheskoe polozhenie Rossii: 2016 god', *Federal'naia sluzhba gosudarstvennoi statistiki*, https://www.gks.ru/free_doc/doc_2016/social/ utoch-osn-12-2016.pdf.

Gabuev, A. (2014). 'Bespokoinoe partnerstvo', *Rossiia v global'noi politike*, 5, http://glo balaffairs.ru/number/Bespokoinoe-partnerstvo-17114.

Gabuev, A. (2015). 'Iskateli privlechenii: kak zarabotat' na proekte Shelkovogo puti', *Forbes*, 15 March, https://www.forbes.ru/mneniya-column/konkurentsiya/284189 -iskateli-privlechenii-kak-zarabotat-na-proekte-shelkovogo-puti.

Gabuev, A. (2015a). 'Kitaitsy ponimaiut, chto Rossiia degradiruet iz-za korruptsii i neeffektivnogo upravleniia: pochemu chast' rossiiskoi elity khochet, chtoby druzhba s

KNR poskoree zakonchilas', *Lenta.ru*, 29 April, https://lenta.ru/articles/2015/04/29/gabuev/.

Gel'bras, V.G. (2001). *Kitaiskaia real'nost' Rossii*. Moscow: Muravei.

Gorod. (2018). 'Gorodok dlia kitaitsev pod Omskom: polnaia istoriia konflikta', 14 December, https://gorod55.ru/news/society/14-12-2018/gorodok-dlya-kitaytsev-pod-omskom-polnaya-istoriya-konflikta.

GPRF (2011). 'Statistika po ubiistvam', *General'naia prokuratura Rossiiskoi Federatsii*, http://crimestat.ru/world_ranking_homicides.

GPRF (2012). 'Statistika po osuzhdennym litsam', *General'naia prokuratura Rossiiskoi Federatsii*, http://crimestat.ru/world_ranking_convicted.

Iukhansen, P. (2017). 'Kitaitsy seichas oboshli russkikh i nekotorye evropeiskie strany. Oni zhivut dol'she, i oni bogache', *InoSMI*, 17 December, https://inosmi.ru/social/20171217/241025042.html.

Ivanov, I. (2011). 'Otchet: chislo bednykh gorozhan v Kitae neuklonno rastet', *Epoch Times*, 5 August, https://www.epochtimes.ru/content/view/50534/4/.

Ivanov, I.S. (ed.) (2013). *Internatsionalizatsiia rossiiskikh vuzov: kitaiskii vektor*. Moscow: Spetskniga.

Khramova, M.N. and Bezverbnyi, V.A. (2017). 'Migratsionnye processy v prigranichnykh regionakh Dal'nego Vostoka v kontekste obespecheniia natsional'noi bezopasnosti', pp. 239–245, in Riazantsev, S.V. (ed.), *Migratsionnye mosty v Evrazii: modeli effektivnogo upravleniia migratsiei v usloviiakh razvitiia Evraziiskogo integratsionnogo proekta*, Moscow: MGIMO.

Kommersant-Vlast'. (2010). 'Russia in figures', 29 March, 10.

Kozykina, N.V. (2010). 'Sovremennaia kitaiskaia migratsiia v Zabaikal'skom krae: osnovnye tendentsii, problemy i perspektivy', *Vestnik Chitinskogo gosudarstvennogo universiteta*, 9(66): 53–59.

Laptev, S. (2002). 'Demograficheskaia ugroza ili upushchennyi shans? Vykhodtsy iz Vostochnoi i Iugo-Vostochnoi Azii v Rossii', *Neprikosnovennyi zapas*, 5: 40–44.

Larin, A.G. (2008). 'Zhizn' v Rossii glazami kitaiskikh migrantov', *Electronic version of the bulletin "Naselenie i obshchestvo"*, http://www.demoscope.ru/weekly/2008/0347/tema06.php.

Larin, A.G. (2008a). *Kitai i zarubezhnye kitaitsy*. Moscow: IDV RAN.

Larin, A.G. (2009). *Kitaiskie migranty v Rossii. Istoriia i sovremennost'*. Moscow: Vostochnaia kniga.

Larin, A.G. (2010). 'Kitaiskie migranty i rossiiskii pravoporiadok', *Aziia i Afrika segodnia*, 4: 34–40.

Larin, A.G. (2013). 'Mirovaia kitaiskaia diaspora i novaia migratsionnaia kontseptsiia Rossii', *Kitai v mirovoi i regional'noi politike. Istoriia i sovremennost'*, 18: 193–222.

Larin, A.G. (2013a). 'Cherkizon, "seraia rastamozhka" i ikh kitaiskoe ekho', pp. 296–307, in Kobzev, A.I. (ed.), *Obshchestvo i gosudarstvo v Kitae*, T. XLIII, Vol. 2. Moscow: IV RAN.

Larin, V.L. (2011). *Tikhookeanskaia Rossiia v kontekste vneshnei politiki i mezhdunarod-nykh otnoshenii v ATR v nachale XXI veka*. Vladivostok: IIAENDV DVO RAN.

Leliukhin, S.E. and Nomokonov V.A. (2009). 'Kitaiskaia organizovannaia prestupnost' na Dal'nem Vostoke Rossii', pp. 160–171, in *Nezakonnaia mezhdunarodnaia migratsiia kak ugroza vseobshchei stabil'nosti i bezopasnosti gosudarstv v XXI veke: Pravovoe obespechenie sotrudnichestva Rossii i prigranichnykh stran*. Vladivostok: DVFU.

Luzianin, S.G. and Larin, A.G. (2017). 'Problema kitaiskikh migrantov v Rossii v kontekste sopriazheniia "EAES – Shelkovyi put'", *Kitai v mirovoi i regional'noi politike. Istoriia i sovremennost'*, 22: 64–75.

Malykhin, M. (2015), 'Studenty iz Kitaia – vtorye po chislennosti inostrantsy v rossiiskikh vuzakh', *Vedomosti*, 11 August, https://www.vedomosti.ru/management/articles/2015/08/11/604362-kitaiskie-studenti-rossiiskih-vuzah.

Mikheev, V. (ed.) (2005). *Kitai: ugrozy, riski, vyzovy razvitiiu*. Moscow: Carnegie Moscow Center.

Molodikova, I. and Diuvel', F. (eds.) (2009). *Tranzitnaia migratsiia i tranzitnye strany: teoriia, praktika i politika regulirovaniia*. Moscow: Universitetskaia kniga.

Motrich, E.L. and Izotov, D.A. (2017). 'Transformatsiia kitaiskoi migratsii na rossiiskom Dal'nem Vostoke', pp. 223–231, in Riazantsev, S.V. (ed.), *Migratsionnye mosty v Evrazii: modeli effektivnogo upravleniia migratsiei v usloviiakh razvitiia Evraziiskogo integratsionnogo proekta*. Moscow: MGIMO.

MVDRF. (2019). 'Kratkaia kharakteristika sostoianiia prestupnosti v Rossiiskoi Federatsii za ianvar'-dekabr' 2018 goda', *Ministerstvo Vnutrennikh Del Rossiiskoi Federatsii*. Available at: https://xn--b1aew.xn--p1ai/reports/item/16053092/.

Nezhdanov, V. (2017). 'Stareiushchii Kitai: kak KNR gotovitsia k privlecheniiu v stranu trudovykh migrantov', *RSMD*, 5 June, http://russiancouncil.ru/analytics-and-comments/columns/sandbox/stareyushchiy-kitay-kak-knr-gotovitsya-k-privlecheniyu-v-stranu-trudovykh-migrantov/#detail.

Nomokonov, V.A. (ed.) (2001). *Transnatsional'naia organizovannaia prestupnost': definitsii i real'nost'*. Vladivostok: Izdatel'stvo Dal'nevostochnogo universiteta.

Panarin, S. (ed.) (2016). *Vostok na Vostoke, v Rossii i na Zapade: transgranichnye migratsii i diaspory*. Saint-Petersburg: Nestor-Istoriia.

Piontkovskii, A. (2015). 'Dialog s petlei na shee', *Radio Svoboda*, 16 April, https://www.svoboda.org/a/26957437.html.

Polonskii, I. (2019). 'Rossiia i Kitai: pliusy i protivorechiia sblizheniia v XXI veke', *Voennoe obozrenie*, 24 June, https://topwar.ru/159342-rossija-i-kitaj-pljusy-i-protivorechija-sblizhenija-v-xxi-veke.html.

Portiakov, V. Ia. (2006). 'Rossiiskii vector v global'noi kitaiskoi migratsii', *Problemy Dal'nego Vostoka*, 2: 11–14.

Prezident Rossii. 'Kontseptsiia demograficheskoi politiki Rossiiskoi Federatsii na period do 2025 goda', http://www.kremlin.ru/acts/bank/26299.

Priemskaia, E. (2019). 'Razlei voda: pochemu v KNR nazyvaiut Baikal svoim "severnym morem"', *Izvestiia*, 27 February, https://iz.ru/847637/evgeniia-priemskaia/razlei-voda-pochemu-v-knr-nazyvaiut-baikal-svoim-severnym-morem.

Repetskaia, A.L. (2012), *Otchet po grantu 'Spetsifika deiatel'nosti kitaiskikh ethnicheskikh prestupnykh grupp v Vostochnoi Sibiri postsovetskogo perioda'*, http://docplayer.ru/31468322-Repeckaya-a-l-finalnyy-otchet-po-grantu-specifika-deyatelnosti-kitayskih-etnicheskih-prestupnyh-grupp-v-vostochnoy-sibiri-postsovetskogo-perioda.html.

Ria novosti. (2015). 'Golodets: RF i KNR nuzhno dovesti do 100 tysiach studentov po obmenu', 9 October, https://na.ria.ru/20151009/1299447658.html.

Riazantsev, S.V. and Rybakovskii, L.L. (2007). *Strategiia demograficheskogo razvitiia Rossii*. Moscow: ISPI RAN.

ToRpPK. (2009). *Primorskii krai: sotsial'no-ekonomicheskie pokazateli*. Vladivostok: Territorial'nyi organ Rosstat po Primorskomu kraiu.

Van, G. (2017). 'Perspektivy rossiisko-kitaiskogo sotrudnichestva v oblasti trudovoi migratsii', *Vestnik Tomskogo universiteta*, 416: 61–68.

Varnavskaia, O. (2019). 'Kitaiskaia ekspansiia. Kitaiskii molokozavod: chto nedogovarivaet chuvashskaia vlast', *Versiia*, 11 July, https://ch.versia.ru/kitajskij-molokozavod-chto-nedogovarivaet-chuvashskaya-vlast.

Vishnevskii, A. (2004). 'Al'ternativy migratsionnoi strategii', *Rossiia v global'noi politike*, 6, http://globalaffairs.ru/number/n_4215.

Vitkovskaia, G. and Panarin, S. (eds.) (2000), *Migratsiia i bezopasnost' v Rossii*. Moscow: Carnegie Moscow Center, Interdialekt+.

VL (2007). 'S Dal'nego Vostoka vernetsia v Kitai do 100.000 kitaitsev', *VL.ru*, 5 April, https://www.newsvl.ru/vlad/2007/04/05/kitajcy/.

VL (2008). 'Ekspert: "Kitaiskogo Kosovo" na Dal'nem Vostoke ne budet', *VL.ru*, 3 April, https://www.newsvl.ru/vlad/2008/04/03/kity/.

VPN (2010). 'Vserossiiskaia perepis' naseleniia 2010', https://www.gks.ru/free_doc/new_site/perepis2010/croc/perepis_itogi1612.htm.

Zaionchkovskaia, Zh. (2010). 'Kogda zhe konchitsia voina s "kitaiskoy ugrozoi"?', *Migratsiia XXI vek*, 2: 14–17, http://migrant.ru/Files/XXIvek/migraciaXXI-02.pdf.

Zaionchkovskaia, Zh. (2011). 'Rossiia i Kitai: partnerstvo na rynke truda', http://www.myshared.ru/slide/85662/.

Zakharov, S.V. (eds.) (2017). *Naselenie Rossii – 2015: 23rd Annual Demographic Report*. Moscow: HSE Publishing House.

Zolotukhin, I.N. (2012). 'Kitaiskaia biznes-diaspora v Iugo-Vostochnoi Azii', *Oikumena. Regionovedcheskie issledovaniia*, 3(22): 103–108.

PART 2

China and Russia in the Changing World: Opportunities and Sources of Competition

∵

Global Shocks, Regional Conflicts and the Quest for Stable Prosperity: Which Way Forward for China and Russia?

Eugenia Baroncelli

Almost two decades into the third millennium, China and Russia have emerged as the main challengers to the US post-unipolar role in an evolving international order. Since the end of the Cold War, limited domestic political representativeness and increasingly liberal market policies, particularly in trade relations with the rest of the world, have coexisted in both countries, with the mix between rising economic performance and repression of domestic dissent through coercive practices becoming a stable – albeit socially regressive- equilibrium. However, while China exerted a stabilizing power on the global economy, leading the worldwide recovery after the crisis (Lin 2011), Russia struggled to recover from post-crisis reduced world demand, and subsequently lower quantitative easing by the main advanced economies. The country's war with Ukraine, and the anti-Russian economic sanctions by the US and EU have further strained its economic situation, triggering a downward spiral in both oil and currency prices. Since 2016, Russia's assertive military intervention in Syria has further complicated the country's relationship with the West. In turn, Washington's unilateralist twist, coupled with the uncertainties of "Brexit EU", has provided multiple occasions for China and Russia to widen the scope of their foreign policy aspirations.

By examining key economic trends, the chapter locates the two countries' relative positions in the global economy, connecting the evidence with the hypothesis of China as an order-maker, and of Russia as an order-taker, respectively (Section 1.2). From this vantage point, it engages the political economy literature on the relation between domestic institutions and economic performance, to question the sustainability of their respective models of development (Section 1.3). Subsequently, the analysis connects such trends to the major simultaneous dynamics in the global political economy. First, based on IR scholarly research on policy roles, an inside-out perspective is adopted to explore the implications of China and Russia's domestic choices for the global economy, and for the broader construction of their foreign policy roles (Section 1.4). The focus then shifts to outside-in dynamics (Section 1.5), to investigate the net effect of key external developments on the evolution of China and Russia's foreign policy roles and performances. The global crisis and recession of 2008–2010, the international responses to the war in Eastern Ukraine, the protracted conflict in the Middle East, North Korea's nuclear challenges, the EU uncertainties and the US unilateralist turn are singled out as particularly consequential occurrences. Speaking to the IR literature on the relation between evolving polarity, norm change and systemic order transition, the chapter concludes on the implications of the dynamic interaction between external drivers and the two countries' policy choices, respectively, for the future international order.

1   **China and Russia in the Global Economy of the Third Millennium: Past Achievements and Future Trajectories**

1.1   *GDP and Growth Patterns: China's Ascendancy and Russia's Setbacks*
China is currently the second largest economy in the world, an upper-middle income country with a share of almost 12% of world GDP (worth US$ 8.91 tn in 2015), second only to the United States (with a GDP worth US$ 16.67 tn, or 24.23% of 2015 world GDP).[1] Accounting for the largest portion of the BRICS (Brazil, Russia, India, China, South Africa) GDP share (US$ 15.62 tn in 2015, or 20.64% of world income), China's contribution is key to bringing the group up to slightly below the EU's share (at US$ 17.96 tn, or 23.73% of world GDP in the same year). Since 2005, Russia too has entered the group of upper middle income countries, but has remained at the lower end of their combined GDP performance (World Bank WDI, 2016). Its economic weight is below the top 10 world economic systems, with the country ranking 11th with a GDP of US$ 1.66 tn in 2015 (2.19% of total world GDP).

With a mean GDP growth of 9.98% between 1991 and 2015, China has outperformed other advanced economies in dynamic terms, as expected according to catching up hypotheses but, more substantially, it has also topped the already impressive performance of other BRICS (Fig. 10.1).[2] The Chinese economy has kept growing at rates below 7% but above 6% between 2016 and 2019, with projections pointing to 6% rates for 2020 and 2021 (World Bank Global Economic Prospects 2020). As discussed below, however, the gradual decline of the Chinese GDP growth rate is likely to have a longer-term impact on regional and global economic trends for the years to come. China has also recorded a

---

1   See Table A1 in the Appendix.
2   For the same period, World Bank data indicate that the mean GDP growth for the US has been 2.56%, and in the EMU region 1.46%. Source: World Bank WDI, 2016.

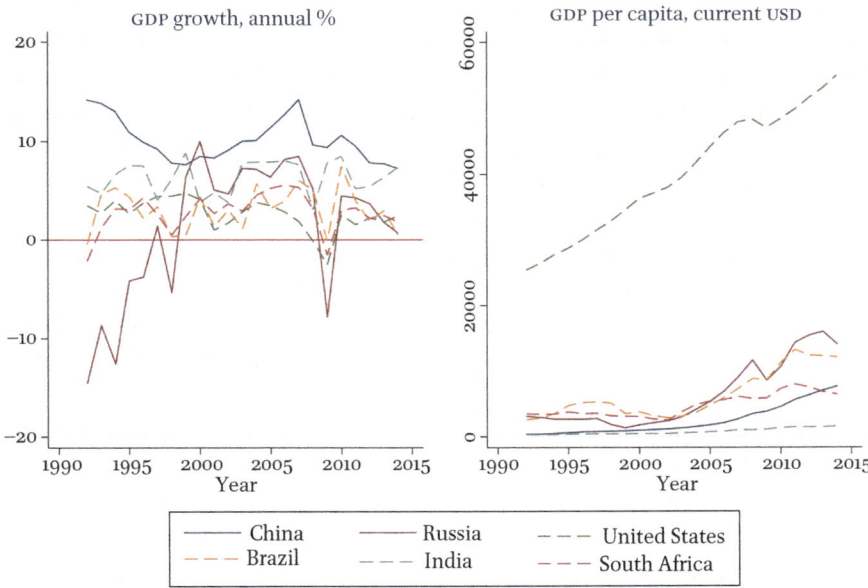

FIGURE 10.1   The BRICS and the US: Trends in GDP growth and GDP per capita
               SOURCE: WORLD BANK WDI 2016

sizable improvement in individual income levels, even discounting for its
spectacular demographic performance, which has brought the country's 600
million citizens in the 1960s to the current 1.3 bn individuals. The shift to 2-digit
GDPpc growth rates occurred between 2005 and 2007, with an average rate of
GDPpc income growth of 12% (World Bank WDI 2016).[3] The evidence points to
a pattern that reconciles population dynamics with other growth drivers, along
a steady path of system-wide economic development. Trends relative to absolute GDPpc also indicate that the average Chinese individual has experienced
a marked improvement in economic security, particularly when compared to
citizens from other BRICS (Fig. 10.1).

Compared to industrialized economies, China's performance in per capita
income levels is even more pronounced. World Bank data indicates that between 1991 and 2015, China's GDPpc growth rate averaged 8.87%. In the same
period, GDPpc has grown on average 1.39% in the US, and 1.44% in the EU.
However, the gap between average individual income levels remains wide for
the two upper-middle income countries of China, Russia and, respectively, the
US (US$ 55,837 in 2015) and the EU (US$ 31,843).

---

3 Calculated as the simple average of growth rates in years 2005 to 2007.

In spite of remarkable results in the yearly GDPpc growth rate in 2007 (8.535%), Russia has conversely plunged into a steep decline, reaching negative 7.821% in 2009, recovering in the following years up to 4.5% in 2010, to experience another precipitous decline (-3.74%) in 2015 (World Bank WDI 2016). Since the end of 2014, the country entered a recession, which closely followed the downturn in oil prices and the economic effects of EU and US sanctions of July 2014. In the second quarter of 2015, Russian GDP growth plunged below -4%. In 2016 the deceleration of the economy slowed down, however, thanks to a dedicated policy response package, including increased flexibility of the exchange rate, cuts in real expenditures and bank recapitalization (World Bank Russia Economic Report 2016). Overall, the country was projected to recover (overall positive 1.5% in 2017, World Bank WDI 2016), and managed to reach 2.3% in 2018 (World Bank 2019). Russia's policymakers have worked on a conservative fiscal rule to consolidate the federal budget, via a three-year budget law (2017–2019) (World Bank Russia Economic Report 2017). Based on low oil price baselines, the fiscal rule brought about cuts in national defence (-1.8% GDP), social policies (-0.5%) and national security (-0.4%), as well as transfers from state controlled companies and increased tax revenue from energy, to get to a -1.2 fiscal balance in 2019, from the -3.7 level of 2016 (World Bank Russia Economic Report 2016). Russia's economic performance has surpassed those expectations, so that the country's trajectory puts its economy just behind that of other OECD mature industrialized economies: its stagnant performance is compatible with that of a mid-income country that is striving to achieve higher status in the world economy. Overall, however, the high dependence of Russian GDP on oil and oil-related exports puts a non-trivial constraint on the country's future process of catching up.

1.2   *China and Russia's Performances in the World Economy: Trade and*
      FDI

Since 2005, China gained two spots in 2015 world trade rankings, surpassing Germany and the US, still topping the list of world exporters with US\$ 2.27 tn and a share of 13.8% in total world exports[4] (Table 10.1 below). While increasing the value of its total world exports (from US\$ 243.80 bn in 2005 to US\$ 340.35 bn in 2015) Russia on the contrary lost two spots from its pre-crisis rank (13th world exporter), shifting to 15th position in 2015.

China also managed to almost double its share of world imports, rising from 5.09% to 9.82% between 2005 and 2015, thus becoming the world's second

---

4   The US and Germany followed with US\$ 1.5 tn, 9.13% of world exports, and US\$ 1.3 tn, or 8% of world exports, respectively (WDI 2016).

TABLE 10.1   Top World Exporters, 2005 and 2015

Country	2015 Rank	2005 Rank	2005–2015 Change in Rank	2005 US$ bn	% WLD 2005	2015 US$ bn	% WLD 2015
China	1	3	2	762	7.25	2270	13.8
US	2	2	0	901	8.57	1500	9.13
Germany	3	1	-2	971	9.24	1330	8.07
Japan	4	4	0	595	5.66	625	3.79
Netherlands	5	6	1	406	3.87	567	3.44
Korea, Rep.	6	12	6	284	2.71	527	3.2
Hong Kong SAR, China	7	11	4	292	2.78	511	3.1
France	8	5	-3	463	4.41	506	3.1
United Kingdom	9	7	-2	391	3.72	460	2.79
Italy	10	8	-2	373	3.55	459	2.78
Canada	11	9	-2	360	3.43	408	2.48
Belgium	12	10	-2	334	3.18	398	2.42
Mexico	13	15	2	214	2.04	381	2.31
Singapore	14	14	0	230	2.18	351	2.13
Russian Federation	15	13	-2	244	2.32	340	2.06
World				10500		16500	

SOURCE: WORLD BANK WDI 2016. TOTAL MERCHANDISE EXPORT VALUES (CURRENT US$)

largest importer after the US and Germany (See Table 10.2 below). With the expected rise in the purchasing power of its growing middle class, China will further expand its potential as a global engine for trade and worldwide growth. In turn, while still the first world importer, the US witnessed a compression of its share over the same period, declining from 15.94% to 13.37%. Russia was the 20th world importer in 2015, accounting for 1.35% of world imports, compared to 1.29% in 2000. Coupled with China's ascendancy in import demand, the US relative decline and Russia's stagnation further confirm that the balance has shifted towards Beijing's end.

In the long run, China and Russia's trade performances replicate dynamics that are similar to those recorded in income levels, respectively, with China experiencing a stellar performance and Russia lagging behind. Along with data on FDI, trade records convey key information about the two countries' patterns of opening to the world economy since their shift to market-based systems.

TABLE 10.2   Top World Importers

Country	2000 USD bn	2005 USD bn	2010 USD bn	2015 USD bn	2016 USD bn	2015 Rank	% WLD 2015	% WLD 2005
United States	1472.63	2030.09	2364.99	2786.28		1	13.37	15.94
China	224.31	648.71	1380.08	2045.76	1950.37	2	9.82	5.09
Germany	595.91	935.13	1266.13	1318.96	1330.30	3	6.33	7.34
United Kingdom	439.26	686.98	752.36	836.05	785.36	4	4.01	5.40
Japan	449.42	594.57	773.86	787.15		5	3.78	4.67
France	370.65	590.22	739.13	759.67	768.01	6	3.65	4.64
Hong Kong SAR, China	208.79	300.02	456.01	598.68	594.47	7	2.87	2.36
Netherlands	247.52	393.12	531.87	537.86	538.96	8	2.58	3.09
Korea, Rep.	184.99	308.73	506.04	530.64	500.17	9	2.55	2.42
Canada	286.68	384.89	499.99	527.48	510.41	10	2.53	3.02
Italy	283.35	458.76	577.11	494.69	490.68	11	2.37	3.60
India	64.97	183.30	448.92	469.97	467.07	12	2.26	1.44
Singapore	169.52	250.28	410.66	451.23	434.37	13	2.17	1.97
Mexico	183.59	242.65	326.64	426.99	418.28	14	2.05	1.91
Belgium	164.68	270.59	360.98	369.81	382.71	15	1.77	2.13
Spain	188.28	343.33	384.02	366.58	371.57	16	1.76	2.70
United Arab Emirates		93.86	229.10	343.72	353.76	17	1.65	0.74
Switzerland	125.12	190.21	311.08	343.37		18	1.65	1.49
Australia	89.08	144.09	233.20	284.29	253.98	19	1.36	1.13
Russian Federation	62.42	164.34	322.37	281.42	263.75	20	1.35	1.29
World	7901.51	12732.48	18438.29	20834.77	20360.40		100	100

SOURCE: WORLD BANK WDI 2016. IMPORTS OF GOODS AND SERVICES (CURRENT USD BILLIONS)

As such, they proxy the ability of the Chinese and Russian leaderships to integrate their countries into global markets. They also convey, however, information on how the global environment has adapted to their domestic changes, with recent adjustments reflecting the rebalancing of the Chinese economy and Russia's response to the glut in fuel.

Since the 1990s, China has moved upward from trade-to-gdp ratios in the range of 30%, doubling openness rates in 2005–2007 above 60%.[5] On average between 2009 and 2014, China's share of merchandise trade in GDP has fallen to 45.42%, declining to 36.41 % in 2015, as the rise in per capita income levels has also opened domestic demand and widened opportunities for Chinese producers to sell in a fast-growing domestic market. In line with this relative contraction, and with the broader compression in world trade values, the yearly percentage growth rate of China's trade value has been negative (–7.58), vis à vis an overall value of –4.43 percentage points in world trade for 2016 (WITS 2018). The decline in import demand from emerging Asian countries is not the only factor that accounts for the relative contraction in world trade (with just 1.7 % increase in merchandise import growth in 2015, down from 3 % in 2014). It seems however that both the fall in commodity prices and China's transition to a new, slower growth pattern (as well as the rebalancing from investment to consumption, and, within investment, from goods to services) have played a major role in that contraction.[6] Lower Chinese demand for manufactured goods (particularly in investment-related import-intensive sectors) from Asian exporters, has been quoted as a main driver in the slowdown in 2015 world trade (also dubbed "the new normal"), as seen above. China is also a major importer of commodities (13 % of world commodities, and up to 40% percent in selected metals), so its lower demand for primary or minimally processed goods has exerted an additional negative impact on world trade values (Constantinescu et al. 2016).

The deterioration in fuel prices since 2014 has further contributed to declining trade values, and has been particularly problematic for Russia and other oil-exporting economies. Reduced supply and import capacity from Russia and other Asian trade partners (namely Kazakhstan among oil producers) account for up to one quarter of the contraction in Chinese exports in 2015 relative to 2014 (Constantinescu et al. 2016). The reduction in China's GDP growth rate and the depreciation of the *renminbi* in July 2015 further contributed to reducing Chinese exports in that year (idem).

---

5   See Table A2 in the Appendix.
6   Other major determinants of the broader slowdown in trade include a slower pace of trade liberalization and maturation of global value chains (Hoekman 2015). In the same period, China's top markets for exports were the US (1), the EU (2) (particularly Germany), Hong Kong (3) and South Korea (4), its main import partners being South Korea (1), the US (2), Asian n.e.s (3) (proxy label for Taiwan, not allowed to report as a country by the UN system for diplomatic reasons), and Japan (3) (WITS 2016).

The potential for trade growth in manufacturing will depend on the further (expected) contraction in Chinese demand. However, the gradual shift from investment to consumption that is taking place in the country will open up opportunities for foreign producers of final-consumer goods. Improvement in income and real wages for Chinese citizens, with the diffusion of enhanced purchasing power to growing numbers, will increase such demand in China, with potential growth for Chinese imports from abroad. Labour dynamics (including internal migration vs migration to neighbouring countries with lower labour costs) may however have contrasting effects on these changes.

Along with Russia and South Africa, China has been on average the most active among the BRICS in pursuing an export-led growth strategy (see Figure 10.2 below). However, while China has been on an upward trajectory since the early nineties, cushioning the post-crisis fall in world demand and regaining some positive margin in trade-to-GDP above 40%,[7] Russia has followed an opposite trend. The country started from very high levels of trade to GDP in the years of its inception in the international system, followed by lows (1997) and highs (2000). Export-wise, though, Moscow has since been on a downward trend, and on a particularly unstable path (see Figure 10.2).[8] Such dynamics can be accounted for by trends in crude oil prices, oil and related products being the main commodities in the country's export basket.[9] According to WTO statistics, in 2014 Russia was the 11th largest exporter of merchandise goods, and the 22nd for commercial services (WTO 2015: 44, 46). This places Russia on the second spot for both trade types when only considering BRICS economies – with China ranking first for both types.[10]

In addition to increasing traded volumes, China has succeeded in diversifying sectors and intensifying the technological sophistication of its export products (Fig. 10.3 and 10.4 below). Behind such performance lies Beijing's enhanced investment in research and development, which has brought the

---

7   See Table A2 in the Appendix.

8   Yearly data are also reported in Table A3 in the Appendix.

9   In 2015, the top 5 products exported by Russia were indeed petroleum oils (crude) (1), oils excluding crude and preparations (2), natural gas (gaseous) (3), bituminous coal (4) and natural gas (liquefied) (5) (WITS 2016).

10   In 2014 China was the leading exporter worldwide for merchandise goods, and the 5th for commercial services. For commercial services, only advanced economies such as the US, the United Kingdom, France, and Germany outperformed China. In 2014, 35% of Russia's exports were accounted for by items in crude petroleum, 20% in refined petroleum, and 8.0% in petroleum gas (Observatory for Economic Complexity – OEC- 2014). In that same year the EU was the main outlet for Russian exports, absorbing 57% of the country's exported goods and services, with the Netherlands, China, and Germany as the three top destinations (idem).

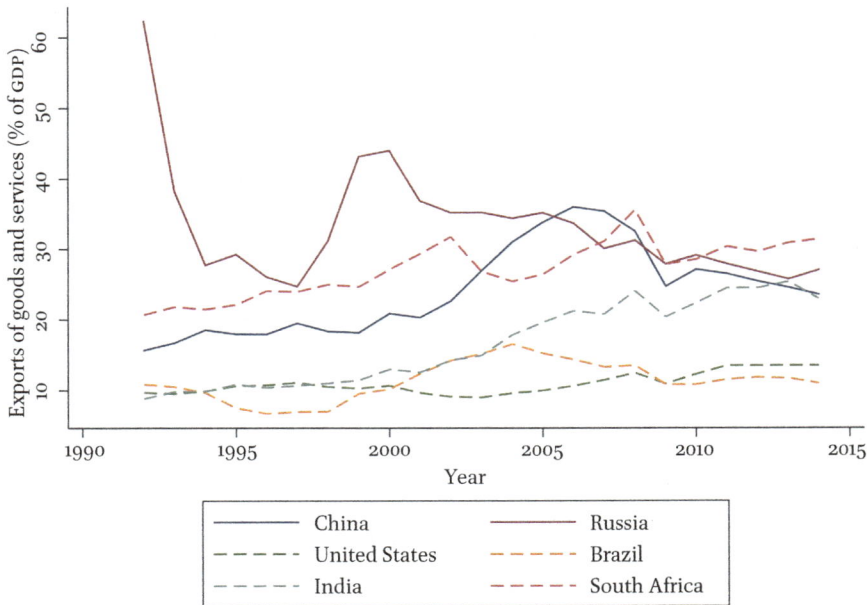

FIGURE 10.2   BRICS and the US: Exports as a share of GDP
SOURCE: WORLD BANK WDI 2016.

country to become the largest investor in R&D among the BRICS in the 2000s. By 2015 China had more than doubled its R&D spending as a share of GDP (2.056%), rising to 1.73% in 2010 from 0.90% in 2000.[11] The evidence suggests that increased volumes of technology-intensive tradables may have responded to strategically placed policy incentives for research (Xiong et al. 2018).

Trends in FDI flows further confirm Beijing's potential to take on the role of global growth engine, as China has been one of the major recipients of long-term investment throughout the past 15 years.[12] At the turn of the millennium it accounted for 2.88% of the world's total FDI inflows and was ranked the 7th recipient of FDI worldwide. In 2015, China moved up to become the second largest recipient of FDI inflows, accounting for 10.44% of world total inflows, worth 242 bn US$ in that year, around half of the US's FDI absorption which accounted for almost 22% of world total FDI inflows (US$ 506 bn). While Russia has also witnessed an expansion of net FDI inflows between 2000 and 2015 (from 2.7 bn to 6.8 bn, with growth in its share from 0.18% to 0.30%), its rank among FDI recipients has declined from 20th to 39th position.

---

11   See Table A4 in the Appendix.
12   See Table A5 in the Appendix.

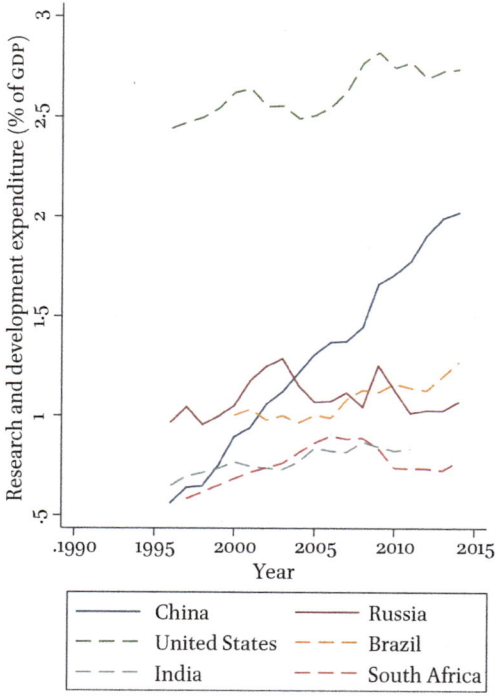

FIGURE 10.3
BRICS vs US: R&D in GDP
SOURCE: WORLD BANK WDI 2016.

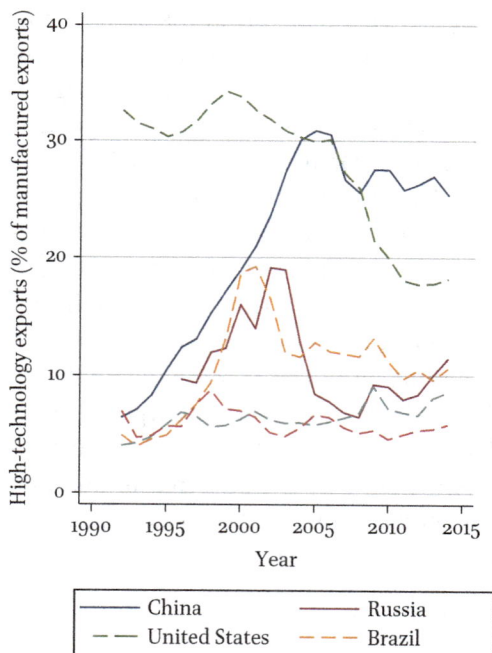

FIGURE 10.4
BRICS vs US: High-Tech Exports in
Manufactured Exports
SOURCE: WORLD BANK WDI 2016.

Particularly relevant in the redefinition of Beijing's foreign policy role, the reach of Chinese foreign direct investment across the globe has constantly expanded, with a jump from US$ 4.6 bn in 2000, when the country ranked 17th among top country sources of FDI, accounting for 0.33% of world total FDI net outflows, to US$ 174.39 bn in 2015, which earned China the third position in the list of top country-sources of FDI, accounting for 9.27% of total world FDI net outflows.[13] As a result, China's level of outward FDI has reached one half of FDI outflows that originate in the US – the top worldwide source. While close to China in 2000, with a total of US$ 3.2 bn in FDI outflows, Russia has remained the 18th FDI supplier worldwide in 2015, even though its share in total net FDI outflows has grown from 0.23% (2000) to 1.17% (2015), almost a sevenfold increase.

Relative to domestic patterns, China has experienced a substantial rise in incoming FDI as a share of its GDP in the first half of the 1990s, and then again between 2000 and 2005 (See Figure 10.5 below). However, the stellar growth in China's GDP rates from 2000 to 2006 have partially compensated for the rise in FDI inflows, that now account for almost 3% of the country's GDP. Outflows have remained relatively more stable over time, accounting for between 1 and 2% of the country's GDP. Conversely, Russia has undergone significant, simultaneous growth in both inflows and outflows of FDI as a share of its GDP, moving from the 0–2 % range in the 1990s to the 2–4 % range in the first decade of the new millennium. After 2010 however, the oil crisis first, and the sanctions of 2014 then, have marked declines in both trends, with more severe deterioration in FDI inflows as a share of GDP post-2014, when the share has reverted to the range of 1%.

Overall, the economic trends reconstructed above appear to corroborate the view of post-Soviet Russia as an order-taker. In the 1990s and 2000s the integration of the country in the global economy has closely followed fluctuations in crude and gas prices, nested in the political contingencies of Moscow's new relations with the transatlantic countries. While the economic reforms adopted by the USSR under Gorbachev had ultimately domestic sources, a notable system-based explanation of the federation's decline can be traced to its failure to keep up with the economic and military competition with the US (Waltz 1993; Oye 1995). Conversely, over the same period, the policy choices of Chinese leaders have significantly contributed to turn the country into an economic order-maker.[14] The long-term key to Beijing's extraordinary

---

13   See Table A6 in the Appendix.
14   Gao (2011) has referred early on to China's wavering among rule-taking, rule-shaking and rule-making in global trade governance; Lee et al. (2011) have questioned the shift from

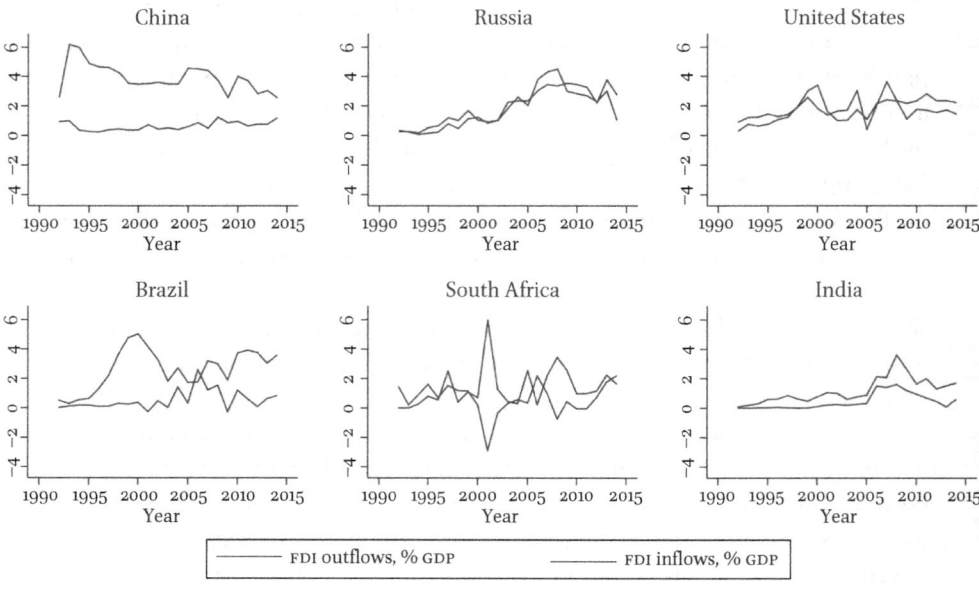

FIGURE 10.5   BRICS vs US: FDI inflows and outflows in GDP (%), 1990–2015
SOURCE: WORLD BANK WDI 2016, VARIOUS YEARS.

growth performance has been premised on chiefly domestic-institutional (as opposed to externally-induced, economic) drivers that were activated over that time span, starting with Deng Xiaoping reforms aimed at the country's transition from a centralized economy to a market-based system.[15] With a forward-looking perspective, the next section investigates the domestic parameters that will likely shape China and Russia's foreign policy aspirations, focusing on the two countries' political-economy systems. The subsequent section, in turn, explores the potential impacts of China and Russia's redefined foreign policy roles on the evolving dynamics of the international system.

2   The Perils of Exclusionary Institutions: Implications for Growth and Democracy in China and Russia

Into the second decade of the third millennium China and Russia have widened their reach of new economic partners, and have pursued differential

---

humanitarian rule-taker to rule-maker relative to China in Darfur. Subsequent elaborations on the concept include Chen (2016) and Caffarena (2017).

15   Zhang (2002) highlights the relevance of domestic drivers in China's growth performance.

strategies to support growth and modernization of their respective domestic systems. Chinese leaders, in particular, have engaged in liberalization reforms, with the country achieving the status of a regional and, post-2008, global engine for growth. In parallel, studies in political economy have started to explore the consequences of the poor quality of institutional development that has accompanied China's economic transition (Pei 2006). Enduring with low protection of economic rights and lagging regulatory reforms, so it is argued, has made it more difficult for the Chinese leadership to adequately respond to bottom-up domestic demands, and to replicate the spectacular growth performance of the past decades (Huang 2016). According to some, these are constraints that may significantly hinder Chinese efforts to overcome a potential mid-income trap (Cai 2014).[16]

The highlights of China's economic performance illustrated in the previous section seem to provide anecdotal evidence of the deeper nexus that exists between institutional evolution and economic growth (Acemoglu & Robinson 2012). Without inclusive institutions, prospects for country-wide growth do not appear sustainable over the long term. One key reason is that, once past the level of early innovation stages, the protracted exclusion of large strata of citizenry from both growth gains and equal voice rights on how to distribute them, deepens inequality in ways that either slow down or altogether impair future development. Far from being a potential driver for innovation, inequality turns into a system-blocking liability. From the standpoint of a rational – selfish-leadership, the key to unlocking the growth potential of a system premised on exclusionary institutions, without unduly relinquishing the incumbent's power, would be to open up the system politically just as much, and just until the (oligarchic) dividend from (institutional) closure equals the advantages of (marginally higher) political opening.

Examples of political closure that have postponed – and in some cases altogether forgone – economic development abound, both in European and post-colonial systems. In the first group, Tsarist Russia and Habsburg Austria-Hungary are two undisputed cases. In the second one, the regressive choices of Ottoman leaders, as opposed to tolerant pre-Ottoman Islamic rulers, are quoted to show the regressive parable of innovators that were best performers (certainly the case for Arabic Islam around the year 1000) and that subsequently lost their competitive edge when confronted with the difficulties of reshaping institutions to balance political and economic freedoms across a large territory and population. Examples from countries in sub-Saharan Africa, that have added to

---

16   A different perspective on China's propensity to fall in a mid-income trap is provided by
      Bulman et al. (2016).

the miseries of colonial subjugation the hardship of exclusionary rule are also manifold, from the Kingdom of Congo, to Ethiopia, or, to an even more serious degree, Somalia. While very different in their specific trajectories, the post-colonial leaders of these countries have antagonised innovation and political openness at once, promoting oligarchic, at times personalistic, discretionary rulemaking. Stateness problems have increased the cost of exclusionary strategies chosen by predatory elites, as the absence of a reference point for law-making, interpretation and application has magnified uncertainty, risks and resorting to self-help by violent means to solve controversies between private parties.[17]

Present-day China does not have the stateness problems of rural, war-torn Somalia, and certainly does not face the development hurdles that Ethiopia or the Democratic Republic of Congo must confront nowadays. Yet in vast rural areas of today's China most citizens are excluded from access to key public goods (health care, liveable environment, basic and secondary education) and are *de facto* denied basic voice rights. The negative impact of those conditions is often muted, as it is more-than-compensated for by the size of the working population that has migrated to China's coastal areas, and that has entered into those productive activities that have contributed so much to the "Chinese miracle" in the past 25 years. The number of poor people living on US\$ 1.90 a day in China has decreased from a mean level of 41.30% between 1995 and 2000 to an average of 16.70% for the period 2005–2010 (See Figure 10.6 below). The trend is even more significant if compared to the achievements of the other BRICS (ibid). China alone does account for most of the decline in the number of the world's total poor population between the 1980s and today (Deaton 2013). Yet, the gap has widened, inside China, between the haves and the have nots (Xie & Zhou 2014).

Anti-poverty measures are being adopted, but inequality between rural and urban areas is still problematic (Tian et al. 2016). Projected over the long run, its effects appear to be even more damaging, as reported by a study on the future effects on Chinese growth of present-day education differentials between children of urban and rural families, respectively (Li et al. 2017). The country's current gradual rebalancing away from industrial manufacturing towards consumption, and from manufacturing to services, discussed in the previous section, will also have implications on domestic inequality, poverty levels and wider socio-political stability. On the one side, the gains in per capita income of the average Chinese consumer will increase his purchasing power, strengthen demand for more diversified consumer goods and services, as well as stimulate further advancements on the scale of technological innovation. On

---

17   On stateness see the seminal Linz and Stepan (1992).

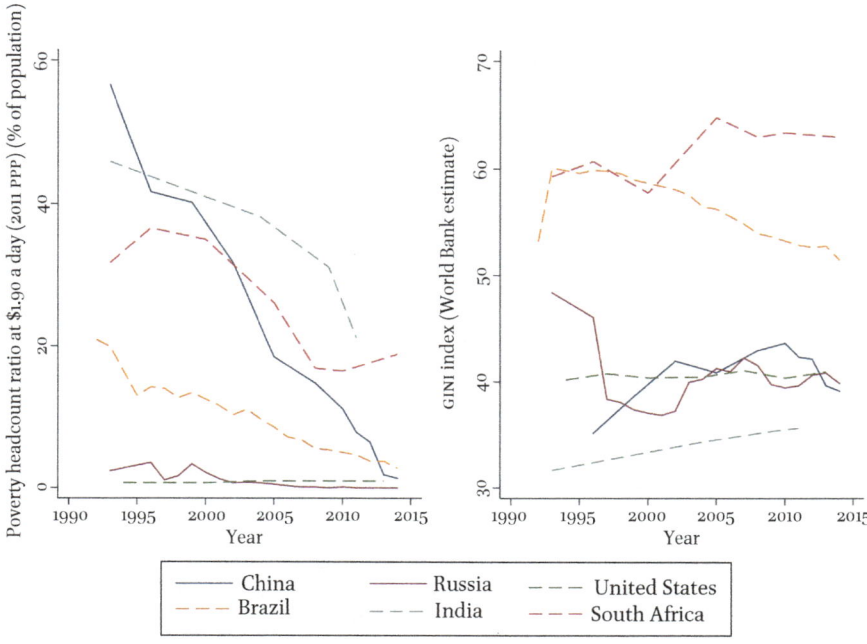

FIGURE 10.6   BRICS Poverty trends
                DATA SOURCE: WORLD BANK WDI 2016.

the other side, the shift to a consumption economy is also likely to increase unemployment and negatively impact domestic wages. Lower wages/increased downward labour market flexibility, and migration to lower cost neighbouring producers are equally, and perhaps jointly, possible outcomes. The stability of the Chinese system will then depend on wider bottom up dynamics: a growing middle-class, better educated and more demanding (increasingly aware of existing opportunities worldwide, particularly in a digital age), may become more difficult for the Party leadership to control.

As a matter of fact, there is little indication that Chinese leaders are heading towards opening the country's political system. According to the Polity index, which provides a numerical proxy for the level of (electoral) democracy in a given country/year, no change has occurred in Chinese political institutions since 1990 (Coppedge et al. 2016). The dataset ranks China as a full authoritarian regime, its score always falling below the -6 threshold, above which the country would enter the "intermediate" category of transitioning regime ("anocracy", i.e. neither a full autocracy, coded -6 or lower scores, nor a fully democratic system, coded 7 or higher scores) (See Figure 10.7 below). Other proxies such as the Freedom House index that combines both political and

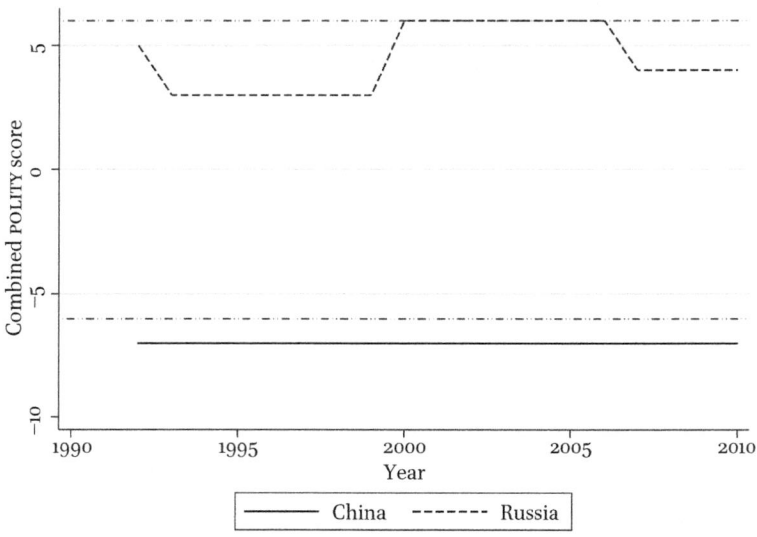

FIGURE 10.7   China and Russia: political openness 1990–2015
                Note: In order to facilitate the comparison between the trajectories of the two
                countries, Polity cutoff points (+6 and -6) have been indicated with a
                punctuated line.
                SOURCE: AUTHOR'S ELABORATION FROM: VARIETIES OF DEMOCRACY
                DATASET (COPPEDGE ET AL. 2016)

civil liberties, also report China as "not free", with the same freedom score –
of 6.5 – that the country had in 1998.

Illiberal practices have unfortunately been adopted also in the formally pro-
market anticorruption program launched by President Xi Jinping. Apparently,
and in spite of official claims, the program has not reached the expected results (Xing & Zhen 2016). Cases of incarceration and death sentencing of several CEOs of domestic companies who were deemed to have behaved fraudu-
lently have also raised suspicions about a surge in state executions to cover
other cases of (state sponsored) corrupt behaviour. The question of whether
capital punishment serves indeed as a diversionary strategy to cover the corruption of "privileged CEOs" that are closer accolades of political elites, and/or
to preserve the appeal of the free-market façade in the eyes of the international community, raises yet another question about the sustainability of the
virtuous link between "capitalist China" and the country's economic prowess
(Pei 2006).

Russia is similarly ranked as "not free" in 2015 by Freedom House, with a deterioration in the level of freedom compared to 1999 levels (when the country

was categorized as "partly free"), as both political rights and civil liberties have been curtailed since the beginning of the Putin era. Based on Polity scores (Fig. 10.7), Russia's illiberal democracy is more open politically compared to Beijing's one-party autocracy. Yet, China's political stability has been instrumental in the country's phenomenal growth in the post-Tiananmen years. Conversely, post-Soviet Russia has undergone multiple phases of political turmoil since the Gorbachev years, with the gains from political opening achieved under Boris El'tsin eroded by the poor results of his privatization programs and collusion choices to the advantage of the oligarchs (Åslund 2007). As discussed in Section 1.2, and in contrast to (relative) economic Chinese stability, Russia has been subject to recurrent economic bottlenecks, largely influenced by the structural volatility of crude prices. Under the current leadership of Vladimir Putin, economic instability has been instrumental in the provision of a peculiarly selective order, much closer to the pre-revolutionary patrimonial-personalistic tsarist regime – according to some, than to the subsequent, allegedly totalitarian, yet more impersonal and certainly more formalized Soviet rule (Shkaratan 2007).[18] Popular dissatisfaction with both the Russian government (80% negative ratings according to 2017 polls) and economic elites, has raised citizens' trust in Putin's charismatic personality. Re-elected in the 2018 spring elections, Putin's discretion is maximum: he enjoys nearly universal support from both elites and the public as the key balancer between corrupted governmental cadres, crooked oligarchs and revolutionaries (*The Economist* 01.04.2017). However, the future of Russia, and particularly the sustainability of its institutional-economic model of development, depends very much on the ability of its leaders to manage the country's recurrent economic instability through more stable, more formalized rules and radically longer-term horizons.

Beyond the choice between patronage and formalized, impersonal rule, Russian and, to a lesser extent, Chinese leaderships will have to decide whether they want their countries to progress further along representative polities that incentivize private entrepreneurship by also backing individual rights, or, on the contrary, choose to endorse growth by banking on the compression of political and civil freedoms. To a wide margin, such a choice impinges on the extent to which it is possible to dissociate long term sustainable growth achieved through free-market capitalistic development from liberal-democratic institutions (Pei 2006). Current critics, those who believe that state capitalism without liberal democracy has worked in the past and does work for countries like China and Russia, note that reversion to higher levels of state intervention in

---

18   The formalization of self-appointed total control of the Communist party by China's president Xi Jinping also points in the same direction.

the economy has been on the rise in mature, industrialized democracies too, since the failure of "pure" Washington Consensus policy prescriptions in the 1990s and 2000s, and particularly after the 2008 crisis (The Heritage Foundation 2018).[19] Yet, counterpoints retort that the sort of intervention pursued post-global crisis by liberal-democratic capitalist systems is different from the gradual centralization (or, in the case of Russia, re-centralization) of an entire economic system in the hands of the state (or of the individuals that control it). They note that in mature industrialized liberal-democracies, basic freedoms have been largely preserved – aside from select cases, in times of crisis and under state-sponsored bailout programs of an emergency nature. A different story would be at play in the "state sponsored" illiberal capitalisms of China and Russia (Kurlantzick 2016).

Retrospectively, a key issue is whether state capitalism is indeed "the factor" that explains China's economic miracle, and Russia's ability to stay afloat even in the midst of major energy shocks, or whether, on the contrary, the Chinese and Russian paths to state capitalism are in fact second-best solutions, devised by domestic incumbents to support the maximum level of growth achievable under relative political closure and exclusionary – or partially exclusionary – institutions. With a forward-looking, systemic perspective, the sustainability of Chinese and Russian illiberal state capitalisms will be key for the future of the global economy, as well as for its governance rules.

3   Inside-out Processes: Foreign Policy Role Projections and Performances

While the economic performance discussed in the previous sections indicates Russia as a *de facto* order-taker and China as an order-maker in the global political economy, their respective leaderships have projected to the outside world different, and peculiar foreign policy aspirations.[20] Both countries are permanent members of the UNSC (United Nations Security Council), and major players in the BRICS group, alongside India, Brazil and South Africa. Through the

---

19   The overall index of economic freedom produced by The Heritage Foundation has declined since 2007 – to regain moderately at the end of the 2010s. The index is a composite indicator of several dimensions of state intervention in the market – including business, investment, trade and public expenditures. A major shift has been recorded by China in terms of freedom of investment, which has marked a downward trend from a peak of 50% in 2007 to 25% in 2018.

20   Chen (2016) labels both present-day China and the EU as order-shapers, speculating about the potential for their cooperation.

BRICS venue, as well as individually, they have claimed enhanced voice rights in major multilateral *fora*, achieving some gains on the boards of the Washington-based IFIs (the IMF and the World Bank) since the quota and voice reform (Baroncelli 2013). Alternatively, they have aggregated other clusters of developing and emerging economies, creating their own financing facilities to support growth at the regional level. Among them, the New Development Bank, also dubbed the "BRICS Bank", in force since 2015, and the Asian Infrastructure Investment Bank (AIIB), operational since 2016. China has also been a participant in the Chiang-Mai Initiative, a bundle of currency swaps launched after the Asian Crisis by some members of the Asian Development Bank, to pool reserves and help member countries to cope with large imbalances without resorting to IMF support. While the Chiang Mai initiative has been subsequently multilateralised, its success during the 2008–10 crisis was rather limited.

China and Russia have also gained greater influence and visibility through their membership in the G20, which has taken the lead on global macroeconomic and financial decision-making since the 2008 crisis.[21] Even if the G20 entry rules still remain obscure to date, China and Russia's sheer economic size in the world economy, coupled with their political reach, made their membership a predictable outcome. However, beyond sharing standard arguments against the bloc-power of western industrialized economies, the two countries have vigorously pursued their respective national priorities, with very distinct foreign policy styles.

Chinese leaders have worked to forge an image of responsible power for their country, softening the tones of geopolitical and economic claims vis à vis Beijing's counterparts, particularly outside East Asia.[22] Putin's Russia has taken the opposite way. After the failed reforms initiated in Soviet times under Mikhail Gorbachev, and pursued in the new Russia towards openly free-market – if largely unregulated and corrupt – ends under Boris El'tsin (McFaul 1995), Vladimir Putin's regime has decidedly married the cause of diversionary and rent-seeking oil politics. Identifying different external threats as the main culprits of domestic failures (during times of oil price slumps), Putin has been able to exploit the convergence between economic hardship and political transition to his advantage. In doing so, he has succeeded in compacting a nationwide consensus (in fairness, a non-trivial task in a pluri-national state born out of the ashes of a federation of multi-national republics) behind the idea that Russia had been left for too long at the margins of international politics,

---

21   Early on, Russia was a member of the G8 group.
22   Breslin (2016) connects China's responsible behavior at the multilateral level to Beijing's assertive pursuit of its interests at the regional level.

and that it was time to regain the stature and place it deserved. Diversionary war and "rally 'round the flag" politics (Levy 1988; Mueller 1973) have been the norm in Putin's post-Soviet Russia. He started with fiercely nationalistic propaganda during the repression of domestic opposition in Chechnya in 1999, and continued with foreign policies of an anti-democratic nature in neighbouring countries: in 2008, in Georgia, followed by military intervention in Ukraine in 2014. In 2016, Russia's military involvement in Syria has unequivocally signalled Putin's will to claim a global role for Moscow. There is little doubt that Putin's revamping of military action and Russia's role in the Middle East have also served the purpose of further cementing his domestic consensus, pushing up ratings polls to that effect.

Russia's aspiration to achieve a global foreign policy role is also reflected in the country's military expenditures, that in relative terms surpass those of the US, the most powerful military actor in current international politics.[23] The evidence is confirmed by trends in military expenditures out of total government spending for the BRICS, the US and selected EU countries (see Figure 10.8 below). Russia has unequivocally reached the highest average levels across the whole 1990–2015 period, leading the rank, followed by India, the US and, since the mid-2000s, by China. Shares of domestic fundamentals (GDP, Government expenditures) provide a raw indication of the country's planned military engagement, based on its own domestic capabilities. As such, they also convey a prima facie indication of the expected breadth of its foreign policy aspirations. However, the gap between role concept (aspiration) and role performance, theorized in the IR literature to also include role acknowledgement by others (Harnisch 2011), casts light on Russia's potential ability to fulfil its self-expectations with role-enactments and ultimately policy results, leaving the issue open to multiple future relational and systemic developments.

In turn, China's military expenditures as a percentage of GDP, stably revolving around 2% (yearly average 1990–2015), suggest commitment to a regional, as opposed to global, foreign policy role. By 2005, China's military expenditures as a share of government spending had reached 15%, on par with lower thresholds of military spending as a percentage of government budgets of the US, Russia and India.[24]

---

23   Taking the average of military expenditures on GDP at 5-year intervals between 1995 and 2015, Russia's 4% goes beyond Washington's 3.68%, with Moscow's share of military spending in GDP even exceeding 5% in 2015. See Table A7 in the Appendix.

24   Paucity of data points and reliability issues suggest particular caution in drawing implications on China's foreign policy roles.

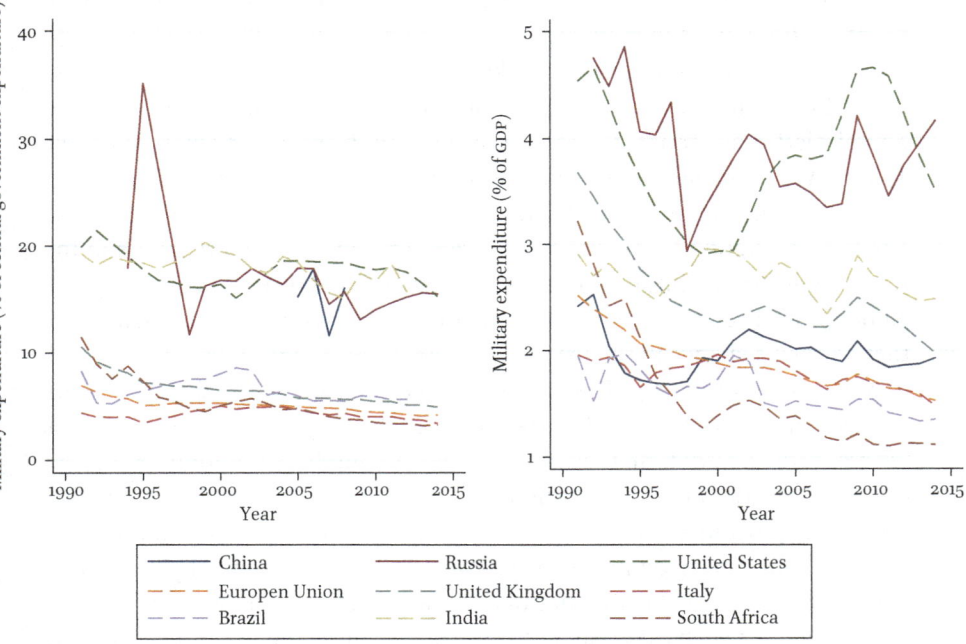

FIGURE 10.8   BRICS, the US and the EU: Trends in military spending
                Left: Military Spending on public expenditure (World Bank WDI 2016)
                Right: Military Spending on GDP (World Bank WDI 2016)

China's foreign policy in Asia, and particularly in the South China Sea, vis à vis Japan and Taiwan, has been assertive and at times aggressive, yet it has never escalated to levels that compare to Russia's interventions in Georgia and Ukraine, and ultimately in Syria. While certainly blunt, a fair comparison would cast China's security policy in line with its (official) aspiration to the status of a regional power, while putting Russia in the group of countries aspiring to a global role. A few key developments in the 2010s, however, indicate that China has started to widen its foreign policy ambitions well beyond Asia. In early 2017, President Xi Jinping has claimed for its country the role of defender of globalization, trade openness and environmentally friendly development, endorsing the Paris agreement on climate change. The country's "Belt and Road" initiative, launched in 2013, projects China's economic clout globally, potentially providing the basis for its future, wider strategic geo-political repositioning (Caffarena 2017). Expected to become the largest infrastructural endeavour in human history, the initiative enlists 68 participating states, is budgeted in the range of tn 6–7 US$, and is set to encompass half of the world's population and 1/3 of world GDP. Over the course of 2017 China has expanded its military ambitions outside Asia, by opening its first military base abroad (Djibouti) and directing its navy to hold exercises in the Baltic sea. The country is not new to maritime operations in regional seas. In the East Chinese Sea, Beijing has opposed Japan's claims over the Senkaku Diaoyou Islands. In the South Chinese Sea, it has been involved in ongoing quarrels over sovereign rights on continental platforms around the Spratly Islands, with the Philippines, Malaysia, Taiwan, Vietnam and Brunei. China has also engaged in openly building artificial islands on atolls and reefs to buttress its reclamation rights on the Spratlys. However, as argued above, beyond the country's military assertiveness in the region, a recurrent feature of its foreign policy, it is the recent surge in Beijing's global projection, attached to the operations in Djibouti and the Baltic Sea, that marked a change in the reach of China's military ambitions.

Meanwhile, China and Russia have settled their territorial divergences by agreeing on the contentious frontier that kept them apart. The reasons for this progress are manifold. On the one side there are the sheer economic gains that the two countries are reaping, and that would have been impaired by further protracting hostilities on territorial claims at the borders. Between the 1990s and 2014, bilateral trade between the two countries has grown by more than twenty times. In 2008 China became Russia's biggest trading partner (WITS 2016), while between that year and 2012 Chinese investment in Russia grew by almost 100% (UNCTAD 2015). On the other side, China's spectacular performance in domestic growth has also spelled an increased demand for energy, which is expected to rise further in the future. In turn, the negative impact of 2014 EU sanctions against Russia on energy deals under negotiation with select EU partners (particularly the North Stream, South Stream and Arctic pipelines) has raised the attractiveness of the eastern option for Moscow. The agreement on a Russian-Chinese contract for the building of the Sila Sibiri gas pipeline, negotiated in July 2017 by Presidents Vladimir Putin and Xi Jinping, is expected to provide 38 bn cubic meters of gas per year over the next 30 years, worth approximately 200 bn euros. This Sino-Russian rapprochement in trade and energy relations, however, does not detract from China's drive towards unilateral ascendancy as the main global contender of the US as the next global economic hegemon. Beijing has indeed stepped up investment to increase its own production of shale gas, totalling 9 bn cubic meters in 2017, with a projected target of 20 cubic meter ceiling by 2020.

4　　Outside-in Dynamics

System-wide developments have occurred since the global economic crisis and recession of 2008–2010, a shock that China absorbed with remarkable resilience, playing a key role in the global recovery that followed. Managing recession has been more difficult for Russia, which was hit hard by the drop in oil prices. In turn, the international responses to the war in Eastern Ukraine (particularly through sanctions against Moscow), and to the militarized conflicts in the Middle East, have led Russia to become more assertive in its search for a wider geo-political reach. The recurring threats agitated by Kim Jong Un's North Korea have also modified the range of options for the Chinese and Russian leaderships. Putin's display of force, through the deployment of strategic bombers in the region at the end of 2017 (a move reminiscent of Russia's once privileged relation with North Korea) has reminded both China and the US of Moscow's symbolic potential to project its global aspirations further eastward.[25]

Exacerbated by the economic consequences of the 2008 crisis, the controversial nature of unipolarity has been magnified since 2017 by the un-presidential assertiveness of the US Trump Administration (Ikenberry 2017). Wary of President Trump's escalating tweets, threateningly alluding to non-diplomatic solutions to the nuclear tests implemented by North Korea, Moscow and Beijing have compacted around a not-so hidden anti-US stabilizing deal in the region, putting aside the claims that had previously strained their relations over the two Koreas.

News on Russian information warfare, and allegations of the country's meddling with the US presidential election in early 2017, and in French, German and British elections later in the year, have not helped the cause of easing the already tense relations between Moscow and Washington, and have embittered bilateral relations between Russia and several EU members. Domestic cleavages have emerged, or compacted, in both EU countries and, particularly, the US, around the significance and reliability of such allegations, showing the relevance of disinformation campaigns in the age of digital globalization (*The Economist* 15.04.2017; 02.12.2017). While Russia's military might was put under strain by the post-crisis fall in oil prices and 2014 economic sanctions, the country has vigorously endured in its policy of robust military spending. Moscow's choice to upgrade its cyberpower, and to add it to modernized nuclear and conventional capabilities, has alerted NATO of the possibility that Russia's role aspirations may not be as distant from actual fulfilment as they were in the past. Deals between apparently odd bedfellows, as in the case of the 2017 agreed sale of S-400 Russian air defence missiles to Turkey, have further spread concerns among transatlantic partners.

---

25   Symbolic gestures that have been further buttressed by Russia, through taking pro-North Korea stances in the UNSC and renewing economic support to Kim Jong Un's regime.

In turn, changes in the direction and tone of US foreign policy under the presidency of Donald Trump, his "America first" rebuttal of commercial cooperation with the EU, as well as reticence in joining the scaling up effort in multilateral lending commitments to the Washington-based IFIs in 2017, indicate that role and power transitions have been further at play on that end too (Birdsall 2017). Non-decisions and outright political mistakes by transatlantic allies in addressing conflict and instability in the Middle East, including the 2017 US decision to support the Netanyahu government and officially recognize Jerusalem as the capital of Israel, have greatly reduced their role as neutral mediators, and have in turn helped Russia in the endeavour.

On the one side, the business mentality of US President Trump, and his relatively carefree approach to human rights issues (Human Rights Watch 2018), have driven him closer to China, the new land of economic opportunity. His convinced praise of Chinese President Xi Jinping and his quiet *placet* to the "Belt and Road" initiative indicate that the "Pacific vocation" of the US may grow further, to the detriment of privileged relations with its European allies. Washington's unilateralism has simultaneously raised concerns of a deepened divide with European partners. Discarding the trade deals that had been envisaged in the Obama-sponsored TTIP, dismissing the role of NATO in the provision of regional and global security, demeaning the role of the EU, and withdrawing from the 2015 Paris Agreement on climate change in 2017, have been among the most tangible moves in that direction.[26] On the other side, an equally unilateral approach has been adopted by the US vis à vis a group of Asian partners, through the scrapping of the TPP (Transatlantic Pacific Partnership) in early 2017, which enhanced the value of cooperation between the latter and their Chinese neighbour instead. Admittedly, the failure of negotiations for a transatlantic mega-regional has revealed inconsistencies on the side of European partners too, where large sections of domestic audiences have fiercely opposed furthering the negotiations on the TTIP well before the US unilateral closure under the new Trump Presidency. Overall, the US unilateralism, coupled with EU indecision and lack of coordination, have magnified the potential for success of Russian military ambitions and Chinese economic expansion. They also point to a handful of opportunities for rising China to

---

26   Across the ebb-and-flow of isolationist calls, and past the long Cold War hiatus, voices supporting US disengagement have gained traction. On pre-Trump US unilateralism see Posen (2014). Elaborating on Layne (1997), Mearsheimer and Walt (2016) have advocated a strategy of US "offshore balancing" again, during the campaign for presidential elections.

upgrade its official aspirations well beyond the regional role that the country has been forging for itself in East Asia for some time.

Compared to the immediate post-Cold War period, international politics is currently marked by a higher dependence of regional and global orders on domestic evolutions in China and Russia. While different in their "order-shaping" abilities, leaders in Beijing and Moscow are keener on claiming expanded roles for their respective countries, assertively at the regional level, but increasingly also in the new global context. The extent to which they are able to follow up on those claims is also premised on their success in credibly projecting authority at the domestic level. First, the endeavour implies a renewed focus on controlling internal centrifugal authority flows, slowing down growth deceleration and reducing inequality for China, and containing audience costs during oil-related downturns in Russia. Both countries will have to devote efforts to pursuing their own economic development, with strategies that may be at times detrimental to regional stability, as shown by the diversionary strategy adopted under Putin's Russia – which continues to subsume economic priorities to foreign policy ambitions.

Second, China's and Russia's ability to fulfil their roles also depends on the response of the other major actors in the international system, the United States and the EU (or, according to some, its main powers – most notably Germany), while also being impacted by the behavior of Japan and of major emerging market economies (most notably India, Brazil, Turkey and Israel). Washington's unipolar moment has been superseded by increased fluidity (Scwheller 2011), and the power transition has reduced the asymmetry between the hegemon and runners-up, followers and challengers (Nye 2017). However, status has not yet adjusted to the power redistribution dynamics underway, which has caused China and Russia, as well as other emerging powers, to claim an increased role in the structures of current multilateral governance. To date, China is the only player that has started – albeit reluctantly – to assume some of the responsibilities that come with enhanced status – particularly through its aid policy, sponsorship of Asian development facilities and, lastly, the "Belt and Road" initiative. Russia, on the contrary, has shirked most of these responsibilities – not least because it is not in a position to sustain economic efforts of that sort. Relative to Moscow, and if the expectation of "hegemonic stability" theorists is right, the wider and more enduring a power-status gap is, the dimmer the chances for peaceful systemic transitions (Doran 1989). The role played by the United States in this process remains crucial. In principle, wise yet vigilant accommodation by Washington to an authority-sharing transition improves the opportunities that key liberal principles of the Bretton Woods order are retained (Ikenberry 2009). In practice, the flimsy foreign policy attitude of the Trump administration, coupled with the norm drifting, role changing and power redistribution dynamics underway, indicate the coming of a multi-order international system (Flockhart 2016). Time will tell how liberal, effective and concerted the new plural order is going to be, and the extent to which its core principles can be shared by future major powers.

5   Conclusion

Through an in-depth overview of their economic performance in growth, trade and investment, this chapter has analysed the prominent role of China and Russia in the global context of the third millennium. The two countries' foreign policies have significantly influenced the redefinition of global equilibria currently underway. However, to locate the source of China and Russia's future potential for redefining the international order, this chapter contends that one should look at their domestic systems, and particularly at the long-term compatibility between their development models and the political formulas devised by respective leaderships.

Against the resilience and shock-absorbing capacity displayed by China after the global crisis, the analysis has contrasted Russia's structural dependency on the fluctuations of oil and gas prices. Exploring the connections between economic growth and institutional development at the domestic level, the chapter has advanced a critical reading of the long-term sustainability of the paths of illiberal capitalisms adopted by the leaders of both countries. Based on the hypotheses advanced by new institutional economics, the chapter has discussed the difficulties that Chinese leaders will face from mounting citizens' demands for opened voice rights and lower inequality, particularly in the age of internal rebalancing and reduced growth that China has experienced since the 2010s. While the phenomenal expansion of China outside East Asia has proceeded mainly through economic means, 2017 developments in the Baltic Sea and Djibouti witness a tangible enlargement of the country's military horizons. The likelihood that China will shift from a responsible power posture, with mainly regional military ambitions and global economic aspiration, to that of a full-fledged aspiring hegemon of the world system in its own right, much depends on the interplay between China's domestic and foreign policy choices, on the one side, and the constraints and opportunities provided by the international context, on the other. In that respect, the US retreat to foreign policy unilateralism and its "America first" economic approach, coupled with "Brexit EU" weaknesses, have provided multiple windows of opportunity for China to undertake a more assertive foreign policy role with a global, as opposed to regional, reach.

Compared to China's cautious moves, that policy void has been exploited more explicitly by Russia under the leadership of Vladimir Putin, who has chosen "rally round the flag" and "diversionary war" tactics to fuel nationalist claims and compact consensus around an increasingly authoritarian regime. While that choice has imposed sustained growth in military expenditures and reduced public resources to meet basic social needs at the domestic level, the widespread popular support to his leadership has so far served Russia's military ambitions in former Republics and the Middle East particularly well. Compared to the immediate post-Cold War period, the coming international order will depend much more on the evolution of China and Russia's domestic and foreign policy choices, consistent with their ascendancy in the new global context. However, the role of outside-in dynamics will remain key. The US contradictory management of North Korea's nuclear threats has indeed provided a further opportunity for Chinese and Russian leaderships to approximate their foreign policies in the area along an anti-US posture. Short of a solid, joint US-EU commitment to the benefits of a rule-based, concerted multilateral order, the logic of balancing will prevail as the key mechanism in the new multipolar context. Admittedly, either global, Kantian-type multilateral cooperation, on the one side, or crude power-based balancing dynamics on the other, are two polar outcomes that appear equally unlikely. While Russia will have to reconcile foreign policy ambitions with its actual capabilities, a more coherent EU and a revamped transatlantic compact could provide substantial impetus to smooth Moscow's revisionist assertiveness. Ultimately, the chance to convene on intermediate solutions, negotiated frameworks premised on concerted criteria, will in no little measure depend on the ability of established industrialized democracies to engage China and Russia in the existing web of multilateral institutions, to cooperate to add legitimacy and representativeness through appropriate reforms of their governance structure, and to provide incentives for old incumbents and rising challengers to profit from the benefits of such a redefined order.

Appendix

TABLE A1   Major World Economies by GDP

2015	Country	GDP 2015, USD tn (constant 2010)	2010	2005	2000
1	US	16.67	1	1	1
2	China	8.91	2	3	5
3	Japan	5.99	3	2	2
4	Germany	3.71	4	4	3
5	France	2.78	5	5	4
6	U.Kingdom	2.71	6	6	6
7	Brazil	2.33	7	8	8
8	India	2.30	9	12	14
9	Italy	2.06	8	7	7
10	Canada	1.80	10	9	9
11	Russian Fed.	1.66	11	11	11
12	Spain	1.42	12	10	10
13	Australia	1.31	13	13	13
14	Korea, Rep.	1.27	14	15	16
15	Mexico	1.21	15	14	12

SOURCE: WORLD BANK, WORLD DEVELOPMENT INDICATORS – HEREINAFTER WDI 2016.
RANKS REFER TO COUNTRY SHARES IN WORLD GDP

TABLE A2   China Trade/GDP Shares 1991–2015

Year	Trade, GDP %	Trade in services, GDP%	Merchandise trade, GDP%
1991	33.00	2.91	35.57
1992	33.69	4.40	38.95
1993	31.73	5.25	44.19
1994	42.06	5.85	42.08
1995	38.44	6.06	38.37
1996	33.72	5.02	33.67
1997	33.95	8.96	33.94
1998	31.63	8.74	31.60
1999	33.15	9.01	33.10
2000	39.36	9.54	39.35
2001	38.25	9.73	38.26
2002	42.46	10.19	42.46
2003	51.61	6.86	51.58
2004	59.45	7.83	59.46
2005	62.90	7.16	62.68
2006	64.77	7.14	64.49
2007	62.28	7.23	61.78
2008	56.80	6.62	56.23
2009	43.59	5.31	43.63
2010	49.38	4.28	49.24
2011	51.14	5.99	48.61
2012	48.67	5.71	45.70
2013	47.14	5.66	43.82
2014	45.09	7.08	41.56
2015	41.20	6.95	36.41

SOURCE: WORLD BANK WDI 2016.

TABLE A3   Russia Trade/GDP Shares 1991–2015

Year	Trade (% of GDP)	Trade in services (% of GDP)	Merchandise trade (% of GDP)
1991	26.26	–	–
1992	110.58	–	–
1993	68.70	–	–
1994	50.95	6.04	29.88
1995	55.18	7.78	35.91
1996	47.92	8.16	40.19
1997	47.26	8.42	39.99
1998	55.77	10.73	49.05
1999	69.39	12.45	58.80
2000	68.09	10.64	57.84
2001	61.11	10.93	50.77
2002	59.71	11.32	48.76
2003	59.13	10.69	49.26
2004	56.58	9.68	47.48
2005	56.71	9.07	48.33
2006	54.73	8.28	47.26
2007	51.71	8.04	44.46
2008	53.38	8.11	45.97
2009	48.44	8.93	40.50
2010	50.36	8.16	42.58
2011	48.37	7.35	41.59
2012	47.98	7.95	40.14
2013	47.64	8.89	38.74
2014	48.45	9.10	39.25
2015	50.74	10.54	40.15

SOURCE: WORLD BANK WDI 2016.

TABLE A4   Research and development Spending as a share
            of GDP (%): BRICS and other advanced economies

Country	2000	2005	2010
Brazil	1.00	1.00	1.16
Russian Federation	1.05	1.07	1.13
India	0.74	0.81	0.80
China	0.90	1.32	1.73
South Africa	n.a.	0.86	0.74
US	2.62	2.51	2.74
United Kingdom	1.72	1.63	1.69
Italy	1.01	1.05	1.22
Germany	2.39	2.42	2.71
France	2.08	2.04	2.18
Canada	1.87	1.99	1.84
European Union	1.74	1.75	1.93
World	2.08	1.99	2.06
Hong Kong SAR, China	0.46	0.77	0.75
Netherlands	1.81	1.79	1.72
Japan	3.00	3.31	3.25

SOURCE: WORLD BANK WDI 2016.

TABLE A5   FDI, net inflows

Country	2015 mn	2015 rank	% WLD 2015	Country	2000 mn	2000 rank	% WLD 2000
World	2322454.03	–		World	1461012.74	–	
European Union	580656.11	–	25.00	European Union	709128.69	–	48.54
US	506161.00	1	21.79	US	350066	1	23.96
China	242489.33	2	10.44	Germany	247986.59	2	16.97
Ireland	203463.37	3	8.76	United Kingdom	164130.33	3	11.23
Hong Kong SAR, China	181047.43	4	7.80	Hong Kong SAR, China	70495.74	4	4.83
Netherlands	129749.72	5	5.59	Canada	68309.24	5	4.68
Switzerland	97577.57	6	4.20	Netherlands	63118.80	6	4.32
Brazil	74693.63	7	3.22	China	42095.3	7	2.88
Singapore	70579.75	8	3.04	France	41382.27	8	2.83
Cayman Islands	63448.12	9	2.73	Spain	40489.48	9	2.77
United Kingdom	58450.56	10	2,52	Brazil	32994.72	10	2.26
Canada	54702.38	11	2.36	Ireland	25501.01	11	1.75
Germany	52576.91	12	2.26	Switzerland	23080.88	12	1.58
India	44009.49	13	1.89	Mexico	18382.28	13	1.26
Australia	36595.01	14	1.58	Singapore	15515.29	14	1.06
France	34968.75	15	1.51	Australia	14892.98	15	1.02
Mexico	33181.27	16	1.43	British Virgin Islands	8097.4	16	0.55
British Virgin Islands	28854.72	17	1.24	Cayman Islands	7626.86	17	0.52
Spain	25299.04	18	1.09	Chile	4860.01	18	0.33
Chile	20468.71	19	0.88	India	3584.22	19	0.25
Indonesia	19779.13	20	0.85	Indonesia	-4550.35	21	-0.31
Russian Federation	6852.97	39	0.30	Russian Federation	2678.03	20	0.18

SOURCE: NET INFLOWS EXPRESSED AS BOP, CURRENT MN USD (WORLD BANK WDI 2016)

TABLE A6   FDI, net outflows

Country	2015 mn	2015 rank	% WLD 2015	Country	2000 mn	2000 rank	% WLD 2000
World	1880685.98	–	–	World	1403427.65	–	–
European Union	562781.73	–	29.92	European Union	908359.27	–	64.72
US	311137	1	16.54	US	186370	1	13.28
Ireland	183213.50	2	9.74	France	173566.13	2	12.37
China	174390.68	3	9.27	Germany	98169.90	3	7.00
Netherlands	136776.81	4	7.27	Netherlands	74510.26	4	5.31
Japan	136410.66	5	7.25	Hong Kong SAR, China	69984.25	5	4.99
Switzerland	131293.83	6	6.98	Spain	59072.42	6	4.21
Germany	112504.18	7	5.98	Switzerland	47305.93	7	3.37
Canada	80619.73	8	4.29	Canada	46651.75	8	3.32
Hong Kong SAR, China	78514.94	9	4.17	Japan	45027.49	9	3.21
British Virgin Islands	76169.4	10	4.05	Sweden	40232.72	10	2.87
Spain	57828.19	11	3.07	British Virgin Islands	37144.6	11	2.65
Cayman Islands	57746.75	12	3.07	Norway	10802.97	12	0.77
Luxembourg	39370.76	13	2.09	Cayman Islands	7238.50	13	0.52
France	33319	14	1.77	Singapore	6848.38	14	0.49
Singapore	31405.23	15	1.67	Korea, Rep.	4842.1	15	0.35
Korea, Rep.	23760.4	16	1.26	Ireland	4628.71	16	0.33
Norway	22134.80	17	1.18	China	4612	17	0.33
Russian Federation	22085.1	18	1.17	Russian Federation	3178.83	18	0.23
Cyprus	17396.31	19	0.92	Cyprus	172.09	19	0.01
Sweden	16779.92	20	0.89	Luxembourg	na	20	na

SOURCE: NET OUTFLOWS EXPRESSED AS BOP, CURRENT MN USD (WORLD BANK WDI 2016)

TABLE A7   Military expenditures: BRICS vs selected transatlantic allies, 1995–2015

Country	Year	Military spending/ Gov't exp.	Military spending, %GDP
China	1995	n.a.	1.72
	2000	n.a.	1.90
	2005	15.27	2.02
	2010	n.a.	1.92
	2015	n.a.	1.98
Russia	1995	35.17	4.07
	2000	16.79	3.55
	2005	17.94	3.58
	2010	14.07	3.85
	2015	n.a.	5.01
Brazil	1995	n.a.	1.82
	2000	8.10	1.73
	2005	6.01	1.52
	2010	5.95	1.54
	2015	n.a.	1.39
India	1995	18.42	2.58
	2000	19.47	2.95
	2005	18.46	2.75
	2010	16.73	2.71
	2015	n.a.	2.42
South Africa	1995	7.35	2.12
	2000	5.10	1.39
	2005	4.82	1.38
	2010	3.51	1.12
	2015	n.a.	1.11
US	1995	17.78	3.64
	2000	16.42	2.93
	2005	18.62	3.84
	2010	17.79	4.67
	2015	n.a.	3.32
United Kingdom	1995	7.24	2.77
	2000	6.53	2.27
	2005	5.78	2.28
	2010	5.50	2.42
	2015	n.a.	1.95

Table A7   Military expenditures: BRICS vs selected transatlantic allies, 1995–2015 (cont.)

Country	Year	Military spending/ Gov't exp.	Military spending, %GDP
European Union	1995	5.11	2.07
	2000	5.34	1.88
	2005	4.97	1.76
	2010	4.46	1.71
	2015	n.a.	1.49

SOURCE: WORLD BANK WDI 2016.

Bibliography

Acemoglu, D. and Robinson, J.A. (2012). *Why Nations Fail: The Origins of Power, Prosperity and Poverty*. New York: Crown.

Åslund, A. (2007). *How Capitalism Was Built: The Transformation of Central and Western Europe, Russia and Central Asia*. Cambridge: Cambridge University Press.

Baroncelli, E. (2013) 'The World Bank', pp. 205–220, in Jørgensen, K.E and Laatikainen, K. (eds.). *Routledge Handbook on the European Union and International Institutions*. Abingdon: Routledge.

Breslin, S. (2016). 'China's Global Goals and Roles: Changing the World from Second Place?', *Asian Affairs*, 47(1): 59–70.

Birdsall, N. (2017). 'Getting to Yes on a World Bank Recapitalization', Views from the Center Blog, July 11, Washington, D.C.: Center for Global Development.

Bulman, D., Eden, M. and Nguyen, H. (2016). 'Transitioning from low-income growth to high-income growth: is there a middle-income trap?', *Journal of the Asia Pacific Economy*, 22(1): 5–28.

Caffarena, A. (2017). 'Diversity Management in World Politics. Reformist China and the Future of the (Liberal) Order', *The International Spectator*, 52(3): 1–17.

Cai, H. (2014). 'Overcoming the Middle-Income Trap in China', pp. 428–432, in Fan, S., Kanbur, R., Wei, S-J. and X. Zhang (eds.), *The Oxford Companion to the Economics of China*. Oxford: Oxford University Press.

Chen, Z. (2016). 'China, the European Union and the Fragile World Order', *Journal of Common Market Studies*, 54(4): 775–792.

Constantinescu, I.C., Mattoo, A. and Ruta, M. (2016). 'Trade Developments in 2015', *Global Trade Watch*, Washington, D.C.: The World Bank Group.

Coppedge, M., Gerring, J, Staffan I.L., Skaaning, S-E., Teorell, J., Altman, D., Bernhard, M., Fish, S., Glynn, A., Hicken, A., Knutsen, C.H., Marquardt, K. McMann, K., Miri, F., Paxton, P., Pemstein, D., Staton, J., Tzelgov, E., Wang, Y. and Zimmerman, B. (2016). 'V-Dem [Country-Year/Country-Date] Dataset v6.2'. (Varieties of Democracy V-Dem Project).

Deaton, A. (2013). *The Great Escape: Health, Wealth and the Origins of Inequality.* Princeton, NJ: Princeton University Press.

Doran, C. (1989). 'Systemic Disequilibrium, Foreign Policy Role, and the Power Cycle', *Journal of Conflict Resolution*, 33: 371–401.

Flockhart, T. (2016). 'The Coming Multi-Order World', *Contemporary Security Policy*, 37(1): 3–30.

Gao, H.S. (2011). 'China's Ascent in Global Trade Governance: From Rule Taker to Rule Shaker, and Maybe Rule Maker?', pp. 153–180, in Deere Birkbeck, C. (ed.) *Making Global Trade Governance Work for Development.* Cambridge, UK: Cambridge University Press.

Harnisch, S. (2011). 'Role theory: operationalization of key concepts', pp. 7–35, in Harnisch, S., Frank, C. and Maull, H. (eds.), *Role Theory in International Relations.* London and New York: Routledge.

Heritage Foundation. (2018). 'Index of Economic Freedom', Washington, D.C.: The Heritage Foundation, https://www.heritage.org/index/.

Hoekman, B. (ed.) (2015). *The Global Trade Slowdown: A New Normal?, A Vox EU E-Book.* London: Center for Economic and Policy Research Press, http://voxeu.org/sites/default/files/file/Global%20Trade%20Slowdown_nocover.pdf.

Huang, Y. (2016). 'Can China Escape the Middle-Income Trap?', *China Economic Journal*, 9(1): 17–33.

Human Rights Watch. (2018). 'US: Trump's First Year Sets Back Rights', 18 January, https://www.hrw.org/news/2018/01/18/us-trumps-first-year-sets-back-rights.

Ikenberry, G.J. (2009). 'Liberal Internationalism 3.0: America and the Dilemmas of Liberal World Order', *Perspectives on Politics*, 7(1): 71–87.

Ikenberry, G.J. (2017). 'The Plot Against American Foreign Policy. Can the Liberal Order Survive?', *Foreign Affairs,* 96(3): 2–9.

Kurlantzick, J. (2016). *State Capitalism – How the Return of Statism Is Transforming the World.* Oxford: Oxford University Press.

Layne, C. (1997). 'From Preponderance to Offshore Balancing: America's Future Grand Strategy', *International Security*, 22(1): 86–124.

Levy, J. (1988). 'Domestic Politics and War', *Journal of Interdisciplinary History,* 18: 653–673.

Li, H., Loyalka, P., Rozelle, S. and Wu, B. (2017). 'Human Capital and China's Future Growth', *Journal of Economic Perspectives,* 31(1): 25–48.

Linz, J., and Stepan, A. (1992). 'Political identities and electoral sequences: Spain, the Soviet Union and Yugoslavia', *Daedalus*, 121(2): 123–139.

Lee, P., Chan, G., and Chan, L. (2011). 'China in Darfur: Humanitarian rule maker or rule taker?', *Review of International Studies*, 38(2): 423–444.

Lin, J. (2011). 'China and the global economy', *China Economic Journal*, 4(1): 1–14.

McFaul, M. (1995). 'State Power, Institutional Change, and the Politics of Privatization in Russia', *World Politics,* 47: 210–243.

Mearsheimer, J., and Walt, S. (2016). 'The Case for Offshore Balancing. A Superior US Grand Strategy', *Foreign Affairs*, 95(4): 70–83.

Mueller, J. (1973). *War, Presidents and Public Opinion*. New York: Wiley.

Nye, J.S. (2017). 'Will the Liberal Order Survive?', *Foreign Affairs,* 96(1): 10–16.

The Observatory for Economic Complexity. (2014). 'Observatory for Economic Complexity Dataset', Cambridge: MIT, https://atlas.media.mit.edu/en/.

Oye, K.A. (1995). 'Explaining the End of the Cold War: Morphological and Behavioral Adaptations to the Nuclear Peace?', pp. 57–84, in Lebow, R.N and Risse Kappen, T. (eds.), *International Relations Theory and the End of the Cold War*. New York: Columbia University Press.

Pei, M. (2006). *China's Trapped Transition. The Limits of Developmental Autocracy*. Cambridge: Harvard University Press.

Posen, B. (2014). *Restraint. A Foundation for US Grand Strategy*. Ithaca: Cornell University Press.

Shkaratan, O. (2007). 'The Russian Transformation: a New Form of Etacratism', in Lane, D. (ed.), *The Transformation of State Socialism. System Change, Capitalism, or Something Else?*. Basingstoke: Palgrave Macmillan.

Schweller, R. 2011. 'Emerging Powers in an Age of Disorder', *Global Governance,* 17: 285–297.

The Economist. (2017). 'Red mist; America and Russia', 2 December, 425 (9069).

The Economist. (2017). 'Shadow puppets; Russian meddling in Europe', 15 April, 423 (9036).

The Economist. (2017). 'The Young and the Restless. Protests in Russia', 1 April, 423 (9034).

The Financial Times (2016). 'China anti-corruption campaign backfires', by Hudson Lockett, 09.10.2016, online edition, accessed at https://www.ft.com/content/02f712b4-8ab8-11e6-8aa5-f79f5696c731.

Tian, X., Zhang, X., Zhou, Y. and Yu, X. (2016). 'Regional income inequality in China revisited: a perspective from club convergence', *Economic Modelling*, 56: 50–58.

UNCTAD. (2015). 'Multiple years. Bilateral FDI Statistics', Geneva: United Nations Publications, http://unctad.org/en/Pages/DIAE/FDI%20Statistics/FDI-Statistics-Bilateral.aspx.

Waltz, K. (1993). 'The Emerging Structure of International Politics', *International Security*, 18(2): 44–79.

WITS (2016). 'China Trade Summary'. Multiple years', Washington: World Integrated Trade Solutions, https://wits.worldbank.org/CountryProfile/en/Country/CHN/Year/LTST/Summary.

World Bank (2016). 'The Russian Economy Inches Forward: Will that suffice to turn the tide?', Russia Economic Report 36, Washington, D.C.: The World Bank Group.

World Bank (2017). 'Russia's Recovery: How Strong Are Its Shoots?', Russia Economic Report 38, Washington, D.C.: The World Bank Group.

World Bank (2019). 'The World Bank in Russia – Overview'. Washington, D.C.: The World Bank Group, https://www.worldbank.org/en/country/russia/overview#3.

World Bank (2020). 'Global Economic Prospects January 2020. Slow Growth, Policy Challenges', Washington, D.C.: The World Bank Group.

World Bank WDI (2016). 'World Development Indicators – WDI. Multiple years'. Washington, D.C.: World Bank Statistical Department, http://databank.worldbank.org/data/reports.aspx?source=world-development-indicators.

WTO (2015). 'International Trade Statistics 2015. Special Focus: World Trade and the WTO, 1995–2014'. Geneva: The World Trade Organization.

Xie, Y. and Zhou, X. (2014) 'Income inequality in today's China', *Proceedings of the National Academy of Sciences of the USA*, 111(19): 6928–6933.

Xiong, Y., Yang, X., and Song, M. (2018) 'Analysis on the Effects of China's Fiscal and Taxation Policy on Exporting Products of Photovoltaic and High-end Equipment Manufacturing Industries', *Journal of Renewable and Sustainable Energy*, 10(1).

Xing, N. and Zhen, L. (2016). 'Perceptions of clean governance: the state of discrepancy and its explanation', *Journal of Public Administration (China)*, 3.

Zhang, B. (2002). 'Gaibian Ziji, Yingxiang Shijie [Transform China itself and influence the world]', *Social Sciences in China*, 1: 6–15.

CHAPTER 11

NATO-Russia Relations through the Prism of Strategic Culture

Nicolò Fasola and Sonia Lucarelli

1   The (Ups and) Downs of NATO-Russia Relations: A Cognitivist Perspective

The destinies of NATO and Russia have been intertwined since the creation of the North Atlantic Treaty Organization (NATO), in 1949. It is no secret that NATO's *raison d'être* was to deter a Soviet attack on the Allies. The Warsaw Pact (1955) was the USSR's response which mirrored NATO's Washington Treaty. The main function of both organizations was collective defence (as defined in articles V of the Washington Treaty and IV of the Warsaw Pact), with a clear enemy in mind, not mentioned in the Washington Treaty but implicitly meant: the other bloc.[1] Both organizations had also a very important intra-bloc function, but the logic of the Cold War imposed emphasis on their deterrent function.

The end of bipolarity and the dissolution of the USSR represented a systemic change with potentially huge implications. NATO seemed to have lost its reason for being and Russia its empire. This opened up what appeared to be a fully new era in NATO-Russia relations, an era of deep transformation of each actor's international role and of possible cooperation between them. This was the reality of the early 1990s, which opened with Russia taking part in the North Atlantic Cooperation Council (1991) and declaring that one of the pillars of Russia foreign policy should be the recognition that respect for human rights and fundamental freedoms is an essential component of peace (Kozyrev 1992). However, this "honeymoon period" did not last long. Its first setback was the North Atlantic Council declaration in December 1994 that NATO would start to evaluate the process of enlargement (Pouliot 2010: 151). The move was interpreted by Russia as a threat to international security and it reacted accordingly.

---

1   The Washington Treaty does not specify an enemy explicitly (neither did NATO's first Strategic Concepts of 1949 and 1953). However, NATO's 1957 Strategic Concept detailed the Soviet threat at length. See: https://www.nato.int/docu/stratdoc/eng/a570523a.pdf. We are grateful to Mark Webber for pointing us to this document.

The transformation of relations was evident in the pages of Russia's new military doctrine, as well as in new practices undertaken by the two actors. Pouliot argues that the revival of Russia's Great Power disposition can be linked to NATO's functional and geographic enlargement which *de facto* started with the declaration of 1994 (Ibid.: 341). Later on, after the Madrid Council (July 1997) in which NATO formally agreed to enlargement, a new "Mechanism for Consultation and Cooperation" was established to cope with tensions relative to NATO's enlargement: the Permanent Joint Council (PJC). The signature of the PJC Founding Act, however, was regarded with suspicion by both Russian and Western observers (Webber et al. 2012). Subsequently, NATO's first geographic enlargement in 1999 (to embrace the Czech Republic, Hungary and Poland) as well as its intervention against Serbia that same year triggered new tensions.

It was only with 9/11 that the perception of a shared global threat led to a relaunch of relations with the creation of the NATO-Russia Council (NRC) (May 2002) and engagement in common operations, such as Operation Active Endeavour (an anti-terrorism operation in the Mediterranean). However, relations were to worsen again with the US invasion of Iraq (2003), NATO's second, and broader enlargement (2004) and eventually Russia's intervention in Georgia in 2008 after G.W. Bush's call for Georgia's membership in NATO. Since then, relations have been on a slippery downwards slope culminating in Russia's unlawful annexation of Crimea in 2014 and the subsequent destabilization of eastern Ukraine. The consequent economic sanctions imposed on Moscow, the suspension of the NRC, as well as Russia's intervention in Syria on the side of Bashar Al-Assad, all indicated a continuing deterioration of relations. The additional accusations by NATO members of Russia's violations of their air space, as well as episodes of cyber interference, have led to the lowest point in the post-Cold war relations between NATO and Russia. Secretary General Rasmussen declared that "Russia's aggression to Ukraine was the gravest threat to European security in a generation" (Rasmussen 2014). How shall we read all this? Was it avoidable?

Several analysts tend to express explicit or implicit support for either NATO or Russia, while blaming the other party for engaging in (or generating) conflict-triggering behaviour. An illustrative example in this sense is J.J. Mearsheimer's "Why the Ukraine Crisis is the West's Fault" (2014). The renowned scholar claims that the seizure of Crimea was not due to Putin's desire to revive the Soviet empire. On the contrary, responsibility lies in the unconsidered policy of eastward expansion carried out by NATO and the EU. "The West had been moving into Russia's backyard and threatening its core strategic interests" for long, disregarding Moscow's justified opposition and its need to preserve a sphere of influence. After the ousting of Ianukovych from power in February 2014, "Putin's pushback should have come as no surprise". Among others, R. Sakwa (2017) sees NATO-Russia post-Cold War relations in a similar light.

However, the view presented above is by no means universally shared (Snegovaya 2014). Indeed, many commentators side with the West, against Russia. Moscow, and not NATO, is the subject truly responsible for this (and other) crises. Starting with liberal assumptions and bringing as evidence the nature of the Russian political regime, this second argument suggests that Russia poses a growing threat to Europe and liberal democracy more broadly (witness the proven interference in the 2016 US elections). It is the case of Larry Diamond (2016), who reconnects Russia's political course to a defined project to rebuild the Soviet empire, by means of aggression and discrediting democratic values. Putin wants to "make the world safe for autocracy", so the argument goes.

The debate has polarised around these two positions, with insufficient attempts to explore the deeper roots of the NATO-Russia confrontation. While Mearsheimer reduces the two actors to "pre-programmed torpedoes" acting and reacting automatically on the basis of fixed material stimuli, Diamond simplifies his judgement according to a sharp ideological line flattening the analysis on a gross division between Good and Evil. But why should Russia consider NATO's eastward expansion so threatening? What makes it dangerous in the eyes of Moscow? By the same token, why has NATO expanded even in the face of Russia's complaints? And why is Moscow's behaviour often so inconceivable for the West? Power politics – the most widely used approach to the case – is not sufficient for understanding what is at stake for the two actors. No security dilemma is brought on by the simple fact that a neighbour gets stronger, as the case of relations among countries within NATO shows. Even if we conceive that the two actors are balancing a "threat" (and not the relative rise in power), we need to account for threat perception: why should a peaceful broadening of NATO's membership be perceived as a threat by Russia? Why should Russia's rhetoric (and practice) of *Russkii Mir* be perceived as a threat to NATO? To answer these questions, we need to look at the two actors' deeper cognitive assumptions and processes.

We claim here that the way NATO and Russia have defined their roles in world politics, have decoded the other's intentions, and have ultimately undertaken certain practices, is deeply embedded in their strategic cultures (Johnston 1995; Gray 1999; Biehl et al. 2013). Here, we use strategic culture as a synonym for *broad cognitive frameworks subsuming an actor's self-perception, worldview, and preferred ways to use force. Self-perception* entails a narrative of the actor's core characteristics and qualities as well as (implicit or explicit) qualifications of difference with respect to a set of relevant Others. In other words, self-perception can be observed through the analysis of self-representation. In the case of a collective actor, self-perception (as it emerges from self-representations) tells the story of its self-identification in terms of "who we are" ("mirror identity") and "who we are not" ("wall identity") (Cerutti 2008: 6). *Worldviews* describe instead an actor's perception of the mechanics characterizing international politics and the legitimate instruments of action. As a corollary, worldviews help to understand how force is intended conceptually and how it would be employed practically. Both self-perception (as it appears in self-representation) and worldview are not given once and for all, but emerge out of processes of historical stratification, social construction and reinterpretation of who we are (also in relation to others) and how we interpret world politics. The process of construction and reconstruction of self-representation and worldviews is by no means only a verbal/linguistic exercise, but interacts closely with *practices*: it is through practices that linguistic narratives acquire practical interpretation and credibility (or not); it is also through the effort to legitimate new practices that self-representation may evolve (Pouliot 2010; Flockhart 2012).

It is very important to note that a cognitivist perspective does not preclude political actors from having material interests nor that the actions occur in response to those interests. But what this perspective does assume is that the way actors interpret their interests and the means of coping with them, as well as the interests and preferences of others, are all influenced by an actor's self-perception and worldviews. At the same time, the way we represent ourselves (self-representation) embeds a communicative message to the other actors about who we are and what we stand for, to which the other reacts.

In this chapter we deal with NATO's and Russia's self-representation and embedded worldviews as they emerge from official documents (strategic concepts and doctrines) and leaders' speeches (particularly by NATO's Secretary Generals Anders Rasmussen and Jens Stoltenberg, and Russian Presidents Dmitrii Medvedev and Vladimir Putin). Addressed to both domestic and international audiences and by no means mere rhetorical exercises, these sources are vocal about NATO's and Russia's self-representations and reinforce their perceptions, values, and worldviews. In this sense, documents and speeches are portraits of the two actors' definitions of "who we are (not)" and help to understand how they construct the borders of their respective communities. We claim here that a fundamental difference between NATO's and Russia's understanding of the community of reference (respectively, *non-ascriptive* and *ascriptive*) explains a lot about the tension between the two actors. In fact, such a difference is at the basis of their perceived "ontological insecurity", that is a sense of unsafety and existential anxiety, due also to lack of trust in other actors.[2]

The analysis will focus particularly on the timespan 2008–2016, a period in which NATO-Russia relations – despite ups and downs – substantially worsened.[3] The conclusions summarize and discuss the findings of this Chapter.[4]

2   NATO's Strategic Culture

The concept of Strategic Culture has been traditionally applied to states, and the few exceptions mainly regard the European Union (Rynning 2003). Very little has been written on NATO and the little that has is directed at assessing the negative implications of different national strategic cultures within the Alliance or with reference to NATO's strategic posture (Yost 2009; Biehl et al. 2013). Here we will claim that in order to understand NATO's strategic culture(s) we need to explore the core elements of NATO's self-representation and its worldviews, as they emerge from its narratives. In the case of a military and political organization like NATO, self-identification also tells the story of what type of use of force is considered legitimate and what worldview underlines its self-representation and legitimacy considerations. Such self-identification has partially changed over time.

Since its creation in 1949, NATO has been more than one thing at once (a defensive alliance, a transatlantic bond, the institution through which post-war Germany was reintegrated into the European political system, etc). Throughout the Cold War, NATO developed at least two functions which were also two self-representations: an alliance of *Collective Defence* and a *Security Community*. The end of the Cold War brought a huge change in NATO as it passed from "the practice of talking" to "the practice of doing" (Flokhart 2012),

---

2   Anthony Giddens defines ontological security as a "person's fundamental sense of safety in the world [which] includes a basic trust of other people [in order to] maintain a sense of psychological well-being and avoid existential anxiety" (Giddens 1991: 38–39). Jennifer Mitzen (2006), Brent J. Steele (2008) and others have developed and applied the concept to international relations, mainly translating the reflection on the individual to the state level.

3   From a methodological viewpoint, these nine years are a good compromise between the willingness to maintain a focus on contemporary events and the necessity to have enough sources to conduct meaningful research.

4   It is worth noting again that the arguments we put forth in the following pages are not tantamount to a justification or endorsement of the conduct of either NATO or Russia. Quite the opposite, we present the two actors' self-representations as they emerge from the words and actions of the actors themselves. On that basis and via the aforementioned theoretical lens, we infer what we think are the credible cognitive themes of NATO and Russia.

transforming the meaning of previous identities and adding new functions which also corresponded to new identities: NATO as an institution of *Collective Security and Crisis Management* and *Global NATO*. Let us explore these different identities in their evolution over time.

Collective Defence, enshrined in article V of the Washington Treaty, was the security guarantee of all member states (in NATO's jargon "Nations") against a possible attack from the USSR. Since collective defence was/is in the first place an act of solidarity among the members of the Alliance, it does not necessarily imply the use of coercive means, and has basically a deterrent function and is designed within the boundaries of international law:

> The Parties agree that an armed attack against one or more of them in Europe or North America shall be considered an attack against them all and consequently they agree that, if such an armed attack occurs, each of them, in exercise of the right of individual or collective *self-defence* recognised by Article 51 of the Charter of the United Nations, will assist the Party or Parties so attacked by taking forthwith, individually and in concert with the other Parties, such action as it deems necessary, *including* the use of armed force, *to restore and maintain the security of the North Atlantic area.*
>
> NATO 1949: §5. Emphasis added

This emphasis on Collective defence points to the use of force justified exclusively as a response to an external attack. "Aggression can only emanate from the outside; NATO itself does by definition pose no threat to any actor" (Behnke 2013: 81): It is clear that what Behnke derives from NATO's post-cold war self-representation has in reality been present since its inception.

NATO developed very early also as a *Community of values*, which resulted in a *Security Community*, that is a community in which peoples and countries would not feel threatened by each anymore, having agreed on norms (and practices) of peaceful resolution of conflict (art 1 of the Washington Treaty), and being bound by a sense of belonging, mutual sympathy and trust.[5] To be clear, NATO has never used the concept of "Security Community" to refer to itself, but the essence of the concept is contained in its documents since the founding Treaty, in which the core elements binding the Nations together are said to be a set of fundamental values: "The Parties [...] are determined to safeguard the freedom, common heritage and civilization of their peoples, *founded*

---

5   The first to name NATO a Security Community was Karl W. Deutsch in 1957. See Deutsch *et al.* (1957).

on the principles of democracy, individual liberty and the rule of law" (NATO 1949: Preamble. Emphasis added). Moreover, "[t]he Parties will contribute toward the further development of peaceful and friendly international relations by *strengthening their free institutions* [… They will also] *seek to eliminate conflict in their international economic policies"* (Ibid.: §2). In NATO's self-representation and worldview, therefore, since the inception, the shape and basic liberal values of the Parties (democracy, individual liberty, economic liberalism, rule of law) are core prerequisites of peaceful relations within the Alliance as well as of security in a broader context. Such principles have been recalled and reinforced at any occasion and particularly in the New Strategic Concepts issued after the end of the Cold War (1991, 1999, 2010), as we shall see below. This element, as pointed out by A. Behnke, is a fundamental one around which NATO defines the identity of the West and, by opposition, identifies what is the Other (Behnke 2013).

The Washington Treaty also established another principle which has remained a characteristic feature of the Alliance: its *open-door policy*. Article 10 states: "The Parties may, by unanimous agreement, invite any other European State in a position to further the principles of this Treaty and to contribute to the security of the North Atlantic area to accede to this Treaty" (NATO 1949). The only limits to being a potential candidate of the Alliance are therefore geographic (being a European State) and "merit" (being able to adhere to NATO's principles and to contribute to its security). Hence, since the beginning, NATO qualified as a largely *non-ascriptive* community:[6] beyond the geographic collocation of the would-be-member, there are no cultural, ethnic or linguistic pre-requisites required to become a member; rather what is required is adherence to a set of liberal values (by definition potentially universal according to the liberal worldview) and the willingness to contribute to European defence.

In the years that followed its inception NATO become a fundamental pillar of the Western bloc's deterrence and at the same time developed as a broadened security community, testified to by the enlargement to West Germany in 1955, which made the country's rearmament possible without triggering significant concerns by the other nations. Moreover, from the Harmel Report on, the Alliance enhanced its political *détente* capacity next to its deterrent one (NATO 1967).

The end of the Cold War put the very existence of NATO at risk and called for a redefinition of NATO's role. Interestingly enough, the process of reinvention was not based on the rejection of the founding Treaty or NATO's core identities,

---

6   An ascriptive community/group is one in which status is based on a predetermined factor such as age, sex, or race, and not on individual achievement.

but rather on the re-interpretation of their content in accordance with the new environmental conditions.

In the first place, NATO's response to the post-bipolar turmoil was a broadening of its understanding of security. "In contrast with the predominant threat of the past" – stated the New Strategic Concept of 1991 – "the risks to Allied security that remain are multi-faceted in nature and multi-directional. [...] Risks to Allied security are less likely to result from calculated aggression against the territory of the Allies, but rather from the adverse consequences of instabilities that may arise from the serious economic, social and political difficulties, including ethnic rivalries and territorial disputes, which are faced by many countries in central and Eastern Europe". Hence, transatlantic security cannot be provided solely by deterrence and defence, but also by providing *"one of the indispensable foundations for a stable security environment in Europe, based on the growth of democratic institutions* and commitment to the peaceful resolution of disputes" (NATO 1991. Emphasis added). In other words, the best way to defend the Alliance (and show its relevance) was extending to its unstable neighbourhood the fundamental elements of the Transatlantic security community: liberal democratic values and institutions (Lucarelli 2005: 85–105).

The first tool to stabilize Central and Eastern Europe and part of the former Soviet Space through democratic socialization, was the Partnership for Peace (PfP). The signatories of the PfP endorsed a Framework Document in which they committed to preserving a democratic society; to respect obligations undertaken in the field of arms control; and to respect the principles of international law. Ultimately, the PfP endorsed the conviction that "stability and security in the Euro-Atlantic areas can be achieved only through cooperation and common action. *Protection and promotion of fundamental freedoms and human rights, and safeguarding of freedom, justice and peace through democracy are shared values fundamental to the Partnership"* (NATO 1994: §2. Emphasis added). Moreover, active participation in the Partnership for Peace was presented as playing a fundamental role "in the evolutionary process of the expansion of NATO" (ibid.). All new NATO members since the end of the Cold War were previously involved in the PfP.

Enlargement was in fact the second (yet the most important) instrument for stabilizing Central and Eastern Europe by means of socialization and norms transfer (Epstein 2005). Any European nation willing to adhere to the non-ascriptive liberal values could potentially become a candidate, as stated in the 1995 *Study on NATO Enlargement* and recalled over and over again in subsequent years, even after the deterioration of relations with Russia: the Final Communique of all NATO Summits since 2009 openly recalled NATO's open door policy.[7] The metaphors used to legitimize the first post-Cold War enlargements are also telling of the view that the sharing of liberal values is regarded by NATO as a fundamental element of belonging to the Western "family". Reference to the notion of "family", noted K. Fierke (1995), introduced the notion of "commitment" and gave to the alliance a sense of stability that alliances usually do not have (see also: Klein 1990). Moreover, the notion of "family" (or home) recreated a clear distinction between Self and Others (inside and outside), between the realm of shared values and that of external challengers.

The "Community of values NATO", "Open doors NATO" and the "Cooperative NATO" become the fundamental, intertwined components of NATO's identity and practices, leading to the identification in the New Strategic Concept of 2010 of a core task called "Cooperative security" (next to "Collective defence" and "Crisis management"), as well as to several enlargements and Partnership programmes (Locatelli 2015).

At the same time, rather soon NATO developed two further functions which were a result of a redefinition of the NATO identity described above: NATO as a *Collective Security* institution and *Global NATO*.

Since NATO's involvement in the war in Bosnia (first to monitor arms embargoes, then to protect the no-fly zone and finally to "enforce peace"), NATO has performed functions in line with or aspiring to be coherent with the UN System of Collective Security. This brought a dramatic change to NATO's practices and saw for the first time NATO engaged in combat operations (Libya) – yet not always authorized by the UN, but claimed to be in line with the UN Charter (Kosovo) – and gaining a role in post-conflict stabilization (Bosnia, Kosovo, Afghanistan, and Iraq).[8] In 2010, creating a self-defining narrative out of a repeated practice, the 2010 Strategic Concept introduced "crisis management" as one of NATO's three core tasks (the others being Collective Defence and Cooperative Security – i.e. Partnerships). In a speech just before the presentation of the 2010 Security Strategy, Secretary General Rasmussen declared that:

> the second area, where we need reform [beyond modernising our defence and deterrence] is crisis management [...]. No other organisation can marshal, deploy and sustain NATO's military power. Which is why I am totally unconvinced by the media suggestions that after Afghanistan,

---

7 The list of NATO Summits and the link to their Final Communiques is available at: https://www.nato.int/cps/en/natolive/events.htm?search=true&event_types=Summit.

8 For a detailed overview of NATO's military operations, see: Sperling & Webber (2018: 887–913).

NATO might never take on another big mission. First and foremost, because I have no doubt that we will succeed in Afghanistan. And second,
because there will be other missions in future for which only NATO can
fit the bill. We will have to be ready.

RASMUSSEN 2010a

These changes contributed to a rediscovered perception of NATO – particularly by Russia – as an *imperial force* and "potentially a hostile power" (Brovkin
1999).

In 2017, approximately 18,000 military personnel are engaged in NATO missions, with operations of several types (from military post-conflict stabilization to anti-smuggling operations and disaster relief operations) in several
parts of the world (Afghanistan, Kosovo, the Mediterranean, support to the
African Union...). This means that NATO has not only become militarily active
on several fronts, but it has also turned *global. Global NATO* has been engaged
in conflicts and partnerships far beyond the traditional geographic area of concern; "partners across the globe" include countries such as Australia, Japan, the
Republic of Korea, New Zealand, Pakistan, Iraq, Afghanistan and Mongolia.
Although NATO has not explicitly used the term "Global NATO" to refer to itself,
the concept has been paraphrased in several documents and speeches, and has
been reinforced by practices. In his first appearance at the Munich Security
Conference in 2010 Secretary General Rasmussen opened his speech with three
points:

> First, that in an age of globalised insecurity, our territorial defence must
> begin beyond our borders;
>   Second, that our success in preserving our shared security – including
> through NATO – increasingly depends on how well we cooperate with
> others;
>   And third, that NATO should become a forum for consultation on
> worldwide security issues.
>   In short, we must take NATO's transformation to a new level – by con-
> necting the Alliance with the broader international system in entirely
> new ways. [...] *Security today is about active engagement, possibly very far
> from our own borders.*
>
> RASMUSSEN 2010

Both new NATOs (*Collective Security* and *Global NATO*) aimed to satisfy the
need of the Alliance to both respond to internal challenges (show its relevance
and legitimacy), and external challenges. Over time however, the different

identities of NATO have generated tension with each other and the allies have engaged in harsh debates on the geographic focus of NATO (East vs South), its main enemy (Russia vs Islamic terrorism) and its core tasks (collective security vs crisis management). Although NATO went global since 2003 (with the mission in Afghanistan), at the beginning there was not that much internal opposition. It was with Russia's intervention in Georgia, in 2008, that an internal debate started on what functions/identities NATO should prioritize. The East European nations feared that a Global NATO would not have enough strength to face and deter Russia's aggressive behaviour. Street demonstrations against Russia's behaviour occurred in several European states and the Eastern countries read Russia's behaviour as "[t]he imperial and forceful enforcement of raw power" not too dissimilar to the USSR's intervention in satellite countries in the Cold War, as Hungarian President Orban underlined (Index 2008). This led to concrete measures (e.g. the instalment of NATO forces in Poland), but not to a full representation of Russia as NATO's "negative Other" on the side of NATO. Dialogue never ceased (Haas 2009) and, on September 2009, Secretary General Rasmussen even spoke of "a new beginning" of NATO-Russia relations (Rasmussen 2009).

Russia's annexation of Crimea in 2014 was running against such principles and, for the first time since the end of the Cold War, the table of cooperation was frozen, sanctions were imposed on Moscow and NATO's self-identification started to be juxtaposed to Russia. A diachronic evolution can be detected in the discourses by Secretary General Rasmussen, who passed from identifying Russia as "a great European Power", to conceiving of Russia as "a danger" (Ališauskas 2015).

Since the annexation of Crimea, despite diverging views among the allies and different communicative styles of Secretary Generals Rasmussen (2009–2014) and Stoltenberg (2014-), looking at both NATO Summits Final Communiques of the Wales and Warsaw Summits, and the Secretary general's discourses, three main trends can be detected in relation to NATO's self-identification:

1. Renewed attention to its collective defence identity (with respect to its Collective security one), yet always with reference to NATO's shared values. As the Wales Declaration stated, "NATO remains the transatlantic framework for strong collective defence and the essential forum for security consultations and decisions among Allies" (NATO 2014). The Warsaw Declaration recalled that "The greatest responsibility of the Alliance is to protect and defend our territory and our populations against attack, as set out in Article 5 of the Washington Treaty. And so renewed emphasis has been placed on deterrence and collective defence" (NATO 2016). Eventually "To protect and defend our indivisible security and our common

values, the Alliance must and will continue fulfilling effectively all three core tasks as set out in the Strategic Concept: collective defence, crisis management, and cooperative security" (ibid.). In the Secretary General's communication there has been a constant attempt to emphasise that collective defence has always been and continues to be at NATO's core. Yet, if Secretary General Stoltenberg has made more than one reference to the need to cooperate with Russia, Secretary General Rasmussen and – more so – the Eastern members of NATO have underlined repeatedly that NATO's core business is Article V and that Russia is the main enemy, whose goal is "the return of the territories and sphere of influence once possessed by the Soviet Union" (Böller 2018, 22).

2. A shift from a predominant focus on *Global* NATO (with Rasmussen), to renewed attention to *Regional* NATO (as called for by the Baltic States and Poland), albeit never abandoning reference to NATO's global responsibilities in the maintenance of the liberal order (see below) (ibid.). Renewed attention to NATO's regional role (and challenges) next to its global role, is present in both Wales and Warsaw Summits' Final Communiques. In the latter, "Russia" is quoted 56 times, while "terrorism" 16. Physical threats to the Alliance territory are spelled out as coming from its Southern and the Eastern borders, more than from general global threats.

3. A confirmation of *Liberal* NATO's identity and the relative identification as the relevant – negative – Other, with respect to this very identity. As example is provided by Rasmussen's talk in Tallinn in May 2014:

> Freedom. Democracy. The rule of international law. The inviolability of borders. And the right of nations to decide their own security arrangements. These values and these norms are essential for our way of life. [...] But now, Russia is violating these very values. [...] I deeply regret that Russia currently seems to view NATO as an adversary rather than as a partner. This is not an approach we favour. But we are ready to meet the challenge.
>
> RASMUSSEN 2014

Talking at the 2014 Munich conference, Stoltenberg conveyed a similar message and underlined NATO's global responsibilities in the defence of the challenged liberal order:

> Last year was a turning point: for European security and for the global order. Here in Europe, we see a dangerous pattern of Russian behaviour: annexation, aggressive actions and intimidation. [...] North Africa and

the Middle East are also in turmoil. [...] But does this mean that the international order is on the brink of collapse? My answer – is no. Not as long as the guardians of the international order remain ready to act to uphold international rules and the vision of a Europe whole, free and at peace. Since its foundation, NATO *has been a resolute guardian of the international order*. That order is being challenged. And we must do our utmost to protect it.

> STOLTENBERG 2015

NATO shared values and principles are recalled in all NATO's documents and the two latest Final Communiques reiterated the concept and linked it to NATOs global role: "NATO Allies form a unique community of values committed to the principles of individual liberty, democracy, human rights, and the rule of law. The Alliance is convinced that these shared values and our security are strengthened when we work with our wide network of partners around the globe".

> NATO 2014

What can we conclude about NATO's strategic culture? In terms of self-identification, NATO has always had several identities that have evolved over time and around which there has been (particularly in recent years) a degree of internal dissent. However, one element more than any other has remained constant in NATO's self-portrait: the liberal-democratic core of NATO's values which make it a non-ascriptive community and a guarantor of the liberal order at the regional and – potentially – at the global level.

NATO's worldview is also based on the idea that its values and institutions are part of the West's identity, but at the same time potentially exportable. NATO's expansion coincides with the endorsement in the alliance of countries sharing the same values and hence belonging to the same family. What is more, the existence of forces who do not share these values is inevitably a threat to the ontological security of the Alliance and its members. At the same time, a potentially global NATO, enlarging and engaging on the basis of guiding values, is analogously a threat to third parties not fully sharing similar values: it can be perceived as a potential "liberal Leviathan" (Ikenberry 2011).

3   Russia's Strategic Culture

If NATO is the Leviathan, then Russia could be the Behemoth. As mentioned in the introduction, the historical divergence between these two actors could not be accounted for by looking merely at material interests. Reciprocal misunderstanding and strategic incompatibilities run deeper than that and emerge from NATO's and Russia's subjective representations of the self, the Other, and the world. As in the case of the Atlantic Alliance, the analysis of official documents and leaders' speeches in the years 2008–2016 unveils a series of elements particularly relevant for the reconstruction of Russia's strategic culture – starting from its self-perception.

The first element of Russia's self-perception is a constitutive sense of *grandeur*. A latent feeling of superiority is central in Russian political cognition and gives rise to Great Power aspirations (Urnov 2014).[9] This self-representation shines through all strategic documents and provides a point of convergence for the different voices of the political-ideological debate at the domestic level. For example, the National Security Strategy (NSS) of 2009 clearly states that Russia has "sufficient potential to [grant] its entrenchment among global leaders" in economic and political terms (Strategii 2009: §9), in order to achieve a role that – according to the Foreign Policy Concept (FPC) of 2008 – is "well-deserved" (Kontseptsiia 2008: Section II). Later editions re-propose the same concept not as a mere aspiration, but as a concrete reality. *Inter alia*, the NSS 2015 stresses "[...] the Russian Federation's role in resolving the most important international problems, settling military conflicts, and ensuring strategic stability" (Strategii 2015: §8). Beyond explicit declarations, the aspiration to *velikoderzhavnost'* transpires from the overall rhetoric of these documents and their description of Russia's interests as certainly greater in scope than those of a small or even medium power (Kontseptsiia 2008: Sections II, IV; Kontseptsiia 2013: §4, 42–94; Kontseptsiia 2016: §3, 49–99; Strategii 2009: §21–24; Strategii 2015: §30–31).

In addition, "greatpowerness" is rendered negatively by communicating a deep dissatisfaction for the international, Western-dominated status quo, which is inherently "inadequate" because it resists Russia's efforts to be recognized as a Great Power (Strategii 2009: §8, 17).[10] Such a sense of "unattended greatness" is widespread in Russian elites' discourses, too. With some differences in style and practical implications, rhetoric showed under both Medvedev and Putin considerable resentment for post-1991 political developments and underlined the need for historical redemption for Russia (Clunan 2009: 114; Mankoff 2012: Chapter 1; Nalbandov 2016: 4–5). More in general, the

---

9   Indeed, all books on Russian foreign policy or identity refer more or less explicitly to Russia's sense of superiority.

10   See also: Kontseptsiia (2008), Sections I, II; Kontseptsiia (2013: §4, 14); Kontseptsiia (2016: §5, 61, 70); Strategii (2015: §15–18, 106). In addition, both versions of the Military Doctrine (see below) list NATO as a danger for Russia.

self-entitlement to shape and manage the global order cuts across the entire political-ideological debate. Liberals, nationalists, and Eurasianists all see the need to carve out a relevant space for Russia in the world, whatever the chosen means (Mankoff 2012: Chapter 2; White & Feklyunina 2014: 101–128).[11]

A second crucial component of Russia's self-perception deals with the sources of the above-mentioned sense of *grandeur*. Russia's *velikoderzhavnost'* has no root in material reality, but rather in historical experiences and a peculiar socio-political constitution. In other words, the Russian quest for greatness is legitimate because it is a consequence of Russia's civilizational might and uniqueness.[12] This point is stressed in all versions of the NSS, where traditions and values are described as the fundamental underpinnings of the country's interests and identity (Strategii 2009: §80–84; Strategii 2015: §76–79, 82). As Putin has stressed more than once, these transcendent elements "made up the moral and spiritual foundation of civilization" and have prominence over the material domain (Putin 2014b).[13]

Moreover, the morality of the Russian Orthodox Church permeates this discourse and brings to bear its ecumenical vision on the formulation of strategic views (Kontseptsiia 2008: Sections II, III.3; Kontseptsiia 2013: §21, 32; Kontseptsiia 2016: §19, 38). Ultimately in fact, Orthodoxy offers a pre-constituted cultural-cognitive layer linking faith, political action, and moral ends (Engström 2014). In so doing, it explicitly elevates Russia above other civilizations and transforms Moscow into a global peacemaker (Nalbandov 2016: 31). The religious interpretation of Russian civilization is the kernel of the Eurasianist discourse and appears, even if scaled down, in the dominant nationalist rhetoric as well. According to both positions, Russia cannot accept unipolarity, Western

---

11 Liberals, nationalists, and Eurasianists are the three categories usually employed to classify the positions in Russia's political debate. With regard to foreign policy, liberals focus on (economic) cooperation and closer relations with the West to harvest absolute gains, while nationalists take a more individualist stance that gives preeminence to Russia's relative gains. Instead, Eurasianist foreign policy has the final aim of reuniting the Eurasian landmass under Russia's control. These are somehow simplified definitions that do not account for all the shades of these ideologies, but an extensive literature could be consulted to gain more precise knowledge on the issue.

12 It could be argued that a material source of Russia's sense of *grandeur* is its status as a nuclear power equal to the United States. However, in cognitive terms this is a consequence, not a cause, of Russia's greatness. It is to say that Russia worked to reach that status because of its own self-perception as a Great Power – and not the other way around. The status as nuclear power is a symbol of Russian might and an instrument to enforce Russia's self-perceptions, but as such it becomes a posteriori with respect to the self-perception itself. Without the latter, to reach nuclear status would be void of meaning.

13 Medvedev has been less vocal about values but has always recognized at least implicitly their importance. See for example his interview for the German newspaper Der Spiegel (2009) (especially "Our values […] live with".).

dominance, or the imposition of others' models of socio-economic development; NATO's practices of cooperative security (from enlargement to partnerships), rather than a means of stability are interpreted as a source of concern.
To drop Russian values would mean to lose Russia's uniqueness and, with it,
the right and duty to shape global affairs (Mankoff 2012: Chapter 2; White &
Feklyunina 2014: 120–128). In other words, Russian nature and aspirations are
necessary and non-negotiable.

Building on these cognitive premises, Russia's self-perception commands
the fulfilment of a special mission: to act "as a counterbalance in international
affairs and the development of the global civilization" (Kontseptsiia 2013: §25;
almost identical in Kontseptsiia 2016: §22). In that light, Moscow develops its
foreign and security policy in order to resist socio-economic contaminations
from outside and to hinder the spread of moral decay and physical destruction –
allegedly thriving beyond the borders of the *Russkii Mir*. The liberal order that
"Global NATO" aims to defend is precisely what Moscow wants to withhold.
Differently from NATO's case, no universalist tension fits in this logic. Clearly,
Moscow's cultural-civilizational outlook implies a paternalistic and possessive
approach towards the former Soviet space. Here, Russia claims special rights
deriving from its duty to defend the super-ethos allegedly unifying the post-Soviet space. According to this perspective, sovereignty seems to be intended by
Russia in cultural – not formal, geographical – terms. The so-called Medvedev
Doctrine already gave a taste of such a view (Vesti News 2008), then confirmed
by Putin's choices about Ukraine (Putin 2014b). By the same token, Moscow's
prerogatives seem to be constricted within defined cultural borders and therefore Russian behaviour acquires a conservative nature, not an expansionist
one. Even the seizure of Crimea in the Russian perspective is not to be considered as annexation. According to Moscow, it was a legitimate act based on
the necessity to defend Russia's reserved dominion, whose borders are cultural
borders. Since the peninsula (and Ukraine at large) falls within such cultural
space, the crisis outcome is not conceived by Russia as an expansion, but as the
reaffirmation of the natural state of things against the threat of dispossession
coming from the West.[14]

However, how to explain the recent entanglement in Syria? It falls out of the
Russkii Mir and seems to be motivated by mere strategic interests. Nonetheless,
the cultural-constructivist reading proposed above still applies. It is worth re-
membering that Russia's self-perception implies the aspiration to *velikoderzhavnost'* and that this latter, coupled with the civilizational outlook and the

---

14   Particularly significant in this sense is the propagandistic documentary "Krym. Put' na
       Rodinu", describing Crimea's "way home" – i.e., its return to Russia. Available on YouTube
       at: https://www.youtube.com/watch?v=c8nMhCMphYU.

syndrome of "unattended greatness", brings about the rejection of US' global supremacy. Moscow cognitively refuses a reality in which only the US acts as a Great Power; by definition, Russia *is* a Great Power and as such should be entitled to the same prerogatives. Citing Skak (2013), this state of things often generates a sort of "copycat behavior". In other words, to satisfy its self-perception, Russia tends to copy the same behaviour as the US – the Great Power *par excellence*. At the same time however, Moscow orients its own actions towards opposite stances – so as to gratify its sense of moral superiority vis-à-vis Washington. This may be the case of the Russian intervention in Syria, where Moscow pretends to play a decisive role but proposes a solution to the conflict different from the US.

It is clear how the Russian logic, however conservative in nature, is also conflict-prone. This leads to the discussion of the second constitutive element of Strategic Culture: *Worldviews*. In general terms, Russia's worldview is mechanistic and holistic. It conceives of international affairs, and social relations at large, as a thick web of interlocked events and cause-effect dynamics that cut across internal and external domains. Everything is bound together in an organic whole regulated à-la Hobbes by the sheer logic of power and where even the most complex features are simplified to a contrast between opposite forces. It is possible to find a trace of this reasoning in the emphasis put on the "competition for resources" and shifts in the "balance of power", as well as the acknowledgement that "problems may be resolved using military force", according to "a rational and pragmatic foreign policy" (Strategii 2009: §12–13. Identical in: Strategii 2015: §13–14).

These statements reflect a zero-sum mentality that fits well within a Realist theoretical framework. It is no surprise, given the fetishization of geopolitical thinking after the collapse of the Soviet system (Sergunin 2004; Solovyev 2004). The dissolution of Socialist ideology created a cognitive vacuum that needed to be filled somehow, in order to regain a route to follow while relating with other subjects of international politics. Classical geopolitics seemed to be apt for this purpose and progressively assumed prominence in Russia, acquiring veins of scientism that are not so different from religious dogmatism – as in A. Dugin's Eurasianist discourse. Indeed, the fortunes of geopolitics in Russia depend precisely on the mechanistic and competitive worldview it conveys, that resonates with Russian strategic culture (Skak 2013: 10–12; Skak 2016).

However, Russia's worldview refutes a purely material focus and thus resembles Realism only superficially. As introduced above when dealing with self-perception, Russia broadly focuses on civilizational and transcendent issues. Similarly, Moscow perceives competition mainly in cultural terms. It is a competition between civilizations, based on opposite moral principles and not on contrasting objective interests. Each edition of the FPC from 2008 to 2016 explicated this view, highlighting the "civilizational dimension" of contemporary global dynamics, endangered by "attempts to impose values on others" in the face of the fact that "cultural and civilizational diversity [...] and multiple development models have been emerging" (Kontseptsiia 2016: §4–5. See also: Kontseptsiia 2008: Sections II, III.3; Kontseptsiia 2013: §13–14). This cultural and often moralistic view of international relations brings about a simplistic model of global affairs in which the easy labels of Good and Evil, oppressor and oppressed, in synergy with the mechanistic framework addressed above, reinforce the popular rhetoric in favour of *mnogopoliarnost'* – multipolarity (Clunan 2009: 54–60, 91–92, 128–130; Medvedev 2011; Mankoff 2012: Chapter 1; Putin 2014a). In such a multipolar setting, Russia would clearly assume the role of civilizational hub and tensions with the West seem to be almost unavoidable not just because of the inescapable zero-sum dynamic of international politics, but also because of NATO's liberal oriented worldview – which is at odds with Russia's "civilizational protectionism".

The holistic component of Russia's worldview is not reflected simply in the intermingling of material and non-material dimensions of reality – both subjected to the same mechanistic, conflictual logic. Holism appears as well in Moscow's identification of perils and relative countermeasures. The Military Doctrines (MDs) of both 2010 and 2014 present the reader with a long list of dangers and threats – the former only potentially causing harm to Russia, while the latter harmful in themselves. Dangers, in addition, are subdivided into two categories: internal and external (Doktrina 2010: §8–10; Doktrina 2014: §12–14). Whatever the formal classification, the two (three) groups of perils are compatible in their substance. All the events and conditions listed could be described as results of the purposeful action of external agents interested in interfering with Russia's unity and (cultural) sovereignty; as such, they could or must require a military response.

Two corollaries are worth mentioning. First, the host of dangers and threats listed in the MDs provides textual evidence for well-known Russian existential anxiety. The old rhetoric of the "besieged fortress" seems to hold true during the timeframe addressed. A constant feeling of precariousness afflicts Russia, as if adverse forces were continuously attempting to undermine its existence and inner constitution, generating perils that could strike at all political levels both within and outside of Moscow's sovereign space. Secondly, and most importantly, in the Russian worldview the very difference between internal and external sources of harm is blurred. Not only because they are put on the same level in Russia's programmatic documents, but also because they all share the same non-Russian origin. This latter characteristic is in line with the self-perception described above, which depicts Russia as lacking internal contradictions possibly leading to spiritual disunity. Even the multi-ethnic and multi-religious nature of the Federation is not a problem, since the *Russkii* super-ethos cuts across these cleavages and allegedly provides stability. Hence, given that Russia is stable by definition, even classically domestic perils such as subversion and revolution necessarily have an external origin. The rhetoric of foreign-led colour revolutions is the product of this logic (Putin 2014; Skak 2016: 324–325, 334–335).

The holistic conception of reality and the intermingling of external and internal domains do not simply ease the externalization of domestic problems, but impact the very concept of force and its use. It shines through the overall phrasing of the MDs that Russia conceives of the use of force as an ordinary instrument to deal with problems. While it is occasionally remembered that military means are last resort options, the use of force is clearly presented as just one of the tools at Russia's disposal. MDs state that "[...] the Russian Federation uses political, diplomatic, legal, economic, environmental, informational, military and other instruments for the protection of national interests". (Doktrina 2010: §4; analogue phrasing in: Doktrina 2014: §5). Military means appear on the same level as other tools more or less coercive in nature, reflecting Russia's broad definition of military security, which has the potential to embrace areas that classically fall outside of its domain (Doktrina 2010: §6; Doktrina 2014: §8). The restrictions applied to the deployment of armed forces do not ensure that Moscow will not use them, because – coherently with what has been discussed so far – the terms "aggression" and "existential threat" may have a different meaning for Russia (Doktrina 2010: §20–22; Doktrina 2014: §22–27). Consequently, NATO should expect Russia to resort to military, coercive means even when this would be inconceivable for Western standards. For Moscow, the empowerment of the Ministry of Defence is not a foreign policy failure: it is just another way to deal with other states, an alternative to the Ministry of Foreign Affairs.

Indeed, in the eyes of Russia this could not be any different, given the perceived characteristics of contemporary conflicts. The MD 2010 already presented a view of conflicts à-la Gerasimov, who invented no doctrine but just took stock of a consolidated opinion among Russian officials (Gerasimov 2013; Galeotti 2014). According to this view, Moscow sees conflict as more than a simple clash between conventional forces on the ground. As for competition in general, conflict falls outside the restricted military domain, inextricably intertwined with the social dimension of politics Russia (Doktrina 2010: §12–14; Doktrina 2014: §15). For Russia, conflict is everywhere, and everything could be an object of conflict (Covington 2016, 26–38). On the theoretical-political side, this means that in Moscow's eyes the barrier between peace and war blur, generating a grey zone in which the conversion between peaceful and conflictual conduct is very rapid and commands a sort of latent, permanent mobilization. On the practical-military side, asymmetric and non-conventional means of conflict and so-called hybrid warfare find their cognitive underpinning. Soft-power, informational war, and non-military tactics are all mentioned in NSSs, FPCs, and MDs both as sources of peril and, more or less explicitly, opportunities for Russia (Doktrina 2010: §12–14, 31–34, 41, 46–47; Doktrina 2014: §15, 36–42; Kontseptsiia 2008: Sections II, III.6; Kontseptsiia 2013: §9–10, 20; Kontseptsiia 2016: §6–9, 17–18; Strategii 2009: §27, 30, 93; Strategii 2015: §12, 21, 41, 43). As a consequence of the perceived social character of conflict and its theoretical-political implications, new instruments and areas of action become available for Defence. Moscow takes advantage of them to hit at the very kernel of the enemy – its society, its values, its organizational centres – before the enemy could do the same to Russia. In other words, Russia uses the same instruments it fears.

4   Conclusion: An Unbearable Clash of Strategic Cultures?

The analysis of the Strategic culture of NATO and Russia, in the double form of self-representations and Worldviews, provides cognitive lenses through which the deep roots of enmity can be analysed. Russia and NATO's Strategic cultures differ quite significantly in several respects. A fundamental one is their understanding of the cultural foundation of the Self, which is also the legitimation of their role as world powers. In the case of NATO, the identity and legitimacy of the organization is built on a set of shared political and civic values with no immediate connection to religious beliefs or to broad cultural roots. The liberal values on which NATO is founded (liberty, democracy, rule of law) by definition are not ascriptive and can be made one's own through a process of socialization (and civilization). Achievement, transformation, and socialization make the broadening of the value-based community possible. Russia's core values are those of an ascriptive community in which the borders of the community of reference (*Russkii Mir*) are defined by language and historically shaped cultural features. The implications in terms of both Self-Other representations and Worldviews are very relevant: the borders of NATO's family are much less objectively defined and subject to broadening through processes of socialization and adaptation. The borders of the *Russkii Mir* are more fixed and defined by the presence of Russian communities. This does not make the *Russkii Mir* a completely closed geographic entity, but implies that no membership by means of socialization is possible. It also implies a specific emphasis on the need to defend the cultural roots of the community of reference. A final implication is the inner relation to the past: although both NATO and Russia have been engaged in a process of "re-actualization of the past" through which they have decoded the other side's practices in light of past experiences, NATO's worldview is *modern* (progress oriented, evolutionary, state-based), Russia's worldview is *pre-modern* (conservative, static, community-based):[15] NATO's ontology is transformative, Russia's ontology is conservative.

Do these differences necessarily imply conflict? Not necessarily, but they can. The transformative and expansive nature of NATO easily clashes with what we have defined above as Russia's "existential anxiety". At the same time, Russia's provocative behaviour in areas of its Cold War sphere of influence, its unrestrained attitude towards the possibility of using force and the blurring distinction between peace and war, are all perceived as a direct threat to the Alliance. In fact, the threat is both to the safety of NATO's nations and to the internal solidarity among Alliance member states (put under strain by Russia's un-conventional means of pressure). If we were to summarize, relations between NATO and Russia in recent years has developed in such a way that each one represents a source of ontological insecurity to the other. Either the two will be able to deconstruct such images by means of real "confidence building measures", or a new Cold War in different clothing risks taking shape.

Acknowledgment

The authors are grateful to James Sperling and Mark Webber for comments and suggestions to a previous version of the chapter.

Bibliography

Al išauskas, T. (2015). 'NATO, Russia and the Discourse of Danger: Analysing the Rhetoric of NATO Secretary General A.F. Rasmussen', *Lithuanian Foreign Policy Review*, 34(1): 34–60.

Behnke, A. (2013). *NATO's Security Discourse After the Cold War. Representing the West.* Abingdon: Routledge.

---

15   Neither of the two actors is *quasi post-modern* (progress oriented, evolutionary, but with a redefined concept of sovereignty in the states and beyond them), as is the European Union.

Biehl, H., Giegerich, B. and Jonas, A. (eds.) (2013). *Strategic Cultures in Europe. Security and Defence Policies Across the Continent*. Potsdam: Springer.

Böller, F. (2018). 'Guardian of the International Order? NATO's Contested Identity, the Discourses of Secretaries General, and the Ukraine Crisis', *East European politics*, 34(2): 217–237.

Brovkin, V. (1999). 'Discourse on NATO in Russia during the Kosovo War', *Demokratizatsiya*, 7(4): 544–560.

Cerutti, F. (2008). 'Why political identity and legitimacy matter in the European Union', pp. 3–22, in F. Cerutti and S. Lucarelli (eds.), *The Search for a European Identity*. London: Routledge.

Clunan, A. (2008). *The Social Construction of Russia's Resurgence: Aspirations, Identity, and Security Interests*. Baltimore: Johns Hopkins University Press.

Covington, S.R. (2016). *The Culture of Strategic Thought Behind Russia's Modern Approaches to Warfare*. Cambridge: Harvard Kennedy School Belfer Center, http://www.belfercenter.org/sites/default/files/legacy/files/Culture%20of%20Strategic%20Thought%203.pdf.

Der Spiegel. (2009). 'Oil and Gas is Our Drug. Spiegel Interview with Russian President Dmitry Medvedev', *Der Spiegel*, 9 November, http://www.spiegel.de/international/world/spiegel-interview-with-russian-president-dmitry-medvedev-oil-and-gas-is-our-drug-a-660114-3.html.

Deutsch, K.W. et al. (eds.) (1957). *Political Community and the North Atlantic Area: International Organization in the Light of Historical Experience*. Princeton: Princeton University Press.

Diamond, L. (2014). 'Russia and the Threat to Liberal Democracy', *The Atlantic*, 9 December, https://www.theatlantic.com/international/archive/2016/12/russia-liberal-democracy/510011/.

Doktrina. (2010). 'Voennaia doktrina Rossiiskoi Federatsii', *Kremlin website*, 5 February, http://kremlin.ru/supplement/461 (English version available at: http://carnegieendowment.org/files/2010russia_military_doctrine.pdf).

Doktrina. (2014). 'Voennaia doktrina Rossiiskoi Federatsii', *Russian Federation MoD website*, 26 December, http://www.mid.ru/documents/10180/822714/41d527556bec8deb3530.pdf/d899528d-4f07-4145-b565-1f9ac290906c (English version available at: https://www.offiziere.ch/wp-content/uploads-001/2015/08/Russia-s-2014-Military-Doctrine.pdf).

Engström, M. (2014). 'Contemporary Russian Messianism and New Russian Foreign Policy', *Contemporary Security Policy*, 35(3): 356–379.

Epstein, R.A. (2005). 'Nato Enlargement and the Spread of Democracy: Evidence and Expectation', *Security Studies*, 14(1): 63–105.

Flockhart, T. (2012). 'Towards a strong NATO narrative: From a "practice of talking" to a "practice of doing"', *International Politics*, 49(1): 78–97.

Galeotti, M. (2014). 'The "Gerasimov Doctrine" and Russian Non-Linear War', *In Moscow's Shadows*, 6 July, https://inmoscowsshadows.wordpress.com/2014/07/06/the-gerasimov-doctrine-and-russian-non-linear-war/.

Gerasimov, V. (2013). 'Tsennost' nauki v predvidenii', *Voenno-promyshlennyi Kur'er*, 27 February, http://vpk-news.ru/sites/default/files/pdf/VPK_08_476.pdf.

Giddens, A. (1991). *Modernity and Self-Identity: Self and Society in the Late Modern Age.* Stanford: Stanford University Press.

Gray, C.S. (1999). 'Strategic Culture as a Context: The First Generation Theory Strikes Back', *Review of International Studies,* 25(1): 49–69.

Haas, M. (2009). 'NATO-Russia relations after the Georgian Conflict', *Clingendael,* 7, https://www.cligendael.org/sites/default/files/pdfs/20090000_cscp_artikel_mhaas.pdf.

Index. (2008). 'Orbánnak 56 jutott eszébe az orosz hadmûveletekrõl', *Index,* 14 August, http://index.hu/belfold/ovgruzorsz08/.

Johnston, A.I. (1995). 'Thinking About Strategic Culture', *International Security,* 19(4): 32–64.

Klein, B.S. (1990). 'How the West Was One: Representational Politics of NATO', *International Studies Quarterly,* 34(3): 311–325.

Kozyrev, A.V. (1992). 'Russia and Human Rights', *Slavic Review,* 51(2): 287–293.

Kontseptsiia. (2013). 'Kontseptsiia vneshnei politiki Rossiiskoi Federatsii', *Kremlin website,* 12 February, http://static.kremlin.ru/media/events/files/41d447a0ce9f5a96bdc3.pdf (English version available at: http://www.mid.ru/foreign_policy/official_doc uments/-/asset_publisher/CptICkB6BZ29/content/id/122186).

Kontseptsiia. (2016). 'Kontseptsiia vneshnei politiki Rossiiskoi Federatsii', *Kremlin website,* 30 November, http://kremlin.ru/acts/bank/41451 (English version available at: http://www.mid.ru/foreign_policy/news/-/asset_publisher/cKNonkJE02Bw/content/id/2542248).

Kontseptsiia. (2018). 'Kontseptsiia vneshnei politiki Rossiiskoi Federatsii', *Kremlin website,* 15 July, http://kremlin.ru/acts/news/785 (English version available at: http://en.kremlin.ru/supplement/4116).

Locatelli, A. (2015). 'Handle With Care: The Limits And Prospects of Nato Partnership Policy', pp. 82–96, in Fassi, E., S. Lucarelli and A. Marrone (eds). *What NATO, for What Threats? Warsaw and Beyond.* Brussels: NATO HQ, http://www.act.nato.int/images/stories/events/2015/acor/ac15_final.pdf.

Lucarelli, S. (2005). 'NATO and the European System of Liberal-democratic Security Communities', pp. 85–105, in Flockhart, T. (ed.), *Socializing Democratic Norms: The Role of International Organizations for the Construction of Europe,* Basingstoke: Palgrave.

Mankoff, J. (2012). *Russian Foreign Policy: The Return of Great Power Politics.* Lanham: Rowman & Littlefield.

Mearsheimer, J.J. (2014). 'Why the Ukraine Crisis is the West's Fault', *Foreign Affairs*, 18 August.

Medvedev, D. (2011). 'Prezident Rossii vystupil na otkrytii Vsemirnogo ekonomicheskogo foruma', *Kremlin website*, 26 January, http://kremlin.ru/events/president/news/10163 (English version at: http://en.kremlin.ru/events/president/news/10163).

Mitzen, J. (2006). 'Ontological Security in World Politics: State Identity and the Security Dilemma', *European Journal of International Relations*, 12(3): 341–370.

Nalbandov, R. (2016). *Not by Bread Alone: Russian Foreign Policy Under Putin*. Lincoln: Potomac Books.

North Atlantic Treaty Organization (NATO) (1967). 'Harmel Report – The Future Tasks of the Alliance', *NATO website*, 13 December, https://www.nato.int/cps/en/natohq/official_texts_26700.htm.

North Atlantic Treaty Organization (NATO) (1994). 'Partnership for Peace: Invitation Document', *NATO website*, January 10, https://www.nato.int/cps/ic/natohq/official_texts_24468.htm.

North Atlantic Treaty Organization (NATO) (1995). 'Study on NATO Enlargement', *NATO website*, 3 September, https://www.nato.int/cps/en/natohq/official_texts_24733.htm.

North Atlantic Treaty Organization (NATO) (2014). 'Wales Summit Declaration', *NATO website*, 5 September, https://www.nato.int/cps/ic/natohq/official_texts_112964.htm.

North Atlantic Treaty Organization (NATO) (2016). 'Warsaw Summit Declaration', *NATO website*, 9 July, https://www.nato.int/cps/en/natohq/official_texts_133169.htm.

North Atlantic Treaty Organization (NATO) (1949). 'Washington Treaty', *NATO website*, 4 April, https://www.nato.int/cps/en/natohq/official_texts_17120.htm.

Pouliot, V. (2010). *International Security in Practice. The Politics of NATO-Russia Diplomacy*. Cambridge: Cambridge University Press.

Putin, V. (2014). 'Obrashchenie Prezidenta Rossiiskoi Federatsii', *Kremlin website*, 18 March, http://kremlin.ru/events/president/news/20603 (English version at: http://en.kremlin.ru/events/president/news/20603).

Putin, V. (2014a). 'Peterburgskii mezhdunarodnyi ekonomicheskii forum', *Kremlin website*, 23 May, http://kremlin.ru/events/president/news/21080 (English version at: http://en.kremlin.ru/events/president/news/21080).

Putin, V. (2014b) 'Poslanie Prezidenta Federaln'omu Sobraniiu', *Kremlin website*, 12 December, http://kremlin.ru/events/president/news/19825 (English version at: http://en.kremlin.ru/events/president/news/19825).

Rasmussen, A.F. (2014). 'Defending Allies, Sharing Responsibility, Upholding Values', *NATO website*, 9 May, https://www.nato.int/cps/en/natohq/opinions_109757.htm?selectedLocale=en.

Rasmussen, A.F. (2010). 'NATO in the 21st Century: Towards Global Connectivity', *NATO website*, 7 February, https://www.nato.int/cps/en/natolive/opinions_61395 .htm.

Rasmussen, A.F. (2010a). 'The New Strategic Concept: Active Engagement, Modern Defence', *NATO website*, 8 October, https://www.nato.int/cps/en/natohq/opin ions_66727.htm.

Rasmussen, A.F. (2009). 'NATO and Russia: A New Beginning', *NATO website*, 18 September, https://www.nato.int/cps/su/natohq/opinions_57640.htm.

Rynning, S. (2003). 'The European Union: Towards a Strategic Culture?', *Security Dialogue,* 34(4): 479–496.

Sakwa, R. (2017). *Russia Against the Rest. The Post-Cold War Crisis of World Order*. Cambridge: Cambridge University Press.

Sergunin, A.A. (2004). 'Discussions of International Relations in Post-Communist Russia', *Communist and Post-Communist Studies,* 37(1): 19–35.

Skak, M. (2016). 'Russian Strategic Culture: The Role of Today's Chekisty', *Contemporary Politics,* 22(3): 324–341.

Skak, M. (2013). 'The Strategic Culture of Russia: One Paradigm, Multiple Strategies', Paper presented at the 13th Aleksanteri Conference on 'Russia and the World', University of Helsinki, 23–25 October, http://pure.au.dk/portal/files/56641059/Alek santeri_PAPER_2013.docx.

Snegovaya, M. (2014). 'The Ukraine Crisis is not the West's Fault', *The Moscow Times,* 15 September, https://themoscowtimes.com/articles/ukraines-crisis-is-not-the-wests-fault-39411.

Solovyev, E.G. (2004). 'Geopolitics in Russia – Science or Vocation?', *Communist and Post-Communist Studies,* 37(1): 85–96.

Sperling, J. and Webber, M. (2018). 'NATO Operations', pp. 887–913, in Meijer, H. and M. Wyss (eds.), *The Handbook of European Defence Policies and Armed Forces*. Oxford: Oxford University Press.

Steele, B.J. (2008). *Ontological Security in International Relations: Self-Identity and the IR State*. London: Routledge.

Stoltenberg, J. (2015). 'Speech by NATO Secretary General Jens Stoltenberg at the Munich Security Conference', *NATO website*, February 6, https://www.nato.int/cps/en/ natohq/opinions_117320.htm.

Strategii. (2009). 'O Strategii natsional'noi bezopasnosti Rossiiskoi Federatsii do 2020 goda', *Russkaia Gazeta*, 19 May, https://rg.ru/2009/05/19/strategia-dok.html (English version available at: http://rustrans.wikidot.com/russia-s-national-security-strategy-to-2020).

Strategii. (2015). 'O Strategii natsional'noi bezopasnosti Rossiiskoi Federatsii', *Russkaia Gazeta*, 31 December, https://rg.ru/2015/12/31/nac-bezopasnost-site-dok.html

(English version available at: http://www.ieee.es/Galerias/fichero/OtrasPublicacio nes/Internacional/2016/Russian-National-Security-Strategy-31Dec2015.pdf).

Urnov, M. (2014). 'Greatpowerness as the Key Element of Russian Self-consciousness Under Erosion', *Communist and Post-Communist Studies*, 47(3–4): 305–322.

Vesti News. (2008).'Polnyi tekst interv'iu Medvedeva rossiiskim telekanalam', *Vesti News website*, 31 August, https://www.vesti.ru/doc.html?id=205510.

Webber, M., Sperling, J. and Smith, M.A. (2012). *NATO's Post-Cold War Trajectory. Decline or Regeneration?*. Basingstoke: Palgrave.

White, S. and V. Feklyunina. (2014). *Identities and Foreign Policies in Russia, Ukraine, and Belarus*. Basingstoke: Macmillan.

Yost, D.S. (2009). 'Assurance and US extended deterrence in NATO', *International Affairs*, 85(4): 755–780.

CHAPTER 12

The Western Decline, Multipolarity and the Challenges of Identity in the Making of Russian Foreign Policy

Stefano Bianchini

Despite a few short periods of smooth cooperation, misperceptions and divergences between Russia and the West have widened since the collapse of the Soviet Union. Some of the most relevant problems in their relationship will be briefly mentioned here below and some are not new in their essence. Unquestionably, however, the Ukrainian crisis has exacerbated the confrontation. As a reaction to the annexation of Crimea and the war in eastern Ukraine, the US/EU sanctions against Moscow, Russia's exclusion from the G8, the strengthened military presence of NATO on Russia's borders (particularly in the Baltic republics and Poland) and the different ideas of modernisation in terms of global governance promoted by the West are just but a few examples of a set of adopted measures aimed at challenging and marginalizing the international role of Russia.

Nevertheless, the Ukraine crisis and its aftermath has occurred in a broader and disorderly context, marked by declining US world authority, growing cacophony in the EU, and the rise of different global players. These circumstances are posing the Kremlin not only with challenges, but also opportunities to avoid marginalisation and reshape its external role, by juxtaposing a multilayered network of international organisations on to traditional western-centric policy. And in fact, Russian diplomacy has engaged in a pragmatic strategy which encompasses both the Eurasian and Euro-Pacific dimensions, while stimulating the search for a global identity profile.

In view of these considerations, and with the aim of understanding Russia's self-perception of its world role, this chapter investigates the most relevant obstacles and potential that Putin's foreign policy is facing in his effort to redefine Russia's place as a recognised great Power in a still disorderly and fluid world.[1]

---

1   This study benefited from a variety of sources, which include recent international literature (reported in the bibliography), Putin's statements, the documents and analysis published by the Valdai Discussion Club, the Carnegie Moscow Center, Russian Direct and others. Additionally, a series of fieldworks with open-ended interviews and qualitative observation were

The chapter is therefore structured in three main parts, focusing respectively on (1) the roots of Russia's disappointment with the West, (2) efforts to design a global strategy of multiple networks, with Russia playing a key role, and (3) the endeavour to construct an attractive, worldwide cultural identity of Russianness.

1   Russia's Disillusion with the West

Once Gorbachev was overthrown, as is well known, El'tsin expected a remarkable improvement in Russia's relations with the West, as a consequence of the role he personally played to put an end to the Soviet Union. The neoliberal economic policy carried out by Egor Gaidar and the neo-Atlantic foreign policy promoted by Andrei Kozyrev contributed to enhancing such expectations between 1992 and 1993 (Tsygankov 2013: 55–79 and 249; Sergounin 2003: 108–112).

Conversely, the West reacted very cautiously to post-Soviet Russian policies in terms of financial investments, trade, and endorsed partnership. This attitude was mostly motivated by the West's firm belief that it was the "obvious winner" of the Cold War, even though Russia continued to be considered a reliable nuclear partner, where it was wise to concentrate the nuclear weapons deployed in Ukraine, Belarus, and Kazakhstan. They, subsequently, transferred the weapons between 1994 and 1996, following a joint protocol signed with Russia and the US.

However, this recognition did not remove the firm belief in the West that Russia was a "defeated country" and a marginal player in international relations, disregarding the fact that the Cold War ended by agreement between the US and the USSR Presidents, Ronald Reagan and Mikhail Gorbachev respectively, after bilateral negotiations and mutual respectful engagement, between 1986 and 1988, as ambassador Matlock extensively explains in his eyewitness account (Jack F. Matlock Jr. 2004: 315–316; Savranskaya & Blanton 2016).

After all, the events that led to the Communist collapse and the demise of the Soviet Union occurred later and were triggered by internal, domestic factors. Honestly, the West had little to do with these developments. Rather, it was caught by surprise and was basically a "gratified witness". That said, the western narrative that prevailed among public opinion and political élites rapidly

conducted with scholars and activists during my study-visits. My special thanks to: Sansar Chakhirmaa, Nataliia Tsvetkova, Igor Gretskii, Konstantin Khudolei, Aleksandra Kuznetsova, Mariia Lagutina, Bulat Mubarashkin, Ilshat Mukhametzaripov, I.R. Nasyrov, Evgenii Rizhkov, Vasil Sakaev, Stanislav Tkachenko, and Oleg Zaznaev.

emphasised the end of European Communism as a patent victory of liberal democracies, paving the way for a radical alteration of the balance of power in Europe.

The image of Russia in the West suffered from additional shortcomings. For example, the brutality that marked the Constitutional crisis of 1993, when the Parliament was disbanded by force following a Presidential decision, provoked hundreds of victims and reinforced the West's unfavourable perception of the Russian post-communist transition. Moreover, the violence perpetrated by the Russian Army in the Chechen war of 1994–96, particularly against civilians, exposed Moscow to the West's strong disapproval. This feeling was strengthened during the second Chechen war at the end of the 1990s. Then, western criticism of the "disproportionate use of force" was raised against Russian reactions to terrorist attacks, such as those that occurred at the Dubrovka theatre in Moscow and in Beslan (Pinder & Shishkov 2002; McFaul et al. 2004).

Similarly, however, Russia's pro-western attitude soon began to decline. The first indication that a sense of humiliation was causing a Russian reaction could be recognised in 1994 when Minister of Foreign Affairs Kozyrev injected, unwillingly, a change of direction toward the CIS countries. Beyond Communist opposition in the Duma, which was still influential in the mid-1990s, Kozyrev was strongly criticised by a number of advisers and policy makers (among those the Chairman of the parliamentary Joint Committee on Foreign Affairs and Foreign Economic Relations Evgenii Ambartsumov), who demanded a more affirmative policy in the so called "near abroad", which they considered Russia's backyard. In this context, the Kremlin's applied version of the "Monroe Doctrine" was the first important step marking the reshaping of Russia's external projection towards its neighbourhood (Migranian 1994; Bianchini 2017: 161).

The American military and diplomatic intervention to stop the war in Bosnia-Herzegovina and its decision to gradually expand NATO eastward became additional sources of concern in Moscow (Itzkowitz Shifrinson 2016).

As a result, in 1996 Minister of Foreign Affairs Evgenii Primakov elaborated for the first time the notion of a multipolar world in opposition to the unipolarity of the US and its allies. By specifically suggesting convergence with India and China, he outlined a strategy of counter-balancing the role of the US and NATO (Primakov 1996; Ambrosio 2005).

These changes in Russia's attitude were in part underestimated and in part neglected by the West. In fact, Russia's role in the Balkans became increasingly marginalised. NATO's illegal attack on Serbia and Montenegro in 1999 strengthened the Kremlin's belief that western military operations were determined by anti-Russian hostility. This view was corroborated not only by the eastward enlargement of the Euro-Atlantic institutions, but also by western support offered to the "colour revolutions" in Georgia and Ukraine between 2003 and 2004. In particular, these revolutions were interpreted by Russia's leadership as anti-constitutional movements, whose aspiration was to overthrow legally elected governments. As a consequence, the Kremlin became persuaded that the West was pursuing regional destabilisation on its borders as a strategy aimed at imposing both external values and US hegemony over Russia (Gretskiy 2016).

The solidification of this belief, however, was not inevitable. Russia's leadership repeatedly manifested the will to develop a constructive partnership with the West. This occurred during El'tsin's presidency when Russia joined the Partnership for Peace program in 1994. Moreover, the Clinton administration offered Russia economic aid in order to cope with economic stagnation, increased bilateral cooperation on space shuttle missions, and succeeded in getting the Senate to ratify the Salt II treaty in 1996. Other agreements were later signed between Russia and NATO with the aim of softening Moscow's resistance to NATO enlargement, although the results achieved remained doubtful. Nevertheless, the war on terrorism declared by the Bush administration after 9/11 offered Putin the opportunity to establish a new dialogue with the US. Russia's inclusion in the G8 political forum in 1997, the creation of the Russia-NATO council in 2002, Russia's support for the American war in Afghanistan, and its enhanced cooperation with the EU, launched in 2001 with the energy summit in St. Petersburg, which was followed by the agreement on the Kaliningrad exclave and the four common spaces in 2003 – all these facts, together with Barack Obama's reset policy, seemed to pave the way for an intense partnership between Russia and the West (Tsygankov 2010: 249–250; Sakwa 2004: 207–213).

Over time however, Putin (but, broadly speaking, a large part of the Russian political élite) increasingly viewed these events as "merely cosmetic operations" which did not modify the West's hostile behaviour toward Moscow. Other developments in fact convinced Putin to revise his relations with the West. Their catalogue is not a short one, but the most important operations that raised alarm in Russia are associated with the decision by the Bush administration to attack Iraq without the support of the Security Council as well as to deploy antiballistic interceptor missiles in Poland and the Czech republic, formally to protect these countries against potential retaliation from Iran, but suspected in Moscow to be actually directed toward Russia.

Moreover, the US (albeit failed) attempt to include both Georgia and Ukraine in NATO in 2008 and the western military intervention in North Africa, when a series of Arabic uprisings occurred beginning in 2011, persuaded Putin that the US and its allies were seriously considering acting beyond NATO defence schemes, and thus potentially threatening the constitutional stability of Russia and its Eurasian space of interest. Reconsidering under this lens the war against Milošević in 1999, Putin concluded that the military operations against "ramp" Yugoslavia were the first test of a new attitude, because they took place outside NATO and when no aggression against its member-states had occurred (Bechev 2017: 58–64).

As a result, concern grew considerably about a potential western destabilisation of Russia through penetration of the CIS area, especially the southern Caucasus and Ukraine.

Alarm began to be visible in August 2008, when Georgian president Saakashvili sought to re-establish control over the secessionist regions of Abkhazia and Southern Ossetia by force, after years of tension and local conflicts. However, he failed to achieve his goal because the Russian army intervened militarily and easily defeated his troops. A few weeks later President Medvedev formally recognised the independence of these two regions, by comparing their situation to Kosovo, which had declared independence earlier in February (Stent 2014).

Similarly, the annexation of Crimea in 2014 was justified by Putin, among other arguments, by Russia's aim to prevent a potential US base on the peninsula, following the Maidan political developments in Ukraine, after weeks of protests supported by the US and the EU.

Consistent with this interpretation of events, Putin made an illuminating statement when he received Erdogan in Moscow on 9 August 2016, after the failure of the coup d'état of 15 July. On that occasion, while manifesting solidarity with the Turkish President, he stressed that Russia has "a position of principle: we are against any illegal overturning of the constitutional order" (Walker & Rankin 2016). The statement referred not only to allegedly hesitation on the part of the West to react during the attempted coup, but was also an evident critique of US and EU military intervention against Ghaddafi in Libya, in support of Syrian insurgents against Bashar al-Assad, the "colour revolutions" in Tbilisi and Kiev, and the post-Maidan events in Ukraine, which Russia interpreted as an anti-constitutional overthrow of duly elected President Ianukovych.

It was thus throughout this chain of events that the Russian leadership manifested a growing assertiveness in international relations. By taking up and enhancing Primakov's policy of world multipolarity, the critique of US unipolarity intensified. Even though the perspective of a partnership with the West was never rejected, and sometimes even revived, it was considered realistically viable only on an equal basis, that is, "not under US and EU conditions".

Soon thereafter, the applied mutual sanctions exacerbated the confrontation with the West and Russian foreign policy turned to the East. Since then, the Kremlin has given priority to (1) its relations with the Asia-Pacific area, including China and the CIS area; (2) a multipolar policy involving targeted countries or international organisations; and (3) a neo-idealist-conservative emphasis on "Russian values". To sum up, the swinging external projection of Russia between Europe and Asia has again moved eastward, although this option was never considered in Moscow as an ultimate decision (Khudoley 2016). In fact, western-centrism (which should not be confused with pro-western orientations) has remained a pillar of Russian foreign policy even if Moscow perceives it simultaneously as a resource and a threat, as Bobo Lo has effectively emphasised (Lo 2015: 198). Nevertheless, within this framework Russia's external agenda is engaging more closely with Asia and the Pacific.

2 The Russian Strategy of Multilayered Networks

The Eurasian Economic Union (EAEU) is key to Moscow's current networking diplomacy. Strictly connected to its "security area of interests", it is being pursued as a bridge for further global initiatives. Their basic aim is to overcome the current world disorder by promoting global stability, which should benefit from both the US's declining authoritative morality and the development of interdependent networks, in which Russia is looking to play a crucial role.

In this perspective, the EAEU was emphatically launched at the beginning of 2015 after years of negotiations, the establishment of a custom union, and governance that in many respects appears reminiscent of the European Economic Community. In a short while it has also rapidly expanded from 3 to 5 member-states.

Although the EAEU is mainly perceived in the West as the "incarnation" of Eurasianism (that is, an imperialist ideology against western values and their stability), the complexity of the relations within this organisation is perhaps barely visible, but nonetheless alive (Subotić 2004; Shlapentokh 2007). Its partnership suffers from significant social, economic, and demographic disparities, deriving from for example the impact of oil and gas low prices, rouble weakness, unbalanced population growth and distribution rates, and the impact of mutual sanctions between the EU/US and Russia because of the Ukrainian crisis. Moreover, multilateral trade has not yet improved, while traditional bilateral trade through Russia still prevails, similar to trade patterns during the Soviet era (Boguslavska 2015: 10; Vinokurov 2017: 59–62).

At the institutional level, Russia has had to accept the positions of Kazakhstan and Belarus on restricting cooperation within the economic sphere, abandoning its original idea of initiating a political union by creating an inter-parliamentary dimension, as a first step. This was because the leaders of the member-states do not necessarily share the Union's agenda (Vasilyeva & Lagutina 2013). On the contrary, their participation in the EAEU in some respects stems from opportunities that are perceived in different ways and often consistently pursued in connection with local, rather than joint interests (Gabuev 2016: 9–11). It seems that Putin has understood this reality since he accepted a "multi-speed and multi-level integration principle" as an essential component of the Union. In so doing, the Russian hope is to enable "open regionalism", and to encourage diversified memberships in the post-Soviet area (Putin 2011). Whether the goal will be achieved remains questionable, but the formulation is vague enough to leave open the way either for unpredictable adjustments of member-states' relations or to new enlargements, not necessarily within the CIS environment.

Meanwhile, relations between Russia and Kazakhstan are formally excellent, but a sort of "shadow competition" is affecting both the EAEU's main leadership (expressed by Putin and Nazarbaev) and the strategic development of the Union. For example, Kazakhstan has tenaciously supported the involvement of Turkey as a full member, in contrast to Russia, which prefers India. This dichotomy temporarily vanished, however, when Armenia, whose controversy with Turkey is well-known, was accepted into the EAEU (Lagutina-Vasileva 2015: 21–22).

In addition, Central Asian developments may become increasingly fragile as most of the leaders are quite elderly. The institutional transition that may start after their deaths is unpredictable. Such fragility has already been experienced in Uzbekistan in the fall of 2016 when Islam Karimov passed away. Putin quickly decided to pay a visit to the country to support political continuity and avoid any vacuum which may provide opportunities for Chinese penetration or Islamic fundamentalist growth. For different reasons, in fact, Moscow worries about both of these perspectives (Gabuev 2016a: 27–29). In 2019 Nazarbaev also resigned, thus starting a transitional phase in which developments are affected by domestic and international uncertainties (particularly given the penetrating role of China).

Furthermore, at the moment the EAEU project corresponds geopolitically to the CIS area. This coincidence has raised suspicion both in the West and in some former Soviet republics that Russia may pursue a "hidden agenda" aimed at re-establishing its predominant role "in its backyard". Admittedly, most of the states that became independent when the USSR collapsed have a young

and fragile statehood, particularly if compared with Russia, whose long imperial experience and great power role during the Cold War show a remarkable
imbalance with the newly independent neighbouring countries. This imbalance leads Moscow to often underestimate the sense of vulnerability of its new
neighbours. For example, El'tsin's declaration of August 27, 1991 about the need
for the USSR constituent republics to adjust their borders, was never forgotten
by the other post-Soviet leaders. Its memory is refreshed every time the word
"restore" appears in the Russian political narrative, even though it refers to economic relations only (The New York Times 1991).

In other words, the mere idea of "restoring" relations is a source of anxiety,
which Russia finds empathically difficult to understand. Consequently, the
fear that Moscow is pursuing expansionist strategies to the detriment of what
Russian policy defines "the near abroad" remains well-rooted in the awareness
of the neighbouring countries. Concerns are manifested in different ways.
Sometimes they are voiced openly and critically, for example in the Baltic republics, Georgia, and Ukraine (Tkachenko 2016). Sometimes they are expressed
latently by EAEU member states which do not fully endorse Russian policies,
for instance regarding the Crimean annexation or the sanctions against the
EU/US. Under these circumstances, they seek to play the role of mediator in
relations between the EAEU and the EU, in hopes of enhancing their autonomous role. Kazakhstan in particular has started to develop its own networks
with Russia, China, and the Islamic world, with the aim of achieving a central
political and economic position.

Meanwhile, military incidents frequently occur between Armenia and
Azerbaijan in the southern Caucasus, where Russia still exerts undeniable
influence, even if it plays a diplomatically embarrassing role. Moscow in fact
supports Armenia as an EAEU member-state, but is also an important arms
supplier of Baku.

All things considered, the beginning of the EAEU seems to be marked more
by centrifugal forces than epitomizing an integrative spirit, as formal political
statements declare.

Nonetheless, both the Kremlin and the other capitals of the Union believe
that globalisation is going to increase competition between macroregional
players. This view is the "glue factor" of the EAEU. It crucially contributes to
preserving its cooperation, while exploring new opportunities beyond the "traditional" CIS geo-economic and cultural framework. Accordingly, a memorandum of understanding was signed with South Korea; a free trade zone came
into force in 2016 with Vietnam, while the final stage with Iran was achieved in
summer 2017. Similar negotiations were successfully concluded with Serbia and
Singapore in 2019. Psychologically, this openness is welcomed by Central-Asian

countries, which see a form of reassurance that Russian temptations to "restore" former domination are weakening. Furthermore, Moscow is engaging in ambitious political activism with international organisations like MERCOSUR, SCO, ASEAN, APEC, and BRICS (Kozyrev 2016; Hartwell 2016; Stadnik 2016).

The diversification of contacts is particularly dynamic in Asia, where Moscow's partnership with China has been developing economically, militarily, and politically, in clear competition with the US. Furthermore, Moscow supports the Chinese strategy of the "one belt, one road", in its land-based and maritime forms. This is extensively analysed by other authors in this book. However, it is important to stress that the intensity of these partnerships is "softened" by a number of factors, as Russia does not intend to play the "junior role" with Beijing, while rivalry in Central Asia may arise due to increasing Chinese investments in the area. Nor does the Kremlin like to depend on Chinese energy imports, despite the crisis with the West. Additional concerns for Moscow derive from the visible asymmetry in economic and social spheres including demographic growth, GDP, industrial development, trade volume, employment, inflation, public debt and so on (Kashin 2016; Gabuev 2016a).

Not surprisingly, Russia's "attraction with moderation" towards China is part of a broader set of Asia-Pacific initiatives. The development of relations with APEC on environmental goods and ASEAN in the fields of infrastructure, trade, and energy demonstrates Moscow's willingness to enhance dialogue with this region (Iwashita, 2007). Although contact with ASEAN dates back to 1991, Russia was formally included in its most important institutions like the East Asia Summit (EAS) and the Asia-Europe Meeting (AEM) only after 2010. Indeed, the visibility of these relationships is still poor, but the Russian proposal for an EAEU-ASEAN free trade agreement in 2016 is an evident effect of the Ukrainian crisis and the conflicts with the EU/US.

An additional, amazing example of dynamism is the development of relations with Japan, marked by reciprocal official visits of Shinzo Abe and Putin since 2016, after decades of disagreement about borders and the absence of a peace treaty at the end of WWII. One result of this dialogue with Tokyo has been the inclusion of the issue of the contested Kuril Islands. A new approach has emerged, paving the way for the potential growth of trade, technological and economic exchanges.

However, the development of partnerships in Asia and the Pacific is considered by Moscow a crucial, but not exclusive opportunity to expand cooperation.

In Europe for example, Serbia has acquired new importance, as the EU enlargement negotiation has suffered from a setback in the whole region and Montenegro joined NATO in 2017 against Moscow's desires. Subsequently, joint military exercises with Belgrade intensified. Moreover, Russia subsidised

Serbia with 6 MIG 29 warplanes and armoured vehicles, while intensifying economic cooperation with Belgrade and EAEU. More recently, in October 2017 Russian diplomacy opened a new channel of communication with Croatia after the Croatian president's visit to Sochi. Energy (pipeline construction) and the future of the big enterprise Agrokor (in the sectors of food, drinks, distribution, and biogas facilities) are new potential business areas for a "two legged" Russian presence in the Balkans, with Zagreb and Belgrade as focal points.

At the same time, Russia is maintaining dialogue with the EU and some EU member-states. For example, in 2016 Gazprom sealed an agreement with Brussels to double the volume of the Nord Stream gas-pipeline. Cordial relations are also developing with Italy and Greece (Khudoley 2016a).

The BRICS summits are also acquiring increasing relevance for Moscow, as Stanislav Tkachenko describes in another chapter of this book. Despite Indian-Chinese tensions, these gatherings (particularly the last one in 2017) relaxed the relations between the two Asian Powers, thus giving new impetus to the *Pancha Shila* (the 5 principles of Peaceful Coexistence that paved the way to the Bandung conference in 1954). This atmosphere has allowed Russia to reinforce its relations with India and South Africa, also bringing Iran closer to this "club" of emerging states with global ambitions. In this perspective, the BRICS is instrumentally viewed by the Kremlin as a vector to help shape the transformation of global normative power, by promoting an alternative to the "Washington consensus" (Sergunin 2014).

Truly, these hopes are still fluid. How they will solidify remains open. Patently, the Russian strategy in support of world multipolarity is being comprehensively pursued by establishing networks of international organisations, the actions of which are expected to challenge US centrality (Ambrosio 2005). Additionally, Russia frames its approach to collective security by suggesting a greater role for the five permanent members of the UN Security Council with respect for "international law" worldwide. Yet this claim is seen as more of a critique of the US wars against Serbia and Montenegro in 1999, Iraq in 2003 and the military intervention in Libya and Syria, than a proposal for an effective reform of the UN. In fact, Moscow also applies double standards in this matter, for instance when it disregarded the Budapest Memorandum on Ukraine's borders (although the document was not formally binding) or when it passed a law establishing the priority of national over international courts in December 2015, in contrast to the Council of Europe and the European Court of Human Rights (Newcity 2015).

Actually, the persistence of equivocal behaviour and understanding (manifested not only by Russia, but also by a plurality of players) vis-a-vis international law and international organisations is an evident manifestation of the new world disorder. Under these conditions Russia's external image remains fragile, affected by domestic social uncertainties, volatile global economic conditions, and friction with the enlarged NATO. Moreover, great fluidity marks relations between the international actors on which Russia is relying. Suffice it to recall the antagonism between China, and Japan and Vietnam, or Turkey and Syria; the institutional, social, and economic weaknesses of Brazil, South Korea, and South Africa; or the potential instability of Central Asia. As a result, Russian cooperation with the EU and US, however contentious it is today, remains a functional perspective and, culturally, in continuity with the dynamic of attraction/rejection of Russian-European relations since the 17th century, as charmingly reconstructed by Dieter Groh in his book *"Russia and the Self-Consciousness of Europe"* (Groh 1961).

Still, the Russian view of a multipolar, global order displays some innovative and post-modern aspects. Particularly, its networking dynamism in different international theatres is worthy of scrutiny. By contrast, the growing world disorder and the intensification of various international players' alternative agendas are challenging Moscow's expectations for stability. In this context, the Russian reputation worldwide becomes crucially important for the magnetism and effectiveness of the new world governance that the Kremlin is advocating. However, its reputation still suffers from a set of serious shortcomings, such as for example corruption, the Ukrainian crisis and the incorporation of Crimea, the contested accountability of the judicial system, restrictions of some new civil rights (such as for the LGBT community) as well as freedom of the press, and persistent suspicion about the reliability of a partnership with Russia. Under these circumstances, an attractive, positive Russian identity is key to achieving the "status seeking" of a recognised global power. At the moment, however, this is an additional, weak aspect of Russia's external projection.

3   The Challenge of Identity Profile: Calling on the Past While Tackling the Future?

In 2003 Dmitrii Trenin suggested a Euro-Pacific identity for Russia. In his view, dissociating the country's image both from "Asia" and the neo-imperialist appeals voiced by Eurasianists would allow Russia to bridge Western Europe and Japan, while positively interacting with American interests in the Atlantic and Pacific theatres (Trenin 2002; Trenin 2003; Klein 2014).

By contrast, other advisors (indeed, quite a few) have emphasised old geopolitical theories inspired by Mackinder and his heartland theory. Rightist and sometimes pro-fascist orientations, embodied in the rediscovered Eurasianist fascination, were propagated by Aleksandr Dugin, whose ideas are frequently quoted with anxiety in the western literature, but also ignored or criticised by Russian academia (Shlapendokh 2007; Laruelle 2008; Beznosiuk 2016: 58–64).

Putin in turn has recurrently addressed the issue of Russian identity and its relation to Europe, especially after 9/11. Speaking at the Bundestag during his visit to Germany on September 25, 2001, he highlighted the idea of a "Greater Europe", which had inflamed the imagination of De Gaulle, Mitterrand, and Gorbachev (Putin 2001). At the time however, cooperation between the EU, US, and Russia seemed to offer unexplored opportunities of development. Conversely, events soon took on a different appearance, and the initial optimistic expectations quickly vanished. Actually, Russian foreign policy never abandoned the idea of exploring synergies between the EU, the EAEU and China. In 2016 during the economic forum of St. Petersburg, Putin envisaged prospectively a "Greater Eurasia" from Lisbon to Beijing. Soon thereafter a similar project was recommended by an important German think-tank, the Bertelsmann Foundation, which published a Focus Paper on free trade from "Lisbon to Vladivostok", suggesting a common free trade area between the EU and the EAEU, with the obvious aim of reducing tensions with Russia and building the conditions for mutual trust (Bluth 2016).

In other words, despite the Ukrainian crisis, Moscow is aware of the geopolitical impact of China's "one belt one road" project, particularly after the failure of both the TTIP (Transatlantic Trade and Investment Partnership) and the TPP (Trans-Pacific Partnership). With the American withdrawal from multilateral trade agreements, Russia is looking to achieve a central role, although major investment in high-speed infrastructure are needed to consolidate the Nizhnii Novgorod-Moscow-St. Petersburg-Helsinki transportation link already in service, and the Moscow-Kazan' connection is still in progress (to be eventually extended to Ekaterinburg and beyond).

In this regard, substantial loans might be offered by China, which can take advantage of both Russia's and the EU's current restricted margins for manoeuvring. However, as China might benefit significantly from this situation, Russia would be willing to establish convergence with the EU (or at least single European states) and the US, because this would help preserve Moscow's autonomy. At the moment this convergence is missing for evident political reasons, but this situation explains Russia's interest in strengthening its "sovereign democracy", by pragmatically designing an identity profile which might help to configure convincing alliances worldwide.

And in fact, Russia does commit itself to defining its identity perimeter, which is perceived as an exclusive, but still European "civilisation", operating in a global context of different, and parallel, "civilisations". In this view, the coexistence and interaction of these "civilisations" embodies the nature of the "new international relations" able, as believed, to restore order in the world (Ray 2014).

So far, efforts at promoting such a vision show great pragmatism which includes a combination of post-modern global methodology, based on multilayered networks as summarised above, and an emphasis on pre-modern, conservative values. This hybridity marks to a large extent how Russianness is advertised worldwide, either through the notion of *Russkii Mir* and the values ascribed to it, or through a certain nostalgia for the "Concert of Nations" from the times of the Vienna Congress, or – even more so – though the special inputs imprinted in the media and digital diplomacy.

This is another unusual mix. On the one hand, the idea that a set of civilisations characterises global dynamics, is partially generated by the appeal that philosophy, literature, and humanities in general have in the Russian cultural approach to reality. On the other hand, it is a way of contesting the universality of western values, their intrinsic aspiration to permeate both the political and legal international order, and US unipolarity. The "Concert of Nations" nostalgia is, therefore, a manifestation of the Kremlin's demand for recognition that multipolarity does exist, it dominates the world economy, and it is weakening the moral authority of the West.

Additionally, Russian "specialness" has been propagated by *Russkii Mir*, a liquid idea originally inspired by the biologist Petr Shchedrovitskii and the businessman Gleb Pavlovskii, who cultivated a philosophical love for Berdiaev and spirituality in general. The outlook of *Russkii Mir* was a mix of marketing and messianic vision of Russia or, differently said, an original attempt to amalgamate the needs of economic globalisation with the legacy of Russian thought (Laruelle 2015: 17).

For more than a decade, *Russkii Mir* was seen as a potentially convincing soft-power instrument, able to improve the Russian image in support of its international competitiveness (both in political and economic terms). The search for an international trademark was ambitiously stimulated by the attractiveness of Francophonie for France, the Commonwealth for Great Britain, liberty for the US, and economic effectiveness for Germany.

With this aim in mind, in 2007 Putin established the *Russkii Mir* foundation (but some Russian economists have complained about its lack of transparency) (Inozemtsev 2015: 15). Furthermore, the Gorchakov Public Diplomacy Fund was invited to coordinate other public institutions dealing with research and studies on humanities, cultural heritage, and Russian language development abroad, in connection with the Moscow Patriarchate. The Gorchakov foundation began to operate, therefore, in a context in which other players were also active, like the Valdai Club, the University MGIMO, the Paris-based Institute for Democracy and Cooperation, the Federal Agency *Rossotrudnich-estvo* for relations with the CIS and Compatriots Abroad. All these institutions were created between 2003 and 2010. Later, Minister of Foreign Affairs Lavrov urged joint activity of the Gorchakov fund with the powerful think-tank "Russian International Affairs Council" (Lutsevych 2016).

However, neither has the search for a brand come to a satisfactory conclusion, nor has the main target of *Russkii Mir* been identified. Activists and scholars involved in the project honestly admitted the uncertainty of the target, which possibly encompasses (a) former Soviet citizens; (b) the Russian diaspora (that is, Russian ethnic minorities, but also Russian speakers living in newly independent post-Soviet countries), or (c) – at least until 2015 – people interested in Russian language and culture.

Affected by multiple, overlapping geographies which increase doubts about priorities, *Russkii Mir* strengthened either hopes for temperate cultural policies or fears/desires of imperial behaviours, aimed at restoring Moscow's control over the post-Soviet space. Also, the appeal to diaspora suffered from several limitations.

At the first world "Convention of Compatriots Abroad" in 2001, Putin stated that *Russkii Mir* should not be related to Russian geographical borders or Russian ethnos. Rather, it was to be understood as a feeling, shared by those who value the "soul and culture" of Russia and appreciate the "spiritual self-determination" of individuals as a powerful transnational morality (Putin 2001a). Nevertheless, the ethnic dimension remains ambiguously included in the Russian narrative. Putin himself praised the "primordial traditional values" of Russians in his address at the turn of the millennium. Subsequently on other public occasions he mentioned the relevance of ethnos, when he justified the annexation of Crimea in 2014 and highlighted Moscow's responsibility toward its minorities abroad. Sometimes however, he softened the tone, particularly during the conventions of the Compatriots, alternatively convened in St. Petersburg and Moscow, when priority was given to the intensification of economic, cultural, and legal ties of the Russian diaspora with the "motherland".

Actually, the addresses to compatriots are understood differently in Russia. For example, the economist Inozemtsev warned about the fact that two categories of "Russians abroad" exist, generating confusion. On the one hand, there are Russians who left the country for new job opportunities or studies, becoming a sort of off-shore élite over the years, often well integrated into their new political reality. On the other hand, there are Russians who suddenly and unexpectedly found themselves as a minority in the newly independent states after the USSR collapse. Not necessarily all of them are likely to integrate or wish to be integrated into the new societies. The Ukrainian context is, according to Inozemtsev, a litmus test of this resistance, which is able to generate, locally, a number of "professionals of the Russian idea". Their aim is to pressurize Moscow and rely on its financial support, in order to create a "Русский мірь" (written in Ukrainian), which is however interpreted, particularly in the Donbas region, as a neo-imperial strategy (Inozemtsev 2015).

Radically different is the perception of *Russkii Mir* in other areas of Russia, for example in Tatarstan. The preferred expression in this republic is *Rossiiskii Mir*, rather than *Russkii*. As is known, the word *Rossiiskii* was introduced by El'tsin with the aim of stressing the civic character of the new post-Soviet Russia, whose formal name is *Rossiiskaia federatsiia*. Understandably, sensitivity toward a civic connotation of the whole project is higher in non-Russian areas (Nasyrov 2007).

Within this context, the importance ascribed to the diaspora captured the imagination of Tatars who have more than one million "compatriots abroad". As a result, they have started to promote their own *Tatarskii Mir*, in agreement with the Ministry of Foreign Affairs of the Russian Federation. Coexisting for centuries with an intercultural population with a variety of religious and ethnic groups living side by side with Russians and Orthodox believers, the Tatars of the Volga region have adopted a flexible and so far effective policy. Thus, their local traditions and diversity are successfully developed within the broader, but inclusive Russian institutional environment. Inspired by Putin's approach to the Russian diaspora and praised by him (Putin 2015), they summoned conventions of Tatar compatriots, discussed the problems of their émigrés, established social networks for youth, launched an on-line program for learning the Tatar language for free, and established joint ventures to promote economic growth in Tatarstan. Furthermore, they built a palace of Tatar culture both in Azerbaijan and Uzbekistan and started celebrating the birthday of the poet Ğabdulla Tukay, the "father" of the modern Tatar language and literature.

A similar initiative was promoted by the republic of Mari, whose population has a Finno-Ugric origin. A networking-cultural Assembly was promoted with the participation of representatives from Finland and Hungary but, admittedly, the impact remained negligible.

In short, *Russkii Mir* has generated contending interpretations in Russia itself. Furthermore, the attractiveness of the "brand" has remained below expectations, both in quantitative and qualitative terms.

Given these unsatisfactory outcomes, the identity focus has shifted to other instruments such as Internet and digital diplomacy. A new strategy was designed to help the advertising promotion of Russian media like *"Sputnik"*,

"*Russia today*" and "*Voice of Russia*", which broadcast in approximately 30 languages. The main concern was to create a "counter-information" environment able to contend on-line the influence of either the media of the Baltic republics and Poland, or the assessments of domestic dissidents and bloggers, whose activism is regarded by Moscow as politically, if not financially, supported by the US and the EU. So, the original strategy was addressed to Russian speakers, including Jewish-Russian émigrés in Israel, where they are still considered Russians. In this case, the aim was to encourage possible repatriation (Konik 2011).

Soon thereafter, however, plans to promote the Russian external projection changed. Russian authorities started supporting information initiatives by relying on social networks and platforms operating in the United Kingdom, Spain, the US and Latin America.[2] This "counter-information" policy soon mixed with the propaganda of Russian "traditional values", both at the domestic and international levels. These values were increasingly identified with state greatness (*derzhavnost'*), patriotism, orthodox religiosity, honour, virility, masculine courage and self-sacrifice, and the heterosexual family. Meanwhile, bilateral contacts with far-right parties in the western world were promoted with the aim of testing a normative and values convergence.

As *Russkii Mir* was disappointing, the networking policy tested with a variety of international organisations was reinforced by digital diplomacy initiatives in selected countries. Interference in the US presidential elections of 2016 or the Austrian parliamentary elections in 2017 are good illustrations of this new strategy, tailored to take advantage of social divisions, while promoting the "asserted effectiveness" of traditional values and conservativism (Trenin 2016). Reference here is not so much to the hackers' role in gaining access to confidential and private documents, as the US Congress is investigating. Rather, the focus is on information and propaganda messages launched to millions of citizens over a number of platforms and concerning social conflicts, as for example racial tensions in the US or the negative impact of migration in Austria. The main goal was to reinforce conservative stances within socially divided societies, where liberal and traditional values antagonise. Undeniably, a remarkable impact has been achieved, while cultural affiliations were undertaken with some far-right wing and populist movements such as the French National Front and the Austrian Freedom Party (Polyakova 2016).

However, the programmatic congruence of these parties is limited, and sometimes even mutually conflictual. Therefore, the expected cultural vicinity with rightist movements does not necessarily meet the Kremlin's needs,

---

2   How Russians used the content posted by Americans is well illustrated by Confessore and
    Wakabayashi (2017).

particularly when the populist agenda includes hate speeches, state partitions, racism, or pro-LGBT policies.

Digital diplomacy is certainly increasing the potential for transnational interference in domestic and international affairs between states, but may also produce unwanted effects through the mechanism of comments, whose circulation risks reinforcing fundamentalist feelings, extreme radicalism, and hatred. The consequences of such behaviours are unpredictable and they are likely to get out of control: for example, the rise of hatred towards Ukraine in Russian Internet channels is already a matter of concern in the Kremlin, illustrating how delicate it is to implement the strategy promoted in Russia to deal with globalisation, strengthen its international role as a recognised great power, and preserve "traditional" stability.

4   Conclusion

The reshaping of the Russian trajectory in the global arena is currently marked by a combination of post-modern networking diplomacy (both traditional and digital) and an emphasis on conservative and traditional values, as expressions of Russia's "specialness". These characteristics stem at least partially from the disappointing status of Russia's relations with the EU and the US. Partially, however, they are also the outcome of a policy which aims to avoid marginalisation in the context of world disorder and whose potentially disruptive implications Putin wishes to avoid at any cost.

This behaviour of the Russian president does not merely go back to Moscow's negative perception of NATO's expansion eastward, the impact of the "colour revolutions", and suspected US interference in the 2011–2013 rallies against Putin, which reached their peak with the Bolotnaia square demonstration in the capital. Actually, Putin's hostility toward mass manifestations dates back to much earlier, at least when the Berlin wall came down. Putin was particularly impressed by the crowded protests that led to the collapse of DDR. Since then he has nurtured the deep belief that mass protests may lead to institutional overthrow, insecurity, and disorder. Later, the Maidan events, the Arab riots, and even the failure of the Turkish coup were perceived as adamant confirmations of this conviction.

Accordingly, the Russian external projection under Putin mirrors this concern, alongside the aspiration to once again achieve great power status. The multilayered networking strategy with international organisations worldwide, like the SCO, BRICS and MERCOSUR, along with its intense cooperation with China, are designed and implemented to avoid the isolation that the western world has pursued since the Russian annexation of Crimea and the war in Ukraine. However, Moscow nurtures another more ambitious goal, that is, the construction of a new international legal order, based on the coexistence and mutual recognition of a variety of "civilisations". Russia's efforts to define the perimeter of its own "civilisation" have produced the *Russkii Mir* project and, later, the construction of a set of "traditional, conservative values". Digital diplomacy is used as a tool to complementing state diplomacy.

In Putin's view, increasing world disorder is a threatening source of social divisions and weakness, whose implications are visible particularly in western societies, where liberal and conservative options confront. Indeed, similar clashes occur in Russian society, but the Kremlin's interpretation of global reality assumes that disorder and weakness are generated by the rejection of "traditional, conservative values", the loss of religious feelings, and the decline of the heterosexual family. Accordingly, Russian authorities wish to prove that their attachment to traditionalism is a source of stability both for the benefit of the world order and the return of Russia to great power status. Under these conditions, and despite the inconsistencies between Russian cultural richness and the Russian official "selective narrative" of its civilisation's "specialness", Moscow's conservativism would ideally be considered – by the Kremlin – as a crucial factor of convergence with western countries, motivated by common Christian roots and a shared "white vicinity" against religious fundamentalism and, potentially, growing Chinese power. Nonetheless, this view is also deterred by the thinness of its boundaries with white racism and anti-Semitism. Although such trends do exist in Russian society (especially against Central-Asian immigrants), the leadership in Moscow does not show interest in seeing them grow stronger, while Russian media regularly broadcasts news about racist clashes in the US with the aim of putting American society in a bad light.

As a result, the Russian conservative agenda remains affected by the weak attractiveness of its arguments, unable to cope with multiple lifestyles, which already coexist in Europe and the US and cannot be rejected or denied. Furthermore, the Kremlin's demand to respect the diversity *of* civilisations cannot suppress the recognition of diversities *within* civilisations. Consequently, the promotion of conservative values, as vectors for reshaping the Russian identity and marking its international trajectory – despite diplomatic innovation –, has limited effects in the dialogue with the West, even if populism and far right movements are growing. For the Kremlin, these discrepancies remain a key source of concern for its aspiration to "make order in the world disorder".

Bibliography

Akihiro, I. (2007). *Eager Eyes Fixed on Eurasia. Russia and Its Eastern Edge.* Sapporo: Hokkaido University.

Ambrosio, T. (2005). *Challenging America's Global Preeminence. Russia's Quest for Multipolarity.* Abingdon: Routledge.

Bechev, D. (2017). *Rival Powers. Russia in Southeast Europe.* New Haven: Yale University Press.

Beznosiuk, M. (2016). 'The roots of Russia's neo-Eurasianism', *New Eastern Europe*, 20(1): 58–64.

Bianchini, S. (2017). *Liquid Nationalism and State Partitions in Europe.* Cheltenham: Edward Elgar.

Bluth, C. (2016). *Free Trade from Lisbon to Vladivostok. A tool for Peace and Prosperity: The Effects of a Free Trade Area between the EU and the Eurasian Region.* Gütersloh: Bertelsmann Stiftung.

Boguslavska, K. (2015). 'The First Steps of the Eurasian Economic Union: Disputes, Initiatives and Results', *Russian Analytical Digest*, 170, 7 July: 9–14.

Confessore, N. and Wakabayashi, D. (2017). 'How US rage was spun into a weapon', *International New York Times*, 14 October, 10–11.

Deriglazova, L., Shukra, A. and Fritsch, S. (eds.) (2007). *EU and Russia: Face to Face.* Tomsk: Tomsk State University Publishing House.

Gabuev, A. (2016). 'Post-Soviet States Jostle for Role in One Belt One Road', *Russian Analytical Digest*, 183, 3 March: 9–11.

Gabuev, A. (2016a). 'Friends with Benefits? Russian-Chinese Relations After the Ukraine Crisis', *Carnegie Moscow Center*, 29 June, http://carnegie.ru/2016/06/29/friends-with-benefits-russian-chinese-relations-after-ukraine-crisis-pub-63953.

Gretskiy, I. (2016). 'Russia's Troubled European Identity', *New Eastern Europe*, 20(1): 32–37.

Groh, D. (1961). *La Russia e l'autocoscienza d'Europa.* Torino: Einaudi.

Gudkov, L. (2011). 'The Nature of "Putinism"', *Russian Politics and Law*, 49(2): 7–33.

Hartwell, C. (2016). 'How to Cure the Woes of the Eurasian Economic Union', *Russia Direct*, 27 January, https://russia-direct.org/opinion/how-cure-woes-eurasian-economic-union.

Inozemtsev V.L. (2015). 'Russkii Mir protiv russkago mira', *Sotsiologicheskie Issledovaniia*, 5: 150–155.

Kashin, V. (2016). 'Takticheskoe partnerstvo ili soiuz velikikh derzhav?', *Kontrapunkt*, 5 September, http://www.counter-point.org/wp-content/uploads/2016/09/kashin_counterpoint5.pdf.

Khudoley, K.K. (2016). 'Russia's Foreign Policy amid Current International Tensions', *Teorija in Praksa*, 53(2): 388–408.

Khudoley, K.K. (2016a). 'Russia and the European Union: The Present Rift and Chances for Future Reconciliation', *Stosunki Międzinarodowe*, 52(2): 195–214.

Klein, M. (2014). 'Russia: A Euro-Pacific Power?', *SWP Research Paper*, https://www.swp-berlin.org/fileadmin/contents/products/research_papers/2014_RP08_kle.pdf.

Konik, S.V. (2011). '"Russkaia ulitsa" Izrailiia kak chast' "Russkogo mira"', *Monitoring obshchestvennogo mneniia*, 3(103), May-June: 98–104.

Kozyrev, V. (2016). 'Russia-Southeast Asia Relations: In China Shadow?', *ASAN Open Forum*, IV: 2, The ASAN Institute For Policy Studies, ASAN Academy, http://www.theasanforum.org/russia-southeast-asia-relations-in-chinas-shadow-2/.

Lagutina, M. (2015). 'A Global Eurasian Region in a "Regiopolar" World-Order', *Russian Analytical Digest*, 170: 5–8.

Laqueur, W. (2015). *Putinism: Russian and Its Future with the West.* New York: St. Martin's Press.

Laruelle, M. (2008). *Russian Eurasianism: An Ideology of Empire.* Washington, D.C.: Woodrow Wilson Press/Johns Hopkins University Press.

Laruelle, M. (2015). *The Russian World.* Washington, D.C.: Center of Global Interest.

Lo, B. (2015). *Russia and the New World Disorder.* London-Washington, D.C.: Chatham House/Brookings Institution.

Lutsevych, O. (2016). 'Agents of the Russian World. Proxy Groups in the Contested Neighbourhood', Chatham House, 14 April, https://www.chathamhouse.org/sites/default/files/publications/research/2016-04-14-agents-russian-world-lutsevych.pdf.

Matlock, Jr. J.F. (2004). *Reagan and Gorbachev: How the Cold War Ended.* New York: Random House.

McFaul, M. (2001). *Russia's Unfinished Revolution.* Ithaca: Cornell University Press.

McFaul, M., Petrov, N. and Ryabov, A. (2004). *Between Dictatorship and Democracy. Russian Post-Communist Political Reform.* Washington, D.C.: Carnegie Endowment for International Peace.

Melville, A. and Shakleina, T. (eds.) (2005). *Russian Foreign Policy in Transition. Concepts and Realities.* Budapest: CEU Press.

Migranian, A. (1994). 'Russia and the Near Abroad', pp. 590–593, in Suny, R.G. (2003), *The Structure of Soviet History, Essays and Documents*, Oxford: Oxford University Press.

Nasyrov, I.R. (2007). *Mezhdunarodnoe sotrudnichestvo regionov. Mirovaia praktika i opyt Tatarstana.* Kazan': Izdatelskii Tsentr Kazanskogo Universiteta.

Newcity, M. (2015). 'Why Russia withdraws from the International Criminal Court?', *Russia Direct*, 24 November, http://www.russia-direct.org/opinion/why-russia-withdraws-international-criminal-court.

Ostrovskii, E. and Shchedrovitskii P. (1999), 'Rossiia – strana kotoroi ne bylo', *Russkii Arkhipelag*, http://www.archipelag.ru/ru_mir/history/history99-00/shedrovicky-possia-no/.

Polyakova, A. (2016). 'Putinism and the European Far Right', *Institute of Modern Russia*, 19 January, https://imrussia.org/en/analysis/world/2500-putinism-and-the-european-far-right.

Pinder, J. and Shishkov, Yu. (2002). *The EU and Russia. The Promise of Partnership*. London: The Federal Trust.

Primakov, E. (1996). 'There is a Multipolar World at the Horizon', *Official Kremlin International News Broadcast*, 22 October.

Putin, V. (2001). 'Speech in the Bundestag of the Federal Republic of Germany', *President of Russia*, http://en.kremlin.ru/events/president/transcripts/21340, 25 September.

Putin, V. (2001a). 'Vystuplenie Prezidenta Rossiiskoi Federatsii V.V. Putina na Kongresse sootechestvennikov', 11 October, http://old.nasledie.ru/politvnt/19_44/article.php?art=24.

Putin, V. (2011). 'The New Integration Project for Eurasia: The Future in the Making', *Izvestiia*, 4 October, http://archive.premier.gov.ru/eng/events/news/16622/.

Putin, V. (2014). 'Address by President of the Russian Federation', *President of Russia*, 18 March, http://eng.kremlin.ru/news/6889.

Putin, V. (2015). 'World Congress of Compatriots: Vladimir Putin took part in the plenary session of the fifth World Congress of Compatriots Living Abroad', *President of Russia*, 5 November, http://en.kremlin.ru/events/president/news/50639.

Robinson, P. (2012). 'Putin's Philosophy. The Russian leader's paradoxical, strong-state "Liberal-conservatism"', *The American Conservative*, 28 March, http://www.theamericanconservative.com/articles/putins-philosophy/.

Sakwa, R. (2007). 'Vladimir Putin and the New Realism in Russian Foreign Policy', pp. 10–33, in Deriglazova, L., Shukra, A. and Fritsch, S. (2007). *EU and Russia: Face to Face*, Tomsk: Tomsk State University Publishing House.

Sakwa, R. (2004). *Putin: Russia's Choice*. London: Routledge.

Savranskaya, S. and Blanton, T. (2016). *The Last Superpower Summits. Conversations that Ended the Cold War*. Budapest: CEU Press.

Sergunin, A. (2003). 'Russia and the World: Changing Paradigms of Russian Foreign and Security Policy under Yeltsin and Putin', pp. 105–173, in Godzimirski, J.M. (ed.), *The Russian Federation – Ten Years of Statehood: What Now?*, Oslo: Norwegian Institute of International Affairs.

Sergunin, A. (2014). 'Understanding Russia's policies towards BRICS: theory and practice', http://web.isanet.org/Web/Conferences/GSCIS%20Singapore%202015/Archive/55c376c8-7911-42be-b13d-22867ff8ea2a.pdf.

Shifrinson, J.R.I. (2016). 'Deal or not Deal? The End of the Cold War and the US Offer to limit NATO Expansion', *International Security*, 40(4): 7–44.

Shlapendokh, D. (2007). *Russia between East and West*. Leiden: Brill.

Silvius, R. (2014). 'The Russian State, Eurasianism, and Civilisations in the Contemporary Global Political Economy', *Journal of Global Faultiness*, 2(1): 44–69.

Stadnik, A. (2016). 'The Eurasian Economic Union continues to focus on global economic integration', *Russia Direct*, 27 January, https://russia-direct.org/opinion/eurasian-economic-union-continues-focus-global-economic-integration.

Stent, A. (2014). *The Limits of Partnerships: US-Russian Relations in the twenty-first century*. Princeton: Princeton University Press.

Subotić, M. (2004). *Put Rusije: evroazijsko stanovište*. Beograd: Plato.

Suny, R.G. (2003). *The Structure of Soviet History, Essays and Documents*. Oxford: Oxford University Press.

The New York Times. (1991). 'Soviet Turmoil; Yeltsin Warns Seceding Republics About Ethnic Russian Minorities', 27 August, https://www.nytimes.com/1991/08/27/world/soviet-turmoil-yeltsin-warns-seceding-republics-about-ethnic-russian-minorities.html.

Tkachenko, S. (2016). 'The EU-Russia relations and their reflections in the Baltic Sea Region', *BSR Policy Briefing*, 2: 1–14.

Trenin, D. (2002). *The End of Eurasia: Russia on the Border Between Geopolitics and Globalization*. Washington, D.C., and Moscow: Carnegie Endowment for International Peace.

Trenin, D. (2003). 'Euro Pacific Nation', *Russia in Global Affairs*, 24 March, http://eng.globalaffairs.ru/number/n_639.

Trenin, D. (2016). 'A Five-Year Outlook for Russian Foreign Policy: Demands, Drivers, and Influences', *Carnegie Moscow Center*, https://carnegieendowment.org/files/Trenin_Russian_FP_TF_clean.pdf.

Tsygankov, A. (2010). *Russia's Foreign Policy. Change and Continuity in National Identity*. Lanham: Rowman and Littlefield.

Vasilyeva, N.A. and Lagutina, L.M. (2013). 'The Eurasian Idea from the Modern Political perspective', *Wschodnioznawstwo*, 7: 257–268.

Vasilyeva, N.A. and Lagutina, L.M. (2015). 'Geopolitical Prospects of the Russian project of Neo-Eurasian Integration', paper presented at the 56th ISA Annual Convention, New Orleans, 18–21 February.

Vinokurov, E. (2017). 'Eurasian Economic Union: Current State and Preliminary Results', *Russian Journal of Economics*, 3: 54–70.

Walker, S. and Rankin, J. (2016). 'Erdoğan and Putin discuss closer ties in first meeting since jet downing', 9 August, https://www.theguardian.com/world/2016/aug/09/erdogan-meets-putin-leaders-seek-mend-ties-jet-downing-russia-turkey.

CHAPTER 13

BRICS and Development Alternatives: Russia and China

Stanislav L. Tkachenko

All states nowadays are in search of new political and economic models, which are able to generate sustained growth. Developmentalism, which is interpreted as rapid economic development of a sovereign state, is one of the most insightful economic ideas of the previous century. The screaming success of a "developing state" came about in the period after the Second World War, especially in the 1960s. In that period projects dealing with accelerated development were actively promoted almost in all regions of the world, including in the format of interstate integration associations. Economic liberalism made a remarkable contribution to the debates on development. It insisted that there was just a single way to achieve sustainable economic growth – via the formation of markets, which should be free of state intervention. That was followed by a rather long period of domination by neoclassical economic theory and neoliberalism policy (1980–2000s). State developmentalism during these decades almost totally disappeared from public debates and survived only in a few regions of the world, including East Asia and Latin America. Nowadays developmentalism is once again on the rise. China and Russia play a remarkable role in elaborating and implementing measures designed to speed up economic growth, improve the quality of social policy and consolidate state sovereignty. The BRICS, as a forum for the leading developing economies, plays a prominent role in these processes. China as the largest economy among the five BRICS states, and Russia as the originator of the forum, are its informal leaders and their cooperation is a crucial prerequisite for the success of the initiative.

In both China and Russia today the notion of "development policy" is not yet clearly defined. There have been lively debates going on for many years in the governments, parliaments and expert communities of China and Russia on development, its aims and stages of implementation, as well as its prospects for promotion across national borders to other states with the same level of socio-economic development. Development policy is seen as the goal-directed activities of a state and its structures aimed at redistributing domestic resources accumulated during previous periods, with the goal of transforming states into independent and self-sufficient centres in world politics and economy.

Another connected aim is to bridge over sharp social problems and reach a high level of welfare. Objects of attention and efforts of the development policy of China and Russia nowadays are traditional branches of industry and their modernisation, the marketisation of agriculture, the privatisation of large-scale inefficient enterprises, problems of regional imbalances, and the extension of transport and logistics corridors. These aims are not unique; dozens of other states face them today. The uniqueness of China and Russia is in fact that both states while designing and implementing their development strategies are trying to create universal models, ready to be copied by other states, neighbouring or located on other continents.

The aim of our research is to elaborate common characteristics and dissimilarities of the development policies of China and Russia as informal leaders of the BRICS. We apply theoretical models from different schools of International Political Economy (IPE) due to the fact that for the complex study of contemporary developmentalism its interdisciplinary approach is the most useful (Tkachenko 2017).

The beginning of economic reforms in China in the fall of 1978 has become one of the most significant events in global economic history since the Second World War. These reforms have been driven by complex domestic processes in China but they were accelerated by sharp socio-economic crisis in the USSR, which ended up in disintegration of the superpower. Our research is based on the analysis of the two states' legislation, statements of leaders representing the executive and legislative branches of power, data on the socio-economic situation of citizens and households, as well as macroeconomic dynamics in the two states.

The IPE approach to comparative analysis of development policy in China and Russia enables us to point out correlations between their economic and social policies while seeing the latter (social policy) as part of a reproduction process in emerging nationally-specific models of market economy and social relationships. This approach does not see a direct correlation between GDP growth and the level of welfare, and it places emphasis on an extended set of factors which influence national socio-economic policies. In our research agenda we put emphasis on how the political authorities in Beijing and Moscow have identified the balance between economic efficiency in the global market system and the optimal volume of social expenditures, which they are able to afford without jeopardizing the whole process of national development.

In the first paragraph we study the role of BRICS in the transformation of the unipolar Washington-run world order into a multipolar model of international security system, in which BRICS states will play a prominent role due to their economic, political and demographic power. The second paragraph deals with an analysis of the main spheres of Russia's socio-economic transformation after the collapse of the USSR, as well as how Russia's example has influenced neighbouring states and the world-wide discussion on the availability of shock therapy instruments for the transition from a planned to a market economy. The third paragraph of our research pays special attention to China's policy of economic reforms since the late 1970s and possibilities for application of the Chinese experience in other countries worldwide. Finally, the fourth paragraph is devoted to identifying prospects for the formulation by BRICS states of a universal model of development policy, which opens a window of opportunities for the Global South states to integrate into the global political and economic system as participants, possessing equal rights with others.

The rapid growth of IPE reflected the genesis of concrete events in the 1960–70s and it is no coincidence that it was preceded by the collapse of European colonial empires and the appearance of about one hundred new sovereign states, which embarked on economic and social development. From the late 1960s to the early 1970s, the crisis of the Bretton Woods system of exchange rates between the major currencies was the most significant development in the world economy. Within two years of President Richard Nixon's unilateral decision to float the US dollar, the OPEC countries decided to use the 1973 Arab-Israeli War to quadruple the asking price of oil. Their success, although short-lived since inflation in the US rapidly devalued the real price of the same oil, led to the demand in developing countries for economic justice (the New International Economic Order or NIEO) and assistance from industrialised countries in matters of trade and aid. This was followed by the long debt crisis of developing states in the 1980s. Once again, this made clear how economic events are triggered by political decisions and that they have highly political consequences. Dividing lines – both those that separate politics and economics and those that separate domestic political economies from the international economy – collapsed. Governments and private companies alike were under pressure as a result of these events. They could not avoid making decisions that affected the distribution of costs and benefits, of risks and opportunities not only within states but also across national frontiers. It is exactly this agenda that prevails in the strategic planning of Chinese and Russian leaders while they are trying to develop consistent and efficient development strategies.

1   BRICS and the Political Economy of Development

Throughout world history, rising great powers have translated their growing economic might into military capabilities as well as into political expansion

via spheres of direct influence or empires. There could be several alternative explanations to that phenomenon, but the most reliable is security
concerns and the wish to sustain rising power via control of the external
environment.

In fact, any conflict between rising and dominant powers in the world system could be considered as a conflict over distribution of great power status
rather than over regional or global security. In today's world of deteriorating
US unipolarity, the BRICS countries could be viewed as revisionist states, those
strategic aims are not to completely transform the world system and replace its
leader but rather to upgrade their status to a global level as centres of multipolar system of international relations.

The following innovations enabled west European and American leadership in international politics and the economic system since the 16th century:
the removal of serfdom and the granting of personal freedoms; the demolition
of neighbouring commons and the enclosure of common land; the emergence
of free towns; the Protestant ethic; universities; freedom of speech and free
circulation of ideas; the supremacy of statute law; the protection of property
rights; relatively free markets and social mobility. Due to these factors, the current standard of development policy has emerged. It is closely connected to
the global extrapolation of Western Europe's practices of industrial revolution,
individualism, ethics and the gradual decline of public authority in managing
national economies. The western model for about one century has been considered as universal and avoiding significant deviations. Nowadays it is in deep
crisis that is why a search for a new standard of development policy is going on
in different regions of the world.

The ongoing debates both in Russia and worldwide are concentrated on the
issue of whether the dynamic BRICS can build on their political and economic
momentum and transform international relations or whether this alliance will
remain in history as a geopolitical fad. Russian diplomat V. Lukov characterised
the BRICS as "...one of the most significant geopolitical events of the new century" (Lukov 2012). At the April 2011 Summit on Hainan Island in China, BRICS
leaders stated that they had reached a broad consensus to improve coordination and strengthen cooperation "...on international and regional issues of
common interest". This statement has been repeated many times at annual
forums of the BRICS since then. The three biggest states in the BRICS (China,
India and Russia) continue to compete for regional favour and resources in
wider Eurasia as well as in some other regions (in the Arctic area, for example).
India and China are quarrelling over borders and different attitudes toward
Pakistan, while Russia and China reportedly disagree with each other over
BRICS and SCO enlargements (Kaukenov 2007: 74–75; Astakhov 2016: 48).

2   IPE Schools on the Concept of Development (Economic
       Transition)

A. Leftwich in his studies of the developmental state concept, came to the conclusion that its success should be measured by six elements: 1) determination
of ruling elites to achieve the aims of development; 2) relative autonomy of
the developmental state; 3) a well-established, well-educated and insulated
bureaucracy; 4) a weak and subordinated civil society; 5) efficient public management of non-governmental economic actors; 6) ability to use effectively
law-enforcement measures according to existing legislation (Leftwich 1995:
400–427). Nowadays, the leading theoretical schools of IPE have different
opinions on the basic aims of development policy and the symptoms of success in its implementation.

2.1   Economic Nationalism

The conviction that development policy should be based on the concept of
economic nationalism has been known for several centuries. Initially, following the success of economic development in such different states as the US,
Germany and Soviet Russia, economic nationalism in the late 19th – early 20th
centuries dominated the field. Later, in the 1980–90s, the popularity of economic nationalism was destroyed by the dogmas of the Washington Consensus. Nowadays, after the 2007–09 global financial crisis, economic nationalism
is returning to the centre stage of debates on development. The newest examples of this type of public policy are China, Russia, Singapore and a few other
states mostly in Asia. For contemporary economic nationalists, the solution to
the catch-up development problem can be found through the establishment
of a "strong state", turning government into a key driver of national socio-
economic reforms. In fact, this refers to entering into a contract between public authorities and society, within the framework of which a state guarantees
citizens steady growth of their prosperity and the build-up of the welfare state
in compensation for the denial of liberal economic policy. As an example, we
may indicate the Kremlin's social contract with the people of Russia, which has
been brought to an understanding in the autumn of 2004 after a number of
antidemocratic reforms in the system of governance in Russia. That contract
collapsed due to the economic crisis of 2014–2016 in Russia and the war sanctions of the US and its allies since the spring of 2014.

For Russian *gosudarstvenniki* (believers in a strong state) the key challenges
today are for the public authorities to reclaim their function as the most important actors in the national economic system, to stimulate growth in the hi-
tech sector, and to overcome the resource curse with import-substitution

policy measures. Academician Sergei Glaziev, intellectual leader of the group of Russian politicians, is arguing for soft monetary policy, extensive investment in national industrial and agricultural enterprises, interstate integration with former Soviet republics and a hard-line foreign policy towards NATO and EU member-states.

Debates on economic nationalism are not popular in contemporary China. Both politicians and experts are trying to avoid looking at national economic policy from the nationalist perspective. Meanwhile, many experts are convinced that we may ignore Beijing's claims of its commitment to the liberal economic model, and should concentrate on an extensive set of measures of government intervention in business life, which are typical of economic nationalism.

2.2   *Liberalism*

Since Adam Smith (i.e. the last quarter of 18th century) liberals have believed that rapid pro-market reforms, which serve the interests of private business, and efficient institutions of a democratic society, are crucial prerequisites for rapid and successful economic development.

Despite of the fact that multiple changes in the previous 40 years have dramatically transformed the Chinese economy, leaders in Beijing prefer to avoid radical reforms and choose step-by-step measures. They started in the fall of 1978 by supporting private initiative in selected rural areas of the country; after that they moved to a decentralisation policy, opening up the domestic market to foreign direct investment and creating a number of "free economic zones" in several coastal regions. The contemporary success of Chinese reforms is a result of several decades of cautious and well-balanced policy actions by the Chinese central government and authorities in different provinces.

For Russian liberals, today's Russian economy is a result of shock-therapy reforms implemented by acting Prime Minister Egor Gaidar in 1991–1992, and extended by President Vladimir Putin in 2000–2003 as well as President Dmitrii Medvedev in 2008–2010. Russian liberals have always had their small number of representatives in the government, parliament and the Presidential Administration of Russia since 1991. They are convinced that the key characteristics of national economy are openness and competitiveness. The major problems, which can be found in contemporary Russian political economy, remained unchanged due to government failure, public authorities' attempts to regain "the commanding heights of the national economy", to establish a system of support for cronies (corporations and selected businessmen), as well as to use protectionist measures in foreign trade to gain unilateral advantages for national business.

2.3   Neo-Marxism and the Theory of the Modern World System

If we eliminate ideological clichés from public speeches and official documents of politicians in China and Russia, it is hardly possible to find convincing evidence of their devotion to the ideology of Marxism in its classical form from the 19th century or in its updated Neo-Marxist version. Still, there should be no doubt that many leaders of the two states share the opinion of Immanuel Wallerstein on the architecture of the contemporary world economy, in which the global northern states are "the core" and the almost 150 sovereign states of the Global South are the "periphery". Moreover, the leaders of China and Russia consider this system unfair and in need of radical transformation. The two states are persuaded of the fact that it is a long-term goal and they should not hasten to achieve it.

Leftist activists in Russia, including supporters of the Communist Party of the Russian Federation (CPRF), believe that for the time being Russian ruling elites are moving towards a more "patriotic" agenda in foreign policy and this is why they don't see antagonism between them and communists. The leadership of the CPRF, at the same time, considers Russia's current economic policy based on liberalism, membership in the WTO and openness of financial markets as wrong and requiring immediate cessation. There is growing evidence that "patriots" in China are dissatisfied with pro-market reforms and China's possible place in the future global political and economic system (Ramzy 2009).[1] But it is hardly possible to hear the voices of Marxist critics of this policy in Beijing or elsewhere around the country.

3   The BRICS Agenda

Today the BRICS Forum is building up a new universal model of development, which fits the realities of the contemporary world. Since the beginning of the new century the US has lost its indisputable leadership in world politics, and meanwhile economic growth in the Global North is slowing down compared to the impressive results of economic advancement in emerging economies. Five BRICS states are working intensively to present their original version of a non-Western welfare system, which will be attractive globally.

The decision of Russian leaders to initiate a discussion on a wide-ranging spectrum of global security issues in the framework of the BRICS Forum is still

---

1   In 2009 a book of five retired journalists and politicians "Unhappy China" should be considered as a manifesto of growing Chinese nationalism, originated from traditional Marxist perspective on class struggle and unfair division of labor in global system.

in its early stages, requiring further research. It took quite some time (2006–2009) before the leaders of China and India appreciated that initiative and met in person on June 16, 2009, in the Russian city of Ekaterinburg for the very first BRIC Summit.

Our analysis of official statements of the original four, and later five BRICS member-states has allowed us to distinguish several topics, which at different stages of the Forum's development were important for its members.

Challenge to US "unipolar moment". This is the most important aim for Russia since the very first days of the Forum's existence. There is no doubt that the gradual eclipse of US leadership is totally in line with China's strategic interests and Beijing's growing involvement in BRICS affairs should be seen from this angle. Still, it is impossible to find any official statement from China which supports this observation. Moreover, Brazil and South Africa, while demonstrating interest in debates on a "post-unipolar" world system, prefer tacit approval of the idea. India in contrast has never supported this idea and it is hardly possible that it will change its position any time soon.

"Parallel UN". All five BRICS members are to different extents dissatisfied with the UN system and are trying to diminish US hegemony in this universal organisation. This is why the thesis that at a certain moment of its genesis the BRICS Forum may evolve into an intergovernmental organisation similar to the UN, should not be neglected, even if there are no official statements or decisions on that nowadays.

Alternative financial infrastructure for global development. In recent years the BRICS have established a number of global financial institutions: the New Development Bank (NDB); the BRICS Contingent Reserve Arrangement (CRA); as well as the BRICS Payment system, an alternative to the SWIFT system. We may conclude that developing states' dissatisfaction with US-controlled international financial institutions (first of all – the IMF and the World Bank) is now transforming into a willingness to establish independent financial institutions and consequently undermine Washington's dominance in world politics.

Alternative monetary system (challenge to US-dollar domination). The 1997 Asian financial crisis demonstrated to what extent the global monetary system with the US dollar as its centre could be dangerous for all of Asia. The 1997 crisis opened the way for the implementation of major initiatives, with the aim of averting such turbulences in the future: the Chiang Mai Initiative (CMI)[2] and

---

2   The Initiative (May 2000) is a multilateral currency swap arrangement among the ten members of the ASEAN, the People's Republic of China, Japan, and South Korea (ASEAN+3).

the Asian Bond Markets Initiative (ABMI).[3] Russia as the leader of the EAEU is taking the same type of action to provide monetary stability for all CIS member-states. The relative decrease in the role of the US dollar in the international financial system fits the strategic interests of Russia and China. Thus Moscow is ready to promote this idea right now, but Beijing is only willing to proceed slowly, as long as it takes to transform China from its current status as an "asymmetric power" into a world hegemonic leader (Womack 2016).

In the contemporary global political economy the BRICS Forum is the most powerful new player and "trouble-maker" for traditional leaders – the US and the states of Western Europe. The transformation of the unipolar system of the 1990s into something totally new will be a long process, and include both the decline in the power of previous leaders and the elaboration of a model of governance of the new leaders (BRICS), which should be universally acceptable and attractive. Neither the old hegemon (USA) is doomed to lose its leadership, nor will the newcomers inevitably take the central position in the global architecture of power later in this century. So, we are studying a dynamic process of global transformation, still in its initial phase.

4   Russia's Socio-Economic Model of Development

4.1   *The Political Economy of Contemporary Russia: Debates on Development*

The Soviet Union turned out to be the first state of the global periphery which was able to close the gap with the West (Europe and the US) – the economic leaders of the global economy since the 19th century. In the period 1930–1960 the GDP per-capita of Soviet citizens grew from 20 to almost 40 percent of the level of the global leader – the US. However, from the 1970s on the gap began to increase again, mostly due to the fact that the Soviet model of import-substitution as a driver of industrial growth had become irrelevant in post-industrial society.

The growth of the Soviet economy since 1945 was ensured by the intensive utilisation of such assets as manpower, cheap energy and plenty of natural resources. It was an ideal combination for rapid growth of heavy industry and

---

3   Another initiative of ASEAN+3 is designed to develop currency bond markets in East Asia and facilitate bond market integration. ABMI was launched in 2002 to strengthen the resilience of the region's financial system by developing local currency bond markets as an alternative source to foreign currency-denominated, short-term bank loans for long-term investment financing.

rehabilitation of areas devastated during the Second World War. The Soviet economy in this period was able to ignore output costs and to categorically deny any positive role of competition. Aging Soviet leaders believed that the problems of harmonious growth of their country could be solved by appropriate socio-economic masterplans. It is no coincidence that in the 1960s the USSR was one step away from joining the leaders of the Information Revolution, as it was on the same level of production of electronic computing machines and their application in the national economy. But in September, 1970 the CPSU Central Committee's Politburo rejected the plan by academician Viktor Glushkov to set up the Statewide Automated Management System for Collection and Processing of Information for the Accounting, Planning, and Management of the National Economy (in Russian, abbreviation, OGAS). From then on the gap in informatics between the Soviet Union and the US began to grow. As a direct consequence, the USSR followed a model of pure quantitative "growth without development". It means that increasing production was not followed by qualitative changes in the socio-economic structure and that led to the establishment of an enclave export industry and a sphere of consumption of luxury goods that was predominantly imported from the Global North states.

For Paul Kennedy, there were three reasons for the crisis and disintegration of the USSR:
– A crisis of political legitimacy of the Soviet system of governance;
– A crisis of economic production and the social security model;
– A crisis of ethnic and cultural interactions (Kennedy 1994).
In the estimation of specialists, up to 30 percent of working time in the USSR was wasted, and the surplus of labour reached 25 percent of the national labour force. All these people produced unneeded goods and were used inefficiently. In its first post-Soviet years, the Russian state budget had to spend about 30 percent of GDP to subsidise loss-making enterprises inherited from the Soviet era.

The intertwining of politics with the economic and social spheres in the USSR meant that any significant change in the country could not limit itself to just one of these segments but would unavoidably penetrate the political system, cultural patterns, and lead to changes in the system of governance. Indeed, since 1991 the almost total destruction of traditional community-conscious institutions has taken place. They were replaced by new institutions of individualism and individual liability, imported from the West.

Reforms in Russia began under the slogan of "Democratisation". This presented the idea of utilizing state budget resources as an instrument for the redistribution of incomes, which had already been accumulated in a country but were used inefficiently. Those who could benefit from above-mentioned *redistribution*, had to join the ranks of democracy supporters. But socio-economic situation in Russia was totally different in early 1990s. It had inherited from USSR a vast and incredibly inefficient "socialist welfare state", which was marked by a high level of public spending. In that situation radical pro-market reforms could not increase the scope of income redistribution via the state budget. On the contrary, for the sake of success in reforming the national economy, measures of social policy had to be terminated. Subsequently, reforms lost almost all support of ordinary people and were considered anti-social.

At the beginning of transition from socialism to the market, a sharp dispute emerged between supporters of radicalism (shock therapy) and gradualism (slow transformation). The idea of *shock-therapy* (introduced by Egor Gaidar, Prime-Minister of Russia in 1991–1992) was based on the belief that the faster reforms were carried out, the quicker new post-socialist (market) economy would become sustainable. Inescapable elements of this "shock-therapy" for Russia were price decontrol and liberalisation of markets, a decline in inflation, fiscal discipline, privatisation, as well as opening of the national economy via convertibility of the national currency and lowering obstacles to trade. *Opponents of shock-therapy* argued for application of the Chinese experience of gradual economic reforms. But at the moment of the collapse of the USSR (December 1991) political reforms in the country had gone so far that they had become totally irreversible via ordinary political processes. Fortunately, the new Russian leaders were not able to commit an act of coercion, following the example of China's leaders during the turmoil at Tiananmen Square in early June of 1989. Still, Russian reformers were acting amid a grave political crisis, initiated by the disintegration of the USSR and difficulties encountered in their search for a new model of governance in post-Soviet Russia.

The results attained after a quarter century of reforms in Russia have been interpreted by a number of schools of thought. Below we would like to present the findings of the most influential among them.

4.2   *Normal Middle Income Economy*

This model has been presented in 2004 by two US scholars – Daniel Treisman and Andrei Shleifer. They argued, that "...although Russia's transition has been painful in many ways, the country has made remarkable economic and social progress since the end of communism" (Shleifer & Treisman 2004). Adherents of this model were inclined to disregard the potential of the Russian economy, its military clout and capability to project its power beyond national borders. Nowadays, after Russian military's successful operation in Syria they have changed their minds and limit their scepticism to merely the economic power of the country and its inability to sustain the Kremlin's great power aspirations.

Treisman and Shleifer reconsider the shock therapy reforms of Egor Gaidar in a positive sense, analyzing all the available data and statistics in order to demonstrate that the socio-economic crisis after the reforms was not so long and tragic as it was depicted. In particular they took into consideration the most important aspects of the Russian economy and Russian society (GDP per capita, life expectancy, consumption of goods and services, mortality rate, etc.) in order to counter all the prejudices and disbelief about Russia. In this way they also open up better perspectives for the future. The bottom-line of their analysis is that even if a number of political developments in Russia since 2000 have pushed the country toward the illiberal end of political spectrum, they do not move it beyond the customary range of politics of middle-income countries and it will take another several decades to fix the problems of transition and convert Russia into a democratic state with efficient institutions of a market economy.

4.3   *Virtual Economy, the System of Informal Rent-Distribution*

US researcher Clifford G. Gaddy is well-known for his invention (together with Barry Ickes) of the term "virtual economy", which he has used to describe the contemporary socio-economic model of the Russian Federation (Gaddy & Ickes 1998). Its main thesis is that nowadays the Russian economy is not able to create new value (i.e. to develop as a normal country). Instead, it is systematically destroying it and that is why a significant segment of the national economy should simply be subject to closure. The main reason for this is systemic and wide-spread corruption. Enterprise directors and their corrupted partners throughout the economy (including government officials and regional leaders) collude to use nonmarket prices and various forms of nonmonetary exchange such as barter to transfer value from resource sectors of the national economy to manufacturing industry.

Supporters of the Virtual economy model believe that informal rents include politically determined price subsidies – oil sells at 31 to 46 percent of the world price in Russia – and informal taxes. The latter class includes bribes, support for the social sector, and excess costs. According to a 2005 study by INDEM, bribes have increased by a factor of nine since 2001. Because of its inconsistent socio-economic policy Russia is suffering from the "Dutch disease". It means that resource exports cause currency appreciation and undermine the competitiveness of domestic manufacturers. But, argues C. Gaddy, Russia suffers from "Russian disease": some parts of the national manufacturing sector actually benefit by charging the resource sector excess costs.

4.4 *"The OPEC Model" and Resource Nationalism*

Russian energy resources have always been a major source of the positive foreign trade balance. But since 1999 natural gas, coal, electricity, but most of all crude oil have become the key drivers of the nation's economic and social revival. In the period 1999–2008 Russia was growing fast, reducing the gap in development level between itself and the western world. This catching-up was interrupted in 2009 and once again in 2014–16 by a landslide of oil prices. Both crises hit Russia a little later than they hit the West, but Russia's striking vulnerability to a fall in the oil price meant that it was hit harder than any other G20 nation.

Some economists argue that the Russian economy is totally dependent on its energy sector and fluctuations of oil prices at global exchanges (Goldman 2008). Others believe that there is no difference between the oil price (plus inflation) and the Russian rouble exchange rate (Kireu & Movchan 2017). As a result, there is no such thing as the "Russian national economy" with its social dimensions. Believers of the OPEC model think that the key reason for Russia's rebirth since 1999 is the use of its ever-expanding energy wealth to reassert its traditional great power ambitions. They also insist: Russia is using its oil-based power as a lever in world politics and its leaders neglect the social sphere as peripheral to Russia's global strategy.

4.5 *"Government Failure" vs. "Market Failure"*

Many political economists since Adam Smith believe that markets regulate the economic development of states by an invisible hand and there is no space for governments in this mechanism. It is an established fact that markets are able to function efficiently only in ideal conditions, which are impossible in today's world: the total absence of externalities, perfect competition, complete information among all actors in the market, a high level of development in all segments of the national economy (goods, services, financial and foreign exchange markets), and even the absence of innovation since the latter upset the equilibrium of actors in a perfect market (Winston 2006: 351–379).

Meanwhile, government interventions are allowed only in extreme cases, in the form of single, unified flat income tax scale as well as equal distribution of government subsidies. It is quite obvious that in contemporary economies these pieces of advice are useless and public authorities have to fine tune national economic policy according to the peculiarities of global and national economic development.

Thus following the recognition of the "market failure" which took place in Russia in the 1990s, experts on Russia nowadays acknowledge that the real problems in the Russian economy originate from "government failure": its inability to timely and massively intervene in economic processes with the aim of directing and stimulating post-socialist socio-economic development. For example, asymmetry in the distribution of incomes from exports as well as of incomes generated inside the country occurs due to the erosion of institutional quality reflected in rampant criminality, dependence of the legal authorities on the executive branch of power, as well as corruption.

Nowadays the issue under consideration (government vs. market) has been solved in Russia in favour of the national government. It is the institutions of the executive branch of power that are working out a policy of economic development and doing their best to minimise market failure as well as prevent players in the market from promoting their egoistic interests if those actions contradict national interests.

5 China's Socio-Economic Development Since 1979: the Chinese Model

Until the mid-20th century the USSR was the only successful example of the "catch-up development" model. But at that moment, when the resources of import-substitution as the key driver of Soviet economic growth were exhausted, a number of Asian states found another model – export-oriented catch-up development. Japan was the first in the 1950s, followed in the 1960s by the Republic of Korea, Taiwan, Hong Kong, Singapore, and since the late 1970s – by China.

Due to the closed nature of its domestic political system and its resistance to attempts of imperial colonisation, China in the 20th century was able to secure traditional community institutions. There were a number of important consequences: negligible growth of income inequality, and preservation of a relatively high savings ratio. Continuity of traditional institutions has allowed them to ensure their high quality as soon as they were restored. China's political history clearly demonstrates that the transfer of institutions is a complex process, which could be successful only if imported institutions can be adjusted to local needs and do not interrupt the institutional continuity in the country under consideration (Polterovich 2001: 24–50). It is exactly this phenomenon (the successful accommodation of new institutions alongside those which are traditional to China) that we are witnessing in this country now.

5.1   *Origin of the Model: The Four Modernisations of Deng Xiaoping*
In the world of Deng Xiaoping, stability was the central characteristic of China's political system and a prerequisite to rapid economic development and interethnic collaboration. It includes international security, and that is why after the USSR's invasion into Afghanistan in December 1979, China turned increasingly towards the West, in particular to the US. This combination of internal demand for reforms and growing cooperation with the most powerful state in the world created a unique moment for launching the "four modernisations" policy of Deng Xiaoping.

The four modernisations of China have been accompanied by its progressive extension towards the outside world. Despite sceptics' expectations, China's opening to the outer world has contributed to the survival of its regime by fuelling vigorous economic growth. Beijing succeeded in reaping the benefits of increasing demand in the US and western Europe for cheap industrial products. In the 1980s social stability in China was maintained through a cautious policy whereby job creation went in tandem with the restructuring of industry and agriculture as well as the efficient redeployment of human resources displaced by intensifying competition domestically as well as internationally. Deng Xiaoping's policy enabled the Chinese authorities to combine the benefits of export-oriented industrialisation, mostly driven by inflows of FDI, with some advantages of China's autarkic economy, informally protected by traditions, customs, institutions and networks.

5.2   *The Beijing Consensus*
The term "Beijing Consensus" emerged in reaction to two phenomena. The first was the decades-long growth of Chinese economy, whose qualitative characteristics varied from previous examples of Japan and South Korea. The second was driven by a bitter dispute between protagonists and opponents of the liberal economic model and the Washington Consensus as a symbol of its global triumph.

US political scientist Joshua Ramo, the author of the "Beijing Consensus" (BC) concept, has formulated three hallmarks which distinguished BC from previous liberal doctrine: (1) a willingness to innovate; (2) equitable growth and sustainable development; (3) a strong belief in a nation's self-determination (Ramo 2004). The preconditions for the export of the BC model were set out by Deng Xiaoping, who asked Chinese leaders to carefully study the legacy of Singapore for its implementation at home.

The BC has an almost balanced combination of political and economic ideas at its foundation. It assumes that the previous model of the Washington Consensus is not the only one possible. The second conviction is that political stability should forego economic liberalisation (Sautman 1992: 72–102). Yet another belief is that national security should be reliably guaranteed. Even economic factors have political value for BC. For example, the peaceful rise of China was oriented toward economic development and was not designed initially (in the 1980s) to challenge US global domination. But the popularity of the BC is so high today that its supporters exceed the protagonists of the Washington Consensus.

5.3   New Structural Economy

The concept of the New Structural Economy (NSE) is closely associated with the Chinese scholar and Ph.D. graduate of the University of Chicago Justin Yifu Lin. He believes that sustainable and inclusive growth should be the driving force for poverty reduction in developing countries and for convergence with developed economies (Lin 2011: 194).

The urgent need for elaboration of a new school on development was based on the recognition of globalisation as a key external factor for all national economies. At the beginning of the current century it became clear that with the exception of a few rapidly growing and politically stable states (mostly in East Asia) there were few examples of successful economic convergence between developed and developing countries. Even the growing scale of international assistance, including the ambitious MDGs (Millennium Development Goals) of the United Nations did not fundamentally change the situation.

The NSE theory is based on the neoclassical economic school, dominant in economic science in the 19th century as well as in the 1980–1990s. Its prime objects of interest are technologies, infrastructure and institutions as determinants of economic structure influencing socio-economic development. The theory emphasises that the starting point for analysing an economy's structure is its endowments (the total budget) as well as the structure of its endowments (factors' relative price that is endogenously defined). The theory demonstrates the structuralist approach to studies of economic policy and argues that national economic development is an evolutionary process, which includes at different stages industries, technologies, infrastructure and institutional mechanisms, in which a "facilitating government" is also indispensable in addition to an "effective market".

According to Daniel A. Bell, China's current leaders hope to achieve a more open and modern Confucian-oriented meritocratic system, which should be based on traditional values and flexible enough to accommodate the challenges of the global economy (Bell 2015). Debates on the China Model and its export together with Chinese technologies and investments touch upon an extremely important issue: is there a future for capitalism and the market economy in an authoritarian state? I.e., is democracy an imperative for building an efficient market economy? There is no answer yet for this question and we may not find it any time soon. Different types of states may preserve a stable balance of their political and economic systems for many years. In recent decades rapid and sustainable take-offs have been accomplished not only in democratic states, but in authoritarian ones as well (Singapore, Republic of Korea). During the period of pro-market reforms these states had clearly authoritarian political regimes. Probably, they were able to secure their success due to subsequent democratic reforms and institutions, but this issue is beyond our research. Until now the example of China, as well as the development of Russia from 1999–2014, demonstrates that an authoritarian political system has its benefits for the genesis of a model of economic development in states with a planned socialist economy.

6   Prospects for the Integration of the Chinese and Russian Models and the Creation of a BRICS's Alternative to the Washington Consensus

China and Russia were able to secure their sovereignty for many centuries throughout their history. Even after the tremendous shocks of the 20th century they are members of the great powers' club with traditional institutions and, until recently, rather homogeneous societies. Many states look upon them as good examples of continuity and change, which has helped to secure sovereignty and a prominent status in global affairs.

Starting from the Emperor Peter the Great (1672–1725), Russia pursued a path of westernisation, which was accelerated by the reforms of Emperor Alexander II (1855–1881) and Prime-Minister Peter Stolypin (1906–1911). The results were controversial: intermittent growth of inequality and the emergence of weak institutions of a market economy. Many of them were imported from western Europe and did not take hold in Russia. Even the socialist experiment in the times of the USSR, which included the resurrection of communal institutions, led to the reduction of poverty, as well as of income and social inequality, but just for a short period of time. This is due to the fact that it was in conflict with the strategic aim of the USSR – to elaborate a universal model of development which ignored the historical experience of Russia.

In the case of China, its 100-year long westernisation in the 19th-20th centuries led the country into a situation of a semi-colony and de-facto break-down in the 1920s. Nevertheless, soon after the Communist Party of China's rise to power in 1949 the country resumed its commitment to "Asian values" and community institutions. We should emphasise that even after Deng Xiaoping's reform, inequality, which re-emerged in the country as a consequence, did not lead to the weakening of institutions' efficiency. Hence Beijing was able to retain the positive dynamics of socio-economic development based on traditions and customary social practices.

From 2008 onward the global political and economic system has been facing both the period of complex and sharp economic crisis represented by the deepening decline of traditional centres of power (the European Union, the US and Japan) and the emergence of new poles in the changing global system, such as the BRICS. The G20 financial Forum took the centre stage in autumn 2008 as a global arena for strategic communication between world leaders and their countries. The G20 Forum made it clear that open and mutually equal debates were much in need in order to balance American power with the realities of the emerging markets of other countries, first of all of those of the BRICS.

The strongest message to the international community at the inauguration of the BRIC Summit (2009) has been focused on the idea that the four countries were not going to challenge or undermine the liberal order of the global economy but see themselves as a balancing element in times of international financial turmoil. At the same time, the four countries positioned themselves outside of a Western-centric order and did not acknowledge the fact that they are actually among the leading beneficiaries of the liberal international system with US at the centre of it.

A comparison of different nations' social policies presupposes treatment of multiple factors and should not be limited to only a few areas. In the table below there are several indicators, which allow us to characterise the recent achievements of China and Russia in the field of social policy.

Our comparison of development policy in China and Russia demonstrates that social processes have remained on the periphery of attempts to modernise the two states and their political and economic systems. The prioritisation of private initiative and the liberal nature of these national economies have led over the long-term to a de-emphasis of social policy measures as instruments of economic support of people at large. Social policy's decentralisation via the functional transfer to subnational structures (regional authorities) as well as business organisations, have led to negative social consequences in China and Russia, at least initially. This is exactly what happened in the 1990s. The negative consequences of the social sphere's degradation (duration of life, access to free medicine, level of pensions) have not been fully addressed in either state.

China and Russia differ in their choice of endogenous factors to implement their social policy. Russia follows global trends while officially recognizing the top-priority goal of the Comprehensive Development Framework for fighting

TABLE 13.1   China and Russia: economic and social indicators (end of 2016)

	China	Russia
Population, millions	1 379	146
Crude birth rate (per 1 000 persons)	12,3	13,3
Infant mortality rate (per 1 000 live births)	12	6,5
Maternal mortality rate (per 100 000 live births)	27	10,8
Unemployment (%)	4,0	5,6
Share of public expenditure on education as % of GDP	4,2	3,8
Public expenditure on health as % of GDP	5,5	3,6

SOURCE: *BRICS JOINT STATISTICAL PUBLICATION, 2016; BRAZIL, RUSSIA, INDIA, CHINA, SOUTH AFRICA.* PRABHAT PUBLICITY, NEW DELHI

poverty and for sustainable development. The Framework was proposed by the World Bank in January 1999 (The World Bank 1999) and includes "good governance" and "second generation reforms" as strategic aims for the future of global development (Wolfensohn 1999). Russia's priority today is to implement new and novel forms of social policy to accomplish a limited number of aims. Democratic institutions are indispensable elements of the model.

In contrast to Moscow, Beijing has so far ignored factors such as "democracy" and democratic institutions. The new priority of its socio-economic policy, which was proclaimed at the 19th CCP National Congress (October 2017) as the highest priority for the next five years, is the achievement of a "moderately prosperous society" (Xi 2017).

Both China and Russia have so far been unable to establish efficient models of social transfers which could provide assistance to those people who are actually suffering from economic and social insecurity. Annually Russia spends about 3 percent of GDP on social benefits, much more than the absolute majority of developing countries. It is one of the global leaders in the variety of these payments and types of relief (Sinnott et al. 2016). Unfortunately, this diverse and expensive assistance is inadequate for fighting Russian poverty. Only 25 percent of social transfers go to statistically poor people, and the share of targeted support in poor families' budgets in the Russian regions is only 2 percent of their total incomes. This is due to the fact that the current model of social transfers gives money to honoured people who are deserving according to the Russian authorities. This is why we should not consider Russia's current model of social policy as efficient, attractive or good for replicating elsewhere.

China's current profile in the social sphere is even less impressive. The problem of designing and implementing social policy is seen as a regional one, and hence until very recently the Government of China did not even have a strategy for social policy. Still, in 1993, the Shanghai Municipal authorities implemented a minimum livelihood guarantee, or *dibao*, a sort of anti-poverty safety net. Since then this program of social entitlements has expanded throughout China and is centrally regulated. Today, it serves as the country's primary social insurance program. Even though it is the largest welfare program in the world, recent decisions at the 19th CCP Congress open new avenues for expanding China's social policy. This is why we can predict a growing interest to the Chinese model of social policy all over the world.

Below we would like to present some observations on common and distinctive features of development policies in China and Russia nowadays.

7   The Search for a Balance between Liberalism and Economic Nationalism

In the last two decades Russia has made its way from a state with an ultraliberal social policy (in the 1990s) to a country with its own original national version of a neo-liberal "welfare state". The model is not 100 percent a liberal one, if we accept recommendations from Walt Rostow's book "The Stages of Economic Growth" (Rostow 1962). Still, we consider the current Russian model of development as semi-liberal. It fits the basic criteria of liberalism and demonstrates major successes in constructing market economy structures and civil society's institutions. In contrast, Chinese leaders remain ignorant about these problems and concentrate on achieving their "moderately prosperous society" agenda as a substitute for substantial debates on the country's current social problems and prospects for their solution.

7.1   *Import Substitution (in Russia) and the Search for Domestic Drivers to Stimulate Internal Demand (in China)*

Despite the Kremlin leaders' numerous statements about their willingness to keep the Russian economy open towards the global market, the basic characteristics of the Russian economy are: 1) the exchange of mineral resources for finished goods and knowledge industry services, and 2) a vigorous import-substitution policy, which is driven by military security concerns and the need to protect the national economy from economic sanctions, imposed by the US and their allies in 2014.

China looks at the same type of challenges differently. As a high-volume exporter of industrial goods, China has to import the newest technologies to produce them and is forced to establish its own industrial enterprises, which have to be competitive internationally to survive. The key driver of economic growth in China today is domestic demand, public investment in infrastructure, science and education.

7.2   *The Search for Sustainability of the Current Socio-Economic Models in Both Countries*

The task of changing its economic strategy from the previous focus on the extensive growth of exports to encouraging domestic demand was recognised in China as the most important political challenge as early as 2012. At the 19th CCP Congress it was officially reiterated by Xi Jinping, as a key element of the new strategy of constructing a moderately prosperous society.

It is too early to present Russia's current socio-economic policy as a unique phenomenon, not yet ready to be imitated outside the BRICS community. Some success with the policy of import-substitution in 2015–2017 did not remove the need for urgent modernisation of the national economy, and the integration of Russian industry into global value chains. The "Pivot to Asia" strategy of foreign policy declared in 2014 was an attempt to delay the substantial modernisation of the Russian economy and survive the period of economic war with European countries – Moscow's previous key economic and trade partners. It appears that Russia is trying to copy the Chinese model of reforms, which manifests itself in building up investments and keeping the "commanding heights" of the national economy under tight government control.

7.3   *Rising Living Standards without Proportional Democratisation*

The ruling political elites in China and Russia do not share liberals' conviction that the rapid growth of a national economy is impossible without strong democratic institutions which are well-grounded in political systems in the two states. More likely, Beijing and Moscow believe that progressive democratisation will be a side-effect of rapid economic growth and gradually rising living standards.

7.4   *The Slowdown of Economic (GDP) Growth and the Search for New Drivers of Economic and Regional Development*

China and Russia face the problem of a massive drop in the rate of economic growth. China's rapid economic development in 1978–2013 remains unprecedented in global history (its average annual growth of GDP was above 9 percent for 36 years). Since 2013 GDP growth in China is less than 7 percent with a downward trend. Annual GDP growth in Russia in 1999–2008 was on average about 7 percent due to the combination of rather unique factors (a low base effect, devaluation of the national currency, the energy price increase, and radical economic reforms in 2000–2003). Since 2013 the Russian economy has hovered between stagnation and slow economic growth. It is very likely that in the future China and Russia will have a similar rate of economic expansion (3–4 percent of GDP) and a totally new socio-economic policy will be required to cope with the consequences of slow economic growth.

7.5   *Dialogue between the Authorities and the Public*

A special feature of current political life in Russia is the escalation of authoritarianism, which could be considered as an attempt to return to traditional values, including community spirit, a negative attitude towards the protection of minority rights, and the significant role of religion in the spiritual life of citizens. Meanwhile, Russian authorities consider the social activism of Russian people as a high-value asset for national socio-economic development. This is why the State budget of Russia in recent years has dramatically increased funding for non-governmental organisations: from 300 million RUR a few years ago to 8 billion RUR in 2018. These efforts coincide with an assertive policy to squeeze out of Russia foreign foundations and NGOs, to constrain the activities of the American media, and to impose some forms of censorship in Russia.

The dialogue between the authorities and civil society in China has witnessed ups and downs in the recent decade. In 2016–2017 there were numerous examples of harassment of NGO activists and journalists. The prioritisation of "stability" in China has as an inevitable consequence the subordination of social and political life to the interests of economic development and a disregard for the interests and human rights of different minorities.

8   Prospects for Integration of the Chinese and Russian Models (Liberal Economy and Authoritarian Political Systems)

8.1   *Liberal Trade System*

China and Russia consider the liberal international trade regime as favourable for their economies. Their recently obtained membership in the WTO confirms this thesis, as well as statistics on their foreign trade in 2000–2016, which far exceeded their GDP growth. The Chinese President Xi Jinping's keynote speech at the World Economic Forum in Davos, Switzerland, on January 17, 2017, entitled "Jointly Shoulder Responsibility of Our Times, Promote Global Growth", became an open claim of China on leadership in the international economic system (Xi 2017a). Those who share the premises of the Hegemonic Stability Theory may come to the conclusion that Beijing already considers itself a global economic leader, and believes, following the example of the Chancellor of the German Empire Otto von Bismarck, that free trade is a weapon of the most powerful nation.

8.2   *Rigid Political System and the Idealisation of Stability*

China's political system has been "frozen" since late 1980s and is becoming increasingly rigid. The same process in Russia started in the autumn of 2011 when Prime-Minister Vladimir Putin declared that he was willing to return to the Kremlin as President of Russia despite the US's adamant opposition to this move (Tkachenko 2017: 116). The rules of behaviour in domestic politics in Russia are becoming tougher and more rigid, and public authorities are making active efforts to marginalise domestic actors who are able to lead opposition movements and become the front-runners of a "colour revolution". The leaders of China and Russia embrace the ideal of stability and consider any reform (either political or socio-economic) as potentially explosive for domestic stability.

8.3   *Democracy within Elite Circles*

Up until the 19th Congress of the CCP there were numerous examples of pluralism among the representatives of the elites at the national and regional levels of power in China. Nowadays this practice is gradually disappearing, and we may expect a less tolerant approach to public political discussions in the media and inside the Chinese political machine. The level of democracy in Russia is historically higher than in China and it includes the political elites. Still, the same process of declining tolerance towards opponents can be found in Russia as well.

9   Conclusion

The idea of economic development was one of the most influential and successful concepts of the previous century. The developmental state model attracted the attention of scholars from the USA and the USSR as opponents in the Cold War.[4] Even "the End of History" and US unilateralism did not prevent

---

4   There is no consensus over what is meant by the developmental state. See, for example: Stubbs, R. (2009). 'What ever happened to the East Asian Developmental State? The unfolding debate', *The Pacific Review*, 22(1): 1–22.

states in different regions of the planet from continuing their search for a set of measures to transform the traditional sectors of the economy into modern ones. There were two major approaches to transformation before China began its reforms: 1) gradual "social-democratic" reforms, associated with western Europe in the mid-20th century; and 2) shock-therapy reforms of former Soviet bloc countries. China in late 1970s started its search for the so-called Third Road of transformation. Russia since the beginning of the 21st century has joined its eastern neighbour, totally unsatisfied with the results of the shock-therapy reforms which originated with the Washington Consensus.

Currently the ruling political parties in China (the Communist party of China) and Russia (the United Russia party) are attempting to change their profile and become more inclusive social democratic parties. They do believe that gradual reforms could spur socio-economic stability and sustainable growth while preserving the ruling elites' authority to rule in China and Russia. The growing role of elections at the subnational level in China, and Russia's willingness to comply with the requirements of the Council of Europe for free and fair elections, make their political systems more open and pluralistic.

Our research demonstrates that until now the Chinese gradualist approach to development has produced multiple winners and a few losers. Russian ruling elites are in the process of adopting Chinese best practices in national economic policy. China (since late 1978) and Russia (since early 2000) have been practicing a mixture of liberal economic reforms and a continuation of the "strong state" security model. Their efforts to achieve peaceful economic development are acquiring normative and political significance among dozens of states in the Global South and emerging economies in Eurasia. Beijing and Moscow are challenging the intellectual foundations of the Washington Consensus and undermining the global political and economic leadership of the US, providing a more equal model of socio-economic development. The two states are also challenging another belief of liberals: that democracy is good for development.

Reforms in China and Russia nowadays are marked by socio-economic growth in a period of prolonged stability, authoritarian domestic political regimes, innovative economic reforms and disregard for the problems of political liberalisation. Still, a new type of social instability is growing in the two countries: widespread discontent over social issues is growing for increasing numbers of low-income groups, forced to survive within the burgeoning market economies of the two states.

While emphasizing the success of reforms in China and their prospects for being transferred around the globe, we should keep in mind the uniqueness of the domestic situation in this country. In the late 1970s China had a large agricultural labour force, a low level of social transfers to the population, a decentralised system of national economy, which allowed the beginning of radical reforms at the regional and sub-regional levels in order to check their sustainability. In contrast to Russia, China is still a large agrarian economy which means that rural areas are able to provide additional labour to sustain economic growth, especially in the private sector of the national economy. Sources of cheap labour inside Russia were exhausted in the 1990s and nowadays either immigration or modernisation may become additional drivers of socio-economic growth in this country.

At the moment there is no optimal development model which is open for duplication worldwide. Copying the development experience of one state by another state is a risky business with no guarantee for success. That is why we see the current role of China and Russia as BRICS members in setting a new agenda for debates on development as twofold: to transform their own economies into global economic leaders and poles in a multipolar economic system, and at the same time to ground their development policies on new principles, different from those which we may have found in the Washington Consensus. A combination of these two factors may establish a new paradigm of development.

Bibliography

Acemoglu, D., Johnson, S., and Robinson, J.A. (2001). 'The Colonial Origins of Comparative Development: An Empirical Investigation', *American Economic Review,* 91: 1369–1401.

Astakhov, E. (2016). 'BRIKS – perspektivy razvitiia', *Vestnik MGIMO-Universiteta,* 1(46): 42–50.

Bator, F.M. (1958). 'The Anatomy of Market Failure', *Quarterly Journal of Economics,* 72, August: 351–379.

Bell, D.A. (2015). *The China Model: Political Meritocracy and the Limits of Democracy.* Princeton: Princeton University Press.

Gaddy, C. and Ickes, B. (1998). 'Russia's Virtual Economy', *Foreign Affairs,* September-October: 53–67.

Goldman, M.I. (2008). *Petrostate: Putin, Power, and the New Russia.* London: Oxford University Press.

Kaukenov, A. (2007). 'Politika Kitaia v Shankhaiskoi organizatsii sotrudnichestva', *Tsentralnaia Asia i Kavkaz,* 3(51): 73–89.

Kennedy, P. (1994). *Preparing for the Twenty First Century.* London: Vintage.

Kireu E. and Movchan, A. (2017) 'Formula rublia. Kak rasschitat' kurs rossiiskoi valiuty v liuboi moment vremeni', Moskovskii Tsentr Karnegi, 28 September, http://carnegie.ru/commentary/73225.

Leftwich, A. (1995). 'Bringing politics back in: Towards a model of the developmental state', *The Journal of Development Studies*, 31(3): 400–427.

Lin, J.Y. (2011). 'New Structural Economies: A Framework for Rethinking Development', *The World Bank Research Observer*, 26(2): 193–221.

Lukov, V. (2012). 'A Global Forum for the New Generation: The Role of the BRICS and the prospects for the future', *BRICS Information Centre: University of Toronto*, 24 January, http://www.brics.utoronto.ca/analysis/Lukov-Global-Forum.html.

Nureev, R.M. (1993). 'Aziatskii sposob proizvodstva kak ekonomicheskaia sistema', pp. 62–87, in Ivanov, N.A. (ed.), *Fenomen vostochnogo despotizma: struktura upravleniia i vlasti*, Moskva: Nauka.

Polterovich, V.M. (2001). 'Transplantatsiia ekonomicheskikh institutov', *Ekonomicheskaia nauka sovremennoi Rossii*, 3: 24–50.

Popov, V. (2012). 'Pochemu Zapad razbogatel ran'she, chem drugie strany, i pochemu Kitai segodnia dogoniaet Zapad? Novyi otvet na staryi vopros', *Zhurnal Novoj ekonomicheskoj assotsiatsii*, 3(15): 35–64.

Ramo, J. (2004). *The Beijing Consensus*. London: Foreign Policy Center.

Ramzy, A. (2009). 'A new book reveals why China is unhappy', *Time*, 20 May, http://content.time.com/time/world/article/0,8599,1886749,00.html.

Rostow, W.W. (1962). *The Stages of Economic Growth*. London: Cambridge University Press.

Sautman, B. (1992). 'Sirens of the Strongman: Neo-Authoritarianism in Recent Chinese Political Theory', *China Quarterly*, 129, March: 72–102.

Shleifer, A. and Treisman, D. (2004). 'A Normal Country', *Foreign Affairs*, March-April: 21.

Sinnott, E., Matytsin, M., Popova, D., and Gorina, E. (2016). *Russian Federation Distributional Impact of Fiscal Policy over the Boom and Downturn*. Washington, D.C: World Bank.

Stubbs, R. 2009. 'What ever happened to the East Asian Developmental State? The unfolding debate', *The Pacific Review*, 22(1): 1–22.

Tkachenko, S. (2017). 'Coercive Diplomacy of Vladimir Putin (2014–2016)', pp. 115–136, in Kanet, R. (ed.), *The Russian Challenge to the European Security Environment*. Basingstoke: Palgrave Macmillan.

Winston, C. (2006). *Government Failure versus Market Failure: Microeconomics Policy Research and Government Performance*. Washington, D.C.: AEI-Brookings.

Wolfensohn, J.D. (1999). 'A Proposal for a Comprehensive Development Framework', 21 January, Washington, D.C.: The World Bank. Available at: http://web.worldbank.org/archive/website01013/WEB/0__CO-87.HTM.

Womack, B. (2016). 'Asymmetric parity: US–China relations in a multimodal world', *International Affairs*, 92(6): 1463–1480.

World Bank. (1999). 'Comprehensive Development Framework (CDF): Progress Report', 14 September (SecM99- 642).

Xi. (2017). 'Secure a Decisive Victory in Building a Moderately Prosperous Society in All Respects and Strive for the Great Success of Socialism with Chinese Characteristics for a New Era', Delivered at the 19th National Congress of the Communist Party of China, 18 October, http://www.xinhuanet.com/english/download/Xi_Jinping's _report_at_19th_CPC_National_Congress.pdf.

Xi. (2017a). 'Jointly Shoulder Responsibility of Our Times, Promote Global Growth. Davos', 17 January. Available at: https://america.cgtn.com/2017/01/17/full-text-of-xi-jinping-keynote-at-the-world-economic-forum.

CHAPTER 14

Engaging with European (Dis-)Integration: Russia in Dialogue with Europe/s

Marco Puleri

> To get a better handle on the fluctuations in EU-Russia bilateral relations, one has to take a closer look at how Russia's proverbial love-hate relationship with Europe vacillates back and forth between two interconnected spheres: the world of political imaginary and the realm of actual decision making.
>
> TORBAKOV 2017: 70

Looking at the recent developments of EU-Russia relations, Igor Torbakov (2017: 76) highlighted the gradual progression of "Russia's mental distancing from Europe" throughout the last years. According to Torbakov, this happened mainly because the EU's enlargement and European integration process "was and is perceived by the Kremlin as particularly worrisome" (ivi: 75): namely, "Russia appears to be confronted by an assertive neighbour whose eastern border is not fixed, but indeed moving steadily further eastward, gobbling up, piece after piece, what used to be parts of the 'outer' and even of the 'inner' Soviet empire" (ivi: 75). It is exactly at the crossroads between the "EU's behavior in Eurasia as [...] a normative and bureaucratic empire that resolves its strategic problems through extending its internal bureaucratic norms and regulations" (Torbakov 2017: 73) – and the "vital and exclusive" Russian national interest in its "near abroad" where the "realm of actual decision making" clashes with the "world of political imaginary":

> The EU has its own "sphere of identity", but its *modus operandi* is diametrically opposed to that of Russia. Being a norms- and values-based entity, the EU cultivates an identity that essentially is not territory-bound. This incompatibility of principles will make an EU-Russia accommodation, in terms of delimitating their respective "spheres", extremely difficult, if not altogether impossible.
>
> TORBAKOV 2017: 73

Nonetheless, throughout the first decades of the 21st century "there has been no shortage of engagement in the EU-Russia relationship" (Greene 2017: 2), even if cooperation between the two geopolitical actors has always been character-ised by unstable dynamics. On the one hand, whereas at the dawn of the 2000s the Prodi Commission led by former Italian Prime Minister Romano Prodi launched the European Neighbourhood Policy, "offering the countries in the neighbourhood the opportunity to participate in 'everything but institutions'" (Bildt 2015: 3), Russia refused the terms of European cooperation and integra-tion, mainly because of "a wish to establish more direct and equal relations with the EU" (ivi). On the other hand, the Ukraine's Orange Revolution in 2004, the Russo-Georgian war and the launch of the Eastern Partnership on the initia-tive of Poland and Sweden in 2008 only postponed the renegotiation of the old Partnership and Cooperation Agreement signed in 1994 and the launch of the new Partnership for Modernisation in 2009–10, which "committed Moscow – at least rhetorically – to using European integration as a means toward its own do-mestic transformation" (Greene 2017: 2) under Dmitrii Medvedev's presidency.

Nonetheless, it was not by chance that throughout Vladimir Putin's third mandate (2012–2018), and the further development of alternative integration platforms such as the Custom Unions (2010–2014) and the Eurasian Economic Union (2014-), Russia – previously "labelled a 'strategic partner'" – came to be a "strategic problem" (Bildt 2015: 9) for the EU. In the Russian "world of political imaginary", Ukrainian "European" integration embodied a direct threat from the EU (and the US) to prevent:

> Basically, Russian governing elites were faced with a tough question: if a European orientation is compatible with Russian identity, then on what grounds is Moscow preventing other post-Soviet nations from joining the EU?
>
> TORBAKOV 2017: 79

While for "about five years (2008–2013), the EU and EaU [i.e. Eurasian Union] developed in a 'soft' way [...], in 2013 both geopolitical projects hardened" (Minakov 2017): the Maidan revolution in the aftermath of the missed signing of the Association Agreement between Ukraine and the EU in the framework of the Eastern Partnership in November 2013, the contested annexation of Crimea to the Russian Federation in March 2014, and the escalating war in Donbas testified then to the "unprecedented level of hostility" (ivi) reached by the two competing geopolitical actors and their colliding integration projects throughout 2014.

Coming to more recent times, as highlighted by John R. Deni (2017) for Carn-egie Europe, over the past years the Western strategy has remained "mostly opaque" and "seems to be to treat Russia as a combination of adversary and partner – to confront Moscow where the West must, but to cooperate where the West can". The reasons behind this impasse in finding a common strategy seem to be clear: on the one side, the Member States of the EU have completely different perceptions and interests in relation to Russia, thus undermining the implemented policies of cooperation (or contestation) between the two actors in a global perspective; on the other hand, "the road forward for Europe vis-à-vis Russia must begin with the recognition that the relationship is geopolitical, and that the primary field of competition is – and will remain for the foreseeable future – the Eastern Neighborhood" (Greene 2017: 4), where the diverging policies of enlargement and partnership promoted respectively by the European Union and the Russian Federation do conflict. Thus, it is exactly their respective competing regional and international projections that affect the possibility of a common space of dialogue and cooperation. While at the end of the 1980's, Gorbachev could prospectively expect the creation of a "common European home", in the light of the years which followed the fall of the Soviet Union we can see that this ambition belonged to "other politics and epochs". Along these lines, nowadays it seems to be just Russia mirroring the disarticulation of European Union policies, while at the same time the unstable relationship between the two actors can reflect the constant change of direction in Russian foreign policy.

In this chapter, we will analyse the recent evolution of relations between the two geopolitical actors, stressing in particular the role played by the different member states of the European Union in promoting, or disapproving, the creation of a common space of cooperation with the Russian Federation. Furthermore, we will pay close attention to the role played by Russia in the movements of integration, or, alternatively, disintegration, of the European Union. As stressed by I. Krastev (2014), nowadays "[t]he EU and Russia are really living in different worlds and the competition this time is not to demonstrate which of these worlds is a better one, it is to demonstrate which of these worlds is the real one".

The research will concern the study of the different outcomes for EU-Russia relations brought on by the two main crises which affected the European Union throughout 2014–17. While in the case of the Ukraine crisis in 2013–14, "despite much criticism, the EU member states have [...] agreed on a still functioning and comprehensive sanctions regime against the Russians" (Härtel 2017: 3) and excluded the latter from debates on the European geopolitical scene, it was the 2015 migration crisis – combined with the crisis within the EU after Brexit in June 2016, along with the outcomes of extra-EU dynamics such as the Russian military intervention in Syria – that "widened room for Russia's return to the European (geo)political scene through a strategy of redefining Europe in more conservative and traditionalist terms, as opposed to the liberal cosmopolitan philosophy of EU's project" (Braghiroli & Makarychev 2017: 1).

Most fundamentally, if during the 2013–14 crisis the different positions assumed by the member states in relation to Ukraine-related sanctions against Russia could still find common ground in a shared security strategy, it was throughout 2015–16 that the EU's quest for "common action" revealed its fragility. As highlighted by Braghiroli and Makarychev in their article emblematically entitled "Redefining Europe: Russia and the 2015 Refugee Crisis", the rise of parties claiming pro-Russian stances in the EU – emerging from both far-right and far-left backgrounds – together with the decline of the mainstream parties in the EU member states, opened new channels for the Russian elite's dialogue with the "other" conservative and pro-security Europe:

> Russia's pragmatic preference to communication with groups adhering to different political worldviews can be seen as a tactical reverse side of the process of mixing and mutating of ideological loyalties in Europe, to which the refugee crisis significantly contributed, in order to eventually advance the process of disintegration/disaggregation of European unity and promote its long-term strategic political and ideological preferences.
>
> BRAGHIROLI & MAKARYCHEV 2017: 2

Russia in dialogue with Europe/s: if through the lens of the Russia policies recently enacted by the EU we witness a more "pragmatic engagement" with Russian elites – i.e. engaging with Russia on a range of selected foreign policy issues, it is only on the side of Russia that a "concrete strategy" in cooperating with conservative forces in Europe is taking shape. Following these lines, we will try to answer the question concerning the assumed Russian efforts to weaken the EU's central power, in the light of the Kremlin's alleged attempt to tighten its relations with the "conservative" and "anti-euro" parties around Europe.

1   Partnership or Rivalry: Russia and the EU in a Polycentric International System

What is truly fascinating is how quickly Russia's official/mainstream perspective on "Europe" has run full circle during the Putin years: from the perception of Russia as a full-blown member of the European community of nations, to the vision of it as a part of a "Greater Europe", to imagining Russia as the "true Europe" and the EU as the "false Europe", to the contention that Russia constitutes a distinct civilization apart from Europe.

TORBAKOV 2017: 80

In the *Foreign Policy Concept of the Russian Federation*, which was approved by Vladimir Putin on November 30, 2016, the recent deterioration of relations between Western powers and Russia is clearly declared: the "containment policy" against Russia adopted by the allies in the aftermath of the Ukrainian crisis runs "counter to the growing need for cooperation and addressing transnational challenges and threats in today's world" (Foreign Policy Concept 2016).[1] Nonetheless, by going further in reading the document, insofar as "the possibilities of the historic West to rule in World Economics and Politics are reducing", the European Union "remains an important partner in economics, trade and foreign politics to Russia" (ivi). If compared to the 2013 Concept, the new document lists the EU countries which Russia intends to develop bilateral relations with: Germany, France, Italy and Spain. Actually, by comparing the two latest *Concepts*, it is significant to observe that in 2016 Russia is no more described "as an integral part of European civilization" (Foreign Policy Concept 2013).

Throughout 2016, following the difficult situation faced by the EU institutions to find a shared position in establishing a common policy on EU-Russia relations, we witnessed the publication of several documents on the debated "Russian question". In the "Global Strategy for the European Union's Foreign and Security Policy. Shared Visions, Common Action: A Stronger Europe", presented in June 2016 by Federica Mogherini, High Representative of the Union for Foreign Affairs and Security Policy, the concept "fails to address such prospective areas for EU-Russia cooperation as fighting terrorism and illegal migration, which are mentioned in the Russian foreign policy doctrine",

---

1 "Systemic problems in the Euro-Atlantic region that have accumulated over the last quarter century are manifested in the geopolitical expansion pursued by the North Atlantic Treaty Organization (NATO) and the European Union (EU) along with their refusal to begin implementation of political statements regarding the creation of a common European security and cooperation framework, have resulted in a serious crisis in the relations between Russia and the Western States. The containment policy adopted by the United States and its allies against Russia, and political, economic, information and other pressure Russia is facing from them undermine regional and global stability, are detrimental to the long-term interests of all sides and run counter to the growing need for cooperation and addressing transnational challenges and threats in today's world" (Foreign Policy Concept 2016).

as stressed by Artem Kureev (2016). Significantly, the Russian case is included only in the section devoted to the prospects for the "European security order":

> Managing the relationship with Russia represents a key strategic challenge. A consistent and united approach must remain the cornerstone of EU policy towards Russia. Substantial changes in relations between the EU and Russia are premised upon full respect for international law and the principles underpinning the European security order, including the Helsinki Final Act and the Paris Charter. We will not recognize Russia's illegal annexation of Crimea nor accept the destabilization of eastern Ukraine [...] At the same time, the EU and Russia are interdependent. We will therefore engage Russia to discuss disagreements and cooperate if and when our interests overlap.
>
> Global Strategy 2016: 33

Throughout 2016 the quest for "common action" stated in the "Strategy" revealed its fragility, as highlighted in the briefing "The EU's Russia policy. Five guiding principles" issued by the European Parliamentary Research Service (EPRS) in October, on the eve of the European Council meeting. The cornerstones of the EU's Russia policy were already identified by the Foreign Affairs Council on 14 March 2016, as follows:
- insisting on the full implementation of the Minsk agreements before economic sanctions against Russia are lifted;
- pursuing closer relations with the former Soviet republics in the EU's Eastern Neighbourhood (including Ukraine) and of central Asia;
- becoming more resilient to Russian threats such as energy security, hybrid threats, and disinformation;
- engaging selectively with Russia on a range of foreign policy issues;
- increasing support for Russian civil society and promoting people-to-people contacts.

While "none of the key points of the Minsk II agreement", which was negotiated by the leaders of Russia, Germany, France and Ukraine in February 2015, "have been fully implemented", at the same time the "annual cost of sanctions and counter-sanctions has been estimated at 0.25% of GDP for the EU, and 2% of GDP for Russia" (EPRS 2016: 3). Furthermore, the EU's Eastern Neighbourhood remains at the crossroads between the Eurasian Economic Union integration process and closer ties to the EU, and a shared solution for EU dependence on Russian energy imports has not yet been found, as the proposed TurkStream and Nord Stream 2 have been harshly opposed by some of the EU member states (see Sytas 2016). Thus, in the aftermath of the worsening situation in Syria, at the European Council meeting in Brussels held on 20 October 2016 Donald Tusk clearly stated that "Russia's strategy is to weaken the EU" (European Council 2016).

This preluded the prolongation of the "EU restrictive measures in response to the crisis in Ukraine" (see European Council), which can be summed up as follows:

- diplomatic measures, including the cancellation of EU-Russia summit, the exclusion of the Russian Federation from G8 (now G7) meetings, and the suspension of negotiations over Russia's joining the Organisation for Economic Cooperation and Development and the International Energy Agency since 2014;
- individual restrictive measures introduced in March 2014 and extended until 15 March 2020. This affects 150 people and 38 entities – including an asset freeze and a travel ban;
- economic sanctions targeting specific sectors of the Russian economy – such as limiting access to EU primary and secondary capital markets for selected Russian banks and companies, an export and import ban on trade in arms and an export ban on dual-use goods for military use in Russia, and restriction of technologies and services for oil production and exploration. This was introduced in July and September 2014, and then extended throughout 2015–2019 until 31 July 2020, following cyclical assessments of the Minsk agreements implementation;
- restrictions on economic relations with Crimea and Sevastopol' until 23 June 2020, including an import ban on goods from these areas and an export ban for selected goods and technologies, a prohibition to supply tourism services, and restrictions on trade and investment.

Considering the different positions assumed by the EU member states in relation to Russia policy in the aftermath of the Ukraine crisis, this is no surprise that a "'universe' of national perspectives" (David et al. 2013: 255) was to arise following the different historical, geographical, and cultural experiences, and the economic and political interests – combined with extra-EU dynamics, and mainly the central role of the USA's policies towards Europe and Russia. Thus, "we have witnessed the full range of possible developments, from turmoil (Finland, partly Baltics) over gradual change (Germany) to consistency (Italy, Greece) or even prioritization (e.g. Sweden), which developed into a 'champion' of related EU policies" (Härtel 2017: 5). Interestingly, as for a reflection on the broader distribution of views within the EU, even the Central and Eastern European countries shared different stances on how to deal with Russia. Whereas the Visegrad Group included the "strong pro-Ukrainian line of Poland on one side, Hungary aligning in a pro-Russian stance on the other and ambivalent positions of Czech Republic and Slovakia" (Brajerčíková & Lenč 2017: 250), the Baltic states clearly "came to favor the common European response to Russia", even if all three countries, Lithuania, Latvia and Estonia, "observed with concern the rapprochement of Russia and the West in the case of Syria and in the fight against the Islamic State" (Vilson 2017: 10). Actually, as emblematically described by the analyst André Härtel in his introduction to the edited issue "National Perspectives on Ukraine Crisis":

> What we see therefore is a largely re-active policy without a clear strategy, especially in regard to future relations with Russia or the final place of Ukraine in European and Atlantic structures. What is more, this policy rests [...] on a fine tuned coalition of member-states. Those coalitions, be it through domestic elections, new found geopolitical priorities or a waning confidence in Ukraine's potential for sustained reforms, can always crumble.
>
> HÄRTEL 2017: 7

Generally, when describing the outcomes of the restrictions implemented by the EU, on the one hand, we can value the way "the EU managed to maintain unity in its sanctions policy – a considerable achievement given the diverse attitudes of member states toward Moscow", while on the other we should still consider that "the price of this unity was diplomatic paralysis" (Lehne 2017).[2] As for the European neighbourhood policy, the emphasis on stabilisation and resilience significantly prevailed in the 2015 Review (see Review of the European Neighbourhood Policy 2015) – and was then stressed again in the 2017 report "Implementing the EU Global Strategy Year 1" (see Global Strategy 2017). This reflects the EU's shift from "being the vanguard of a new liberal order" to "a focus on threats and interests" (Lehne 2017), following the new trends in international relations triggered in the second half of 2016 by Brexit in Europe and the victory of Donald Trump in the United States presidential election. This also came to affect the stagnation of the eastward integration process, whereas still in 2015 Alexander Baunov wondered why the Eastern Partnership made "increasingly less sense".[3]

---

2   As emblematically highlighted by Stefan Lehne: "Just two EU member states, Germany and France, participated in the Normandy format negotiations on the Ukrainian conflict, but they were unable to overcome the stalemate" (ivi).

3   "So what is the purpose of this organization? It is not a stepping stone on the way to Europe, nor can it condemn and oppose Russia with a single voice" (Baunov 2015).

Looking at the measures implemented by Russia in response to EU policies, the complex dynamics of Moscow's approach – as proposed by Ivan Krastev (2015) – can be best explained as "reverse engineering": "They are trying to reconstruct and imitate what they believe the West is doing". Yet throughout 2017, on several occasions the Russian minister of Foreign Affairs Sergei Lavrov highlighted the Russian position vis-à-vis the EU:

> What do we think about future EU-Russia relations? The creative potential for cooperation – from trade to the countering of new challenges and threats – is truly enormous. It is important to use it correctly. Russia is consistently advocating the formation of a common space of peace, security and partnership [...] Aware of this objective reality, the EAEU (Eurasian Economic Union) is actively stepping up dialogue with dozens of countries and associations on all continents. We will welcome the EU's joining this work. We share a continent. To begin with, we hope to receive a reply to the proposal to establish contacts between the EAEU and the EU [...] We consider it counterproductive when two neighbouring integration associations do not have direct contacts.
>
> MFARF 2017a

While in 2014 the competitive Eurasian integration project was launched, with the ratification of the establishment treaty by the leaders of Belarus, Kazakhstan and Russia in May and the accession treaties of Armenia and Kyrgyzstan respectively in October and December, the direct response to the EU's sanctions came in August, mirroring the EU's decision by imposing "counter-sanctions". The Russian elites' symmetrical answer consisted of introducing travel bans for EU political and military leaders – an official blacklist was first released in May 2015 – and blocking imports of selected categories of western agro-food products from the EU, the US, Australia and Japan (see The Russian Government 2014).[4] The latter measure in particular had a huge impact on public opinion and political debate in the West, whereas two years after the implementation of the bilateral sanctions in 2016, "the lack of progress on implementing the Minsk agreements and the heavy cost of sanctions" were already "reflected in growing parliamentary opposition to their continuation" (EPRS 2016: 3). Leaving aside the real economic impact of these restrictive

---

4 The Russian counter sanctions were then prolonged until the end of 2019, in response to the prolongation of the EU's sanctions against the Russian Federation.

measures on bilateral trade flows between the EU and Russia,[5] it is still worth stressing the political and symbolic value of these measures for the Kremlin. As emblematically highlighted by Andrei Movchan (2017):

> Sanctions do have a big impact in one area – Russian domestic politics. The government-controlled media […] blames Russia's current economic decline on the United States and European Union […] For Putin, the sanctions are useful in helping him alienate the public from any Western-backed opposition leaders or from those who still proclaim that the West is a model for Russia's future development.

Furthermore, while within the EU the refugee crisis was dramatically affecting the European political debate, especially in the aftermath of the EU Commission's proposal to relocate refugees across the member states in September 2015, the emerging intra-EU splits "created new contexts and opened new opportunities for Russia's relations with European governments" (Braghiroli & Makarychev 2017: 8), also leading to a diversification of "foreign policy instruments of Russia to include direct appeals to non-governmental actors and different social and political groups abroad" (ivi: 3). Significantly, as outlined by Braghiroli and Makarychev (2017: 4), these international trends paved the way for new points of convergence between the narratives implemented by political actors in the EU and Russia: on the one hand, these dynamics "reshaped the main lines of political distinction within Europe between the proponents of *solidarity* and *security*", whereas "a value-based, liberal, supranational and multicultural Europe" confronts "a traditional Europe, based on its religious and historical ancestral characteristics, with inter-governmental and (mostly) national policy mechanisms" (ivi: 5); on the other, "Russia's strategy of re-entry" to Europe was pervasively "accompanied by narratives of othering today's Orientalized Europe and salvaging it from liberal tolerance, political correctness and cultural fragmentation" (ivi: 2).[6]

---

5   For further analysis on the issue, see the monitoring of the Economic situation in Russia published in April 2016 by the Russian Presidential Academy of National Economy and Public Administration (RANEPA 2016) and the Center for European Policy Studies reports issued in July 2017. Drawing on data on EU-Russian trade flows, these reports seem to agree that the EU's market share in total Russian import "decreased very little and only gradually since the implementation of bilateral sanctions" (Gros & Di Salvo 2017: 3).

6   Sergei Lavrov upheld such position in an interview published in the Italian newspaper Libero: "We are concerned about the existing trend in a number of Western countries towards substituting universal human values with quasi-liberal ones and this not only within their national borders. There is no end to the attempts to aggressively export [these new values],

2   For the Sake of Europe(s): The Information War

> [...] we hear allegations that Russia is interested in a weak EU and is try-
> ing to divide it. This is untrue [...] In turn, we will be open to develop co-
> operation at a pace and to an extent suitable for our EU colleagues. Natu-
> rally, in the process we will continue our multi-vector foreign policy of
> consolidating diverse cooperation with those states that have got rid of
> ideological blinkers in their economic relations with foreign partners.
> These states form an overwhelming majority (MFARF 2017a).
>
> S. LAVROV

There is no doubt that throughout the years following the migration crisis
"the growing divide between and within EU member states and Union's dis-
coherence" (Braghiroli & Makarychev 2017: 3) affected the directions undertaken by governmental actors in the face of internal contestation, and tensions
within the ruling coalitions.[7] Significantly, among the dominant discourses in
Europe, Russia is frequently described as "an eventual beneficiary of the whole
migration impasse" (Braghiroli & Makarychev 2017: 9) in the EU.

It is no coincidence that of the five guiding principles of the EU's Russia policy identified in 2016, the quest to "become more resilient to Russian threats" has
recently taken centre stage in the political debate, namely as regards so-called
"hybrid threats" and disinformation. Whereas the alleged Russian-meddling
in the 2016 US elections found its European counterpart in the allegations by
French President Emmanuel Macron on Russia's use of "organs of influence
and propaganda" (see McAuley 2017) on the occasion of the 2017 presidential
elections, and British former Prime Minister Theresa May's accusations of the
Kremlin's interference in elections and fake news (see Mason 2017), already
in 2015 the European External Action Service East StratCom Task Force was
established within the EU: this was "an action plan on strategic communication in order to address Russia's ongoing disinformation campaigns", directed
at "the overall media environment in the Eastern neighborhood and in EU
member states" (ESCTF 2017).

---

which are being increasingly resisted by other nations seeking to preserve their lifestyles as
    well as their own national identity" (MFARF 2017).

7   Still in 2017, this divide could be traced even between diverging political dynamics in Eastern
    and Western Europe: "In Western Europe, the securitization of the refugee debate is orches-
    trated by identitarian and national conservative parties, while in Poland, Hungary or Slova-
    kia, key actors are the national governments" (Braghiroli & Makarychev 2017: 7).

On the one hand, this has been followed by numerous reports published by US-based non-profit policy institutes and think tanks, such as the Center for European Policy Analysis[8] and the Atlantic Council, claiming the return in the EU's post-2014 information landscape of Russian "active measures" – i.e, "tools of political warfare once used by the Soviet Union that aimed to influence world events through the manipulation of media, society and politics" (Polyakova 2016: 3). On the other, the approval in December 2016 of the new Doctrine of Information Security of the Russian Federation clearly traced the reactive stance in defending Russia's "national interest" in the face of growing "external threats":

> There is a trend among foreign media to publish an increasing number of materials containing biased assessments of State policy of the Russian Federation. Russian mass media often face blatant discrimination abroad, and Russian journalists are prevented from performing their professional duties. There is a growing information pressure on the population of Russia, primarily on the Russian youth, with the aim to erode Russian traditional spiritual and moral values.
>
> Doctrine of Information Security 2016

Among the Russian national interests in the information sphere, the document lists significantly the need for "providing the Russian and international community with reliable information on the State policy of the Russian Federation and its official position on socially significant events in Russia and in the world, and applying information technologies to ensure the national security of the Russian Federation in the sphere of culture" (ivi).

It is worth stressing that the development of international information platforms funded by the Russian government in the face of the so-called "information war with the West" is strictly connected to the escalating conflict of the integration processes implemented by the two actors throughout the 2000s. Its origins can be traced back to 2008, when, as suggested by Anton Shekhovtsov, "many Russian politicians, experts and officials discussed one particular paradox: Russia easily won the Russian-Georgian war, but lost the information war, implying that it failed to convince the international community of the righteousness of Moscow's invasion of Georgia" (Shekhovtsov 2017).

Whereas the Russia Today TV channel was launched in 2005, and then re-framed in RT in 2009, it was only at the end of 2013 that the international information agency *Rossiia Segodnia* was established. The former aims to cover

---

8   See: http://infowar.cepa.org/index/.

"stories overlooked by the mainstream media, provides alternative perspectives on current affairs, and acquaints international audiences with a Russian view point on major global events",[9] providing contents in English, Arabic, Spanish and Russian. As for the description included in the RT website, the channel "enjoys its largest regional audience in Europe, with more than 36 million people watching RT weekly in 10 European countries, placing it among the top 5 pan-regional news channels". *Rossiia Segodnia* was created in December 2013, following Russian President Vladimir Putin's Executive Order "On Measures to raise efficiency in the work of State Mass Media Outlets", with the main purpose of providing "information on Russian state policy and Russian life and society for audiences abroad" (President of Russia 2013). The main project promoted by the new agency for international broadcasting was Sputnik News[10] – eventually launched in November 2014: it is available in over 40 languages and relies on local media outlets, since, as outlined by the *Rossiia Segodnia* Editor-in-Chief Margarita Simonian, it was "absolutely clear to us that trying to broadcast in foreign languages and win over foreign audiences from Moscow is not a productive approach" (RT 2014).

On several occasions both the information platforms have been accused in the West of perpetuating so-called "fake news" and conspiracy theories, thus capitalizing "on specific weak spots in a united Europe and – addressing European audiences – aggravating problematic areas such as the cohesion of the eurozone, immigration or the integration of minorities" (Shekhovtsov 2017). These allegations have been labelled by Russian media as the product of "Russophobic hysteria", whereas so-called "Russian disinformation" has been described in RT as "the kind of news the Western establishment doesn't want the public to see" (RT 2016), or, as for the Sputnik slogan, as "telling the untold".

In the global information security scene, this clash of narratives has then been followed by the implementation of restrictive measures on both sides. This is the case of the RT America affaire, highlighting the triangulation of the "information war" between the EU, the USA and Russia, and its peculiar "reactive" traits. On November 13, 2017 the US Justice Department (2017) officially requested the American arm of RT to register as a "foreign agent" under the umbrella of FARA (Foreign Agents Registration Act). Only two days later, Russia's State Duma passed amendments to the law on information and the law on media, signed by the President Vladimir Putin on November 25, which enabled the Russian government to brand news media outlets as "foreign agents"

---

9   See: https://www.rt.com/about-us/.
10   See: https://sputniknews.com/.

(President of Russia 2017). These amendments have been emblematically described by Viacheslav Volodin, Chairman of the Russian Federation State Duma, as a "mirror measure" (Tikhonov 2017) answering the US provision. Eventually, this also came to affect the position assumed by the European External Action Service on November 26, whereas "the 'foreign agent' legislation [...] and the extensions of its scope to foreign media, in addition to its existing application to Russian NGOs" has been described as "a further threat to free and independent media and to access to information, and yet another attempt to shrink the space for independent voices in Russia" (EEAS 2017).

Looking at these dynamics, as stressed by Peter Pomerantsev, we witness how the main "implications of this frame is to reduce all discourse to a conflict between two sides, with no 'good' or 'bad'", and eventually to the conclusion that "all information is war" (Pomerantsev 2017). Furthermore, in the context of the diplomatic paralysis which has followed the recent West-Russia crisis, the current information war and accusations concerning Russian disinformation and election meddling in the US and the EU has paradoxically disappointed many westward-leaning Russians, because this "seems to be mimicking some of their own country's least appealing traits" (Higgins 2017).

3   Towards a Decentralisation of Europe-Russia Relations: The "Convenience Axis"

In order to evaluate the allegations concerning the alleged Russian destabilisation of the EU, it is worth analysing the broader frame of strategies implemented by the Russian establishment in promoting a "multi-vector foreign policy". Specifically, in the aftermath of the Ukraine crisis "as mainstream politicians and officials in western countries gradually withdrew their political support for Putin's regime, the latter started looking for non-mainstream political allies in the West" (Shekovtsov 2018: 222). These bilateral relations "tend to transcend the traditional left-right and liberal-conservative dichotomies" (Braghiroli & Makarychev 2017: 2) and "can be described as 'mutually-aware' (or of bidirectional interest), with Moscow gaining access to the European public [...] while the latter obtains access to material and immaterial resources of support" (ivi: 14). In dialogue with "the new language of European populism", this convergence of narratives develops in the West into what has been described by Brubaker as "civilizationism" (Brubaker 2017), i.e. "a paradoxical combination of 'identitarian' Christianity, secularism, philo-Semitism, Islamophobia, and even some elements of liberalism such as support for gender equality and gay rights" (ivi). More than "genuine ideological connections" between "civilizationist" groups in the West and Russia, as suggested by Marlene Laru-elle, we can identify the rise of a "convenience axis":

> After the Ukrainian crisis, and Crimean annexation, Russia lost most of its political connection to mainstream parties in Europe [...] If Russia could interact more with the mainstream, they would prefer the main-stream over the far right [...] That is the convenience axis. But then you have a real, genuine, more ideological connection about, for example, be-ing anti-NATO, anti-U.S., anti-liberal values – that is a shared agenda – promoting what they call Christian or conservative values, being very anti-establishment, anti-EU, criticizing the political correctness.
>
> Carnegie Council 2017

At the crossroads between the convenience axis and concrete ideological connections,[11] we thus witnessed the rise of intense contacts of Russian elite with "EU's centrifugal forces" (Braghiroli & Makarychev 2017: 13), including "civilizationist" groups from western Europe[12] and some Central European governments.[13] As described by Braghiroli and Makarychev (2017: 13), this dia-logue provides the Russian Federation with a channel for proposing "itself as the counter-hegemonic herald of an alternative model of integration".

Similar dynamics are reflected in the case of the position assumed by the leaders of Italy's Northern League – since December 2017 just the League – throughout 2013–17, shedding further light on the new framework of decen-tralised relations between Western European and Russian political actors. The recent initiatives promoted by the party in relation to the leadership in the Russian Federation, emblematically, run parallel with the progressive deterio-ration of EU-Russia relations. Under Matteo Salvini, who was elected Federal Secretary in December 2013, the League "embarked on a major rebranding of the party", reframing the traditional separatist stances "into a right-wing

---

11   "Civilizationism has been adopted by the Netherlands' Party for Freedom, Denmark's People's Party, Norway's Progress Party, Finland's True Finns, Sweden's Sweden Demo-crats, France's National Front, and, to a certain extent, Belgium's Vlaams Belang, Austria's Freedom Party, and Italy's Northern League (although not by the Alternative for Germany, which remains closer to the traditional nationalist far right)" (Brubaker 2017).

12   A comprehensive study of the relations between anti-establishment parties, such as France's National Front, Austria's Freedom Party, and the Alternative for Germany, in the EU and Russia has been undertaken by Anton Shekhovtsov (2018).

13   The positions assumed by Hungarian PM Viktor Orbán in Hungary, Slovak PM Robert Fico (2012–18) and the Czech President Milos Zeman in relation to EU sanctions against Russia go in this direction. For further reading, see Byrne 2017; Ereli 2017; Jancarikova & Muller 2016.

nationalist, populist and sovereignist force, similar to Le Pen's National Front"
(Germani & Iacoboni 2017). Throughout the Ukraine crisis and beyond, the
party promoted a strong pro-Russian orientation, which finally found visibility
in the Russian media, such as RT and Sputnik (see Bertolasi 2015, 2016). As for
platforms developing the party's relations with Russian political and economic
elites, in February 2014 the Lombardy-Russia Cultural Association was created:
as we can read in the mission statement, "the need for a new association arises
from the fact that despite millions of Europeans sympathizing with Russia
and its President, the whole press is in a manner of prejudice against Moscow
and it is impossible to find an objective source for information".[14] Among the
members of the Association board, there are representatives of the League,
such as Claudio D'Amico and Gianluca Savoini, and prominent Russian figures
such as Alexey Komov, the World Congress of Families Regional representative
for Russia and the CIS. Throughout 2014–17 the League party affiliates visited
Crimea and Moscow on several occasions, and in March, 2017 Salvini was in
Moscow to sign a cooperation agreement between his party and the Russian
President's party United Russia (see Edinaia Rossiia 2017). In a 2017 interview
with RT, Matteo Salvini, who will then serve as Deputy Prime Minister of Italy
from June 2018, clearly confirmed his stance on the Russian Federation and
the EU:

> The EU is a problem not only for the northern regions of Italy but for all
> European countries. It is the European Union that imposes sanctions on
> Russia, crippling our agricultural sector and robbing Italy of €7bn a
> year. Today, we advocate the unity of Italy, but with autonomy for the
> regions and federalism. We do so, first and foremost, to defend ourselves
> against the onslaught of the EU and multinational corporations which
> are simply seeking to annihilate us [...] EU headquarters is a place
> where you can find only people who are interested in business and don't
> care about values, culture, identity, family or any existing differences be-
> tween nations and cultures at all. Again, Europe either changes or ceas-
> es to exist.
>
> RT 2017

Salvini's stance reflects how the "convenience axis" between "EU's centrifugal
forces" and Russian political actors can play an important role even *within* EU
institutions, namely the EU Parliament in Strasbourg and Brussels, especially

---

14   See: http://www.lombardiarussia.org/index.php/associazione/lo-scopo.

in debating and voting Russia-related resolutions.[15] As highlighted by Shek-hovtsov (2018: 221), this cooperation has assumed a relevant role since the beginning of the European Parliament's eighth term in July 2014. Nonetheless, it features a decentralised character and – "rather than being a top-down demand from Putin" – is often the result of "a bottom-up offer to the Kremlin made by those Russian actors who want to consolidate their own positions", which can be useful in giving Moscow access to the European public. This decentralisation and diversification of relations between European political actors and Russian elites testifies to new trends, representing at this stage the main alternative for Russia in the face of diplomatic paralysis.

4   Scenarios for Future Developments: Looking for a Third Way?

> The European Union must now rethink its whole project for integration. Even if it eventually overcomes its systemic crisis, with the EU becoming more a "Europe of Individual States" than a "European Union" per se, it is unlikely to become a full-fledged global player. However, the EU will continue to wield significant influence, especially in adjacent territories. As a result, if competition increases, the EU will not so much "export stability" as it will foster conflicts on the European periphery.
>
> BARABANOV et al. 2017: 10–11

In the section emblematically entitled "A class with no teacher", included in the 2017 report "The Importance of Being Earnest: How to Avoid Irreparable Damages" issued by the Valdai Discussion Club, a Moscow-based think tank, the prominent role of the European integration project conducted by the EU is clearly contested in light of "its systemic crisis": as we read in the document, "if competition increases, the EU will not so much 'export stability' as it will foster conflicts on the European periphery". The need for a "new big deal among the key geopolitical players to restore the international order and reduce international tensions between the United States and the EU, on the one side, and

---

15   At the time of interview, Salvini served as Member of the European Parliament (MEP; July 2014-March 2018). In his analysis of the voting in the European Parliament in 2014–16, Shekhovtsov (2018) observed that "many far-right MEPs demonstrated a relatively balanced approach toward Russia-related issues", voting against critical Russia-related resolutions, such as "The State of EU-Russia relations" on June 2015, in a more consistent and homogeneous way than in the past.

Russia, on the other" has been highlighted also by Mikhailo Minakov (2017). According to the Ukrainian political analyst, "the deterioration of the international order, democratic development, and internal stability in postcommunist Europe" represents the main challenge for both the integration process and security prospects in Europe. The key factors in this unstable situation are clearly outlined as follows: "Eastern European countries are squeezed between two regional unions, the EU and the Eurasian Union" (Minakov 2017). Following the diplomatic paralysis between these global actors, "Eastern Europe has been losing its regional interstate channels of communication and conflict resolution", whereas the rise of identity politics in the region has led further to a "deterioration of stability, international order and democratic development" (Minakov 2017).

These processes are mainly affected by the decline of a common European integration perspective for the region. On the one hand, the failure of the Eastern Partnership Summit in Vilnius in November 2013, which preceded the Ukraine crisis, and the 2015 Riga "survival" Summit, as it was defined by the Latvian minister of Foreign affairs hosting the event, testified to the need for revamping this cooperation format. As emphasised by the chairman of Eurasia Group Cliff Kupchan for Valdai Club, "the time for formal association mechanisms that clearly define which countries are 'in' or 'out' of a given regional grouping has passed" (Kupchan 2017). Regarding this trend, the analyst highlights the case of China's Belt and Road Initiative "that allows states to flexibly join parts of an initiative without necessarily committing to it irreversibly" and managing "to coexist with Russia's own Eurasian Economic Union (EAEU) across overlapping geographies". Furthermore, the emerging model of "Europeanization without accession to membership" laid the groundwork for the recent development of an integration process "at different paces", not only within the EU – as stated in the Rome Declaration of March 2017, but even in the Eastern Partnership format. As emerged from the European Parliament recommendation of 15 November 2017 in the run-up to the fifth Eastern Partnership Summit in Brussels,

> significant progress has been made since the last [2015] Summit, notably with the conclusion and entry into force of three Association Agreements (AAs) including a Deep and Comprehensive Free Trade Area (DCFTA) with Georgia, Moldova and Ukraine, as well as visa-free regimes with Georgia and Ukraine since 2017 (and with Moldova since 2014), the conclusion of negotiations on a Comprehensive and Enhanced Partnership Agreement with Armenia (which serves as an example of how membership of the Eurasian Economic Union and participation in the EU's

neighbourhood strategies can coexist), the launching of negotiations on a new comprehensive agreement with Azerbaijan, the adoption of major reforms in a number of these countries with the political, technical and financial support of the European Union, and the continuation of the critical engagement policy towards Belarus.

European Parliament 2017

The diversification of "integration speeds" finds further confirmation in the joint declaration of the November 2017 Eastern Partnership Summit in Brussels whereas, the document opens to "cooperation on a case-by-case basis" to "third countries", reaffirming "the sovereign right of each partner to choose the level of ambition and the goals to which it aspires in its relations with the European Union" (Council of the European Union 2017). A promising example of the search for "a third way" may come from the Armenian case, leading to a new frame of relations between the European Union and the Eurasian Economic Union. While in September 2013 President Sargsyan refused to sign the EU association agreement and announced Armenia would be joining the Eurasian Customs Union (then, the Eurasian Economic Union), the new Comprehensive and Enhanced Partnership agreement signed in November 2017 with the EU (EEAS 2018), as highlighted by Sergei Markedonov (2017), "does not contain free trade arrangements in order to respect the EEU's [Eurasian Economic Union] trade jurisdiction", symbolically suggesting that – rather than an "'either/or' approach to integration, the EU and Russia are gradually moving in a 'both/and' direction". Generally, the South Caucasus case testifies to the diversification of foreign policies implemented by third countries, whereas this "cannot be reduced to a diametric choice between Russia and the West, or a competition of value systems" (Markedonov 2017).

Bilateral relations and cooperation between third countries and both the EU and the Eurasian Economic Union could work as a constructive example for the next developments in EU-Russia relations. Nonetheless, at the time of writing (July 2018) the state of affairs is still tense. While on the one hand, in the frame of the 2017 Eastern Partnership summit in Brussels European Council president Donald Tusk warned that "cyber-attacks, fake news, hybrid war" (Rankin 2017) on the side of Russia are among Europe's real problems – thus confirming the new funding of the East Stratcom taskforce from the EU budget for 2018–20, on the other hand the Minister in charge of the Development of Integration and Macroeconomics of the Eurasian Economic Union in October 2017 pointed out how "Brussels, unfortunately, is not yet ready for official dialogue with the Eurasian Union" (Akchabar 2017). The most promising path for both geopolitical actors in implementing their integration processes seems to be to work on a strategic "multilateral-to-multilateral basis" (Greene 2017: 5), leaving aside "the world of political imaginary" and re-entering "the realm of actual decision making" (Torbakov 2017: 70). Eventually, a different approach from the EU that takes "greater stock of Europe's own interests and that understands the potential for a socially and economically deeper relationship with Russia – could yield a more effective conditionality and, while not devoid of conflict, would potentially lay the foundation for a more robust and genuinely strategic EU-Russia relationship" (Greene 2017: 2). On the other hand, while in search for "practical solutions within the existing system of political coordinates", as symbolically emphasised by the Director General of the Russian International Affairs Council Andrei Kortunov "Russia's new relationship with the EU could be that of a hybrid vehicle that can run either off the old internal combustion model of East-West geopolitical division or off the new system of global, regional, and sub-regional regimes that preserve and expand the 'shared spaces' of Russia and Europe" (Kortunov 2017).

Bibliography

Akchabar. (2017). 'Za tri goda tovarooborot EAES i EC upal vdvoe', 26 October, https://www.akchabar.kg/news/za-tri-goda-tovarooborot-eaes-i-es-upal-vdvoe/.

Barabanov, O. et al. (eds) (2017). *The Importance of Being Earnest: How to Avoid Irreparable Damage*. Moscow: Valdai Discussion Club, http://valdaiclub.com/files/15788/.

Baunov, A. (2015). 'Not Against Russia: Why the Eastern Partnership Makes Increasingly Less Sense', *Carnegie Moscow Center*, 1 June, http://carnegie.ru/commentary/60256.

Bertolasi, E. (2015). 'Matteo Salvini a Mosca: lotta al terrorismo e fine delle sanzioni contro la Russia', *Sputnik Italia*, 21 December, https://it.sputniknews.com/politica/201512211762938-Salvini-conferenza-a-Mosca-lotta-terrorismo-fine-sanzioni/.

Bertolasi, E. (2016). 'Salvini a Mosca: "No" alle sanzioni', *Sputnik Italia*, 19 November, https://it.sputniknews.com/opinioni/201611193655509-salvini-a-mosca-sanzioni-no-referendum/.

Bildt, C. (2015). 'Russia, the European Union and the Eastern Partnership', *ECFR Riga Series*, 19 May, http://www.ecfr.eu/article/commentary_russia_eu_and_eastern_partnership3029.

Braghiroli, S. and Makarychev A. (2017). 'Redefining Europe: Russia and the 2015 Refugee Crisis', *Geopolitics*, 3 November, https://doi.org/10.1080/14650045.2017.1389721.

Brajerčíková, S. and Lenč, M. (2017). 'Walking on Thin Ice: Slovak Perspective on Ukraine Crisis', *The Ideology and Politics Journal*, 1(7): 235–256.

Brubaker, R. (2017). 'The New Language of European Populism', *Foreign Affairs*, 6 December, https://www.foreignaffairs.com/articles/europe/2017-12-06/new-language-europe an-populism.

Byrne, A. (2017). 'Orban joins Putin in attack on Russia sanctions', *Financial Times*, 2 February, https://www.ft.com/content/f1f4482a-e96b-11e6-893c-082c54a7f539.

Carnegie Council. (2017). 'Marlene Laruelle on Europe's Far-Right Political Movements', 9 November, https://www.carnegiecouncil.org/studio/multimedia/20171109-far-right-france-europe-marlene-laruelle.

Council of the European Union. (2017). 'Joint Declaration of the Eastern Partnership Summit (Brussels, 24 November 2017)', http://www.consilium.europa.eu/media/31758/final-statement-st14821en17.pdf.

David, M., Gower, J. and Haukkala, H. (2013). *National Perspectives on Russia: European Foreign Policy in the Making?*, Abingdon: Routledge.

Deni, J.R. (2017). 'More of the Same in Response to Russia?', *Carnegie Europe*, 23 November, http://carnegieeurope.eu/strategiceurope/74811.

Doctrine of Information Security. (2016). 'Doctrine of Information Security of the Russian Federation', *The Ministry of Foreign Affairs of the Russian Federation*, 5 December, http://www.mid.ru/en/foreign_policy/official_documents/-/asset_publisher/CptICkB6BZ29/content/id/2563163.

Edinaia Rossiia. (2017). '"Edinaia Rossiia" zakliuchila soglashenie o sotrudnichestve s italians'koi partiei "Liga Severa"', 6 March, https://er.ru/news/152403/.

EEAS. (2017). 'Statement by the Spokesperson on the Russian law allowing the registration of foreign media as "foreign agents"', *European Union External Action Service*, 26 November, https://eeas.europa.eu/headquarters/headQuarters-homepage/36222/statement-spokesperson-russian-law-allowing-registration-foreign-media-%E2%80%9Cforeign-agents%E2%80%9D_ro.

EEAS. (2018). 'EU-Armenia Comprehensive and Enhanced Partnership Agreement (CEPA)', *European Union External Action Service*, 3 January, https://eeas.europa.eu/sites/eeas/files/eng_cepa_factsheet_armenia_digital.pdf.

EPRS. (2016). 'The EU's Russia policy: Five guiding principles', *European Parliament Research Service*, October, http://www.europarl.europa.eu/RegData/etudes/BRIE/2016/589857/EPRS_BRI(2016)589857_EN.pdf.

Ereli, A. (2017). 'Is the Czech Republic Falling Under Putin's Shadow?', *Foreign Policy*, 10 October, http://foreignpolicy.com/2017/10/10/is-the-czech-republic-falling-under-putins-shadow/.

ESCTF. (2017). 'Questions and Answers about the East StratCom Task Force', *European Union External Action*, 8 November, https://eeas.europa.eu/headquarters/headquarters-homepage/2116/-questions-and-answers-about-the-east-.

European Council. 'EU restrictive measures in response to the crisis in Ukraine', http://www.consilium.europa.eu/en/policies/sanctions/ukraine-crisis/.

European Council. (2016). 'European Council discussed relations with Russia', 21 October, https://eeas.europa.eu/delegations/russia/12646/european-council-discussed-relations-russia_en.

European Parliament. (2017). 'European Parliament recommendation of 15 November 2017 to the Council, the Commission and the EEAS on the Eastern Partnership, in the run-up to the November 2017 Summit', 15 November, http://www.europarl.europa.eu/sides/getDoc.do?pubRef=-//EP//TEXT+TA+P8-TA-2017-0440+0+DOC+XML+V0//EN&language=EN.

Foreign Policy Concept. (2013). 'Concept of the Foreign Policy of the Russian Federation', *The Ministry of Foreign Affairs of the Russian Federation*, 18 February, http://www.mid.ru/en/foreign_policy/official_documents/-/asset_publisher/CptICkB6BZ29/content/id/122186.

Foreign Policy Concept. (2016). 'Foreign Policy Concept of the Russian Federation (approved by President of the Russian Federation on November 30, 2016)', *The Ministry of Foreign Affairs of the Russian Federation*, 1 December, http://www.mid.ru/en/foreign_policy/official_documents/-/asset_publisher/CptICkB6BZ29/content/id/2542248.

Germani, L.S. and Iacoboni, J. (2017). 'Italy. Is the turn to Russia reversible?', pp. 11–19, in Polyakova, A. et al. (eds.), *The Kremlin Trojan Horses 2.0: Russian Influence in Greece, Italy and Spain*, Washington, D.C.: Atlantic Council Eurasia Center, http://www.atlanticcouncil.org/publications/reports/the-kremlin-s-trojan-horses-2-0.

Global Strategy. (2016). 'Shared Vision, Common Action: A Stronger Europe. A Global Strategy for the European Union's Foreign and Security Policy', *European Union External Action*, June, https://eeas.europa.eu/archives/docs/top_stories/pdf/eugs_review_web.pdf.

Global Strategy. (2017). 'Implementing the EU Global Strategy Year 1', *European Union*. 19 June, https://europa.eu/globalstrategy/en/implementing-eu-global-strategy-year-1.

Greene, S.A. (2017). 'Conditionality Beyond Sanctions. Identifying and Pursuing Interests in the EU-Russia Relationship', *PONARS Eurasia*, Policy Memo N. 460, February, http://www.ponarseurasia.org/sites/default/files/policy-memos-pdf/Pepm460_Greene_Feb2017_0.pdf.

Gros, D. and Di Salvo M. (2017). 'Revisiting Sanctions on Russia and Counter-Sanctions on the EU: The Economic Impact three years later', *CEPS*, 13 July, https://www.ceps.eu/publications/revisiting-sanctions-russia-and-counter-sanctions-eu-economic-impact-three-years-later.

Härtel, A. (2017). 'EU member states national perspectives on the "Ukraine Crisis": Introductory Remarks', *The Ideology and Politics Journal*, 1(7): 3–7.

Higgins, A. (2017). 'Why Putin's Foes Deplore U.S. Fixation on Election Meddling', *The New York Times*, 23 November, https://www.nytimes.com/2017/11/23/world/europe/russia-vladimir-putin-liberals.html.

Jancarikova, T. and Muller R. (2017). 'EU should drop Russia sanctions, Slovak PM says after meeting Putin', *Reuters*, 26 August, https://www.reuters.com/article/us-ukraine-crisis-slovakia/eu-should-drop-russia-sanctions-slovak-pm-says-after-meeting-putin-idUSKCN1111A1.

Kortunov, A. (2017). 'Hybrid Cooperation: A New Model for Russia-EU Relations', *Carnegie Moscow Center*, 7 September, http://carnegie.ru/commentary/73030.

Krastev, I. (2014). 'Russia's Revolt Against Globalisation', *Eutopia*, 24 November, http://www.eutopiamagazinearchive.eu/en/ivan-krastev/issue/russia%E2%80%99s-revolt-against-globalisation.html.

Krastev, I. (2015). 'Ivan Krastev: Russia is "reverse engineering" Western foreign policy', *The Graduate Institute of Geneva*, 18 November, http://graduateinstitute.ch/home/relations-publiques/news-at-the-institute/news-archives.html/_/news/corporate/2015/ivan-krastev-russia-is-reverse-e.

Kupchan, C. (2017). 'EU's Neighborhood Policy: Revamping Fundamentals', *Valdai Discussion Club*, 29 November, http://valdaiclub.com/a/highlights/eu-neighborhood-policy-revamping-fundamentals/.

Kureev, A. (2016). 'Decoding the changes in Russia's new foreign policy concept', *Russia Direct*, 9 December, http://www.russia-direct.org/opinion/decoding-changes-russias-new-foreign-policy-concept.

Lehne, S. (2017). 'Is There Hope for EU Foreign Policy?', Carnegie Europe, 5 December', *Carnegie Europe*, 5 December, http://carnegieeurope.eu/2017/12/05/is-there-hope-for-eu-foreign-policy-pub-74909.

Markedonov, S. (2017). 'Armenia's "Both/And" Policy for Europe and Eurasia', *Carnegie Moscow Center*, 7 December, http://carnegie.ru/commentary/74938.

Mason, R. (2017). 'Theresa May accuses Russia of interfering in elections and fake news', *The Guardian*, 14 November, https://www.theguardian.com/politics/2017/nov/13/theresa-may-accuses-russia-of-interfering-in-elections-and-fake-news.

McAuley, J. (2017). 'French President Macron blasts Russian state-owned media as "propaganda"', *The Washington Post*, 29 May, https://www.washingtonpost.com/world/europe/french-president-macron-blasts-russian-state-run-media-as-propaganda/2017/05/29/4e758308-4479-11e7-8de1-cec59a9bf4b1_story.html?utm_term=.758dd2b7b135.

MFARF. (2017). 'Foreign Minister Sergey Lavrov's Interview with the Libero, Italy, published on November 30, 2017', *The Ministry of Foreign Affairs of the Russian Federation*, http://www.mid.ru/en/web/guest/maps/it/-/asset_publisher/y8qQ47DsHQYD/content/id/2971828.

MFARF. (2017a). 'Foreign Minister Sergey Lavrov's remarks at a meeting with members of the Association of European Businesses in Russia Moscow, October 31, 2017', *The Ministry of Foreign Affairs of the Russian Federation*, http://www.mid.ru/en/foreign_policy/news/-/asset_publisher/cKNonkJE02Bw/content/id/2927175.

Minakov, M. (2017). 'Big Aims for a Deal in Eastern Europe', *Kennan Institute-Focus Ukraine*, 13 November, http://www.kennan-focusukraine.org/big-aims-for-a-deal-in-eastern-europe/.

Movchan, A. (2017). 'How the Sanctions Are Helping Putin', *Politico Magazine*, 28 March, https://www.politico.com/magazine/story/2017/03/how-the-sanctions-are-helping-putin-214963.

Polyakova, A. (2016). 'Introduction: The Kremlin's Toolkit of Influence in Europe', pp. 3–6, in Polyakova, A., Laruelle, M., Meister, S. and Barnett, N. (eds.), *The Kremlin's Trojan Horses: Russian Influence in France, Germany and the United Kingdom*, Washington, D.C.: Atlantic Council Dinu Patriciu Eurasian Center, http://www.atlanticcouncil.org/publications/reports/kremlin-trojan-horses.

Pomerantsev, P. (2017). 'Beware the Russian Elephant', *The American Interest*, 20 November, https://www.the-american-interest.com/2017/11/20/beware-russian-elephant/.

President of Russia. (2013). 'Executive order on measures to make state media more effective', 9 December, http://en.kremlin.ru/events/president/news/19805.

President of Russia. (2017). 'Amendments to the law on information and the law on the media', 25 November, http://en.kremlin.ru/acts/news/56179.

RANEPA. (2016). 'Operativnyi Monitoring Ekonomicheskoi Situatsii v Rossii: Tendentsii i vyzovy sotsial'no-ekonomicheskogo razvitia', 6(24), April, http://www.ranepa.ru/images/docs/monitoring/2016_6-24_april.pdf.

Rankin, J. (2017). 'EU anti-propaganda unit gets €1m a year to counter Russian fake news', *The Guardian*, 25 November, https://www.theguardian.com/world/2017/nov/25/eu-anti-propaganda-unit-gets-1m-a-year-to-counter-russian-fake-news.

Review of the European Neighbourhood Policy. (2015). 'Joint Communication to the European Parliament, the Council, the European Economic and Social Committee and the Committee of the Regions. Reviews of the European Neighbourhood Policy', *European Union External Action*, 18 November, http://eeas.europa.eu/archives/docs/enp/documents/2015/151118_joint-communication_review-of-the-enp_en.pdf.

RT. (2014). 'Sputnik launched to news orbit: Russia's new intl media to offer alternative standpoint', 11 November, https://www.rt.com/news/204231-sputnik-news-agency-launched/.

RT. (2016). 'Save the West! Russophobic hysteria hits new heights', 7 October, https://www.rt.com/op-ed/361943-save-west-russophobic-hysteria/.

RT. (2017). 'EU must change or cease to be', 9 October, https://www.rt.com/shows/sophieco/406084-catalan-crisis-referendum-italy/.

Shekhovtsov, A. (2017). 'Conventional bedfellows: The Russian propaganda machine and the western far right', *Eurozine*, 27 October, https://www.eurozine.com/conventional-bedfellows-the-russian-propaganda-machine-and-the-western-far-right/.

Shekhovtsov, A. (2018). *Russia and the Western Far Right: Tango Noir*. Abingdon-New York: Routledge.

Sytas, A. (2016). 'EU leaders sign letter objecting to Nord Stream-2 gas link', *Reuters*, 16 March, https://uk.reuters.com/article/uk-eu-energy-nordstream/eu-leaders-sign-letter-objecting-to-nord-stream-2-gas-link-idUKKCN0WI1YV.

The Russian Government. (2014). 'On amending the list of good, raw materials and foodstuffs, the export of which intor Russia is banned for a period of 12 months', 20 August, http://government.ru/en/docs/14392/.

Tikhonov, R. (2017). 'Zerkal'naia mera: Vladimir Putin podpisal zakon o SMI-inoagentakh', *RT*, 25 November, https://russian.rt.com/russia/article/452976-putin-zakon-smi-inoagenty.

Torbakov, I. (2017). 'Russia-Europe Relations in Historical Perspective: Investigating the Role of Ukraine', *Insight Turkey*, 19(4): 69–83.

US Justice Department. (2017). 'Production Company Registers Under the Foreign Agent Registration Acts as Agent for the Russian Government Entity Responsible for Broadcasting RT', 13 November, https://www.justice.gov/opa/pr/production-company-registers-under-foreign-agent-registration-act-agent-russian-government.

Vilson, M. (2017). 'Baltic Perspectives on the Ukraine Crisis: Europeanization in the Shadow of Insecurity', *The Ideology and Politics Journal*, 1(7): 8–46.

CHAPTER 15

Looking at the EU from the Russian and Chinese Perspectives

Vitaly Kozyrev

Nearly three decades have passed since the liberal dreams of a common European home without fault lines and walls brought new inspirations to the minds of politicians, strategists, philosophers, economists and entrepreneurs in both West and East. At the turn of the 21st century both China and Russia established multifarious relationships with the EU based on a series of core agreements and basic bilateral declarations. For the major Eurasian powers, the evolution of the European Union served as a model of effective economic integration, political harmonisation, and a new approach to security, different from the traditional type of great power hegemony. While Russia remained euro-centric politically and economically, and considered Europe as the *yardstick* for Russia's civilisational belonging (Laruelle 2016: 278), China was also inspired in 2003 to upgrade its relationship with the EU to the status of a "comprehensive strategic partnership" so that the years 2003–2004 were considered a honeymoon period in the relationship between the two parties.[1]

However, over the decade since 2005–2006 one could regretfully observe growing instability within the anticipated multipolar setting in Eurasia with EU-Russia-China relations at the core. As Europe strengthened transatlantic cohesion and solidarity and enhanced the values-based component of its foreign and security policy in 2007–11, Russia's strategic interests in Europe, despite all its efforts to become a part of it, were increasingly perceived as fundamentally in conflict with those of the West (Lo 2009). At present Russia and China are increasingly seen in the West as joining forces and offering an authoritarian alternative to prevailing liberal international institutions, creating the greatest threat to the existing global order (Diamond 2016). Fear spreads across Europe that, as the US retreats from world affairs under the Trump administration and democracies worldwide have grown fragile, China and

---

1 In 2003 the Chinese government issued its first "EU Policy Paper" which stressed the importance of China-EU relations stating that there was no fundamental conflict of interest between China and the EU and neither side posed a threat to the other. See EU Policy Paper 2003.

Russia are ready to step in to replace the US leader, split the West and ignore European interests and the EU perspective (Walt 2016).[2]

These negative developments in East-West relations require a thorough examination of the parties' mutual perceptions, the sources of conflict and specifically attitudinal aspects in the policymaking of the major great powers in Eurasia. Since the possibility of preserving the "strategic partnership paradigm" between Russia, China and the EU by conventional means seems to remain illusionary, observers are calling for "a more realistic and sober approach" and "a new foundation" to restore Russian-EU partnership and cooperation (Bordachev 2016: 561; Khudoley 2016: 195, 211).

This chapter explores the ongoing evolution of Chinese-Russian views towards the EU resulting from structural shifts in the international system, namely, the crisis of American leadership and neoliberal globalisation, inherent shocks within the global capitalist system, the poor performance of international governance institutions, the rise of non-Western powers, new trends in regional (and transregional) integration, and the return of geopolitics to international affairs. *The first section* provides an outlook for China-Russia-EU relations highlighting both the significance of the EU for China's and Russia's post-Cold War evolution and the ambivalent character of these partnerships. *In the second section*, the rifts in China-EU and Russia-EU relations are examined in the context of the structural crisis of the post-Cold War capitalist system which explains Western aggressiveness and also the radicalisation of Russian-Chinese views toward the EU as a result of Beijing-Moscow's "securitisation of identities"[3] and their opposition to the neoliberal transformation of the West including the EU's post-sovereign agenda. In *the third section*, the changing attitudes in Russia and China toward Europe are examined in the context of a heated systemic contestation among the great powers for leadership in the era of *re-globalisation*. The latter is perceived in this chapter as the process that does not reverse globalisation but revises its neoliberal component stressing instead domestic economic effectiveness and governance or the institutional and functional resources of key individual actors, which determine their capacity to exercise global leadership in the era of "civilizational geopolitics" (Tsygankov 2017). Finally, *the last section* explores the feasibility of a new Russo-Chinese "Greater Eurasia" project as a novel strategy which aims

---

2   In an interview, German Foreign Minister Sigmar Gabriel famously declares that Moscow, Beijing and Washington "don't value the European Union" and even "disregard it". See Hoffmann & Brinkbäumer 2018.

3   On the securitisation of identity in Russia's new foreign policy thinking see Zevelev (2016: 2).

to "embrace Europe" by initiating a profound structural change in the Eurasian space and establishing a more integrated relationship with the EU.

The paper demonstrates that in the era of foreign policy *ideologisation* Russo-Chinese attitudes toward the EU are driven by their pessimistic views on the West-dominated global capitalist system and "securitisation of identities". However, the era of *re-globalisation* gives them a chance to develop some novel institutional approach to engage the EU. The successful realisation by Russia and China of a "Greater Eurasia" project seems to be increasingly instrumental for their re-engagement with Europe. Beijing's ability to implement a variety of "Silk Road" projects with the EU is crucial for the joint Sino-Russian effort to reorder Eurasia and can help to modify the existing European economic and institutional construction. Given the deterioration in Moscow's relationship with the West, the Greater Eurasia initiative might provide Moscow with another chance to assert its leadership in Northern Eurasia and engage with Europe on new ground, now as part of the Chinese-Russian condominium.

1 China-Russia-EU Relations in the Post-Cold War Era: From Idealistic Romanticism to Systemic Contradictions

After the fall of the Berlin wall the rise of the European Union marked the dawn of a new era of regionalism and economic integration symbolizing globalisation and the emergence of a post-sovereign world. The normative consensus formed after the end of the Cold War set the framework for global transformation characterised by the imperative of homogenisation, internalisation of new global norms, domestic structural reforms and the formation of a post-sovereign identity.

The vicissitudes of US global strategy in the G.W. Bush era drove the European polity away from power politics, in Robert Kagan's words, "beyond power into a self-contained world of laws and rules and transnational negotiation and cooperation", (Kagan 2002) and this fuelled, for a short time, Sino-Russian sentiments toward Europe as a "different West" or a "benign Europe" (Vershbow et al. 2005: 25). However, many new developments in the 2000s – Russo-Chinese opposition to "colour revolutions" in Eurasia, their doubts about NATO's enlargement and extra-regional missions, rifts over regional security, state sovereignty, and international humanitarian norms and principles, along with intense friction between the EU and China over human rights, political reforms, arms embargoes and fair trade policies – created *political distrust* between these major actors.

Since the outbreak of the Ukraine crisis and the implementation of Western sanctions policy against Russia, earlier hopes to transform Russia into a post-imperial nation-state, "to find its place on the global map as a Euro-Pacific nation" (Trenin 2011) dissipated as strategic stability in Europe was disrupted,[4] and Russia moved toward the Chinese orbit and wiped out its traditional image of Europe as an independent global actor and as an example to follow (Lo 2015: 166). Despite China-EU bilateral relations being upgraded to "a comprehensive strategic partnership" in 2003, the China-EU "honeymoon" was short-lived, and hopes for a China-EU "strategic axis" to oppose US unilateralism after the Iraq war dissipated over the following years. In 2007 and 2008 serious disputes erupted between China and a number of EU countries over human rights and Tibet (Chen 2012). China's anxiety grew as the Obama administration announced its "pivot to Asia" and started a new course toward mega-regionalism in Asia and Europe. In 2009–2016 the US embarked on a new global course seeking to change the rules of trade and constrain China's economic capabilities[5] and "outrun" the growing trade superpower by upgrading existing WTO norms and principles (Tellis 2015). As a result, the China-EU relationship in 2003–2016 became more pragmatic, and, despite a series of high level strategic documents addressed to each other (the White Papers issued by the Chinese State Council and two Communications published by the EU Commission), analysts argued that the future between both still looked "challenging and potentially highly complex" (Brown 2016).

After the 2008 global financial and the EU's debt crises in 2011–13 public debates were launched in China and Russia to analyse the prospects of the capitalist system. Government columnists observed that the 2008 global recession exposed the many profound fallacies of the capitalist system, which were manifested in slow economic growth, increasing inequality, political polarisation, populism, trade protectionism, and right-wing extremism. The EU's economic performance and slow recovery, along with the crisis of political institutions

---

4   Fedor Luk'ianov described Russia's strategies in Eurasia before the Ukraine crisis as an attempt to create just the "second pole of the European world" (Luk'ianov 2016: 476). Russian expert Sergei Karaganov characterises the current strategic situation in Europe as the one which is "much worse than it was 30 or 40 years ago" (Karaganov 2016).

5   Prior to President Trump's retreat from the Obama-era trade policy, the Trans-Atlantic Trade and Investment Partnership agreement (TTIP), along with the Trans-Pacific Partnership (TPP), had been seen in Beijing as threatening China's foreign trade and investment, since it had aimed at slowing down China's upward momentum in the global industrial chain and compromising China's existing development model by raising concerns about the status of SOEs, government subsidies, government procurement and ownership and market transparency. See Cui 2013.

(Krastev 2012; Youngs 2013) have been considered in both China and Russia as a negative factor affecting their own regional strategies (The People's Daily 2017).

2 Neoliberal Transformation and the Radicalisation of Sino-Russian Views toward the West: Europe as a Weak Link in the System

Since the outbreak of the 2008 global recession, grim forecasts of the future of capitalism have gained popularity in the Chinese and Russian media and academia.[6] In his examination of the crisis of laissez-faire capitalism, leading CCP expert Zhou Rongguo contends that inefficient Western institutions seem to be unable to cope with the crises of legitimacy exacerbated by the impact of modern networked social platforms, which lead to "political gambling", widen societal gaps, create ideological chaos and impede progress and healthy economic growth (Zhou 2017). As prominent Singapore expert Zheng Yongnian suggests, the current crisis of capitalism is related to the globalisation-induced weakening of state power, rather than the power of market capitalism per se. This explains the need for a principal shift in government strategies and state regulation, which is driving the new era of re-globalisation (Zheng 2012).

Chinese and Russian experts have drawn heavily on the multiple critical narratives of capitalism, American "imperialism" and the liberal order produced by various theoretical schools – from left-wing scholars and economists (Immanuel Wallerstein, Richard D. Wolff, Wolfgang Streeck, Robert H. Parks, Slavoj Žižek) to staunch advocates of the revision of the global liberal normative consensus to revamp the existing order in the era of de-globalisation and power shifts.[7]

The idea of a post-American world and the decline of the West have been powerful drivers of Russian and Chinese strategic and political thought. Donald Trump's presidency in the US is widely seen in Beijing and Moscow as the manifestation of the crisis of neoliberalism, which has led to contradictions uncontrolled by the capitalistic class. Chinese experts predict that Trump's policy of imperial retreat could shake the positions of the capitalist regimes

---

6 In the recent decade commentaries produced by some well-known Russian "anti-liberal" economists – Andrei Fursov, Mikhail Khazin, Mikhail Deliagin, Valentin Katasonov, and the like – predicting the imminent collapse of the Western capitalist system – have been dominant in the Russian press. See Fursov & Fursov 2014; Fursov 2015; Katasonov 2016.

7 Chinese views on the matter may be found in: Reference News Online 2012. On the advocates of the liberal consensus see: Transatlantic Academy 2014. In 2017 the Foreign Affairs magazine initiated an interesting debate on the future of the liberal order (Haass 2017; Nye 2017; Niblett 2017; Mazarr 2017).

that depend on America – including the Gulf monarchies and the European Union, which might slide into another political and economic crisis (BBS Forum 2017). Another related conceptual premise that informs Russian-Chinese attitudes toward the EU (and the West in general) has been the thesis of Western aggressiveness caused by unprecedented shifts in the global hierarchy (Miller & Luk'ianov 2017). Hence, it is the US role in the world and particularly in Europe that becomes the major target of Russo-Chinese balancing.[8]

These changes have caused pessimism among Russian and Chinese elites with regard to prospects for East-West relations and the world order in general. It is noteworthy that Western assertiveness drives China and Russia closer to each other and toward a new type of "strategic partnership" (Savic 2016). In both countries' worldviews and attitudes toward the consolidated West, the role of power balancing and security concerns has grown dramatically. China has developed a certain hierarchy of strategic priorities (Kozyrev 2016), and Russia has been increasingly driven by the process known as "securitisation of identity". As Igor Zevelev contends, the Kremlin stresses "a strong link between sovereignty and the preservation of national identity threatened by globalization and a decadent West which rejects its traditional roots including the Christian values and moral principles of Western civilization" (Zevelev 2016).

This new polarisation however looks more like a hybrid, low intensity conflict than direct confrontation. Both Beijing and Moscow increasingly portray themselves as the guarantors of global stability and global public goods providers, thus jointly assuming special responsibility for shaping a more democratic and just world order. For more than a decade Moscow has justified its standing as a self-declared responsible great power, participating in the process of a forming a new world order.[9] China seeks a tiny balance between interests and fairness in world affairs which would solidify China's new role as a responsible regional power (Heath 2018).[10] But, given the intensity of tensions with the West and lack of mutual trust, Russia's and China's constitutive roles within

---

8   In their new report published by the Council on Foreign Relations, Robert D. Blackwill and Philip H. Gordon contend that "Putin has apparently concluded that a larger Russian regional and global role depends on the decline of American power projection" (Blackwill & Gordon 2018).

9   Vladimir Putin's recognition of the country's responsibility for global and socio-economic development announced at the meeting with the Russian diplomatic corps in June 2006 signalled about the change in Kremlin's strategic worldview. See Putin 2006.

10   See Zheng 2017. To implement the correct concept between justice and interest, Beijing needs to find an optimal correlation between peaceful development and the protection of China's core interests, avoiding hegemonic behaviour and preserving the international order (Qin 2014).

the international system could not be secured simply by conventional diplomatic means attributable to great power management. A new set of overarching inclusive concepts – regional and global – is needed to secure peaceful transition to a new order.

3   Beijing-Moscow's Search for "Structural Power" in the Era of "Re-Globalisation", and the Role of the EU

In the era of great power realignment, Russia-EU and China-EU relationships have become an essential component of the new Sino-Russian effort to shape a new world order. In their assessment of the current change in the capitalist system with Europe as an important constituent component, the Chinese strategists draw heavily on the new popular ideas of global structural readjustment, proposed by Klaus Schwab, the founder and Executive Chairman of the World Economic Forum. Schwab calls for reforms in capitalism's technical components and new approaches to economic theory and practical policies. Being concerned about the imbalance *between finance and the real economy,* Schwab suggests that competitiveness in the changing system depends on nations' ability to successfully reform regulation and social welfare systems, flexible labour and capital markets simultaneously. According to Schwab, capitalism has to be transformed into a "servant rather than the master of a socially responsible market economy", in compliance with Michael Porter's principle of "shared value creation" for the broader community (Schwab 2012).

In this "shared-value creation" process, the role of the EU seems to be different from expansionist America, since both Russian and Chinese leaders consider Europe a "weak link" in the declining Western community – the one that remains one of the major targets of the Russo-Chinese joint effort to reshuffle the regional and international order in compliance with some new principles and norms dictated by the imperative of re-globalisation. While on the bilateral level, the Russian-EU split seems to be irreversible, and Russia "is no longer the eastern flank of the failed Greater Europe" in the emerging new geopolitical reality (Ivanov 2015), the EU's prospective involvement in a larger project with Russia might "broaden the scope of Russia-EU cooperation and even assist the EU in its deeper positive transformation" (Kortunov 2017) in the era of re-globalisation.

Contrary to the popular notion of de-globalisation which entails a "return to geopolitics", re-globalisation marks the beginning of a new stage of globalisation which Marcos Troyjo labels "local contentism" which leads to "clashes for competitiveness" (Troyjo 2017). This is a new game in which countries compete in the sphere of their domestic organisation, governance, technological innovation and productivity, rather than simply improving the rest of the world in the neoliberal fashion with the hope that this would make the West more advanced and more developed. In the global arena key global actors are moving from the "relational power" approach, which considers power as a capacity to extract advantage within the established framework of activity, toward a "structural power" approach, in which power is the ability to gain by rewriting the rules of the game determines the structures of the global political economy and shapes frameworks within which states relate to each other (Strange 1988; Pustovitovskij & Kremer 2012).

Despite these new parameters of the era of "re-globalisation" and America's recent shift toward a more pragmatic policy in Europe, Chinese and Russian leaders remain assured that the US is still the key factor in European affairs and the European policy making process. As Miller and Luk'ianov assert, the "EU's transformation will continue within the framework of the same Atlantic paradigm, and Russia would not fit this framework" (Miller & Luk'ianov 2017). Therefore, any attempts to improve ties with the EU on the principle of equality and mutual benefit would require some novel approaches and incentives.

In the situation of "alienation without confrontation" with the West, Russia has been going through a painful process of "undoing" its EU-centeredness and deviating from its European self-identification. Unable to change Europe's strategic orientation in its favour (Miller & Luk'ianov 2017), Russia's major objective in Europe has therefore been to solve the "security dilemma" between Russia and NATO, redesign its ties with Europe and re-establish Russia as a close partner of Europe in the long run, though an equal one and as the carrier of a unique Eurasian identity. The Russia-led Eurasian Economic Union (EAEU), formally established in January 2015, has been so far the only instrument of Moscow's potential re-engagement with the EU. Established as an "open project" in the former Soviet space, the Eurasian Union was formed on principles similar to those of the EU – including free movement of goods, services and capital and also coordination in economic and currency policies.[11] Moreover, by stimulating effective cooperation between the member-states' governments, the project has been designed to increase the competitiveness of

---

11   Designed as an instrument to improve competitiveness of member-states (Armenia, Russia, Belarus, Kazakhstan, Kyrgyzstan), the EAEU has been economically oriented to industrial-innovative development, unified industrial policy, and exposed toward external markets to secure its role as a bridge between the European and Asian zones of development. Prior to the Ukraine crisis, this integration project was supposed to be compatible with European and Asia-Pacific integration models, and aimed at the formation of an associate relationship with the EU. See: Putin 2011; EAEU Treaty 2011.

Eurasian economies in the age of re-globalisation. However, since the introduction of Western sanctions against Russia, the EAEU has been suffering from internal discrepancies and is no longer seriously regarded in Europe as a viable mechanism for cooperation.[12]

As for Beijing, the major conflict stems from the growing gaps between China and the EU in the sphere of political institutions, values, and the fundamentals of an emerging new normative consensus. In search of new approaches and new mechanisms in its relations with the EU, China, unlike the Russians whose policies remain more procedural than substantive (Trenin 2017), has developed a variety of concepts, policies, and holistic transregional initiatives that position the Asian giant more favourably vis-à-vis Europe.

Beijing's first paradigm attributable to China-EU relations is based on Xi Jinping's formula of "a new type of relationship between major countries in the 21st century" (新型大国关系), which implies "mutual understanding and strategic trust", "respecting each other's core interests", "mutually beneficial cooperation", and "enhancing cooperation and coordination in international affairs and on global issues" (Xi 2012). Prominent expert in China's great power diplomacy Wang Fan points to Chinese official documents in which ties with the EU are qualified as an example of the new type of the relationship between great powers – based on mutual respect of sovereignty, the choice of social systems, appreciation of each other's interests, and coordination in world affairs (Wang 2016: 271–272, 274).

Another instrumental idea behind China's attempts to engage Europe has been setting up a linkage between the "China Dream" and the "European Dream" (Kuhn 2013). Since 2013 China and the EU have been seeking new areas and mechanisms of cooperation, to further implement the two parties' comprehensive strategic partnership in the era of China's transition to the "new normal" (新常态) and Europe's economic reconstruction. During his visit to Europe in March 2014 Xi Jinping proposed "Four Big Partnerships" (peace, growth, reforms, and civilisation) to deepen Sino-EU cooperation based on the perceived proximity of Chinese and European "dreams".[13]

---

12   One Russian political observer Semen Uralov maintains that the priority of Eurasian integration is restoration of a mighty and efficient state (Uralov 2013). Anna Kuznetsova asserts that in the eyes of most Europeans, the EAEU is a flawed project (Kuznetsova 2017). Only some publications suggest that some sort of EU–EAEU engagement could give a new forum to continue economic dialogue with Russia even under difficult circumstances (Khitakhunov et al. 2017).

13   Chinese expert Tian Dewen examines the commonalities and differences between the "China Dream" for the great rejuvenation of the Chinese nation and the "Europe Dream"

To conjoin the "two dreams" Beijing in 2015 launched another key initiative – the development of a Production Capacity Network in Eurasia to integrate China's enormous production capacity with advanced technology offered by developed countries, which will in turn help developing countries in infrastructure construction and industrialisation. In Beijing's view, Europe would play an important role in implementation of this plan since the "EU economy boasts the most advanced and valuable technologies urgently needed by China to update its equipment and manufacturing capacities" (Li 2015). In less than two years since its implementation, the framework cooperation on production capacity has been formed with more than 30 countries, reinforcing the economy of each of the countries involved (Xi 2017).

Beijing's mega-plan to construct a new integrated economic order in Eurasia based on the unique "division of labour" between China, Eurasian economies, and Europe, contains another key component of Chinese strategy – China's cooperation with 16 Central and Eastern European states (CEEC, 16+1).[14] Beijing assures the Europeans that one of the goals of this plan is to contribute to more balanced development within Europe and accelerate European integration on the base of the CEE countries' re-industrialisation and modernisation (Li 2015a). Some experts believe that for China, Central and Eastern Europe represents its "bridge to Europe", and that is true in both a political and logistical sense (Tiezzi 2015). In a single Eurasian economic space which would be regulated by much more transparent rules and more effective transnational (or supranational) institutions, the CEE countries may be incentivised to partake in China's transformation in greater Eurasia while backing up a more flexible investment regulatory regime in Europe and even potentially recognizing China's "market economy" status (Li 2017).

Finally, China's most significant continental integration mechanism – related to the "industrial capacity network" effort – is China's "Belt and Road Initiative" (BRI, including its continental component – the Silk Road Economic Belt). The BRI has been structured to meet the mixed economic and geopolitical objectives through careful coordination of the domestic and external dimensions of Beijing's policies. Michael Clarke maintains that "geopolitically, BRI with its focus on developing trans-Eurasian connectivity centred on China, speaks to Beijing's desire to construct a viable strategic and economic

---

of integration, arguing that the two dreams are common in their goal of peace and development and that the "Dream Fusion" opens up new opportunities in Eurasia (Tian 2016).

14   This format brings together leaders from China and 16 Central and Eastern European states: Albania, Bosnia and Herzegovina, Bulgaria, Croatia, Czech Republic, Estonia, Hungary, Latvia, Lithuania, Macedonia, Montenegro, Poland, Romania, Serbia, Slovakia, and Slovenia. See more details at the official website: http://www.china-ceec.org/eng/.

alternative to the current international order" (Clarke 2017: 72). Scott Kennedy holds that the BRI has become an integral part of China's economic policy to cushion the effect of the domestic economic doldrums and "to help make use of China's enormous industrial overcapacity and ease the entry of Chinese goods into regional markets" (Kennedy 2015). With the EU as the major destination of the new Silk Road initiative, the Chinese leadership will utilise its new connectivity project to solidify China's geoeconomic influence vis-à-vis the US in Europe (Lim 2016: 118).

There are two key aspects of China's integration projects that attract Moscow and drive these two countries together toward even larger trans-regional partnerships grounded on their strategic quasi-alliance.[15] Firstly, China's "creative engagement" approach is based on the principles of amity, sincerity, mutual benefit, and inclusiveness (亲诚惠容) toward other actors and develops cooperation but avoids interference in other countries' internal affairs and dominance over regional affairs or spheres of influence (Yang 2014). Secondly, the validity of the Chinese developmental model which supports global economic liberalisation while stressing the principle of diversity and the preservation of sovereignty. Beijing's smart management of the Eurasian space implies equal dialog, attention to national sentiments, frequent interaction, much real action.[16] These ideas lay the groundwork for a Greater Eurasian project which targets the EU as an indispensable component of the future pan-Eurasian construction.

4   The New "Greater Eurasia" Project and the EU: Will the East Embrace the West?

The Greater Eurasian Project (GEP) was proposed by Russian President Vladimir Putin at the 20th St. Petersburg International Economic Forum in June 17,

---

15   Some Western observers contend that in Eurasia, it is clear that China does not aspire to undermine Russia's sociopolitical and security influence in the region, while Russia in turn is not resisting China's economic encroachment into the region. It might be a stretch to call the relationship symbiotic, but it is certainly mutually tolerant. See Gapak et al. 2015.

16   In his report to the 19th congress of the Chinese Communist Party in October 2017 President Xi Jinping highlighted the role of the Chinese model for the new era, saying his country had developed its economy without imitating Western values, and that this model would offer a new option for other countries and nations who "want to speed up their development while preserving their independence". (Xi 2017a). Some special commentaries on the party congress reflect this Chinese leadership's approach (Buckley & Bradsheroct 2017).

2016, and this mega-project since then has been central to Russo-Chinese Eurasian strategies (RBTH 2016). The project has been further promoted as the formation of a common space for economic, logistic, and information cooperation, and for peace and security from Shanghai to Lisbon and from New Delhi to Murmansk.[17] Chinese analyst Liu Fenghua believes that this integration initiative opens up a new chapter in Eurasian regionalism. In November 2016 the Chinese and Russian premiers agreed to produce a detailed greater Eurasian project feasibility plan (Liu 2017).

Despite the stronger emphasis on Russia's relations with Asia in order to solidify this new mega-association, the "Greater Eurasian" initiative is tailored to reactivate ties with Europe, on a new basis. Russia's success in Eurasia has long been considered a prerequisite for a more productive relationship with the EU (Klepatskii 2008). In his comments on the prospects of the GEP Putin explained that Russia "would welcome the participation of European colleagues, of European Union states in a partnership of this kind. In this case it will become truly harmonised, balanced and all-encompassing" (ITAR-TASS 2017). It is noteworthy that Russian strategists consider GEP a new geo-political phenomenon, since Russia would no longer represent the greater European identity, being itself a centrepiece of a common space between Europe, Russia, and Asia with a new status as an independent centre of power. Moscow persistently demonstrates its devotion to the principles and norms which include commitment to the prosperity of all member states by developing a transcontinental free trade area regionally and globally, avoiding the bloc mentality, fragmentation and politicisation, and exercising respect for sovereignty, non-interference and territorial integrity, cultural and political pluralism, securing the right of each nation to choose its own path for development and way of life (Karaganov 2016a).

In a new Greater Eurasian construction, the relationships between the EAEU and the China-sponsored Silk Road Economic Belt will serve as the major pillar (Suslov 2016: 10). To coordinate multiple economic integration projects, the role of the SCO is highlighted, especially after the 2017 enlargement of the organisation (Li 2016). The potential for deeper and more expansive SCO economic cooperation remains huge as regional cooperation starts to expand from project development to synergy in economic strategy, especially over the China-proposed Belt and Road Initiative. In addition to enhanced transport

---

17   Geographically, the project is likely to encompass countries that participate in the Eurasian Economic Union (EAEU), the Shanghai Cooperation Organisation (SCO), the Association of Southeast Asian Nations (ASEAN), and countries involved in the integration of the Silk Road, including Turkey, Iran, Israel, and Egypt (Kuznetsova 2017).

connectivity, an SCO trade facilitation agreement is considered an important step to deepening regional economic cooperation (Xinhua 2017). Interestingly, while Russia seeks its central role in the new mega-project, China observers also notice Beijing's growing ambitions to secure its own special status as "the Atlantic-Pacific power" in the Greater Eurasian space (Wang & Zhu 2017).

In the normative sphere, China is strengthening its focus on the universal character of Chinese values, the human-centred approach, and the role of social stability that Europe badly needs. The Russian leadership believes that since the West is losing its moral leadership and its military dominance, the appeal of its material prowess is diminishing as other effective economic models emerge. Russia's influential Eurasianist Aleksandr Dugin believes that Russia should rescue Europe from the "modernity trap" by "saving Europe from its liberal elites, and … the struggle with liberalism lies in Eurasia", justifying Moscow's ambitions to establish a protectorate over the European Union (Dugin 2017). Speaking about the democratic nature of the model of our Eurasian Economic Union, the former Speaker of the Russian State Duma's lower chamber Sergei Naryshkin invited European countries to use the Eurasian model of cooperation "until it is too late".[18] Many publications discuss the prospect of "Europe without Eurasia" which would be detrimental for the EU (Belov 2016; Akopian 2017). One Russian analyst warned the EU that in the future Europe would have to deal with the SCO which might not be interested in cooperating with Eurasia's western appendix. Europe's real choice is seen as its ability to recognise itself as part of Eurasia or not (Baranchik 2017).

Many experts however remain sceptical about the future of Europe's involvement in the "Greater Eurasian Partnership". Timofei Bordachev contends that an integral approach of the Greater Eurasia project hardly corresponds to the fragmentary nature of current relations in the current Greater Europe project, so the priority for now is an extensive dialogue between the EAEU and China (Bordachev 2016a). Dmitrii Suslov denies any possibility of joining the models of relations which have emerged in Greater Europe or Eurasia since the EU accepts only the EU-centric model of integration which requires other countries' full accommodation of European norms and regulatory rules, and in Russia's case this process is impossible without a fundamental change of Russia and its foreign policy (Suslov 2016a). Dmitrii Trenin acknowledges that creating a new regional order with China, India, Iran, Turkey and others will not

---

18   Naryshkin pointed to the importance of the sovereignty principle within the EAEU saying that the "goals of the Eurasian Economic Union (EAEU) are absolutely transparent, its rule are more democratic than those of the European Union, the activities of its bodies directly depend on the will of nations that are members of that union" (Naryshkin 2015).

be easy, but, since the EU and Ukraine are also part of Grand Eurasia, the "mission will not be accomplished before Europe and Russia reach a new normal based on empathy in diversity" (Trenin 2017a).

Overall, the outcome of the Russo-Chinese joint effort to engage the EU depends primarily on China's ability to successfully promote its integration and connectivity projects, helping Russia to modernise and find an optimal niche in the implementation of trans-regional initiatives. Beijing needs to reassure Europe of its benign intentions with regard to the BRI and reaffirm its support of the EU's unity (Wemer 2019). In the era of "re-globalisation" it is the two Eurasian powers' domestic efficiency and stability that would secure the formation of new institutions and practices in Eurasia, raising their competitiveness and opening up more opportunities for the EU's involvement.

5   Conclusion

In their attempt to reshape the world order China and Russia have aligned to provide an alternative to the failing Western system of neoliberal capitalism and promote "re-globalisation". While the West has embarked on a new era of political consolidation, institutional reforms and regional realignment, the emerging powers are looking for ways to set a new global economic agenda while avoiding the drastic breakup of global production chains and alienation of the West. The decline of the West provides the Eurasian giants with the chance to partner with the EU in an emerging multipolar format. The EU is seen as the Achilles hill of the waning American neoliberal hegemonic project, and Beijing and Moscow are searching for new levers to win the EU vis-à-vis the US. The struggling European Union, which is encountering a series of ongoing financial, economic, social, and political crises, is increasingly becoming the focus of new integration initiatives in Greater Eurasia.

The EU will remain a very important and essential balancing element of a new configuration in Eurasia. But the extent of its involvement in the new continental processes significantly depends on Beijing's ability to assume leadership as the driver of Eurasian connectivity. To demonstrate its new credentials, the Chinese leadership will ensure the non-hegemonic character of its regional supremacy, promoting multilateral trade liberalisation, "open regionalism", and building mutual trust and a spirit of cooperation. China's calls for synergies between EU policies and China's "Silk Road Economic Belt" initiative may indeed be seen as the manifestation of an unfolding China-US competition for the EU markets and influence in Eurasia. Russia will contribute to China's grand strategic effort to win the EU over from the US and capitalise on its prospective participation in the rule-making process that will shape the future regional and world order.

Bibliography

Akopian, A. (2017). 'Strategicheskii tupik EAES. Kak Rossii "zavoevat" Evropu'?', *Eurasia Daily*, 13 December, https://eadaily.com/ru/news/2017/12/13/strategicheskiy-tupik-eaes-kak-rossii-zavoevat-evropu.

Baranchik, Iu. (2017). 'Evraziia-ShOS poglotit appendiks-Evropu', *Regnum News Online*, 11 June, https://regnum.ru/news/polit/2286920.html.

BBS Forum. (2016). 'Trump's Victory and the Crisis of Global Capitalism' (特朗普胜选与世界资本主义的危机), *BBS Forum*, 10 November, http://bbs.pinggu.org/thread-4933123-1-1.html.

Belov, S. (2016). 'Berevka Putina dlia Evropy. Mozhno povesit'sia, a mozhno spastis', *Regnum News Online*, 22 September, https://regnum.ru/news/polit/2183316.html.

Blackwill, R.D. and Gordon, P.H. (2018). 'Containing Russia. How to Respond to Moscow's Intervention in U.S. Democracy and Growing Geopolitical Challenge', *Council on Foreign Relations Special Report*, 80, January, https://www.cfr.org/sites/default/files/report_pdf/CSR80_BlackwillGordon_ContainingRussia.pdf.

Bordachev, T. (2016). 'Russia and the European Union: Lessons Learned and Goals Ahead', *Strategic Analysis*, 40(6): 561–572.

Bordachev, T. (2016a). 'Some Important Questions and Points Regarding Russia's EU Strategy', *The Valdai Discussion Club*, 15 March, http://valdaiclub.com/a/highlights/questions-and-points-regarding-russia-eu-strategy/.

Brown, K. (2016). 'China EU Relations: Where to Now?', *Note D'actualité*, 11/16 (September), l'Observatoire de la Chine, cycle 2016–2017, http://www.defense.gouv.fr/content/download/487437/7798438/version/1/file/OBS_Chine_201609-NA11-China+EU+Relations+Where+to+Now.pdf.

Buckley, C. and Bradsheroct, K. (2017). 'Xi Jinping's Marathon Speech: Five Takeaways', *The New York Times*, 18 October, https://www.nytimes.com/2017/10/18/world/asia/china-xi-jinping-party-congress.html.

Chen, Z. (2012). 'Results, Regrets and Reinvention: Premier Wen's last China-EU Summit', *European Strategic Partnerships Observatory Policy Brief*, 6, October, https://www.files.ethz.ch/isn/153954/PB_6_Last_China_EU_summit.pdf.

Clarke, M. (2017). 'The Belt and Road Initiative: China's New Grand Strategy?', *Asia Policy*, 24, July, The National Bureau of Asian Research, Seattle, Washington, D.C., http://www.nbr.org/publications/element.aspx?id=941.

Cui, H. (2013). 'The Transatlantic Trade and Investment Partnership: Origins, Objectives and Impact', *China Institute of International Studies*, 7 November, http://www.ciis.org.cn/english/2013-11/07/content_6440336.htm.

Diamond, L. (2016). 'Russia and the Threat to Liberal Democracy', *The Atlantic*, 9 December, https://www.theatlantic.com/international/archive/2016/12/russia-liberal-democracy/510011/.

Dugin, A. (2017). 'Russians Must Save Europe from the Liberal Elite, Interview to Foglio', *Geopolitica.ru*, 25 April, https://www.geopolitica.ru/en/article/russians-must-save-europe-liberal-elite.

EAEU Treaty. (2011). 'Treaty on the Eurasian Economic Union', The United Nations Web Site, 18 November, http://www.un.org/en/ga/sixth/70/docs/treaty_on_eeu.pdf.

EU Policy Paper. (2003). 'China's EU Policy Paper (2003/10/13)', Permanent Mission of the People's Republic of China to the United Nations Office at Geneva and Other International Organizations in Switzerland, 19 April, http://www.fmprc.gov.cn/ce/cegv/eng/ljzg/zgwjzc/t85896.htm.

Fursov, A.I. and Fursov, K.A. (2014). 'World Capitalist System: New Scenarios of Development', *Knowledge. Understanding. Skill Journal*, 1, http://www.zpu-journal.ru/en/journal/contents/2014/1/Fursov_World-Capitalist-System/.

Fursov, A.I. 2015. 'The Downfall of the Capitalist System Will be Marked By a World War, Just As Its Rise Was', *DEN TV*, 28 June, https://www.sott.net/article/298445-Andre-Fursov-The-downfall-of-the-capitalist-system-will-be-marked-by-a-world-war-just-as-its-rise-was.

Gapak, D., Kosnazarov, D. and Browring, G. (2015). 'China and Russia – Allies Not Frenemies in Central Asia', *The Financial Times Blogs*, 11 March, http://blogs.ft.com/beyond-brics/2015/03/11/guest-post-china-and-russia-allies-not-frenemies-in-central-asia/.

Haass, R. (2017). 'World Order 2.0', *Foreign Affairs*, 96(1), January: 2–9.

Heath, T.R. (2018). 'China Prepares for an International Order After U.S. Leadership', *RAND Corp.*, 2 August, https://www.rand.org/blog/2018/08/china-prepares-for-an-international-order-after-us.html.

Hoffmann, C. and Brinkbäumer, K. (2018). 'Germany's Foreign Minister: We Are Seeing What Happens When the U.S. Pulls Back', *Der Spiegel Online*, 8 January, http://www.spiegel.de/international/germany/sigmar-gabriel-we-are-seeing-what-happens-when-the-u-s-pulls-back-a-1186181.html.

ITAR-TASS. (2017). 'Putin favors creation of big Eurasian partnership', *ITAR-TASS Daily*, 14 May, https://dlib.eastview.com/browse/doc/48741213.

Ivanov, I. (2015). 'The Sunset of Greater Europe', *Russian International Affairs Council*, 16 September, http://russiancouncil.ru/en/analytics-and-comments/analytics/zakat-bolshoy-evropy/.

Kagan, R. (2002). 'Power and Weakness', *Policy Review*, 113, June/July, http://www.esi2 .us.es/~mbilbao/pdffiles/rkagan.pdf.

Karaganov, S. (2016). '"We Are Smarter, Stronger and More Determined". Interview with Kremlin foreign policy advisor Sergey Karaganov', *The Spiegel Online*, 13 July, http:// www.spiegel.de/international/world/interview-with-putin-foreign-policy-advisor- sergey-karaganov-a-1102629.html.

Karaganov, S. (2016a). 'S Vostoka na Zapad, ili Bol'shaia Evraziia', *Rossiiskaia Gazeta*, 241, 25 October, https://dlib.eastview.com/browse/doc/47574095.

Katasonov, K. (2016). 'Katasonov: Mirovoi kapitalizm obrechen. Rossiiu spaset tol'ko avtarkiia', *Kolokol Rossii,* 2 September, http://kolokolrussia.ru/globalizaciya/ka tasonov-mirovoy-kapitalizm-obrechen-rossiu-spaset-tolko-avtarkiya#hcq=Ew8 mAJq.

Kennedy, S. (2015). 'Building China's "One Belt, One Road"', *Center for Strategic and International Studies*, 3 April, http://csis.org/publication/building-chinas-one-belt- one-road.

Khitakhunov, A., Mukhamediyev, B. and Pomfret, R. (2017). 'Eurasian Economic Union: Present and Future Perspectives', *Economic Change and Restructuring*, 50(1), February: 59–77.

Khudoley, K. (2016). 'Russia and the European Union: The Present Rift and Chances for Future Reconciliation', *Stosunki Międzynarodowe – International Relations*, 2(52): 195–213.

Klepatskii, L. (2008). 'Strategiia otnoshenii Rossii i Evrosoiuza', *Mezhdunarodnaia zhizn'*, 4: 88–104.

Kortunov, A. (2017). 'Gibridnoe sotrudnichestvo. Kak vyiti iz krizisa v otnosheniiakh Rossii i ES', *Russian International Affairs Council*, 30 August, http://russiancouncil .ru/analytics-and-comments/analytics/gibridnoe-sotrudnichestvo-kak-vyyti-iz- krizisa-v-otnosheniyakh-rossii-s-es/.

Kozyrev, V. (2016). 'Harmonizing "Responsibility to Protect": China's Vision of a Post- Sovereign World', *International Relations*, 30(3): 328–345.

Krastev, I. (2012). 'Europe's Democracy Paradox', *The American Interest*, 7(4), 1 February, https://www.the-american-interest.com/2012/02/01/europes-democracy-paradox/.

Kuhn, R.L. (2013). 'Xi Jinping's Chinese Dream', *The New York Times*, 4 June, http://www .nytimes.com/2013/06/05/opinion/global/xi-jinpings-chinese-dream.html.

Kuznetsova, A.. (2017). 'Greater Eurasia: Perceptions from Russia, the European Union, and China', *Russian International Affairs Council*, 1 September, http://russiancoun cil.ru/en/analytics-and-comments/analytics/greater-eurasia-perceptions-from- russia-the-european-union-and-china/#detail.

Laruelle, M. (2016). 'Russia as an Anti-Liberal European Civilization', pp. 275–297, in Kolstø, P. and Blakkisrud, H. (eds.), *The New Russian Nationalism. Imperialism, Ethnicity and Authoritarianism, 2000–15*. Edinburgh: Edinburgh University Press.

Li, K. (2015). 'Premier Li Keqiang Talks about International Capacity Cooperation', 2 July, http://english.gov.cn/premier/photos/2015/07/02/content_281475138798021 .htm.

Li, K. (2015a). 'Remarks by H.E. Li Keqiang Premier of the State Council of the People's Republic of China at the Fourth Summit of China and Central and Eastern European Countries, Suzhou', 24 November, *Ministry of Foreign Affairs of the People's Republic of China*, http://www.fmprc.gov.cn/mfa_eng/zxxx_662805/t1318260.shtml.

Li, K. (2017). 'Chinese Premier Li Keqiang has vowed to bring cooperation between China and the 16 Central and Eastern European countries (CEEC) and relations between China and Hungary to a higher level', *Secretariat for Cooperation between China and Central and Eastern European Countries*, 27 November, http://www .china-eec.org/eng/zdogjhz_1/t1514065.htm.

Li X. (2016). 'The Docking of Silk Road Economic Belt and Eurasian Economic Union: Building a Eurasian Common Economic Space' [李新, 丝绸之路经济带对接欧亚经济联盟: 共建欧亚共同经济空间], *Northeast Asia Forum* [东北亚论坛], 43(4): 15–23.

Lim, W.X. (2016). 'China's One Belt One Road Initiative: A Literature Review', pp. 113–131, in Lim, T.W., Chan, H.H.L., Tseng, K.H.-Y. and Lim, W.X., *China's One Belt One Road Initiative*. London: Imperial College Press.

Liu, F. (2017). 'Eurasian Partnership: New Agenda for China-Russia Cooperation', [欧亚伙伴关系:中俄合作新议程], *Northeast Asia Tribune* [东北亚论坛], 4: 78–86, http://www.sohu.com/a/163905843_825949.

Lo, B. (2009). 'Medvedev and the New European Security Architecture', *Centre for European Reform Policy Brief*, July, http://www.cer.eu/sites/default/files/publications/ attachments/pdf/2011/pbrief_medvedev_july09-741.pdf.

Lo, B. (2015). *Russia and the New World Disorder*. London: Chatham House; Washington, D.C.: The Brookings Institution.

Luk'ianov [Lukyanov], F. (2016). 'A Failed New World Order and Beyond: Russian View', *Strategic Analysis*, 40(6): 474–485.

Mazarr, M.J. (2017). 'The Once and Future Order', *Foreign Affairs*, 96(1): 25–32.

Miller, A. and Luk'ianov, F. (2017). 'Sderzhannost' vmesto naporistosti', *Russia in Global Affairs*, 24 August, http://www.globalaffairs.ru/number/Sderzhannost-vmesto-naporistosti-18927.

Naryshkin, S. (2015). 'Naryshkin predrekaet krakh integratsionnoi modeli Evrosoiuza', *TASS News Agency*, 28 June, http://tass.ru/politika/2077939.

Nye, J.S. (2017). 'Will the Liberal Order Survive?', *Foreign Affairs*, 96(1): 10–16.

Niblett, R. (2017). 'Liberalism in Retreat', *Foreign Affairs*, 96(1): 17–24.

The People's Daily. (2017). 'The People's Daily Explores Systemic Crisis of Capitalism: Its Roots and How to Asses it', [人民日报探析资本主义系统性危机: 根源、如何

看待], 22 January, http://news.xinhuanet.com/politics/2017-01/22/c_1120360641 .htm.

Pustovitovskij, A. and Kremer, J.-F. (2012). 'Towards a New Understanding of Structural Power: "Structure Is What States Make of It"', pp. 59–78, in Fels, E., Kremer, J.-F. and Kronenberg, K. (eds.), *Power in the 21st Century: International Security and International Political Economy in a Changing World*. Berlin, Heidelberg: Springer.

Putin, V. (2006). 'Speech at Meeting with the Ambassadors and Permanent Representatives of the Russian Federation', President of Russia, 27 June, http://en.kremlin.ru/ events/president/transcripts/23669.

Putin, V. (2011). 'Novyi integratsionnyi proekt dlia Evrazii – budushchee, kotoroe rozhdaetsia segodnia', *Izvestiia*, 3 October, http://izvestia.ru/news/502761.

Qin, Y. (2014). 'The Correct View on the Concept of Righteousness-Justice and Interests: Innovative Ideas and Practical Principles of Chinese Foreign Policy in the New Era' [秦亚青，正确义利观:新时期中国外交的理念创新和实践原则], *The Quest* [求是], 12, 16 June, http://www.qstheory.cn/dukan/qs/2014-06/16/c_1111103905 .htm.

RBTH (2016). 'Putin Proposes Formation of a "Great Eurasian Partnership"', *Russia Beyond the Headlines*, 17 June, https://www.rbth.com/news/2016/06/17/putin-pro poses-formation-of-a-great-eurasian-partnership_603985.

Reference News Online. (2012). 'Euro-American Capitalistic System Falls into a Comprehensive Crisis [欧美资本主义制度陷入全面危机]', 16 March, http://column .cankaoxiaoxi.com/2012/0316/18511.shtml.

Savic, B. (2016). 'Behind China and Russia's "Special Relationship"', *The Diplomat*, 7 December, https://thediplomat.com/2016/12/behind-china-and-russias-special-relationship/.

Schwab, K. (2012). 'The End of Capitalism – So What's Next?', *The Huffington Post*, 13 April (Updated 27/01/2016), https://www.huffingtonpost.com/klaus-schwab/end-of-capitalism----_b_1423311.html.

Strange, S. (1988). *States and Markets*. London&New York: Bloomsbury Publishing.

Suslov, D. (2016). 'Regionalization and Chaos in Interdependent World: Global Context by the Beginning of 2016', *Valdai Paper*, 3(43), 25 January, http://valdaiclub.com/ publications/valdai-papers/regionalisation-and-chaos-in-interdependent-world-global-context-by-the-beginning-/.

Suslov, D. (2016a). 'V raznykh prostranstvakh: novaia povestka dnia dlia otnoshenii Rossiia- ES', *Valdai Discussion Club Newsletter*, 49, June, http://ru.valdaiclub.com/ files/12497/.

Tellis, A.J. (2015). 'The Geopolitics of the TTIP and the TPP', pp. 93–120, in Baru, S. and Dogra, S. (eds.), *Power Shifts and New Blocs in the Global Trading System*. New York: Routledge.

Tian, D. (2016). 'China Dream and European Dream: the Study of China-EU Relations in the New Era' [田德文, "中国梦"与 "欧洲梦": 新时期中欧关系研究], *European Studies* [欧洲研究], 4: 131–144.

Tiezzi, S. (2015). 'China's "Belt and Road" Reaches Europe', *The Diplomat*, 26 November, https://thediplomat.com/2015/11/chinas-belt-and-road-reaches-europe/.

Transatlantic Academy. (2014). 'Liberal Order in a Post-Western World', *Transatlantic Academy Report*, Washington, D.C., May, http://www.gmfus.org/publications/liberal-order-post-western-world.

Trenin, D. (2011). 'What Russian Empire?', *The New York Times*, 23 August, http://www.nytimes.com/2011/08/24/opinion/24iht-edtrenin24.html.

Trenin, D. (2017). 'Looking out Five Years: What Should Washington and Its European Allies Expect From Moscow?', *Russian International Affairs Council*, 30 August, http://russiancouncil.ru/en/analytics-and-comments/comments/looking-out-five-years-what-should-washington-and-its-european-allies-expect-from-moscow/.

Trenin, D. (2017a). 'Russia Has Grand Designs for the International Order', *The Moscow Times*, 24 October, https://themoscowtimes.com/articles/russias-formative-plan-c-foreign-policy-59357.

Troyjo, M. (2017). 'The Clash Between Deglobalization And Reglobalization', *The Huffington Post*, 5 January, http://www.huffingtonpost.com/entry/the-clash-between-deglobalization-reglobalization_us_586e8e2de4boa5e600a78907.

Tsygankov, A. (2017). 'Towards a New Strategy of Civilizational Concentration', *Russia in Global Affairs*, 2, 6 June, http://eng.globalaffairs.ru/number/Towards-a-New-Strategy-of-Civilizational-Concentration-18758.

Uralov, S. (2013). 'Istoricheskii smysl i politicheskie tseli integratsii Evrazii', *Odnako Online*, 10 December, http://www.odnako.org/blogs/istoricheskiy-smisl-i-politicheskie-celi-integracii-evrazii/.

Vershbow, A., Odom, W., and Kozyrev, V. (2005). 'Reevaluating Russia's Role in the World', *The Yale Journal of International Affairs*, Summer/Fall, http://yalejournal.org/wp-content/uploads/2011/01/051102vershbow-odom-kozyrev.pdf.

Walt, S.M. (2016). 'The Collapse of the Liberal World Order', *Foreign Policy*, 26 June, http://foreignpolicy.com/2016/06/26/the-collapse-of-the-liberal-world-order-european-union-brexit-donald-trump/.

Wang F. (2016). *China's Great Power Diplomacy* [王帆，大国外交， 北京联合出版公司]. Beijing: Beijing United Publishing Co., Ltd.

Wang, S. and Zhu, Y. (2017). 'The Great Eurasian Partnership: A Multidimensional Analysis' [王树春; 朱燕, 大欧亚伙伴关系: 多维视角下的深度解析], *Russian Studies Journal* [俄罗斯研究], 7(2): 17–43.

Wemer, D.A. (2019). 'Skepticism Casts a Shadow Over China's Belt and Road Summit', *The Atlantic Council Commentary*, 25 April, https://www.atlanticcouncil.org/blogs/new-atlanticist/skepticism-casts-a-shadow-over-china-s-belt-and-road-summit.

Xi, J. (2012). 'Xi Jinping's Speech at the National Committee on U.S.-China Relations and U.S.-China Business Council Luncheon, Washington, D.C.', 15 February, http://www.ncuscr.org/programs/luncheon-honor-vice-president-xi-jinping.

Xi, J. (2017). 'Work Together to Build the Silk Road Economic Belt and The 21st Century Maritime Silk Road. Full text of President Xi's Speech at Opening of Belt and Road Forum', *Xinhua News*, 14 May, http://news.xinhuanet.com/english/2017-05/14/c_136282982.htm.

Xi, J. (2017a). 'President Xi Jinping's Address to the 19th CPC Congress', [习近平在中国共产党第十九次全国代表大会上的报告], *The People's Daily Network* [人民网-人民日报], 28 October, http://cpc.people.com.cn/n1/2017/1028/c64094-29613660.html.

Xinhua. (2017). 'Economic Watch: SCO Summit Highlights Potential For Expanded Cooperation', *Xinhua Net*, 11 June, http://news.xinhuanet.com/english/2017-06/11/c_136357431.htm.

Yang, J. (2014). 'Jointly Undertake the Great Initiatives With Confidence and Mutual Trust', Speech by H.E. Yang Jiechi at the Session of 'Reviving the Silk Road: A Dialogue with Asian Leaders' at the Boao Forum for Asia Annual Conference 2014, http://english.boaoforum.org/u/cms/www2/201411/03101933vp5r.pdf, 34–41.

Youngs, R. (2013). 'The EU Beyond the Crisis: The Unavoidable Challenge of Legitimacy', *Carnegie Europe*, 8 October, http://carnegieeurope.eu/2013/10/08/eu-beyond-crisis-unavoidable-challenge-of-legitimacy-pub-53242.

Zevelev, I. (2016). 'Russian National Identity and Foreign Policy', *Center for Strategic and International Studies Report*, 12 November, https://www.csis.org/analysis/russian-national-identity-and-foreign-policy.

Zheng, S. (2017). 'China Expanding Global Clout as US, EU Retreat From Global Stage, Says Report', *The South China Morning Post*, 30 November, http://www.scmp.com/news/china/diplomacy-defence/article/2122219/china-expanding-global-clout-us-eu-retreat-global-stage.

Zheng, Y. (2012). 'The Crisis of Capitalism or the Crisis of State Power?' [郑永年:资本主义危机还是国家权力危机?], *Finance News Network* [财经网], 25 April, http://finance.ifeng.com/opinion/zjgc/20120425/6372348.shtml.

Zhou, R. (2017). 'Real Dilemmas of Contemporary Capitalism, Internal Debates, and Future Trends' [周荣国，当前资本主义的现实困境、内部争论和未来走势], *Contemporary World Journal* [当代世界], 1, 10 February, http://www.cwzg.cn/theory/201702/34174.html.

CHAPTER 16

The Fight against Human Trafficking in the European Union and Russia

Marco Borraccetti

Trafficking in human beings is a serious form of crime that consists in a grave violation of fundamental human rights and with an extremely pernicious and highly lucrative form of organised crime, above all with transnational characteristics. It affects countries and regions worldwide. Human trafficking and smuggling of migrants are linked but are not the same; in this respect, trafficked persons are always victims of the crime of trafficking, while smuggled migrants are not victims of smuggling but they could be victims of crimes, that is, of violence during their journey. Multiple aspects and factors of insecurity within countries of origin, transit and destination make trafficking in persons a human security issue (Friman & Reich 2007: 150; Kreidenweis 2015: 67). Vulnerability, the use of violence – physical and psychological – and exploitation are characteristics of this phenomenon (Clark 2003: 247).[1]

Despite the recent legislative and political developments to prevent, fight and prosecute trafficking in human beings, a comprehensive framework embracing human security aspects is still lacking. Especially the lack of legislation, on the one side, and the effects of interpretation of the existing norms, on the other side, put the protection of victims at risk, foremost their access to rights, and the prosecution of their exploiters (Borraccetti 2017: 187). This particularly egregious criminal activity is characterised by the intention of perpetrators to exploit the vulnerabilities of potential victims for personal gain, frequently by exploiting conditions of poverty or forced migration due to civil unrest or the collapse of economic systems: economic, political and social factors can all contribute to creating a heightened status of insecurity among certain segments of a population. Strategies of traffickers aim at identifying and targeting these individuals who can be characterised as vulnerable, thereby ensuring greater success for themselves.

---

1 Clark pointed out that growth of trafficking in human beings has reached such proportions as to present a significant human rights crisis in countries of origin, transit and destination; certain populations are specifically at risk for being exploited because of their particular vulnerabilities.

The economic and social impact of the global financial crisis, the migration crisis and the security threats posed by organised crime groups further exacerbate vulnerabilities, and therefore require stronger action at both national and EU levels. Such action must continue to pursue a human rights-based, gender-specific and child-sensitive approach, and their implementation needs to be coordinated within the EU and externally, as well as across various policy fields. In a human security framework, both national and international dimensions have to be considered. The States are fully expected to maintain the security not only of their national borders, but also of the individuals living within those borders. They are held responsible for protecting the people living in their territory from external conflict and harm and they are also expected to ensure that those citizens enjoy a wide range of rights and are able to live their lives with a sense of dignity and an absence of fear. A human security framework will therefore provide a basis for specific policy and institutional changes necessary to protect vulnerable populations from the risk of being trafficked in their countries of origin as well as in countries of transit and destination. Hence, in Europe, EU actions and the legal framework on trafficking in human beings has undoubtedly an added value, since trafficking is a transnational threat to human security.

As highlighted by the Office of the High Commissioner for Human Rights "the human rights of trafficked persons shall be at the centre of all efforts to prevent and combat trafficking and to protect, assist and provide redress to victims".[2] According to the 2005 Human Security Report, trafficking in human beings is "so widespread and so damaging to its victims that it has become a cause of human insecurity"[3] on a global scale (Friman & Reich 2007: 154).[4] Being linked with the exploitation of vulnerable persons human security has implications and is related to the greater discourse on mobility, irregular and regular migration. Vulnerable migrants – i.e. women, children[5] and persons in poor economic conditions or undocumented (Friman 2007: 143) – are at heightened risk to be trafficked, to be exploited in domestic work, in the agricultural sector or in the sex industry (Koser 2005) because of their particular

---

2 Office of the United Nations High Commissioner for Human Rights (2010), *Recommended Principles and Guidelines on human rights and human trafficking Commentary.*

3 *Human Security Report* (2005), released by the Human Security Centre, http://www.human-securityreport.info/.

4 Friman and Reich are pointing out (2007: 154) that the human security approach to human trafficking "remains underutilized and its potential underrealized".

5 See European Parliament LIBE Committee, Press Release of 21.4.2016, *Fate of 10,000 missing refugee children debated in Civil Liberties Committee.*

conditions. In particular, in the current context of the "migration crisis",[6] part of the migrants that reached the EU territory have been confronted with human trafficking by becoming victims or experiencing violence during their journey.[7]

In light of intensifying insecurity regarding illegal movement across European borders, the most obvious way to prevent such illegal movement is to provide security to the most vulnerable populations, who are invariably most likely to become victims of human trafficking (Ball 2015).

1   International and Regional Dimensions: The Palermo Protocol and the CoE Convention against Trafficking in Human Beings

The international legal framework against trafficking in human beings has a double dimension, international and regional. In the first one, the Protocol to Prevent, Suppress and Punish Trafficking in Persons Especially Women and Children to the Convention of Palermo on the organised crime as to be considered; the regional dimension developed its action against trafficking with the Council of Europe Convention on Action against Trafficking in Human Beings, adopted by the Committee of Ministers of the Council of Europe on 3 May 2005. The European Union and Russia signed and ratified the first; Russia is currently not bound by the second.[8]

The international community decided to implement actions against traffickers with a Protocol to the Convention of Palermo on the organised crime.[9] In particular, according to the Protocol to Prevent, Suppress and Punish Trafficking in Persons Especially Women and Children,[10] trafficking in persons shall mean:

---

6   Report from the Commission to the European Parliament and the Council, Report on the progress made in the fight against trafficking in human beings (2016), COM(2016: 267).

7   Violence along the trip is not an exclusive of trafficking; in fact, migrants can be victims of violence also in the case of smuggling. The important distinction of the two phenomena is not simple.

8   Russia signed and ratified the Convention and the Protocol of Palermo (2000–2004) but it didn't sign the Council of Europe Convention on Action against Trafficking in Human Beings (https://www.coe.int/en/web/conventions/full-list/-/conventions/treaty/197/signatures?p_auth=vov5i1Yr).

9   *United Nations Convention against Transnational Organized Crime.* Adopted and opened for signature, ratification and accession by General Assembly Resolution 55/25 of 15 November 2000 (Palermo Convention on Organised Crime).

10   *Protocol to Prevent, Suppress and Punish Trafficking in Persons Especially Women and Children*, supplementing the Palermo Convention on Organised Crime (Protocol on trafficking

the recruitment, transportation, transfer, harbouring or receipt of persons, by means of the threat or use of force or other forms of coercion, of abduction, of fraud, of deception, of the abuse of power or of a position of vulnerability or of the giving or receiving of payments or benefits to achieve the consent of a person having control over another person, for the purpose of exploitation. Exploitation shall include, at a minimum, the exploitation of the prostitution of others or other forms of sexual exploitation, forced labour or services, slavery or practices similar to slavery, servitude or the removal of organs.[11]

The approach adopted by the Protocol does not require only the use of force as a constitutive element of the crime of human trafficking, but leaves space for other forms of so called "means" such as traffickers taking advantage of the vulnerability of their victims using psychological violence or deception. The definition is comprehensive in its description of the three main characteristics: what are the acts, as recruitment, transportation, transfer, harbouring, receipt; what are the means, as threat, use of force, other forms of coercion, abduction, fraud, deception, abuse of power, abuse of a position of vulnerability, receiving or paying of benefits; what are the purposes, as exploitation, in particular of the prostitution of others, other forms of sexual exploitation, forced labour or services, slavery or practices similar to slavery, servitude and removal of organs. Punishing not only traffickers, but also the exploiters, that are not part of the organisation but are benefitting of their activity is crucial. For example, in countries where prostitution is legal, women victims of trafficking are marketed through the legalized sex industry. An action against the exploiters would complete in a reasonable way the legal framework.

Effective anti-trafficking legislation should be based upon two core principles. The first is the criminalization of the act of trafficking, and the second is the victims' protection. The recognition of the trafficked persons as a victim of a crime is a necessary step to ensuring their protection. The fact that victims are frequently criminalized for being in possession of illegal papers or for having been involved in prostitution, and that their families and communities will no longer accept them, helps us to point out the importance of a human

---

or Protocol on Trafficking in Persons or Protocol on trafficking in Human Beings). According to Ruggeri (2014), *The European Legal and Policy Framework: impact on human Trafficking*, Lambert Academic Publishing, the Protocol is using both human right approach and criminal justice approach to define trafficking in human beings; however, the two theories are not considering the prevention approach.

11   Palermo Protocol on Trafficking in Persons, art.3 (a).

security approach, where a victim is at the core of the legislation, irrespective of the status in the receiving country.

In particular, the need of better access to rights and to justice – for example not requiring victims to testify against their alleged traffickers – is a key factor for the victims that should not have to decide between deportation and protection. In this respect, the lack of unconditional access to support and protection puts victims at risk of criminalization and potential deportation, thereby denying them right of access to an effective remedy.[12] Furthermore, access to effective and appropriate remedies is an obligation on States,[13] confirmed by United Nations organs and a range of regional and international policy instruments.[14] In a nutshell, unconditional assistance to victims would constitute a fundamental element for a trafficking approach to correlate with the notion of human security.

The Council of Europe Convention on Action against Trafficking in Human Beings entered into force on 1 February 2008, following its 10th ratification.[15] While building on existing international instruments, the Convention goes beyond the minimum standards agreed upon in them and strengthens the protection afforded to victims, having a comprehensive scope of application, encompassing all forms of trafficking -whether national or transnational, linked or not linked to organised crime- and taking in all persons who are victims of trafficking, i.e. women, men or children.

The Convention covered all the forms of exploitation; including, at a minimum, sexual exploitation, forced labour or services, slavery or practices similar to slavery, servitude and the removal of organs. Its main added value is the human rights perspective and the focus on victims' protection: the Preamble defines trafficking in human beings as a violation of human rights and an offence

---

12   As stressed by the Office of the United Nations High Commissioner for Human Rights in the Recommended Principles and Guidelines, cit., the Human Rights Committee has noted that for trafficked women who "are likely to be penalized for their illegal presence [...] by deportation", apprehension "effectively prevents these women from pursuing a remedy for the violation of their rights under article 8 of the Covenant", Concluding Observations of the Human Rights Committee (1998): Israel (CCPR/C/79/ Add.93, para.16).

13   Recognizing the multifaceted nature of this right, guideline 9 of the Recommended Principles and Guidelines on Human Rights and Human Trafficking, issued by the Office of the High Commissioner for Human Rights in 2002, recommends the States to consider "[e]nsuring that victims of trafficking have an enforceable right to fair and adequate remedies, including the means for as full a rehabilitation as possible". See further ECHR, n. 25965/04, Rantsev v. Cyprus and Russia, ECLI:CE:ECHR:2010:0107JUD002596504.

14   For example, see also the Brussels Declaration on Preventing and Combating Trafficking in Human Beings (2002), para. 16; ECOWAS Initial Plan of Action against Trafficking in PERSONS 2002–2003 (2001), P. 3, PARA. 6.

15   Council of Europe Treaty Office: http://conventions.coe.int/Treaty/en/Treaties/Html/197 .htm.

to the dignity and integrity of the human being. Consequently, a series of rights are provided for victims of trafficking, in particular the right to be identified as a victim, to be protected and assisted, to be given a recovery and reflection period of at least 30 days, to be granted a renewable residence permit, and to receive compensation for the damages suffered.

Furthermore, the added value of the Convention comes from the monitoring system set up to supervise the implementation of the obligations contained in it, which consists of two pillars: the Group of Experts on Action against Trafficking in Human Beings (GRETA) and the Committee of the Parties.

Even if an international treaty in the contest of the Council of Europe, the Convention is not restricted only to its member states; non-members states and the European Union also have the possibility of becoming Party to it.[16]

Finally, another European regional act could be included in the group of the instruments useful in the fight against THB: the Istanbul Convention on Preventing and Combatting Violence against Women and Domestic Violence, entered into force in August 2014. Considering a 2014 report from the UN Office on Drugs and Crime[17] found that 49% of trafficking victims were women, and 20% girls, the Istanbul Convention would seem to extend to trafficking. Article 12, which sets forth general obligations, states that "Any measures taken pursuant to this chapter shall take into account and address the specific needs of persons made vulnerable by particular circumstances and shall place the human rights of all victims at their centre".

Given the use of the term "vulnerable" in the Council of Europe Convention on THB (specifically in articles 4, 5, and 12), the proposition that the Istanbul Convention at minimum calls for interaction with, if not outright bolsters, the Convention against Trafficking in Human Beings does not seem too far-fetched. It is itself quite clear in creating an obligation for Parties to undertake measures to combat trafficking, especially in articles 5 through 7.

2 The EU Action against Human Trafficking

The Rantsev v Cyprus and Russia[18] judgment provides a decisive human rights benchmark with clear obligations for Member States to take the necessary steps to address different areas of trafficking in human beings. These include

---

16 Given the possibility, the State of Belarus ratified the Convention in 2013.

17 UNODC, Global Report on Trafficking in Persons 2014, http://www.unodc.org/documents/data-and-analysis/glotip/GLOTIP_2014_full_report.pdf.

18 ECHR, n. 25965/04, Rantsev v. Cyprus and Russia, cit.; Jean Allain, Rantsev v Cyprus and Russia: The European Court of Human Rights and Trafficking as Slavery, HRLR 10 (2010: 546–557).

recruitment, investigation, prosecution, protection of human rights, and providing assistance to victims. Once the authorities are aware of a case of human trafficking, or that an individual risk being a victim of human trafficking, they are obliged to take appropriate measures.[19]

Moreover, trafficking in human beings is a priority crime threat area in the 2018–2021 EU Policy Cycle on Organised and Serious International Crime.[20] In addition, the political commitment to stepping up EU action against trafficking in human beings, within the EU and around the world, is supported by the Global Strategy on the European Union's Foreign and Security Policy (EUGS) and by relevant European Parliament resolutions.[21]

The importance of the fight against trafficking is part of the EU legal order: Under Article 5(3) of the EU Charter of Fundamental Rights, trafficking in human beings (THB) is prohibited and has to be seen in connection with forced or compulsory labour, slavery, and servitude.[22] Hence, the fight against trafficking is a way to respect and protect human dignity, and if need be to restore the victims' dignity (Borraccetti 2017b: 281). Furthermore, the fight against human trafficking is part of the general aims of the EU. This is set forth in particular in Article 2 TEU, on the respect for human dignity and human rights, and Article 3(2) TEU, on the existence of an area of freedom, security, and justice, with appropriate measures for a common action in preventing and combating crime.

In the Treaty on the Functioning of European Union (TFEU), the fight against human trafficking figures among the actions needed to develop an area of freedom, security, and justice. In this case, it has to be seen from a twofold perspective. On the one hand, the legal basis for counteracting irregular migration is included in Article 79 as an independent task within migration policy,

---

19   Communication from the Commission, The EU Strategy towards the Eradication of Trafficking in Human Beings 2012–2016, 19.6.2012, COM (2012) 286 final.

20   Council of the European Union, 2018–2021 EU Policy Cycle on Organised and Serious International Crime, 4.10.2017, n. 12811/17.

21   European Parliament resolution of 5.7.2016 on The fight against trafficking in human beings in the EU's external relations; European Parliament resolution of 10.2. 2010 on preventing trafficking in human beings.

22   According to the "Explanations relating to the Charter of Fundamental Rights", OJ C 303 of 14 December 2007, Art. 5(3) "takes account of recent developments in organised crime, such as the organisation of lucrative illegal immigration or sexual exploitation networks". It links the definition of trafficking to the Annex to the Europol Convention, which includes a definition referring to trafficking for the purpose of sexual exploitation: "'Traffic in human beings' means subjection of a person to the real and illegal sway of other persons by using violence or menaces or by abuse of authority or intrigue with a view to the exploitation of prostitution, forms of sexual exploitation and assault of minors or trade in abandoned children".

with particular attention to victims as vulnerable persons, especially women and children.

On the other hand, trafficking in human beings and the sexual exploitation of women and children – as serious form of criminality – are included in cooperation in criminal matters. In that case, Article 83 TFEU recognizes the EU competence to have common rules concerning the definition of criminal offences and sanctions in the areas of particularly serious crime with a cross-border dimension.

In the EU legal framework, different directives interact in view of the aim of protecting victims and enabling them to exercise their rights. In a chronological order, we need to consider the Residence Permit Directive,[23] the Trafficking Directive,[24] and the Victims' Rights Directive.[25] Their territorial application is patchy by the fact that the legal framework has no application in the Kingdom of Denmark, and the Residence Permit Directive has no application in Ireland.[26] The differential application between the other Member States and these countries could create a situation of inequality and a risk of less favourable conditions, depending on the standard of internal legislation,[27] as well as on the lack of jurisprudence by the EU Court of Justice.

Despite the human rights and the gender approaches – and generally speaking a victims-oriented approach – the EU legal framework still continues to have legislative gaps or difficult hypotheses of application, with room for differential treatment. All these types of situations are jeopardising the real protection of victims, and hence their human security, in case they are denied the assistance they need to live and escape their terrible conditions. Access to victims' rights is part of the protection pillar, one of the so-called "four Ps"

---

23 Directive 2004/81/EC of 29 April 2004, on the Residence Permit Issued to Third-Country Nationals Who Are Victims of Trafficking in Human Beings or Who Have Been the Subject of an Action to Facilitate Illegal Immigration, Who Cooperate with the Competent Authorities. OJ L 261, p. 19.

24 Directive 2011/36/EU of 5 April 2011, on Preventing and Combating Trafficking in Human Beings and Protecting Its Victims, and Replacing Council Framework Decision 2002/629/JHA. OJ L 101, p. 1.

25 Directive 2012/29/EU, of 25 October 2012, on Establishing Minimum Standards on the Rights, Support and Protection of Victims of Crime, and Replacing Council Framework Decision 2001/220/JHA. OJ L 315, p. 57.

26 The Trafficking Directive and the Victims' Rights Directive, by contrast, do find application in both the UK and Ireland.

27 Incidentally, Denmark, Ireland, and the UK are members of the Council of Europe and are subject to the Convention on Action against Trafficking in Human Beings, CETS No. 197, adopted by the Committee of Ministers on 3 May 2005. It entered into force on 1 February 2008 (DK), 1 April 2009 (UK), and 1 November 2010 (IRL).

(Fukuda Parr 2003: 167) developed by the international community in the Protocol against Trafficking, annexed to the Palermo Convention against Organised Crime.[28]

The main source of secondary law in the fight against THB is the Trafficking Directive, which aims at more rigorously preventing the phenomenon, at prosecuting traffickers, and at protecting victims. It establishes minimum standards concerning the definitions of criminal offences and sanctions in the area of THB; it applies to victims and recognizes the gender-specific nature of the phenomenon of trafficking. For that reason, EU action is characterized by a fundamental rights approach, a gender approach, and a victims' protection approach. Furthermore, victims have to be protected from prosecution of crimes committed as a direct consequence of being subject to trafficking. In this way victims' human rights are safeguarded, and victims are encouraged to act as witnesses against the perpetrators of those crimes.

The directive specifies the meaning of vulnerability and of forms of exploitation, shaping the definition of trafficking in human beings. A "position of vulnerability" is one in which "the person concerned has no real or acceptable alternative but to submit to the abuse involved"; whereas exploitation "shall include, as a minimum, the exploitation of the prostitution of others or other forms of sexual exploitation, forced labour or services, including begging, slavery or practices similar to slavery, servitude, or the exploitation of criminal activities, or the removal of organs".

The system stands on different pillars with a common horizontal approach, including particular attention to women and children, and pointing out the fundamental importance of the victims-centred approach in the effort to root out the phenomenon.

In particular, the victim's consent to exploitation is deemed irrelevant in prosecuting the offence (Art. 2 of the Trafficking Directive), this owing to the

---

28   "Protocol to Prevent, Suppress and Punish Trafficking in Persons, ESPECIALLY Women and Children", supplementing the United Nations Convention against Transnational Organised Crime (hereinafter the Palermo Protocol on Trafficking, or simply the Palermo Protocol), UN General Assembly resolution 55/25 of 15 November 2000. The importance of the Protocol has been pointed out in A.T. Gallagher, "Two Cheers for the Trafficking Protocol", *Anti-Trafficking Review* 4 (2015): 14–32: "Without the Protocol, arguments around definitions would have continued to block the evolution of principles and rules. Without the Protocol it is likely that the human rights system would have continued its shameful tradition of side-lining issues such as forced labour, forced sex, forced marriage and the ritual exploitation of migrant workers through debt. Most critically, the Protocol provided the impetus and template for a series of legal and political developments that, over time, have served to ameliorate some of its greatest weaknesses, including the lack of human rights protections and of a credible oversight mechanism".

situation of vulnerability and its abuse by the traffickers; furthermore, in this same manner, competent authorities may choose not to prosecute victims for their involvement in criminal activities carried out under duress (Art. 8). Because of the weakness and vulnerability and its abuse by traffickers, investigation or prosecution need not be dependent on reporting or accusation by a victim, and a criminal proceeding may move forward even if the victim has withdrawn his or her statement (Art. 9), so as to safeguard the private life from pressures inflicted on victims and on members of their family even in their country of origin.

The position of vulnerability makes the victims more hesitant to file criminal complaints, considering the threats that they and their families are highly likely to come under from traffickers seeking to make them withdraw what they report to the authorities. That is why consent is irrelevant, and why it is essential that they be allowed to continue to stay, thus enjoying the benefit of support and assistance.

Sanctions apply to both individuals and legal entities; however, if the Trafficking Directive provides for criminal sanctions only against traffickers, there are no similar provisions against users of victims' services. In fact, under Article 18(4), a Member State shall only "consider taking measures to establish as a criminal offence the use of services which are the objects of exploitation", without compulsory provisions in that connection. In this respect, it is imperative for States not to leave open dangerous loopholes that could be exploited by traffickers: "a liberal prostitution policy does not lead to better protection and, in some cases, legalized prostitution can be detrimental to protecting victims of human trafficking" (Cho 2016: 321). Indeed, States need to be able to prosecute any type of crime related to THB if the crime is committed, even only in part, in the national territory or, without any limitation, if it is committed its own citizens. For that reason, States have the ability to extend their jurisdiction over different situations, as when the victim is someone who habitually resides in their territory, or when the benefit is for a legal person based in the territory, or when the offender habitually dwells in its territory.

Protection, assistance, and support for victims have to be provided as soon as the authorities have reasonable grounds for believing that the person might have been subject to any of the offences related to THB.[29]

---

29   Trafficking Directive, Art. 11 and Whereas 18. In the judgment in *L.E.* v *Greece* of 21 January 2016, n. 71545/12, the European Court of Human Rights held unanimously that there had been violations of Arts. 4, 6(1), and 13 of the Convention because a woman, "officially recognised as a victim of human trafficking for the purpose of sexual exploitation", "had nonetheless been required to wait more than nine months after informing the authorities of her situation before the justice system granted her that status".

The act focused on the guarantee to assist and support the victims before, during, and for an appropriate period after the conclusion of criminal proceedings, this in order to enable them to exercise the rights set forth in the Victims and Trafficking Directives. In particular, assistance and support mean an adequate standard of living, safe accommodations, material assistance, medical treatment, and translation and interpretation services.

Access to victims' rights is part of the abovementioned protection pillar (Fukuda-Parr 2003: 167) developed by the Palermo protocol (Gallagher 2015: 14);[30] none of these rights are made conditional on the victim's willingness to cooperate in the criminal investigation, prosecution, or trial, but the express reference to such cooperation without prejudice of the Residence Permit Directive could affect the real benefit to victims (Borraccetti 2017: 281). However, the question comes up as to whether the expiration of a residence permit or the lack of such a permit means that one can no longer access to assistance.

From another perspective, assistance also has a protective implication in criminal investigations and proceedings: legal counsel and representation have to be guaranteed in any case without delay, with an opportunity to be cleared of charges. Furthermore, victims can request compensation, appropriate individual protection based on individual risk assessment, and specific treatment to prevent secondary victimization. In this respect, access to a scheme of compensation for victims of violent crimes has to be included.

3   The Russian Dimension of THB

As mentioned before, Russia signed the UN Convention Against Transnational Organized Crime and the Protocols thereto, including the Protocol to prevent, suppress and punish trafficking in persons, especially women and children. However, it didn't sign the Council of Europe Convention: a decision that affects the fight to this serious form of crime in the Russian territory.

Russia is a source, transit, and destination country for men, women, and children subjected to forced labour and sex trafficking; the first one remains

---

30   Gallagher pointed out the importance of the protocol: "Without the Protocol, arguments around definitions would have continued to block the evolution of principles and rules. Without the Protocol it is likely that the human rights system would have continued its shameful tradition of side-lining issues such as forced labour, forced sex, forced marriage and the ritual exploitation of migrant workers through debt. Most critically, the Protocol provided the impetus and template for a series of legal and political developments that, over time, have served to ameliorate some of its greatest weaknesses, including the lack of human rights protections and of a credible oversight mechanism".

the predominant problem with workers coming from Russia and other countries in Europe, Central Asia, and Southeast Asia, including Vietnam and Democratic People's Republic of Korea (DPRK). Furthermore, women and children from Europe, predominantly Ukraine and Moldova, Southeast Asia, primarily Vietnam, Africa, and Central Asia are reportedly victims of sexual exploitation.[31]

In the meanwhile, Russian women and children are reportedly victims of sex trafficking in Russia and abroad, including in Northeast Asia, Europe, Central Asia, Africa, the United States, and the Middle East.[32] Something confirmed by Eurostat in its Report 2016, Russian citizens are the third group of registered victims of THB in the EU, which since the collapse of communism has seen a dramatic increase in the number of persons trafficked into and through the region, being one of the largest source in the world for victims of human trafficking (Hughes & Denisova 2004: 43), due to the socio-economic conditions in the region and high profits from trafficking (Bartilow 2008: 1).

In addition to the listed above, experts highlight such forms of THB as marriages for the purpose of exploitation, including the use of "mail-order brides"; as forced commercial surrogacy; THB for use in armed forces, as well as the use of soldiers and prisoners for forced labour (Tiurukanova 2006: 22).

Traffickers are exploiting people's poverty and helplessness, lack of awareness of the law, willingness to trust, and desire to earn "easy money", as well as inadequate state support. Some population groups in Russia experience particularly high rates of poverty, labour market segregation, and limited access to effective employment, education, and welfare; essentially, anyone employed informally, without standard social protections, runs the risk of being subject to forms of labour exploitation that verge on human trafficking. Also, since Russia is richer than its neighbour countries, it serves as a more attractive destination point for migrants from neighbourhood countries.

The Palermo Protocol had more influence on policy development in the early 2000s, but Dean suggests that over time the influence of this protocol dissipated (Dean 2017; Shelley 2005: 291; Avdeyeva 2007: 877). Policy adoption was impeded by bureaucratic factors and state capacity, where bureaucratic reforms slowed policy adoption and made it difficult to identify the lead ministry for human trafficking policy development. At the same time, as it happened

---

31   International Organization for Migration, *Prevention of Human Trafficking in the RF* (2006–2008), https://www.iom.int/jahia/webdav/site/myjahiasite/shared/shared/mainsite/events/docs/Project_Concept_rome.pdf.

32   U.S. Department of State, 2017 Trafficking in Persons Report (http://www.state.gov/j/tip/rls/tiprpt/2016/index.htm).

worldwide, monetary burdens on member states with Palermo Protocol compliance is another internal factor determining policy adoption (Hathaway 2002: 1935). In fact, preventative policies such as criminalization statutes were identified as the most popular form of international treaty compliance regarding human trafficking because they are the cheapest (Cho & Vadlamannati 2011: 249).

In terms of policy variation, Russia's trafficking policy is consisting of one policy tool: a statute that criminalizes human trafficking. In particular, Russia has the lowest number of legal frameworks in place to fight trafficking in the entire post-Soviet region, with only one human trafficking policy tool: two criminal code articles criminalizing human trafficking. According to Dean, Russia lacked a better human trafficking policy simply because it was not among the government's priorities; at the same time, NGO's action was important in the successful attempt, in cooperation with international organisations for the incorporation of these two criminal code articles (McKarthy 2011: 221; McKarthy 2010b: 1).

Though human trafficking might appear to be an apolitical issue that no one but the traffickers themselves would oppose, the anti-trafficking discourse and often the human rights discourse demonstrate that there is no consensus on the issue in international policymaking (Dean & Dovgaia 2017). It probably happened also in Russia, and it could be related to the international pressure in somehow; in the country an estimated one million people are involved, it seems that the Russian government has made the task of assisting trafficking victims a political one.

At the same time, some legislative decision had a positive effect, in particular considering an external dimension. In fact, to reduce some migrant labourers' vulnerability, the government made it easier for citizens of some countries to obtain work permits, though it charged fees upfront that effectively excluded many of the most vulnerable from obtaining the permits. New legislation limited the amount of time an employer can send employees to work for other firms and required these outsourced employees to earn the same amount as permanent employees. These regulations may reduce the vulnerability of temporary workers loaned to other companies, a practice known as "out staffing".[33] According to Tyuryukanova (2006: 22), the initiatives of the Russian NGOs and international organizations had a serious impact on the revitalization of the Government activity in this area, as well as on the rise of awareness of the general public and groups at risk. If the attention of the public and the media focuses on trafficking for the purpose of sexual exploitation, the extent of

---

33   U.S. Department of State, 2017 Trafficking in Persons Report, cit.

trafficking for other forms of forced labour is disproportionately higher due to a significantly larger numbers of migrants exposed to this type of exploitation (Mukomel 2013: 4).

From a law enforcement perspective, the Government of Russia does not fully meet the minimum standards for the elimination of trafficking and is not making significant efforts to do so, without developing a national strategy or assigning roles and responsibilities to government agencies. Furthermore, it is far in the development of a victims' protection programs, because the government offered no funding or programs for trafficking victims' rehabilitation, while several privately-run shelters ceased operations during the reporting period due to lack of funding and the government's crackdown on civil society.[34]

In December 2003, Articles 127.1 "Trafficking in Human Beings" and 127.2 "The use of slave labour", which criminalized the use of slave labour, were introduced into the Criminal Code of the Russian Federation. From that moment onwards, the law enforcement agencies obtained legal tools to combat trafficking in human beings. In parallel, public authorities were establishing cooperation with international organizations; In order to improve understanding, coordination and cooperation in the implementation of initiatives to combat human trafficking, a joint working group with the participation of the UN and the IOM agencies was set up in March 2004. The UN participation in the Working Group was represented by such agencies as the ILO, the UNICEF, the UNDP, the UNFPA, the UNODC and the Office of the UN Resident Coordinator in the Russian Federation.

The national legislation broadly complies with the obligations arising from the Palermo Protocol. The reclamation of international organizations generally comes to two points. First, the federal law does not provide for specific grounds for the extension of stay on the territory of the Russian Federation for the victims that are foreign citizens and persons without citizenship, which is in conflict with Article 7 of the Protocol. Second and more important, there are no specialized programs for the prevention of trafficking and protection of victims of trafficking, which follows from the obligations under Article 9 of the Protocol.

In Russia, a considerable positive experience in preventing and combating trafficking in human beings is accumulated, which manifests itself in the adoption of relevant legislation, creation of corresponding structures within the law-enforcement agencies, and elaboration of practices for effective interdepartmental and international cooperation between the law enforcing agencies, as well as between the state authorities, local authorities and the

---

34   Ibid.

NGOs. The main problems stem from the lack of a national strategy (program) to combat trafficking in human beings and assist victims of trafficking, and from the lack of mechanisms to support of the Russian NGOs that work in this direction.

The Russian government did not collect and share information on trafficking cases or maintains comprehensive statistics about criminal cases, making it difficult to assess the adequacy or effectiveness of law enforcement efforts.[35] Media reports and publicly available data reveal some details on trafficking cases investigated and prosecuted during the reporting period, although this limited number of cases reported did not appear to constitute an adequate law enforcement response compared to the estimated prevalence of trafficking in Russia. From the limited available information, authorities pursued trafficking suspects through articles 127.1 and 127.2 of the criminal code, which prohibit sex trafficking and forced labour, although they also cover non-trafficking offenses. These articles prescribe punishments of up to 10 years' imprisonment, which are sufficiently stringent and commensurate with punishments prescribed for other serious crimes, such as rape.

The government generally did not undertake efforts to protect victims and it did not provide funding or programs for protective services dedicated to them. Without specific legislation differentiating victims of trafficking and victims of other crimes, government agencies claimed they had neither the means nor authority to provide assistance programs specifically for trafficking victims. Finally, the government did not make available official statistics on the number of victims identified or assisted by its authorities.

4   The External Dimension: THB in the Dialogues EU-Russia

THB has an internal dimension and a transnational one. Given that the dimension of the crime and the higher involvement of Russian citizens, it should be important to set it as a priority in the Russia-EU relations. Unfortunately, there are not evidences that it happened in the common political debate even if the external dimension of the EU fight against THB was explicit in the Strategy 2012–2016 and there is strong evidence that criminal networks could exploit the situations. Not only, the risk to have THB as a form of refuelling terrorist organization fosters human trafficking as a matter of security.

---

35   US Department of State, 2017 Trafficking in Persons Report, cit.

In 2006, a multilateral program was funded by the European Union, Switzerland, and the United States to combat trafficking in Russia on several levels. First, it aims to raise awareness about trafficking among high-risk groups as women, migrant workers and children; second, it will upgrade the Russian national legislation with better capacity to enforce laws and detect, investigate, and prosecute trafficking crimes. Third, it seeks to develop cross-border cooperation between Russia, CIS, and EU countries and between governmental and nongovernmental organizations. In the field, the program will help establish a first-of-its-kind rehabilitation centre for medical and reintegration support to victims, focusing on three crucial regions: Moscow Oblast, Karelia, and Astrakhan.

The cooperation with the competent authorities of other foreign countries was expanded. In 2010 changes were introduced into the model draft agreement:

> on cooperation between the Ministry of Internal Affairs of the Russian Federation and the Ministry of the Interior (competent authority) of a foreign state, in which special attention was paid to the cooperation in prevention, detection, suppression and prosecution of crimes in the area of trafficking in persons, especially women and children, as well as human organs and tissues.[36]

From a security perspective, the management of the mobility between Russia and the EU could have a positive impact if driven in a proper way, creating and implementing a framework where legal channel of migration and mobility are guaranteed. The key problem here is not the tightening of Russian borders; combatting cross-border crime, human trafficking and illegal immigration remain key challenges. This, however, requires modernization of the border infrastructure and closer co-operation between police and justice authorities on both sides of this border and police cooperation in the victims' protection system, even supporting the fight by the Russian police against internal corruption.

---

36 Resolution, Postanovlenie Pravitel'stva Rossiiskoi Federatsii O Vnesenii izmenenii v tipovoi proekt soglasheniia o sotrudnichestve mezhdu Ministerstvom vnutrennikh del Rossiiskoi Federatsii i Ministerstvom vnutrennikh del (kompetentnym vedomstvom) inostrannogo gosudarstva [*Resolution of the Government of the Russian Federation on Amending the standard design of a cooperation agreement between the Ministry of Internal Affairs of the Russian Federation and the Ministry of the Interior (competent authority) of a foreign state*] from 12 April, 2010, N 227.

5   Conclusion

The EU, with the action developed by the Commission in cooperation with the European External Action Service, should continue to ensure that an anti-trafficking angle is systematically included in all aspects of its relations with non-EU countries and in all relevant policy areas, including human rights, security and organised crime.

Commitments on trafficking in human beings set out in the New York Declaration should be implemented in the Global Compact on Migration through political and operational cooperation, promoting enhanced bilateral and regional cooperation with relevant partners and other organisations by means including targeted financing under relevant instruments.

In the meanwhile, relevant actors in EU and non-EU countries will be encouraged to tackle issues including protecting victims and reintegrating them into society in their initiatives on prevention, education and shelters, and to address the situation of vulnerable women, children and other groups.

Russia could be an important player supporting the EU action and developing a strengthen cooperation in preventing and tackling trafficking in human beings, building strong law enforcement and prosecution.

In addition, the EU will step up its external action targeting criminal organisations involved in THB, developing an efficient action that could also have effect in the international action against terrorism.

Perpetrators and abusers exploit people's vulnerabilities, exacerbated by factors such as poverty, discrimination, gender inequality, male violence against women, lack of access to education, conflict, war, climate change, environmental degradation, and natural disasters, for the purposes of sexual or labour exploitation, begging, criminal activities and more.[37]

As traffickers' modus operandi is constantly evolving, both Russia and the EU need to tackle the links between trafficking in human beings and other crimes, including migrant smuggling, terrorism, corruption, drug trafficking, cybercrime and online sexual exploitation, production of material involving the sexual abuse of children, financial crime, document fraud, credit card fraud, and benefit fraud.

Mutual cooperation would be the added value in this sector: upgrade the capacities of the law enforcement authorities to effectively prevent, detect, investigate and prosecute this serious form of crime through diversified training;

---

37   Communication from the Commission to the European Parliament and the Council, *Reporting on the follow-up to the EU Strategy towards the Eradication of trafficking in human beings and identifying further concrete actions*, 4.12.2017, COM (2017) 728 final.

sharing best practices and exchange visits, involving high and mid-ranking, as well as promoting international operational and judicial cooperation between the Russian law enforcement authorities and their counterparts abroad.

Bibliography

Avdeyeva, O. (2007). 'When do states comply with international treaties? Policies on violence against women in post-communist countries', *International Studies Quarterly*, 51(4): 877–900.

Ball, K.M. (2015). 'Surrounding Human Trafficking and the Conflict in Ukraine', https://ilg2.org/2015/02/25/the-troubling-silence-surrounding-human-trafficking-and-the-conflict-in-ukraine/.

Banerjee, P. (2010), *Borders, Histories, Existences. Gender and Beyond*. London: SAGE Publications.

Bartilow, H. (2008). 'Gender Representation and the Sex Trade: Domestic Sources of International Compliance against Human Trafficking', paper presented at the 49th International Studies Annual Convention, San Francisco, 26–29 March.

Borraccetti, M. (2017), 'Trafficking in Human Beings and Human Security: a comprehensive approach', pp. 187–210, in Salomon, S. et al. (eds), *Blurring Boundaries: Human Security and Forced Migration*. Leiden: Brill.

Borraccetti, M. (2017b). 'Human Trafficking, Equality, and Access to Victims' Rights', pp. 281–293, in Rossi, L.S. and F. Casolari (eds.), *The Principle of Equality in EU Law*, Cham: Springer.

Cho, S.Y. (2016). 'Liberal Coercion? Prostitution, Human Trafficking and Policy', *European Journal of Political Economy*, 41: 321–348.

Cho, S.Y. and Chaitanya, V. (2011), 'Compliance with the Anti-Trafficking Protocol', *European Journal of Political Economy*, 28: 249–265.

Clark, M.A. (2003). 'Trafficking in Persons: An issue of human security', *Journal of Human Development*, 4(2): 247–263.

Dean, L.A. (2017). 'The Diffusion of Human Trafficking Policies in the Post-Soviet Region: A Comparative Analysis of Policy Adoption in Ukraine, Latvia, and Russia', *Journal of Comparative Policy Analysis: Research and Practice*, 19(5): 1–16.

Dean, L.A. and A. Dovgaia, (2017). 'The Politics of Russia's approach to human trafficking', https://www.wilsoncenter.org/blog-post/the-politics-russias-approach-to-human-trafficking.

Friman, H.R. and S. Reich (2007). *Human Trafficking, Human Security and the Balkans*. Pittsburgh: University of Pittsburgh Press.

Fukuda-Parr, S. (2003). 'New Threats to Human Security in the Era of Globalization', *Journal of Human Development*, 4(2): 167–179.

Gallagher, A.T. (2015). 'Two Cheers for the Trafficking Protocol', *Anti-Trafficking Review*, 4: 14–32.

Hathaway, O.A. (2002). 'Do human rights treaties make a difference?', *The Yale Law Journal*, 111(8): 1935–2042.

Hughes, D.M. and Denisova, T.A. (2004). 'The transnational political criminal nexus of trafficking in women from Ukraine', pp. 43–67, in J.O. Finckenauer and J.L. Schrock (eds.), *The Prediction and Control of Organized Crime: The Experience of Post-Soviet Ukraine*. New Brunswick: Transaction Publishers.

Koser, K. (2005). 'Irregular migration, state security and human security', *Global Commission on International Migration*, September, https://www.iom.int/jahia/webdav/site/myjahiasite/shared/shared/mainsite/policy_and_research/gcim/tp/TP5.pdf.

Kreidenweis, A. and Hudson, N.F. (2015). 'More than a Crime: Human Trafficking as Human (In)Security', *International Studies Perspectives*, 16: 67–85.

Mukomel, V. (2013). 'Combatting Human Trafficking: The Russian Federation', CARIM-East Explanatory Note 13/30, Migration Policy Center.

McCarthy, L.A. (2011). 'Human Trafficking and the New Slavery', *Annu. Rev. Law. Soc. Sci.*, 10: 221–242;

McCarthy, L.A. (2010). 'Beyond corruption: an assessment of Russian law enforcement's fight against human trafficking', *Demokratizatsiya*, 18(1): 1–27.

Ruggeri, D. (2014). *The European Legal and Policy Framework: impact on human Trafficking*, Lambert Academic Publishing.

Shelley, L. (2005). 'Russia's law against trade in people: A response to international pressure and domestic coalitions', pp. 291–305, in F. Feldbrugge and R. Sharlet (eds.), *Public Policy and Law in Russia: In Search of a Unified Legal and Political Space*. Leiden, Brill.

Tiurukanova, E. (2006). 'Human trafficking in the Russian Federation inventory and analysis of the current situation and responses', UNICEF, ILO, CIDA, 22–25.

PART 3

Russia and China in Contested Regional Theatres: Some Case Studies

∴

CHAPTER 17

The Disputed Ukrainian Knot

Francesco Privitera

Since the collapse of the Soviet Union in 1991, the precarious relationship between Russia and Ukraine represents the cornerstone of a complex set of processes which imprinted the post-Soviet transition in both successor states. Yet
the tragic events which marked the 2013–14 crisis and the following developments were driven mostly by external actors/factors.

Clearly, domestic factors interacted together with the external dimension
of the Ukrainian affair, but in the end it was the "ambiguity" of Ukraine's geopolitical location, as a buffer zone between the enlarged EU and NATO, and
the Russian Federation, which mobilised the competing powers (the US, the
EU and Russia) in a zero sum game. The Ukrainian affair in turn has in many
respects replaced the process of Yugoslav dissolution. The dramatic collapse of
the Yugoslav Federation in 1991 paved the way for a set of interpretations among
policy makers and experts, about the right to get access to self-determination.
Different interpretations markedly divided the international community, at
first the US/EU on the one side and Russia (and China) on the other (Huttenbach & Privitera 1999). Hence, the national question (and all its implications)
remains the main political issue on the agenda of European affairs, since the
Balkan question is still open (Bosnia and Kosovo remain divisive issues within
the international community), as well as in the post-Soviet space. In addition,
the EU itself has started to be affected by national questions, since the Scot-
tish/Brexit issue and the Catalan self-determination process have triggered a
set of crises which are affecting the stability of the Union as never before.

1   The National Question in Post-Soviet Times: The Russia-Ukraine Nexus

"Without Ukraine, Russia ceases to be a Eurasian Empire", stated Zbigniew
Brzezinski (1996). From the very moment of the Soviet Union's demise, the relationship between Ukraine and Russia became crucial. Already, Kiev declared
its own self-determination in the aftermath of the putsch in Moscow, as did
Georgia and the Baltics definitively. On the 6th of September 1991 the Baltics
were out, but El'tsin was trying to preserve ties between Russia and Ukraine. As

© KONINKLIJKE BRILL NV, LEIDEN, 2020 | DOI:10.1163/9789004428898_018

the USSR under Gorbachev's leadership was moribund, El'tsin, at the peak of his power, joined an agreement with the Belarusian and Ukrainian leaders to create a new entity, the Commonwealth of Independent States (CIS). The presidents of the three republics declared the USSR terminated on the 8th of December. On December 21st the remaining republics, except Georgia, adhered to the CIS, and on December 25th Gorbachev resigned and the red flag flew over the Kremlin for the last time.

The existence of the CIS was problematic from the very beginning. Although the partners recognised each other's existing borders and agreed on a common currency, on joint control of nuclear power and on a single economic area, de facto each of them moved in opposite directions. Yet the international treaties and obligations of the former USSR remained valid and Russia took responsibility for all of them, at least initially. Russia got the USSR's place on the Security Council and the UN recognised all the successor states. However, quarrels among the members about minority issues, economic cooperation, and territorial disputes troubled the CIS during 1992, and it was unable to exercise any form of coordination. A CIS summit meeting in January 1993 failed to find compromises on the different controversies within the Commonwealth. Gradually, Russia reaffirmed control over the other member states, using its economic leverage and taking advantage of the instability in some of them (Tajikistan first of all). Although the CIS failed to replace the USSR, it still managed to preserve cooperative relations between Russia and Ukraine, at least at the beginning of the 1990s.

In the early 1990s El'tsin and Ukrainian president Kravchuk were able to manage the tricky issue of the 12 million Russian inhabitants of Ukraine, avoiding a possible crisis similar to the Moldovan one and the creation of a separatist Russian republic (as in the case of Dniestr republic). Both leaders agreed to soften any possible nationalist attitude, as well as broad autonomy for the Crimean province. El'tsin proved to be consistent with his policy, repulsing the attempt by some Russian nationalists both in Russia and the Crimea to push for the province's independence, and for it to re-join the Russian federation. Hence El'tsin was assessed by his opponents as too moderate and unable to properly protect Russian minorities in neighbouring countries.

Quite surprisingly, if compared with the situation after 2014, in 1991 relations between Russians and Ukrainians in Ukraine were relaxed and cooperative. The results of the referendum showed massive participation by Russians in favour of Ukrainian self-determination. In Moscow people were a bit shocked by this outcome, as if a certain frustration about Soviet centralism was understandable; such a desire for independence and loyalty to Kiev was quite unexpected. Interestingly enough, very few Russian Army officials (including ethnic

Russians) left, as the absolute majority preferred to be loyal to the new Ukrainian State. Pro-independence support in the referendum in the mining areas of Donets'k, where Russians represented (and represent) the majority, was 83.9%, in Odesa 85.3%, and in Kharkiv as a whole 86.3% (Steele 1994: 214).

Leonid Kravchuk was able to successfully manage the self-determination process amid the demise of the Soviet Union thanks to his ability to use anti-Soviet frustration not as an ethnic narrative (as was happening between Serbs and Croats in the framework of the demise of Yugoslavia). On the contrary, both the old Communist elite and the new Ukrainian nationalists prevented a split along ethnic lines, and ordinary Ukrainians and Russians in Ukraine remained calm.

Ukrainian nationalism emerged late during *perestroika* when compared to other Soviet republics (the Baltics or Georgia). It started, similar to other cases, as an environmental protest before taking on a political form. At the beginning, it was an understandable reaction to the Chernobyl tragedy in April 1986. The search for political responsibility moved intellectuals to first organise a form of protest, asking for the area to be cleaned up. Then an ecological movement was created called *Zelenyi Svit* (Green World), with the goal of organizing a political framework, and this moved very rapidly into the raising of the Ukrainian issue. Chernobyl became the symbol of the Soviet Union's exploitation of Ukraine. Moving from ecological protection to cultural and language protection were the next logical steps. The Ukrainian environment could only be protected if the cultural heritage and the linguistic freedom (of the Ukrainian language, as the official language of expression) became the pillars of the new Ukrainian state.

Like El'tsin, Kravchuk was a pragmatic nationalist; he understood quite rapidly that the national question was the only narrative capable of mobilizing a very primordial civic society in the struggle for power. Promoting Ukrainian sovereignty became the password of the local communist leadership, mitigated by a vague understanding of a renewed Soviet federation. For those communists educated under the ideological constraints of the Leninist approach to the national question (albeit revised by Stalin in the Thirties), the concept of sovereignty was quite familiar, although this concept was mostly theoretical, it was compatible with a federative understanding of the new state.

El'tsin, like Gorbachev, was aware that preserving unity with Ukraine would be of paramount importance for Russia, for several reasons: control over nuclear weapons, economic interdependence (Russia depended on Ukraine for the production of engines for missiles, while Ukraine depended on Russia for energy), but also because of the cultural and symbolic ties between the two. In the end, without Ukraine the whole architecture of any possible Confederation,

Union or Commonwealth among the remaining Soviet entities (as the Baltics were already moving westward) would not be politically credible.

In any case El'tsin's attempt to overcome the disintegration of the Soviet Union by setting up of new Commonwealth failed immediately, since the nuclear issue was solved very soon through specific negotiations with the US. Full access to sovereignty for Belarus, Ukraine and Kazakhstan was compensated for by the dismissal of their nuclear weapons, returned to Russia to be dismantled, as stated in the Budapest agreement brokered by the US. Without nuclear constraints, the level of cooperation among the four successor states decreased immediately, and different nationalist domestic visions prevailed, at first in Russia. Embarking on a very difficult and exhausting transition to a market economic system, Russia with its unclear system of checks and balances, precipitated into two years of instability. In 1993 the bombing of the White House in Moscow "celebrated" the end of the tumultuous years of the demise of the Soviet Union and the beginning of a new phase of El'tsin's rule over Russia. Advocating extended executive power to the president, El'tsin got enormous (personal) power. After two years of political struggle between the President (Yeltsin) and the Duma (set up mostly by Communist party members, led by Rutskoi) Russia reformed its constitution, offering extended powers to the President following the French model of the 2nd Republic.

Similarly, in Ukraine the chaotic early 1990s were followed by the recovery of state power by President Leonid Kuchma, with the adoption of a new Constitution in 1996. Technically, the system was semi-presidential, though with a longer presidential period by Kuchma (1994–2005; 2010–2014), alternating with a premier–presidential system in 2006–2010 and after 2014. The state is unitary with one federal unit of Crimea, which worked well enough as a compromise until 2014 (Pikulicka-Wilczewska & Sakwa 2015).

According to the constitution the state language of Ukraine is Ukrainian. Russian is widely spoken, especially in eastern and southern Ukraine. In the 2001 census 67.5% of the population declared Ukrainian as their native language and 29.6% declared Russian. Most native Ukrainian speakers know Russian as a second language. Russian was the *de facto* official language of the Soviet Union but both Russian and Ukrainian were official languages in the Soviet Union and in the schools of the Ukrainian Republic learning Ukrainian was mandatory. Effective in August 2012, a new law on regional language was passed and any local language spoken by at least a 10 percent minority was declared official within that area. Russian was downgraded as a regional language in several southern and eastern provinces and cities. Russian can now be used in these cities'/oblasts' administrative offices and documents. On 23 February 2014, following the 2014 Ukrainian Revolution, the Ukrainian Parliament voted to repeal the law on regional languages, making Ukrainian the sole state language at all levels; however, the repeal was not signed by then acting President Turchynov or the current President Poroshenko.

Ukrainian is mainly spoken in western and central Ukraine. In western Ukraine, Ukrainian is also the dominant language in the cities. In central Ukraine, Ukrainian and Russian are equally used in cities, with Russian being more common in Kiev, while Ukrainian is the dominant language in rural communities. In eastern and southern Ukraine, Russian is more widespread in the cities, and Ukrainian is spoken in the rural areas.

For a large part of the Soviet era, the number of Ukrainian speakers declined from generation to generation, and by the mid-1980s usage of the Ukrainian language in public life had decreased significantly. Following independence, the government of Ukraine began to restore the Ukrainian language through a policy of "Ukrainisation". Today for example, most foreign films and TV programs, including Russian ones, are subtitled or dubbed in Ukrainian.

According to the Constitution of the Autonomous Republic of Crimea Ukrainian was the only state language of the Republic. However, the republic's constitution specifically recognised Russian as the language of the majority of its population and guaranteed its usage "in all spheres of public life". Similarly, the Crimean Tatar Language – the language of 12.1 percent of the population of Crimea, according to the last Ukraine Population Census of 2001 (UPC 2001) – was guaranteed special state protection, as well as the "languages of other ethnicities". Since unification with Russia the rights of the Crimean Tatars have been drastically reduced. Russian speakers constitute an overwhelming majority of the Crimean population (77 percent), with 11.4% Crimean Tatar speakers and just 10.1% Ukrainian speakers (Statdata 2019). But in everyday life the majority of Crimean Tatars and Ukrainians in Crimea use Russian. Yet the Ukrainisation process moved Ukraine into the ethnicisation process of identity.

El'tsin too was very pragmatic in using nationalism as a political tool. El'tsin's main goal was to overthrow the communist federations, not because of ideological reasons but because they were no longer functional for his own political project.

In the Soviet case, El'tsin used nationalism in the political struggle against Gorbachev in order to weaken the Soviet leader. Supporting self-determination processes in the Baltics (or in Georgia) as El'tsin did, would increase Russian legitimacy in relation to its own sovereignty. From El'tsin's perspective this was the only way to achieve the goal of the reforms as promoted within the so-called "500 days of shock therapy", in order to introduce a fully functioning market system. Like the Bolsheviks (Lenin), El'tsin was unable to implement the reform process at large, across the entire Soviet space. So, he used the

national question to focus it on Russian soil only (like Lenin did, see Huttenbach & Privitera 1999). As Russian identity was based on the Soviet landscape,
political mobilisation could only be accomplished by adopting a victimisation
perspective, transforming Russians into the first victims of the Soviet Union.
As victims themselves, Russians must be generous with other peoples (like in
the Baltics), supporting their own self-determination processes. Nevertheless,
while El'tsin was contributing to destroying the Soviet Union, on the other
hand he was supporting Gorbachev in the final attempt to transform it into a
Union, and then a Commonwealth of sovereign states. El'tsin remained confident that a certain type of cooperation would remain in force among the post-
Soviet states and that Russia would remain its own centre of gravity, naturally.
This would happen because of Russia's size, economic interdependence, cultural ties, and last but not least, because many of the leaders came from the
same Communist party elite with a long history of common relations and
mind-set.

Thus, in the end El'tsin did not use any significant form of assertiveness in
Russia's relations with its neighbouring post-Soviet countries (except for the
Baltics, between 1992/93). In the Baltic case independence was achieved not
only through a strong anti-Soviet approach, but an anti-Russian one too. Baltic
nationalisms were constructed along the ethnic division between us vs. the
Russians, which moved into a very rapid deterioration of the mutual relations
between the Baltic States and Russia, while El'tsin (as well as the Russians in
the Baltics) was supportive of the local self-determination processes at the
beginning.

This is the key: Russian nationalism (in El'tsin's mode) was not based on
ethnicity, but on the imperial/Soviet landscape, providing a sense of power
and superiority over the other communities, similar to the relationship between the centre and the colonial periphery. The main issue in the current
Ukrainian affair is that for the first time, Russian identity is also going to be
based on the ethnic dimension. In the end the Ukrainian conflict has promoted the ethnicisation of the Russian identity; as for the Ukrainian one, the process started earlier.

2   Behind the 2014 "Ukraine Crisis": An Historical, Economic and
         Political Background

In order to understand the origins of the national question in Ukraine within
the framework of the 2014 crisis, it is useful to refer to some historical matters. The Dnieper River roughly divides the two main geographical areas of

Ukrainian identity: the right bank (as the river flows), and the left bank. The left bank (the east side of Ukraine), which includes the current regions of Crimea, Dnipropetrovs'k, Donets'k, Kharkiv, Kherson, Luhans'k, Odesa, Mykolaïv, and Zaporizhzhia, represents a relatively compact ethnic and cultural area that is distinguished by the strong influence of Russian culture, even though the majority of the population still defines itself as Ukrainian. The right bank (the western side of Ukraine) includes Galicia and the Cossack hetmanate and represents a relatively compact ethnic area that is the Ukrainian speaking area, mostly supportive of Ukrainian nationalism. The division of Ukraine into these two areas has also been reproduced by electoral patterns. Since 1994 voting has been quite stably split between these two electoral groups, which usually vote for opposing candidates of parties referring to a pro-Russian or pro-Ukrainian perspective (Petro 2018).

From the beginning the main political issue has been the country's international position, reflect in the domestic political arena. For east Ukrainians (mostly Russian speakers) the country has to preserve its ties with the Russian Federation and possibly the rest of the former Soviet community. On the opposite side, western Ukrainians prefer the establishment of strong connections with the EU and western countries at large.

Such different perspectives remained contained up until the 2014 crisis, as they reflected the political alternation of cabinets and presidencies representing the two visions. However, such a political division produced a highly consociational and corrupt political system ruled by oligarchs representing the two main communities.

A brief overview of electoral trends in the period 1994–2014 may represent the stability of the electoral pattern, but also external factors which influenced the vote. In connection to this matter, Western Ukrainians neglect of the Russian-speaking community and the Russian identity of those of the left bank, by introducing the "Ukrainisation" of the country, did not contribute to increasing mutual respect and understanding (Petro 2016).

The language issue became one of the first challenges to the unity and integrity of the country. The two groups started to divide themselves into two parallel societies with opposite goals. Evidence of this arose during the so-called "Euromaidan".

According to the western perspective, the current crisis originated in an attempt by Ukrainians to free themselves of centuries-old Russian colonial oppression, while Moscow has resisted it in every way, and "as soon as Ukraine would go, European values would triumph in Kiev". The main misunderstanding in the western perception of the self-determination processes that occurred in post-communist societies is that those processes have to be understood as a vehicle for the promotion of democratisation and civic values. On the contrary, nationalism is not a vehicle for democracy per-se, due to its intrinsic assertive/ oppressive dimensions.

During the Euromaidan crisis the western approach encouraged the inflexibility of the position of the Kiev government which came to power riding the wave of protest, and that in turn contributed to the loss of Crimea and to the civil war in the Southeast. Similarly, when Croatia declared its own independence in 1991, western support increased the rigidity of the Croat government against the Serb minority, contributing to the civil war in Krajina and Slavonia.

Russians in Ukraine do not represent such a distinctive national group as other large minorities in other countries. The issue is that both contemporary Russians and Ukrainians (at least inhabitants of the lands of the former Russian Empire, that is the majority of contemporary Ukraine) originate from people with a common identity (All-Russian, "orthodox"), where the differences between Great Russians ("Russians") and Little Russians ("Ukrainians") were rather of a regional sub-ethnic nature. It would be more correct to consider Russians, alongside Ukrainians, as a state-constituting nation of Ukraine within its 2013 borders, and not a national minority (Pikilcka-Wilcezewska and Sakwa 2015).

In any case, it is clear that the polarisation in Ukraine originated with the political manipulation of two main issues: the status of the Russian language and the preferred direction of integration (to the West or to the East). It is no accident that the pretext for the beginning of mass protests in autumn 2013 was Ianukovych's decision to delay the signing of the Association and Free Trade Agreement with the EU. The first issue on the agenda of the Ukrainian parliament on the day of the Ianukovych's ousting on 22 February 2014 was the repeal of the liberal Kolesnichenko-Kivalov language law, which triggered protests in the Southeast, that were later called "the Russian Spring". In addition, in the past year another topic has joined the two, further contributing to the split in the Ukrainian society, namely the preferred form of power structure in Ukraine: unitary state or federation.

During its independence Ukraine has been one of worst governed states in Europe, led by a group of rapacious oligarchs organizing a very delicate elite balance first managed by President Kuchma. As Wilson correctly analyses, in contrast to Russia, Ukraine is not a resource state but a rentier state, as it does not have the abundant energy resources of Russia (or Azerbaijan). It has energy transit and raw materials, and a model of steel and chemical production based on rents from subsidised state inputs. So, Ukraine has enough rent for a corrupt elite, but not enough to pay for a social contract, like Russia, or even using Russian money, like in Belarus (Wilson 2014: 104).

In Soviet times the economy of Ukraine was the second largest in the Soviet Union, an important industrial and agricultural component of the country's planned economy. With the dissolution of the Soviet system the country moved from a planned economy to a market economy. The transition was difficult for the majority of the population, which plunged into poverty. Ukraine's economy contracted severely following the years after the Soviet dissolution. Day-to-day life for the average person living in Ukraine was a struggle. A significant number of citizens in rural Ukraine survived by growing their own food, often working two or more jobs and buying the basic necessities through the barter economy.

In 1991 the government liberalised most prices to combat widespread product shortages and was successful in overcoming the problem. At the same time, the government continued to subsidise state-run industries and agriculture by uncovered monetary emission. The loose monetary policies of the early 1990s pushed inflation to hyperinflationary levels. For the year 1993, Ukraine holds the world record for inflation in one calendar year.

Those living on fixed incomes suffered the most. Prices stabilised only after the introduction of the new currency, the hryvnia, in 1996. The country was also slow to implement structural reforms. Following independence, the government created a legal framework for privatisation. However, widespread resistance to reforms within the government and from a significant part of the population soon stalled the reform efforts. A large number of state-owned enterprises were exempt from privatisation.

In the meantime, by 1999 GDP had fallen to less than 40% of its 1991 level. It recovered considerably in the following years, but in 2014 had yet to reach its historical maximum. In the early 2000s the economy showed strong export-based growth of 5 to 10%, with industrial production growing more than 10% per year. Ukraine was then hit by the economic crisis of 2008 and in November, the IMF approved a stand-by loan of US$ 16.5 billion for the country.

The country imports most of its energy, especially oil and natural gas, and to a large extent depends on Russia as its energy supplier. While 25% of the natural gas in Ukraine comes from internal sources, about 35% comes from Russia and the remaining 40% from Central Asia through transit routes that Russia controls. At the same time, 85% of Russian gas is delivered to western Europe through Ukraine.

Growing sectors of the Ukrainian economy include information technology (IT), which topped all other Central and Eastern European countries in 2007, growing some 40 percent. In 2013, Ukraine ranked fourth in the world for the number of certified IT professionals after the United States, India and Russia.

As Wilson says: "Ukraine is a new state with many underlying divisions of ethnicity, language, and religion, although the most powerful division of all is regional and regional-based patronal networks. These well-known internal divisions would have been less of a factor in the break-up of the country if Ukrainian politicians had been brave enough or competent enough to transcend them. Instead, they have exploited and exacerbated them to stay in power. Moreover, it was politicians from eastern Ukraine who did most of the polarising. Ideology and the idea of a European destiny were stronger forces in western Ukraine, so public opinion was harder to manipulate, although there were many nationalist politicians capable of alienating voters in the East. But a post-Soviet culture of paternalism, social atomisation, and Soviet Ukrainian mythology was still strong in the East and South, where politicians were able to win and retain power with a mixture of welfare and patronage and so-called "political technology" that exploited anti-Western Ukrainian stereotypes" (Wilson 2014: 105).

Ianukovych's presidency was not capable of maintaining such a mixture. More precisely, its ability to distribute even limited economic benefits was increasingly circumscribed. Ianukovych's predatory state destroyed growth in Ukraine and even the ruling Party of Regions began to lose support in their East Ukrainian heartlands and was increasingly dependent on fraud and political technology to divide and corrupt the opposition to stay in power.

3   Conclusion

As emerges from this historical reconstruction, defining the identity of Russia and Ukraine today is extremely complicated as both countries are still involved in their own state-building processes. Indeed, the intimate intricacy of the common past between Russians and Ukrainians since the Middle Ages, makes the issue impossible to solve.

The Russian Federation is a legacy of its imperial past and the absence of a genuine Russian nation–state. It was created in the 1920s from the territories left over after the borders of the non-Russian Union republics had been determined. More than 25 million Russophones live in bordering countries and still Russia does not have a state with uncontested borders. Moreover, the conceptualisation of the Russian nation remains rooted in the socialist concept articulated by Aleksandr Herzen in the 1840s and 1850s (Tolz 2001: 272). Within the socialist definition of national community, the symbolic elevation of the "masses" to the level of sole representative of the nation went hand in hand with the view of the idea of Russian uniqueness, from religious to linguistic patterns. This implies that membership in the Russian nation could not be voluntary. Consequently, it is not conducive to democratisation either. Only recently did the phenomenon of a democratic concept of a civic nation of equal citizens, with voluntary membership, enter the discourse of Russian political elites (Tolz 2001: 273). In any case, the 2018 presidential elections in Russia and the confirmation of Putin's post shows that the crucial period of Russian nation-building is still far from over, and it remains unclear, whether or not this is the destination of Russia's post-communist transition.

"Putin has described Ukraine as an "artificial state" whose territory has often changed in the course of the twentieth century. More importantly, Putin has repeatedly stated that "the Russian and Ukrainian people are practically one people", with "common historical roots, and a common destiny, we have a common religion, a common faith, we have a similar culture, language, tradition, and mentality" (Wilson 2014: 148–149)

If this is so, as reported by the BBC, a "common destiny" implies that Ukraine can only have a future alongside Russia – not outside Russia's sphere of influence in Europe – "while Putin's conservative values project is promoted with Europe and the West vilified as decadent and a lower civilisation compared to Russia" (Ukraine BBC Monitoring 2014).

Kuzio's consideration confirms: "Controlling Ukraine is not only a strategic objective for Russia to regain its great power status, but an important component of its national identity that has always stressed the unity of the three Eastern Slavic peoples, beginning in Kievan Rus' and continuing to Tsarist Russia and the USSR, with the CIS Customs Union-Eurasian Union their natural home (not NATO or the EU). Spiritual unity is provided by the Russian Orthodox Church, which has a greater number of parishes in Ukraine than in the Russian Federation" (Kuzio 2016: 118).

As Kuzio states again, "Putin came to power soon after NATO's bombardment of Yugoslavia, the detachment of Kosovo into a future independent state, and the Bulldozer revolution in Serbia that was the first of what became called coloured or democratic revolutions. Kosovo had never been a Yugoslav republic and therefore, unlike the fifteen Soviet and six Yugoslav republics, it had no right under international law to become an independent state, a fact that Russian leaders have continually raised in their justification of the annexation of the Crimea" (Kuzio 2016: 119).

In this sense, Putin is genuinely convinced that coloured revolutions are orchestrated by the West (including the mass protests in Russia in 2011 against Putin's regime) in order to overthrow the current Russian regime. The Ukraine affair has been perceived by Moscow as an attempt to push Russia into turbulent times, with the intent by the West to shake Russian stability and prevent its own power from being renewed. What appears to be a novelty in the Ukrainian crisis is the ethnicisation of the conflict, which represents on the Ukrainian side the "natural outcome" of the two-decades long Ukrainisation process, and on the Russian side, similarly, the need to reinforce their self-identity like the Serbs and Croats in the mixed areas of Croatia and Bosnia-Hercegovina. In light of the so-called Ukraine Crisis, today it is the increasing ideological competition that still reveals the permeability of the nation-building process in Russia and Ukraine.

As Petro argues in his essay "The Tragedy of Ukraine", the path to peace, both inside Ukraine and between Ukraine and Russia, is thus one and the same – dialogue and reconciliation. Ukrainians, regardless of their religion, language, and cultural heritage, embrace the whole country. Apparently, this is the message that millions of voters sent at the last presidential election in 2019, as Volodymyr Zelens'kyi, a Russophone comedian, was elected as the President of Ukraine, with massive votes in most of the regions, thus overcoming the traditional polarisation between the West and the East. Whether Zelens'kyi and Putin will be able to settle the "Ukrainian Knot" remains to be seen, but it is the only possible solution.

Bibliography

Bianchini, S. (2017). *Liquid Nationalism and State Partitions in Europe*. Cheltenham: Edward Elgar Publishing.

Beissinger, M.R. (2002). *Nationalist Mobilization and the Collapse of the Soviet Union*. Cambridge: Cambridge University Press.

Boffa, G. (1995). *Dall'URSS alla Russia. Storia di una crisi non finita*. Bari: Editori Laterza.

Brzezinski, Z. (1996). *Russia and the Commonwealth of Independent States: Documents, Data and Analysis*. New York: Routledge.

Brown, A. (1997). *The Gorbachev Factor*. Oxford: Oxford University Press.

Clowes, E.W. (2011). *Russia on the Edge. Imagined Geographies and Post-Soviet Identity*. Ithaca and London: Cornell University Press.

Huttenbach, H. and Privitera, F. (eds) (1999). *Self-Determination. From Versailles to Dayton the Historical Legacy*. Ravenna: Longo Editore.

Kemp, W. (1999). *Nationalism and Communism in Eastern Europe and the Soviet Union. A Basic Contradiction?* London: MacMillan Press.

Kuzio, T. (2016). *Ukraine*. London and New York: Routledge.

Lavigne, M. (1995). *The Economics of Transition. From Socialist Economy to Market Economy*. New York: St. Martins Press.

Magocsi, P.R. (1996). *A History of Ukraine*. Toronto, Buffalo, London: University of Toronto Press.

Nahaylo, B. (1999). *The Ukrainian Resurgence*. Toronto, Buffalo: University of Toronto Press.

Petro, N.N. (2018). 'The Tragedy of Ukraine. Hard Lessons to Learn from Classics', *Russia in Global Affairs*, 16(4): 52–71.

Petro, N.N. (2018). 'Are We Reading Russia Right?', *The Fletcher Forum of World Affairs*, 42(2): 1–24.

Pikulicka-Wilczewska, A. and Sakwa, R. (eds.) (2015). *Ukraine and Russia: People, Politics, Propaganda and Perspective*. Bristol: E-International Relations Publishing.

Polian, P. (2004). *Against their Will: The History and Geography of Forced Migrations in USSR*. Budapest, New York: CEU Press.

Puleri, M. (2016). *Narrazioni Ibride Post-sovietiche. Per una letteratura ucraina di lingua russa*. Firenze: Firenze University Press.

Rothschild, J. (1993). *Return to Diversity*. Oxford: Oxford University Press.

Rothschild, J. (1974). *East Central Europe between the Two World Wars*. Seattle and London: University of Washington Press.

Statdata. (2019). 'Naselenie Kryma i Sevastopolia: Chislennost', natsional'nyi sostav', 13 September, http://www.statdata.ru/naselenie-krima-i-sevastopolya.

Steele, J. (1994). *Eternal Russia*. London: Faber and Faber.

Tolz, V. (2001). *Russia. Inventing the Nation*. London: Arnold.

UPC. (2001). 'All-Ukrainian population census. State Statistics Service of Ukraine', http://www.ukrcensus.gov.ua/eng/.

Wilson, A. (2014). *Ukrainian Crisis. What it Means for the West*. New Haven and London: Yale University Press.

Woodward, S. (1995). *Balkan Tragedy. Chaos and Dissolution after the Cold War*. Washington, D.C.: The Brookings Institution.

CHAPTER 18

Central Asia in China's Energy Strategy

Antonio Fiori

In the last three decades the People's Republic of China (PRC)'s economic performance has been extraordinary. The country has enjoyed double-digit annual economic growth since the launch of economic reforms and openings at the end of the 1970s until 2010, becoming the second largest economy in the world. China's nominal GDP climbed from US$ 440 billion in 1993 to approximately US$ 13,400 trillion in 2019 (IMF 2019). This record growth, which has allowed China to become the world's largest exporter and manufacturer, is commonly attributed to factors such as market-oriented reforms, enterprise ownership changes, and the adoption of an export-oriented and foreign direct investment (FDI)-led development strategy.

This growth, however, needs to be adequately and constantly nurtured by a reliable energy supply. In parallel with its economic development, China's presence in world energy markets has increased as rapidly as its energy needs, especially since the turn of the millennium. In 2010, the PRC surpassed the US as the world's largest energy consumer, accounting for 23 percent of global energy consumption and contributing 27 percent to global energy demand growth in 2016 (BP 2017). In 2009, Chinese energy consumption per capita was just 20 percent of US per capita use; however, over the past decade Beijing's per capita use has risen sharply, by over 130 percent (Cohen & Siu 2012). Based on the country's rapid urbanization trend, the United Nations projections indicate that already by 2030, the Chinese urban population will total close to 1 billion people (UN 2018). This scenario would generate a potentially dramatic increase in per capita energy consumption, with severe environmental consequences mainly in terms of an average increase in CO_2 emissions per capita. As a matter of fact, the rapid rise in China's demand for energy has been mainly met by "dirty sources", which is an undesirable yet unavoidable option (Cohen & Siu 2012; Wang & Li 2005). Coal, in particular, is still the major source of energy in China, accounting for 59 percent of its energy consumption, even though this is the lowest share on record (Daly & Xu 2019). Beijing's demand for every primary energy sources is forecasted to increase over the next decades but the basic structure of the country's energy mix is not expected to alter significantly, unless a series of political and technological changes were to make other fuels more competitive. Though oil accounts for only 20 percent of its

© KONINKLIJKE BRILL NV, LEIDEN, 2020 | DOI:10.1163/9789004428898_019

total energy consumption, China is highly dependent on crude oil supplies –
the dependency ratio rose to more than 70 percent in 2018, the highest in
history – whose stability has not yet been adequately secured (Shuo 2018; EIA
2015). Oil is the PRC's second-largest energy resource and it has become vital to
the support of the industrial and building sectors, as well as transportation in
the context of China's current transformation of the automotive business
model.

Given China's reliance on hydrocarbons, the country's growing oil deficit is
at the heart of its energy insecurity. As a result, the PRC's foreign policy has
been largely influenced by efforts to reduce its dependence on oil imports and
to secure and diversify energy supplies. Although China is the world's fifth largest producer of petroleum and oil-related products (EIA 2018), the domestic
output of which has increased thanks also to improved drilling technology, the
country has gone from being one of the top exporters of oil outside the Organization of the Petroleum Exporting Countries (OPEC) in the late 1980s, to im-
porting half of its oil needs by 2012. Indeed, two years later China became the
largest net oil importer and its dependence on foreign provisions is estimated
to rise from 71 percent in 2015 to 79 percent in 2035 (BP 2017a) as demand is
expected to grow faster than domestic crude supply. The Chinese market alone
is responsible for 40 percent of the global increase in oil demand since 2000.
Domestic oil demand is projected to steadily increase at an annual rate of 2.7
percent through 2020, slowing to 1.2 percent through 2030 (Reuters 2017). Since
China's largest oil fields are mature and production has peaked, leading companies have shifted their focus to developing largely untapped reserves in the
western interior provinces and offshore fields. Acceleration in internal exploration and production led domestic oil production to reach an all time high of
almost 4.5 million barrels per day (bbl/d) in 2016, then decreasing to the actual
3.89 bbl/d (Trading Economics 2019). Nevertheless, these improvements will
only slightly offset declining internal production and imports will continue to
play a necessary role in meeting the PRC's demand for oil. Against this background, China's national oil companies (NOCs) will face immense pressures,
particularly due to the lack of a sufficient Strategic Petroleum Reserve (SPR),
the dramatic fluctuation of global energy prices and rising domestic energy
prices (Global Times 2019).

1   The NOCs "Go Out" in Search of Diversification

At the beginning of the 1990s, China was confronted with a dramatic new reality: to sustain its outstanding economic performance over the course of the

previous decade, the country was no longer "self-sufficient" with respect to oil, and found itself incapable of meeting its needs solely with domestic production. In 1993, China's oil demand outstripped domestic supply and the country transitioned from being an oil exporting country to a net oil importer. This situation fundamentally altered China's entire energy outlook and pushed the country to be more actively involved in foreign energy markets. In addition, after having entered the group of oil-importing nations, China officially became a net energy importer in 1997 and a net gas importer in 2007 (in addition, rising demand drove the country to become a net importer of coal in 2009) (EIA 2015).

Against this background, Beijing had to come up with a strategy to stabilize and secure its access to foreign energy resources in line with the CCP's guiding principle of opening China to the outside world. Already in 1982, Hu Yaobang, then CCP Secretary general, had announced that the Secretariat of the Central Committee had unanimously concluded that "to achieve modernization, China must utilize two types of markets, domestic and foreign markets, and master two types of skills – organizing domestic construction and developing foreign economic relations" (CCCPC 1982). Two years later, the Third Plenum of the 12th CCP Central Committee adopted the strategy enunciated by Hu as the framework for China's economic reforms. China's President, Jiang Zemin, endorsed this position, followed by Premier Li Peng who summed up the guidelines for the development of the country's petroleum industry in an article titled "China's Policy on Energy Resources", making clear that "the development of the petroleum industry [in China] should place its basis at home and gear toward the world" (Li 1997). The Chinese leadership believed that not only was the energy market characterized by instability, but also that the system was created and dominated by Western powers. Therefore, the implementation of a different plan, according to which it was possible to purchase direct control of imports, or of the transport systems through which China would import oil, was deemed necessary.

As a result, the Chinese government adopted the "going out" (*Zǒuchūqū Zhànlüè*) strategy, encouraging its oil companies to share overseas oil and gas resources (Xu 2006: 44–45), which reflected the general reform policies set in motion in the 1980s aimed at converting loss-making state-owned enterprises into a modern enterprise system through corporatization and the formation of large groups.

In 1982, China had established the China National Offshore Oil Corporation (CNOOC) to handle offshore exploration and joint contracts with foreign oil companies; the following year, the China Petroleum & Chemical Corporation (SINOPEC) was created under the State Council by merging petrochemical assets from the Ministry of Petroleum Industry (MPI) and the Ministry of

Chemical Industry (MCI), and in 1988 the MPI was dismantled to form the China National Petroleum Corporation (CNPC). These NOCs were among the first groups encouraged to expand into world-class corporations and to pursue direct control over the oil produced in a given country (Lieberthal & Herberg 2006). They have been involved in acquiring equity stakes in a number of foreign oil exploration and production projects, building pipelines and setting up long-term supply contracts, with the aim of enhancing direct control over energy supply (Chen 2008). The "going out" policy envisions government support for foreign investments on the part of NOCs that secure oil resources at the source and/or are involved in oil exploration and production. Consequently, China's overseas equity oil production has dramatically increased, from 140,000 bbl/d in 2000 to over 1.742 million bbl/d in early 2018 (Reuters 2017). Many Chinese think tanks and energy experts thus strongly recommend approaches that secure direct control of oil (Lewis 2007). One of the results of the "going out" initiative was that NOCs established footholds in Africa, Central Asia, and Latin America, in addition to strengthening their presence in the Middle East, thereby exponentially increasing the number of foreign upstream projects. In most cases, NOCs have shown the ability to choose their foreign ventures and acquisitions, based on business interests, and even when faced with deals involving low commercial feasibility but high strategic benefit, NOCs have closed them thanks to the government's encouragement and support.

The "going out" strategy was carried out also through "summit diplomacy" since the Chinese leaders understood that they had to strengthen relations with other oil-producing nations. Indeed, China attaches utmost importance to leadership summits and bilateral meetings, through which it proves a high level of commitment to its energy projects. Back in 1995, the PRC was almost completely dependent on just two regions – the Persian Gulf and Asia Pacific – upon which it relied for fully 88 percent of its crude oil imports (Downs 2006). By 2005, however, China had begun to diversify its mix: the African continent accounted for 31 percent of China's imports, with an additional 10 percent coming from the Americas and Russia; hence, all three regions became significant sources of China's energy supply. However, this important development has not solved the PRC's overall vulnerability, as Beijing is still heavily reliant on the Middle East, which is its main source of energy supplies. Because of that, China has dramatically increased its dependence on the Strait of Malacca, through which 80 percent of its oil imports must pass en route to the mainland. Due to its geographic conformation, however, the Strait represents a sort of bottleneck beset by numerous hindrances such as piracy, traffic jams, collisions (Lai 2009), and the concrete possibility of eventually being controlled or blocked by another, more powerful, actor.

China's over-reliance on the Strait of Malacca and other sea lines of communication (SLOCs) is a key cause of anxiety for the central government. Therefore, strenuous efforts have been made to devise and execute policies to reduce dependence, including diverting transport routes away from the SLOCs and emphasizing land-based options, such as pipelines, over maritime shipping because they are thought to be both cheaper and more secure as well as implementing policies to alleviate existing threats to strategic transport routes.

The bulk of China's oil pipeline infrastructure serves the more industrialized coastal markets and the north-eastern region, but several long-distance pipeline links have been built or are under construction to deliver oil supplies from the north-western region or from downstream refining centres to more remote markets in the central and southwestern regions (EIA 2015). In 2017, PetroChina managed a total of 82.374 km of domestic pipelines (51.315 km of gas, 11.389 km of refined products and 19.670 of oil pipelines) (PetroChina 2017).

Through the implementation of the "going out" strategy, the PRC has sought to diversify its energy import structure in order to decrease its dependence, expand its portfolio of crude oil suppliers and deal with transportation vulnerability by improving its domestic pipeline network. Moreover, Beijing has significantly increased NOCs refining capacities, which are crucial to the country's efforts to unlock its resources buried by geology and gain greater control over the oil production process. Therefore, the strategy clearly reflects worries over the reliability of international markets and oil price fluctuations as Chinese leaders believe that equity oil can be useful in times of market disruption or during price hikes to mitigate negative impacts on the domestic economy. In addition, the Chinese government hopes its NOCs will eventually increase the scope of their activities to the point where they can influence international energy markets and help Beijing have a much greater say in global energy trade. Finally, much of Beijing's financing of the global expansion of NOCs has relied on the State's foreign-exchange reserves, valued at US$ 3.13 trillion in February 2018, in an attempt to diversify them and internationalize its currency (Kong and Gallagher 2016).

2   China's Relations with Central Asia at the Sunset of the USSR

The political transformation caused by the dissolution of the Soviet Union created an unprecedented situation in political, economic and strategic terms for regional powers and China immediately tried to benefit from the origination of a *new* Central Asia. Unsurprisingly, the first reaction of Beijing was to reaffirm that the developments were to be considered "internal affairs" and a respectable choice of the people of those countries. On 27 December, 1991, the government of the PRC recognized the independence of Kazakhstan, Kyrgyzstan, Tajikistan, Turkmenistan and Uzbekistan: a gesture that did not go unobserved by the new leaderships in Central Asia. Beijing's promptness in launching this "charm offensive" was due to the fear that the collapse of the Soviet Union could cause instability in the region and, eventually, have domestic repercussions for the Xinjiang Uighur autonomous region, given the militant Islam which was spreading in the area (Chu 2012). At the same time, China wanted to dispel every possible doubt and suspicion regarding its intentions and also prevent any possible recognition of Taiwan by the newly established republics by promoting its One China policy (Umarov & Pashkun 2006: 4). Diplomatic relations with the newly born republics were established without any hesitation between January 2nd and the 7th: China promptly sent a delegation headed by Li Lanqing, then Minister of Foreign Economic Relations and Trade, with the task of paving the way for close commercial relations and mutual cooperation (Zhu 2010: 122).

In March 1992 the President of Uzbekistan, Islam Karimov, made the first official visit to China of a leader from the ex-Soviet republics since their independence, followed in May and November by those of President Akayev of Kyrgyzstan and President Niyazov of Turkmenistan, respectively (Tian 1994: 317–320). Shortly after, Chinese Foreign minister Qian Qichen reciprocated the visits to Kazakhstan, Kyrgyzstan, and Uzbekistan, along with Russia. High-level visits from Central Asia continued throughout 1993: in March the leader of Tajikistan, Rahmanov, visited Beijing, where he met with the Chinese President, Yang Shangkun. The two issued a joint statement regarding the basic principles for "mutual relations" with the central message that "the two sides should not engage in any hostile actions against the opposite side, and neither side should allow a third country to use its territory to impinge upon the sovereignty and security of the other" (Clarke 2011: 110). The Chinese government decided to grant thirty million *renminbi* in aid and three million in humanitarian aid, even though Beijing's economic relations with Tajikistan remained limited throughout the first phase of Sino-Central Asian relations. The main reason was most likely the civil war in the country, which kept Chinese entrepreneurs at a distance. Unlike China's cold relations with Tajikistan, the first state visit to China of Kazakhstan President Nursultan Nazarbayev contributed to further consolidating relations between the two countries. Nazarbayev had already visited China in July 1991 as a member of a delegation from the USSR: sensing what was going to happen in the Soviet Union, the Chinese had given him special treatment, predicting how important this politician could be for the future of bilateral relations (Aitken 2009: 125). After having reassured

Beijing that his official position saw Taiwan as an integral part of the PRC, Nazarbayev paid his first presidential visit to China in October 1993. The ratification of a joint declaration promoting regional cooperation with Xinjiang represented the visit's quintessence. China not only had become the most important Kazakhstan's partner in economic cooperation, but it had made Beijing very pleased by emphasizing cooperation in the fight against organized crime, drug trafficking, and international terrorism (Karrar 2010). This steady attitude between the leaders of the PRC and Kazakhstan, elucidated by Nazarbayev's declaration according to which the two figuratively "spoke the same language", was not matched by a similar feeling in the relations between Astana and Moscow. In the early 1990s, in fact, relations were turbulent, even though Nazarbayev managed to maintain a cordial entente with El'tsin. The particular attention reserved by Beijing to Astana, apart from geographic and demographic reasons–Kazakhstan being the country in the region that shares the longest border with China and the second in terms of population–was justified by the fact that Kazakhstan had been less peripheral to Moscow than the other republics.

Beijing's concerns about Kazakhstan's policy were rooted in the fear that promotion of Kazakh nationalism would inflame Uighur separatist groups in Xinjiang. These groups had been quite active in Kazakhstan since the late 1980s and had coordinated a few terrorist acts in big cities, including Urumqi (Dillon 1997: 141). In the early 1990s their assertiveness grew and in some Kazakh newspapers they began to claim that their struggle was not moved by the will to gain autonomy but to establish the Uighur's "motherland" (Liao 2006: 41). These continuous manifestations of unrest, such as the protest of thousands of Uighurs outside the Chinese embassy in Almaty in April 1993, complicated relations between China and Central Asia: Premier Li Peng's visit to the region, scheduled for April-May 1993, was deferred. Immediately, Central Asian states' leaderships understood to what extent these obstacles could hamper the development of relations with Beijing, which were highly beneficial from the economic and political perspective.

In April 1994, Li Peng made his previously postponed trip to Kazakhstan, Kyrgyzstan, Turkmenistan, Uzbekistan and Mongolia, leaving Tajikistan aside because of the beginning of the civil war. In his speech before the Uzbek parliament Li mentioned the need to improve infrastructural connections (citing the "New Silk Road") and economic cooperation. In Turkmenistan, he investigated the possibility of constructing a gas pipeline to connect Turkmen gas fields with China, in this way counterbalancing the strategies of both Russia and the United States (Andrews-Speed et al. 2005: 58). In Kyrgyzstan, the Chinese Premier was interested in testing Bishkek's position on pro-independence

Uighur political organization, settling the demarcation issue and starting trade and economic relations. In Almaty, the final destination of his tour, Li Peng summarized the important principles that characterized Sino-Central Asia relations: equality and mutual benefits acting according to economic laws; diversifying the types of cooperation; proceeding from the actual situation and making full use of local resources; improving the conditions of communication and transportation; providing modest economic aid to the Central Asian countries as an expression of friendship; developing multilateral economic cooperation, and promoting common prosperity (Li 1994; Qian 1995: 5). These concepts testified to the importance that Central Asia was assuming for China and the fact that economic cooperation was pivotal to their relationship as confirmed by the large delegation of businessmen that had embarked on Li's trip, accompanying for the first time a high-level government representative abroad (Burles 1999: 15–16). The result was the signature of various agreements and letters of intent for mutual cooperation in a vast number of fields. With Nazarbayev, Li Peng discussed several important themes: from economic cooperation to China's nuclear facility at Lop Nor, including the Kazakh minority in Xinjiang (Clarke 2011: 113). The visit was also an opportunity to talk about border demarcations, an issue that had taken shape soon after Almaty gained independence, and that was crucial to other important matters of common concern, such as the sharing of water resources. A boundary accord was signed on 21 March, just ahead of Li's visit, and entered into force in September, resolving all but a small segment of Sino-Kazakh borders and further enhancing mutual cooperation in some crucial sectors.

The disappearance of the Soviet Union created opportunities for China's cooperation with Central Asia; however, it did not mean that Russia had lost its strong influence in the region. For this reason, Premier Li was careful to stress that China was engaging with Central Asia on the basis of equality and non-interference with sovereignty. In addition, Beijing was successful in the strategic dimension of the cooperation: Central Asian leaders unanimously declared that Taiwan was an inalienable part of the Chinese territory and that they opposed any attempt to modify this state of things with the creation of "two Chinas" or "one China, one Taiwan".

Since concerns about security were the main motives behind China's initial engagement with the Central Asian republics, during the first phase economic relations remained modest: total trade with Kazakhstan, China's largest economic partner in the region, amounted to US$ 363 million in 1992, while in 1995 it totalled US$ 391 million (IMF 2017); with the other countries in the region it was even more negligible. The reasons were to be found in the recent past of the five republics: on the one side, the collapse of the Soviet Union had caused massive inflation, the closure of factories and a drop in the purchasing power of the population; on the other side, the fact that these countries had traditionally contributed to the Soviet Union's economy had limited their productive capacity, and consequently the range of goods they could export. It must be highlighted, however, that unofficial trade or "shuttle trade", mainly performed by merchants in Xinjiang markets (contributing to the increase in this province's foreign trade) that had made their appearance after Central Asian republics had achieved their independence, equalled the official one (Paramonov & Strokov 2007; Peyrouse 2007). At a later stage these border markets appeared in many other cities in Central Asia. As a consequence, China started to be considered by the Republics' leaderships as an important economic actor. Despite poor transport infrastructure between China and Central Asia, in 1992, Beijing decided that Urumqi had to be given the same status as Chinese coastal areas to attract foreign investment: this contributed enormously to the infrastructural and economic development of Xinjiang province, beyond pushing for its integration with the external world.

While China's overall strategy toward Central Asia had followed the pathway of bilateral relations, in 1992 an intergovernmental discussion began with a joint delegation from Kazakhstan, Tajikistan, Kyrgyzstan and Russia meeting with their Chinese counterparts in order to discuss the issue of enhancing military confidence-building measures along shared borders (Dillon 1997: 136). This multilateral diplomatic initiative represented the backbone of the important "Agreement on Confidence-Building in the Military Sphere in the Border Areas", signed on 26 April, 1996 by the above-mentioned five countries, usually referred as the "Shanghai Five". This agreement marked an important moment in cooperation between China and Central Asia: the increase in trade was sharp and important steps in the pacific settlement of border disputes had been made. The "Shanghai Five mechanism", as named by Wang Li, was based on a gradualist approach: in the beginning, specific attention had to be given to confidence-building measures in the border areas, which were to be substantiated in the "mutual non-use of force or threat of force" and a "renunciation to obtain unilateral military superiority" (Dillon 1997: 136). This understanding was an important step from several points of view: first of all, it was conducive to transparency in military activity along the border areas; secondly, it brought border security to the forefront of diplomatic relations; and thirdly, it finally established a multilateral mechanism between China, Russia and the Central Asian republics, covering a wide spectrum of regional and global issues. What is more, the agreement represented an important step forward in regional cooperation, also given the fact that by that time Beijing and Moscow had started to criticize the persistence of United States "hegemonism". In this regard, the day before the Shanghai meeting, presidents Jiang Zemin and Boris El'tsin announced their intention to bring the mutual partnership from a "constructive" (as declared during a meeting between the two heads of state in September 1994) to a "strategic" one, making special reference to state sovereignty, ethnic minorities and, above all, to the necessity to reorient the international system in a multipolar way (Wishnick 2001; Wilson 2015).

The creation of this multilateral mechanism did not terminate bilateral diplomatic initiatives, which in fact continued with the visit to Central Asia by Jiang Zemin in July 1996. In a speech to the Parliament in Kazakhstan, Jiang reaffirmed the need to broaden cooperation with Central Asia, by invoking "south-south cooperation" between developing countries with similar economic, political and social structures (Syroezhkin 2002: 180), based upon full respect for the principle of non-interference in the other country's internal affairs, which was essential for the good development of relations, implying the necessity not to offer any support to Uighur aspirations for independence. In this regard, the leaders of Central Asian states were deeply sensitive to China's demands and, since they had nothing to gain from supporting Uighur activities in their countries, crackdowns on separatists were frequent and vehement.

The summit held in Almaty in June 1998 was crucial since in its communiqué the members stressed the need for the development of transport infrastructure, the construction of oil and gas pipelines, and placed emphasis on regional security, singling out terrorism, separatism and extremism. The need to deepen regional cooperation in military and security terms was the result of a convergence of interests among the organization members. China was extremely preoccupied by the intense activity of trans-national Islamic movements and minority unrest in Xinjiang, while Kazakhstan, Kyrgyzstan and Tajikistan were becoming more concerned in light of the offensive launched by the Islamic Movement of Uzbekistan (IMU) in the late 1990s and the attempt to assassinate President Karimov. The following summit, in Bishkek in the summer of 1999, definitely marked a shift from issues concerning border demarcation and economic cooperation to a more pronounced regional response to trans-national Islamic movements, drugs and weapons trafficking and border security (Karrar 2010). Both the Bishkek summit and the following in Dushanbe, in 2000, testified to an intense Sino-Russian convergence on strategic interests–such as countering the "three evil forces" of separatism, terrorism and extremism–and on the vision of a "multipolar" international political and economic order, always based on respect for national sovereignty and non-interference in national affairs (People's Daily 2000). Despite efforts for greater cooperation, terrorist incursions from Islamic movements were not completely eradicated. On the contrary, following China's initiatives to involve its

Central Asian neighbours in the crackdown on Uighur separatists, violence and terrorist act took place in Kyrgyzstan.

3   China's Multilateralism in Central Asia: The Shanghai Cooperation Organization

On 15 June, 2001 the Shanghai Five countries, with the addition of Uzbekistan, institutionalized this multilateral mechanism with the creation of the Shanghai Cooperation Organization (SCO). As stated in its founding declaration, the new organization aimed to strengthen "mutual trust and good-neighbourly and friendly relations", and encourage "effective cooperation...in the political, trade-economic, scientific-technical, cultural, educational, energy, transportation, ecological and other areas" (People's Daily 2001). It should also be noted that the SCO "adheres to the principles of openness", and was not directed against any country. The element of transparency was meant to reassure other countries of the non-antagonistic nature of the organization: this was a crucial factor for the Central Asian republics, for which cooperation with the West, especially in the energy sector, was highly relevant and profitable. Additional documents were released including the one entitled "Shanghai Covenant on the Suppression of Terrorism, Separatism and Extremism" which stated the provisions for the creation, in 2003, of the Regional Anti-Terrorism Structure (RATS) to coordinate antiterrorist activities. In order to convince everyone that there were no indigenous reasons for unrest in Xinjiang, Chinese scholars declared that instability in the region was mainly fuelled by the conflict in Afghanistan, the civil war in Tajikistan, and the insurgency in Uzbekistan.

The events of September 11, 2001 attenuated the influence of the SCO. Rumsfeld's "sustained engagement" implied forging new military alliances and for Kyrgyzstan and Uzbekistan, in particular, cooperating with the United States was important in order to curtail internal opposition and as a source of funding (Karrar 2010): the airbases of Karshi-Khanabad, in southern Uzbekistan, and Manas International Airport in Bishkek were provided to the Americans, officially free of charge, but in reality in exchange for military support and substantial aid packages. Nonetheless, China's tolerance was due to the fact that it was not seeking an exclusive sphere of influence in Central Asia and fully understood that, along with Russia, it did not have the ability either to stop the US in the region or to impede the deployment of American troops in Central Asia. On the contrary, most likely China welcomed the US presence in Central Asia as beneficial for bringing instability in Xinjiang under control. Nonetheless, China's purpose was to enhance its own influence in the region at a measured pace. For this reason, Beijing's decision to accept the US presence in entral Asia could be intended more as a pragmatic move than a capitulation.

A few months after the terrorist attacks against the US homeland, however, China's concern about Washington's unilateralist policies and, above all, the possibility that it would expand the "war on terror" to the Middle East, grew noticeably. In this regard, Beijing's insistence on the primacy of the United Nations was a demonstration of the Chinese desire that eventual US-led military action would not go unconstrained, as reiterated in its opposition to the "Bush doctrine", and the consequent war against Iraq, which created a deep fracture between Washington and Beijing. In mid-2002 however, the US Deputy Secretary of State, Armitage, during a visit to China, declared that the East Turkestan Islamic Movement (ETIM) was to be classified by both the US and the UN as a foreign terrorist organization (People's Daily 2002). While some have seen in this move an attempt to gain China's support in Iraq, Washington strongly denied this assertion, clarifying that ETIM had links and financial relations with Al-Qaeda.

In 2002, whereas Uzbekistan had become an intimate ally of Washington in Central Asia, China and Kyrgyzstan announced they would conduct joint military exercises, officially to test anti-terrorism coordination, the first in a long series China steered with Central Asian countries.

Central Asia's reorientation towards the United States, however, was short-lived. In 2005, Washington's support for the "Tulip Revolution" that toppled President Akayev in Kyrgyzstan and its insistence on an internal investigation into Uzbekistan's suppression of the Andijan uprising pushed Central Asia rulers away from American democracy and human rights promotion and again into the arms of the SCO and its vision of shared interests, economic development, stability and state sovereignty, intertwined with Beijing's emphasis on "non-interference".[1] In the following SCO summit in Astana, in July 2005, disillusionment with the United States' conduct in the region became palpable, and it was reinforced by Uzbekistan's decision to terminate its agreement with Washington concerning the concession of the Karshi-Khanabad air base

---

1 In the events that the Uzbek government called an Islamist riot, while many others define as peaceful protests, hundreds of people gathered in the central square of Andijan were attacked by Uzbek security forces (OSCE, 2005). While the nature of both the demonstrations and the subsequent violence is unclear, the deaths of hundreds of demonstrators led to a noticeable cooling of relations between Uzbekistan and many western countries, and e.g. the European Union placed sanctions on Uzbekistan for the next several years (Castle 2009). To garner support for his regime, Karimov visited both Russia and China.

(Paton Walsh 2005). The rhetoric that had both security cooperation among the members of the SCO and anti-US sentiment at its core did not change at subsequent SCO summits in Shanghai in 2006 and in Bishkek in 2007, highlighting China's and Russia's concern over the threat of the US military presence to their interests in the region.

4   China's Energy Policy in Central Asia

Strategically and geographically, Central Asia's proximity provides Beijing with secure access and obvious advantages in transportation efficiency. Politically, China is involved in the SCO and it shares good relations with these states on crucial political issues, which can certainly influence the Central Asian governments' decisions on energy developments. Economically, the prospects are mixed though. Central Asia is blessed with rich natural resources, but one significant economic disadvantage is the tendency for these states to delay investment in the transport infrastructure needed for an efficient energy trade network. The quality of rail and road connections remains the real Achilles' heel of the region, as land-based transit is the only route option, therefore limiting the volume of energy trade. From Central Asian governments' point of view, four key issues form their core domestic and foreign policy interests: nationhood, political stability, economic development, and reduced dependence on Russia. Natural resources are perceived to be the key to economic growth in Central Asia; hence, the rapid exploration, development, and export of crude oil, as well as natural gas, are priorities for these countries. Due to their landlocked status, building the infrastructure needed to export petroleum is an expensive proposition; however, the lack of such infrastructure is a major constraint to the full realization of their potential. Before the collapse of the USSR little was done to develop Central Asia's petroleum reserves; after gaining independence, these states sought investment from foreign countries and explored a wide range of possible export routes. In this context, China has gained importance as a crucial partner for Central Asian states.

4.1   *Kazakhstan*
The relationship between Kazakhstan and China in the field of energy started in 1994 when the CNPC acquired 60.3 percent of the shares in the Kazakh company Aktobemunaj Gaz (Niquet 2006). This interest grew deeper in 1997, when the CNPC won a tender to develop and operate two oil fields in Akhtubinsk and one in Uzen, outbidding American oil companies Texaco and Amoco and the Russian Yuzhnimost (Andrews-Speed et al. 2005). This conspicuous investment

was of US\$ 4.3 billion over 20 years and an agreement to build a cross-border oil pipeline from Kazakhstan to China was also reached. Beijing was also given exclusive rights over Kazakhstan's second largest oil field, Aktobe, even though breaking the virtual monopoly Russia had on Central Asian energy exports was particularly complicated. Indeed, Central Asian countries continued, for a decade, to sell most of their oil and gas production to Moscow, which resold it to Europe at a higher price, making significant profits. The most important outcome of this relationship was the oil pipeline that connects Alashankou, on the western borders of the Xinjiang region, to Atyrau, the northern harbour of the Caspian Sea in Kazakhstan. This pipeline, completed through a triple-step construction (the first one from Aktobe to Atyrau completed in 2003; the second from Atasu to Alashankou in 2005; and the third line from Kenki-yak to Kumkol in 2009), has an overall length of more than 2,228 kilometres, and it was jointly built by CNPC and the Kazakh oil company KazMunayGas. Through this pipeline, China is provided with 200,000 bbl/d, but the expansion of the Atasu-Alashankou section nearly doubled capacity in 2013 (EIA 2015). In Alashankou, the pipeline is connected with the Alashankou-Dushanzhi crude oil pipeline, constructed by the CNPC and operational since December 2005, which has a capacity of 10 million tons of oil per year and mainly supplies the Dushanzhi refinery.

In 2005, CNPC also took over PetroKazakhstan, an international petroleum company registered in Canada with all of its assets in Kazakhstan, for an exorbitant amount of money, US\$ 4.18 billion, financed by China Development Bank (China Daily 2005). The deal marked the first case in which a Chinese oil company acquired an overseas listed energy company (Wang 2005). PetroKazakhstan was at the time the largest private oil company in Kazakhstan with 12 percent of the country's oil output and listed on various stock markets all around the world. Moreover, its oil output was basically equal to the entire overseas oil reserves that CNPC had at that time. In April 2009 CNPC purchased 50 percent of MangistauMunaiGaz, as part of a US\$ 10 billion loan-for-oil deal with Astana (PetroChina 2009). These moves were inspired less by the commercial attractiveness of the company than by the opportunity to further consolidate CNPC's position in the Kazakh oil sector. Against this backdrop, in February 2011 Kazakh President, Nazarbayev, visited China and he discussed with Hu Jintao about CNPC participation in the development of Urikhtau gas deposit in Western Kazakhstan: the gas would be exported to the PRC via a new pipeline already under construction. Among other investments for different projects, China promised its support with a US\$ 5 billion loan to Kazakhstan to construct a petroleum refinement facility on the shore of the Caspian Sea (Pannier 2011).

During Xi Jinping's tour in September 2013, Kazakhstan and China signed several energy deals worth US$ 30 billion and CNPC purchased, defeating India's interest, an 8.33 percent stake in Kazakhstan's Kashagan Caspian offshore field: this represents China's first offshore and largest acquisition in the Caspian Sea basin (Reuters 2013). Through the recently constructed Beineu-Bozoy-Shymkent domestic pipeline, Kazakhstan in 2016 also started to export its gas to China (up to 10 bcm/y) using Line-C, the third additional stage of the Central Asian Gas Pipeline (KazTransGas 2019). In addition, the construction of an additional pipeline, Line-D, is currently underway: it will connect Beineu to Shymkent and from here the gas will be directed to Turpan in Xinjiang, providing China with an additional 15 bcm/y (Aliyeva 2018). This broad picture testifies to the fact that China is interested in energy resources all over Kazakhstan, and not only in its western hydrocarbon regions.

4.2   *Turkmenistan*

At the dawn of Central Asia's opening in 1992, CNPC and Mitsubishi proposed exporting Turkmen oil to China and two years later they worked together with Exxon on a feasibility study regarding the possible construction of a pipeline connecting Turkmenistan's gas fields with China (Andrews-Speed et al. 2005). Even though the project was not implemented at that time, it demonstrated the political and strategic significance the region had not only for Beijing but also for the United States. China's energy cooperation with Turkmenistan had grown significantly by the mid-2000s driven by China's newfound interest in Central Asian gas. For the purpose of increasing the domestic proportion of clean energy through greater use of natural gas, China decided to partner with Turkmenistan, the largest producer of gas in the region and starting around from 2010 the PRC had taken over Russia's position as the main gas buyer of Ashgabat (Shustov 2017). The most important development in this relationship remains the 1,883 kilometres long Central Asian-China gas pipeline connecting Turkmenistan, Uzbekistan and Kazakhstan with Xinjiang, whose construction started in 2007. The pipeline, with an estimated cost of US$ 7.31 billion, totally financed by CNPC, allowed China to receive 21.3 bcm/y of gas from Turkmenistan in 2012: about half of Ashgabat's total gas exports and about half of China's total imports (Smith Stegen and Kusznir 2015: 102). The following year China and Turkmenistan agreed to expand pipeline capacity to 40 bcm/y by 2015, and in 2013 the two decided on a new expansion to 65 bcm/y by 2020. However, the completion of the fourth line of the pipeline has been continuously delayed, to the detriment of Turkmenistan, for which the PRC is the only customer (Eurasianet 2017).

In 2009, China provided a US$ 3 billion loan for the initial development of the South Yolotan gas field (Eurasianet 2009), the world's second largest infrastructure of this kind with proven reserves of seven trillion cubic meters, and two years later China added a US$ 4.1 billion loan. The PRC has been the sole foreign importer of Turkmen gas since Russia halted gas imports from the country in 2016 and gas supplies to Iran stopped due to a payment dispute in early 2017 (Khatinoglu 2018). Beijing has also become Ashgabat's main trade partner, and this was further secured by Xi Jinping's visit in 2013.

4.3 *Uzbekistan*

Uzbekistan is particularly attractive for China due to its oil and gas reserves and its importance as a transit country, but mature political and economic cooperation with China started only in the 2000s. Until that moment, in fact, the volume of bilateral trade cooperation amounted to less than US$ 100 million, which was about seven times less than Uzbekistan's total trade with Russia or with OECD countries. In 2002 bilateral trade cooperation drastically accelerated and, within 10 years, in 2014, China had managed to overtake not only the West (or OECD countries) that had attempted to establish strong cooperation with Uzbekistan in the 1990s, but also Russia. In 2005, after the "divorce" from the United States, Uzbekistan decided to "marry" Beijing, with whom it signed the Treaty on Friendly and Cooperative Partnership. The same year, CNPC and Uzbekneftegas signed deals related to 23 oil fields: China decided to invest US$ 600 million (Energy-pedia 2005). In July, when Wu Yi, the Chinese Deputy Prime Minister, visited Uzbekistan to further stimulate trade and economic cooperation, the other Chinese company, Sinopec, signed an agreement with Uzbekneftegas to create a joint venture for oil exploration and development of existing fields in the country. Karimov described China as a trustworthy friend and energy became one of the core interests of this renewed alliance that allowed CNPC to open its office in Tashkent in 2006. The company became involved in the development of Uzbekistan's oil and gas fields in the eastern and western areas of the country, including the onshore blocks of the Aral Sea and the Mingbulak oil field in the Fergana valley. In 2008, CNPC, together with Uzbekneftegas, the national energy company, started working on the construction of the Uzbek segment of the Central Asia-China gas pipeline, which became operational in 2009. Apart from oil and gas, China has also invested in other sectors in Uzbekistan including railways and electricity. When Xi Jinping visited Central Asia in 2013, China and Tajikistan, Uzbekistan and Kyrgyzstan decided to sign an agreement for the further development of the Central Asia-China gas pipeline, but as already highlighted, this effort has been delayed.

Given Uzbekistan's limited resources for export, if compared to Turkmenistan and Kazakhstan, Chinese interest in the country is better explained by geostrategic and security factors–that is, its degree of industrialization, geographic location, and its being the most populous country in the region–than by pure economic motives (Paramonov 2014).

4.4   Tajikistan

Tajikistan was the poorest and most underdeveloped part of the Soviet Union until 1991; since the end of the civil war (1992–1997), the country has experienced steady economic growth, mainly in agriculture, construction and services. Strategically important because of its long border with Xinjiang, China has developed infrastructure in Tajikistan including roads–the Dushambe-Chanak highway, for example–and power lines and hydropower plants. China is also providing the Central Asian country with a huge development loan package which, according to many, will be not easily paid back, augmenting the risk for Tajikistan of being caught into a debt trap (Kley 2017). According to Takijistan's Minister of Finance, Faiziddin Qahhorzoda, China remains the country's largest creditor. As of February 2018, Tajikistan owes more than US$ 1.2 billion to the Export-Import Bank of China (Asia-Plus 2018). In 2012 it was announced that ten new deals signed by the Tajik president would bring in about US$ 1 billion in Chinese investments, loans and aid. In 2013, testifying to the growing importance Tajikistan has for Beijing, Xi Jinping signed a joint announcement with President Rakhmon on the establishment of a strategic partnership aimed at boosting mutual cooperation (China Daily 2013).

4.5   Kyrgyzstan

Kyrgyzstan was one of the most important satellites of the USSR, and it has remained loyal to Moscow, even though China's growing influence has challenged Russia's dominant position. In 2016, for example, China's exports to Kyrgyzstan totalled US$ 1.6 billion, nearly double the value of Russia's. While in the early 1990s the Chinese invested in property and industry construction in Kyrgyzstan, over the last ten years highway repair and energy have become pivotal for investments. Though Kyrgyzstan lacks hydrocarbons, it has major renewable energy potential, particularly hydropower that accounts for over 90 percent of *electricity* generation (AIIB 2017). One of the most relevant energy projects jointly built with China was the reconstruction of the Bishkek power station, for which Beijing allocated US$ 386 million; recently, however, the plant experienced major problems, and the Chinese company responsible for its modernization was harshly criticized and came under scrutiny in Kyrgyzstan (Putz 2018). Moreover, China's State Power Investment Corporation and the Kyrgyz government held negotiations on the construction of the Kazarman chain of hydropower plant on the Naryn River, which, if implemented, is expected to become Beijing's biggest investment in the Kyrgyzstan's energy (Taldybayeva 2017; Du 2018).

5 The New Silk Road: Eurasia in China's Grand Strategy

Six months after becoming president, in 2013, Xi Jinping embarked on a diplomatic tour that brought him to four of the five republics of Central Asia. The relevance of the trip appeared crystal clear during his visit to Kazakhstan, where, on 7 September, the new leader gave a speech at Nazarbayev University whose main argument was centred around a "strategic vision" to realize a "New Silk Road" in order to foster regional cooperation (MFA 2013). The term was carefully chosen: what was traditionally known as the Silk Road–a watchword introduced in 1877 by Baron Ferdinand Von Richthofen to describe the "channel" that ran from the Middle Kingdom to Europe through Central Asia–essentially came into being in the 1st century BC, following China's efforts to develop overland trade and cultural exchanges across Eurasia (Fallon 2015). Xi, in any case, was not the first to refer to the Silk Road: the term had already been used by the Chinese leadership in the 1990s and the 2000s, without being linked to any project in particular. In this specific moment, on the contrary, it became a symbolic element that was needed to project a corpus of future infrastructural plans, offered firstly to Central Asian nations and later to Europe, and to complement the official diplomatic approaches implemented by previous Chinese administrations, like the "Shanghai Spirit" by Jiang or the "peaceful rise" by Hu. The New Silk Road envisioned by Xi was a land-based economic belt with the main aim of "opening up the transportation channel from the Pacific to the Baltic Sea" (MFA 2013). The colossal project was to be completed, as described by Xi Jinping less than one month later during a visit to Indonesia, by the creation of a "21st Century Maritime Silk Road" that would run from China to the Indian Ocean, with ramifications for South Asia and Southern Africa, via Southeast Asia. The maritime project was inspired by historical sea-based trade routes from China's coastal areas through the South China Sea and beyond. As for the land-based leg, the main emphasis of the maritime Silk Road was placed on stronger economic and infrastructural cooperation, the enhancement of security collaboration, and the strengthening of the "maritime economy, environment, technical and scientific cooperation" (MFA 2013).

These two pivotal speeches, although scarcely covered by the Chinese media, convinced the Chinese Communist Party to endorse the idea of investing in infrastructure connecting Beijing with its periphery. Gradually the initiative has gained greater attention domestically and internationally, becoming in 2016 the most discussed topic in the People's Daily (Rolland 2017). Despite the initial lack of details, Xi's words were of the utmost importance for the development of the so-called Belt and Road Initiative (BRI), the denomination that is now widely used to define it.

While the main focus of the BRI is on building transportation networks between multiple locations, it must be clarified that China's 21st-century revival of the Silk Road is not limited to the construction of physical infrastructures but, as announced by Xi, focuses on "win-win" cooperation projects. 'Connectivity' has become the buzzword, seen in terms of improving transports, communications and energy infrastructures to remove trade and investment barriers as well as to facilitate information and people-to-people exchanges (NDRC 2015). Three land routes have been planned: the Northern one (Beijing-Russia-Germany-Northern Europe); the Middle one (Beijing-Xi'an-Urumqi-Kazakhstan-Hungary-Paris); and the Southern one (Beijing-Kashi-Pakistan-Iran-Turkey-Italy-Spain). These will be complemented by two maritime routes: the first one starting from southern Chinese ports west to the Indian Ocean, Europe, and Africa while the second one from ports in South Fujian to the South Pacific. As a result, the BRI has come to be depicted as part of China's "grand strategy", using all elements of national strength to "assert [China's] influence and reshape at least its own neighbourhood" (Rolland 2017a: 136).

While several Chinese ministries and agencies bear responsibility for implementing the BRI, the lack of a structure of its own poses several risks. On the one hand, as one of China's leading thinkers, Wang Jisi, first suggested, the BRI might be perceived by some of the countries involved as a unilateral move pursued by a neo-colonialist actor (Wang 2012); on the other, the absence of any kind of formal membership stems from Beijing's intention to reassure countries about the open and inclusive nature of the initiative. From the point of view of economic sustainability the New Silk Road should rely principally, from the Chinese side, on the Silk Road Fund, the Asian Infrastructure Investment Bank, and a few private-public holdings.

Central Asia is the core of the land-based component of the New Silk Road and could act as a "testing ground" for the BRI as a whole (Lain 2018: 3). Since the project was announced, most Chinese investment projects or loans, both existing and new, have been placed under the Silk Road Economic Belt umbrella, representing an amplification of China's existing economic policy in the region. For now, China's financial presence has taken the form of "connectivity-specific" investments in physical infrastructure, relying on Central Asia as a gateway to bring energy and natural resources from the Middle East and to conduct trade with Europe. Given China's vital energy security interests in accessing energy supplies, protecting the overseas investments and activities of its NOCs and securing overland oil and natural gas pipeline supplies from across Eurasia, Xi Jinping's signature policy promises to substantially affect future trade and investment dynamics across Eurasia, with significant geopolitical implications (Downs et al. 2017).

From the political point of view, Beijing's main reasons for pursuing the BRI initiative are found in the need to respond to the American "pivot to Asia" strategy, launched under the presidency of Barack Obama, and to support the economic development of its peripheral regions Tibet and Xinjiang to better integrate them into the unitary nation-state of China. With regard to the latter in particular, the BRI could help China's long-standing attempt at a "double-opening", that is, to simultaneously integrate Xinjiang with Central Asia and China in economic terms, while establishing security and cooperation with Central Asian neighbours (Clarke 2015). It goes without saying that the economic priorities of the Xinjiang province go hand in hand with Beijing's necessity to control separatist and terroristic groups, which represent a danger for the security and territorial integrity of the state.

6 Conclusion

The "New Great Game", referring to the struggle in Central Asia spurred on by the collapse of the USSR for control over hydrocarbons resources, transit routes and political influence, has largely benefitted China to the detriment of other actors, especially Western ones. Since then, guaranteeing continuous energy supplies and access to other mineral resources in Central Asia has been a matter of high priority for Beijing. Indeed, China's rapid economic growth could only be sustained by diversifying its sources of energy imports, and Central Asia immediately appeared in this regard as a perfect interlocutor. In the wake of the emergence of Central Asian states, China was also anxious about its domestic stability and above all about the vulnerabilities that could spill over into the Xinjiang province. The different Central Asian ethno-nationalistic identities, and the resurgence of Islam and militant Islamic extremism, could have contributed to the inflammation of separatist sentiments among China's ethnic minorities, endangering the unity of the country. This issue has been faced through the creation of the Shanghai Cooperation Organization, a platform for diplomatic contacts with the Central Asian region and a tool to encourage the alignment of those nations' interests with those of China.

In the last few years, China's "New Silk Road" plan has become the primary driver of Beijing's engagement with Central Asia states. In many ways, this initiative is an extension of the pre-existing framework of the SCO: even though security arrangements were not initially mentioned explicitly, Chinese officials are beginning to expand the narrative to included common security interests in the development of BRI. From the Chinese leadership perspective, BRI reflects the region's geopolitical significance for China's interests, therefore supporting its ambition to extend its influence in the area while inevitably undermining Russia's role within the post-Soviet space. As a result, of all BRI recipients, Central Asian states are the most affected by its socio-economic and political implications.

In conclusion, BRI entails potentially enormous benefits in the post-Soviet space as China finances and invests in new energy projects that will help spur local economic growth. At the same time, the initiative might be perceived as the expression of a mercantilist agenda, allowing China to increasingly shape the future of Central Asia in line with its own domestic and international needs, while Beijing broadens its energy footprint.

Bibliography

Aitken, J. (2009). *Nazarbayev and the Making of Kazakhstan: from Communism to Capitalism*. London: Bloomsbury Academic.

Aliyeva, K. (2018). 'Kazakhstan to Increase Gas Supplies to China', *Azernews*, 15 January, https://www.azernews.az/region/125507.html.

Andrews-Speed, P., Liao, X., and Dannruther, R. (2005). 'The Strategic Implications of China's Energy Needs', *Adelphi Paper 346*, Oxford: Oxford University Press.

Asia-Plus (2018). 'Tajikistan's Public Debt-to-GDP Ratio Exceeds 51 Percent', 6 March, https://www.news.tj/en/news/tajikistan/economic/20180306/tajikistans-public-debt-to-gdp-ratio-exceeds-51-percent.

Asian Infrastructure Investment Bank (AIIB) (2017). 'Republic of Tajikistan. Nurek Hydropower Rehabilitation Project Phase I', *AIIB Project Document*, 31 May, https://www.aiib.org/en/projects/approved/2017/_download/tajikistan/document/document_nurek-hydropower-rehabilitation-project.pdf.

British Petroleum (BP) (2017). *Statistical Review of World Energy 2017*, https://www.bp.com/content/dam/bp/en/corporate/pdf/energy-economics/statistical-review-2017/bp-statistical-review-of-world-energy-2017-china-insights.pdf.

British Petroleum (BP) (2017a). *BP Energy Outlook-China*, 2017, https://www.bp.com/content/dam/bp/pdf/energy-economics/energy-outlook-2017/bp-energy-outlook-2017-country-insight-china.pdf.

Burles, M. (1999). *Chinese Policy Toward Russia and the Central Asian Republics*, Santa Monica, CA: RAND Corporation, https://www.rand.org/pubs/monograph_reports/MR1045.html.

Castle, S. (2009). 'Europe Ends Its Attempt to Penalize Uzbekistan', *The New York Times*, 28 October, https://www.nytimes.com/2009/10/28/world/asia/28uzbek.html.

CCCPC Party Literature Research Office (ed.) (1982). *San Zhong Quan Hui Yi Lai Zhong Yao Wen Xian Xuan Bian* [Important File Selection Since the Third Plenary Session of the Eleventh CPC Central Committee], Changchun, Jilin: Renmin Chubanshe.

Chen, S. (2008). 'Motivations behind China's Foreign Oil Quest: A Perspective from the Chinese Government and the Oil Companies', *Journal of Chinese Political Science*, 13(1): 79–104.

China Daily (2013). 'China, Tajikistan Establish Strategic Partnership', 20 May, https://www.chinadaily.com.cn/china/2013-05/20/content_16513300.htm.

China Daily (2005). 'CNPC Completes Acquisition of PetroKazakhstan', 27 October, http://www.chinadaily.com.cn/english/doc/2005-10/27/content_488314.htm.

Chu, C. (2012). 'Phases in the Development of the Shanghai Co-Operation Organization', pp. 384–393, in M. Beeson and R. Stubbs (eds.), *Handbook of Asian Regionalism*, London: Routledge.

Clarke, M.E. (2015). 'Beijing's March West: One Belt, One Road and China's Continental Frontiers into the 21st Century', *Orbis*, 60(2): 296–313.

Clarke, M.E. (2011). *Xinjiang and China's Rise in Central Asia – A History*, London: Routledge.

Cohen, A.J. and Siu, R. (2012). 'Sustainable Growth in China: Spotlight on Energy', *Global Markets Institute Report*, Goldman Sachs, 13 August, http://www.goldmansachs.com/our-thinking/archive/archive-pdfs/sustainable-growth-china-cohen.pdf.

Daly, T. and Xu, M. (2019). 'China's 2018 Coal Usage Rises 1 percent, but Share of Energy Mix Falls', *Reuters*, 28 February, https://www.reuters.com/article/us-china-energy/chinas-2018-coal-usage-rises-1-percent-but-share-of-energy-mix-falls-idUSKCN1QH0C4.

Dillon, M. (1997). 'Central Asia: the View from Beijing, Urumqi and Kashghar', pp. 133–148, in M. Mozaffari (ed.), *Security Politics in the Commonwealth of Independent States*. London: Palgrave Macmillan.

Downs, E. et al. (2017). 'Asia's Energy Security and China's Belt and Road Initiative', *NBR Special Report*, no. 68, Washington, D.C.: The National Bureau of Asian Research.

Downs, E. (2006). 'China', The Brookings Foreign Policy Studies, Energy Security Series, December, https://www.brookings.edu/wp-content/uploads/2016/06/12china.pdf.

Du, Y. (2018). 'One Belt One Road: Realizing the China Dream in Central Asia?', pp. 193–214, in D.L. Burghart and T. Sabonis-Helf (eds), *Central Asia in the Era of Sovereignty. The Return of Tamerlane?*. Lanham. MD: Lexington Books.

Energy Information Administration (EIA) (2018), *International Energy Statistics*, https://www.eia.gov/beta/international/.

Energy Information Administration (EIA) (2015). *China*, 14 May, https://www.eia.gov/beta/international/analysis_includes/countries_long/China/china.pdf.

Energy-pedia (2005). 'Uzbekistan and China to Sign $600 Million Oil Deal', *Energy-pedia*, 25 May, https://www.energy-pedia.com/news/uzbekistan/uzbekistan-and-china-to-sign-usd600-million-oil-deal.

Eurasianet (2017). 'Central Asia-China Gas Pipeline Expansion Delayed Again', *Eurasianet*, 3 March, https://eurasianet.org/central-asia-china-gas-pipeline-expansion-delayed-again.

Eurasianet (2009). 'Turkmenistan: China Loans $3 Billion for Gas Field Development', *Eurasianet*, 8 June, https://eurasianet.org/turkmenistan-china-loans-3-billion-for-gas-field-development.

Fallon, T. (2015). 'The New Silk Road: Xi Jinping's Grand Strategy for Eurasia', *American Foreign Policy Interests*, 37(3): 140–147.

Global Times (2019). 'With High Dependency on Imported Oil, China Needs to Continue Strategic Petroleum Reserve Buildup', 28 March, http://www.globaltimes.cn/content/1143813.shtml.

International Monetary Fund (IMF) (2019). *World Economic Outlook Database*, https://www.imf.org/external/pubs/ft/weo/2019/01/weodata/weorept.aspx?pr.x=41&pr.y=16&sy=2017&ey=2021&scsm=1&ssd=1&sort=country&ds=.&br=1&c=924&s=NGDPD%2CPPPGDP%2CNGDPDPC%2CPPPPC%2CPCPIPCH&grp=0&a=#cs1.

International Monetary Fund (IMF) – Direction of Trade Statistics (DOTS) (2017). data.imf.org.

Karrar, H.H. (2010). *The New Silk Road Diplomacy: China's Central Asian Foreign Policy since the Cold War*. Vancouver: UBC Press.

KazTransGas (2019). 'Projects of Export Gas Pipelines', http://www.kaztransgas.kz/index.php/en/37-project.

Khatinoglu, D. (2018). 'Iran Gas: Where Does it Go?', *Natural Gas World Magazine*, 3(1), January, https://www.naturalgasworld.com/ngw-magazine-vol-3/1-irans-gas-where-does-it-go-57876.

Kley, D. (2017). 'Can Central Asia's Poorest States Pay Back Their Debts to China?', *The Diplomat*, 1 December, https://thediplomat.com/2017/12/can-central-asias-poorest-states-pay-back-their-debts-to-china/.

Kong, B. and Gallagher, K.P. (2016). 'The Globalization of Chinese Energy Companies: The Role of State Finance', *Global Economic Governance Initiative*, Boston University, June, https://www.bu.edu/pardeeschool/files/2016/06/Globalization.Final_.pdf.

Lai, H. (2009). 'Security of China's Energy Imports', pp. 49–77, in H. Lai (ed.), *Asian Energy Security: The Maritime Dimension*. Basingstoke, UK: Palgrave Macmillan.

Lain, S. (2018). 'The Potential and Pitfalls of Connectivity along the Silk Road Economic Belt', pp. 1–10, in M. Laruelle (ed.), *China's Belt and Road Initiative and its Impact in Central Asia*. Washington, D.C.: The George Washington University.

Lewis, S.W. (2007). 'Chinese NOCs and World Energy Markets: CNPC, Sinopec and CNOOC', paper presented at the Carnegie Endowment event 'The Changing Role of National Oil Companies in International Energy Markets', 8 March, https://www .bakerinstitute.org/media/files/page/95afd6a6/noc_cnooc_lewis.pdf.

Li, P. (1997). 'China's Policy on Energy Resources', *Xinhua, 28* May.

Li, P. (1994). 'China's Basic Policy Towards Central Asia', *Beijing Review*, 37(18), 2–8 May, 18–19.

Liao, J.X. (2006). 'A Silk Road for Oil: Sino-Kazakh Energy Diplomacy', *The Brown Journal of World Affairs*, 12(2): 39–51.

Lieberthal, K. and Herberg, M. (2006). 'China's Search for Energy Security: Implications for U.S. Policy', *NBR Analysis*, 17(1), April.

Ministry of Foreign Affairs of the PRC (MFA) (2013). 'President Xi Jinping Delivers Important Speech and Proposes to Build a Silk Road Economic Belt with Central Asian Countries', 7 September, http://www.fmprc.gov.cn/mfa_eng/topics_665678/ xjpfwzysiesgjtfhshzzfh_665686/t1076334.shtml.

National Development and Reform Commission of the PRC (NDRC) (2015). 'Visions and Actions on Jointly Building Silk Road Economic Belt and 21st Century Maritime Silk Road', 28 March, http://en.ndrc.gov.cn/newsrelease/201503/t20150330_669367 .html.

Niquet, V. (2006). 'China and Central Asia', *China Perspectives*, 67: 2–11.

Organization for Security and Co-operation in Europe (OSCE) (2005). 'Preliminary Findings on the Events in Andijan, Uzbekistan', 13 March, https://www.osce.org/ odihr/15653.

Pannier, B. (2011). 'Kazakh President Energized After China Trip', *Radio Free Europe/ Radio Liberty*, 23 February, https://www.rferl.org/a/kazakh_president_energized_ china_trip/2318634.html.

Paramonov, V. (2014). 'China's Economic Presence in Uzbekistan: Realities and Potentials', *Uzbekistan Initiative Papers*, no. 5, February, https://app.box.com/s/vecd1 meo4wtt3ppmirh8kbkozmnlu6w2.

Paramonov, V. and Strokov, A. (2007). 'Economic Involvement of Russia and China in Central Asia', Conflict Studies Research Center, Central Asian Series, 7 December, https://www.files.ethz.ch/isn/92590/07_Mai.pdf.

Paton Walsh, N. (2005). 'Uzbekistan Kicks US Out of Military Base', *The Guardian*, 1 August, https://www.theguardian.com/world/2005/aug/01/usa.nickpatonwalsh.

People's Daily (2002). 'China Appreciates US Decision to Put ETIM on Terror List', 28 August, http://en.people.cn/200208/28/eng20020828_102193.shtml.

People's Daily (2001). 'Declaration of Shanghai Cooperation Organization', 15 June, http://en.people.cn/english/200106/15/eng20010615_72738.html.

People's Daily (2000). 'Shanghai Five Nations Sign Joint Statement', 6 July, http://en.people.cn/200007/06/eng20000706_44803.html.

PetroChina Company Limited (2017). *Sustainability Report*, http://www.petrochina.com.cn/petrochina/xhtml/images/shyhj/2017kcxfzbgen.pdf.

PetroChina Company Limited (2009). 'CNPC and KazMunayGas Acquire 100% of MangistauMunaiGas Shares Through Open Trade on Kazakhstan Stock Exchange', 25 November, http://www.petrochina.com.cn/ptr/xwxx/201404/0a30577fe3d0452e9d618a66ea6dd95c.shtml.

Peyrouse, S. (2007). 'Economic Aspects of the Chinese-Central Asia Rapprochment', Central Asia-Caucasus Institute & Silk Road Studies Program, http://isdp.eu/content/uploads/publications/2007_peyrouse_economic-aspects-of-the-chinese-central-asia-rapprochement.pdf.

Putz, C. (2018). 'Bitter Cold Hits Bishkek, Chinese-Repaired Power Plant Breaks Down', *The Diplomat*, 30 January, https://thediplomat.com/2018/01/bitter-cold-hits-bishkek-chinese-repaired-power-plant-breaks-down/.

Qian, Q. (1995). 'Shizhong Buyu de Fengxing Duli Zizhu de Heping Waijiao Zhengce [Forever Implementing a Peaceful Foreign Policy of Independence and Self-reliance]', *Qiushi Zazhi* [Seeking Truth], vol. 12.

Reuters, (2017). 'China's Energy Demand to Peak in 2040 as Transportation Demand Grows: CNPC', 16 August, https://www.reuters.com/article/us-china-cnpc-outlook/chinas-energy-demand-to-peak-in-2040-as-transportation-demand-grows-cnpc-idUSKCN1AW0DF.

Reuters, (2013). 'China, Kazakhstan to Ink Deals Worth $30 Billion on Saturday', 7 September, https://www.reuters.com/article/us-kazakhstan-china-deals/china-kazakhstan-to-ink-deals-worth-30-billion-on-saturday-idUSBRE98608320130907.

Rolland, N. (2017). *China's Eurasian Century? Political and Strategic Implications of the Belt and Road Initiative*. Washington, D.C.: National Bureau of Asian Research.

Rolland, N. (2017a). 'China's 'Belt and Road Initiative': Underwhelming or Game-Changer?', *The Washington Quarterly*, 40(1): 127–142.

Shustov, A. (2017). 'Why China Will Remain Turkmenistan's Main Gas Buyer', *Russia Beyond,* 26 January, https://www.rbth.com/business/2017/01/26/why-china-will-remain-turkmenistans-main-gas-buyer_689386.

Shuo, Z. (2018). 'Crude Imports to Increase 7.7%', *China Daily*, 17 January, http://www.chinadaily.com.cn/a/201801/17/WS5a5e8b3ea310e4ebf433e29a.html.

Smith Stegen, K. and Kusznir, J. (2015). 'Outcomes and Strategies in the "New Great Game": China and the Caspian States Emerge as Winners', *Journal of Eurasian Studies*, 6(2): 91–106.

Syroezhkin, K. (2002). 'Central Asia Between the Gravitational Poles of Russia and China', pp. 169–207, in B.Z. Rumer (ed.), *Central Asia: A Gathering Storm*. Armonk, NY: M.E. Sharpe.

Taldybayeva, D. (2017). 'Prospects for China – Kyrgyzstan Economic Relations in the Framework of the Silk Road Economic Belt Project', *HKTDC Research*, 28 March, http://china-trade-research.hktdc.com/business-news/article/The-Belt-and-Road-Initiative/Prospects-for-China-Kyrgyzstan-Economic-Relations-in-the-Framework-of-the-Silk-Road-Economic-Belt-Project/obor/en/1/1X000000/1X0A9JIX.htm.

Tian, Z. (ed.) (1994). *Gaige Kaifang Yilai De Zhongguo Waijiao* [China's Diplomacy Since its Reform and Opening], Beijing: Shije Zhishi Chubanshe.

Trading Economics (2019), *China Crude Oil Production*, https://tradingeconomics.com/china/crude-oil-production.

Umarov, A. and Pashkun, D. (2006). 'Tensions in Sino-Central Asian Relations and their Implications for Regional Security', Conflict Studies Research Centre, Central Asia Series, 6 February, https://www.files.ethz.ch/isn/92580/06_Jan.pdf.

United Nations, Department of Economic and Social Affairs, Population Division, (2018). *World Urbanization Prospects: The 2018 Revision*, https://population.un.org/wup/Country-Profiles/.

Wang, F. and Li, H. (2005). 'Environmental Implications of China's Energy Demands', pp. 180–200, in K.A. Day (ed.), *China's Environment and the Challenge of Sustainable Development*. Armonk, NY: M.E. Sharpe.

Wang, J. (2012). 'Xijin: Zhongguo Diyuan Zhanlue De Zai Pingheng [Marching West, China's Geo-strategic Re-balancing]', *Huanqiu Times*, 17 October, http://opinion.huanqiu.com/opinion_world/2012-10/3193760.html.

Wang, Y. (2005). 'CNPC Eyes Oil Empire in Kazakhstan 2005', *Caijing Magazine*, 5 September, http://english.caijing.com.cn/2005-09-05/100043185.html.

Wilson, J.L. (2015). *Strategic Partners. Russian-Chinese Relations in the Post-Soviet Era*. Abingdon, UK: Routledge.

Wishnick, E. (2001). 'Russia and China. Brothers Again?', *Asian Survey*, 41(5): 797–821.

Xu, F. (2006), 'Shiyou Daqiao Zhongguo Qiye De An'ge'la Wubu [Oil Builds Bridges for Chinese Enterprises in Angola]', *Nan Feng Chuang* [Window for the Southern Wind].

Zhu, Z. (2010). *China's New Diplomacy. Rationale, Strategies and Significance*. Farnham, UK: Ashgate.

CHAPTER 19

The Convergence of Differences: Russia and China in the Middle East and North Africa

Massimiliano Trentin

This chapter reviews Russia and China's engagement with the Middle East and North Africa (MENA) since the 1990s. In the early post-Cold War context, Russia and China had quite different footholds and postures in the region because of resource endowment, domestic development and foreign policy trajectories. However, during the 2000s the combination between rising investments in the region and the perception of Western failures, or outright hostility, developed into political cooperation between Moscow and Beijing in supporting the "stability" and "sovereignty" of existing regimes, whatever their foundations and features. Such development accelerated since the Arab Uprising of 2011 and was welcomed by local elites in their struggle to survive social upheavals and political crisis across the region, as well as against uncertainties over Western policies.

On the background of the review of the existing literature and the analysis of official statistics, the two countries are analysed and compared along the topics of economy and diplomacy in order to assess the factors for cooperation as well as competition in the region.

1 Economy: Differences that Make the Difference

The relevance of the Middle East and North Africa in the international economy of modern times lay in their strategic location at the crossroads of major trading routes, their artisanship before industrial revolutions and, since early 20th century, the presence of energy commodities for global industrial growth, namely oil and natural gas. Hence, from historical perspective, the area might be valued for its role in global transit trade, the production, processing and export of energy raw materials and last, but not least, for its share in the world purchase of military commodities (SIPRI 2016; Findlay & O' Rourke 2007; Owen & Pamuk, 1998).[1] Despite their commonalities in society and culture, as

---

1 According to Stockholm International Peace Research Institute (SIPRI) estimates, the Middle and North Africa accounts for some of the highest military spending both as percentage

well as their complementarity in economic endowment, obstacles to integrate the different territories into a regional, economic space proved too great to be overcome, and local, national specificities took the priority in the setting the development policies of the different ruling regimes. As a result, the economy of the Middle East and North Africa ranks among the less integrated within the regional framework, and one of the most outward-oriented of the world (World Bank 2009; World Bank 2010; Mustapha 2010). The globalization waves of late 20th and early 21st centuries have underlined existing cleavages, fostering a differential integration of highly-selected centres, like the Arab Gulf and Mediterranean coasts, against the marginalisation of peripheries, notably rural, inland territories (Romagnoli & Mengoni 2014: 73, 122).

Russia and China have been acting within such a framework and grasped the opportunities provided by competing markets. In particular, they entered the markets of the Middle East and North Africa as long as these have been trying to diversify their international economic relations beyond their traditional partnerships with close neighbours as well as with European countries and the United States of America. In a remarkable difference with the previous oil shocks in the "long Seventies" (1969–1986), the recent "long 2000s" one (2001–2014) witnessed the diversification and increase of trade relations between MENA and Asia regions, as well within the MENA region, whereas in the past, oil shocks led to an outward-oriented development process that favoured mostly Western industrial countries (World Bank 2017; Trentin 2014). Energy is the commodity that has provided the basis for economic interaction between the MENA region, Russia and China. Since mid-2000s most of the energy flows from the Gulf moved to the consumption markets of Eastern and South Asia, rather than Europe or North America: since 2013, China has become the largest importer of oil from the Gulf area. In order to offset the trade deficits, Asian manufacturing, industrial and financial products entered the area massively, now framed in the Beijing's *One Belt, One Road* (OBOR) project. Russia has continued to expand its partnership as for energy-production technology. This process had constructed a wider and deeper web of economic relations that might be already described as "structural interdependencies" (Davidson 2010).

Differently from Central Asia, Russia and China moved along their own specific assets and never really entered in direct competition (Carlsson et al. 2015: 59–65). Sitting at the opposite sides of production and consumption, both countries have agreed so far to the principle of stability in energy markets, and not of maximisation of short-term gains through prices hikes, which has

---

of Government spending (between 10 and 20%, except for lower figures in Egypt and Turkey) and share of GDP (between 4 and 6 per cent); Saudi Arabia and Israel rank among the first countries spending on military items.

granted Moscow the Chinese acquiescence to its engagement with MENA governments. Occasional competition might arise between respective public and private companies as for contracts in the region but, given that both countries have largely benefitted so far from trade diversification in the area, it is likely that they will prevent competition from turning into rivalry.

2   Russia: Assets and Limits of Specialization in Energy and Technology

After the collapse of the Soviet Union in 1991, Russia withdrew from MENA markets and resorted to minimal trade relations with those countries with which it still had strategic partnerships, like Syria or Algeria, or direct connections, like Turkey and Iran. However, beginning in the early 2000s Russia returned the MENA region as a relevant economic actor in four specific fields: energy, weaponry, tourism and food industry. Russia is as a net importer of food products, particularly from Turkey and Iran, whereas Moscow is a major exporter of commodities in all other three sectors, and registered constant surpluses in its balance of trade: from 147 million US$ in 1992 to 3 billion in 2002 and 12 billion in 2015. Its exports to MENA countries increased from 1,19 billion US$ in 1992 to 3,31 billion in 2002 and 13,7 billion US$ in 2015. Trade value with the Middle East is six times higher than with North Africa (IMF 2018).[2] Among the most important trade partners of Russia one might figure out a first ring of countries, including Turkey, Iran, Iraq, Israel and the United Arab Emirates, followed by a second ring composed by Syria, Egypt, Algeria and Saudi Arabia (IMF 2018).

As a major world producer and exporter of hydrocarbons, Russia has returned the MENA markets with its own technology for exploration, refining and transport facilities for oil and natural gas. Again, previous relations, dating back to the Soviet era, rank first for exports, like Syria and Algeria, as well as Libya until Qadhafy's death; since late 1990s Russia stroke big deals for the development of Iraqi oil production, which implied Moscow advocating for the lifting of the UN sanctions regime.

Russia contributes to the development of the nuclear energy production capacities of Iran, in particular the nuclear site in Busher, which stands as the hallmark of Russian-Iranian partnership. Relations with Teheran have steadily improved since 1991: first of all, for reciprocal interest in the stability of both countries, given their geographical and historical proximity. However, Moscow

---

2   Values are expressed in US$ at the average annual exchange rate for every single, national currency.

has proven cautious on Iranian strategic projects in order to defuse tensions with neighbouring Arab countries. For example, in 2008 Russia, signed with Kuwait and Qatar a memorandum on the peaceful use of nuclear energy.

A fresh, new start occurred instead between Russia and the Arab Gulf Monarchies. Beside Kuwait, which had full relations since the 1960s, Moscow entered the GCC markets only after the demise of the Soviet Union in 1991 but made significant inroads only during the 2000s (IMF 2018; Oskarsson & Yetiv 2013). Between 2005 and 2007 a whole range of permanent institutions have been set up in order to facilitate trade with the Arab Gulf states: the Russian-UAE Business Council in 2005 presiding over trade and Emirates' hedge funds investments in transport facilities in Russia; the Russian-Kuwaiti Business Council and the Russian-Bahraini Business Council in 2007.

Between 2008 and 2012 dozens of agreements were signed between Gulf and Russian energy companies in Iran, Iraq, Kuwait, Saudi Arabia, the UAE, Bahrain and Oman. In November 2011, Moscow inaugurated the GCC-Russian Strategic Dialogue, which would enhance political dialogue on strategic issues for the economy, like trade, investments, technology and culture. Russia exported technology for energy production while it imported capitals for its booming real estate sector, as well as for the much-needed development of oil and gas fields in Siberia and the Urals.

While the re-nationalization of Russian energy industry since the 2000s has proved challenging for Western investors, the Gulf partners were not to deterred by, not least because all state-owned energy enterprises (SOE) have adopted similar patterns of corporate governance, based on efficiency and profit-making criteria (Hertog 2010).

Despite efforts "to modernize and diversify" (Kremlin 2011), Russian economy still depends largely on revenues from energy exports. As a consequence, Moscow has been trying to face competitors by both confronting and reaching out at them, namely Qatar, Algeria and Iran, in order to coordinate policies and investments, stabilize prices and market shares (Oskarsson & Yetiv 2013). Russian efforts, like the Gas Exporting Countries Forum, have reached mixed results: though agreeing on stabilizing prices, Iran is reluctant to let Moscow oversee any coordination policy that would hamper its exports projects, like the delivery of its natural gas straight to Europe through Iraq, Syria and the Mediterranean, which might compete with Russian supplies to the EU.[3] Similar dynamics apply to the relations with Algeria and Qatar, the world-largest producer of Liquified Natural Gas (LNG). Since mid-2000s, the Gulf

---

3 Moscow stood firm in its political and military presence in Syria just at the endpoint of the planned Iranian pipeline, proving several times its leverage on the Iranian ally Author's interviews in Moscow, April 2017.

country has increased its exports of LNG to European countries: these, in turn, work to diversify their energy imports out of Russia's prominence. The development of oil and gas shale in North America, the conflict in Ukraine and tensions with NATO are all factors that contribute to the decline of Russia's market share in Europe.

More difficult have been the efforts by Moscow to engage Gulf exporters as for oil prices are concerned. The price collapse in spring 2014 hugely reduced Russian revenues and Moscow tried to set out an arrangement with OPEC members, and particularly with Saudi Arabia, but divergence on relations with Iran and Syria disrupted efforts until 2016. As soon as Riyad too faced recession, they resorted to dialogue and cooperation to stabilize oil prices back at profitable levels for all exporting countries (Kuznetsov 2017; Dubovikova 2017). Here again, Moscow tries to engage MENA producers in a common framework that would balance competition with the stability that cooperation might provide: within this, the state would act as an effective player in shaping the "market" in accordance to its development goals.

In quite a sharp difference with the Soviet era, marked by low mobility, the growth of a middle and wealthy upper-class in Russia since the 2000s was followed by major real estate investments in tourism across the Mediterranean coasts of Tunisia, Egypt, Israel, Lebanon and Turkey. Though minor in quantitative terms, Russian tourism in the region contributed to re-balancing the large trade-deficits between MENA countries and Russia, as well as to increase and diversify the networks of knowledge, which were once monopolized by state and party officials (Kessler & Zilberman 2017; ITE 2017).

The overall increase in economic interdependency between Russia and the Middle East and North Africa was largely welcomed among partners as a contribution to diversify. However, the primary role played by energy and state policies in fostering partnership proved vulnerable to the instability provoked by the Arab uprisings in 2011 and the fall of oil prices in 2014: trade exchange witnessed a significant decline since then. Because of diplomatic disputes on the Syrian conflict, major contracts with Saudi Arabia, the United Arab Emirates and Qatar were halted: in all three cases, trade exchange diminished by one third of its value. Quite different, the military-led government in Egypt resumed partnership in the name of the fight against "Islamist terror": Russia exports jumped from 2,5 to 4,9 and 3,6 billion US\$ from 2013 to 2015. The crisis with Turkey over Syria in 2015 lowered trade exchange by one third, but their mutual desire to safeguard and expand the economic partnership, which so far has benefitted both countries in terms of diversification led soon to rapprochment: Russian exports to Turkey jumped from 10 billion to an average of more than 20 billion US$ between 2005 and 2015, while imports ranged to around 5,5 billion US$ for the same period (IMF 2018). In all cases, political differences had a direct, short-term impact: in fact, both Turkey and Gulf monarchies were later to resume relations within one or two years after the crisis, with business following suit once state guarantees were provided.

On the whole, Russia still represents a minor economic partner for most of Middle East and North African countries as for trade and investments are concerned. Mainly focused on energy and security sectors, Russia and MENA countries do not contribute much to the diversification of production and consumption of their respective economies. However, in a hydrocarbon-rich and conflict-ridden region, where political elites often base their survival on rent-distribution and armed coercion, Russia has two major assets to play with.

3 China: Massive Investments beyond Energy

Up to 2017 Chinese and MENA officials have mostly focused their partnership on economic issues, namely how to stabilize energy flows and increase Beijing's investments in the region, framed into the 2004 China-Arab States Cooperation Forum (CASCF) and the "strategic dialogue" between Beijing the Gulf Cooperation Council inaugurated in 2010 (Scobell & Nader 2016; Brown 2014; Ezzat 2016).

As for economic relations, the People's Republic of China presents a different set of characteristics compared to Russia because it is a net importer of energy and a net exporter of consumption and industrial commodities. Oil is the major factor impacting on trade exchange with the MENA region: since 1993 China has become a net importer of oil and in 2014, 51% of its oil imports came from the Middle East and North Africa, while since 2013 Beijing ranks as the largest importer of oil from the Gulf area (Varij and Chen 2014; Brown 2014). When oil prices declined in the 1990s, Beijing scored trade surplus between 1 and 2 billion US$ with the Middle East and North Africa countries whereas, as oil prices increased between 2000 and 2014, China registered trade deficits between 3,4 billion US$ and 2,6 trillion US$ respectively. When oil prices halved in 2015, Beijing returned to a surplus of 29,9 billion US$ (IMF 2018).[4]

---

4 Since almost all its energy imports originate from the Gulf area, China has always registered large surpluses with North African partners: from a tiny 183 million US$ in 1992 to 14.5 billion in 2015.

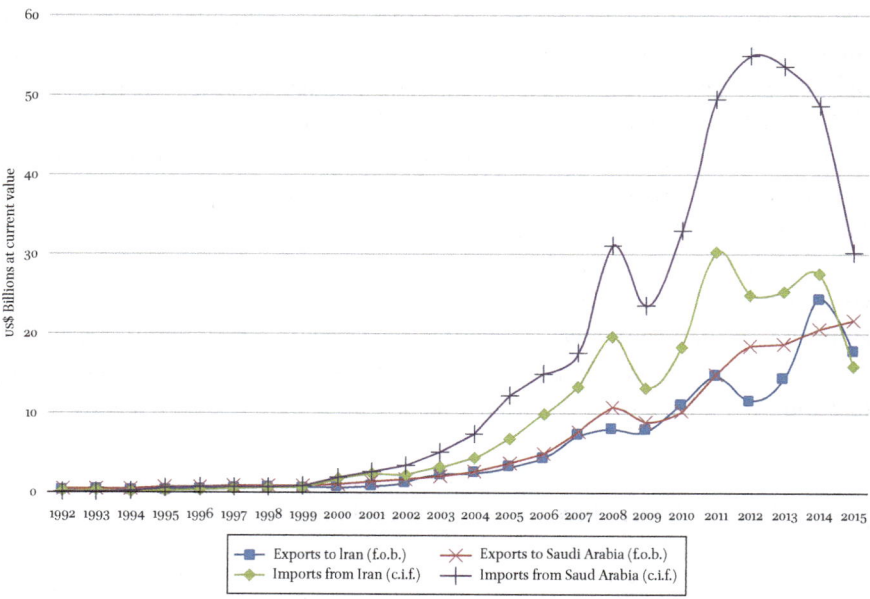

FIGURE 19.1   China's export and import to Saudi Arabia and Iran (1992–2015)
                 SOURCE: DATA ELABORATED FROM INTERNATIONAL MONETARY FUND,
                 DIRECTION OF TRADE STATISTICS, 1980–2015; US$ EXPRESSED AT
                 CURRENT VALUE; LAST ACCESSED NOVEMBER 2018

Among the main economic partners of China, Saudi Arabia and Iran rank first
and second thanks to the energy trade with Beijing. Chinese exports to Saudi
Arabia moved from less than one billion US$ during the 1990s to 21,6 billion
US$ 2016, while imports jumped from 127 million US$ in 1992 to a peak of 48,6
billion US$ in 2014. Though on a lower scale, Chinese trade with Iran followed
a similar path, marked by a steady increase since 2000s and a general deficit up
to 2014 (IMF 2018). However, Iran enjoys a major asset for Beijing because it is
a strategic logistical gateway for the "New Silk Road" initiative on the way to
Eastern Mediterranean. Saudi Arabia and the United Arab Emirates, instead,
are worth being the main energy and political stakeholder and logistical hub,
respectively, of the GCC (Scobell & Nader 2016). Egypt represents a large consumption market and a strategic hub to Europe for maritime trade, where Chinese exports moved from 174 million US$ in 1992 to 11,9 billion US$ in 2016.
Similarly, Turkey is valued for its large and expanding consumption market
and location towards Europe: Chinese exports to Turkey moved from 68,8 million US$ in 1992 to 18,6 billion US$ in 2016 (IMF 2018).

    The cases of Iraq and Libya are worth mentioning because they proved Chi-
nese capacities in the energy market. In Iraq, Beijing could profit from the

security guarantees provided by both US and Iranian forces deployed in the south in order to secure contracts in the energy sector. Beijing was less successful in Libya, where Chinese companies encountered major difficulties in exploiting offshore fields, much to the dismay of former ruler Mu'ammar Qadhafy (Sotloff 2012; Feng 2015).

Since 2001, when China entered the World Trade Organisation, Beijing has become one of the largest importers of oil and gas from the Gulf Cooperation Council (GCC), and one of the most important partners for the supply of consumption products and infrastructural projects in the whole region. Chinese exports helped stabilizing the balance of payments between the Asian country and the region throughout the 1990s and the 2000s: in order to pay back for its energy imports, Chinese authorities engaged with MENA countries first by selling consumption and manufacturing products, like light industrial products, textiles, clothing, machinery and automobiles. Later, in the 2000s, Beijing invested heavily in the energy sector through the state-owned Sinopec, Petrochina, Chinese Offshore Overseas Oil Corporation. Still in 2010, Saudi Arabia was the main recipient of Chinese FDI with 9,19 billion US$, compared to the 774 million in the UAE, 715 in Iran, 483 in Iraq, 337 million in Egypt, 185 in Yemen and 189 million US$ in Israel (Brown 2014).[5]

Beijing climbed fast high in the chain of value by supplying capital investments in infrastructural projects connected to energy and logistics: in particular, the renewal of maritime ports in the Gulf and the Mediterranean, and railroads connecting the main productive and consumption centres of the region (Davidson 2010; Neill 2014). The programmes of the "Silk Road Economic Belt" and "21st Century Maritime Silk Road", announced in 2013 and referred to as "One Belt, One Road" (OBOR), would consolidate further the penetration of Chinese investments in the region, whose stability and development are not just instrumental to trade with Europe but a goal in itself (Scobell 2016). The "China's Arab Policy Paper" of January 2016, which provides the official framework of engagement, adopted the "1+2+3" formula: "to take energy cooperation as the core, infrastructure construction and trade and investment facilitation as the two wings, and three high and new tech fields of nuclear energy, space satellite and new energy as the three breakthroughs" (PRC 2016).

According to conventional approaches the "One Belt, One Road" initiatives are eventually directed to secure Beijing's transit trade to and from Europe. However, this is only partially true because China has been developing a more

---

5 OECD, Chinese Foreign Direct Investment Stock in the MENA, 2010, reported in Brown, Mixed Signals: 4. Chinese investments in Israel concern high-technology programs connected to military and civilian security.

area-fit approach too, which would combine the assets of local forces with their strategic location in global trade routes. By sub-contracting certain productive segments to the area, it hopes exploiting both labour abundance and the preferential trade agreements between the EU and neighbouring Mediterranean countries: China contributed to increase by one-third the ports' activities in Egypt, Algeria, Morocco and Turkey between 2008 and 2014, which would match with Chinese shares in the ports of northern Mediterranean, notably in Greece and Italy (Kowalski 2015; UnctadStat 2017). In Egypt, China focused on the construction of the Chinese-led Suez Economic and Trade Cooperation Zone (SEZ) in 2009, and the high-speed railway connecting the urban centres of Cairo and Alexandria in 2012. Though most of the FDI to the region still originate from the European Union, the Gulf states and the US, MENA governments highly welcomed Chinese investments because they resort to local labour, and thus help meeting the urgent need for employment opportunities (Alessandrini 2012: 3–4; Aita 2011).[6]

On the whole, the economic presence of China in the Middle East and North Africa is still based on the massive consumption of energy, whose stability in delivery has prompted Beijing to move with much caution in the regional politics. However, all along the 2000s China has expanded fast into sectors like industry, logistics and infrastructures, which involve quite a degree of competition with local firms as well as with more traditional foreign actors. In fact, now MENA leaders hold China as a major economic partner that can be leveraged against their European, US, Japanese or South Korean partners in order to either diversify relations or strike better deals (Fandy 2004; Alessandrini 2012).

Last but not least, both ruling elites and popular masses in MENA countries view China as an effective partner for development against the disillusionment, or distrust, towards the US and Europe. On the one side, during the last two decades ruling elites grew wary of Western efforts to link economic liberalizations to political reforms, which might disrupt existing state-business networks. On the other side, social movements criticized Western powers for supporting those neoliberal reforms that impacted heavily on popular and middle classes. On the search for new references, they depict China as an alternative model, conjugating a market-based economy with a strong developmentalist state, which retains the ultimate control over the "commanding heights" of the economy, and to the benefit of people as well (Zambelis & Gentry 2008; Abdel-Malek 2004). Such views often pay lip service to the complexity of Chinese

---

6   If that came as a relief for MENA rulers, it also required state guarantees for labour discipline
     and efficiency, which have been negotiated in bilateral agreements.

development, but they actually match the interests of China, namely to act as a sovereign, independent actor in world economy, as well as the interests of MENA elites, to rejuvenate the legitimacy of their command over state power.

4   International Politics: Diplomacy and Institutions

The Middle East and North Africa have provided major opportunities for the strategic projections of Russia and China in terms of resources, partnerships, and alliances but it represents also a difficult area to engage with as international political actors. In fact, the commonalities in languages, religions, political cultures, migration flows and natural resources that bound these spaces together as a region are not matched by common political institutions that would make them cohesive and effective as for inner governance and foreign relations. As a matter of fact, social integration has mostly translated into political rivalry among elites, with the consequence of preventing the consolidation of any leading pole or consensual institution that might develop the de facto regionalization into a working regionalism; balance of power, anti-hegemonic alliances and bandwagoning with external powers are some of the most salient features of regional and international politics in MENA (Hinnebusch 2003; Börzel & Risse 2016).

The Middle East and North Africa host some of the long-standing conflicts since WWII, whose complexity has both enhanced and exhausted the diplomacy or hegemonic ambitions of world powers, like the late European colonialism or Cold War superpowers (Khalidi 2009; Westad 2017). As such, both Moscow and Beijing are extremely wary of direct engagement in the Middle East and North Africa, and have been generally cautious to move within the consensual frameworks of either the United Nations or bilateral agreements (Charap 2014; Neill 2014).

The main differences between Moscow and Beijing's approaches stem from their geographical and historical proximity to the Middle East and North Africa, which heavily condition interests and perceptions of security. For Russia, the Middle East is a "proxy" area: a neighbourhood laying on the contested "near abroad" of the Caucasus and Black Sea, and linked to its own citizens by transnational ties, like Islam, Orthodox Christianity, and remnants of socialist and nationalist networks. For China, instead, the Middle East is located in the "third" circle of Beijing's foreign policy, which is concerned with energy supplies and, more recently, the impact of political Islam among its own Muslim communities in Xinjiang.

Nonetheless, since the late 1990s Moscow and Beijing have converged on some basic principles and patterns of action: the development of multipolar world where hierarchical politics preside over economic globalization; the primacy of state institutions, as the pillar of domestic and international legitimacy; the primacy of intergovernmental bilateralism as for defence partnership, and multilateralism as for conflict-resolution; the rejection of any kind of regime-change strategy and, after NATO interventions in Kosovo in 1999 and Libya in 2011, heavy caution towards humanitarian interventions; the aversion against militant Political Islam, which might boost dissent within their own territories; the focus on armed forces as the primary actor in the defence of state legitimacy against "instability" (PRC 2016; Foreign Policy Concept 2016).

Such a convergence on general, basic principles was first tested in Central Asia during the 1990s, and institutionalized in the Shanghai Cooperation Council. Later on, as long as both Moscow and Beijing deepened their involvement in the region and conceived US and western policies in Eastern Europe and East Asia as increasingly inimical, they began to act along a de facto division of labour in the MENA region: Russia being at the forefront of diplomatic and security initiatives, while China supporting the latter's actions at multilateral and bilateral levels.

Regional political elites played at full length in the Russian and Chinese engagement in order to offset those policies by Western powers, or local rivals, that might run against their own interests. However, MENA leaders found difficult to draw both countries into the sands of regional rivalries because Moscow and Beijing stood firm against endorsing their local partners' interests as their own, namely aligning on the Arab-Israeli conflict or the disputes between the Gulf Arab monarchies and Iran (Charap 2014). As such, compared to Western countries, and the US in particular, both Russia and China have shown so far a higher degree of autonomy towards their local partners.

Relations with the United States heavily conditioned Russian and Chinese policies in the MENA region: to some respect, the region stood as a sort of test case for the relations with Washington. This latter massive involvement in the region offered Moscow and Beijing the chance to adopt either a cooperative or confrontational stance: Russia and China provided support whenever their strategic interests were not challenged or even converged with NATO's ones, like in the early stages of the "Global War on Terror" against transnational Islamic terrorist organisations in 2011; they even provided occasional "exit-strategies" from crisis, like the provision of goods and services by China in war-torn Iraq after 2003, or the dismantling of the Syrian WMD arsenal in summer 2013. However, they shifted to critical, if not confrontational postures when the instability that followed Western interventions threatened their regional and domestic policies, like in the cases of Iraq (2003), Libya (2011) and Syria (2011–2017).

Cooperation between Moscow and Beijing expanded in parallel with the partial disengagement by the United States from their "moment" in the Middle East and North Africa since 2008 (Fawaz 2012): the "pivot to Asia" was seen as an opportunity to enlarge their presence as well as a source of uncertainty, because the assertiveness of regional players and the search for a new balance of power would ignite rivalry and conflict, along the "New Middle East Cold War" (Valbjørn & Bank, 2012; Hanau Santini 2017). Quite consistent, Moscow and Beijing presented themselves as agents of stability, legitimacy and pragmatism, which actually ran counter the tide of political change during the Arab Uprisings in 2011 but was praised either by the conservative counterattacks and or during wars since 2013 (Lynch 2016; Hokayem & Wesser 2014).

5   Russia: From Withdrawal to Renewed Engagement

At the 2007 Security Summit in Munich President Vladimir Putin shifted to a more confrontational approach against Western foreign policies, and since then Russian moves in the Middle East and North Africa have been framed within the "new Cold War" discourse, which conveys a zero-sum dynamic underneath the Kremlin's decisions. However, if some rhetoric are reminiscent of past rivalry, which still proves useful to mobilize domestic constituencies, a closer scrutiny shows a more limited, neo-realist strategy: today's Russia thinks and acts as a leading actor in an "unstable" world, whose "legitimate" return at the top of power hierarchies is first instrumental to domestic development, and second profitable to other rising powers in terms of diversification and defence of sovereignty (Lavrov 2016). In the Middle East and North Africa, this translates in the defence of domestic political order against transnational movements, the conquest of profitable market shares in all countries of the region, and the assertion of Russia as a reliable partner against Western liberalism (Vasiliev 2018; Dannreuther 2012; Milosevich 2019).

Russian elites and society conceive the region as a close neighbourhood, whose control or stability has a direct impact on their own territories: over a quarter of Tsarist Russia, then the Soviet Union and today's Russia is composed of Muslim people, largely Sunni; with the formal exception of the USSR, Moscow has claimed for the "protection" of Orthodox Christianity in the region; after 1991, it has forged strong ties with Israel through the Jewish citizens of Russian origin (Kreutz 2007: 52–53). If such transnational networks provided Russia with multiple channels for business and foreign policy, processes of

Islamic radicalization in the region spilled over to Russia through transnational links, as it was the case with Islamic insurgencies in the Caucasus during the 2000s (Charap 2014; Hegghammer 2006).

In order to offset criticism against military campaigns, as well as to advocate for moderation in Islam, Moscow appealed to Muslim citizens by embedding Islamic authorities within the nationalist discourse, where Islamic principles have their own historical, and legitimate role to play in the development of Russia (Naumkin 2006; Dannreuther 2010). A major breakthrough in Islamic legitimacy came with the admission of Russia to the Organization of the Islamic Conference in 2005, with an observer status, which marked the high point of warming relations with Saudi Arabia and the GCC.

The scale and depth of Russian engagement in the region developed along territorial proximity to its borders. The relations between Russia and its two direct neighbours, Turkey and Iran, follow their long history of cooperation and confrontation: geographical and social proximity, couple here with assertive political independence, forge wary partnerships between states that all share imperial legacies, top-down modernizations, and revolutionary experiences in the case of Russia and Iran. After the end of the Cold War, relations improved on the basis of respect of political sovereignty and mutual interests on market interdependency, as witnessed by the "Treaty on Principles of Relations and Principles of Cooperation" signed by Russia and Iran on March 2001 (Pravda 2001; Dannreuther 2014; Freedman 2000; Akturk 2006; RIAC 2016).

The new pattern of relations endured different, serious crisis. In particular, the war in Syria (2011–2017) showed how a major conflict prompted cooperation with Iran and confrontation with Turkey, and yet it never developed into a full-fledged Russian-Iranian alliance, or a full-fledged armed conflict between Russia and Turkey (Azizi 2017; RIAC 2016). In all cases, bilateral cooperation has been championed whenever tensions grew with European states, and the US in particular, which adds an instrumental nuance against the West to such bilateral relations.

Moving to the Arab world, a high degree of consistency might be detected in the posture of post-Soviet Russia. The disillusionment of Soviet leaderships against Arab nationalist regimes moved Moscow since the early 1970s towards pragmatic realism: namely, supporting non-aligned postures in the region by diplomacy; forging ties with military leaderships by way of export of military technology; advocating diplomatic solutions to armed conflicts in multilateral fora.

The "retreat" from international politics during the 1990s further scaled down any engagement and maintained a minimal presence in those countries with long-standing ties, like Syria, Algeria or, partially Libya. Since early 2000s, partnership was renewed with Iraq as well as new engagements started with Gulf States. Moscow's regional standing was valued on the one hand as a viable supplier of advanced military and energy technology; on the other hand, as an effective international supporter of state legitimacy, which would secure the incumbent ruling elites whatever their political features (Primakov 2009; Cherif 2019).[7]

The export of military technology has often been described in Russia as a merely exchange of commodities along commercial criteria. In fact, different from Soviet patterns of barter or clearing agreements, military export has been conducted on commercial basis, and along financial transactions. The need for hard currency, especially after Western sanctions and oil prices collapse in 2014, is a major factor for Moscow to sell expensive weaponry abroad: especially, air-defence systems, tanks and transport vehicles (SIPRI 2017). From 1992 to 2015, Algeria ranked first as for purchase of military technology with 8,27 billion US$, followed at distance by Iran with 3,4 billion US$, the United Arab Emirates with 1,7 billion, Egypt with 1,65 billion, Syria with 1,5 billion, Iraq with 1,13 billion and Yemen with 1,18 billion US$ (SIPRI 2018). However, the political relevance of such commodities is proven by the synchronization between diplomatic agreements and arms deals: without a political understanding, if not partnership, no major arms deals were ever made.

Moreover, Western failures, or shortcomings, provided Moscow with major opportunities to assert its standing in the region. This was the case of Russian exports to Iran after the Treaty of Cooperation in 2001 and the failed Israeli war against Hizballah in Lebanon in 2006; Russia doubled arms sales to Baghdad following the US-led invasion of Iraq (SIPRI 2017a). Distrust for Western efforts to reach out at civil society or opposition forces or selective conditionality on the respect of human rights led Arab ruling elites to look at Moscow, even among long-standing Western allies like Saudi Arabia and Turkey. The search for additional partners was then amplified by the partial disengagement of the US from the region along Obama's "pivot to Asia" and Western responses to the Arab Uprisings of 2011 (Dodge, Hokayem, 2014). Military-led Egypt has been a remarkable case since 2014, or Turkey and the Gulf Monarchies since 2015.

Ultimately, the Russian leadership plans to re-gain the Soviet-era market share of nearly one-third of military purchases in the MENA region, which would involve a massive political campaign in all countries, not just traditional

---

7   A closer look would find out the relevance of former Prime Minister Evgenii Primakov in resetting Russian foreign policy on the backdrop of its long-standing experience as Middle East expert and diplomat during the Soviet era.

allies.[8] In this sense, Russia's specialization in the export of military and energy facilities is a major reason for Moscow to accord a leading role to state authorities, in the development and governance of economic relations: not surprisingly, the Kremlin does converge with MENA ruling elites in subordinating market dynamics, based on private actors, to an important but overall subaltern role (Hartwell 2019).

If continuities between late USSR and current Russia's posture in the Middle East are easy detect, there are also major differences. For example, once the Cold War was over, Russia re-established strong relations with Israel, and the massive flow of Russian Jews to Israel allowed Moscow to recover from a major political gap in the region.[9] Most important, both out of conviction and capacities, Russia abstains from championing any universal patterns for development or any precise institutional setting (Dannreuther 2012; Baev 2015). As champion of socialist internationalism, the USSR advocated for strong centralized states, together with mass organizations like parties and unions, which would act as the main engine for social development and political power. Now Moscow is cautious on intervening in topics like institutional building, which let Moscow overcome previous suspicion by conservative elites (Aita 2011; Teti 2015).[10] Additionally, in order to consolidate its "hard power" in the region, Moscow also tried to appeal to a broader public by conveying an image of muscular masculinity, benevolent patriarchy and strong connection between national and religious identities, which would distance Russia from the "moral decay of the West" caused by liberalism. Accordingly, such a discourse was to set Moscow in tune with nationalist and conservative forces in the region, both secular and religious-oriented (Zvjagel'skaja 2016; Akl 2019).

However, facing the rapid change ushered by the Arab Uprisings of 2011, and more urgently by the direct engagement in Syria, Libya as well as Iraq since 2015, Moscow began to figure out some preferences over the patterns of political development in the region. Russian officials opt for a strong central government, on the line of a presidential republic wherever possible, because this would enhance the cohesiveness of leadership that, on the one hand, presides over fragmented societies through state channels and patronage, and, on the other hand, it would present a unique, legitimate partner for foreign dealings.

---

8   Interviews held in Moscow, Russia, April 2017.

9   While abiding to international law and UN resolutions as for the Palestine question, as well as abstaining from any major initiative on the conflict, Russia hopes getting recognized as a legitimate actor by all parties concerned.

10   The topic was left to the EU advisory missions working in the framework of Association Agreements or the EU Neighbourhood Policy.

On the ground, especially in the Arab world, this preference fitted well with political leaderships originating from regular armed forces, like in Egypt and Algeria, and would appeal to regimes featuring close relations between civilian and military elites as well, like in Syria or, partially, Iraq. In a historical perspective, such a preference would not depart much from those hold by the Soviet Union since the late 1970s (Kreutz 2007; Kramer 2011). However, given the social and cultural complexity of Middle Eastern societies as well as the disruption of state institutions by wars, Moscow also argued for robust local autonomy as a suitable solution to pacify post-conflict societies: preventing secession or exhausting guerrilla warfare, decentralization would give a stake to those forces that retain effective control over territories (Sputnik 2016; Harb & Atallah 2015: 229–234). If territorial integrity was a basic principle of Russian foreign policy, the domestic articulation of the state was an issue to be negotiated case by case.

The hard experience made by the Soviets in the Third World, and in the Caucasus during the 1990s, led Russian experts and officials to pay more attention to non-state actors, like tribes, religious and ethnic communities, as meaningful forces to deal with in case of military interventions, negotiations and state-building processes. Such attention proved the more useful as soon as Russia engaged in Syria, central Iraq, Libya or the Arabian Peninsula. Hence, if Russian policy in the region still retains the state as the exclusive, legitimate institution of sovereignty, it also acknowledges trans- and subnational social groups as relevant political actors to deal with (Chuprygin et al. 2019).[11]

6   China: Assets and Limits of Free-Riding in Politics

The People's Republic of China has kept a low-profile in the international politics of the Middle East and North Africa, both out of willingness and necessity. On the one hand, it has focused on East Asia, North America and Europe as leading areas for growth and development, while MENA has been instrumental for energy supplies. On the other hand, the systematic interventions of Western powers have suggested the PRC to abstain from direct engagement. So far, such a posture has allowed Beijing to expand its economic presence, but the more recent, massive round of investments under the One Road One Belt Initiative has stirred up international competition with Western and local companies and would likely require a more pro-active engagement in regional politics in order to secure the support of MENA elites.

---

11   Interviews with Russian academics and analysts, Moscow, April 2017.

The political and cultural heritage of early postcolonial politics, in the forms of respect of sovereignty, non-alignment and developmentalism, remains the pillar of Sino-Arab and Sino-Iranian relations. Meanwhile, the growing assertiveness of Chinese leadership on the global stage is legitimized by references to Chinese, Persian, Islamic and Arab "civilizations", whose heritage are now being held by current "nations" (PRC 2016; Shichor 1979).

Similar to Russia, Chinese engagement in the Middle East and North Africa stems from different factors, the most important being those concerning the domestic priorities set by the Chinese Communist Party: namely, economic development and political stability. Since the 1980s, Chinese politics and diplomacy were to serve the interests of economic interdependence, namely developing trade relations and securing energy flows from the Gulf area; non-interference in domestic politics, "neutrality" on regional disputes, and political "stability" were the principles for Chinese engagement in the Middle East and North Africa. A prerequisite for Beijing has always been the support for the "One China Policy", that is the non-recognition of Taiwan's independence (Brown 2014: 2).

More recently, the risks of spillovers of conflicts and religious radicalism originating in the Middle East, North Africa or Central Asia are a source of deep concern in Beijing because they might spark instability among already restive communities in West China, and hamper the inland trade routes connecting Chinese coasts to the interior, Central and Western Asia. The domestic concern over secessionist movements by Muslim Uighur communities in the Xingjian region prompted Beijing to converge first with the US "War on Terror" in 2001 and later with Russia, under the Shanghai Cooperation Organization policy against "terrorism, separatism, extremism" in 2006. As shown by the case of the organisation of the Islamic State, China endorsed all kinds of interventions by the US and Russia since 2014, which would help containing the impact of Chinese "foreign fighters". Once again, the reliance on foreign partners spared Beijing from direct intervention in the Middle East and North Africa.

In fact, during the 1980s and the 1990s, China profited from the role of power broker played by the US in the Middle East, which guaranteed Chinese economic presence without the costs of major political or security expenditures. However, US partial disengagement since 2008 stirred up rivalry for leadership among Turkey, Iran or Saudi Arabia, and Beijing tried to stay neutral as much as possible while converging with Russian policies: this time again, to minimize the risks of direct intervention (Feng 2015: 3).

Only, under the leadership of President Xi Jinping, China began advocating for deeper engagement in the Middle East and North Africa. In December 2015

Beijing established the Middle East Foundation for Peace and Development (MEFPD); in January 2016 the "China's Arab policy Paper" provides the official framework for Chinese partnership under the keywords of "peace" and "development"; soon after, in May 2016, Beijing and the China-Arab States Cooperation Forum founded the Middle East Peace Forum (PRC 2016b).[12] Accordingly, the MENA region lays in the "third circle" of Chinese foreign policy, where Beijing abstains from binding treaty alliances, prefers bilateral agreements as for economics while uses multilateral fora for debating all sides' domestic priorities, especially economic development.

As for arms trade, China is a minor partner for Middle East and North Africa embattled countries. From 1950 to 2015 the total amount of Chinese exports to MENA countries amounts to 13 billion US$, which is just a percentage of the 121 billion US$ of Russian exports to the region (SIPRI 2017b). Since the 1990s Iran has become steady importer of Chinese military technology, like Algeria or Saudi Arabia bought weapons from Beijing only occasionally, in 1987 and 1988. Conversely, China imported military technology, in particular for unmanned-vehicles like drones, from Israel between 1990 and 2001, for a total amount of 350 million US$ (SIPRI 2017c; Zambelis & Gentry 2008).

Concerning the main conflicts in the Middle East and North Africa during the 2000s, China abstained from taking definitive side on the long-standing rivalries. Beijing supported Palestinian movements since the 1950s for the establishment of an independent, viable Palestinian state on the pre-1967 borders, and condemned Israeli occupation at the United Nations; it stood up to Israeli and US criticism for inviting Hamas officials at the Chinese-Arab States Cooperation Forum in 2006, after the Islamist movement won national elections. Officially, it stood by Russia in supporting peaceful, negotiated solutions to the conflict while advocating for the respect of territorial integrity of both states (Liang 2017). Meanwhile, China developed relations with Israel in the 1990s, as Tel Aviv became a supplier of advanced military technology. While this angered Washington on several occasions, China, Arabs and Iran officially downplayed the dossier as long as Beijing continued to support Arab stances on the Israeli-Palestinian conflict (Brown 2014; Pang 1997).[13]

---

12   The issue came in concomitance of a major round of visit by PRC President Xi Jinping in Saudi Arabia, Iran and Egypt.

13   The visit by Taiwanese President to Arab countries in 1994 was a largely symbolic, occasional retaliation for Sino-Israeli military partnership.

As for the rivalry between Iran and the Saudi Arabia, Beijing supported the multilateral negotiated solution to the "nuclear question" concerning Iran in July 2015 and, like Russia, was reluctant to impose sanctions because Teheran is pivotal to its energy supplies and the Silk Road Economic Belt. In order to prevent military interventions by either the US or Israel in 2014, Beijing promoted "security and defence" cooperation with Iran in 2014. And yet, Beijing is cautious against the Iranian elites' bid for leadership in the region: in fact, it constantly advocates moderation towards Arab neighbours in the Gulf as well as the United States in Iraq (Scobell & Nader 2016). In early 2016 Beijing offered mediation between Riyad and Teheran, which was kindly rejected by both partners, which still do not conceive China as a relevant diplomatic actor in the region (Ezzat 2016).

In Syria, Beijing endorsed Russian stances on the conflict, and increased its public support for the official Government after Moscow's intervention in September 2015, which tilted the military balance in favour of the Damascus and would be rewarded in the post-war context (Dacrema 2017). Libya proved to be a peculiar case: having huge investments in the energy and infrastructural sectors, Beijing was caught off-guard by NATO extensive use of UN Security Council resolution n. 1973 in 2011 to overthrow Qadhafy's regime. However, Beijing displayed effective logistical capacities in the fast repatriation of tens of thousands of Chinese citizens trapped in the war-torn country in 2011, which was a successful showcase for long-distance intervention that might easily turn into military operations (Parello-Plesner & Duchâtel 2015; Collins & Erickson 2011).

7   Conclusion

Russia withdrew from MENA politics in the early 1990s, following the collapse of the Soviet Union. However, the effort to regain a major role in world politics and in energy markets led Moscow to engage back with the region, which is also a political space where conflict and cooperation with Western countries would be tested to defend specific interests as well as international standing.

Russia looks at the Middle East and North Africa as lucrative markets mainly for weapons, technology and energy industry in exchange for food and consumption products. Since the 2000s Russia has championed the principles of "raison-d'état", the primacy of state institutions, whose stability is ultimately guaranteed by armed forces, and the fight against Islamic militancy: this was the rationale of Moscow in Iraq in 2003, in Egypt in 2012 as well as in Syria, Libya and Yemen, which reminds to the Soviet Union's turn to realpolitik since the 1970s. Quite different, China has been looking for hydrocarbons to fuel its economic growth which, coupled with the decline of Western consumption, contributed to re-direct MENA energy flows from Europe to Asia. In order to balance strategic imports, Beijing embarked on major investments in infrastructural projects and energy industry. Meanwhile, by standing firm to the principles of sovereignty and multilateralism, it keeps a low profile in regional politics in order not to compromise its economic stakes, and let the front stage to other partners that, from different standpoints, fit well with China's goals: namely, the United States in the 1990s and Russia after the mid-2000s.

Russia and China's postures have gained foothold in the region thanks to both domestic and international factors. First of all, the attention by those embattled, ruling elites in MENA countries who welcome diversifying international relations and aspire to combine the monopoly of political power with the dividends of market economies. Last but not least, their distrust, if not outright rejection, of economic and political liberalism as it has been branded and conveyed by Western powers since the 1980s through direct interventions or conditionalities.

Recent events like the Arab Uprisings in 2011 or wars in Syria, Iraq, Libya and Yemen have translated the general convergence on principles into a working cooperation between Moscow and Beijing. If their support for regional "stability" currently means opting for a conservative status quo, it also provides fuel and strength for the revision of the international relations of the Middle East and North Africa: that is, the provision of additional partnership out of the prominence enjoyed by Western powers since last century. If, up to now, the "old" and "new" engagements have not involved any major alternatives in terms of patterns of economic and political development, they nonetheless raise concerns among NATO countries, and the US in particular. The risk of the region spiralling into the previous patterns of Cold War rivalry, looms large on a region featuring all the cleavages of rapid social change, contemptuous politics and institutional resilience.

Bibliography

Abdel-Malek, A. (2004). 'China's Message to the Arabs', *Al-Ahram Weekly*, 708.

Akl, Z. (2019). 'Russia and Post-Arab Spring Political Elites in Egypt, Libya and Syria', pp. 54–69, in C. Lovotti and V. Talbot (eds.), *The Role of Russia in the Middle East and North Africa Region. Strategy or Opportunism?*, Euromesco Joint Policy Studies, 12.

Aita, S. (2011). *Les travailleurs arabes hors-la-loi. Emploi et droit de travail dans les Pays arabes de la Mediterranée*. Paris: l'Harmattan.

Akturk, S. (2006). 'Turkish-Russian Relations after the Cold War (1992–2002)', *Turkish Studies*, 7(3): 337–364.

Alessandrini, S. (2012). 'Foreign Direct Investments (FDI) to the Middle East and North Africa Region: Short- and Medium-Term Developments', Policy Brief (Washington, D.C., Torino: The German Marshall Fund of the United States, Istituto Paralleli): 3–4.

Azizi, H. (2017). 'Is Iran following Russia's Lead in Syria?', *Al-monitor.com*, 8 January, https://www.al-monitor.com/pulse/originals/2017/01/iran-turkey-russia-syria-cease-fire-kurds-raqqa-assad.html.

Baev, P.K. (2015). 'Russia as Opportunist or Spoiler in the Middle East?', *The International Spectator*, 50(2): 8–21.

Börzel, T.A. and T. Risse (eds.), (2016). *The Oxford Handbook of Comparative Regionalism*. Oxford: Oxford University Press.

Brown, K. (2014). 'Mixed Signals: China in the Middle East', Policy Brief 190 (Fride – Hivos): 2.

Carlsson, M., Oxenstierna S., and Weissmann M., (2015). 'China and Russia – A Study on Cooperation, Competition and Distrust', Report n. FOI-R – 4087 – SE (Stockholm: Swedish Defence Research Agency): 59–65.

Charap, S. (2014). 'Is Russia a Putside Power in the Gulf', pp. 185–204, in T. Dodge and E. Hokayem (eds.), *Middle Eastern Security, the US Pivot to Asia and the Rise of ISIS*. London: Routledge-IISS.

Cherif, Y. (2019). 'The Interests of Putin's Russia in the MENA Region in Historical Perspective', pp. 12–29, in C. Lovotti and V. Talbot (eds.), *The Role of Russia in the Middle East and North Africa Region. Strategy or Opportunism?* Euromesco Joint Policy Study, 12.

Chuprygin, A., Chuprygina, L., Matrosov, V. (2019). 'Key Actors in the Libyan Conflict. Friends and Foes of the Libyan Political Milieu', *Russia in Global Affairs*, 25 December.

Collins, G. & Erickson, A.S. (2011). 'Implications of China's Military Evacuation of Citizens from Libya', *China Brief*, 11(4), 11 March.

Dacrema, E. (2017). 'Will China get the lion's share in Syria Reconstruction?', Syria Untold, 16 September, https://syriauntold.com/2017/09/16/52977/.

Dannreuther, R. and March, L. (2010). *Russia and Islam. State, society and radicalism.* New York: Routledge.

Dannreuther, R. (2012). 'Russia and the Middle East: a New Cold War?', *Europe-Asia Studies,* 64(3): 543–560.

Dannreuther, R. (2014). 'Russia and the Middle East', in H. Carter and A. Ehteshami (eds.), *The Middle East's Relations with Asia and Russia*. London: Routledge.

Davidson, C. (2010). *The Persian Gulf and Pacific Asia. From Indifference to Interdependence.* London: Hurst&Co.

Dubovikova, M. (2017). 'Saudi-Russian relations reach new heights', *Arab News*, 6 October, https://www.arabnews.com/node/1173081/middle-east.

Ezzat, D. (2016). 'China in the Middle East', *Al-Ahram*, 20 January, http://weekly.ahram .org.eg/News/15302.aspx.

Fandy, M. (2004). 'Energy Security: Implications for U.S.-China-Middle East Relations', (The James A. Baker III Institute for Public Policy of Rice University).

Fawaz, G.A. (2012). *Obama and the Middle East: the End of America's Moment*. New York: Palgrave-MacMillan.

Feng, C. (2015). 'Embracing Interdependence: the Dynamics of China and the Middle East', Policy Briefing, Brookings Doha Center, April.

Findlay, R. and O' Rourke, K. (2007). *Power and Plenty. Trade, War and Economy in the Second Millenium*. Princeton: Princeton University Press.

Foreign Policy Concept. (2016). 'Foreign Policy Concept of the Russian Federation (approved by President of the Russian Federation on November 30, 2016)', *The Ministry of Foreign Affairs of the Russian Federation*, 1 December, http://www.mid.ru/en/for eign_policy/official_documents/-/asset_publisher/CptICkB6BZ29/content/ id/2542248.

Freedman, R.O. (2000). 'Russian–Iranian Relations in the 1990s', *Middle East Review of International Affairs*, 4(2): 65–78.

Harb, M. and Atallah, S. (2015). 'An Assessment of Decentralization and Service Delivery in the Arab World', pp. 229–234, in Harb, M. and Atallah, S. (eds.), *Local Governments and Public Goods: Assessing Decentralization in the Arab World*, Beirut: The Lebanese Center For Policy Studies.

Hanau Santini, R. (2017). 'A New Regional Cold War in the Middle East and North Africa: Regional Security Complex Theory Revisited', *The International Spectator*, 52(4): 93–111.

Hartwell, C.A. (2019). 'Russian Economic Policy in the MENA Region: A Means to Political Ends', pp. 90–114, in C. Lovotti and V. Talbot (eds.), *The Role of Russia in the Middle East and North Africa Region. Strategy or Opportunism?* Euromesco Joint Policy Study, 12.

Hegghammer, T. (2006). 'Global Jihadism After the Iraq War', *Middle East Journal*, 60(1): 12–32.

Hertog, S. (2010). 'Defying the Resource Curse. Explaining Successful State-Owned Enterprises in Rentier States', *World Politics*, 62(2): 261–301.

Hinnebusch, R. (2003). *The International Politics of the Middle East*. Manchester: Manchester University Press.

Hokayem, E. and Wesser, R. (2014). 'The Gulf States in an Era of American Retrenchment', *Adelphi Series*, 54(477–78): 135–164.

International Monetary Fund, (2018). Direction of Trade Statistics (Washington, D.C.), last access, November 2018. UK Data Service, DOI: http://dx.doi.org/10.5257/imf/ dots/2016-11.

ITE, (2017). 'Russian Outbound Tourism. Where Next?', October.

Kessler, O. and Zilberman B. (2017). 'Russia's Charm Offensive in North Africa', *Foreign Affairs*, 3 April.

Khalidi, R. (2009). *Sowing Crisis. The Cold War and American Dominance in the Middle East*. Boston: Beacon Press.

Kremlin. (2011). 'Meeting of Commission for Modernisation and Technological Development of Russia's Economy', *President of Russia*, 26 September, http://en.kremlin .ru/events/president/news/12824.

Kowalski, P. et al. (2015). 'Participation of Developing Countries in Global Value Chains: Implications for Trade and Trade-Related Policies', OECD Trade Policy Papers. Paris: OECD Publishing, 179: 54.

Kramer, M. (2011). 'The decline in Soviet Arms Transfer to the Third World', pp. 46–100, in A. Kalinovsky and S. Radchenko (eds.), *The End of the Cold War and the Third World. New Perspectives in Regional Conflicts*. London: Routledge.

Kreutz, (A). (2007). *Russia in the Middle East. Friend or Foe*. London: Praeger.

Kuznetsov, V. (2017). 'How Moscow-Riyadh rapport fits into the Mideast scene', *al-Monitor*, 11 June, https://www.al-monitor.com/pulse/ru/originals/2017/06/russia-saudi-arabia-gcc-alliances-qatar-middle-east.html.

Lavrov, S. (2016). 'Russia's Foreign Policy: Historical Background', Russia in Global Affairs, Moscow: Ministry of Foreign Affairs of the Russian Federation, 3 March.

Lynch, M. (2016). *The New Arab Wars. Uprisings and Anarchy in the Middle East*. New York: Public Affairs.

Milosevich, M. (2019). 'The 2010s: Grand Strategy or Tactical Opportunism', pp. 30–53, in C. Lovotti and V. Talbot (eds.), *The Role of Russia in the Middle East and North Africa Region. Strategy or Opportunism?*, Euromesco Joint Policy Study, 12.

Liang, L.Y. (2017). 'Experts split over China's moves in the Middle East following Trump's decision on Jerusalem', *Straits Times*, 12 December, https://www.straitstimes.com/asia/east-asia/experts-split-over-chinas-moves-on-the-middle-east-following-trumps-decision-on.

Mustapha, R. (2010). *Economic integration in the Mashreq*. Washington, D.C.: World Bank.

Naumkin, V. (2006). 'Evroislam kak naslednik dzhadidizma', pp. 307–312, in Mukhetdinov, D. (ed.), *Forumy Rossiiskikh musul'man na poroge novogo tisiacheletiia*, Nizhnii Novgorod: Medina.

Neill. A. (2014). 'China and the Middle East', pp. 205–224, in Dodge, T. and Hokayem E., *Middle Eastern Security, The US Pivot and the Rise of ISIS*, Abingdon: Routledge.

Oskarsson, K. and Yetiv, S.A. (2013). 'Russia and the Persian Gulf: Energy, Trade and Interdependence', *The Middle East Journal*, 67(3): 381–403.

Owen, R. and Pamuk, S. (1998). *A History of Middle East Economy in the Twentieth Century*. London: I.B. Tauris.

Pang, G. (1997). 'China's Success in the Middle East', *Middle East Quarterly*, December: 35–40.

Parello-Plesner, J. and Duchâtel, M. (2015). *China's Strong Arm: Protecting Citizens and Assets Abroad*, London: Adelphi Papers, IISS.

People's Republic of China (PRC) (2016). 'China's Arab Policy Paper', *Xinhua.net*, January, https://www.fmprc.gov.cn/mfa_eng/zxxx_662805/t1331683.shtml.

People's Republic of China (PRC) (2016a). 'Chinese foundation launches Middle East peace forum in Cairo', *Xinhuanet.com*, 16 May, http://www.china.org.cn/world/Off_the_Wire/2016-05/16/content_38458592.htm.

Pravda (2001). 'Russian State Duma Has Ratified Treaty On Cooperation With Iran', *pravda.ru*, 12 December, http://english.pravda.ru/news/world/19-12-2001/24746-0.

Primakov, Y. (2009). *Russia and the Arabs. Behind the Scenes in the Middle East from the Cold War to the Present.* New York: Basic Books.

Russian International Affairs Council (RIAC) (2016). 'New Stage of Russia-Turkey Economic Relations', RIAC: Moscow, Report n. 28.

Russian International Affairs Council (RIAC), The Institute for Iran-Eurasian Studies, (2016). 'Russia-Iran Partnership: an Overview and Prospects for the Future', RIAC: Moscow, Report n. 29.

Romagnoli, A. and Mengoni, L. (2014). *The Economic Development Process in the Middle East and North Africa.* London: Routledge.

Scobell, A. and Nader, A. (2016). *China in the Middle East. The Wary Dragon.* Santa Monica: Rand Corporation.

Shichor, Y. (1979). *The Middle East in China's Foreign Policy, 1949–1977.* Cambridge: Cambridge University Press.

SIPRI, (2016). 'Military Expenditure Data, 1988–2015'.

SIPRI, (2017). 'Transfers of major conventional weapons: sorted by supplier. Deals with deliveries or orders made for year range 1950 to 2015'.

SIPRI, (2017a). 'Trend indicators value (TIVs), 1950–2015, values expressed in US$m at constant (1990) prices'.

SIPRI, (2017b). 'China export to MENA countries, TIV, 1992–2015'.

SIPRI (2017c). 'Israel export to China, TIV, 1992–2015'.

SIPRI, (2018). 'Russia to Middle East Countries. Transfers of major conventional weapons: sorted by supplier. Deals with deliveries or orders made for year range 1950 to 2015'.

Sotloff, S. (2012). 'China's Libya Problem', *The Diplomat*, 14 March, https://thediplomat.com/2012/03/chinas-libya-problem/.

Sputnik, (2016). 'The Country We Used to Know is no More: Possible Scenarios for Post-War Syria', *Sputnik International*, 19 August, https://sputniknews.com/middleeast/201608191044434991-syria-future-analysts/.

Teti, A. (2015). 'Democracy Without Social Justice: Marginalization of Social and Economic Rights in EU Democracy Assistance Policy after the Arab Uprisings', *Middle East Critique*, 24(1): 9–25.

Trentin, M. (2014). 'Boom e Crisi. Lo sviluppo economico dei MENA negli anni Duemi-la a confronto con i lunghi anni Settata', pp. 71–86, in B. Airò and M. Zaccaria (eds.), *I confini della cittadinanza nel nuovo Medio Oriente*. Pavia: Asia Major.

UnctadStat, 2017. 'Container Port Throughput, Annual, 2008–2014', January.

Valbjørn, M. and Bank, A. (2012). 'The New Arab Cold War: Redescovering the Arab di-mension of the Middle East regional politics', *Review of International Studies*, 38(1): 3–22.

Vasiliev, A. (2018). *Russia's Middle East Policy. From Lenin to Putin*. Abingdon: Routledge.

Westad, O.A. (2017). *The Cold War. A World History*. New York: Basic Books.

World Bank, (2009). *Economic Development and Prospects, 2008. Regional Integration for Global Competitiveness*. Washington, D.C.: World Bank.

World Bank, (2010). *Economic integration in the Gulf Cooperation Council*. Washington, D.C.: World Bank.

World Bank, (2017). 'World Development Indicators, Merchandise imports and exports of all MENA, 1960–2015'.

Zambelis, C. and Gentry, B. (2008). 'China through Arab Eyes: American Influence in the Middle East', *Parameters*, 38(1): 60–72.

Zvjagel'skaja, I. (2016). ''Russia, the New Protagonist in the Middle East', p. 75, in A. Fer-rari (ed.) *Putin's Russia: Really Back?*. Milano: ISPI.

CHAPTER 20

The Chinese Penetration in Sub-Saharan Africa: The Case of Tanzania

Arrigo Pallotti

The African states have long been portrayed as weak, dependent and vulnerable actors within the international relations literature. In spite of the high expectations raised by the independence of a large number of African countries in the late 1950s and the early 1960s, the military vulnerability of the newly independent African governments and the many difficulties they encountered in consolidating their state institutions led William Zartman already in the late 1960s to conclude that: "African states have little capability of influencing the decisions of other African and non-African states. (...) Africa does not have the power to protect itself and promote its own goals" (Zartman 1967: 550, 554).

During the 1970s the disappointing results of the import substitution industrialization policies pursued by the African governments and their growing authoritarian tendencies pushed some scholars to stress "the influence of external interests, demands, and models in manipulating African "development" strategies" and political trajectories (Shaw & Grieve 1978: 7). While Francophone Africa was depicted as the victim of France's neo-colonial ambitions (Amin 1973), scholars pointed to the weakness of the African capitalist class and the ambiguous role played by multi-national corporations (MNCs) within the newly independent countries in order to explain the fact that "political independence in Africa has not brought economic independence or development to the continent; rather, it has intensified the inheritance of economic dependence" (Shaw & Grieve 1978: 11). As Langdon and Mytelka remarked: "the symbiosis of MNCs with African petit bourgeois forces that existed after independence blocked developmental responses to [the historical problems of poverty and inequality and] the industrialization that occurred [worked] mainly to the advantage of small minorities" (Langdon & Mytelka 1979: 207).

In the 1980s, the debt crisis and the donor consensus on the need for new and radical solutions to the economic difficulties of the developing countries left the African governments with no option but to ask for assistance from the World Bank (WB) and the International Monetary Fund (IMF). However, the neo-liberal economic reforms the African governments were required to implement in order to get access to the loans provided by the WB and the IMF

© KONINKLIJKE BRILL NV, LEIDEN, 2020 | DOI:10.1163/9789004428898_021

failed to restore economic growth in Africa. The political, economic and social crisis of the African countries led some scholars to argue that the African states lacked the basic requirements of state sovereignty.

Jackson and Rosberg argued that after independence a perverse notion of juridical sovereignty had shielded the African governments from "the competitive pressures and dynamics of the international system to bring about political and economic development to retain their statehood". As a consequence, international organizations such as the United Nations and the Organization of African Unity (OAU), and the same African governments had coalesced to bring about "a new international underclass of mendicant states which have come to depend very heavily not only on legal recognition but, increasingly, on foreign aid as well" (Jackson & Rosberg 1986: 2–3, 28). While in the mid-1980s the analysis of the development cooperation between Africa and the European Economic Community led John Ravenhill to conclude that the African governments behaved as "clients" of the European countries (Ravenhill 1985), almost twenty years later Bayart noted that the African agency in global affairs had been historically limited to the manipulation of the continent marginal and dependent position through a "strategy of extraversion, at the heart of which is the creation and the capture of a rent generated by dependency" (Bayart 2000: 222)

The end of the Cold War, together with the failure of the international peace operations in Somalia and Rwanda reduced Africa's strategic relevance at the international level. While in the mid-1990s Christopher Clapham wrote that the African states were "at the bottom on any conventional ordering of global power, importance and prestige" (Clapham 1996: 3), Khadiagala and Lyons observed that "the leverage of African actors [had] decreased" after the end of the Cold War (Khadiagala & Lyons 2001: 10). As development aid was now made conditional upon implementation of both economic and political reforms, the African countries, which "existed on the periphery of world politics since their independence" (Harbeson & Rothchild 1991: 1), had now been transformed into "choiceless democracies" (Mkandawire 1999).

During the 1990s the outbreak of violent conflicts, the impasse of the democratic transition processes in many African countries, and growing poverty were considered as evidence of the fact that the end of the Cold War had left "Africa in chaos" (Ayittey 1998), and had laid bare the "fiction" of the African state (Hentz 2001: 188). Within this context, while some scholars argued that the study of Africa's international relations would better focus on non-state actors such as "warlords, non-governmental organizations or ethnic groups" (Smith 2012: 28. See also Dunn 2001), others suggested the need for the African governments to cede part of their sovereign rights to the multilateral institutions in order to speed up the development of their countries (Callaghy 1995).

Due to the intense international competition for Africa's natural resources during the last two decades, the view of the African countries as "victims" of global forces and actors remains a dominant one within the African international relations literature. Although some scholars suggest that closer relations between Africa and the emerging powers have strengthened the African governments' bargaining power in the international fora (Rocha 2007: 32), the recent literature on the "new scramble" for Africa has mainly depicted African governments as "pawns" in the hands of the old and new powers competing for access to oil and gas deposits and consumer markets on the continent (Bond 2006; Lee 2006).

In addition to these two perspectives, a third one has emerged, which if on the one side acknowledges the "political agency" of the African governments, on the other side recognizes the "structural pressures" bearing on them (Taylor & Williams 2004: 2). Factors such as the dependency on foreign aid and the vulnerability of the African countries to the fluctuations in the international prices of primary commodities substantially limit the political leverage of the African governments. According to Roger Southall, "in the wake of rapid globalisation and IMF and World Bank entrenchment of neo-liberal economics, African leaders now have little option but attempt to make capitalism work for their countries under highly unfavourable conditions" (Southall 2009: 31). Brown and Harman have recently pointed to an "increased African agency" within the context of the war against international terrorism and the boom in international commodity prices, but have cautioned that when "exploring (...) agency in international politics, Africa serves as something of a limit case" (Brown & Harman 2013: 3, 10).

This chapter aims at putting into question the mainstream view of the African states as passive actors within the international system by investigating the historical evolution of relations between Tanzania and China during and after the Cold War. In so doing, this chapter takes up the challenge raised by the editors in the introduction to this volume of exploring the multiple ways through which relations between developing and emerging countries have historically helped them to achieve their political and economic goals at both the national and international level.

One of Africa's poorest countries at independence, in the mid-1960s Tanzania adopted an unorthodox socialist development strategy whose implementation was politically and materially supported by communist China. During the Cold War the Tanzanian government actively tried to achieve its own political and economic goals at the national, regional and international level by forging close ties with China. The latter, in its turn, tried to project it political influence in Eastern and Southern Africa in competition with the United States and the Soviet Union by actively cooperating with Tanzania. Within the context of what president Julius Nyerere defined "a friendship between most unequal equals" (Hutchison 1975: 261), and contrary to Western fears, during the Cold War the Tanzanian authorities always maintained their own autonomy with respect to the Chinese government. Tanzania only partially realized its development goals, as the country remained heavily dependent on the export of few primary commodities, but the Tanzanian government did play a relevant role in the decolonization of Zimbabwe (Pallotti 2017).

During the 1980s, while Tanzania entered a serious economic crisis that compelled its government to abandon socialism and start to implement a structural adjustment program supported by the IMF and the WB, China was busy implementing its own internal reforms. As a consequence, the reduction in the Chinese aid budget deprived Tanzania of Peking's support at a very critical juncture in the country history. After the end of the Cold War, against the backdrop of China's renewed interest for Africa, relations between China and Tanzania intensified again. China's development aid and, more importantly, concessional loans to Tanzania helped the latter's government to pursue its own development vision and maintain its control over the country's state and society. On its own part, Beijing has maintained strong ties with Tanzania for both political and economic reasons.

1   Revolution in Zanzibar and Development of Tanzania-China Relations

In spite of the fact that Tanzania was "China's closest friend in Africa" during the 1970s (Bailey 1975: 41), at Tanganyika's independence in December 1961 the development and consolidation of close ties between the two countries was not a foregone conclusion. On the one side, the government of Julius Nyerere – Tanganyika's prime minister (1961–1962) and president (1962–1964), and then Tanzania's president (1964–1985) – soon recognized communist China, but adopted a "cautious" (Hoskyns 1968: 453) or "realist" (Bjerk 2011: 216) foreign policy, and maintained a "close association with Britain" (Pratt 1978: 90), which had ruled the country after Germany's defeat in the First World War. On the other side, in the late 1950s China primarily directed its attention to Zanzibar in the East Africa, and established close links with the Zanzibar National Party (ZNP) and, in particular, with its secretary-general, Abdulrahman Mohamed Babu.

Paradoxically, the revolution in Zanzibar on 11–12 December 1964 played an unexpected and crucial role in fostering relations between Tanzania and China.

The revolution, which was initiated by the Youth League of the Afro-Shirazi Party (ASP) with the support of some African policemen who had been retrenched by the Zanzibar government soon after independence in December 1963 (Glassman 2011: 64), brought about an international crisis. The British and American governments, which had hesitated to recognize the new Zanzibar regime in spite of the pressing requests by Abeid Karume, the leader of both the ASP and the Zanzibar Revolutionary Council, saw with growing concern the appointment of Abdullah Hanga, a trade unionist with strong links with the Soviet Union, as prime minister, and of Babu as minister for external affairs, and the decision of the Soviet Union, China and some other communist countries to immediately recognize the new Zanzibar government. In particular, the Americans thought that the "main purpose of [the] accelerated Commie interest [in] Zanzibar [was to] establish [a] strategic foothold off [the] East African coast [in] order [to] unleash [an] intensified campaign [of] subversion and infiltration [of] important mainland countries in East Africa".[1]

Nyerere considered the presence of the Chinese in Zanzibar as a "double menace" since, as he explained to the Americans, "their threat is not only subversion. They are a worse threat if they make success of Zanzibar (...). Then what happens to what I stand for in Tanganyika and what happens to this country?".[2] He thus proposed to Karume the formation of a union between Tanganyika and Zanzibar.[3] According to Nyerere, the merger of the two countries would forestall the realization of any pro-communist revolutionary plan and secure the leadership of Karume on the isles (Wilson 1989: 73).

Babu, who after his release from prison in April 1963 had left the ZNP to form the ultra-leftist Umma Party, did not play an active role in the overthrow of the Sultan's government (on the night of the revolution he was reportedly in Dar es Salaam), but then tried to transform a "lumpen, in many ways apolitical uprising into [an] anti-imperialist revolution" (Babu 1991: 245), and prevented the latter "from taking a racial character" (Wilson 1989: 13). Moreover, as foreign minister of the new Zanzibar government, Babu soon tried to establish

---

1 *Telegram from Department of State to American Embassy Nairobi*, 14 March 1964, National Archives of the United States, College Park, Maryland, United States (NARA II), General Records of the Department of State, Subject Numeric File 1964–66, Box 3043, Folder: POL 23 Internal Security ZAN.

2 *Telegram from American Embassy Dar es Salaam to Department of State*, 22 February 1964, NARA II, General Records of the Department of State, Subject Numeric File 1964–66, Box 3043, Folder: POL 16 Independence Recognition ZAN.

3 According to a report by the CIA, Karume's initial response "was not enthusiastic". It was only when Nyerere threatened to withdraw the Tanganyikan police contingent – whose "support [Karume] needed against Babu" – from Zanzibar that Karume accepted the formation of the Union. Central Intelligence Agency, *Zanzibar: The Hundred Days Revolution*, ESAU XXX, 21 February 1966, 123–124, https://www.cia.gov/library/readingroom/docs/esau-28.pdf (accessed on 15 March 2017).

diplomatic relations with a number of communist countries, and solicited economic aid from them. Few weeks after the revolution, China, East Germany and the Soviet Union had already offered some economic aid to Zanzibar.[4]

On 22 April 1964 Nyerere and Karume signed the Articles of the Union, which established the United Republic of Tanzania. Zanzibar not only maintained its president and government, but also retained a broad autonomy within the Union, as the latter had (at least initially) exclusive jurisdiction on a limited number of matters (foreign policy, defence, external trade, etc.). As Babu was nominated Minister of Trade and Cooperatives in the Union government and moved to Dar es Salaam, Karume could strengthen his leadership within the Zanzibar Revolutionary Council and establish a personal dictatorship on the archipelago (Pallotti 2016), which Nyerere purposefully avoided to publicly criticize due to his fear that Karume could split the Union in revenge.[5]

If the removal of Babu from Zanzibar aimed at reducing communist influence in the archipelago, paradoxically his appointment to the Union Cabinet played a crucial role in the radicalization of Tanzania's development vision and foreign policy, as Babu worked to promote the consolidation of relations between Tanzania and communist China. While soon after the revolution China had established cordial relations with the Zanzibar Revolutionary Council in spite of its past association with the ZNP, Peking welcomed the creation of the Union and tried to establish close ties with the Union government in order to extend its influence on Tanzania and East Africa.

As Tanzania's Minister of Trade and Cooperatives, Babu took part in Vice-President Rashidi Kawawa's official visit to China in June 1964. Together with the signing of an Agreement on Economic and Technical Cooperation between China and Tanzania, the Chinese government offered Tanzania a US$ 42 million concessionary loan (a quarter of it to be spent in Zanzibar) (Yu 1975: 131). Then, in early February 1965 Babu went to China just before Nyerere's first official visit to the country. Babu not only negotiated with the Chinese authorities a new US$ 14 million trade agreement, but discussed also the possibility for Peking to finance and build a railway line between Tanzania and Zambia. The project aimed at providing Zambia with an alternative route to the Indian

---

4　In February 1964 the Chinese government provided the new Zanzibar government with a US$ 14 million interest-free loan and a US$ 500,000 grant. *Countering Chinese Intrusion – Tanzania*, 18 May 1965, NARA II, General Records of the Department of State, Bureau of African Affairs 1958–1966, Box 34, Folder: Political Affairs and Relations: Tanganyika-Chicoms Affairs.

5　*Tanzania: Nyerere and His Problems*, Research Study, Bureau of Intelligence and Research, Department of State, 6 October 1973, NARA II, General Records of the Department of State, Subject Numeric Files, 1970–73, Political and Defense, Box 2617, Folder: POL.

Ocean, and reducing its economic dependence on the colonial and racist regimes of Southern Africa. Thus, during Nyerere's visit to China in late February 1965 the Chinese leaders raised the topic of the construction of the railway line between Tanzania and Zambia, and offered to finance and build it (Coulson 1982: 143).

In September 1967, after London and Washington had refused to finance the railway project because of its uncertain economic sustainability, and Kaunda had visited Peking, a tripartite agreement between China, Tanzania and Zambia was signed. The Chinese government committed itself to constructing the railway line and financing it through an interest-free loan of £ 160 million to Zambia and Tanzania. The two countries were to repay the debt over a thirty-year period (starting from 1983) (Hall & Peyman 1976: 100). The construction of the railway line, which had a total length of around 1,800 kilometres, began in 1970 and finished in 1974, one year before scheduled (Monson 2009: 35–70). In late 1973, it was estimated that 17,000 Chinese workers were employed in the construction of the railway line in Tanzania.[6]

While the presence of Babu in the Union government played a central role in fostering relations between Tanzania and China, the international repercussions of the revolution in Zanzibar indirectly helped to cement them.

After the formation of the Union, the government of West Germany raised with Nyerere the problem of the presence of the embassy of East Germany in Zanzibar. In accordance with the "Hallstein Doctrine", Bonn asked the Tanzanian government to order the closure of the embassy, or face the political consequences of Tanzania's diplomatic links with East Germany. The Tanzanian president tried to find a compromise solution. The embassy of East Germany in Zanzibar was closed, but an East German consulate was opened in Dar es Salaam. However, Bonn adopted an intransigent position, and in February 1965 it suddenly terminated its military cooperation with Tanzania. In response, Nyerere publicly denounced West Germany's blackmail and ordered the suspension of all West German cooperation activities in Tanzania (Pratt 1978: 140–141).

Relations between Tanzania and the Western countries further worsened in the mid-1960s after the expulsion of two US diplomats in early 1965 and the Tanzania's decision to break off diplomatic relations with London in December 1965 in protest against the British policy towards Southern Rhodesia's

---

6   *Airgram from American Embassy Dar es Salaam to Department of State*, 6 November 1973, NARA II, General Records of the Department of State, Subject Numeric Files, 1970–73, Political and Defense, Box 2016, Folder: POL.

Unilateral Declaration of Independence. In retaliation, the British government froze the disbursement of a £ 7.5 million loan already allocated to Tanzania, and in 1968 all British technical assistance to the country was terminated too (Pallotti 2009).

While in the short term China contributed to filling the void left by the suspension of West German and British aid to Tanzania by proving the latter with some limited military and economic assistance (while Canada started to train the Tanzanian army and air force (Godefroy 2012), Peking took over the training of the Tanzanian naval force, and offered the Tanzanian government a new £ 2 million loan together with a £ 1 million grant), in the longer term relations with China helped Tanzania to pursue its policy of non-alignment internationally, promote the liberation of Southern Africa from racialism and colonialism regionally, and implement the socialist development policy of *ujamaa* internally.

In the mid-1960s the deterioration in Tanzania's relations with the Western powers and the disappointing results of the development plans implemented by the government after independence pushed Nyerere to undertake an indepth reassessment of Tanzania's development strategy. In February 1967 the National Executive Council of TANU adopted the Arusha Declaration, a policy manifesto that committed the government to implementing *ujamaa*, a socialist development policy centred on the promotion of small-holder agriculture, state intervention in the economy, and self-reliance. As the American Embassy in Tanzania observed in the early 1970s, "*ujamaa* provides the nation-building mystique around which this country is organizing itself [and] is articulated by one of the most attractive and persuasive leaders in the Third World".[7]

While, as Lal remarked, "Tanzania and China shared a political language of anti-colonialism and self-reliance, and their domestic agendas both valorised the countryside as the primary site of economic and ideological transformation" (Lal 2014: 99), Nyerere was of the opinion that Tanzania "should be able to admire certain things which have been done in China, Russia, Korea, Yugoslavia, and so on, without assuming that any of these countries provide a model for us" (Nyerere 1968: 20). Besides some military aid (Mathews 1981: 155), Israel offered Tanzania some economic assistance (Peters 1992: 17). Thus, if relations with China represented a central pillar of Tanzania's non-alignment policy, during the 1970s Nyerere consolidated the latter by negotiating development

---

7   *Airgram from American Embassy Dar es Salaam to Department of State*, 19 January 1973, NARA
    II, General Records of the Department of State, Subject Numeric Files, 1970–73, Political and
    Defense, Box 2017, Folder: POL 12 TANZAN.

assistance programs with a wide number of bilateral and multilateral donors (Crouch 1987; Rugumamu 1997; Hyden & Mukandala 1999).

China actively promoted the economic development of Tanzania by funding and implementing some rural and industrial projects in the country. While agricultural projects such as the construction of the Ruvu State Farm and the Mbarali Rice Farm in Mbeya Region in the mid-1960s aimed at introducing modern production techniques and reinforcing food security in Tanzania, industrial projects such as the building of the Urafiki Textile Mill and the Ubungo Farm Implements Factory in Dar es Salaam in the late 1960s were meant to sustain the diversification of the national economy (Ping 1999; Brautigam & Tang 2012: 5–9). Moreover, since 1968 Chinese medical teams started working in both Tanzania Mainland and Zanzibar.

In the early 1970s Tanzania had become the largest recipient of Chinese aid in Africa.[8] Peking also emerged as the largest and most successful aid donor in Zanzibar,[9] not least because of the many practical difficulties the implementation of the Soviet, East German and Bulgarian aid programs encountered on the archipelago.[10] In the early 1980s, however, development cooperation between China and Zanzibar had almost come to an end, as "all the Chinese industrial projects had now been handed over to the Zanzibaris".[11]

When the military cooperation agreement with Canada expired in 1970, the Tanzanian government resolved not to renew it, apparently because the Canadian government had refused to provide sophisticated weapons to the Tanzanian army.[12] In this way, China could broaden its military cooperation with Tanzania. Since the early 1970s Peking not only trained the Tanzanian army, air force and naval force, but sold also some arms to the country.

The political and military cooperation between Tanzania and China was further strengthened by their shared commitment to the liberation of Southern

---

8   Department of State, Bureau of Intelligence and Research, *Tanzania: Nyerere and His Problems*, Research Study, 6 October 1970, NARA II, General Records of the Department of State, Subject Numeric Files, 1970–73, Political and Defense, Box 2017, Folder: POL.

9   *Airgram from American Embassy Dar es Salaam to Department of State*, 20 October 1972, NARA II, General Records of the Department of State, Subject Numeric Files, 1970–73, Political and Defense, Box 2016, Folder: POL 2 TANZAN.

10   *Airgram from American Consulate Zanzibar to Department of State*, 27 September 1968, NARA II, General Records of the Department of State, Subject Numeric File 1967–69, Box 2516, Folder: 17 TANZAN; *Airgram from American Consulate Zanzibar to Department of State*, 22 December 1969, NARA II, General Records of the Department of State, Subject Numeric File 1967–69, Box 2515, Folder: POL 15-1 TANZAN.

11   *High Commissioner's Visit to Zanzibar*, 6 June 1980, The National Archives of the United Kingdom, London (TNA), FCO 31/2878 (file 16).

12   *Hart to Holmes*, 21 April 1972, TNA, FCO 31/1295 (file 13).

Africa from racialism and colonialism, which according to the Americans "reflect[ed] a coincidence of goals, rather than necessarily an ideological compatibility".[13] Part of the Chinese military aid to Tanzania found its way to the Southern African liberation movements hosted in military camps in the country.

Since the early 1960s several Southern African national liberation movements, such as the Movimento popular de libertação de Angola (MPLA), the South West Africa's People Organization (SWAPO), the African National Congress (ANC), the Frente de libertação de Moçambique (FRELIMO), the Pan-Africanist Congress of Azania (PAC), the Zimbabwe African People's Union (ZAPU) and the Zimbabwe African National Union (ZANU) had established political offices, military training camps and refugee settlements in Tanzania. The country's role in the liberation of Southern Africa had been reinforced in 1963 by the decision of the Organization of African Unity to locate in Dar es Salaam the headquarters of the Liberation Committee it had created for coordinating Africa's assistance to the national liberation movements (Kisanga 1981).

Since "Nyerere [was] a fanatic on the question of Southern Africa's liberation",[14] relations with Tanzania "served the vital function of establishing and maintaining China's revolutionary credibility" internationally (Yu 1975: 39), and supported Peking in its competition with the Soviet Union for influence over the Southern African liberation movements.

More generally, the close ties with Tanzania, whose unorthodox socialist development strategy was seen with suspicion by the Soviet Union,[15] reinforced China's international projection and, in Nyerere's words, helped it "to break out from the isolation in which other nations were endeavouring to confine her" (Nyerere 1971[1973]: 328). In 1971 the large majority of the African governments voted for the recognition of Peking as the legitimate representative of China at the United Nations.

Although the Western governments saw with suspicion the relations between Tanzania and China, British and American diplomats shared the opinion

---

13   Department of State, Bureau of Intelligence and Research, *Tanzania and Zambia: Campaign against Southern Africa*, Research Study, 24 March 1971, NARA II, General Records of the Department of State, Subject Numeric Files, 1970–73, Political and Defense, Box 2016, Folder: POL TANZAN.

14   Central Intelligence Agency, *African Response to the Rhodesian Rebellion*, Intelligence Memorandum, 3 January 1966, NARA II, CIA Records Search Tool.

15   *Telegram from American Embassy Moscow to Department of State*, 9 October 1969, NARA II, General Records of the Department of State, Subject Numeric File 1967–69, Box 2514, Folder: POL 7 TANZAN.

that there was no evidence that "China has any direct influence or control over Tanzanian affairs",[16] or that "the Chinese [government] intend to exploit [its position in the country] by actively subverting Tanzania".[17]

Nyerere constantly rejected any accusation that Tanzania had abandoned non-alignment to side with the communist bloc in the Cold War. Time and again, Nyerere explained that after independence Tanzania had just "moved from [its] position as a member of the Western bloc, to the position where [it is] really independent in international affairs" (Nyerere 1971[1973]: 325). As the US State Department recognized, it was disingenuous to argue that Tanzania was a communist country because it accepted military aid from China and the Soviet Bloc for the Southern African liberation movements, since it was "Nyerere's commitment to the liberation of Southern Africa, rather than pro-communist leanings, that [had] caused him to accept massive aid from Communist China".[18] As the Tanzanian president remarked, since the "African state are not manufacturers of weapons" and "no country of the Western Bloc is willing to make arms available to the [Southern African] nationalist movements", the African governments were obliged to turn to "the Eastern Bloc and China [for help, as they] are willing to supply arms to these movements" (Nyerere 1976[2011]: 90).

2   From Crisis to New Cooperation Patterns

In the early 1980s the Tanzanian economy plunged into a dramatic crisis. Some observers argued that the causes of the economic crisis had to be found in the contradictions inherent in the government's development policy. According to Babu, "though the economy generated less and less revenue, the government expanded the welfare sector on borrowed money. [These] reckless populist policies [...] ruined the country almost irreparably" (Babu 1991a: 121–122). Others contended that external factors, and in particular the oil shocks, had a tremendous impact on the fragile economy of Tanzania (Bryceson 2015).

---

16   *Airgram from American Embassy Dar es Salaam to Department of State*, 3 April 1967, NARA II, General Records of the Department of State, Subject Numeric File 1967–69, Box 2517, Folder: POL TANZAN – US.

17   *The Chinese in Tanzania*, Diplomatic Report No. 254/72, 11 April 1972, TNA, FCO 31/1295 (file 1).

18   US Department of State, *Tanzania: Nyerere and His Problems*, Research Study, Bureau of Intelligence and Research, Department of State, 6 October 1973, NARA II, General Records of the Department of State, Subject Numeric Files, 1970–73, Political and Defense, Box 2617, Folder: POL.

When in the late 1970s the Tanzanian government approached the Western donors with an urgent request for financial aid, most of them refused to provide it with further assistance until it had committed itself to implementing an extensive economic reform program under the tutelage of the international financial institutions (Snook 1999: 95). However, negotiations with the IMF soon proved very difficult. While the IMF insisted on the need for the Tanzanian government to devalue the Tanzanian Shelling as a precondition for accessing new foreign loans, Nyerere accused the IMF of attempting to violate the sovereignty of Tanzania and stubbornly refused to devalue the Tanzanian Shelling (Edwards 2014: 96–101). As a consequence, relations with most Western donors soured in the first half of the 1980s. Only the Nordic countries continued to provide Tanzania with economic aid, but in the mid-80s they also decided to make the release of new grants conditional upon adoption of a structural adjustment program by the Tanzanian government in line with the demands of the IMF.

Together with the external pressures, the failure of the home-made economic reform programs that the Tanzanian government implemented in the early 1980s and the emerging divisions within the ruling party on how to solve the economic crisis pushed Nyerere to announce that he would not stand for re-election in 1985. The election of Ali Hassan Mwinyi, the president of Zanzibar, to the Union presidency opened the way to an agreement with the International Financial Institutions. The adoption of the neo-liberal Economic Recovery Programme in 1986 spelt the end of the *ujamaa* experiment, as the government committed itself to an extensive process of economic liberalization.

If the international financial institutions and Western donors played a crucial role in Tanzania's turn to neo-liberalism in the mid-1980s, after the end of the Cold War the Chama cha Mapinduzi (CCM), Tanzania's ruling party since independence,[19] retook the political initiative. In the early 1990s, CCM decided to abandon the one-party state system established in 1965 and to re-introduce multipartism before international pressures had forced it to do so. In this way, CCM controlled the pace and shape of the democratic transition in the country, and transformed itself from a single into a dominant party.

Starting in the late 1970s China also undertook a program of economic reforms that aimed at liberalising the internal market and attracting foreign direct investments (Samarani 2017). The economic reforms had a relevant impact on

---

19   CCM was formed in 1977 through the merger of the Tanganyika African National Union
      (TANU), in power on the Mainland since Tanganyika's independence in 1961, and the Afro-
      Shirazi Party (ASP), the only legal party in Zanzibar since the 1964 revolution.

China's development cooperation with the African countries. During the 1980s the Chinese government not only reduced its development aid to Africa, but also stressed "mutual development" as one of the main goals of its financial assistance to the continent. As the Chinese premier Zhao Ziyang explained during his visit to Tanzania in December 1982, from then on development cooperation with Africa would be guided by four principles: "equality and mutual benefits, stress on practical results, diversity in form, and common progress" (Brautigam 2009: 53). Finally, the rehabilitation of already concluded projects became a central component of the Chinese development policy on the continent.

Since the late 1980s the Chinese government embarked on a strategy of closer relations with the African countries, as it aimed at breaking through the international isolation caused by the events of Tiananmen Square (Taylor 2006: 4), and fostering its economic development. Africa rapidly became a critical source of primary commodities for the Chinese industries, and an export market for their manufactured goods. Trade between Africa and China recorded a dramatic increase (Dollar 2016), and Africa also became an important destination of Chinese investments. China's development aid to Africa also increased. In particular, the Chinese authorities used concessional loans and development aid as key instruments to strengthen economic and political cooperation with the African governments and create new business opportunities for the Chinese companies on the continent.

During the last decades the relations between China and Tanzania broadly followed the general pattern of Chinese-African relations. In the 1980s Peking provided Tanzania with very limited financial aid. China's assistance mainly focused on the rehabilitation of aid projects realized in the past. In 1983 Tanzania and China signed an agreement for the rehabilitation of around sixty development projects implemented in the previous decades (Brautigam 2009: 57). In the same year, the Zambian and Tanzanian governments asked Peking for help in the management of the TAZARA (ibidem: 83–85). Given Tanzania's and China's economic difficulties, the two countries negotiated a barter trade agreement in 1984 (Kamata: 2013: 91–92). In the early 1980s, also Chinese military aid to Tanzania significantly decreased.[20]

Contrary to claims that after the end of the Cold War Peking lost interest for Tanzania (Cabestan & Chaponnière 2016), during the 1990s relations between Tanzania and China entered a new phase, which was shaped by the realities of the post-Cold War international (dis)order and their national interests and priorities.

---

20   TNA, *Codrington to Heckle*, 1 September 1982, FCO 31/3672 (file 5).

In Southern Africa, after the demise of the apartheid regime, Peking developed close relations with South Africa, to the point that China insisted for Pretoria's inclusion within the BRICS countries (Pallotti & Zambernardi 2016). Moreover, Angola received a US$ 2 billion loan from China in 2004 and a second one of the same amount in 2007 to rehabilitate its infrastructure after a civil war of almost thirty years (Corkin 2015), and in 2016 it became China's first oil supplier.

During the last decades, in spite of the Chinese growing ties with other Southern African countries, relations between China and Tanzania continued to play a relevant political and economic role for the authorities of both countries. Thus, by constantly referring in their official speeches to the historical friendship between Tanzania and Peking, the Chinese leaders have tried to foster the memory of the role played by Peking in both the promotion of economic development and the fight against racialism and colonialism in Southern Africa, and to legitimize China's contemporary policy in Africa.

During his visit to Tanzania in February 2009, former Chinese president Hu Jintao mentioned the important role the cooperation between China and the African governments played in the decolonization of Southern Africa, and then stressed the fact that after the end of the Cold War the promotion of economic development had become the overarching goal of the Sino-African cooperation. In the words of Hu Jintao: "In the 1950s and 1960s, people of China and Africa fought shoulder-to-shoulder against the colonial rule in order to achieve national liberation on the African continent. (...) Now in this new century, we are working together to attain the Millennium Development Goals (MDGs) and bring about development (...) of China and Africa".

Hu Jintao further explained that the "New Chapter of China-Africa Friendship" that had opened in the early 1990s had been characterized by a growing economic interaction between China and the African continent. "China", Hu Jintao remarked, "will continue to promote trade with Africa, accommodate Africa's concerns as best as it can, and adopt preferential measures to increase imports from Africa. The Chinese Government encourages and supports the efforts of more and more established Chinese companies to invest in Africa, create more jobs for the local people and transfer more technologies to their African partners".[21]

---

21   Hu J., *Work Together to Write a New Chapter of China-Africa Friendship*, Speech delivered in Dar es Salaam, 16 February 2009, http://www.fmprc.gov.cn/mfa_eng/wjdt_665385/zyjh_665391/t538257.shtml (accessed on 24 October 2017).

Similar ideas were expressed by Chinese president Xi Jinping during his visit to Tanzania – tellingly, the first African country he visited after becoming president of China – in March 2013: "We each view the other's development as our own opportunity, and we each seek to promote the other's development and prosperity through closer cooperation". So, after paying tribute to the historical cooperation between China and Tanzania in the liberation of Southern Africa from racialism and colonialism, Xi Jinping added that: "China has worked and will continue to work with African countries to take concrete measures to properly address problems in our economic cooperation and trade, and enable the African countries to gain more benefits from the cooperation. At the same time, we sincerely hope that African countries will facilitate Chinese enterprises and citizens in their cooperation activities in Africa".[22]

On the Tanzanian government's side, relations with China help it to maintain a certain degree of political autonomy from the Western donors (Kamata: 2013: 94), reinforce its security apparatus (China is the largest provider of weapons to Tanzania) (Cabestan & Chaponnière 2016: 14), and also get the financial resources to pursue a development strategy that currently aims at promoting the industrialization of the country and reducing its dependence on the export of primary commodities to rest of the world and, unsurprisingly, to China. This economic strategy marks an incipient shift from the the Post-Washington Consensus to a new development vision (strongly influenced by the Chinese experience), which calls for "a more proactive state [that brings] economic transformation forward" (Wuyts & Kilama 2016: 319). Within the context of Tanzania's predominant party system (Pallotti 2017a), the success of this development vision would inevitably strengthen the political legitimacy of the ruling party and its control over Tanzania's state and society.

Since the early 1990s economic relations between Tanzania and China rapidly intensified. The fast expanding Tanzanian economy (in the period 2007–2014 the Tanzanian economy recorded an annual average growth rate of 6.5%) attracted the interest of the international investors and the Chinese business community. In 2016 China accounted for the largest share of Tanzania's imports (33,9%). As the value of Tanzania's exports to China was US$ 317 million and the value of Tanzania's imports from China amounted to US$ 3,5 billion, in 2016 China recorded a consistent trade surplus with Tanzania. Moreover, while Tanzania mainly exports primary commodities to China, the latter exports

---

22   Xi J., *Trustworthy Friends and Sincere Partners Forever*, Speech delivered in Dar es Salaam, 25 March 2013, http://www.fmprc.gov.cn/mfa_eng/wjdt_665385/zyjh_665391/t1027951. shtml (accessed on 24 October 2017).

primarily manufactured products to Tanzania.[23] As a consequence, the structure of trade between the two countries tends to reinforce Tanzania's dependence on the export of primary commodities (Moshi & Mtui 2008: 16).

During the last two decades Chinese investments in Tanzania have also recorded a dramatic increase. According to some estimates, in 2016 the stock of Chinese investments in Tanzania exceeded US\$ 6,2 billion (The Guardian 2017). Chinese companies are active in the manufacturing sector (Brautigam 2009: 209), in agriculture (Brautigam 2015: 102–106), in services and trade, and also play a relevant role in the building of infrastructures. Peking has vigorously supported the expansion of Chinese economic interests in Tanzania, to the point that recently the World Bank warned the Tanzanian government that "while the increased economic ties [with China] have resulted in increased economic growth, they have also increased Tanzania's vulnerability to downturns in China's business cycles" (World Bank 2016: 19). In 2013 EXIM Bank provided the Tanzanian government with a US\$ 1.3 billion loan for the construction of a gas pipeline from Mtwara to Dar es Salaam. The pipeline, which was built by the China Petroleum Technology and Development Corporation, was officially inaugurated in October 2015 (The Guardian 2016). In 2013 the Tanzanian government signed a US\$ 10 billion agreement with China Merchant Holding International and Oman's State General Reserve Fund to build a new port and a Special Economic Zone in Bagamoyo (The Guardian 2017a).

Tanzania's need for financial resources to fund its infrastructure development programme has not translated into a passive attitude towards the foreign donors in general, and China in particular. In early 2017 Tanzanian president John Magufuli cancelled a US\$ 9 billion contract signed by his predecessor, Jakaya Kikwete, with a consortium of Chinese companies to build a new railway line between Dar es Salaam and Western Tanzania because of irregularities, and then turned to the Turkish government for a new concessional loan to build the railway line (The East African 2017).

During the last decades Peking has also provided limited financial aid to Tanzania. As in most other African countries, the delivery of Chinese aid aimed at fostering cordial relations between Peking and Tanzania and reinforcing a positive image of China in the eyes of the local population. The Chinese government has supported some small-scale agricultural development projects in the country (Brautigam & Tang 2012: 9–17), has built the new Tanzanian parliament in Dodoma and a new stadium in Dar es Salaam, and in 2016 announced

---

23   All trade data are taken from the Atlas of Economic Complexity. See: http://atlas.cid.harvard.edu/.

the intention to donate a new US$ 40 million library to the University of Dar es Salaam.

3   Conclusion

Contrary to the prevailing view within the international relations literature of the African governments as weak and passive actors of the international system, this essay has shown that the Tanzanian government has always maintained a high degree of autonomy in its relations with China.

While soon after independence the Tanganyikan government established diplomatic relations with China, it was only after the revolution in Zanzibar and the creation of the Union that the consolidation of relations with Peking became a priority of the Tanzanian government. During the Cold War China critically supported president Nyerere's development vision and foreign policy. The political, military and economic cooperation with Peking helped the Tanzanian government to implement its development plans, strengthened the country's non-alignment, and contributed to the liberation of Southern Africa from racialism and colonialism.

While in the early 1980s the cooperation with China did not prevent Tanzania from experiencing a serious economic crisis that brought about the end of *ujamaa* (but did not seriously endanger CCM's uninterrupted rule in the country), after the end of the Cold War trade between Tanzania and China rapidly increased and the Chinese investments in the country surged to unprecedented levels. Today, the Chinese concessional loans to the Tanzanian government also play a crucial role in financing the realization of the latter's development vision, with its emphasis on economic diversification and industrialization.

Although the close ties with China have contributed to accelerate Tanzania's economic growth and helped the Tanzanian government to diversify its sources of development assistance, some limits and contradictions have clearly emerged. On the one side, it remains to be seen how far China will go in supporting the industrialization of Tanzania, given its need for raw materials, and what impact the Tanzanian growing debt with China will have on the economic prospects of the country. On the other side, there is a risk that, contrary to expectations, the Tanzanian government's development policy will heighten the (already visible) contradiction between the high rates of economic growth and the pervasive poverty in the country. This pattern of "growth without prosperity" (Lewis 2008) would further erode CCM's political legitimacy, and would put at risk its already uncertain commitment to democratization.

Bibliography

Amin, S. (1973). *Neo-Colonialism in West Africa*. New York: Montly Review Press.

Ayittey, G. (1998). *Africa in Chaos*. New York: St. Martin's Press.

Babu, A. (1991). "The 1964 Revolution: Lumpen or Vanguard?', pp. 220–249, in Sheriff, A. and Ferguson, E. (eds.) *Zanzibar Under Colonial Rule*. London: James Curry.

Babu, A. (1991a). 'The Limits of Populist Nationalism: The Case of Tanzania', in Campbell, H. and Stein, H. (eds.) *The IMF and Tanzania*. Harare: Sapes Trust.

Bailey, M. (1975). 'Tanzania and China'. *African Affairs*, 74: 39–50.

Bayart, J.-F. (2000). 'Africa in the World: A History of Extraversion', *African Affairs*, 99: 217–267.

Bjerk, P. (2011). 'Postcolonial Realism: Tanganyika's Foreign policy under Nyerere, 1960–1963', *International Journal of African Historical Studies*, 44: 215–247.

Bond, P. (2006). *Looting Africa*. London: Zed Books.

Brautigam, D. (2009). *The Dragon's Gift: The Real Story of China in Africa*. Oxford: Oxford University Press.

Brautigam, D. (2015). *Will Africa Feed China?*. Oxford: Oxford University Press.

Brautigam, D. and Tang, X. (2012). 'An Overview of Chinese Agricultural and Rural Engagement in Tanzania', January, https://deborahbrautigam.files.wordpress.com /2014/02/brautigam_china-in-tanzania.pdf.

Brown, W. and Harman, S. (2013), 'African Agency in International Politics', pp. 1–15, in Brown, W. and Harman S. (eds.) *African Agency in International Politics*, London: Routledge.

Bryceson, D.F. (2015). 'Reflections on the Unravelling of the Tanzanian Peasantry, 1975–2015, pp. 9–36, in Ståhl, M. (ed.) *Looking back, Looking ahead – Land, Agriculture and Society in East Africa. A Festschrift for Kjell Havnevik*. Uppsala: Nordiska Afrikainstitutet.

Cabestan, J.P. and Chaponniére, J.R. (2016). *Tanzania-China All-Weather Friendship from Socialism to Globalization: A Case of Relative Decline*. Stellenbosch: Centre for Chinese Studies, University of Stellenbosch, http://www.ccs.org.za/wp-content/up loads/2016/05/CCS_DP_1_2016_TANZANIA-CHINA-ALL-WEATHER-FRIENDSHIP-FROM-SOCIALISM-TO-GLOBALIZATION.pdf.

Callaghy, T. (1995). 'Africa and the World Political Economy: Still Caught Between a Rock and a Hard Place', pp. 41–68, in Harbeson, J. and Rothchild D. (eds.) *Africa in World Politics*. Boulder: Westview Press.

Coulson, A. (1982). *Tanzania. A Political Economy*. Oxford: Clarendon Press.

Crouch, S. (1987). *Western Responses to Tanzanian Socialism, 1967–1983*. Aldershot: Avebury.

Dollar, D. (2016). *China's Engagement with Africa. From Natural Resources to Human Resources*. Washington, D.C.: Brookings Institution.

Edwards, S. (2014). *Toxic Aid. Economic Collapse and Recovery in Tanzania*. Oxford: Oxford University Press.

Glassman, J. (2011). *War of Words, War of Stones: Racial Thought and Violence in Colonial Zanzibar*. Bloomington: Indiana University Press.

Godefroy, A. (2012). 'The Canadian Armed Forces Advisory Training Team Tanzania 1965–1970', *Canadian Military History*, 11: 31–47.

Hall, R. & Peyman, H. (1976). *The Great Uhuru Railway. China's Showpiece in Africa*. London: Victor Gollancz.

Harbeson, J. and Rothchild, D. (1991). 'Africa in post-Cold War International Politics: Changing Agendas', pp. 1–15, in Harbeson, J. and Rothchild D. (eds.) *Africa in World Politics*. Boulder: Westview Press.

Hentz, J. (2001). *Reconceptualizing US Foreign Policy: Regionalism, Economic Development and Instability in Southern Africa*. Basingstoke: Palgrave Macmillan.

Hoskyns, C. (1968). 'Africa's Foreign Relations. The case of Tanzania', *International Affairs*, 44: 446–462.

Hutchison, A. (1975). *China's African Revolution*. London: Hutchinson.

Hyden, G. & Mukandala, R. (eds.) (1999). *Agencies in Foreign Aid*, London: Macmillan.

Jackson, R. & Rosberg, C. (1986). 'Sovereignty and Underdevelopment: Juridical Statehood in the African Crisis', *Journal of Modern African Studies*, 24: 1–31.

Kamata, N. (2013), 'Perspectives on Sino-Tanzanian Relations', in Adem S. (ed.) *China's Diplomacy in Eastern and Southern Africa*. Aldershot: Ashgate.

Khadiagala, G. and Lyons, T. (2001). 'Foreign Policy Making in Africa: An Introduction', pp. 1–13, in Khadiagala, G. and Lyons T. (eds.) *African Foreign Policies. Power and Process*, Boulder: Lynne Rienner.

Kisanga, E.J. (1981). 'Tanzania and the Organization of African Unity (O.A.U.)', pp. 97–122, in Mathews, K. and Mushi S. (eds.) *Foreign Policy of Tanzania, 1961–1981. A Reader*. Dar es Salaam: Tanzania Publishing House.

Lal, P. (2014). 'Maoism in Tanzania. Material Connections and Shared Imaginaries', pp. 96–116, in Cook A. (ed.), *Mao's Little Red Book. A Global History*. Cambridge: Cambridge University Press.

Lee, M. (2006). 'The 21st Century Scramble for Africa', *Journal of Contemporary African Studies*, 24: 303–330.

Langdon, S. and Mytelka, L.K. (1979). 'Africa in the Changing World Economy', pp. 165–191, in Legum, C., Mytelka, L., Zartman, I.W. and Langdon, S. (eds.) *Africa in the 1980s. A Continent in Crisis*. New York: McGraw-Hill.

Lewis, P. (2008). 'Growth without Prosperity in Africa', *Journal of Democracy*, 19: 95–109.

Mathews, K. (1981). 'Tanzania and the Middle East', in Mathews, K. and Mushi S. (eds). *Foreign Policy of Tanzania, 1961–1981. A Reader*. Dar es Salaam: Tanzania Publishing House.

Mkandawire, T. (1999). 'Crisis Management and the Making of Choiceless Democracies', pp. 119–136, in Joseph R. (ed). *State, Conflict and Democracy in Africa*. Boulder: Lynne Rienner.

Monson, J. (2009). *Africa's Freedom Railway: How a Chinese Development Project Changed Lives and Livelihoods in Tanzania*. Bloomington: Indiana University Press.

Moshi, H. and Mtui, J. (2008). 'Scoping Studies on China-Africa Economic Relations: The Case of Tanzania', Nairobi: AERC, http://dspace.africaportal.org/jspui/bit stream/123456789/32075/1/Tanzania-China.pdf.

Nyerere, J.K. (1968). 'Introduction', in Nyerere, J.K., *Freedom and Socialism – Uhuru na Ujamaa*, Dar es Salaam: Oxford University Press.

Nyerere, J.K. (1971) [1973]. 'Ten Years after Independence', in Nyerere, J.K., *Freedom and Development – Uhuru na Maendeleo*. Dar es Salaam, Oxford University Press.

Nyerere, J.K. (1976) [2011]. 'Nationalism in Southern Africa', in Nyerere, J.K., *Freedom and Liberation*, Dar es Salaam: Oxford University Press.

Pallotti, A. (2009). '*Post-colonial Nation-building and Southern African Liberation: Tanzania and the Break of Diplomatic Relations with the United Kingdom, 1965–1968*'. *African Historical Review*, 41: 60–84.

Pallotti, A. (2016). '*La rivoluzione mancata. Zanzibar tra autoritarismo e povertà*', pp. 149–171, in Pallotti, A., Tornimbeni, T. and Zamponi M. (acd). *Sviluppo rurale e povertà in Africa australe. Le sfide del millennio*, Soveria Mannelli: Rubbettino.

Pallotti, A. (2017), 'Tanzania and the 1976 Anglo-American Initiative for Rhodesia'. *Journal of Imperial and Commonwealth History*. 45: 800–822.

Pallotti, A. (2017a). 'Lost in Transition? CCM and Tanzania's Faltering Democratisation Process'. *Journal of Contemporary African Studies*. 35: 544–564.

Pallotti, A. and Zambernardi, L. (2016). 'Twenty Years After: Post-Apartheid South Africa, the BRICS and Southern Africa', pp. 220–239, in Pallotti, A. and Engel, U. (eds). *South Africa after Apartheid: Policies and Challenges of the Democratic Transition*. Leiden: Brill.

Peters, J. (1992). *Israel and Africa. The Problematic Partnership*. London: British Academic Press.

Ping, A. (1999). 'From Proletarian Internationalism to Mutual Development: China's Cooperation with Tanzania, 1965–95', pp. 156–201, in Hyden, G. and Mukandala R. (eds). *Agencies in Foreign Aid: Comparing China, Sweden and the United States in Tanzania*. New York: St. Martin's Press.

Pratt, C. (1978). *The Critical Phase in Tanzania 1945–1968. Nyerere and the Emergence of a Socialist Strategy*. Oxford: Oxford University Press.

Ravenhill, J. (1985). *Collective Clientelism. The Lomé Conventions and North-South Relations*. New York: Columbia University Press.

Rocha, J. (2007). 'A New Frontier in the Exploitation of Africa's Natural Resources: The Emergence of China', pp. 15–34, in Manji, F. and Marks S. (eds), *African perspectives on China in Africa*. Cape Town: Fahamu.

Rugumamu, S. (1997). *Lethal Aid. The Illusion of Socialism and Self-reliance in Tanzania*. Trenton: Africa World Press.

Samarani, G. (2017). *La Cina contemporanea. Dalla fine dell'impero a oggi*. Torino: Einaudi.

Shaw, T. and Grieve, G. (1978). 'The Political Economy of Resources: Africa's Future on the Global Environment', *Journal of Modern African Studies*, 16: 1–32.

Smith, K. (2012). 'Africa as an Agent of International Relations Knowledge', pp. 15–34, in Cornelissen., S., Cheru, F. and Shaw T. (eds). *Africa and International Relations in the 21st Century*. Basingstoke: Palgrave Macmillan.

Snook, S. (1999). 'As Agency under Siege: USAID and its Mission in Tanzania', pp. 68–115, in Hyden, G. and Mukandala, R. (eds). *Agencies in Foreign Aid*. London: Macmillan.

Southall, R. (2009). 'Scrambling for Africa? Continuities and Discontinuities with For-mal Imperialism', pp. 1–35, in Melber, H. and Southall, R. (eds). *A New Scramble for Africa: Imperialism, Investment and Development in Africa*. Scottsville: University of KwaZulu-Natal Press.

Taylor, I. (2006). *China and Africa: Engagement and Compromise*. London: Routledge.

Taylor, I. and Williams, P. (2004). 'Introduction: Understanding Africa's Place in World Politics', pp. 1–22, in Taylor, I and Williams P. (eds). *Africa in International Politics. External Involvment on the Continent*. London: Routledge.

The East African (2017). 'Tanzania's Turn to Turkey for SGR Funds Leaves China in Limbo', 30 January, http://www.theeastafrican.co.ke/business/Tanzania-SGR-fun ds-/2560-3793116-m75574/index.html.

The Guardian (2016). 'Mtwara-Dar Gas Pipeline Cost Soars to 3 Trillion', 25 April, http:// www.ippmedia.com/en/news/mtwara-dar-gas-pipeline-cost-soars-3-trillion.

The Guardian (2017). 'Chinese Firms' Investment in Tanzania Exceed USD 6,62bn', 24 April, http://www.ippmedia.com/en/news/chinese-firms'-investment-tanzania-ex ceed-usd662bn.

The Guardian (2017a), 'Bagamoyo Port Project now Revived', 24 November.

World Bank (2016). 'The Road Less Travelled: Unleashing Public Private Partnerships in Tanzania', Tanzania Economic Update, 8. Dar es Salaam: World Bank.

Wilson, A. (1989). *US Foreign Policy and Revolution. The Creation of Tanzania*. London: Pluto Press.

Wuyts, M. and Kilama, B. (2016). 'Planning for Agricultural Change and Economic Transformation in Tanzania', *Journal of Agrarian Change*. 16: 318–341.

Yu, G. (1975). *China's African Policy. A Study of Tanzania*. New York: Praeger.

Zartman, I.W. (1967). 'Africa as a Subordinate State System in International Relations', *International Organization*, 21: 545–564.

CHAPTER 21

Relations with the West: The Case Study of the EEC-USSR, as Viewed by the Community (1950–1991)

Giuliana Laschi

The initial process of European integration was greeted with profound hostility by the Soviet Union, fundamentally provoked by ideological motives and related to the two-sided confrontation and the Cold War (Rey 2005, Gori & Pons 1996). Such opposition is hardly surprising as the Soviet Union had been hostile to any form of European cooperation and unity from as early as September 1914, when Lev Trotskii published "The War and the International" (Piccardo 2015). European unity had to be opposed because it would strengthen Western capitalism and support transatlantic relations. Yet over time this clear early opposition started to mute, until during the Gorbachev era the view had become explicitly positive and west European cooperation was considered almost as a model to emulate. Despite high initial expectations however, following the implosion of the Soviet Union relations between Russia and the European Union have become uncertain (Piccardo 2012). Nevertheless, relations between the USSR and the EEC have developed and are an interesting case study of the difficult rapport between the two Cold War blocks.

A diachronic reading of EEC/EU-Soviet relations shows us the variety and changeability that has developed over the decades, well beyond the now outdated narrative of two blindly opposed blocs. Over the decades many attempts were made to bring them closer and these attempts often reverted to rigid opposition. It is interesting to note, however, that relations between Europe and the Soviet Union were direct, despite attempts by the US to strictly control them. The complexity of these relationships is often undervalued by contemporary international observers and prevents us from fully understanding current relations between Russia and the EU. Historical analysis shows the full complexity of these relations, providing multiple interpretative tools.

One of the main objectives of this chapter is precisely to create a link between current relationships and the history that produced them. The superficial reading that simply sees two opposing blocks, in which Europe disappears completely, is no longer convincing. Indeed, in this chapter the different national positions of the European Community member countries are analysed, in particular France and Germany, returning to Europe its actual role in the international sphere.

This alternating relationship has naturally been reflected in the geo-political sphere, with a move from a strong, common European identity, despite differences,[1] to a full and manifest alterity. Until the fall of the Berlin Wall the separation and contraposition were clear, yet reference to a shared identity, anchored in the geographical location within Europe, was frequent. Indeed, being part of the same sub-continent created a substantial closeness that was not only geographic, but also political. Khrushchev, above all, continuously referred to this common European identity and the fact of cohabitation on the same sub-continent in an effort to create a split, or at least a crack, in Western Europe's relations with the United States. He underlined, by contrast, a natural convergence of interests, especially regarding peace and peaceful coexistence. Moreover, geography may indicate a European Russia, though only half of the State falls within Europe, divided as it is by the Urals that form the natural boundary of geographical Europe. Yet the two areas are undoubtedly linked by history and especially their cultures, whether literature, art or, music, undoubtedly share common roots.

It is particularly interesting to note how the sense of a common identity was present and alive until the fall of the Berlin Wall. Yet the collapse of the Wall seems to have created an abyss, a truly profound cleavage. One of the aims of this chapter is to attempt to understand how the integration process actually reinforced this split, both in the diplomatic sphere and at the level of bilateral relations between the Member States and the USSR, and between the latter and the Community as a whole. Many scholars have analysed the issue of relations between the Community and the USSR solely within the context of the Cold War, thus taking for granted the existence of a lasting and irresoluble cleavage. Furthermore, most of Cold War historians awarded a residual role to the integration process, consequently adopting a more Atlantic than European geopolitical vision. Instead, while it is true that after 1917 a split was created and increased, thus necessitating a defensive cordon, historical relations and primarily the fact of belonging to the same continent have given rise to a complex situation influenced by the areas' proximity. In the following pages I will try to understand how the Community and its member countries interpreted

---

1   From the earliest attempts to define the geographical spaces and identity of Europe, reference was made to Russia, albeit clearly opposed at the political level. See European Union Historical Archives -ASUE, European Parliamentary Assembly, Session documents, "Report presented on behalf of the Political and Institutional Committee on Membership and Association to the Community", Rapporteur: Willi Birkelbach, 15 January 1961. See also Foucher 1998.

and reacted to the Soviet opposition to the Common Market, how they used this opposition in an ideological way and how they have tried to overcome it to achieve better relations. France stood out among the Member States as being the true leader of the Community in its first twenty years, though by the early 1960s it had been flanked by an increasingly-strong Germany. Archival research, especially in the historical archives of the French Ministry of Foreign Affairs regarding the Embassies of Moscow and Brussels, has enabled us to investigate in depth the relations between the USSR and Western Europe. Although these relations were complex, they remained present and important and were underpinned by a greater desire for détente and dialogue than the Cold War historians have previously shown. For reasons of security, but also of contiguity, identity and for economic motives, the Member States shared the goal of strengthening détente and cooperation on the European continent; they laboured, however, against a backdrop of total opposition and contrast promoted through the Soviet media.

The beginning of greater cooperation between the six states of western Europe that commenced following the Schuman declaration of 9 May 1950, pleased neither Stalin nor his entourage. Yet Stalin's initial reactions to the Schuman plan, and then through the beginning of the integration process, were rather bland. In fact, he believed that these attempts at economic cooperation were destined to failure as any such cooperation could not be achieved in capitalist countries. Yet by the time of the founding of the European Coal and Steel Community (ECSC) and the European Defence Community (EDC), Soviet opposition to the European project was already clear and definitive (Zubok 1996). Not surprisingly the EDC was the target of the harshest criticism as it was considered to be the West's attempt to re-arm Germany against the countries of the communist bloc.[2] Thus, when seeking an interlocutor on the western side, the Soviets attempted dialogue with France, which was the country that had most to fear from German rearmament (Soutou & Hivert 2008).

In the first years after Stalin's death, the concept of peaceful coexistence, the search for peace and the need to halt western rearmament began to dominate Soviet international political discourse. Security was therefore at the heart of the USSR's European policy (REY 1997: 121–136) and the Warsaw Pact of 1955 was presented to the world as a reaction to western aggression (Kennedy-Pipe 1995).

---

2 For a more in-depth analysis of the Soviet position on the EDC see AHMAE, Amb. Moscou, 448PO/B/78, "Text du jour, Déclaration du Ministère des Affaires étrangères de l'URSS sur le reject de la CED par la France (9 septembre 1954), 11 septembre 1954.

The Soviet Union clearly opposed the signing of the treaties of Rome, as expressed in the document *On the creation of the Common Market and Euratom,* known as the *17 theses on the Common Market* (Leonardi 1977: 185). The Communities were defined as the extension of the US imperialist will to control Europe, a slavish expression of American capitalism; essentially nothing of the new Communities was exempt from criticism. The integration process was not interpreted as an attempt at pacification at least in Western Europe, but rather as a tool to enable the economic recovery and rearmament of Federal Germany. Soviet opposition was the expression not only of an ideological barrier, but also of their deep fear that the integration process could strengthen the European West.

Yet Soviet experts in European politics believed that this experiment was destined to early failure due to the many divergences and contrasts among the Member States. This would be a short-lived pacifist project. Nevertheless, it was still an iniquitous project because it was piloted by the United States and as such it had to be resisted as much as possible.

In the 1960s the Gaullist position regarding Europe's role in the international panorama dominated in the Community. Europe was to have a powerful role, free of excessive pressure from the United States, and necessitated an increase in political strength, obviously at an intergovernmental level, that would permit greater investment in European security, including atomic power (Laschi 2015). This position prevailed not because it was shared by all the European partners, and certainly not by the Benelux countries[3] or with the overtones of "grandeur" to which De Gaulle aspired, but because the leading position of De Gaulle's France prevented other forms of international policy. While France foresaw the Community developing into a sort of confederation, the Benelux countries aspired to an increasingly supranational community.[4] These positions were therefore irreconcilable, both at a national and international level. The only position shared by all the Member States in that period related to Eastern Europe (Winand et al. 2015): greater openness and a new détente were necessary both for political and economic reasons, but above all for the security of Western Europe.

At the same time the USSR considered Germany to be the core of European politics and the Federal Republic of Germany was therefore the focus of Soviet

---

3   The following secret document is interesting: AHMAE-Nantes, RP, 122PO/D/136,"Incontro tra Couve de Murville e M. Spaak", Bruxelles, 1 May 1961.

4   On the position of the Belgian Foreign Minister Wigny, who was said to love "European mystic": AHMAE-Nantes, RP, 122PO/D/136, Reports of the French Ambassador to the Minister of Foreign Affairs, on 19 and 21 September, 23 and 26 November 1960.

action as it attempted to win it over and separate it from the other western powers in the European Community. The goal was that of a Germany at the centre of a pacified European system and an international system based on peace, détente[5] and peaceful coexistence in line with the main elements of Leninist doctrine (Roberts 1999). Most of the documents of the French Ministry of Foreign Affairs referring to the thinking and actions of the Soviet Union in the early 1960s, essentially relate to these main objectives and to the absolute predominance of the concept of peaceful coexistence. Khrushchev devoted much of his activity on the domestic front to the goal of describing such relations with Western Europe. It was also the key theme of his first speech broadcast on Soviet radio and television on 1 June 1961, in response to the report Kennedy had made to the Americans after the Vienna talks. It was a profound innovation in the use of communication tools that surprised both Westerners and the Soviets: it was the first time that he had addressed the people directly without the intermediation of the party organs and the state.

The content was much less innovative than the form of communication: according to the Soviets the Westerners did not want to disarm because the monopolies were unwilling to give up the huge profits that the arms race produces for them. For the Soviet Union it was already clear in the early 1960s that the European Community had no economic objectives, but "under the direction of Hallstein, this organization had rapidly appeared as a direct link to the political integration of Europe."[6] And this was the real danger for Soviet supremacy on the European continent.

1   The Years of Confrontation

The early sixties saw a reaction by the Soviet Union to the development of the Common Market and to the process of European integration, and the attempt by the USSR to give a rational and incontrovertible form to the distortions caused by the EEC. The Community was portrayed as an economic tool of NATO, of its neo-colonialist policy; a market managed by monopolies, an autarchic block, with an agricultural policy that favoured only large property

---

5   In the AHMAE-Nantes 448PO/B/76 e 77 files there are many documents on détente as the main objective of the Soviet Union towards Europe. An interesting document in 76 of 1956 specifies the content and objectives of this policy. In ibidem, from the chargé of French affairs in the USSR to the French Foreign Minister Pinay, "De la politique de détente envisagée du point de vue soviétique", 3 Janvier 1956.

6   AHMAE-Nantes, Ambassade Moscou, 448P/B/314, Diplomatie Paris, "Le Marché commun et le réarmement allemande", 3 aout 1962.

holders.[7] Furthermore, it was an imperialist economy that increased unemployment and exploited the workforce. Thus, a wide-ranging critique that took the form of an all-out attack backed up by press campaigns.

One of the most important attacks launched by the USSR was conducted with a virulent press campaign to coincide with the first British application for entry to the Community. On this occasion, in the period from the summer of 1961 and throughout 1962, the Soviet press orchestrated a vast campaign claiming that Great Britain was merely a tool of American imperialism. In fact, this line was then taken up by European public opinion and mentioned several times by De Gaulle himself. The British application was described as a kind of capitulation and the interventions of the Member States during the negotiations underlined the indignity of acceptance. The challenging work of diplomacy and the so-called Monnet method were portrayed by the Soviet press as an internal struggle of the imperialist states for the conquest of power.[8]

Soviet hopes that the EEC might implode were dashed by the results achieved throughout the early 1960s in which the young Community began to shape its first common policies: the trade and agricultural policies. With the former, the Commission assumed the mandate to negotiate autonomously for the six Member States, accelerating the move towards integration. The Common Agricultural Policy founded in 1962, after an exhausting round of negotiations, was established in a completely supranational way. Characterized by the openness of the internal market, and robust tariff protection towards those outside, it projected the image of a strong Community in search of a powerful international role. This image was soon strengthened by early clashes on agriculture with the American allies. In 1962 Soviet information and propaganda responded by upping the heat, multiplying interventions both in the specialized press and in widely circulated newspapers: not only was the Community born, but it was developing and strengthening.[9]

According to European diplomacy, Soviet criticism was undeniably ideological and unacceptable: "The doctrinal approach to the problems posed by the Common Market is unbending, most of the articles start by repeating a number of statements of principle: the EEC is the modern incarnation of

---

7   The most complete document is in AHMAE-Nantes, Ambassade Moscou, 448PO/B/313, Commission de la Communauté economique européenne, Principales critiques sovietiques à l'egard du marché commun et reponses, Octobre 1962.

8   In all the files present at the AHMAE-Nantes of the Embassy of Moscow, there are many documents that report (also verbatim, actual translations) articles of the Soviet press on the EEC. But on this period see in particular the file 448P/B/314.

9   AHMAE-Nantes, Amb. Moscou, 448P/B/314, "La presse soviétique et le Marché Commun", 8 aout 1962.

imperialism, whose guideline is that of dictatorship, the use of force, slavery, inequality and of monopoly privileges. The economy of the Common Market is largely directed towards the objectives of war and remains the infrastructure of NATO."[10]

Whenever an opportunity arose, the Soviet Union tried to divide the Member States. For example, during a meeting in the summer of 1964 between the Italian foreign minister and Khrushchev, the latter tried to convince his counterpart of the necessity for Italy to leave the European Economic Community.

The crisis of the Community was emphasized by Pravda in a very long article by Maievski on 11 November 1964, which analysed the reasons that had led the Western powers to this stalemate. The article once again presents the familiar themes of the aggression of the Atlantic block as against the peaceful policies of the USSR. However, a new theme is introduced: that of the British membership application to the Common Market and, therefore, a possible opening to the American monopolies. The only positive comments in the analysis concerned the policy implemented by General De Gaulle, his vetoing of the British application and the reaffirmation of what the article defined as "Euro-Gaullism" against the Atlanticism of the other five Member States.[11] The enlargement of the Community, and the success that made it attractive, was naturally fought as far as possible by the Soviet Union. The danger was twofold: on the one hand, the strengthening of the European West through the extension of the boundaries of the Community and the single market, on the other hand the highlighting of the Community's undeniable capacity to drive the economic development of its Member States. Interventions in the press and by political leaders as well as Soviet diplomacy continued to increase throughout the 1960s, in an attempt to discredit the policy of Community enlargement.

In addition to passive reactions to enlargement as seen in the case of Great Britain, the Soviet Union also tried to dissuade some European countries from association or membership of the Community. This occurred in the case of Austria which had approached the Community in 1964 with a view to association,[12] but then decided to desist to avoid compromising its neutrality and relations with Eastern Europe. In some cases, this abandonment took on apocalyptic tones, as reported in an exchange of information between the

---

10   Ibidem, p. 5.

11   AHMAE-Nantes, Ambassade Moscou, 448P/B/314, Telegramme "Diplomatie Paris", Moscou 12 novembre 1964.

12   On the modalities and objectives of the tool of association with the Community, in which Austria was fully included, see Historical Archives European Commission-Brussels, BAC 1/1971, n. 19/2, Considérations sur les principes d'une politique d'association de la Communauté, Bruxelles, 30 avril 1960.

Austrian and French Embassies: an association agreement between the Community and Austria could be interpreted by the USSR "as a step towards a new *Anschluss*. The close economic interdependence between Austria and the Federal Republic constitutes, with the common language, clear indicators in the eyes of the Soviets and it is unclear how we might reassure them."[13] The Soviet concern was such as to fear that this was just the first step towards a German recovery of aggressive *grossdeutsch* aims towards central Europe, starting with Czechoslovakia.[14] This concern obviously had repercussions on the policy of the six Member States that consequently put a brake on the negotiations to avoid exacerbating tension with the Soviet Union. Moreover, the attack launched by the USSR, including that of the media, was very strong as evidenced by a statement from the TASS agency of March 1963, which indicated the reasons for Soviet opposition to Austria's association: "The Common Market is an appendix of NATO; led by West Germany and France, it is an unequal group that does nothing to hide its political and military objectives. The Treaty of State, which prohibits *Anschluss*, would be violated."[15] Basically, it was considered an act against the neutrality of Austria, which the Soviet Union intended to respect as laid down in the Treaty. This statement is undoubtedly among the most explicit on Moscow's position towards Vienna. In this case, Soviet pressure proved decisive and prompted the Austrian government to desist from association to the Community which, for its part, appeared unwilling to open an international dispute over respect for Austrian neutrality.

The non-association of Austria, as well as the French decision to prevent the Community's first enlargement, prompted Professor Arzoumanian, defined by the French ambassador in Moscow as the leading Russian specialist on the European Community, to publish a long article in Pravda on the failure of the common policy.[16] The article, entitled "The crisis of imperialist integration", was published just a few days after the meeting in Brussels of the communist parties of the six Member States where they discussed strategies to counter the economic and military integration of Western Europe. The development of the Community had produced a clash between the Western imperialist

---

13 AHMAE-Nantes, Ambassade Moscou, 448P/B/314, telegramme Diplomatie Paris, Moscou 4 aout 1964. In the same file, many other documents report the negative opinion and concern of the USSR in view of a possible association of Austria to the Community.

14 AHMAE-Nantes, Ambassade Moscou, 448P/B/314, Embassy of Prague to the Minister of Foreign Affairs, "association of Austria to the common market", Prague, 3 aout 1964.

15 AHMAE-Nantes, Ambassade Moscou, 448P/B/314, Diplomatie Paris, 2 mars 1963.

16 The article was published on 8 and 9 March 1963 on Pravda. See AHMAE-Nantes, Ambassade Moscou, 448P/B/314, From the Ambassador in Moscow De Jean to Minister Couve de Murville, "Article de Arzoumanian sur le Marché commun", 16 Mars 1963.

monopolies: with Great Britain, but also with the United States, which had not initially understood that the EEC would create serious problems for the American economy. Moreover, America was in decline as the communist doctrine had predicted, foreseeing that after reaching the peak of its power a downward trend would begin in 1961. Although America remained the strongest capitalist power, Europe was by no means a simple appendage as it had been at the end of the Second World War. Despite this, the process of integration was certainly not what the "bourgeois ideologues" wanted people to believe, namely that an international organization of monopolies could manage to "breathe new life into a decrepit and dying system and that it could tip the scales on the side of capitalism in the competition with the socialist system". It was now evident that the Common Market exacerbated the contradictions between "the bourgeois monopolists of the imperialist countries and weakened the position of capitalism towards socialism". These positions were not easy to argue in the midst of the economic boom being experienced by the six members of the European Community.

In addition to these instruments of dissuasion, the Soviets also tried to make a positive change by creating an alternative project to which they asked Western Europe to adhere. From 1960, they began working on a pan-European ideal.

2   Openings and State Visits

The Community had greeted the changes made by Khrushchev, i.e. the important swing in foreign policy aimed at establishing stronger relations with the West, with a mixture of optimism and scepticism. In the early 1960s this need contrasted with the persistence of very weak and tense relations, made especially complex by the fallout from the Berlin crisis and the prolonging of the German problem. The division of Germany and Berlin was actually the tip of an iceberg; however, for both the Soviets and the West it was beginning to appear as overwhelming and disastrous for Europe. The Soviet perception of the European Community, therefore, underwent a radical transformation. Moreover, it was now clear that the Community was consolidating and despite Soviet forecasts, economic integration was becoming increasingly dynamic and successful, as evidenced by the birth of the Common Agricultural Policy (CAP). Thus, in December 1962, Khrushchev decided to radically evolve his thinking on the EEC and published an article in "Kommunist" in which, for the first time since 1957, he recognized the "vitality" of the Community (Bertoncini et al. 2008).

This change was also the result of the deepening of relationships with Western European leaders. In this regard, Khrushchev's state visit to France from 23 March to 3 April 1960 is of great interest. According to most European newspapers the effects of this visit, like other visits by Soviet leaders, strengthened European politicians while the Soviets did not cut a great figure. In this case, the press emphasized the dominance of General De Gaulle, while Khrushchev appeared to have little influence even on the French Communist Party partly, it was claimed, due to the verbosity of his public interventions, especially the radio and television broadcast he made before departing. His speech was indeed lengthy and dull and far removed from European-Western standards. On the Soviet side, of course, the political outcomes were instead emphasized on several occasions, "in every word spoken by the head of the Soviet government, people felt the immense power of truth,"[17] as Pravda stressed. Thus, the reading of the meaning and results of the visit differed, seen more as a comparison of opposing stances than any effective strengthening of relationships.

Khrushchev had presented the visit during the meeting of the Supreme Soviet on 14 January 1960, explaining the need to express solidarity with the French people, who had fought a major war of resistance against Nazism, and to pay tribute to the eminent role of France in both culture and the sciences.[18] During their stay, the Soviets travelled briefly through France, and learnt something of French policies in the industrial, agricultural, scientific and cultural sectors. They also had the opportunity to meet the representatives of various French economic, political and cultural circles. Some themes touched upon by Khrushchev were taken up favourably by De Gaulle and had a positive effect, especially the Soviet people's desire for peace and the unwillingness on both sides of the Iron Curtain to engage in aggression. Naturally their visions diverged radically when Khrushchev spoke of the inevitable universal extension of communism. No mention was made, even in passing, of the European Economic Community; indeed, Khrushchev avoided speaking of it even during his meetings with the French trade unions.

A joint communiqué was issued at the end of the visit, together with the announcement of trade and cultural agreements and atomic energy cooperation for peaceful purposes. The importance of the visit was also demonstrated by the numerous influential figures accompanying Khrushchev, such as Minister of Foreign Affairs Gromyko, the vice-president of the Council of Ministers, the head of the Atomic Energy Directorate, in total about a dozen political

---

17   The words of Pravda of 4 April are reported in AHMAE-Nantes, Embassy in Moscow, 448PO/B/135, "Visit of Khrushchev to France", 23 April 1960.

18   Ibidem.

heavyweights. What caused a sensation and produced politically divergent reactions, was the size of the entourage accompanying Khrushchev at the ex-
pense of Soviet citizens: in addition to the 10 major figures, he brought his wife
and four children and 43 other people, including service staff and 13 guards. Of
course, the tabloids and the more strongly anti-communist press went to town
on this in all the Member States. As was to be expected, on his return to the
USSR Khrushchev recounted the experience of his visit to the Soviet people,
reunited en masse in Lenin stadium on 4 April.

An important turning point that aroused great attention was De Gaulle's
visit to the Soviet Union, preceded by that of Couve de Murville in 1965. It was
a visit that caused a sensation and had enormous media coverage throughout
Europe and within the Community. On the one hand, there were high expectations for a political and economic opening which was certain to produce extraordinary results for all the countries of the Community. At the same time,
however, the visit created considerable fear and anxiety, because many worried that De Gaulle's visions of "grandeur" could distance France from its Community partners and from the whole of the European West. The newspapers of
the six Member States followed each aspect of the visit with great interest.[19]
Firstly, the psychological significance of the event was highlighted: "the primary result of the visit that General De Gaulle is making to the USSR is psychological. The Kremlin has succeeded, thanks to its willingness to stage the event,
in creating a climate that has never been seen during previous visits by western
heads of state […] because De Gaulle is De Gaulle and the circumstances seem
favourable, the event has taken on the dimensions of history."[20]

Apart from the exaggeration of the importance of this visit, it surely represented also De Gaulle's desire to send a signal to his European partners in the
Community, which was recently emerging from a deep crisis marked by the
stance of De Gaulle himself, the so-called "empty chair crisis". De Gaulle made
it clear that European interests were not the only ones that France was developing and that his country maintained a prominent international role and had
by no means disappeared from the international system. The warning was directed particularly to Germany, which was not to imagine itself as the only
player to maintain an interest in Central and Eastern Europe.

Surprisingly in the 1960s, a complex modification of the concept of integration was advanced by the Soviet intellectual elite that from 1965 onwards began

---

19   A file on the visit is present in AHMAE-Nantes, AHMAE-Nantes, RP-Bruxelles,
      122PO/D/136. In addition to extensive documentation it also contains a rich European
      press review.
20   "Le Soir" of 27 June 1966.

to converge around the Academy of Sciences Institute of the World Economy and International Relations (IMEMO). The Academy rejected the idea that the process of integration was only a creation of capitalism aimed at strengthening and consolidating this system, as had always been argued by the Soviet Union. Instead it was a project that united the peoples of Europe and their States in a common project; it was essentially an evolution of capitalism itself, but it also contained a drive for deep union (Baranovsky 1994: 61–62).

A setback to the opening of possible dialogue between the EEC and the USSR was produced by the Soviet reaction to the Prague Spring (Van Ham 1993), as had occurred following the 1956 revolt in Hungary (Békés 2016). "The entire press underlines the considerable regression in the policy of détente caused by the occupation of Czechoslovakia. This signals the downfall of all efforts towards bringing the two blocs closer."[21] The Member States accused the Soviet government of irresponsible and reckless behaviour, leading to the strengthening of the two military blocs and undermining the peaceful coexistence on which the USSR had insisted since 1956, thereby jeopardizing all the progress made by international cooperation. Indeed, the armed reaction to the Prague Spring had abruptly halted the many outcomes of European and Soviet diplomacy, which during the 1960s had led to the signing of a range of agreements of a primarily cultural and scientific nature.[22]

All the reactions in Brussels were strongly negative, to the extent that the Councillor of the Soviet Embassy had to pay an urgent visit to the French Councillor to clarify the nature of the USSR's military intervention with the other Western allies as well. However, the reasons put forward by the Councillor proved to be so realist and so totally unacceptable that both the French Embassy and public opinion as a whole were even more shocked by the unusually bloody repression. Moscow's intervention was justified not through what is known as *jus gentium*, but by an ideological and strategic stance that envisioned Moscow as the guardian of socialism and thus determined the impossibility of allowing a liberal regime to be installed in Czechoslovakia, heralding an unacceptable "contamination".[23] The decision to intervene so abruptly had prevented the occurrence of greater risks and above all that of a propagation of Germany's action against the USSR to the satellite countries.

---

21   AHMAE-Nantes, RP Bruxelles, 122PO/D/133, Report on the reaction of the Belgian press, 22 August 1968.

22   Cultural agreement between Belgium and Hungary of 11 February 1965.

23   AHMAE-Nantes, RP Bruxelles, 122PO/D/133, Embassy Report of 9 September 1968.

3   European and International Détente

The 1970s brought significant changes in relations between the Community and the Soviet Union, because these were the years of détente, both at a global level thanks to the moves of the United States brought about by Nixon and Kissinger, and at a European level in line with the desires of most of the Western European countries and expressed most strongly in the Ostpolitik of German Chancellor Brandt (Loth, Gorbachev 2005: 45–59). For the Europeans détente was not only desirable from the political and ideal point of view, but much more interesting for the Community than the sharp clash of the Cold War. For the EEC Member States such an approach was also fundamental for their security because they lacked sufficient means to resist a possible military threat from the Soviets: "we must therefore work towards détente and cooperation, with prudence and vigilance."[24]

Détente was also the only possibility that the Community's Member States had to measure their strength independently of the United States and to signal autonomy from their great allies, because dependence weighed heavily particularly in the early 1970s. In the words of Pompidou: "Quand M. Brejnev m'a demandé à Moscou si l'Europe pouvait se dégager de l'influence américaine, je lui ai répondu: cela dépend surtout de vous et de votre attitude."[25]

By the late 1960s and early '70s the choice of a strategy of détente on the European continent had become focused and reinforced, especially following Nixon's unilateral cancellation of the direct international convertibility of the United States dollar to gold. "Europe's problem is that of its relations with the United States and with the East."[26] As regards the East, Western Europeans wanted détente and the development of trade, partly because it was evident that in the event of a threat from the communist area, they would be unable to resist Soviet military power with their own means. Détente was thus an integral part of the active defence policy of the Community's Member States. It was a strategic requirement for the Community, to be sought with caution and constancy. Détente and cooperation with the East were also necessary steps to regain full independence as Europeans, because the economic, cultural and,

---

24   Archives Historiques du Ministère des Affaires Etrangères Francoise-Nantes (AHMAE), Ambassade Bruxelles, Minutes of the meeting between the President of the French Republic and the Belgian Prime Minister on 25 May 1971, 4 June 1971. A very interesting document on the relationship between the EEC and the USA and the need for détente in Europe.

25   Ibidem.

26   AHMAE-Nantes, RP, 122PO/D/136, Minutes of the meeting between the President of the French Republic and the Belgian Prime Minister, Brussels, 25 May 1971.

obviously, military influence of United States on the continent was excessive.[27] "Each of the six countries certainly does what it can". This attempt to redefine an area of European autonomy, especially at the level of defence, did not imply a counterposition to the United States, on which Europe was still largely dependent, rather it encompassed the need to reaffirm the European identity and that "Europe exists, distinct from the rest of the world and exists as such."[28] In an ever-changing international system, European security was firmly on the agenda and security on the continent needed to be strengthened through détente and the development of social, intellectual, economic, scientific and political relations with Eastern Europe. Yet vigilance remained high because the Soviet Union "may be compared to Etna; it tends to advance where it finds empty spaces in its path."[29]

The United States was reassured on several occasions and at the same time Nixon repeatedly reaffirmed American support for a strong Western European community, although this created considerable problems in US trade: "the political advantages of a solidly established European Community dominate over all other considerations."[30] Not only that, Nixon also reaffirmed the political importance of Western European cooperation and of its expansion through enlargement. At the same time, the Six claimed that the European integration policy was indispensable to détente.[31]

On the other hand though, neither Nixon nor, to a greater extent, Kissinger liked European détente and they asserted their right to make political and international choices in the bipolar sphere.

The whole Community focused considerable attention on Pompidou's visit to the Soviet Union in September 1970, which reassured Westerners facing the possible fear that Germany would acquire a privileged role in Russian diplomatic relations with the West.

---

27   The following explanation given by the Belgian Prime Minister Harmel: "The king asked me yesterday what we depend on America for; I answered: everything; in the space of one or two years, the habits, the customs pass from one shore of the Atlantic to the other; American civilization imposes itself on our continent; the large American companies established in Europe control a considerable part of the European economy". Ibidem.

28   Ibidem.

29   AHMAE-Nantes, RP, 122PO/D/136, Minutes of the meeting between the President of the French Republic and the Belgian Prime Minister, Brussels, 25 May 1971.

30   AHMAE-Nantes, AHMAE-Nantes, RP, 122PO/D/136, Azores Conference, strictly confidential, 22 December 1971.

31   "Pompidou adds that the consolidation of a united Western Europe is an indispensable element for the policy of détente and agreement with the East, for which we have taken the initiative". Ibidem.

Brezhnev's visit to France, in November 1971 also aroused much interest.[32] It was widely considered to be a true diplomatic success that led to positive political and economic results. A common declaration of principle was signed; this document was of extreme importance, especially for the Soviets, because it represented a precedent in their relations with non-communist countries. Nevertheless, France had succeeded in conducting the negotiations without in any way compromising the solidarity of the Western world, as the Soviets would have liked.

In the 1970s, in the wake of the German agreements, the other members of the EEC also began a rapprochement towards the Eastern European countries and the number of visits and commercial and cultural agreements multiplied. In 1973, moreover, the Member States of the EEC signed mutual recognition treaties with the German Democratic Republic and the respective Embassies were opened simultaneously, marking an epochal change in the relations between the two Europes divided by the Iron Curtain and hence crowning continental détente.[33] Although no shared strategic choice existed on this issue, there were frequent meetings between the nine Ambassadors in Brussels, both to inform each other of developments in individual relations, and to attempt an approach that if not actually common, was at least concerted.

While the action of the German Federal Republic had paved the way towards the resumption of relations between the two sides divided by the Iron Curtain, the Helsinki Conference had strengthened the desire for relations and peaceful coexistence (Romano 2009). The importance of the Conference for the process of European integration and for the external action of the Community has been underlined by historians, above all because on this occasion the Nine were able to act with a strong commonality of ideas and political objectives and to speak with a single voice, as they almost never had before or were to do again. For the European Community and its conception of foreign policy and the international system, détente was essential. Based on military balance, it was to create an atmosphere of stability, necessary for a constant political dialogue between the two blocs in Europe. Détente aimed to secure a situation in Europe, and in the world, that excluded war as a solution to international controversies and its success depended on the degree of peaceful coexistence guaranteed by states belonging to different political systems. The

---

32   A whole file is dedicated to this visit and there are many interesting documents that analyze the visit and the declarations of the Secretary General of the Soviet Communist Party and of the main French and European leaders. In AHMAE-Nantes, AHMAE-Nantes, RP, 122PO/D/136.

33   Extensive documentation in AHMAE-Nantes, RP-Bruxelles, 122PO/D/231.

cardinal principles of détente were peace and security and cooperation and there would be no development unless these were assured. For the Community, the final act of the Helsinki Conference thus became a set of rules to be followed to create an international system based on the political rights and objectives pursued by the Community itself.

In fact, although this détente was of limited duration, it did create a space of interesting relations between the two Europes on each side of the Iron Curtain and between the EEC and the Soviet Union, which as mentioned above, culminated in the Helsinki Accords in 1975 (Rey 2008).

Brandt's foreign policy, which set in motion the actual process of détente in Europe, was questioned not only by the United States, but also created strong suspicion in Europe, mainly because of the positive reaction of the Soviet Union. The fear was that once Germany resumed its role as an international power, it might choose a closer concord with the USSR and could even aim for the German reunification that had always been supported by the communist camp[34] but would have compromised the success of the Community in which Germany would have assumed a hegemonic role. One solution to this extremely risky situation was Britain's accession to the European Community that would counterbalance Germany's power and prevent it from gaining too much economic and political space that the other Member States, especially the small Benelux countries, would never have been able to control.

In an attempt to clarify the German position and reassure the other members of the Community, various political leaders made a series of interventions. One such was the president of the parliamentary group of the Federal Social Democratic party Erler, who held a conference in the prestigious Flemish circle of Brussels. While expressing criticism towards Ulbricht, he spoke of the need to attempt a resolution of the German problem and stated that for such an outcome the best interlocutor was the Soviet Union. At the same time, he spoke positively about Poland, which explained the later decision to resume trade. The direct attack was on the trade bloc against the countries of Eastern Europe, which he considered not only inappropriate, but also meaningless.[35]

In 1972, the year in which the EEC decided on its first enlargement and set up the European currency snake to respond in a communitarian form to the financial shock created by Nixon's declaration ending dollar convertibility,

---

34   Along these lines the article signed by Charles Rebuffat in the Belgian newspaper "le Soir" of 30 November 1968, entitled "Le meme bateau".

35   AHMAE-Nantes, Ambassade Bruxelles, 122PO/D/133, Conference de M. Erler, 19 Mars 1965.

Brezhnev recognized the right of the EEC to work and to proceed in a positive way despite being a grouping of capitalist countries.

In fact, the 1970s marked a period of change in diplomatic relations between the Community and the USSR. While until then relations had been mainly bilateral, the 1970 Davignon Report proposed a European Political Cooperation project (EPC), laying the foundations for Community members to speak with a single voice on foreign policy. In fact, regular meetings were held by the foreign ministers of the Member States to adopt coherent and common policies.[36]

The Soviet Union no longer had any interest in disavowing the economic development of the EEC, given its desire to escape the economic stagnation that had affected the Soviet Union since the mid-1960s. The USSR was in search of trade and transfers of technology, and this explains the increased interest in the EEC and the fact that economic exchanges between the USSR and the Community saw significant growth. In the years 1971–74, the proportion of Soviet trade with the EEC rose from 8.5% to 16%. Thus, together with the softening of ideological barriers, important economic and commercial interests increased, ensuring that the dialogue established during détente was maintained despite any international tensions that might arise.

4   Conclusion

This rapprochement between Western Europe and the Soviet Union did not, however, resist the resumption of the Cold War in the years 1979–81 and there would be no full détente again until Gorbachev came to power (Zubok 1996). His ascent, in fact, marked a new phase in Soviet politics, aimed at moving beyond the politics of the opposing blocs and working on both parts of Europe, to start a process that would lead to the construction of the "Common European Home" (Spetschinsky 2005). The scope of the European Community is broad in this project, since the most natural rapprochement would have been between Comecon Member States and those of the European Community. This was Gorbachev's approach in supporting the joint declaration of June 1988, which established official relations between the two bodies. Gorbachev increased his positive vision of the role of the EEC from late 1988, when he clarified that the project for rapprochement was not to be based solely on respect for the differences but based rather on the very values that until then had

---

36   Bulletin of the European Communities. November 1970, n° 11. Luxembourg: Office for Official Publications of the European Communities. "Davignon Report (Luxembourg, 27 October 1970)", p. 9–14.

been ascribed to Western Europe, namely respect for human rights and democracy based on political pluralism. This was therefore a radical change of
position: from the refusal of the integration process to the recognition of the
EEC as a bearer of values to be shared. Important treaties were signed in this
new perspective: in December 1989 a first agreement on trade and economic
cooperation and in November 1990 the signing of the treaty of reduction of
conventional weapons in Europe and the Charter of Paris for a New Europe.

The position of Gorbachev was maintained by Boris El'tsin who repeatedly
referred to the European characteristics of Russia in public speeches, until the
entry into force in 1997 of the partnership and cooperation agreement between
the EU and Russia. The agreement, which was signed during the Corfu European Council in June 1994, was of great strategic and political importance,
since it defined Russia and the European Union as "strategic partners" and entered into force with the end of hostilities with Chechnya, in December 1997.[37]
The preamble of the agreement even made reference to "the importance of the
historical links existing between the Community, its Member States and Russia
and the common values that they share", while a full resumption of relations
was indicated among the final objectives and the aim "to provide an appropriate framework for the gradual integration between Russia and a wider area of
cooperation in Europe". Based on the respect for human rights established at
Helsinki, full political consultation, increased trade and investment and economic cooperation were hoped for. In the same year, the Treaty of Amsterdam
introduced the common strategies and new policy tools for joint action between the EU and Russia.

With the election of Putin to the Russian presidency in 2000 (Dundovich
2005), Russian policy towards the European Union changed again, though not
immediately in a direct and formal manner. The first obvious symptom was the
non-renewal of the ten-year partnership agreement, because Putin showed no
interest in such close relations with the Union. Moscow showed a similar lack
of enthusiasm for the European Neighbourhood Policy launched during the
Prodi Commission in 2002 to bring Europe closer to Russia and the former Soviet Republics. Russia's subsequent foreign policy choices have further distanced the European sub-continent's two powers mainly because of tensions
in the former Soviet area, which had repercussions in Russian-European relations, especially from 2008 onwards and the Russian conflict with Georgia that
followed the invasion of Ossetia, which had proclaimed independence.

---

37   Official Journal of the European Communities, L 327, vol. 40, 28 November 1997, Agree-
      ment on Partnership and Cooperation establishing a partnership between the European
      Communities and their Member States and Russian Federation.

In an attempt to prevent new wars and international tensions in the area, the EU launched the Eastern Partnership with Azerbaijan, Belarus, Georgia, Moldova and Ukraine. It was precisely the request for ratification of this agreement that triggered the Ukrainian crisis of 2013–14. The difficulties that followed, also in Crimea, have complicated the situation between the European Union and Russia and the EU is unable to propose particularly stringent policies or common strategies, partly because of the divisions and the detached position of the Russians.

Relations between Europe and Russia through the EEC and the EU have therefore been complex and unstable, but both sides have sought to maintain relations, considering them fundamental for their foreign policy. The Community, which was inevitably caught up in the Cold War though it tried to emancipate itself in order to develop both politically and economically, has sought a privileged interlocutor in the USSR and Russia, by starting from those parts of Eastern Europe from which it was dramatically split in the aftermath of the Second World War. Like the Soviets, the Europeans have also used the two-sided confrontation to render the process of European integration indispensable or at least very important. However, at the same time they have sought stronger relations that would allow the European continent to develop economically and to create a level of independence from the United States. An autonomous relationship, therefore, between the Community and the USSR, which goes beyond the simple constraints imposed by the Cold War and the super powers, and in which Europe has played a leading role.

Bibliography

Baranovsky, V. (1994). 'The European Community as seen from Moscow: rival, partner or model?', pp. 61–62, in N. Malcolm (ed.), *Russia and Europe: an end to confrontation*, London: Burn & Oates.

Békés, C. (2016). 'Hungary, the Soviet Bloc, the German question and the CSCE Process, 1965–1975', *Journal of Cold War Studies*, 18(3): 95–138.

Bertoncini, Y., Chopin, T., Dulphy, A., Kahn, S. and Manigand, C. (eds.) (2008). *Dictionnaire critique de l'Union européenne*. Paris: Armand Colin.

Dundovich, E. (2005). 'Goodbye Europa: la Russia di Putin e il difficile rapporto con Bruxelles', *Studi urbinati di scienze giuridiche politiche ed economiche*, 3: 539–547.

Foucher, M. (1998). *The Geopolitics of European Frontiers*. London: Pinter.

Gori, F. and Pons, S. (eds.) (1996). *The Soviet Union and Europe in the Cold War, 1943–53*. London-New York: MacMillan.

Kennedy-Pipe, C. (1995). *Stalin's Cold War: Soviet Strategies in Europe, 1943 to 1956.* Manchester: Manchester University Press.

Laschi, G. (2015). *L'Europa e gli altri. Le relazioni esterne della Comunità dalle origini al dialogo Nord-Sud.* Bologna: Il Mulino.

Leonardi, S. (1977). *L'Europa e il movimento socialista. Considerazioni sui processi comunitari: CEE e COMECON.* Milano: Adelphi.

Loth, W. (2005). 'Mikhail Gorbachev, Willy Brandt, and European Security', *Journal of European Integration History*, 11(1): 45–59.

Piccardo, L. (2012). A*gli esordi dell'integrazione europea. Il punto di vista sovietico nel periodo staliniano.* Pavia: Polo interregionale di Eccellenza Jean Monnet di Pavia.

Piccardo, L. (2015). 'Le relazioni tra Unione Europea e Federazione russa: collaborazione o competizione?', pp. 140–150, in Belluati, M. and Caraffini, P. (eds.), *L'Unione europea tra istituzioni e opinione pubblica.* Roma: Carocci.

Rey, M.-P. (1997). 'L'URSS et la sécurité européenne des 1953 à 1956', *Communisme*, 49–50: 121–136.

Rey, M.-P. (2005). 'Le retour à l'Europe? Les décideurs soviétiques face à l'intégration ouest-européenne, 1957–1991', *Journal of European Integration History*, 11(1): 7–27.

Rey, M.-P. (2008). 'The USSR and the Helsinki Process, 1969–1975. Optimism, doubt or defiance?', pp. 65–81, in Wenger, A., Mastny, V., Nuenlist, C. (eds.), *Origins of the European Security System: The Helsinki Process Revisited, 1965–75,* London: Routledge.

Roberts, G. (1999). *The Soviet Union in World Politics. Coexistence, Revolution and Cold War, 1945–1991.* London: Routledge.

Romano, A. (2009). *From Détente in Europe to European Détente. How the West Shaped the Helsinki CSCE.* Brussels: Peter Lang.

Soutou, G.-H. and Hivert, E.R. (2008). *L'URSS et l'Europe de 1941 à 1957.* Paris: PUPS.

Spetschinsky, L. (2005). 'De la «maison commune européenne» aux espaces communs euro-russes. Une idée au cœur des bouleversements de la scène européenne de 1985 à nos jours', *Journal of European Integration History*, 11(1): 61–81.

Van Ham, P. (1993). *The EC, Eastern Europe and European Unity: Discord, Collaboration and Integration since 1947.* London-New York: Pinter.

Winand, P., Benvenuti, A. and Guderzo, M. (2015). *The External Relations of the European Union.* Bruxelles: Peter Lang.

Zubok, V. (1996). 'The Soviet Union and European Integration from Stalin to Gorbachev', *Journal of European Integration History*, 2(1): 85–92.

CHAPTER 22

Postface: Europe's Response to Challenges from China and Russia

Michael Leigh

China and Russia are widely perceived as deploying a range of instruments, from military force to investment and disinformation, to achieve political and economic goals and to influence opinion in Europe and the United States. Some have described this kind of multifaceted power projection, rather flatteringly, as "sharp power" (Walker & Ludwig 2017).

European Union (EU) policy makers and analysts need to consider carefully the distinct challenges and opportunities posed by current Chinese and Russian initiatives. This postface compares challenges to Europe posed by the two countries and draws attention to asymmetries between them. It concludes by suggesting principles that could guide European countries and the EU in responding to these challenges.

1 China and Russia Unpacked

Both countries possess daunting but fundamentally different geopolitical attributes – size, location, population, resources – which bring diverse strengths and weaknesses. Both have authoritarian systems rooted in national and Leninist traditions, though Russia maintains the semblance of competition for power among different political parties. Both are in the grip of personality cults, recalling those of the Cold War years. The rule of law is weak in both countries, frustrating many of their own citizens and discouraging all but the most avid international investors, attracted by Russia's raw materials and by China's large market as well as its, hitherto, low cost labour market.

Both countries possess nuclear weapons, are permanent members of the United Nations Security Council and draw on historical awareness and experiences that are different from our own and condition their view of the world. For Russians, encirclement in the Cold War happened yesterday. The invasions and vast destruction by Napoleon and Hitler, both western rulers, are part of the fabric of memory; they are not forgotten in the mists of history.

© KONINKLIJKE BRILL NV, LEIDEN, 2020 | DOI:10.1163/9789004428898_023

The Chinese live with the memory of colonialism and unequal treatment by western countries. Both view the United States, and to some extent Europe, as adversaries, intent on weakening their sovereign rights by military, political, psychological or economic means. Both see European countries as rivals for influence, access to resources and business opportunities around the world but also, for the present at least, as a source of technology, know-how and management skills. Chinese and Russian leaders are dissatisfied with the international status quo and seek to change it in their favour.

Chinese and Russian representatives speak as though they have history on their side, while they see Europe and the west as in decline. Before 2008 some Chinese viewed the EU as a welcome partner in building a more multipolar world; now they see it as a shaky mechanism for managing decline. Like Russia, they seek mainly to influence national capitals rather than EU institutions in Brussels and Strasbourg. China and Russia both increasingly project power beyond their own borders, by different means, and to different degrees, and are a troubling presence within our own societies.

The Chinese are investing in infrastructure, technology, telecommunications and other strategic sectors of our economies on a massive scale. They offer inducements to regional groups, involving NATO and EU countries, such as the 16+1 meetings between China and Central and Eastern European countries, which began in 2014, with a headquarters in Budapest (China-CEEC 2017). A scarcely remarked "China-Regional Leaders" meeting took place in Northern Ireland in December 2017, while public attention was focused on the Brexit negotiations.[1]

This meeting, the third such, based on an agreement between former British Prime Minister David Cameron and President Xi Jinping in 2015, was followed by the announcement the following month that Mr Cameron would himself take a leadership role in an investment fund set up to support China's "Belt and Road" initiative (Feng & Mance 2017). Mr Cameron had been widely criticised, as prime minister, for ignoring broader strategic interests and human rights issues in pursuit of commercial advantage.

Like former German Chancellor Gerhard Schröder, Mr Cameron laid the groundwork while in office for a subsequent position boosting commercial links with a country widely viewed as an adversary. He was excused from respecting the normal "decent interval" – of two years – after leaving office, before taking up his new post (Malnick 2017), to much criticism. Conservative members of the German parliament described Mr Schröder's appointment in

---

1   See The Executive Office: https://www.executiveoffice-ni.gov.uk/news/northern-ireland-ho sting-prestigious-china-summit-milestone-relationship.

2017 as Chairman of Rosneft, the Russian oil company, which is under EU and US sanctions, as reprehensible (Foy & Chazan 2017). Thus, both China and Russia see advantages in poaching ex-leaders of major European countries to reinforce their business interests. This has had the active or tacit support of the German and British authorities.

So, China and Russia, each in their distinct manner, currently seek to exercise military, political, economic and "sharp" power to influence outcomes in Europe. In their dealings with China and Russia, European governments need to balance more carefully strategic, political and commercial interests as well as the protection of interests rooted in values.

There is a growing awareness in Europe that interests and values largely coincide, in the protection of a rules based international economic order. The corrosive effects of ignoring rules, standards and principles, in international economic relations are quite quickly felt close to home. This is particularly the case for the European Union for which a principled approach to foreign and security policy was treated for decades as an existential issue. Yet the 2015 migration crisis, and the rise of "populism" in Europe, is now testing the EU's commitment to this and has given rise to such contortions as "principled pragmatism" (Global Strategy 2016) to describe the EU's "global strategy".

2   New Narratives

Beijing and Moscow are developing new strategic narratives to mobilize support at home and abroad. In the case of China these narratives include, principally for domestic consumption, "Xi Jinping Thought on Socialism with Chinese Characteristics for a New Era", which sets the Chinese leader on a pedestal along with Mao Zedong and Deng Xiaoping, and the "Belt and Road Initiative", which is a euphemism for China's will to geopolitical and economic pre-eminence. The current Chinese President's personality cult has been reinforced by moves to put aside current term, and implicitly, age limits on the top positions he occupies (Bader 2018).

Russia's narratives are far less compelling. A current favourite in Russian policy circles is the "Great Eurasia" in which China and Russia are depicted as equal partners in building a geopolitical model that will dominate the 21st century. Sergei Karaganov, veteran Russian policy adviser, academic and polemicist puts it this way:

> We (Russia) and China are the main providers of security in the world today. We have warded off a war in Europe by upsetting plans on Ukraine. In Syria we have stopped, among other things, a series of colour revolutions

that had destabilized huge regions. China is providing economic security; we are providing military-strategic security. Unfortunately, there are almost no other security providers. Europe is increasingly focused on itself, while Americans are destabilizing the world in an apparent bid to shirk the responsibility they assumed, for they think that this responsibility costs them too dearly and imposes too many restrictions upon them.

KARAGANOV 2017

Both Moscow and Beijing are busy projecting narratives of themselves as rising powers. However, only the Chinese narrative has some credibility while the Russian version rings hollow. China is indeed a rising power that will pose major challenges to the West throughout the 21st century. But Russia, despite its nuclear weapons, is a declining power by almost any measure. Its proclivity for cyberwar, fake news, regional conflict and interference in democratic electoral processes disguises strategic weakness and is at worst an irritation to western countries.

Mr Karaganov and other Russian representatives affect to be surprised and flattered that Europeans and Americans attribute to Russia almost devilish skill in interfering with their own political systems and are ready to spend public money countering disinformation. Europeans should not play into the hands of Russian leaders by talking up the threat from disinformation and fake news. At the same time, they should take firm measures where there is a genuine threat to strategic national interests.

The Chinese tell the Russians that the "belt and road" initiative is a "win-win" strategy for both. But Russia is the junior partner and raw materials provider in this relationship. Chinese investors will only provide finance to Russia for major infrastructure projects in exchange for bargain basement access to Russian resource assets. China has recruited Russia as an advocate of the initiative, to attract other participants, such as India, which hesitates because of bilateral differences with China. In return, China supports Russia's foreign policy stance, whenever this does not conflict with its national interests, and President Xi shows Mr Putin the respect that few in the West are ready to accord.

European observers do not take the Eurasian narrative seriously but see it as a way of papering over the growing inequality between China and Russia. Russia's share of global GDP is set to fall from 3.68% in 2012, at purchasing power parity, to 2.84% in 2022. Over a similar period, China's share is set to rise from 15.18% to over 19.76%.[2] The Russians are struggling to be taken seriously,

---

2   See Statista: https://www.statista.com/statistics/270439/chinas-share-of-global-gross-domestic-product-gdp/.

knowing that their economy – which is roughly the size of Italy's – has not diversified away from oil and gas and is declining.

Russia's military is modernizing but its defence budget is still less than 10% of NATO's, measured at nominal exchange rates, and is comparable to defence spending by the UK alone. Russia's desperation to retain a place as a credible player has proved dangerous and de-stabilizing, as in the Crimea, eastern Ukraine and Syria. Russia has been agile in filling the gaps left by inept western diplomacy, which shares responsibility for human suffering and political setbacks in Eastern Europe, the Middle East and North Africa. Russians are nervous about growing Chinese influence in Central Asia and about Chinese interest in the vast and largely empty expanses of Siberia and the Russian Far East.

The Chinese know that they pose a formidable challenge to the US in both economic and military terms (especially the threat to the US Navy in East Asia); this encourages them to act with growing self-assurance. Japan, Australia and other allies in Asia-Pacific are worried about American commitments, particularly after the Trump administration's abandonment of the Trans-Pacific Partnership (TPP), and its erratic response to threats in the South China Sea and from North Korea. Europeans are unsure about whether America will stand by Article 5 of the North Atlantic Treaty and there is revived interest in the notion of building up Europe's "strategic autonomy" to defend its own interests, without the United States, if necessary. European fears and aspirations as well as Brexit account for the current flurry of interest in embryonic EU security and defence projects. But Europe's response to new challenges to the East is clouded in uncertainty. For now, there are more questions than answers.

3   Europe's Response

Should Europe embrace Belt and Road, the Asian Infrastructure Investment Bank, (AIIB) and other Chinese regional cooperation initiatives, or should Europeans hold them at arm's length, championing instead the somewhat frayed rules-based international institutions that have sustained the liberal international economic order over past decades, and, supporting the Comprehensive and Progressive Agreement for Trans-Pacific Partnership, which, on Japan's initiative, replaced the original "TPP" following US withdrawal.

How should we view strategic investment from China, whether in the port of Piraeus, Trieste, or the Hinkley Point nuclear power station in Somerset, England? Are such investments a useful way of recycling China's record trade surplus with the European Union or do they threaten our independence? With Britain's likely departure, will the EU remain largely open to Chinese trade and investment, or will Germany support the trend towards a "Europe which protects", as advanced by French President Emmanuel Macron, with tighter scrutiny of strategic investments and greater recourse to trade defence instruments? Several EU capitals in central Europe now lean towards accommodating Moscow.

With Brexit on the horizon, will the EU maintain sanctions on Russia, following its annexation of Crimea, and continuing military presence in eastern Ukraine, or will it gradually shift towards accommodation, even without fulfilment of the now side-lined Minsk agreements? Those who have received Russia's largesse or who yearn for a new Ostpolitik prefer the latter course. The French President advocates steps towards re-engagement with Russia. Will tough American sanctions laws that potentially target European companies and individuals encourage Germany and other EU countries to move away from sanctions?[3] How will future governments in Berlin, facing a more fragmented domestic political environment, manoeuvre between East and West? Such questions will be debated over the coming months and years.

Meanwhile several considerations should be borne in mind when crafting responses to challenges from a rising China and a declining but recalcitrant Russia. The EU should provide support to neighbouring countries that have the genuine will and capacity to adopt and implement pro-democracy reforms, without encouraging unrealistic hopes of their joining western institutions in the foreseeable future. European countries and the EU should not doggedly pursue policies derived from values when they conflict with interests, or when the political will and resources to enforce respect for values are lacking.

The EU and its members should be robust in scrutinizing strategic investments which may affect national or EU interests. They should be alert to strategic investments in neighbouring regions, such as the Balkans or North Africa, that may affect European interests. But the notion of "a Europe that protects" should not become the pretext for protectionism that runs counter to economic interests.

Where there are real mutual interests, Europeans should be ready to engage with China or Russia, whether on trade liberalization, infrastructure investment, energy, environment, counterterrorism or other global challenges. Europeans should show that they have the will to ensure their own security and defence, less through new EU structures, which may be useful but minor complements to NATO, than through sufficient expenditure on real military capabilities.

---

3   See Countering America's Adversaries Through Sanctions Act, https://www.congress.gov/bill/115th-congress/house-bill/3364/text.

The EU needs to develop a new vision and a new narrative that is rooted in reality and can capture the imagination of somewhat jaded European citizens who are tempted by populism. It is no longer enough to claim that the EU promotes "stability, security and prosperity" or to propound various "unions" – banking, security, energy etc. – that are at best works in progress, with little impact on daily life. The recourse to "human rights" as the lowest common denominator on which member states can agree, in principle, is not a sufficient guide in formulating the EU's response to China and Russia, especially when the member states generally pursue business as usual.

The EU needs to be realistic about its influence on neighbouring countries. Contrary to widely held beliefs, or wishful thinking, within the Brussels beltway, the EU may no longer be a normative power, whose model has a magnetic appeal to others. Certainly, it is a model neither for China nor for Russia. Its brief hope of providing a model to countries in North Africa and the Eastern Mediterranean following the Arab uprisings soon faded. Even countries in the Western Balkans, like Serbia, that have been promised EU membership, tilt towards Moscow when this suits their short-term interests.

At the same time, the EU is not a military power, and will not become one, despite current interest in creating a "security union". Initiatives to stimulate cooperation on armaments production and on police missions, mainly in Africa, are a useful complement to NATO not a step towards creating a European Army.

Let us not pretend that we are back in the Cold War as a way of simplifying our policy choices. Today's global challenges, which have reverberations within our own societies, have more to do with income inequality, demography, religion, climate change and migration than with the East-West conflict of yore. The EU needs to get past Brexit and crises over eurozone governance and migration to develop a new and convincing vision of itself as a civilian power, using its economic and regulatory instruments effectively to address its own and global challenges. This will reinforce the Union's credibility and give it greater leverage with Russia and China when they appear to challenge European interests.

Bibliography

Bader, J.A. (2018). '7 things you need to know about lifting term limits for Xi Jinping', *Brookings*, 27 February, https://www.brookings.edu/blog/order-from-chaos/2018/02/27/7-things-you-need-to-know-about-lifting-term-limits-for-xi-jinping/.

China-CEEC. (2017). 'Promising 16+1 cooperation helps boost European development, integration', 29 November, http://www.china-ceec.org/eng/zdogjhz_1/t1514944.htm.

Feng, E. and Mance H. (2017). 'David Cameron takes senior role in China infrastructure fund', 16 December, https://www.ft.com/content/07a05ac2-e238-11e7-97e2-916d4 fbacoda.

Foy, H. and Chazan, G. (2017). 'Gerhard Schröder appointed chairman of Rosneft', *Financial Times*, 29 September, https://www.ft.com/content/100db270-a518-11e7-9e4f-7f5e6a7c98a2.

Global Strategy. (2016). 'Shared Vision, Common Action: A Stronger Europe. A Global Strategy for the European Union's Foreign and Security Policy', *European Union External Action*, June, https://eeas.europa.eu/archives/docs/top_stories/pdf/eugs_re view_web.pdf.

Karaganov, S. (2017). 'A Cold War: A forecast for tomorrow', 22 October, http://kara ganov.ru/en/publications/462.

Malnick, E. (2017). 'David Cameron given special dispensation to broker talks between Britain and China in new role leading £750m investment fund', *Daily Telegraph*, 16 December, http://www.telegraph.co.uk/news/2017/12/16/david-cameron-set-750m -uk-china-investment-fund/.

Walker, C. and Ludwig, J. (2017). 'The Meaning of Sharp Power: How Authoritarian States Project Influence', *Foreign Affairs*, 16 November, https://www.foreignaffairs .com/articles/china/2017-11-16/meaning-sharp-power.

CHAPTER 23

Concluding Remarks

Stefano Bianchini and Antonio Fiori

Since the turn of the new millennium the world's geopolitical balance has been under stress. Bobo Lo (2015) unequivocally speaks of "World disorder". The decline of the West's moral authority is increasingly recognized, particularly by liberal media in the US, as a crucial factor determining a prospectively different scenario, after the predominant unipolarity of the 1990s.

Succinctly, the deconstruction and reshaping of the post-cold war context is in progress. According to Zygmunt Bauman (2000), this process could be described as the *liquefaction* of pre-existing social links, of the sense of belonging, of the awareness of individuals and groups, waiting for new solid bodies whose forms cannot be predicted yet.

It is under these circumstances of world disorder that both China and Russia have re-emerged as *land empires* in the centre of Eurasia. This setting constitutes, therefore, the main focus of the book. As recurrently pointed out by the authors, the dynamism of the two states' foreign policies has acquired a new stance in the international arena, including assertive and sometime aggressive external projections, which has been manifested in a variety of world domains. Albeit for different reasons, these events pose key challenges to the existing neoliberal order, which shows increasing signs of decay. Under these circumstances, the Russian and Chinese challenges impact not only domestic policies (by promoting "conservative" frames and norms) but also external projections (in terms of values, trade, the balance of power, and the management of the international laws, covenants, and conventions).

On the one hand, Russia openly opposes the post-1989 global unipolarity of the US and its allies. Not surprisingly, especially in recent years, Moscow's confrontation with the West has deepened, although not with the same intensity and not necessarily towards a homogeneously perceived "Western world". Relations with the US and NATO, for example, follow a different pattern if compared with the EU, whose multifaceted context offers multiple alternatives, particularly with some member-states (Giles 2019; Makarychev 2014). On the other hand, China has increasingly started to assert a more pronounced and active role in the international political and economic proscenium, as clearly evidenced by the robust defence of global free trade President Xi Jinping offered in occasion of the World Economic Forum in Davos in 2017, marking his departure from Trump's considerations aimed at rewriting the rules of global commerce. Consistently, Beijing nurtures great ambitions, even greater than Russia, with the goal of representing *the* global alternative at a moment in which Western democracies are facing innumerable deficiencies, beset by flagging economic growth, worsening public security, a widening gap between rich and poor, and the rise of terrorism and populism.

Russia and China definitely possess distinct identities and forms of legitimacy. Their behaviour and commitment follow specific rationales stemming from different historical and cultural legacies. Nonetheless, they also share similarities, based in particular on powerful state traditions and the twentieth century experience of a socialist society inspired by the Marxist-Leninist model, even if differently interpreted and carried out over time.

However, their bilateral relations frequently suffered from ups and downs, either great cohesion or deep political crises and border skirmishes. Ultimately, a temporary marriage of convenience prevailed whenever closeness was diplomatically or politically emphasized. By contrast, a stable, long-term alliance was never achieved, most probably because both countries see their international position as those of great powers, being therefore unprepared to play the role of subordinates in bilateral relations (Stronski & Ng 2018).

Despite this fluctuating historical legacy, this book assumes – as mentioned in the Introduction and in several chapters – that a U-turn convergence between Moscow and Beijing surfaced particularly from 2012 onwards, that is the year when Putin was sworn in as President for the third time and Xi Jinping was elected General Secretary of the Chinese Communist Party (CCP). These developments opened a new window in current international affairs, although divergences and points of mutual reservation or mistrust persisted – and still persist – between the two land powers.

The studies conducted by the authors of this book adamantly show how the reshaping of particular domestic policies in the perspective of building a "strong state" is strictly interconnected with the remodelling of the Russian and Chinese external projection. From both a domestic and an international perspective, China and Russia's proximity but also the two countries' parallel, autonomous policies are manifesting a significant impact on the world balance. Moreover, they will potentially greatly influence the development of international relations, especially if the global agenda will include growing American trade protectionism, deteriorating EU-US cooperation, and the weakening of the European integration process.

Under these circumstances, we should not underestimate the fact that in both the Chinese and Russian cases – despite peculiarities and diversities – the state exercises deep influence in both domestic and foreign affairs. In both countries in fact, the state acts as a gatekeeper, determining interactions with the outside world, which is frequently seen as threatening. The strength of the state, epitomized by Putin and Xi under the frame of the "strong state" notion or model, is marked by the state's deep penetration of society. Moreover, a certain degree of permeability of its institutions by society is also tolerated, while emotional consent is often mobilized, with the leverage of nationalized patriotism. At the same time, both countries have very distinct cultures, largely different from Western Europe, even though Russia's interaction with the European continent as a whole (particularly since the eighteenth century) has transformed the Russian state into a sort of hybrid with a variety of self-identities, which encompass a strong attractive European identification as well as rejections.

From the economic point of view, both Russia and China have suffered from their backwardness when compared to the West. But due to substantial reforms – the adoption of a market economy in Russia and the opening to foreign trade and investments in China – these two actors are now legitimized as relevant players in the global economic sphere, although their performances are differently assessed.

Actually, climate change and paradoxically, even western sanctions have increased Russian agricultural production, which reached a world record in 2017 and 2018, and vastly improved its food exports, in addition to the export of energy commodities, weapons, and military equipment. On the other hand, as seen in a number of chapters, China's economy has achieved a leading role in many sectors worldwide not only in terms of trade and domestic market opportunities for foreign investors, but also in terms of investment in various types of infrastructure in Asia, Africa, East-Central Europe and even Latin America. Its most ambitious project is the well-known "Belt and Road Initiative" (BRI), designed to improve "connectivity" between Beijing and Europe (World Bank 2018). As a result, despite Russia's economic progress – which still suffers from weaknesses owing to the volatility of commodity prices – China has definitely become the second largest economy in the world, with the potential of surpassing the US shortly (World Bank 2018a).

Following further considerations in our volume about the nature of Russian and Chinese "strong state" remodelling, a special relevance should be ascribed to some respective historical legacies and geopolitical positioning. This can be perceived in terms of timeline and impact of specific events, as for example the aftermath of the Golden Horde Empire vs. the Peter the Great modernization for Russia, or in the case of China, the clash between the Chinese Empire and western colonialism, which gave birth to the "century of humiliation". But the legacy of the past has an additional, powerful effect in terms of identity and geopolitical positioning, assigning a range of interpretations to categories like "Europe", "Eurasia" or "Greater Eurasia".

As a result, China and Russia have nurtured a cultural and historical experience which over time has accentuated the dichotomy between encountering and rejecting the western world. Partially perceived as their own "Other", for China and Russia the West has become a key factor against which they measure themselves and their identities either in terms of confrontation or as a lever for their social growth, progress, and development. This dichotomy also has a geopolitical dimension. For example, Russian territory stretches from Central Europe to the Pacific Ocean: for Russian élites and the Russian population at large, this simple fact has originated multiple identities, often realized in controversial and painful ways. On the other hand, China in its millenary history has also manifested both trade attractiveness and the denial of European colonialism, which recently has not hindered Beijing from calling for the resurgence of the traditional Silk Road by carrying out its colossal BRI project.

Undoubtedly, different degrees of hybridity still mark some dynamics within the Eurasian Economic Union (EAEU), whose member states – geopolitically and culturally located between Russia and China, with distinct authoritarian systems that coexist with a market economy – do not reject bilateral or multilateral relations with the European Union and its member states, as for example in the case of Armenia, whose membership in the EAEU did not prevent it from signing a partnership agreement with Brussels in 2017. Russia too is preserving, if not developing, its cooperation with Germany and Italy, directly or through Turkey (despite the fact that all of these countries are important NATO member states). China is also deeply penetrating into the Balkans and has signed an agreement with Italy, conducive to the implementation of its aforementioned BRI plan.

In other words, an increasing number of players around the world (including fundamentalist and terrorist movements, cyber competitors, and organized criminality) is challenging the pre-existing order, which for decades was based on a bipolar confrontation – at the time of the Cold War – and later on the supremacy of the US. Meanwhile, the relevance still recently ascribed by a number of international organizations to shared values, free trade policies, and democratization matters less and less in comparison with the emergence of new transnational networks, alternative financial and geopolitical convergences, declining political moralities, multiple normative suggestions, and growing protectionist vs. neo-globalist trends, as the volume has emphasized in numerous chapters.

Under these circumstances, the Chinese and Russian "fraternity" has recently gained momentum, despite their tumultuous relations in the 1950s that led to a complete breakdown in the following decade lasting more or less until the end of the 1980s. On the contrary, since the beginning of the Ukraine crisis, China has opposed the West's imposition of sanctions following Moscow's annexation of Crimea in March 2014 and Russian support for separatist movements in the Ukrainian regions of Donets'k and Luhans'k (Gabuev 2016). This opposition clearly demonstrates that China aims to circumvent Western sanctions to take advantage of trade and economic cooperation with Moscow. Another reason that well explains such conduct is the desire to preserve Russia as a bulwark against US dominance in the international community.

However, despite some common interests, multiple points of friction remain between the two states, showing the limits of their relationship, as seen both in the second and the third sections of the book. Once again, the 30-year gas deal with Moscow, negotiated in 2014, may be a good example, if the estimated agreed price of US$ 400bn for 38bn cubic meters each year is lower than Russia had aspired for, while being much more favourable for China (Koch-Weser & Murray 2014; Luhn & Macalister 2014). Another example may be seen in the gas pipeline China opened in cooperation with Turkmenistan, Uzbekistan and Kazakhstan in 2009, breaking Russia's traditional monopoly on Central Asian gas exports. These are just two simple examples of cooperation formulae that have generated serious concerns in Moscow about the possibility of becoming an "appendix" of Beijing.

Moreover, there are clear signs of divergence at the regional level. Indeed, both actors oppose the existing order in their respective regions, but signs of integration are unobservable.

Still, what strongly emerges from the pages of this volume is the *new global mapping* drawn by Russia and China in the last decades, how they are trying to promote "re-globalization", or a different form of globalization, based on a new economic agenda, new normative frameworks, new conceptions of the state and identity models. Moreover, our interest has focussed on how boundaries may shift not only geopolitically, but also culturally, socially and economically, according to the converging, or diverging, perspectives pursued by these two great powers in the regional and global arenas.

In the end, we deeply believe that these dynamics deserve further monitoring in order to understand the medium and long-term potential developments not only of these two great land powers, but more broadly, of the future of international relations, their normative remodelling, and the construction of a new balance of power after a presumably long period of social, political and cultural *liquidity* of both domestic and foreign policies of the growing number of players around the world.

Bibliography

Bauman, Z. (2000). *Liquid Modernity*. Cambridge: Polity Press.

Gabuev, A. (2016). 'Friends with Benefits? Russian-Chinese Relations After the Ukraine Crisis', *Carnegie Moscow Center*, 29 June, http://carnegie.ru/2016/06/29/friends-with-benefits-russian-chinese-relations-after-ukraine-crisis-pub-63953.

Giles, K. (2019). *Moscow Rules: What Drives Russia to Confront the West*. Washington, D.C. and London: Brookings Inst. Press and Chatham House.

Koch-Weser, I. and Murray, C. (2014). 'The China-Russia Gas Deal: Background and Implications for the Broader Relationship', U.S.-China Economic and Security Review Commission, 9 June, https://www.uscc.gov/sites/default/files/Research/China%20Russia%20gas%20deal_Staffbackgrounder.pdf.

Lo, B. (2015). *Russia and the New Worlds Disorder*. London/Washington, D.C.: Chatham House and Brookings Institution Press.

Luhn, A. and Macalister, T. (2014). 'Russia signs 30-year deal worth $400bn to deliver gas to China', *The Guardian*, 21 May, https://www.theguardian.com/world/2014/may/21/russia-30-year-400bn-gas-deal-china.

Makarychev, A. (2014). *Russia and the EU in a Multipolar World*. Stuttgart: Ibidem.

Stronski, P. and Ng, N. (2018). 'Cooperation and Competition: Russia and China in Central Asia, the Russian Far East and the Arctic', *Carnegie Endowment for International Peace*, 28 February, http://carnegieendowment.org/2018/02/28/cooperation-and-competition-russia-and-china-in-central-asia-russian-far-east-and-arctic-pub-75673.

World Bank (2018). 'China Overview', April, http://www.worldbank.org/en/country/china/overview.

World Bank (2018a). 'Connectivity Along Overland Corridors of the Belt and Road Initiative', Discussion Paper n. 6, October, http://documents.worldbank.org/curated/en/264651538637972468/pdf/Connectivity-Along-Overland-Corridors-of-the-Belt-and-Road-Initiative.pdf.

Index

AEM (Asia-Europe Meeting)   257
AICHR (ASEAN Intergovernmental
      Commission on Human Rights)   62n5
AIIB (Asian Infrastructure and Investment
      Bank)   93, 203, 474
APEC (Asia Pacific Economic
      Cooperation)   56, 83, 257
Arab uprisings (2011)   404, 408, 415–419, 423,
      476
ARF (ASEAN Regional Forum)   83
Armenia   31, 255–256, 306, 315–316, 330,
      356n, 481
ASEAN   9, 62n5, 72, 83, 257, 278n, 279n, 334n
Asia-Pacific (region)   9, 254, 257, 330n, 381,
      474
Asian Financial Crisis (1997)   278
Asian values   62, 287
Authoritarianism   1, 6, 19n6, 79, 82, 292
      Authoritarian modernisation   8, 100, 112
      Authoritarian welfare state   100, 287
      Authoritarian regime   4–5, 82, 93, 135,
         141–144, 199, 211

Beijing Consensus   79, 90, 285
Belarus   30, 31, 250, 255, 306, 330n, 349n16,
      368, 372, 468
Berdiaev, Nikolai   23, 25, 29n, 261
Brezhnev, Leonid   464, 466
Brexit   185, 210, 300, 305, 365, 471, 474, 475,
      476
BRI (Belt and Road Initiative)   4, 205, 208,
      209, 315, 332–334, 336, 396–398,
      471–473, 480–481
BRICS   7, 8, 17, 18, 93, 186–187, 192, 192–194,
      196, 198–199, 202–205, 215, 218, 219,
      257–258, 265, 271–295, 442

Capitalism   8, 45, 81, 201–202, 286, 327, 329,
      336, 431, 450, 453, 458, 461
Censorship   90, 144, 292
Central Asia   7, 9, 164, 257, 259, 303, 355, 373,
      378–398, 405, 414, 420, 474
Chechen war   251

China
   CCP (Chinese Communist Party)   3, 41,
      49–51, 54, 57, 75n, 79–88, 93, 94, 147,
      150, 289–293, 327, 380, 479
   Century of humiliation   2, 40, 48–51, 53,
      480
   Chinese dream (also China dream)   40,
      53–54, 331
   Chinese Economy   82, 94, 186, 190, 276,
      285
   Chineseness   41, 47
   Civil society   41, 85, 292
   Confucianism   48–49, 286
   Demography   161–162, 176–177, 188, 257,
      384
   Energy outlook   257, 378–398
   FDI   188–196, 216–217, 285, 378, 411
   'Go Out' policy   379–382
   Great Rejuvenation   8, 40, 52–56, 84, 90,
      331n13
   Human Rights   4, 8, 51, 61–64, 66–68,
      72–76, 292, 325–326
   Military Expenditures   204, 218
   Nationalism   42, 47, 54, 56–57, 277n
   NOCs (National Oil Companies)   379,
      381–382, 397
   Patriotism   41n, 42
   Poverty   74, 75n32, 80, 161, 176, 198–199,
      287–290
   Socialist market economy   82, 90
   Strong State   2–5, 8, 79–94, 294, 479–480
CICA (Conference on Interaction and
      Confidence-Building Measures in
      Asia)   83
CIS (Commonwealth of Independent
      States)   29, 171, 176, 251, 253–256, 262,
      279, 313, 359, 366, 375
Cold War   41, 185, 208n, 223, 227, 229–230,
      233, 243, 250, 256, 293, 325, 413, 415, 416,
      418, 423, 431–432, 439–442, 445,
      450–468, 470, 476, 481
CoE (Council of Europe)   61, 62n3, 68, 258,
      294, 346, 348, 349, 351n27, 354

Corruption   2, 33, 50, 81, 84, 86, 91, 143, 172,
     177, 200, 259, 282, 284, 359–360
CSCAP (Council on Security Cooperation in
     Asia and Pacific Region)   83
CSTO (Collective Security Treaty
     Organisation)   9

De Gaulle, Charles   10, 260, 453, 455–456,
     459–460
Democratic People's Republic of Korea
     (DPRK, North Korea)   176, 207, 355,
     474
Democratisation   280, 291, 372, 375
     Liberal democracy   5, 201, 225
     Electoral democracy   5, 199
     Sovereign democracy   19, 260
Deng, Xiaoping   2, 4, 50, 79–82, 87, 90, 92,
     140, 196, 285, 288, 472
Developmentalism   271–272, 412, 420

EAEU (Eurasian Economic Union)   8, 31, 157,
     254–260, 279, 303, 306, 315–316, 325,
     330–332, 334–335, 481
EAS (East Asia Summit)   257
ECHR (European Convention on Human
     Rights)   62, 68–72, 348n13, 349n18
Economic Crisis (2008)   117, 123–124, 164, 176,
     206, 288, 373
Economic Nationalism   275–276
ECtHR (European Court of Human
     Rights)   62, 69–71, 258, 349n18,
     353n
EEC (European Economic Community)   254,
     430, 450–468
El'tsin, Boris   5, 98, 201, 203, 250, 252, 256,
     263, 365–370, 384, 387, 467
EU (European Union)   1, 6, 9–10, 17, 31–32,
     170, 173, 185–188, 191, 192n, 202, 204–211,
     215–217, 219, 227, 243n, 249, 252–254,
     256–260, 264–265, 276, 288, 298–308,
     310–317, 323–337, 344–361, 365, 371–372,
     375, 389, 407, 412, 418n10, 450, 451n,
     467–468, 470–476, 478–479, 481
     Court of Justice   351
     Refugee (migration) crisis   300–301,
          307–308, 345–346, 472
     Treaty on the Functioning of European
          Union (TFEU)   350–351

Eurasia   19, 27, 31–32, 274, 294, 298, 323–325,
     326n, 332, 333n, 334–336, 395, 397, 478,
     481
     Eurasianism   31, 237, 239, 254, 259, 335
     Greater Eurasia   260, 324–325, 332–333,
          335–336, 481
     Greater Eurasia Project   324–325, 333,
          335
     Neo-Eurasianism   31

Fake news   308, 310, 316, 473
FORGO (Foundation for Civil Society
     Development)   25
Four Modernisations   50, 285
France   189, 190, 192, 212, 215, 216, 217, 261,
     302–303, 305n, 451–453, 457, 459–460,
     464

Gaidar, Egor   250, 276, 281, 282
GCC (Gulf Cooperation Council)   407,
     409–411, 416
Gender equality   7, 98–113, 311
Georgian War   129, 204, 205, 224, 233, 309,
     467–468
Germany   30n, 188–190, 191n, 192n, 209, 212,
     215, 216, 217, 227, 229, 260, 261, 275, 302,
     303, 304, 305n2, 396, 434, 435, 451–454,
     457, 458, 460, 463, 465, 475, 481
Globalisation   57, 100, 102, 256, 261, 265, 286,
     324–325, 327, 329–331, 336, 431
Gorbachev, Mikhail   10, 90, 195, 201, 203, 250,
     260, 300, 366, 367, 369–370, 450, 462,
     466–467

Hong Kong   4, 7, 81, 189, 190, 191n6, 215, 216,
     217, 284
Hu, Jintao   42, 82–84, 391, 442
Human Trafficking   344–361
Hybrid regime   1, 6, 19, 141
     Hybridity   5–6, 19, 261, 481
     Hybrid system   6, 93–94, 99

India   1, 9, 122, 186, 187, 190, 193, 194, 196, 199,
     202, 204, 205, 209, 212, 215, 216, 218, 251,
     255, 258, 274, 278, 335, 373, 473
Information war   207, 308–311
International Law   1, 61–76, 174, 228, 230, 234,
     258, 303, 375, 418n

Iran 1, 7, 10, 252, 256, 258, 334n, 335, 393, 396, 406–408, 410–411, 414, 416–417, 420–422

Iraq 224, 231, 232, 252, 258, 326, 389, 406–407, 410–411, 414–415, 417–419, 422–423

ISEPR (Institute for Socio-Economic and Political Studies) 25–26

Japan 9, 41–43, 48–49, 51, 53–58, 189, 190, 191n, 205, 209, 212, 215, 217, 232, 257, 259, 278n, 284, 285, 288, 306, 474

Jiang, Zemin 4, 42, 50–52, 82–83, 88, 380, 387

Kazakhstan 31, 191, 250, 255–256, 306, 330n, 368, 383–387, 390–392, 394–396, 482

Khrushchev, Nikita 451, 454, 456, 458–460

Kozyrev, Andrei 250–251

Kravchuk, Leonid 366–367

Kyrgyzstan 31, 171, 306, 330n, 383–389, 393–395

Land power 1, 7, 479, 482

Lavrov, Sergei 27, 262, 306, 307n6, 308

Lenin, Vladimir 3, 369–370

Liberalism 79, 81, 94, 229, 271, 276–277, 290, 311, 335, 415, 418, 423, 440

Libya 7, 231, 253, 258, 406, 410–411, 414–416, 418–419, 422–423

Macron, Emmanuel 308, 475

Mao, Zedong 4, 49, 79–80, 82–83, 87, 472

Market Economy 99, 107, 112, 272–273, 281–282, 286–287, 290, 329, 332, 373, 480–481

Marxism 22, 80, 98, 277

May, Theresa 308

Medvedev, Dmitrii 6, 117–133, 226, 236, 237n13, 238, 240, 253, 276

MENA (Middle East and North Africa) 404–423, 474

Middle East 9, 186, 204, 207–208, 211, 235, 355, 381, 389, 397, 404–409, 412–413, 415, 417n7, 418–423, 474

Migration 8, 159–171, 173–177, 192, 199, 264, 308, 344–345, 350, 359–360, 413, 476

Illegal migration 162, 169–170, 173, 175, 302

Labour migration 163–164

Migration crisis 300, 308, 345–346

Modernisation 6, 8, 19, 45, 50, 79, 88, 100, 112, 117–120, 122–126, 128–133, 161, 197, 249, 272, 285, 291, 299, 332, 359, 380, 416, 480

Multipolarity 7, 240, 253, 258, 261

Multipolar world 211, 251, 259, 414

Nationalism 18n4, 19, 20n8, 40–47, 41n1, 46n3, 49–54, 56–58, 82, 176, 275–276, 277n1, 283, 290, 367, 369, 371–372, 384

NATO (North Atlantic Treaty Organisation) 9, 52, 207–208, 223–225, 227, 227n4, 238, 241–243, 249, 251–253, 259, 276, 302n1, 312, 330, 375, 408, 414, 422–423, 454, 456–457, 471, 475–476, 478, 481

Strategic culture 227–235

Naval'nyi, Aleksei 33–34, 34n20

NEACD (Northeast Asia Cooperation Dialogue) 83

Near Abroad 29–30, 251, 256, 298, 413

Neo-familism 100, 111–112

Neo-Marxism 277

New Silk Road 333, 384, 395, 398, 410

NGO (Non-Governmental Organisation) 22, 25, 147, 292, 311, 356, 358–359, 430

North Africa 234, 252, 404, 404n1, 405–406, 408–409, 412–413, 415, 419–423, 474–476

OHCHR (Office of High Commissioner on Human Rights) 62n4, 74n30

OPEC 273, 283, 379, 408

PECC (Pacific Economic Cooperation Council) 83

Perestroika 101, 367

Populism 20, 20n7, 266, 311, 326, 472, 476, 479

Post-Soviet transition 365

Primakov, Evgenii 251, 417n7

Putin, Vladimir 2–3, 6, 18, 18n3, 20, 23, 23n12, 25–27, 29–31, 34, 98, 108, 118, 120, 125, 129–130, 201, 203, 211, 225–226, 236–237, 240, 252–253, 255, 260–262, 265, 276,

293, 301–302, 307, 310, 314, 328n8,
   333–334, 375–376, 415, 467, 473,
   479–480
P4M (Partnership for Modernisation)   6

Regionalism   68, 255, 325, 334, 336, 413
Resource nationalism   283
Russia
   Civil society   25, 303, 357, 417
   Conservatism   19, 21–25, 28–32
   Demography   98, 100–101, 108, 157,
      159–162, 176, 254, 257
   Digital Diplomacy   261, 263–266
   Energy   119, 121, 124–125, 132, 188, 202, 206,
      252, 257–258, 279, 283, 292, 303–304,
      367, 372–373, 405–409, 418, 422–423,
      459
   FDI   189, 193, 195
   Foreign Policy Concept   236, 302, 302n1
   Human Rights   5, 8, 61–66, 68–72, 75, 223,
      258, 292, 349, 356, 417
   Military Expenditures   204–205, 211, 218
   National Identity   18, 24, 27, 68, 72, 75,
      328, 375
   Orthodoxy   3, 24, 30, 35, 237, 263–264,
      372, 375, 413, 415
   Patriotism   3, 20n8, 28, 264, 480
   Power vertical   131
   Russian Idea   3, 19, 28–29, 263
   Russian World (Russkii Mir)   19, 27,
      29–30, 225, 238, 242, 261–264, 266
   Russian values   69–70, 238, 254
   Russianness   18, 29–30, 250, 261
   Strategic culture   225, 235–242
   Strong state   2–5, 8, 19, 98, 113, 275, 294,
      479–480
   Trade Balance   283
   Traditional values   18, 20n9, 21, 23, 262,
      264–265, 292
   Tsarism   5

Salvini, Matteo   312–313, 314n15
Sanctions   6, 163, 185, 188, 195, 206–207, 224,
      233, 249, 254, 256, 275, 291, 300–301,
      303–307, 306n4, 307n5, 312n13, 313, 326,
      331, 351–353, 389n1, 406, 417, 422, 472,
      475, 475n3, 480, 482
SCO (Shanghai Cooperation
      Organisation)   9, 257, 265, 274,
      334–335, 334n17, 388–390, 398

Singapore   81, 189–190, 216–217, 256, 275,
      284–285, 287, 327
Social Protest   8, 135–140, 149, 152
Socialism   51, 75, 81, 82, 83, 84, 93, 281, 432,
      458, 461, 472
South China Sea   7, 54, 205, 395, 474
South Korea   43, 56, 81, 191n6, 256, 259,
      278n2, 285
Sovereignty   4, 6, 40, 43n2, 53, 63–64, 66–67,
      71, 238, 240, 243n15, 271, 287, 325, 328,
      331, 333–334, 335n18, 367–369, 383, 385,
      387, 404, 415–416, 419–420, 423, 430,
      440
Stalin, Iosif   3, 367, 452
State capitalism   8, 201–202
State nationalism   45, 47, 50, 52
sub-Saharan Africa   2, 9, 197
Syria   7, 34, 74n29, 185, 204–205, 224,
      238–239, 258–259, 282, 300, 304–305,
      406–408, 407n3, 415–419, 422–423, 472,
      474

Taiwan   43, 48–49, 54, 81, 191n6, 205–206,
      284, 383–385
Tajikistan   171, 366, 383–384, 386–388,
      393–394
Tanzania   431–445
Terrorism   224, 233–234, 252, 292, 360, 384,
      387–389, 420, 431, 479
Tiananmen (movement, protests)   41, 48,
      50–51, 55, 57, 73, 81, 87–88, 103, 140, 152,
      201, 281, 441
TPP (Trans-Pacific Partnership)   208, 260,
      326n5, 474
Turkmenistan   383–384, 392–394, 482

Ukraine
   Crimea   21, 23–27, 23n12, 30, 33, 35, 224,
      233, 238, 249, 253, 259, 262, 266, 299,
      303–304, 313, 366, 368–369, 371–372,
      375, 468, 474–475, 482
   Donbas   26n14, 27, 34, 263, 299
   East Ukraine   22, 374
   Language   367, 369
   Maidan Revolution (Euromaidan)   253,
      265, 299
   Minsk Agreements   303–304, 306, 475
   Ukraine (Ukrainian) Crisis   23–26, 32–33,
      224, 249, 300, 304–305, 311, 313, 315, 326,
      330n11, 370, 376, 482

UN (United Nations)
    Convention Against Transnational
        Organised Crime   346n9, 352n28, 354
    Security Council   7, 202, 252, 258, 366,
        422, 470
US
    Obama, Barack   208, 326, 326n5, 397
    Washington Consensus   90, 94, 202, 258,
        275, 285, 287, 294–295, 443
    Washington Treaty   223, 228–229, 233
    Trump, Donald   1, 4, 9–10, 207–208, 210,
        305, 323, 474
USSR (Soviet Union)   3, 61, 104, 120, 122, 157,
        162, 166, 195, 223, 228, 250, 255–256, 262,
        272–273, 280–281, 284, 287, 293, 366,
        375, 382–383, 390, 394, 397, 415, 418,
        450–457, 460–461, 465–466, 468
Uzbekistan   171, 255, 263, 383–384, 387–389,
        392–393, 482

Valdai Discussion Club   20n10, 24, 31, 249n1,
        262, 314, 315
Virtual economy   282

Warsaw Pact   223, 452
Welfare state   8, 98–103, 109, 111–113, 275, 281,
        290
World Bank   160, 186–188, 203, 205, 278, 289,
        405, 480
World Economic Forum   58, 292, 329, 478
WTO (World Trade Organisation)   83, 192,
        277, 292, 326

Xi, Jinping   4, 75n33, 84, 200, 201n18,
        205–206, 208, 291, 331, 333n16, 393–395,
        420, 421n12, 443, 471–472, 478–479

Yemen   7, 411, 417, 422, 423
Yukos   70–71, 70n17

Zanzibar   432–435, 437, 440, 445
Zhao, Ziyang   80, 441

Printed in the United States
By Bookmasters